서아쌤의 토익 비밀과외 기출 VOCA

시원스쿨어학연구소 지음

시원스쿨 LAB

초판 1쇄 발행 2025년 11월 25일

지은이 시원스쿨어학연구소
펴낸곳 (주)에스제이더블유인터내셔널
펴낸이 양홍걸 이시원

홈페이지 www.siwonschool.com
주소 서울시 영등포구 영신로 166 시원스쿨
교재 구입 문의 02)2014-8151
고객센터 02)6409-0878

ISBN 979-11-7550-036-5 13740
Number 1-110107-30183000-02

이 책은 저작권법에 따라 보호받는 저작물이므로 무단복제와 무단전재를 금합니다. 이 책 내용의 전부 또는 일부를 이용하려면 반드시 저작권자와 ㈜에스제이더블유인터내셔널의 서면 동의를 받아야 합니다.

머리말

안녕하세요. 최서아 선생님입니다.

영어 시험 준비에서 단어는 목표 점수에 도달하기 위한 기본이자 토대이며 본질입니다. 하지만 단어 암기는 지루하고, 외운 듯해도 금세 잊히며, 답답할 만큼 늘지 않는 듯한 경험을 누구나 합니다. 토익 학습자들과 늘 함께해온 제가 그 어려움을 잘 알고 있기에, '어떻게 하면 단어를 좀 더 효율적으로 오래 기억하고, 실제 문제풀이에 바로 적용할 수 있을까?'라는 고민을 오랫동안 이어왔습니다. 그리고 그 연구의 결실로, 시원스쿨랩 연구진과 함께 이 교재를 기획하게 되었습니다.

이 책은 단순한 암기용 자료가 아닌, 실전 전략과 전문성이 결합된, 점수로 직결되는 단어장입니다. 토익 시험에서 자주 출제되는 단어들을 파트별로 분류하고, 각 표제어에는 기출 문장을 기반으로 한 간결한 예시를 수록했습니다. 외우기 쉽도록 문장을 짧게 만들되, 시험장에서 문제를 보는 순간 정답을 고를 수 있도록 기출 정수를 예문에 녹여냈습니다. 또한, '단어는 외웠는데 문제에 적용이 안 돼요'라는 고민에 대한 실질적인 해답으로, 모든 표제어마다 기출 변형 문제를 함께 실었습니다. 그래서 여러분은 단어 암기와 동시에 약 1,500개의 문제 풀이까지 하게 되는 특별한 학습을 하게 될 것입니다. 파트별 분류, 짧은 기출 예시, 실전 문제 적용, 빈출 Collocation까지 엄선하여 모두 자동 암기되도록 설계했으며, 저의 진심을 고스란히 담은 보카 강의까지 함께 합니다.

이 교재와 강의가 여러분을 목표 점수로 이끄는 가장 강력한 엔진이 되리라 확신합니다. 여러분은 혼자가 아닙니다. 여러분의 목표를 향한 여정에 저와 시원스쿨랩 연구진이 함께하고 있다는 것을 느끼셨으면 합니다.

제가 끝까지 응원하겠습니다. 좋은 결과 있기를 바랍니다.

최서아 드림

목차

- 왜 『서아쌤의 토익 비밀과외 기출 VOCA』인가? 006
- 이 책의 구성과 특징 008

WEEK 01   011

- DAY 01 [P1]   사람 사진 빈출 어휘
- DAY 02 [P5,6] 명사 ①
- DAY 03 [P5,6] 명사 ②
- DAY 04 [P5,6] 콜로케이션
- DAY 05 [P7]   기출 동의어 ①

WEEK 01 실전 TEST

WEEK 02   079

- DAY 01 [P1]   사물 사진 빈출 어휘
- DAY 02 [P5,6] 명사 ③
- DAY 03 [P5,6] 명사 ④
- DAY 04 [P5,6] 콜로케이션
- DAY 05 [P7]   기출 동의어 ②

WEEK 02 실전 TEST

WEEK 03   151

- DAY 01 [P2~4] LC가 잘 들리는 어휘 ①
- DAY 02 [P5,6] 동사 ①
- DAY 03 [P5,6] 동사 ②
- DAY 04 [P5,6] 콜로케이션
- DAY 05 [P7]   기출 동의어 ③

WEEK 03 실전 TEST

WEEK 04   223

- DAY 01 [P2~4] LC가 잘 들리는 어휘 ②
- DAY 02 [P5,6] 동사 ③
- DAY 03 [P5,6] 동사 ④
- DAY 04 [P5,6] 콜로케이션
- DAY 05 [P7]   기출 동의어 ④

WEEK 04 실전 TEST

WEEK 05 295

DAY 01	P2~4	LC가 잘 들리는 어휘 ③
DAY 02	P5,6	형용사 ①
DAY 03	P5,6	형용사 ②
DAY 04	P5,6	콜로케이션
DAY 05	P7	독해가 쉬워지는 어휘 ①

WEEK 05 실전 TEST

WEEK 06 369

DAY 01	P3,4	기출 패러프레이징 ①
DAY 02	P5,6	형용사 ③
DAY 03	P5,6	형용사 ④
DAY 04	P5,6	콜로케이션
DAY 05	P7	독해가 쉬워지는 어휘 ②

WEEK 06 실전 TEST

WEEK 07 443

DAY 01	P3,4	기출 패러프레이징 ②
DAY 02	P5,6	부사 ①
DAY 03	P5,6	부사 ②
DAY 04	P5,6	콜로케이션
DAY 05	P7	독해가 쉬워지는 어휘 ③

WEEK 07 실전 TEST

WEEK 08 517

DAY 01	P3,4	기출 패러프레이징 ③
DAY 02	P5,6	전치사
DAY 03	P5,6	다품사
DAY 04	P5,6	다의어
DAY 05	P7	독해가 쉬워지는 어휘 ④

WEEK 08 실전 TEST

무료 온라인 부가자료 (lab.siwonschool.com)

MP3	미국 성우 vs. 영국/호주 성우 골라 듣기
복테영상	무한 회독을 위한 복습 TEST 영상
실전 TEST	Part 5, 6 어휘 기출 변형 문제와 해설
굿노트자료	태블릿으로 편리하게 학습 관리

왜 『서아쌤의 토익 비밀과외 기출 VOCA』인가?

1 스타강사 서아쌤의 초밀착 코칭 인강
- 토익 최신 기출 어휘를 완벽히 꿰뚫고 있는 서아쌤의 정답 어휘 핵심 강의
- 단순 단어 설명이 아닌 토익 기출 기반의 출제 포인트/전략 강의
- 가장 효율적인 토익 어휘 학습 방법 밀착 코칭
- 누구나 쉽게 끝까지 할 수 있도록 동기 부여 팍팍!

2 한 번 시작하면 안 밀리고 끝까지 하게 되는 기출 VOCA
- 주 5일 학습 진도로 구성 ▶ 주말 이용해 밀린 진도 보충 가능
- Weekly Test로 1주일의 학습을 마무리하는 재미와 성취감
- 매주 새로운 학습을 시작하므로 이전 학습이 미흡했더라도 다음 진도를 따라가기 용이

3 지루함 NO! 다양한 방식으로 재미 있게 학습하는 기출 VOCA
- 처음부터 끝까지 똑같은 지겨운 사전 나열식 보카는 이제 그만!
- 매주 전 파트 어휘를 각기 다른 방식으로 학습하기 때문에 재미 UP 암기력 UP
- 유튜브로 제공되는 복습 TEST 영상을 보며 무한 복습 가능

4 점수가 바로 오르는 토익 기출 VOCA

- 매주 토익의 모든 파트를 골고루 학습하도록 구성 ▶ 균형 있는 실력 향상

    `Part 1` 만점에 꼭 필요한 어휘/표현

    `Part 2~4` 모르면 안 들리는 대화/담화 필수 어휘

    `Part 3~4` 정답으로 직행하는 패러프레이징 어휘

    `Part 5~6` 1초 컷 정답 어휘, 콜로케이션

    `Part 7` 최빈출 동의어 문제 정답, 독해가 쉬워지는 어휘

- 읽기 귀찮은 예문 대신 긴장감을 주는 기출변형 문제 제공 ▶ 실전 적응력 수직 상승
- 100% 최신 기출 변형 문제/예문, 최근 어려워진 Part 3, 4, 7 강화 ▶ 고득점 직행
- Part 5, 6 어휘 실전 TEST 및 해설 제공 (온라인)

5 무료 온라인 부가 자료 (lab.siwonschool.com)

- `교재 MP3` 미국 성우 vs. 영국/호주 성우 골라 듣기
- `복테영상` 무한 회독을 위한 복습 TEST 영상
- `실전 TEST` Part 5, 6 어휘 기출 변형 문제와 해설
- `굿노트자료` 태블릿으로 편리하게 학습 관리

이 책의 구성과 특징

점수가 바로 오르는 기출 VOCA

어느 한 파트에만 치우치지 않고 토익 전 파트를 고르게 다룹니다. 각 파트의 고득점에 결정적인 어휘를 빠짐없이 학습해 전 영역의 점수를 고르게 끌어올릴 수 있습니다.

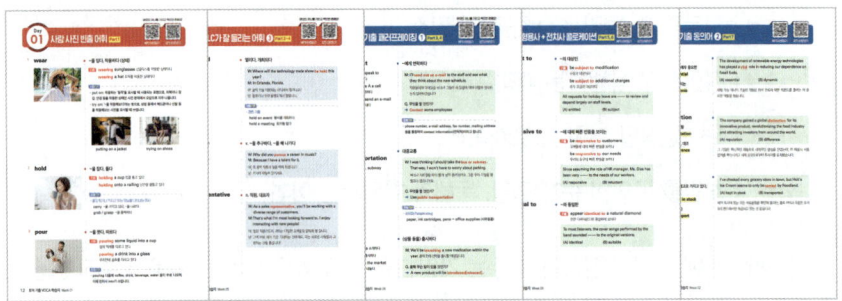

밀리지 않고 꾸준히 학습하도록 주 단위 학습 진도 구성

주 5일 학습 구성으로 밀리지 않고 꾸준히 학습할 수 있으며, 매주 학습을 마칠 때마다 성취감과 완주의 즐거움을 느낄 수 있습니다. 학습 날짜와 진행 상황을 기록하며 끝까지 완주해 보세요.

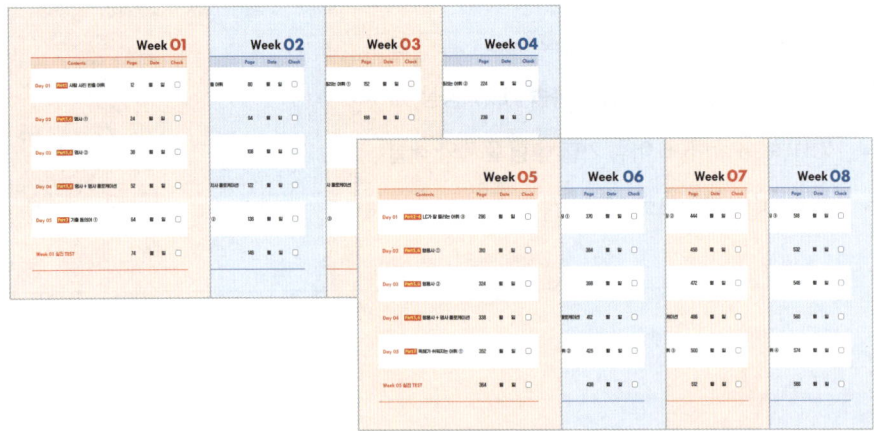

지루한 사전식 암기 NO!
재미있게 학습하는 기출 VOCA

파트별 기출 어휘를 다양한 방식으로 학습해 지루하지 않게, 효과적으로 익힐 수 있습니다. 특히 Part 5 어휘의 경우, 틀에 박힌 예문 대신 기출 변형 실전 문제를 바로 풀어 보며, 정답 어휘가 자연스럽게 머릿속에 각인되도록 구성했습니다.

Daily Quiz와 실전 TEST로
완벽한 복습

Day 학습을 마치면 Daily Quiz로 주요 어휘 암기 여부를 점검하고, Week 학습이 끝나면 실제 토익 시험과 동일한 난이도의 실전 TEST 문제풀이를 통해 실전 응용력을 강화할 수 있습니다.

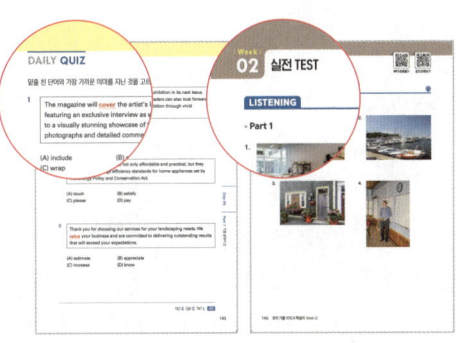

편리한 QR코드 학습

각 Day의 시작 부분에 있는 QR코드를 통해 표제어와 기출표현의 발음을 미국식 vs. 영국/호주식 중에 선택하여 들어볼 수 있습니다. 또한, 서아쌤의 토익 비밀과외 기출 VOCA 유료 인강을 편리하게 수강할 수 있습니다.

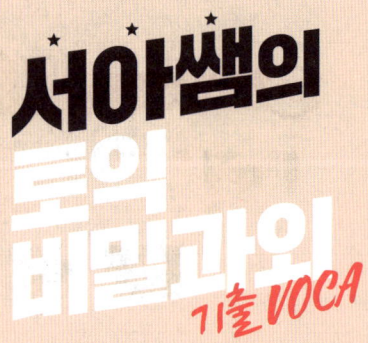

Week 01

Contents		Page	Date	Check
Day 01	**Part 1** 사람 사진 빈출 어휘	12	월 일	☐
Day 02	**Part 5, 6** 명사 ①	24	월 일	☐
Day 03	**Part 5, 6** 명사 ②	38	월 일	☐
Day 04	**Part 5, 6** 명사 + 명사 콜로케이션	52	월 일	☐
Day 05	**Part 7** 기출 동의어 ①	64	월 일	☐
Week 01 실전 TEST		74	월 일	☐

Day 01 사람 사진 빈출 어휘 Part1

MP3 바로듣기

강의 바로보기

QR코드 하나를 가리고 찍으면 편해요!

1 wear

● ~을 입다, 착용하다 (상태)

기출 **wearing** sunglasses 선글라스를 착용한 상태이다
wearing a hat 모자를 착용한 상태이다

만점 TIP
- put on: 착용하는 '동작'을 묘사할 때 사용되는 표현으로, 의복이나 장갑, 안경 등을 착용한 상태인 사진 문제에서 오답으로 자주 나옵니다.
- try on: '~을 착용해보다'라는 뜻으로, 상점 등에서 헤드폰이나 신발 등을 착용해보는 사진을 묘사할 때 쓰입니다.

putting on a jacket

trying on shoes

2 hold

● ~을 잡다, 들다

기출 **holding** a cup 컵을 들고 있다
holding onto a railing 난간을 붙들고 있다

만점 TIP
- 들고 있거나 가지고 있는 모습을 나타내는 동사
  carry ~을 가지고 있다, ~을 나르다
  grab / grasp ~을 움켜쥐다

3 pour

● ~을 붓다, 따르다

기출 **pouring** some liquid into a cup
컵에 액체를 따르고 있다
pouring a drink into a glass
유리잔에 음료를 따르고 있다

만점 TIP
- pouring 다음에 coffee, drink, beverage, water 등이 주로 나오며, 이때 전치사 into가 쓰입니다.

4 leaning against/over/on

- ~에 기대다, 몸을 기울이다

  기출 **leaning against** a wall 벽에 기대어 있다
  leaning over a railing 난간 쪽으로 몸을 기울이고 있다
  leaning on his elbow 팔꿈치에 기대어 있다

  만점 TIP
  - 기대고 있는 모습을 묘사할 때 동사 rest(기대다, 받치다)를 쓰는 정답도 종종 출제됩니다.
    resting against a railing 난간에 기대어 있다

5 kneel

- 무릎을 꿇다

  기출 **kneeling** (down) on the floor
  바닥에 무릎을 꿇고 있다

  만점 TIP
  - crouch: 몸을 웅크리고 있는 모습을 묘사할 때 쓰이며, 최근 시험에 정답으로 등장하였습니다.

6 push

- ~을 밀다

  기출 **pushing** a wheelbarrow 외바퀴 손수레를 밀고 있다
  pushing a cart 카트를 밀고 있다

  만점 TIP
  - pull: 여행가방을 끌고 가는 모습을 묘사할 때는 동사 pull(~을 끌다)을 써서 pulling a suitcase라고 표현합니다.

7 wait

● 기다리다

기출 waiting in line 줄 서서 기다리고 있다
waiting for a train 기차를 기다리고 있다

만점 TIP
- waiting in line이 압도적으로 자주 출제되며, 기차역이나 공항 등에서 사람들이 대기하는 모습을 묘사할 때 waiting area(대기실)도 종종 등장합니다.

8 examine

● ~을 자세히 들여다보다

기출 examining some clothing
옷을 자세히 들여다보고 있다

examining a document
문서를 자세히 들여다보고 있다

만점 TIP
- 자세히 들여다보는 모습을 묘사하는 표현
  inspecting an engine 엔진을 들여다보고 있다
  studying a drawing 그림을 들여다보고 있다

9 wipe

● ~(의 표면)을 닦다

기출 wiping a countertop 카운터 윗면을 닦고 있다
wiping the table 테이블을 닦고 있다

만점 TIP
- 닦는 동작을 묘사하는 표현
  washing a window 창을 닦고 있다
  cleaning a door 문을 닦고 있다
  clearing off a windshield 자동차 앞유리를 닦아내고 있다
  polishing the floor 바닥에 윤을 내고 있다

10 face

- ~을 향하다

  기출 **facing** each other 서로 마주보고 있다
  facing a shelving unit 선반 쪽을 향해 있다

  만점 TIP
  - facing away from each other는 서로 등지고 있는 모습을 묘사합니다.

11 bend

- 몸을 구부리다

  기출 **bending** over a table 테이블 위로 몸을 구부리고 있다
  bending down 아래쪽으로 몸을 구부리고 있다

  만점 TIP
  - 매우 자주 출제되는 표현이므로 꼭 알아 두세요.

12 gather

- 모이다, ~을 모으다

  기출 **have gathered** in a circle 원형으로 모여 있다
  be gathered around a desk 책상 주위에 모여 있다

  만점 TIP
  - 자동사(모이다), 타동사(~을 모으다) 둘 다 쓰이기 때문에 능동태인 have gathered, 수동태인 be gathered 두 가지 형태 모두 잘 나옵니다.

13 be seated

- 착석하다, 앉아 있다

  기출 **be seated** in an outdoor dining area
  야외 식사 구역에 앉아 있다

  be seated across from one another
  서로 마주 보고 앉아 있다

  만점 TIP
  - 앉아 있는 모습을 묘사할 때 동사 sit(앉다)를 쓰는 정답도 종종 출제됩니다.

    sitting on a bench 벤치에 앉아 있다

14 purchase

● ~을 구매하다

기출 **purchasing** some groceries 식료품을 구매하고 있다
purchasing some plants 식물을 구매하고 있다

만점 TIP
• 물건을 구매하고 있는 모습의 사진에서 paying for some items, paying for one's purchase, making a payment 등도 정답으로 등장합니다.

15 place

● ~을 (…에) 놓다, ~을 (…에) 위치시키다

기출 **placing** an item on a shelf 선반에 물건을 놓고 있다
placing a box on a cart 수레에 상자를 놓고 있다

만점 TIP
• 동사 put도 같은 의미로 쓰입니다.
putting an item into a basket 바구니 안에 물건을 넣고 있다

16 load

● ~을 싣다, ~에 싣다

기출 **loading** some items into a vehicle
차량에 물건들을 싣고 있다

loading a cart with boxes
수레에 상자를 싣고 있다

만점 TIP
• 짐을 내리는 동작은 동사 unload를 써서 unloading materials from a vehicle(차량에서 물건들을 내리고 있다)처럼 표현합니다.

17 distribute

● ~을 나눠주다, 배부하다

기출 **distributing** papers 서류를 나눠주고 있다

만점 TIP
• hand out은 distribute와 같은 뜻으로 쓰입니다.
handing out brochures 브로슈어를 나눠주고 있다
• 동사 hand(~을 건네다)를 함께 알아 두세요.
handing an item to a customer 손님에게 물건을 건네고 있다

18 look in(to)

- **~을 들여다보다**

  기출 **looking in** a bag 가방 안을 들여다보고 있다
  looking into a display case
  진열장 안을 들여다보고 있다

  만점 TIP
  - 동사 look(보다)은 무엇을 보는 동작을 나타내며, 뒤에 주로 「전치사 + 보고 있는 대상」이 옵니다.
    looking at a magazine 잡지를 보고 있다
    looking out a window 창밖을 보고 있다

19 trim

- **~(나뭇가지 등)을 다듬다**

  기출 **trimming** some bushes 관목을 다듬고 있다
  trimming a tree 나무를 다듬고 있다

  만점 TIP
  - 나무가 등장하는 사진에서 A tree is being trimmed.가 오답으로 잘 나옵니다.
  - 최근 시험에서는 A bush is being trimmed.가 정답으로 나온 적 있습니다.

20 climb

- **~을 오르다**

  기출 **climbing** a ladder 사다리를 오르다
  climbing some stairs 계단을 오르다

  만점 TIP
  - 계단 사진에 잘 나오는 표현
    steps = stairs = staircase 계단
    going up a staircase 계단을 올라가고 있다
    going down some stairs 계단을 내려가고 있다

21 board

● ~을 타다, ~에 오르다

기출 **boarding** an airplane 비행기에 오르고 있다
　　　boarding a train 기차에 오르고 있다

만점 TIP
• getting into a car(차에 타다), getting on a boat(보트에 오르다)도 함께 알아 두세요.

22 sweep

● ~을 (긴 빗자루로) 쓸다

기출 **sweeping** a walkway 보도를 쓸고 있다
　　　sweeping the floor 바닥을 쓸고 있다

만점 TIP
• 대걸레로 바닥을 닦는 동작은 동사 mop을 써서 표현합니다.
　mopping the floor 대걸레로 바닥을 닦고 있다

23 prepare

● ~을 준비하다

기출 **preparing** some food 음식을 준비하고 있다

만점 TIP
• 요리하는 여러 가지 모습(cooking food, cutting vegetables 등)을 preparing some food라고 묘사하는 정답이 종종 나옵니다.

24 step

● 발을 내딛다

기출 **stepping** onto a dock 부두에 발을 내딛고 있다
　　　stepping down from a boat 보트에서 내리고 있다

만점 TIP
• 발을 내딛어 올라설 때는 stepping onto, 발을 떼서 내릴 때는 stepping off, stepping down from의 표현을 씁니다.

25 enter

~에 들어가다

기출 **entering** a building 건물로 들어가고 있다

26 stroll

천천히 거닐다

기출 **strolling** along a path 오솔길을 따라 걷고 있다
strolling side by side 나란히 걷고 있다

> **만점 TIP**
> • 걷고 있는 동작과 관련하여 walking along(~을 따라 걷고 있다), walking toward(~쪽으로 걷고 있다) 등의 표현도 자주 출제됩니다.

27 adjust

(장치 등을) 조정하다, 조절하다, 맞추다

기출 **adjusting** some equipment
장치를 조정하고 있다

adjusting the window shade
창문 가리개를 조정하고 있다

adjusting a camera 카메라를 조정하고 있다

28 arrange

~을 정렬하다, 정리하다

기출 **arranging** products on a shelf
선반 위에 제품들을 정리하고 있다

> **만점 TIP**
> • 상점 진열대의 물건들을 정리하고 있는 모습의 사진이 자주 출제되는데, 이때 물건들을 products, materials, items, merchandise, goods 등으로 지칭하며, 모두 시험에 자주 출제됩니다.

29 lift

● ~을 들어올리다

기출 **lifting** a box 상자를 들어올리고 있다
lifting some furniture 가구를 들어올리고 있다

만점 TIP
• 물건을 줍거나 주워드는 동작을 묘사할 때는 picking up을 씁니다.

30 rest

● 휴식을 취하다(= relax)

기출 **resting** on the steps 계단 위에서 쉬고 있다

만점 TIP
• rest는 '~을 …에 기대게 하다, ~을 …에 두다'라는 뜻으로도 출제됩니다.
resting arms on a counter 팔을 카운터에 기대고 있다

31 cross

● ~을 건너다

기출 **crossing** the street 길을 건너고 있다

만점 TIP
• 길을 건너는 모습을 묘사할 때 길에 있는 사람을 pedestrian이라고 합니다. 자주 나오는 명사이니 꼭 알아 두세요.

32 tie

● ~을 묶다, 매다

기출 **tying** his shoelaces 신발끈을 매는 중이다
tying an apron 앞치마를 매는 중이다

33 reach

- 손을 뻗다

  기출 **reaching** for a book 책에 손을 뻗고 있다

  reaching into a drawer 서랍 안으로 손을 뻗고 있다

34 point at/to

- ~을 가리키다

  기출 **pointing at** a screen 화면을 가리키다

  pointing to a map 지도를 가리키다

  만점 TIP
  - 가리키는 대상 앞에 전치사 at 또는 to를 쓰는데, 둘 사이에 의미상 차이는 없습니다.

35 dine

- 식사하다

  기출 **dining** at a restaurant 식당에서 식사 중이다

  만점 TIP
  - '식사하다'는 동작을 having a meal, eating 등으로 표현할 수 있습니다.
  - 마시는 동작을 묘사할 때 drinking 외에 sipping(조금씩 마시다)도 자주 출제됩니다.
  - '식사하는 사람'을 diner라고 합니다.

36 remove

- ~을 꺼내다, 빼다

  기출 **removing** an item from a shelf
  선반에서 물건을 꺼내고 있다

  removing mail from a mailbox
  우편함에서 우편물을 꺼내고 있다

  만점 TIP
  - 옷이나 모자, 안경 등을 벗는 동작을 묘사할 때도 동사 remove를 씁니다.
    removing a hat 모자를 벗는 중이다

37 stand

- 서 있다

  기출 **standing** on a platform 플랫폼에 서 있다

  만점 TIP
  - 인물이 서 있는 위치를 나타내는 전치사구를 잘 들어야 합니다.
    next to a chair 의자 옆에   behind a counter 카운터 뒤에
    near a building 건물 근처에   in front of a desk 책상 앞에

38 pose

- 포즈를 취하다

  기출 **posing** for a photo
  사진을 찍기 위해 포즈를 취하고 있다

  만점 TIP
  - 이 모습을 '사진 찍히고 있다'라고 표현할 수도 있겠죠.
    Some women are being photographed by a man.
    남자가 여자들의 사진을 찍고 있다.

39 work

- 작업하다

  기출 **working** on a machine 기계로 작업하고 있다
       working behind a counter
       카운터 뒤에서 작업하고 있다
       working in a garden 정원에서 작업하고 있다

  만점 TIP
  - 기계를 만지는 모습, 컴퓨터로 일하는 모습, 공사장이나 정원 등에서 일하는 모습 등을 모두 work(작업하다)로 표현할 수 있습니다.

40 pack

- 짐을 싸다, 가방을 꾸리다

  기출 **packing** a suitcase 여행가방을 싸고 있다
       packing merchandise into boxes
       물건을 상자에 포장하고 있다

  만점 TIP
  - '짐을 풀다'는 동사 unpack을 써서 표현합니다.

DAILY QUIZ

🎧 음원을 듣고 사진을 바르게 묘사한 문장을 골라보세요.

1
(A)　　(B)

2

(A)　　(B)

3

(A)　　(B)

4

(A)　　(B)

5

(A)　　(B)

6

(A)　　(B)

정답 1 (B) 2 (B) 3 (A) 4 (B) 5 (B) 6 (A)

Day 02 명사 ❶ Part 5, 6

 MP3 바로듣기    강의 바로보기

---

1 **delivery** ● 배송, 배달

deliver v. 배송하다, 배달하다

[기출] **allow three days for delivery**
배송에 3일의 여유를 주다

the launch of a unique delivery service
특별한 배송 서비스의 출시

When ordering by phone or through our app, please allow 30 to 45 minutes for ------- of your pizza.
(A) delivery   (B) method

---

2 **equipment** ● 장비, 기기

equip v. 장비를 갖추다
equipped a. (장비를) 갖춘, 장착된(with)

[기출] **laboratory safety equipment**
실험실 안전 장비

heavy earthmoving equipment
토목 중장비

Assembly line workers at AMJ Manufacturing are trained to use safety ------- in the factory.
(A) equipment   (B) treatment

---

3 **resource** ● 자원, 재원

resourceful a. 자원이 풍부한, 재치있는

[기출] **an invaluable resource for**
~에게 매우 소중한 자원

Taco Queen Inc. supplies all the ------- that franchise owners need to set up a restaurant.
(A) descriptions   (B) resources

4 addition

add v. 추가하다, (말을) 덧붙이다
additional a. 추가적인, 여분의
additionally ad. 게다가

• 추가 (인원), 추가물

기출 a valuable addition to
~에게 소중한 충원 인력

a welcome addition to the collection
소장품에 대한 반가운 추가물

> The ------- of customer reviews to business Web sites can help boost a company's reputation.
>
> (A) comment　　　　(B) addition

5 applicant

• 지원자, 신청자

기출 Most applicants possess ~.
대부분의 지원자들은 ~을 가지고 있다.

business loan applicants
사업 대출 신청자들

> Most ------- have at least three years of experience in the fashion industry.
>
> (A) consumers　　　　(B) applicants

6 requirement

require v. 요구하다, 필요로 하다

• 요구 조건, 자격요건, 필요

기출 a requirement for the position
그 직책의 요구 조건

meet the requirements for
~에 대한 자격요건에 부합하다

> Knowledge of modern graphic design software is a ------- for the online content editor position.
>
> (A) requirement　　　　(B) replacement

7 candidate

● 지원자, 후보자

기출 qualified **candidates** from around the world
전 세계에서 모인 훌륭한 지원자들

external **candidates**
외부 지원자들

> Last summer, numerous highly promising ------- applied for the intern program at our company.
>
> (A) supporters   (B) candidates

8 employment

employ v. 고용하다
employee n. 직원

● 채용, 일자리, 취업

기출 recent inquiry about **employment** with
~에서 진행하는 채용에 대한 최근 문의

currently look for **employment**
현재 일자리를 찾는 중이다

> Margaret Raines recently moved to Los Angeles and is actively seeking ------- in the city.
>
> (A) employment   (B) registration

9 approval

approve v. 승인하다

● 승인

기출 final **approval** from
~로부터의 최종 승인

receive **approval** to hire new employees
신입직원들을 고용하도록 승인을 받다

> Formal ------- from the accounting department is necessary before employees may use a corporate credit card.
>
> (A) approval   (B) decision

10 productivity

produce v. 생산하다
productive a. 생산적인

• 생산성

기출 increase employee **productivity**
직원 생산성을 높이다

improve the designer's **productivity**
디자이너의 생산성을 향상시키다

Since installing chat programs on the office computers, Ryder Corporation has seen a worrying decrease in staff -------.
(A) tendency (B) productivity

11 proposal

• 제안(서)

기출 write a business **proposal**
사업 제안서를 작성하다

detailed **proposal**
상세한 제안서

Mr. Lowe's ------- for an expansion of the city library was accepted by the city's planning department.
(A) proposal (B) approval

12 facility

• 시설(물)

기출 sign up for a guided tour of the **facility**
가이드가 안내하는 시설 견학을 신청하다

be welcome to use company **facilities**
회사 시설물을 이용하는 것을 환영하다

In addition to around 250 stores, Premier Mall houses a cinema and several other -------.
(A) facilities (B) conventions

Week 01   27

13 **payment**

pay v. 지불하다

● 지불(금)

기출 avoid delays in **payment**
지불 연체를 피하다

payment of the rent for
~에 대한 임대료의 지불

------- of the security deposit should be made when checking in to your room at the Portman Hotel.

(A) Renovation (B) Payment

14 **opportunity**

● 기회

기출 have the **opportunity** to do
~할 기회를 가지다

a career **opportunity**
채용 기회

Don't miss this **opportunity**.
이 기회를 놓치지 마십시오.

After being enrolled in the advanced marketing workshop, Mike thanked his supervisor for the ------- to broaden his skill set.

(A) event (B) opportunity

15 **procedure**

proceed v. 진행하다, 나아가다

● 절차, 과정

기출 follow the standard **procedures**
표준 절차를 따르다

The following **procedures** are to do ~.
다음의 과정들은 ~하기 위한 것이다.

All kitchen staff must follow the proper ------- when preparing restaurant orders.

(A) procedures (B) qualifications

16 effort
노력, 수고, 시도

effortlessly ad. 쉽게, 힘들이지 않고

기출 in an **effort** to do
~하려는 노력의 일환으로

ongoing **effort**
계속되는 수고

> In an ------- to reduce operating expenses, we are changing our current plastic packaging to more affordable paper boxes.
>
> (A) effort　　　　　(B) account

17 instruction
안내, 설명(서), 지시

instruct v. 알려 주다, 지시하다

기출 provide step-by-step installation **instructions**
단계적인 설치 안내를 제공하다

find detailed **instructions** on
~에 대한 상세한 설명서를 찾다

> Before using the scientific calculator, please read the detailed ------- printed on the back of the box.
>
> (A) qualifications　　　(B) instructions

18 maintenance
유지(보수)

maintain v. 유지하다, 관리하다

기출 undergo a routine[regular] **maintenance**
정기적인 유지보수를 받다

negotiate a contract for **maintenance**
유지보수 계약을 협상하다

> Triton Engineering agreed to a five-year contract for ------- of the elevators in the Apex One office building.
>
> (A) maintenance　　　(B) application

19 promotion

● 승진, 홍보 (행사), 촉진

기출 offer a **promotion**
승진을 제안하다

This **promotion** ends on May 31.
이 홍보 행사는 5월 31일에 끝난다.

Bramble Bistro is running a ------- that allows its diners to order a free dessert with any main course dish.
(A) destination　　(B) promotion

20 merchandise

● 상품

기출 purchase discounted **merchandise**
할인된 상품을 구매하다

merchandise displayed on our Web site
저희 웹 사이트에 전시된 상품

Most ------- displayed near the store entrance is discounted as part of our Winter Sale.
(A) merchandise　　(B) retails

만점 TIP
• 명사 merchandise는 셀 수 없는 명사로 단수 동사와 함께 사용된다.

21 registration

register v. 등록하다

● 등록

기출 advanced **registration**
사전 등록

registration process
등록 과정

If you join our gym during the advanced ------- period, you will receive a 25 percent discount on the monthly membership fee.
(A) organization　　(B) registration

22 **advancement**

advanced a. 상급의, 진보한, 첨단의

advance n. 전진, 진보
v. 전진하다, 진보하다

● 승진, 발전, 향상

기출 **advancement** to management positions
관리직으로의 승진

the widespread **advancement** in
~ 부문의 광범위한 발전

> The HR manager has compiled a list of six employees who would be suitable for ------- to supervisor roles.
>
> (A) advancement (B) transmitting

23 **responsibility**

responsible a. 책임이 있는

● 책임, 직무, 담당 업무

기출 It is A's **responsibility** to do ~.
~하는 것은 A의 책임이다.

the description of your new **responsibilities**
귀하의 새 직무에 대한 설명

> It is each passenger's ------- to secure their personal belongings when leaving the tour bus.
>
> (A) permission (B) responsibility

24 **replacement**

replace v. 교체하다, 대신하다

● 교환(품), 교체, 후임

기출 request a refund or **replacement**
환불이나 교환을 요청하다

train one's **replacement**
후임을 교육시키다

> Within the one-year warranty period, customers may request a refund or ------- for any Tarsus laptop computer.
>
> (A) receipt (B) replacement

25 **assistance**

assistant n. 조수, 보조

● 지원, 도움

기출 give financial **assistance** to
~에게 재정적 지원을 하다

Our organization provides valuable financial ------- to a wide range of start-up businesses.
(A) assistance　　　(B) association

26 **agreement**

agree v. 동의하다
agreeably ad. 흔쾌히, 기분 좋게

● 계약, 합의, 동의

기출 negotiate a long-term **agreement** with
~와 장기 계약을 협상하다

Ferny Fruit Farm has negotiated mutually beneficial ------- with several shipping companies.
(A) agreements　　　(B) effects

27 **period**

periodic a. 정기적인
periodically ad. 정기적으로

● 기간, 시기

기출 during the promotional **period** 판촉활동 기간 동안
for a **period** of one year 1년의 기간 동안

The financial audit of Herdmont Investment will be conducted over a ------- of three weeks.
(A) period　　　(B) session

28 **identification**

identify v. 찾아내다, 확인하다
identifiable a. 알아볼 수 있는

● 신분증

기출 a valid form of **identification**
유효한 신분증

Make sure one's **identification** is visible.
~의 신분증이 확실히 보이도록 해주십시오.

Attendees are required to present valid photo ------- to claim their tickets at the box office.
(A) identification　　　(B) specification

29 property
재산, 대지

- **기출** other company **property**
  그 밖의 회사 재산

  purchase some **property**
  대지를 약간 매입하다

  > Laptops, flash drives, and other company ------- must be returned when employees leave the company.
  > (A) material (B) property

  만점 TIP
  • 명사 property에는 '특성, 속성'의 의미도 있지만 토익에서는 이 의미로 거의 출제되지 않는다.

30 advice
충고, 조언

advise v. 충고하다, 조언하다

- **기출** accurate and timely **advice**
  정확하고 시기적절한 충고

  hear specific **advice** from
  ~로부터 구체적인 조언을 듣다

  > The Greenacre Landscapers Convention gives attendees a chance to hear expert -------.
  > (A) case (B) advice

31 preference
선호(하는 것), 취향

prefer v. 선호하다
preferable a. 더 좋은
preferred a. 선호하는

- **기출** an increasing **preference** for online shopping
  온라인 쇼핑에 대한 증가하는 선호

  indicate one's food **preference**
  ~의 음식 취향을 표시하다

  > Video game players aged between 15 and 25 are displaying a rising ------- for mobile gaming.
  > (A) amount (B) preference

Week 01 33

32 expertise

expert n. 전문가
a. 전문적인

- 전문 지식, 전문 기술

  기출 require a great deal of mechanical **expertise**
  많은 기계적인 전문 지식을 요구하다

  have the technical **expertise**
  기술적 전문 지식을 지니다

  > Mr. Reynolds admitted that he does not have the management ------- to supervise the new branch office.
  > (A) expense   (B) expertise

33 condition

conditional a. 조건부의

- 상태, 조건

  기출 in excellent **condition**
  훌륭한 상태로

  in its original **condition**
  원래와 같은 상태로

  > All items sold through our online auction are in nearly-new ------- and come with a 30-day money back guarantee.
  > (A) location   (B) condition

34 option

optional a. 선택적인

- 선택지, 선택(사항)

  기출 have an array of **options** to choose from
  ~에서 선택할 수 있는 다수의 선택지가 있다

  provide A with several **options** for
  ~에 대한 몇 가지 선택사항들을 A에게 제공하다

  > The east coast of the island provides tourists with numerous ------- for shopping and sightseeing.
  > (A) receptions   (B) options

35 **inquiry**

inquire v. 묻다

- 문의, 질의

  기출 address the customer **inquiries**
  고객 문의를 해결하다

  I am responding to one's **inquiries** about ~.
  저는 ~에 대한 문의에 답변드리고 있습니다.

  > Because we want to provide excellent customer service, all ------- must be handled in a prompt manner.
  >
  > (A) inquiries　　　(B) positions

36 **statement**

state v. 말하다, 진술하다, 명시하다

- 성명, 진술, 명세서

  기출 in a **statement** given yesterday
  어제 주어진 성명에서

  > In a ------- released this morning, the CEO of Graxley Inc. outlined the firm's national recruitment program.
  >
  > (A) performance　　　(B) statement

37 **suggestion**

suggest v. 제안하다, 암시하다

- 제안(사항), 제시, 암시

  기출 collect **suggestions** from
  ~로부터의 제안사항들을 취합하다

  suggestion to improve the service
  서비스를 향상시키자는 제안사항

  > The council has posted an online poll to gather ------- on the best use for the land opposite Skyway Stadium.
  >
  > (A) suggestions　　　(B) attendees

38 permission

permit n. 허가증
permissive a. 허용하는, 관대한

● 허가, 승인

기출 obtain one's **permission**
~의 허가를 받다

without **permission** from
~로부터의 승인 없이

> All workers must obtain the manager's ------- before taking an extended lunch break.
> (A) admission   (B) permission

만점 TIP
• 명사 permission은 불가산명사, 명사 permit은 가산명사이다.

39 cooperation

cooperate v. 협력하다
cooperative a. 협력하는
cooperatively ad. 협조적으로

● 협조, 협력

기출 appreciate the employees' **cooperation**
직원들의 협조에 감사하다

Thank you for your **cooperation**.
귀하의 협조에 감사드립니다.

> The building manager appreciates the residents' ------- regarding the new cleaning schedule for communal areas.
> (A) cooperation   (B) convention

40 admission

admit v. 인정하다, 허가하다
admissible a. 인정되는, 허용되는

● 입장 (허가), 허가, 시인

기출 receive free **admission** to
~에 대해 무료 입장 허가를 받다

from the date of **admission**
허가일로부터

> Members of the Kennedy Business Institute receive half-price ------- to all seminars.
> (A) admission   (B) exchange

DAILY QUIZ

단어와 그에 알맞은 뜻을 연결해 보세요.

1 facility　　•　　　　　•　(A)　제안(사항), 제시, 암시

2 promotion　•　　　　　•　(B)　승진, 홍보 (행사), 촉진

3 suggestion　•　　　　　•　(C)　시설(물)

빈칸에 알맞은 단어를 선택하세요.

4 a career -------
　　채용 기회

5 give financial ------- to
　　~에게 재정적 지원을 하다

(A) assistance
(B) cooperation
(C) opportunity
(D) period

6 Thank you for your -------.
　　귀하의 협조에 감사드립니다.

앞서 배운 단어들의 뜻을 생각하면서, 다음 문제를 풀어보세요.

7 The escalators in Dixie Shopping Mall will be turned off while they undergo routine -------.

　　(A) preference　　　　　(B) maintenance
　　(C) instruction　　　　　(D) transfer

8 According to company policy, baskets, shopping carts, and other supermarket ------- may not be taken outside the store's parking lot.

　　(A) offers　　　　　　　(B) quality
　　(C) property　　　　　　(D) competitors

정답 1 (C) 2 (B) 3 (A) 4 (C) 5 (A) 6 (B) 7 (B) 8 (C)

Day 03 명사 ❷ Part 5, 6

1 complaint
complain v. 불평하다

● 불만(사항), 불평

기출 frequent complaint
잦은 불만사항

receive increasing complaints
불만사항이 증가하다

> One common ------- library members make is that there are not enough group study rooms.
> (A) opinion (B) complaint

2 enrollment
enroll v. 등록하다

● 등록(자 수)

기출 complete the online enrollment form
온라인 등록 양식을 작성 완료하다

Your enrollment entitles you to A.
귀하의 등록은 귀하에게 A라는 자격을 드립니다.

> Fill out the online ------- form by May 31 if you wish to attend our business management workshop.
> (A) enrollment (B) inventory

3 feedback

● 의견, 피드백

기출 provide feedback to
~에게 의견을 제공하다

receive positive feedback on
~에 대한 긍정적인 피드백을 받다

> Alpha Sportswear has received negative ------- regarding its new television advertisements.
> (A) feedback (B) influence

4 investment

투자(금)

invest v. 투자하다
investor n. 투자자

기출 initial **investment** 초기 투자금

An expert in foreign -------, Arthur Sanders, has become wealthy from purchasing shares in international corporations.
(A) investments   (B) travels

5 source

원천, 출처

기출 the main **source** of inspiration 영감의 주요 원천
the **source** of the data 그 자료의 출처

Singer Richard Prince stated that the birth of his child was the primary ------- of inspiration for his new album.
(A) group   (B) source

6 inspection

점검, 검사

inspect v. 점검하다, 검사하다
inspector n. 검사관

기출 carry out the annual **inspection** of the factory
공장에 대한 연례 점검을 수행하다

The health and hygiene officer will visit our restaurant today to conduct the yearly ------- of our kitchens.
(A) opinion   (B) inspection

7 figure

수치, 인물

기출 This **figure** covers both A and B.
이 수치는 A와 B 둘 다 포함합니다.

update our sales **figures**
우리의 매출 수치를 업데이트하다

Ms. Rondell will report on the company's annual ------- after receiving sales reports from all twenty branches.
(A) measures   (B) figures

8 response

responsive a. 반응하는
respond v. 반응을 보이다, 응답하다

• 반응, 응답

기출 based on the **response** to
~에 대한 반응을 기반으로

in **response** to
~에 응답하여

In ------- to increased demand from consumers, Ryzen Appliances has doubled production of its refrigerators.
(A) contrast   (B) response

9 selection

select v. 선택하다
selective a. 선택적인, 까다로운

• 선택(지)

기출 make a **selection**
선택하다, 선정하다

have a limited **selection** of
~에 대한 제한된 선택지를 가지고 있다

Mangrove Beach Resort offers a ------- of water-based activities, such as jetskiing and snorkeling.
(A) selection   (B) preference

10 variety

various a. 다양한

• 다양성

기출 add greater **variety** to the menu
메뉴에 더 많은 다양성을 추가하다

a wide **variety** of health-care services
매우 다양한 종류의 의료 서비스

The new Funland complex will offer an extensive ------- of entertainment facilities when it opens this summer.
(A) condition   (B) variety

11 invitation

invite v. 초대하다, 요청하다

• 초대(장), 초청

기출 receive an **invitation** to attend
~에 참석하도록 초대를 받다

invitations to the awards banquet
수상 연회에 대한 초청

Ms. Sanchez has been given an ------- to attend the Katrina Velasquez fashion show in Milan next week.
(A) honor　　　　　(B) invitation

12 expansion

expand v. 확장하다

• 확장

기출 **expansion** into overseas markets
해외 시장으로의 확장

to discuss the **expansion** of
~의 확장을 논의하기 위해

Bluefire Games hopes to acquire Taneka Software as part of its ------- into the Asian market.
(A) expansion　　　(B) process

13 appreciation

appreciate v. 감사하다, 이해하다
appreciative a. 감사하는

• 감사, 이해

기출 express one's **appreciation** for
~에 대해 감사를 표하다

in **appreciation** for
~에 감사하여, ~의 답례로

In ------- of his 30 years of service to the company, Primex Inc. presented Mr. Richards with an expensive wristwatch.
(A) response　　　(B) appreciation

Week 01 / Day 03 / Part 5, 6 명사 (2)

14 recognition

recognize v. 인지하다, 인정하다

● 인지(도), 인정

기출 gain national **recognition** for
~로 인해 전국적인 인지도를 얻다

in **recognition** of one's contribution to
~에 대한 헌신을 인정하여

> Ms. Yeats was offered an improved contract in ------- of her outstanding efforts and contributions to our firm.
>
> (A) recognition (B) acceptance

15 ceremony

● 의식, 예식

기출 annual award **ceremony**
연례 시상식

during a **ceremony** at the end of the year
연말 기념식 동안에

> Next month's country music awards ------- will be broadcast nationally on Channel 11.
>
> (A) ceremony (B) product

16 receipt

receive v. 받다, 받아들이다

● 영수증, 수령

기출 turn in **receipts** for reimbursement
환급을 위해 영수증을 제출하다

upon **receipt** of the parcel
소포 수령 즉시

> Sales executives who attended the conference in Manila last week should hand in ------- for reimbursement.
>
> (A) procedures (B) receipts

17 series

- 시리즈, 일련

  기출 annual **series** of musical performances
  연례 음악 공연 시리즈

  sponsor a **series** of public lectures
  일련의 공개 강의를 후원하다

  > Every September, the Richfield Institute hosts a ------- of workshops led by successful business owners.
  > (A) scheme (B) series

18 priority

- 우선순위, 우선 과제

  기출 a top **priority**
  최우선순위

  take **priority** over all other work
  다른 모든 일들보다 우선순위로 두다

  > Nitro Beverages Inc. has made increasing its domestic market share its highest ------- for this year.
  > (A) rate (B) priority

19 supervision

supervise v. 감독하다, 관리하다
supervisor n. 감독관, 상사

- 감독, 관리

  기출 under the **supervision** of Mr. Kane
  케인 씨의 감독 하에

  > Greengro Supermarkets' branch in Allcroft has been under the ------- of Max Hargraves for the past six months.
  > (A) attendance (B) supervision

20 fee

- 요금, 수수료

  기출 charge A a processing **fee** for
  A에게 ~에 대한 처리 요금을 부과하다

  reduce its **fee** for access
  이용권에 대한 수수료를 낮추다

  > The pharmaceutical conference registration ------- covers accommodation and transportation costs.
  > (A) fee   (B) fare

21 competition

competitive a. 경쟁력 있는
compete v. 경쟁하다

- 경쟁, (경연) 대회

  기출 **competition** between businesses
  사업체들 간의 경쟁

  rising **competition** from the overseas education market
  해외 교육 시장에서의 증가하는 경쟁

  > Increasing ------- between mobile game developers has led to a significant improvement in the quality of games.
  > (A) challenge   (B) competition

22 contribution

contribute v. 기부하다, 기여하다, 기고하다
contributing a. 기여하는
contributor n. 기부자, 기여자, 기고가

- 기부(금), 기여, 공헌

  기출 your generous **contributions**
  귀하의 후한 기부

  significant **contributions** to our charity fund
  저희 자선 기금에 대한 의미 있는 기부금

  > The Heritage Trust expressed its gratitude to all individuals who have made valuable ------- to the organization.
  > (A) contributions   (B) evaluations

23 description
- 설명(서)

  기출 a detailed **description** of the position
  그 직책에 대한 상세한 설명

  technical **descriptions**
  기술 설명서

  > Mr. Lane's report includes not only a brief ------- of the technology but a thorough analysis of its benefits.
  > (A) description　　(B) schedule

24 concentration
concentrate v. 집중하다
- 밀도, 밀집, 집중

  기출 boast the largest[highest] **concentration** of
  ~의 높은 밀도를 자랑하다

  > Fifth Avenue is home to the largest ------- of antiques stores in the city.
  > (A) conference　　(B) concentration

25 transportation
transport v. 운송하다
- 교통(편), 운송

  기출 for more information about **transportation**
  교통편에 대한 더 많은 정보를 위해서

  > If you require -------, please view the shuttle bus schedule on the convention Web site.
  > (A) transportation　　(B) lodging

26 transaction
- 거래

  기출 bank **transactions**
  은행 거래

  > All mobile ------- for amounts over $800 must be approved by using the banking app.
  > (A) representatives　　(B) transactions

Week 01　45

27 **intention**

intentional a. 의도적인
intentionally ad. 고의로

- 의도, 의사

  [기출] announce one's **intention** to retire
  은퇴한다는 ~의 의도를 알리다

  have no **intention** of -ing
  ~하려는 의도가 없다

  > During the staff meeting, Mr. Forbes announced his ------- to apply for the Operations Manager position.
  > (A) method (B) intention

28 **advantage**

advantageous a. 이로운, 유리한

- 장점, 유리한 점

  [기출] publicize the **advantages** of the product
  그 상품의 장점을 광고하다

  take **advantage** of
  ~을 이용하다

  > If you would like to take ------- of store discounts, sign up for a Ritz Department Store membership today.
  > (A) advantage (B) merit

29 **destination**

- (여행) 목적지, 도착지

  [기출] premier **destination** for tourism
  관광을 위한 최고의 목적지

  > Located near several major bus routes, Adventure Land's accessibility by public transportation makes it a convenient -------.
  > (A) destination (B) connection

30 task

업무, 직무

기출 handle the **task** of updating the content
컨텐츠를 업데이트하는 업무를 다루다

This **task** is particularly demanding.
이 직무는 특히 힘들다.

Mr. Marlowe has been given the ------- of responding to customer complaints by e-mail.
(A) version　　　　(B) task

31 purpose

purposely ad. 고의로

목적

기출 Do not use it for any other **purpose**.
어떤 다른 목적을 위해 그것을 사용하지 마십시오.

The **purpose** of this report is to do ~.
이 보고서의 목적은 ~하는 것입니다.

The ------- of this inspection is to ensure the factory is operating at full capacity and efficiency.
(A) purpose　　　　(B) indication

32 commitment

committed a. 헌신적인, 전념하는

헌신, 전념

기출 show remarkable **commitment** to
~에 대한 놀랄 만한 헌신을 보여주다

express one's full **commitment** to
~에 대한 완전한 헌신을 표현하다

Ms. Singh has shown an impressive ------- to our company over the past two decades.
(A) commitment　　　　(B) collaboration

33 **difficulty**

difficult a. 어려운, 곤란한

• 어려움, 곤란, 곤경

기출 have **difficulty** -ing
~하는 데 어려움을 겪다

because of several **difficulties** with the new software
새로운 소프트웨어에 대한 여러 어려움 때문에

The music festival has been postponed because of ------- with the online ticketing system.
(A) selections　　　　(B) difficulties

34 **ability**

able a. 능력 있는, 할 수 있는

• 능력

기출 have the **ability** to do
~할 능력을 지니다

the artistic and sporting **abilities** of
~의 예술적 그리고 스포츠 능력

The Fitmate Smartwatch has the ------- to monitor heart rate, breathing rate, and sleep patterns.
(A) decision　　　　(B) ability

35 **transition**

transitional a. 과도기의

• 전환, 이전

기출 make a successful **transition** to
~로의 성공적인 전환을 하다

The **transition** is scheduled to begin next week.
다음 주에 이전이 시작되기로 예정되어 있다.

Chen's Noodle Shop has made a profitable ------- to using a more affordable delivery service.
(A) location　　　　(B) transition

36 occasion

occasional a. 가끔의
occasionally ad. 가끔, 때때로

● 사건, 경우

기출 mark an important **occasion**
중요한 사건을 기념하다

for any **occasion**
어떠한 경우라도

We have been in business for ten years, and to mark this important -------, we will be hosting a party on November 22.
(A) opening   (B) occasion

37 itinerary

● 여행 일정표

기출 a copy of the travel **itinerary**
여행 일정표의 사본

the **itinerary** for your trip
귀하의 여행 일정

The ------- for Ms. Pellberg's sightseeing tour includes visits to several famous museums and galleries.
(A) position   (B) itinerary

38 inventory

● 재고, 물품 목록

기출 deal with excess **inventory**
과도한 재고를 처리하다

inventory management software
물품 목록 관리 소프트웨어

In an effort to sell its surplus -------, Smith's Camping Goods is marking down some prices by up to 50 percent.
(A) inventory   (B) capacity

39 accomplishment
● 성과, 성취

accomplish v. 성취하다, 달성하다
accomplished a. 뛰어난

> **기출** Mr. Smith's many **accomplishments** include ~.
> 스미스 씨의 많은 성과는 ~을 포함한다.

Mayor Pembroke's many ------- include implementing an environmentally friendly monorail system.

(A) capabilities   (B) accomplishments

40 compliance
● 준수

comply v. 준수하다 (with)

> **기출** ensure **compliance** with regulations
> 규정 준수를 보장하다
>
> in **compliance** with standards
> 기준을 준수하여

Many of the manufacturing machines at Rydell Inc. had to be modified in order to be in ------- with safety regulations.

(A) compliance   (B) arrangement

50 서아쌤의 토익 비밀과외 기출 VOCA

DAILY QUIZ

단어와 그에 알맞은 뜻을 연결해 보세요.

1. receipt • • (A) 등록(자 수)
2. competition • • (B) 영수증, 수령
3. enrollment • • (C) 경쟁, (경연) 대회

빈칸에 알맞은 단어를 선택하세요.

4. deal with excess -------
   과도한 재고를 처리하다

5. update our sales -------
   우리의 매출 수치를 업데이트하다

   (A) inventory
   (B) contributions
   (C) figures
   (D) series

6. your generous -------
   귀하의 후한 기부

앞서 배운 단어들의 뜻을 생각하면서, 다음 문제를 풀어보세요.

7. Ms. Grey was presented with a gold watch in ------- of her forty years of service to the company.

   (A) development (B) collaboration
   (C) recognition (D) achievement

8. Michael Akona coordinates wildlife conservation efforts in ------- such as Kenya and Uganda.

   (A) volunteers (B) donations
   (C) destinations (D) initiatives

정답 1 (B) 2 (C) 3 (A) 4 (A) 5 (C) 6 (B) 7 (C) 8 (C)

Day 04 명사 + 명사 콜로케이션 Part 5, 6

* 출제된 「명사 + 명사」 콜로케이션 조합을 빠르게 암기할 수 있도록 관사를 포함하지 않았습니다.

1 product manual ● 제품 설명서

[기출] safety **manual** 안전 설명서
   employee **manual** 직원 안내서

The product ------- includes detailed assembly instructions and diagrams.
(A) receipt   (B) manual

2 budget requirements ● 예산 요건

[기출] quality **requirements** 품질 요건
   age **requirement** 연령 요건

Please check that you fulfill the budget ------- before submitting an application form for the support fund.
(A) requirements   (B) qualities

3 employee productivity ● 직원 생산성

[기출] team **productivity** 팀 생산성
   worker **productivity** 직원 생산성

Since introducing performance-based pay raises last year, Huzzah Technology has seen a dramatic increase in employee -------.
(A) tendency   (B) productivity

4 travel expenses

- 출장 비용

  기출 transportation **expenses** 운송 비용
  living **expenses** 생활비

  The board has agreed to allocate $5,000 per month for travel -------.
  (A) expenses   (B) descriptions

5 building permit

- 건축 허가(증)

  기출 parking **permit** 주차 허가(증)

  After months of preparation, the construction project finally got underway once the city issued the building -------.
  (A) office   (B) permit

6 control system

- 통제 시스템

  기출 ticketing **system** 발권 시스템

  The IT team intends to upgrade the central control ------- at company headquarters.
  (A) places   (B) systems

7 manager position

- 관리자 직책

  기출 assistant **position** 보조 직책
  editor **position** 편집자 직책

  Mr. Jones is the most qualified candidate for the production manager -------, with more than 15 years of experience in the industry.
  (A) control   (B) position

8. assembly process

- 조립 과정

  기출 manufacturing **process** 제조 과정

  > The replacement of our old machines has already increased the efficiency of our assembly ------- by 10 percent.
  >
  > (A) process (B) location

9. operating cost

- 운영비, 운영 비용

  기출 fuel **costs** 연료 비용
  business **costs** 사업 비용
  cost estimates 비용 견적서

  > Due to an increase in operating -------, Bluesky Airlines has decided to suspend some of its Asian routes.
  >
  > (A) systems (B) costs

10. office space

- 사무 공간

  기출 parking **space** 주차 공간
  work **space** 근무 공간

  > Mr. Edwards told the realtor that he requires enough office ------- to accommodate 300 employees.
  >
  > (A) project (B) space

11. population increase

- 인구 증가

  기출 price **increase** 가격 인상
  salary **increase** 급여 인상

  > The population ------- in the urban areas has led to greater demand for public services.
  >
  > (A) statistic (B) increase

12 planning committee

- 기획 위원회

  기출 hiring **committee** 고용 위원회
  search **committee** 조사 위원회

  > The planning ------- will gather on Tuesday to discuss the candidates for the senior management position.
  > (A) schedule (B) committee

13 vacation request

- 휴가 요청

  기출 catering **request** 음식 공급 요청
  customer **request** 고객 요청

  > For all employees at Kaye Department Store, vacation ------- must be approved by the HR department.
  > (A) suggestions (B) requests

14 renewal application

- 갱신 지원서

  기출 employment **application** 고용 지원서
  business **application** 사업 지원서
  loan **application** 대출 신청서

  > Food vendors who wish to participate in the city fair again should submit a renewal ------- for a permit.
  > (A) specification (B) application

15 service charge

- 서비스 요금

  기출 shipping **charge** 배송 요금
  penalty **charge** 벌금 (부과)

  > Stenhouse Furniture adds a higher service ------- to orders delivered outside the city limits.
  > (A) charge (B) supplier

16 improvement project

- 개선 프로젝트

  기출 research **project** 연구 프로젝트
  repair **project** 수리 프로젝트

  Glenfield City Council has secured extensive funding for its urban improvement -------.
  (A) statement (B) project

17 conference registration

- 컨퍼런스 등록

  기출 convention **registration** 총회 등록
  registration form 등록 양식

  Conference ------- will begin on May 4 and continue until the end of the month.
  (A) registration (B) ideal

18 shipment delay

- 운송 지연

  기출 transportation **delay** 교통 지연
  construction **delay** 건축 지연

  A recent sharp rise in the prices of auto parts has resulted in shipment ------- of two weeks or longer.
  (A) items (B) delays

19 management role

- 관리자 역할, 관리 직무

  기출 volunteer **role**
  자원봉사자 역할

  Once he is formally promoted on Thursday, Mr. Riley will take on the management ------- immediately.
  (A) production (B) role

20 privacy policy

- 개인정보 보호정책

  기출 **security** policy
  보안 정책

  insurance policy
  보험 정책

  travel policy
  출장 정책

  > According to the company's privacy -------, customer information is never shared with third parties.
  > (A) policy (B) tasks

21 expiration date

- 만료 일자, 유통 기한

  기출 **publication** date 출간일

  opening date 개장일

  > The expiration ------- is clearly stated on each subscriber's account page on our Web site.
  > (A) date (B) amount

22 shipping contract

- 배송 계약

  기출 **employment** contract
  고용 계약

  maintenance contract
  유지보수 계약

  > Mr. Tyrell has renegotiated the shipping ------- in an effort to lower expenditure.
  > (A) vessels (B) contract

23 training session
- 교육 시간

  기출 information **session**
  설명회

  orientation **session**
  오리엔테이션 시간

  > The HR manager has scheduled four training ------- to ensure all new recruits are fully prepared for their roles.
  >
  > (A) materials   (B) sessions

24 publicity campaign
- 홍보 캠페인

  기출 advertising **campaign**
  광고 캠페인

  marketing **campaign**
  마케팅 캠페인

  > Xcell Digital Solutions has created successful online publicity ------- for clients in a wide range of industries.
  >
  > (A) campaigns   (B) influences

25 working environment
- 근무 환경

  기출 workplace **environment**
  근무지 환경

  work **environment**
  근무 환경

  > To create a more productive working -------, Bitfour Technologies provided all staff with new ergonomic office furniture.
  >
  > (A) environment   (B) position

26 construction site
• 건축 현장

기출 work **site** 근무 현장
plant **site** 공장 현장

Before visitors are permitted to enter the construction -------, they must put on the required safety gear.
(A) site   (B) industry

27 art exhibition
• 미술 전시회

기출 photography **exhibition** 사진 전시회
sculpture **exhibition** 조각품 전시회

At the opening night of the art ------- at Privet Gallery, Lynda Carranza spoke to attendees about her work.
(A) exhibition   (B) guide

28 award ceremony
• 시상식

기출 graduation **ceremony** 졸업식
opening **ceremony** 개장식

This weekend's Young Filmmakers of the Year awards ------- will be held at Seaforth Auditorium.
(A) ceremony   (B) advice

29 customer loyalty
• 고객 충성도

기출 **loyalty** bonus 고객 보상 보너스
loyalty program 고객 보상 프로그램

In order to improve customer -------, Majestic Catering now offers discounts to long-term clients.
(A) loyalty   (B) honesty

30 government restriction

● 정부 규제

기출 budget restriction
예산 규제

size restriction
규모 규제

> Strict government ------- on several rare food items have caused their prices to soar recently.
> (A) authorities (B) restrictions

31 distribution plan

● 분배 계획

기출 distribution area
분배 지역

information distribution
정보 분배

distribution rights
분배 권리

> Mr. Barr is determining the financial needs of the sales, marketing, and HR departments in order to finalize the budget ------- plan.
> (A) distribution (B) assortment

32 safety regulation

● 안전 규정

기출 tax regulation 세금 규정
company regulation 회사 규정
dress regulation 복장 규정

> All staff must adhere to the restaurant's health and safety ------- or face disciplinary action.
> (A) regulations (B) limitations

33 floor renovation

바닥 보수공사

기출 building **renovation** 건물 보수공사
renovation work 보수공사 작업

The floor ------- will take roughly three months and will increase the building's floor space by 15 percent.
(A) agenda   (B) renovation

34 tourist destination

관광지

기출 travel **destination** 여행지
vacation **destination** 휴가지

Carlito Torres organizes food-themed excursions to tourist -------, such as Indonesia and Malaysia.
(A) destinations   (B) ambitions

35 bank transaction

은행 거래

기출 business **transaction** 사업 거래

For certain bank ------- that exceed a certain amount, we ask that customers meet with the bank manager in person.
(A) representatives   (B) transactions

36 processing fee

처리 비용

기출 registration **fee** 등록 비용
service **fee** 서비스 비용

The embassy charges a processing ------- for all passport renewals and replacements.
(A) fee   (B) check

37 delivery receipt

• 배송 영수증

기출 store **receipt** 매장 영수증
sales **receipt** 판매 영수증

Before submitting a delivery -------, be sure to check that all items listed are in good condition.
(A) receipt　　　　　(B) announcement

38 sales figures

• 매출 수치

기출 production **figures** 생산 수치
accounting **figures** 회계 수치

The CEO will announce our annual sales ------- at the year-end banquet on December 29.
(A) measures　　　　(B) figures

39 telecommuting option

• 재택근무 선택권

기출 menu **option** 메뉴 선택권
investment **option** 투자 선택권

Telecommuting ------- provide many employees with the flexibility to work from home or other remote locations.
(A) statements　　　(B) options

40 meal period

• 식사 시간

기출 peak **period** 성수기
warranty **period** 보증 기간

Employees at all Bob's Burgers branches are entitled to a two-hour meal ------- for their lunch.
(A) period　　　　　(B) box

DAILY QUIZ

콜로케이션과 그에 알맞은 뜻을 연결해 보세요.

1 product manual •   • (A) 건축 현장

2 construction site •   • (B) 처리 비용

3 processing fee •   • (C) 제품 설명서

빈칸에 알맞은 단어를 선택하세요.

4 transportation -------
   운송 비용

5 parking -------
   주차 허가(증)

6 building -------
   건물 보수공사

(A) expenses
(B) period
(C) permit
(D) renovation

앞서 배운 콜로케이션들의 뜻을 생각하면서, 다음 문제를 풀어보세요.

7 Customers should check the expiration ------- before consuming any of our dairy products.

   (A) price   (B) amount
   (C) date   (D) bottle

8 Ms. Welling will announce our daily sales ------- after compiling the data from our San Diego office.

   (A) measures   (B) grounds
   (C) instructions   (D) figures

정답 1 (C) 2 (A) 3 (B) 4 (A) 5 (C) 6 (D) 7 (C) 8 (D)

Day 05 기출 동의어 ❶ Part 7

1 back up

❶ 도움을 주다, 지원하다
→ **support**

❷ 복사본을 만들다
→ **copy**

> The results of a recent customer survey **backed up** our decision to expand our Customer Services Department.
>
> (A) copied   (B) supported
>
> 최근의 한 고객 설문조사 결과가 고객서비스부를 확장하기로 한 우리의 결정을 뒷받침해 주었습니다.

2 critical

❶ 매우 중요한
→ **essential, crucial, very important, vital**

❷ 부정적인, 못마땅해하는
→ **negative, disapproving**

❸ 위급한, 심각한
→ **urgent**

> Some **critical** figures regarding last quarter's profits were missing, so you'll need to redo the report.
>
> (A) urgent   (B) essential
>
> 지난 분기의 수익과 관련된 일부 중요한 수치 자료들이 빠져 있었기 때문에 당신은 보고서 작업을 다시 해야 할 것 같습니다.

3 take

❶ (손으로) 잡다
→ **grab, grip**

❷ 필요로 하다, 요구하다
→ **require**

❸ 제거하다
→ **remove**

> The update for our accounting software is enormous, so it **took** five hours to download and install it.
>
> (A) grabbed   (B) required
>
> 우리 회계 소프트웨어의 업데이트가 너무 방대해서, 그것을 다운로드하고 설치하는 데 다섯 시간이 소요되었습니다.

4 release

❶ ~을 풀어주다, 석방하다
→ **set free, let go**

❷ ~을 발표하다, 공개하다
→ **make available, issue**

The company spokesperson <u>released</u> an update on the ongoing project, detailing the latest developments and some challenges that have arisen during the testing phase.

(A) set free　　　(B) made available

회사 대변인은 진행 중인 프로젝트에 대한 최신 소식을 발표했는데, 최근의 개발 사항과 시험 단계에서 발생한 몇 가지 문제점들을 자세히 설명했습니다.

5 feature

❶ 특징, 특성
→ **characteristic**

❷ 특집 기사
→ **a special article, story**

Don't miss the latest issue of our magazine, which includes a special <u>feature</u> on emerging trends in artificial intelligence.

(A) characteristic　　　(B) story

저희 잡지의 최신 호를 놓치지 마세요. 이번 호에는 인공지능의 떠오르는 트렌드에 관한 특별한 특집 기사가 포함되어 있습니다.

6 regarding

❶ ~에 관한
→ **concerning, about**

❷ 존경하는
→ **admiring**

We would like to address any questions or issues you might have <u>regarding</u> your recent purchase.

(A) about　　　(B) admiring

귀하의 최근 구매와 관련하여 갖고 계신 그 어떤 문의사항 혹은 이슈사항들을 처리해 드리고자 합니다.

7 stress

❶ 불안, 염려
→ **anxiety**

❷ 강조
→ **focus, emphasis**

A therapist is coming to the office on Friday to give a presentation about coping with <u>stress</u> in the workplace.

(A) emphasis　　　(B) anxiety

한 치료 전문가가 직장 내에서의 스트레스에 대처하는 일에 관한 발표를 하기 위해 금요일에 사무실로 찾아올 예정입니다.

8 draw

❶ ~을 끌어들이다
→ **attract**

❷ ~을 그리다
→ **sketch**

❸ ~을 뽑다, 골라내다
→ **pick, take out**

> The café is a popular spot for several celebrities, so it also **draws** crowds of fans eager to see their favorite star.
> (A) attracts   (B) sketches

그 카페는 여러 유명 인사들에게 인기 있는 장소이기 때문에, 좋아하는 스타의 모습을 볼 수 있기를 갈망하는 팬들로 구성된 많은 사람들 또한 끌어들입니다.

9 run

❶ 달리다
→ **move**

❷ (업체·서비스 등을) 운영하다
→ **operate, manage**

❸ (기계가) 움직이다, 돌아가다
→ **function, work**

❹ 지속되다
→ **last**

> The local bookstore **runs** a promotion every summer, encouraging readers to explore new genres and authors with incredible discounts and special events.
> (A) moves   (B) operates

지역 서점에서는 매년 여름 프로모션을 진행하여 엄청난 할인과 특별 이벤트를 통해 독자들이 새로운 장르와 작가를 탐색할 수 있도록 장려합니다.

10 significant

❶ 중요한, 뜻깊은
→ **important, meaningful**

❷ 상당한
→ **large enough, enormous**

> The golf tournament is one of the most **significant** fundraisers for the charity because some influential donors come to participate.
> (A) important   (B) enormous

그 골프 대회는 몇몇 영향력 있는 기부자들이 참가하러 오기 때문에 그 자선단체에 있어 가장 중요한 모금 행사 중 하나입니다.

11 rest

❶ 나머지
→ **remainder**

❷ 휴식
→ **break**

> Keep in mind, the <u>rest</u> of the event's budget will be donated to Belle Valley Children's Hospital.
>
> (A) remainder   (B) break

행사 예산의 나머지는 벨 밸리 아동 병원에 기부된다는 점을 기억해 주시기 바랍니다.

12 current

❶ 동시대의, 현재의
→ **contemporary, present**

❷ 습관적인, 관습의
→ **customary**

❸ 흐름
→ **moving, flow**

> *Central Art* magazine has been a leading source of information on <u>current</u> artists and styles for the past fifteen years.
>
> (A) contemporary   (B) customary

<센트럴 아트> 잡지는 지난 15년 동안 당대의 미술가들과 화풍에 관한 정보를 제공하는 앞서가는 매체였습니다.

13 level

❶ 정도, 양
→ **degree, amount**

❷ 층
→ **story, floor**

❸ 지위
→ **position, rank**

> The latest customer surveys indicate a high <u>level</u> of satisfaction with our current product offerings and overall customer service.
>
> (A) degree   (B) position

최근의 고객 설문조사 결과는 현재의 저희 제품 제공과 전반적인 고객 서비스에 대해 높은 수준의 만족도를 나타냅니다.

14 fair

❶ 공정한
→ **just**, **honest**

❷ 타당한, 합리적인
→ **reasonable**

❸ 날씨가 맑은
→ **fine**, **clear**

> We offer high-quality tour services at a **fair** rate. Contact our agency today via e-mail or phone, and we will get back to you promptly.
>
> (A) just   (B) reasonable

저희는 고품질의 여행 서비스를 합리적인 요금에 제공합니다. 저희 대리점에 오늘 이메일이나 전화로 연락 주시면, 신속히 고객님께 다시 연락 드리겠습니다.

15 handle

❶ 만지다
→ **touch**

❷ 다루다, 처리하다
→ **manage**

> If we don't hire more servers, the restaurant staff will not be able to **handle** the Sunday lunch rush.
>
> (A) touch   (B) manage

우리가 더 많은 종업원들을 고용하지 않는다면, 레스토랑 직원들은 일요일에 몰려드는 점심 식사 손님들을 처리할 수 없을 것입니다.

16 entry

❶ 출품(물)
→ **submission to a contest**

❷ 입구
→ **doorway**

❸ 입력
→ **input**

> It is my pleasure to let you know that your **entry**, "Dusk at the Lake", is a finalist for the prestigious photography award this year.
>
> (A) submission to a contest   (B) doorway

귀하의 출품작인 <호수의 황혼>이 올해 권위 있는 사진 상 최종 후보에 올랐음을 알려드리게 되어 기쁩니다.

17 refer

❶ 살피다, 참조하다
→ **check**

❷ 보내다
→ **direct**

Please **refer** any questions regarding your payment to Mr. Keller, the company accountant.
(A) check　　　　(B) direct

귀하의 지불 금액과 관련된 모든 질문은 회사의 회계 담당자이신 켈러 씨께 전달하시기 바랍니다.

18 go with

❶ 동행하다
→ **accompany**

❷ 선택하다
→ **select**

The hotel has decided to **go with** another contractor to do the renovations because the previous contractor's bid was significantly higher than expected.
(A) accompany　　　(B) select

그 호텔은 기존 계약업체의 입찰액이 예상보다 상당히 높았기 때문에, 개조 공사를 하기 위해 다른 계약업체를 선택하기로 결정했습니다.

19 good

❶ 좋은
→ **high quality**

❷ 유효한
→ **valid**

The discount code "DC1468" is **good** through July for a 10% discount on any online order.
(A) high quality　　(B) valid

할인 코드 "DC1468"은 어떠한 온라인 주문품에 대해서도 10퍼센트의 할인을 받을 수 있으며 7월 한 달 내내 유효합니다.

20 dimension

❶ 차원, 특징
→ **characteristic**, **aspect**, **feature**

❷ 크기, 규모
→ **proportion**, **measurement**, **size**

> The advent of virtual reality technology has added another **dimension** to the gaming experience, immersing players in realistic and interactive virtual worlds.
>
> (A) aspect　　　　　(B) proportion

가상 현실 기술의 출현으로 게임 경험에 또 다른 차원이 추가되어 현실적이고 상호 작용하는 가상 세계에 플레이어를 몰입시킵니다.

21 maintain

❶ 유지보수하다
→ **repair**, **service**

❷ 유지하다
→ **keep**

> Due to customer complaints about the store being too hot, the temperature will now be **maintained** at 19°C rather than 22°C.
>
> (A) repaired　　　　(B) kept

매장이 너무 더운 것에 대한 고객들의 불만으로 인해, 실내 온도는 이제 섭씨 22도가 아닌 19도로 유지될 것입니다.

22 register

❶ 등록하다
→ **enroll**

❷ 기록하다
→ **record**

> Check your pay statement to make sure the attendance software accurately **registered** your overtime hours for last month.
>
> (A) enrolled　　　　(B) recorded

출근 확인 소프트웨어가 지난달에 대한 여러분의 초과 근무 시간을 정확히 기록했는지 확실히 할 수 있도록 여러분의 급여 명세서를 확인해 보시기 바랍니다.

23 observe

❶ 관찰하다
→ **monitor**, **watch**

❷ (법 등을) 준수하다, 지키다
→ **comply with**

> To prevent accidents, it is crucial to **observe** safety regulations when using power tools.
>
> (A) monitor　　　　(B) comply with

사고를 예방하기 위해서는 전동 공구를 사용할 때 안전 규정을 준수하는 것이 중요합니다.

24 reflect

❶ 깊이 생각하다, 숙고하다
→ **consider**

❷ 보여주다, 나타내다
→ **represent, show**

I have e-mailed you an invoice for your first month of classes, which **reflects** both the instruction fee and the cost of your equipment.

(A) represents (B) considers

귀하의 첫 달 수강에 대한 청구서를 메일로 보내 드렸으며, 그것에는 강의료와 기기 비용이 모두 나타나 있습니다.

25 matter

❶ 물질
→ **substance**

❷ 상황, 문제
→ **situation, issue**

Employees who have a complaint about a supervisor can speak with an HR representative to resolve the **matter**.

(A) substance (B) situation

상사에 대해 불만이 있는 직원들은 해당 문제를 해결하기 위해 인사부 직원과 이야기할 수 있습니다.

26 over

❶ ~ 위에
→ **above**

❷ ~동안
→ **during**

After learning the surprising news that Wire World is going out of business, we expect that our market share will grow by 10% **over** the next year.

(A) above (B) during

와이어 월드 사가 폐업할 예정이라는 놀라운 소식을 들은 후로, 우리는 앞으로 1년 동안 우리의 시장 점유율이 10퍼센트 증가할 것으로 예상합니다.

27 model

❶ 본보기
→ **example**

❷ 판
→ **version**

The newest **model** in their popular line of smart phones features an improved camera and a crystal-clear screen resolution.

(A) example (B) version

인기 있는 스마트폰 제품 라인에 속해 있는 이 최신 모델은 개선된 카메라와 수정같이 맑은 화면 해상도를 특징으로 합니다.

28 treat

❶ 다루다
→ **manage, handle**

❷ 간주하다
→ **consider**

❸ 접대하다, 대접하다
→ **entertain**

> My family has been using the same veterinarian for 10 years because she always **treats** our pets with care.
> (A) handles   (B) considers

우리 가족은 10년 동안 동일한 수의사를 이용해 왔는데, 그분은 항상 우리의 애완 동물들을 세심하게 다뤄주시기 때문입니다.

29 suspect

❶ 생각하다, 추정하다
→ **think, believe**

❷ 의심하다, 불신하다
→ **distrust**

> The board members **suspect** that the CEO will soon announce his retirement, and they are preparing to search for a suitable successor.
> (A) believe   (B) distrust

이사회 임원들은 CEO가 곧 은퇴를 발표할 것으로 생각하고, 적절한 후임자를 물색할 준비를 하고 있습니다.

30 tentative

❶ 잠정적인, 임시의
→ **not finalized**

❷ 머뭇거리는
→ **hesitant**

> The music festival has released a **tentative** schedule for all of the performances that will take place over the weekend in Mallory Park.
> (A) not finalized   (B) hesitant

그 음악 축제는 주말 동안에 걸쳐 말로리 공원에서 열릴 모든 공연들에 대한 잠정적인 일정을 발표했습니다.

DAILY QUIZ

밑줄 친 단어와 가장 가까운 의미를 지닌 것을 고르세요.

1
> The IT department is facing a **critical** situation with the server outage, requiring immediate attention to restore major services. The team is working tirelessly to resolve the issue and minimize downtime.

(A) essential
(B) negative
(C) urgent
(D) creative

2
> The upcoming tennis championship is generating immense anticipation as the event is expected to **draw** thousands of tennis fans from all over the country. With top-tier players competing for the title, spectators are eager to witness thrilling matches and breathtaking displays of skill.

(A) promote
(B) attract
(C) sketch
(D) remove

3
> At our store, we take pride in ensuring that our customers receive the best products and services at affordable prices. Our prices are **fair** and carefully evaluated to offer the utmost value to our clientele.

(A) objective
(B) reasonable
(C) generous
(D) light

/ Week / 01 실전 TEST

MP3 바로듣기

강의 바로보기

LISTENING

• Part 1

1.

2.

3.

4.

READING

Part 5

5. Jackson & Lee Health Supplies assures ------- of its nutritional supplements within three days of purchase.

    (A) delivery
    (B) sale
    (C) advance
    (D) expense

6. Ms. Beaumont's proposal to establish a monthly staff training workshop received ------- from the board members this morning.

    (A) approval
    (B) experience
    (C) invitation
    (D) election

7. Ms. Jimenez and Mr. Wu are in ------- regarding the location and activities for this year's staff workshop.

    (A) comprehension
    (B) verification
    (C) fulfillment
    (D) agreement

8. Munster Corporation provides employees with a ------- of career advancement opportunities and regular training programs.

    (A) position
    (B) salary
    (C) variety
    (D) promotion

9. Sheraton Road is home to the largest ------- of fine dining establishments in the city of Hartford.

    (A) reservation
    (B) appointment
    (C) concentration
    (D) review

10. The Five Starz can prepare a setlist of various songs appropriate for any -------.

    (A) occasion
    (B) chance
    (C) vacancy
    (D) schedule

11. Roper Corporation announced the opening of a brand-new office ------- in the Gillman Building on Spalding Street.

    (A) project
    (B) space
    (C) report
    (D) worker

12. Interviews will be held all week for the assembly line manager ------- at Reilly Manufacturing.

    (A) participation
    (B) outline
    (C) arrangement
    (D) position

Part 6

Questions 13-16 refer to the following e-mail.

To: <manager@housingconnection.com>
Subject: Available Apartments

Dear sir/madam,

I am writing in **13.** ------- to your advertisement in last week's edition of our university newspaper. I understand that your company specializes in finding affordable housing options for students, and I'm interested in using your services. **14.** -------.

First, I need an apartment that is within walking distance of the campus **15.** ------- I don't currently own a vehicle. Next, I am hoping to share the rent with two of my friends, so a three-bedroom apartment would be ideal. Finally, I have a cat at my parents' home that I would love to take back with me next year.

Please send a reply to this address if you think you could help me find a suitable place. I would also need to know what type of **16.** ------- you typically charge for consultations. I look forward to hearing from you.

Sincerely,

Reggie MacDonald

---

13. (A) respond
 (B) responses
 (C) response
 (D) responsive

14. (A) I am pleased with the service so far.
 (B) I do have a few criteria.
 (C) Thank you for sending the article.
 (D) The apartment is ready for inspection.

15. (A) as
 (B) though
 (C) therefore
 (D) due to

16. (A) property
 (B) device
 (C) fee
 (D) position

Part 7

Questions 17-18 refer to the following article.

Vortex Entertainment CEO Buys New Airplane

By Colin Morrow

LOS ANGELES (July 30)- Martin Bianucci, CEO of the music and film production company Vortex Entertainment, has purchased himself a Slip Stream 500 private jet, which he has named "Bianucci One." He boarded it for the first time yesterday when he flew into New York for an awards ceremony.

The "Bianucci One" boasts two Rankin Mark engines that produce a total thrust power of 13,900 lbs. Although its powerful engine makes more noise than those of some other planes, you cannot hear it in the cabin at all because of the newly equipped, advanced sound-absorbing system. When the aircraft is full of crew and passengers, it can travel impressive distances of up to 8,065 kilometers.

Mr. Bianucci's new jet may not seat as many people as his old one, but it comes with a wide array of modern amenities and technologies. However, the cost of running the airplane will total approximately $1 million per year.

17. How is Mr. Bianucci's new airplane different from his old one?

(A) It has more powerful engines.
(B) It produces more sound in the cabin.
(C) It can fly for longer durations.
(D) It accommodates fewer passengers.

18. The word "running" in paragraph 3, line 3, is closest in meaning to

(A) traveling
(B) boarding
(C) operating
(D) approving

서아쌤의
토익
비밀과외
기출 VOCA

Week 02

Contents		Page	Date	Check
Day 01	Part 1 사물 사진 빈출 어휘	80	월 일	☐
Day 02	Part 5, 6 명사 ③	94	월 일	☐
Day 03	Part 5, 6 명사 ④	108	월 일	☐
Day 04	Part 5, 6 명사 + 전치사 콜로케이션	122	월 일	☐
Day 05	Part 7 기출 동의어 ②	136	월 일	☐
Week 02 실전 TEST		146	월 일	☐

Day 01 사물 사진 빈출 어휘 Part 1

QR코드 하나를 가리고 찍으면 편해요!

MP3 바로듣기

강의 바로보기

---

1 aisle

● 통로

기출 Some bookshelves are separated by an **aisle**. 책장들이 통로로 나뉘어 있다.

만점 TIP
• 발음에 유의하세요. [s]가 묵음으로, [아일]이라고 발음합니다.

---

2 rack

● (물건을 거는) 걸이, (물건을 올려 두는) 선반

기출 Some clothes are hanging on a **rack**. 옷들이 옷걸이에 걸려 있다.

만점 TIP
• 시험에 나오는 또 다른 rack

luggage rack

bicycle rack

---

3 level

● 층, 단

기출 A bicycle rack has two **levels**. 자전거 보관대가 2단으로 되어 있다.

만점 TIP
• '층'을 의미하는 또 다른 표현 : story

A building is several stories tall. 건물이 여러 층 높이이다.

4 (cash) register

● 금전 출납기, 상점의 계산대

> [기출] A **cash register** drawer is open.
> 금전 출납기 서랍이 열려 있다.

> [만점 TIP]
> • 상점 사진에서 계산대를 checkout counter라고 표현하는 문장도 나옵니다.

5 walkway

● 통로, 작은 길

> [기출] A **walkway** is lined with benches.
> 통로에 벤치들이 줄지어 있다.

> [만점 TIP]
> • '길'을 나타내는 기출 어휘
> pathway / path 보도
> trail 산길, 오솔길
> road (특히 차가 다니는) 도로
> street 일반적인 길, 도로

6 patio

● 파티오, 테라스 자리

> [기출] A roof has been built over an outdoor **patio**.
> 야외 테라스 위에 지붕이 설치되어 있다.

> [만점 TIP]
> • Part 2에도 자주 나오는 단어입니다.
> [패디오우 (미) / 패티오우 (영)] 발음에 유의하세요.

7 potted plant

● 화분에 담긴 식물

> [기출] A **potted plant** is positioned in a corner.
> 화분이 구석에 놓여 있다.

> [만점 TIP]
> • 시험에 가장 자주 출제되는 사물 중 하나입니다.

8 container

- 그릇, 용기

  기출 Some **containers** have been filled with food.
  용기들이 음식으로 가득 차 있다.

  > **만점 TIP**
  > • 배에 싣는 화물 수송용 컨테이너만을 연상하기 쉬운데, Part 1에서는 '그릇, 용기'를 나타내는 명사로 잘 나옵니다.

9 be stacked

- 쌓여 있다

  기출 Boxes **have been stacked** on the floor.
  상자들이 바닥에 쌓여 있다.

  Some packages **are stacked** on a cart.
  짐꾸러미들이 카트 위에 쌓여 있다.

  > **만점 TIP**
  > • be piled도 쌓여 있는 모습을 묘사할 때 쓰이며, 정답으로 자주 나옵니다.
  > • 사물의 현재 상태를 묘사할 때 「be동사+p.p.」나 「have been p.p.」를 쓸 수 있는데, 둘 사이에 의미 차이는 없습니다.
  > • stack, pile이 명사로 쓰일 때는 '더미'라는 뜻입니다.
  >   a pile[stack] of dishes 접시 더미, 접시가 쌓여 있는 것

10 be propped against

- ~에 기대어 있다

  기출 A ladder **has been propped against** the wall.
  사다리가 벽에 기대어 있다.

  Tools **are propped against** a wall.
  연장들이 벽에 기대어 있다.

  > **만점 TIP**
  > • 동사 prop의 뜻은 '~을 (받침대 등으로) 받치다, 떠받치다'라는 뜻으로, The door is propped open.은 문에 무엇인가를 받쳐서 열어 놓은 상태를 묘사합니다.

11 be suspended

● 매달려 있다

기출 Some light fixtures **are suspended** from the ceiling.
조명 기구가 천장에 매달려 있다.

Some wires **are suspended** over a road.
전선이 길 위쪽에 매달려 있다.

만점 TIP
• 조명 기구나 장식용 식물이 천장에(from the ceiling) 매달려 있는 모습의 사진이 자주 출제됩니다.

12 be displayed

● 진열되어 있다

기출 Products **are displayed** on shelves.
제품들이 선반들에 진열되어 있다.

Some clothing **is being displayed**.
옷이 진열되어 있다.

만점 TIP
• display(~을 진열하다)는 명사(진열, 전시)로도 쓰이기 때문에 진열되어 있는 모습을 be on display로 묘사할 수도 있습니다.
Food is on display in a cafeteria.
구내 식당에 음식이 진열되어 있다.

13 be arranged

● 정렬되어 있다, 정리되어 있다

기출 Some clothes **have been arranged** for display.
몇몇 옷가지들이 진열되어 있다.

Some merchandise **is arranged** on shelves.
상품이 선반들 위에 정리되어 있다.

만점 TIP
• 정렬되어 있는 형태를 나타내는 부사구도 함께 알아 두세요.
in a circle 원형으로
in a row 한 줄로
in rows 여러 줄로

14 be hanging

● 걸려 있다

기출 Some artwork **is hanging** on a wall.
예술 작품이 벽에 걸려 있다.

Clothing **is hanging** on racks.
옷이 옷걸이들에 걸려 있다.

만점 TIP
- hang은 '~을 걸다'라는 동작을 나타낼 때도 쓰입니다.
  hanging up a sign 표지판을 걸고 있다
- '걸려 있다'라는 뜻의 is hanging은 is hung으로 바꾸어 쓸 수 있습니다.

15 be placed

● (~에) 놓여 있다

기출 Some potted plants **have been placed** outside.
화분들이 바깥에 놓여 있다.

Some spoons **have been placed** in a cup.
숟가락들이 컵에 놓여 있다.

만점 TIP
- be put, be positioned도 같은 의미로 쓰입니다. 물건 등이 어떤 위치에 놓여 있는 상태를 묘사하는 사진에서 정답으로 잘 나옵니다.

16 be built

● (건물, 구조물 등이) 지어져 있다, 세워져 있다

기출 A wooden structure **has been built** outdoors.
나무 구조물이 바깥에 세워져 있다.

A bridge **has been built** over a harbor.
다리가 항구 위로 건설되어 있다.

17 line

● ~에 줄지어 있다

> 기출 Some trees **line** a walkway.
> 나무들이 통로에 줄지어 있다.
>
> Some windows **line** a brick wall.
> 창문들이 벽돌로 된 벽에 줄지어 나 있다.

만점 TIP
- 줄지어 있는 모습을 묘사할 때 be lined up도 자주 쓰입니다.
  Picnic tables are lined up in a row.
  피크닉 테이블들이 한 줄로 늘어서 있다.

18 be prepared

● 준비되어 있다

> 기출 A table **has been prepared** for a meal.
> 테이블에 식사 준비가 되어 있다.
>
> A dining area **has been prepared** for customers.
> 식사 구역이 손님을 위해 준비되어 있다.

만점 TIP
- 주로 식사 준비가 된 모습을 묘사할 때 정답으로 나옵니다.

19 be set up

● 설치되어 있다, 놓여 있다

> 기출 A seating area **has been set up** outside.
> 좌석 구역이 바깥에 설치되어 있다.
>
> Two computers **are set up** next to each other.
> 두 대의 컴퓨터가 나란히 설치되어 있다.

만점 TIP
- 함께 자주 쓰이는 장소/위치 부사구
  side by side / next to each other 나란히
  in front of a building 건물 앞에
  near a wall 벽 근처에

20 be stocked

● 채워져 있다

기출 Shelves **have been stocked** with items.
선반들이 물건들로 채워져 있다.

Products **have been stocked** on shelves.
제품들이 선반들에 채워져 있다.

만점 TIP
• restock(~에 물건을 다시 채워 넣다)이라는 동사가 오답으로 자주 등장합니다.

21 be covered with

● ~로 덮여 있다

기출 The roof of a building **is covered with** snow.
건물 지붕이 눈으로 덮여 있다.

만점 TIP
• cover(~을 덮다)를 능동 형태로 쓴 문장이 출제된 적 있습니다.
An arched roof covers a building.
아치형 지붕이 건물을 덮고 있다.

22 be located

● ~에 위치해 있다

기출 Buildings **are located** along a shoreline.
건물들이 해안을 따라 위치해 있다.

An athletic field **is located** near some trees.
운동장이 나무들 근처에 위치해 있다.

23 be docked

● (배가) 정박되어 있다

기출 Some boats **are docked** at a pier.
보트들이 부두에 정박되어 있다.

만점 TIP

• 배가 정박되어 있는 사진 관련 어휘
  pier / dock 부두, 선창
  harbor 항구
  be docked (배가) 부두에 정박되다
  be tied to ~에 묶이다
  be secured to ~에 고정되다

24 stop

● 멈추어 있다

기출 A train **has stopped** at the station.
기차가 역에 정지해 있다.

만점 TIP

• 기차나 차량(vehicle) 등이 멈춰 있는 모습을 나타낼 때 stop 또는 be stopped를 씁니다.

25 grow

● (풀, 나무 등이) 자라다

기출 Some trees are **growing** alongside a building. 나무들이 건물을 따라 자라고 있다.

만점 TIP

• 식물이나 나무가 자라는 모습을 be planted(심어져 있다)로 묘사하는 문장도 정답으로 잘 나옵니다.

  Some trees have been planted near a building.
  나무들이 건물 근처에 심어져 있다.

26 be parked

● (탈것이) 세워져 있다, 주차되어 있다

기출 Some bicycles **are parked** near a curb.
자전거 몇 대가 연석 근처에 세워져 있다.

Some vehicles **are parked** in front of a fence.
차량 몇 대가 울타리 앞에 세워져 있다.

만점 TIP
- 자전거나 차량 등이 세워져 있는 모습과 관련해 연석(curb), 차고(garage), road sign(도로 표지판) 등의 명사가 자주 출제되니 알아 두세요.

27 be mounted

● ~이 장착되어 있다, 올려져 있다

기출 Some light fixtures **are mounted** on a wall.
조명 기구들이 벽에 붙어 있다.

만점 TIP
- be mounted는 특히 벽에 벽시계(clock)나 장식품(decorations), 화면(screen) 등이 달려 있는 모습을 묘사할 때 나옵니다.
- There is/are 구문을 이용해서 There is a clock mounted on a wall.이라고 표현한 문장도 정답으로 나온 바 있습니다.

28 be left

● 놓여 있다

기출 Dishes **have been left** in the sink.
접시들이 싱크대에 놓여 있다.

A drawer **has been left** open.
서랍이 열린 채로 있다.

만점 TIP
- 서랍이나 상자, 문 등이 열려 있는 모습을 묘사하는 be left open이 자주 출제됩니다.

29 be scattered

• 흩어져 있다

기출 Leaves **are scattered** on the ground.
나뭇잎들이 땅에 흩어져 있다.

만점 TIP
• 서류나 책들이 펼쳐져 있는 모습을 be spread out(펼쳐져 있다)을 써서 묘사한 문제도 여러 차례 출제되었으니 함께 알아 두세요.

Some papers are spread out on a table.
서류들이 테이블 위에 펼쳐져 있다.

30 lie

• 놓여 있다

기출 Some rope is **lying** on the ground.
줄이 땅에 놓여 있다.

There are some power cords **lying** on a desk. 전선이 책상 위에 놓여 있다.

만점 TIP
• 현재진행형으로 표현할 때 현재분사 lying을 씁니다.

31 run

• (길 등이) 뻗어 있다, 나 있다

기출 Some tracks **run** alongside a road.
트랙이 길을 따라 나 있다.

A street **runs** parallel to the water.
길이 강과 나란히 나 있다.

만점 TIP
• run을 '뛰다, 달리다'의 뜻으로만 알고 있으면 이 문장을 듣고 제대로 이해하기 어렵습니다.

32 lead to

- (길 등이) ~로 이어지다

  기출 Some stairs **lead to** water.
  계단이 강으로 이어져 있다.

  A pathway **leads to** a parking lot.
  길이 주차장으로 이어져 있다.

33 be paved

- (길이) 포장되어 있다

  기출 A pathway **is paved** with stones.
  길이 돌로 포장되어 있다.

  A path **has been paved** with bricks.
  길이 벽돌로 포장되어 있다.

  > **만점 TIP**
  > • 포장되어 있는 길을 pavement라고 합니다.

34 be posted

- 게시되어 있다

  기출 A sign **has been posted** in front of a building. 표지판이 건물 앞에 게시되어 있다.

  > **만점 TIP**
  > • 사람이 표지판을 거는 모습을 묘사할 때는 posting a sign, hanging up a sign 등의 표현을 씁니다.

35 occupied

- 이용 중인, 점유된

  기출 All the seats **are occupied**. 모든 좌석이 이용중이다.

  > **만점 TIP**
  > • 이용하지 않고 있는 상태는 unoccupied라고 합니다.
  > An office is unoccupied. 사무실이 비어 있다.
  > Some of the chairs are unoccupied.
  > 의자들 중 일부가 비어 있다.

36 be installed

● 설치되어 있다

기출 A railing **has been installed** next to some stairs. 난간이 계단 옆에 설치되어 있다.

만점 TIP
• 창문, 타일, 가로등 등이 설치되어 있는 모습을 '설치되는 중이다(is being installed)'라고 묘사하는 오답이 자주 등장합니다.

37 overlook

● ~을 내려다보다

기출 Some skyscrapers **overlook** a park. 높은 건물들이 공원을 내려다보고 있다.

38 in the distance

● 멀리

기출 Some trees are visible **in the distance**. 멀리 나무들이 보인다.

만점 TIP
• 자주 출제되지는 않지만 나온 경우 정답이었습니다.

39 be separated

● 나뉘다

기출 Workstations **are separated** by partitions. 작업공간들이 파티션으로 나뉘어 있다.

40 be filled with
● ~로 가득 차 있다

기출 A drawer has been filled with folders.
서랍이 폴더로 가득 차 있다.

만점 TIP
• '(어떤 공간이) 사람들로 가득 차 있다'를 표현할 때는 be crowded with를 씁니다.

DAILY QUIZ

🎧 음원을 듣고 사진을 바르게 묘사한 문장을 골라보세요.

1

(A)　　　(B)

2

(A)　　　(B)

3

(A)　　　(B)

4
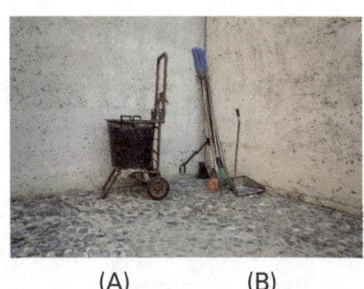
(A)　　　(B)

5

(A)　　　(B)

6

(A)　　　(B)

정답 1 (A) 2 (B) 3 (B) 4 (A) 5 (A) 6 (B)

1 defect

● 결함, 하자, 흠

기출 eliminate any product **defects**
어떠한 제품 결함도 없애다

find physical **defects**
물리적 하자를 찾다

Our quality assurance officer checks for any manufacturing ------- before products are shipped out to customers.
(A) defects　　　　　(B) launches

2 output

● 생산량, 출력

기출 high agricultural **output**
높은 농업 생산량

Over the past ten years, palm oil ------- from our factory in Indonesia has more than doubled.
(A) quantity　　　　(B) output

3 product

produce v. 생산하다

● 제품

기출 a **product** that may not meet one's expectations
기대에 미치지 못하는 제품

contain a full listing of all the **products**
모든 제품의 전체 목록을 포함하다

Our Web site contains a full listing of all the ------- that we sell at our various branches throughout Europe.
(A) consumers　　　(B) products

4 attendee
참석자

attend v. 참석하다
attendant n. 안내원, 종업원

기출 **Attendees** must sign up by March 28.
참석자들은 반드시 3월 28일까지 등록해야 한다.

To make communication more convenient, ------- must pick up a name tag at the welcome desk.
(A) attendees (B) configurations

5 appliance
기기

기출 be dissatisfied with the **appliance**
기기에 대해 불만족하다

boldly colored **appliances**
과감한 색감의 기기들

If you have problems with any Zeletron -------, please contact our technical support team.
(A) alternative (B) appliance

6 renovation
보수 (공사), 개조

renovate v. 보수하다

기출 the planned **renovation** 계획된 보수공사
be closed for **renovation** 개조를 위해 폐쇄되다

The gym's sauna facilities will be closed for ------- and are expected to reopen in early June.
(A) renovation (B) magnification

7 event
행사, 경우, 사건

기출 prior to the **event** 행사 전에
in the **event** that ~하는 경우에

In the ------- that customers wish to be removed from our mailing list, please pass their details on to our marketing team.
(A) event (B) display

8 participant

participate v. 참가하다

● 참가자

기출 Workshop **participants** will learn how to apply
워크숍 참가자들은 ~을 응용하는 방법을 배울 것이다

limit the number of **participants** to 200
참가자 수를 200명으로 제한하다

> At this year's Bridgewater Marathon, the number of ------- is likely to exceed 20,000.
> (A) participants　　　(B) performers

9 stage

● 단계

기출 in the production **stage**
생산 단계에서

the most time-consuming **stages** in
~에서 가장 시간이 많이 드는 단계

> The product development team is in the final ------- of designing the outer casing of our new tablet computer.
> (A) stages　　　(B) scenes

10 competitor

compete v. 경쟁하다
competitive a. 경쟁의
competitiveness n. 경쟁력

● 경쟁자

기출 be well ahead of one's **competitors**
경쟁자들보다 월등히 앞서다

> Mr. Howell's knowledge of market trends has allowed EXA Software to stay well ahead of its ------- in the industry.
> (A) suppliers　　　(B) competitors

11 recommendation

recommend v. 추천하다, 권하다

추천, 권고

기출 make a **recommendation** for
~을 위해 추천하다

if you have a **recommendation** for
~에 대해 추천해주실 수 있다면

Mr. Brown made a ------- for Ms. Yeoman to be given an opportunity to lead the upcoming project.

(A) recommendation   (B) progression

12 duty

근무, 의무, 직무

기출 complete regular **duties**
정규 근무를 완료하다

Additional **duties** may be assigned.
추가 근무가 배정될 수 있다.

The hotel manager insisted that the housekeeping team complete daily ------- more efficiently.

(A) competitors   (B) duties

13 production

produce v. 생산하다
producer n. 생산자

생산(량)

기출 reduce our **production** time by 30 percent
생산 시간을 30퍼센트 줄이다

Thanks to the advanced training courses, we have managed to lower our ------- time by 25 percent.

(A) expectation   (B) production

14 arrangement

arrange v. 준비하다, 기획하다

- 준비, 기획

  기출 make an **arrangement** to do
  ~하기 위해 준비하다

  make **arrangements** for the client
  고객을 위해 기획하다

  > The company's founder made ------- to transport the new clients from the airport to their hotel in the downtown area.
  > (A) arrangements   (B) achievements

15 expectation

expect v. 기대하다, 예상하다

- 기대(치), 예상

  기출 exceed one's **expectations**
  ~의 기대치를 넘다

  meet one's **expectations**
  ~의 기대에 부응하다

  > At the Shangri-La Restaurant, we work hard to ensure the food, service, and ambience exceed your -------.
  > (A) demonstrations   (B) expectations

16 confirmation

confirm v. 확인해주다

- 확인(증)

  기출 serve as **confirmation** of
  ~의 확인증으로서 기능하다

  await one's **confirmation** of
  ~의 확인을 기다리다

  > If you wish to cancel the annual maintenance service, you must provide written ------- to our client support team.
  > (A) confirmation   (B) termination

17 regulation

regulate v. 규정하다, 규제하다

• 규정, 규제, 규칙

기출 follow the **regulations**
규정들을 준수하다

All businesses must follow the ------- listed in the government's Greener Future handbook.

(A) advantages   (B) regulations

18 warranty

warrant v. 보증하다

• 보증 (기한)

기출 extend the **warranty** on
~에 대한 보증 기한을 연장하다

include an extended **warranty**
연장된 보증 기한을 포함하다

By registering your product on our Web site, you can extend the three-year ------- on your laptop computer.

(A) warranty   (B) supply

19 authority

authorize v. 허가하다, 승인하다

• 권한, 전문가, 당국자

기출 have the most **authority** on the committee
위원회에서 가장 많은 권한을 가지고 있다

While Mr. Jacobs is away at the conference, the assistant manager, Ms. Dawkins, has the most ------- in the office.

(A) permission   (B) authority

20 aspect

측면, 양상, 외관

기출 the most challenging **aspect** of
~의 가장 어려운 측면

apply to every **aspect** of marketing
마케팅의 모든 측면에 적용되다

> This staff orientation will cover every ------- of employment at Sirius IT Solutions.
> (A) aspect   (B) reference

21 technician

technically ad. 기술적으로

기술자, 전문가

기출 **technicians** trained in
~에서 훈련받은 기술자들

an experienced **technician**
숙련된 전문가

> Only a highly skilled ------- would be able to repair the manufacturing robot within two days.
> (A) technician   (B) generator

22 analysis

analyst n. 분석가
analyze v. 분석하다

분석

기출 the **analysis** of monthly sales figures
월간 매출에 대한 분석

according to the **analysis**
분석에 따르면

> The ------- of staff attendance figures is essential to ensuring that annual productivity goals are reached.
> (A) destination   (B) analysis

23 means

● 수단, 방법

기출 the preferred **means** for
~에 대해 선호되는 수단

operate by **means** of GPS technology
GPS 기술에 의해 작동하다

> Teleconferencing is an effective ------- of conducting discussions between colleagues based all over the world.
> (A) technique　　　(B) means

24 consideration

considerate a. 사려깊은, 배려하는

● 고려, 배려

기출 take A into **consideration**
A를 고려하다

show **consideration** for A
A를 배려하다

> The building manager will take tenants' opinions into ------- when deciding how to use the rooftop area.
> (A) consideration　　　(B) participation

25 factor

● 요인, 요소

기출 based on a number of **factors**
많은 요인들에 근거하여

a key **factor** in
~에서의 중요한 요소

> The host city for the sporting event was chosen based on several -------, including infrastructure and public safety.
> (A) factors　　　(B) portions

26 completion

complete a. 완전한
       v. 완료하다
completely ad. 완전히

● 완료, 완성

기출 in the **completion** of an education degree
학위 과정의 완료에

upon **completion** of program requirements
프로그램의 요건을 충족한 후에

> Upon ------- of the probation period, successful employees will be provided with a full-time contract.
> (A) admission   (B) completion

27 exception

except v. 예외로 하다
      prep. ~을 제외하고는
exceptional a. 예외적인

● 예외, 제외

기출 make an **exception**
예외를 두다

with one **exception**
하나를 제외하고

> Almost all board members approved the proposal to relocate to Texas, with the only ------- being Mr. Tasker.
> (A) separation   (B) exception

28 consultation

consult v. 상담하다
consultant n. 상담사

● 상담

기출 will be unavailable for **consultation**
상담을 이용할 수 없을 것이다

complimentary **consultation**
무료 상담

> The payroll manager will be available for ------- on payroll-related issues after 4 PM every day this week.
> (A) reputation   (B) consultation

29 accordance

accord v. 일치하다, 조화하다
accordingly ad. 그에 맞춰, 그리하여

- 일치, 합의, 조화

  기출 in **accordance** with the company guidelines
  회사 안내지침에 따라서

  > It is crucial that the extension of our head office be constructed in ------- with the city's building regulations.
  >
  > (A) accordance　　　(B) regards

30 nomination

nominate v. (후보로) 지명하다
nominee n. 지명자, 후보

- (수상) 후보, 지명

  기출 **nominations** for Employee of the Year award
  올해의 직원상의 후보들

  > ------- for the Best Film of the Year award will be considered by a panel consisting of 25 noted film critics.
  >
  > (A) Performances　　　(B) Nominations

31 confidence

confident a. 자신감 있는, 확신하는

- 자신감, 확신

  기출 express **confidence** in
  ~에 대한 자신감을 표하다

  have **confidence** in one's ability
  ~의 능력에 대해 확신을 가지다

  > Ross Ogilvie's talk at Sala Technology's year-end banquet increased employees' ------- in the company's success.
  >
  > (A) assertion　　　(B) confidence

32 **reminder**

remind v. 상기시키다

- 상기시키는 것, 알림

  기출 This is just a **reminder**.
  이것은 그저 상기시켜드리는 글입니다.

  send A an e-mail **reminder**
  A에게 이메일 알림을 보내다

  > This is a ------- that your parking section has been changed from D5 to E3.
  > (A) request　　　　(B) reminder

33 **preparation**

prepare v. 준비하다

- 준비

  기출 in **preparation** for
  ~을 준비하면서, ~에 대비해

  > In ------- for the grand opening event, the owners of the Starburst Mall are sending invitations to local celebrities.
  > (A) presentation　　(B) preparation

34 **precaution**

- 예방 조치, 조심, 경계

  기출 take every **precaution** to ensure that
  ~라는 것을 확실히 하기 위해 모든 예방 조치를 취하다

  safety **precautions**
  안전 예방 조치

  > BC Hiking Expeditions takes every ------- to ensure that participants stay properly hydrated and free from injury.
  > (A) precaution　　　(B) advice

35 component

- 구성 요소, 부품

  기출 central **component** of the economy
  경제의 중심이 되는 구성 요소

  Worn-out **components** can be replaced easily.
  닳은 부품은 쉽게 교체될 수 있다.

  > Celebrity endorsement is a primary ------- of the company's global marketing strategy.
  > (A) component (B) policy

36 patience

patient a. 인내심 있는, 참을성 있는

- 인내(심), 참을성

  기출 We appreciate your **patience**.
  저희는 귀하의 인내(심)에 감사드립니다.

  Thank you for your **patience**.
  귀하의 참을성에 감사드립니다.

  > While the swimming pool is closed for cleaning, we appreciate your ------- and encourage you to enjoy the hotel's other amenities.
  > (A) recommendation (B) patience

37 congestion

- 정체, 혼잡

  기출 avoid **congestion** on major roads
  주요 도로에서의 정체를 피하다

  > The proposed widening of Fourth Avenue would drastically reduce ------- on downtown roads.
  > (A) congestion (B) direction

38 connection

connect v. 연결하다, 접속하다
connected a. 연결된

- 연결(성), 접속, 관계

  기출 create a strong **connection** between A and B
  A와 B 사이에 강한 연결성을 만들다

  give A a **connection** with B
  A에게 B와의 연결성을 주다

  The art critic noted a firm ------- between Paul Noonan's work and that of Luca Bergoni.

  (A) development (B) connection

39 shortage

- 부족 (현상), 결핍

  기출 face a serious **shortage** of
  ~의 심각한 부족에 직면하다

  because of a **shortage** of
  ~의 부족 때문에

  As the cost of importing oil continues to soar, motorists in Europe should prepare for a major ------- of fuel.

  (A) shortage (B) exaggeration

40 presence

present a. 출석한, 현재의

- 출석, 존재(감)

  기출 request your **presence** at a meeting
  귀하의 회의 출석을 요청하다

  reestablish its **presence** in
  ~에서의 존재감을 재확립하다

  Mr. Barker has requested your ------- at the press conference that will be held at 3 o'clock this afternoon.

  (A) occurrence (B) presence

DAILY QUIZ

단어와 그에 알맞은 뜻을 연결해 보세요.

1 completion •   • (A) 완료, 완성
2 production •   • (B) 일치, 합의, 조화
3 accordance •   • (C) 생산(량)

빈칸에 알맞은 단어를 선택하세요.

4 eliminate any product -------
   어떠한 제품 결함도 없애다

5 This is just a -------.
   이것은 그저 상기시켜드리는 글입니다.

(A) renovation
(B) reminder
(C) output
(D) defects

6 be closed for -------
   개조를 위해 폐쇄되다

앞서 배운 단어들의 뜻을 생각하면서, 다음 문제를 풀어보세요.

7 All newly installed Electra boilers come with an extended ------- to cover technical faults.

   (A) record   (B) operation
   (C) budget   (D) warranty

8 Mayor Buchanan prefers small-scale public forums because they help her foster a better ------- with local constituents.

   (A) suggestion   (B) connection
   (C) profession   (D) policy

정답 1 (A) 2 (C) 3 (B) 4 (D) 5 (B) 6 (A) 7 (D) 8 (B)

1 notification

notify v. 알리다

● 통지, 알림

기출 send a written **notification** of one's plan
~의 계획에 대해 서면 통지를 보내다

Property renters who do not wish to renew their lease must send a written ------- to the landlord.
(A) introduction   (B) notification

2 consequence

consequently ad. 그 결과, 따라서

● 결과

기출 as a **consequence** of
~의 결과로서

Mr. Olback has seen sales of his music album rise as a ------- of his appearance on a popular podcast.
(A) timing   (B) consequence

3 pressure

press v. 누르다, 압박하다

● 압박, 압력

기출 be under a lot of **pressure** to get
~을 얻기 위해 많은 압박 하에 있다

increasing **pressure** to do
~해야 한다는 증가하는 압박

Mr. Dyer is under ------- to fill ten positions before the fast food outlet opens next Monday.
(A) difficulty   (B) pressure

4 portion • 부분, 몫

기출 a major **portion** of the shopping mall's design
쇼핑몰 디자인의 주요 부분

a **portion** of all sales
모든 매출의 한 부분

A ------- of all proceeds from ticket sales for music festivals will be donated to charity.
(A) quality (B) portion

5 interruption • 중단, 방해

interrupt v. 중단시키다, 방해하다
interrupted a. 가로막힌, 중단된

기출 a brief **interruption** in
~의 일시적인 중단

avoid possible **interruption** of your service
혹시 있을지 모르는 서비스 중단을 피하다

Due to scheduled maintenance, there will be a brief ------- in the office's Internet connection at 11 AM tomorrow.
(A) statement (B) interruption

6 investigation • 조사, 수사

investigate v. 조사하다, 수사하다

기출 a thorough **investigation**
철저한 조사

conduct an **investigation** into
~에 대한 수사를 실시하다

A government agency recently carried out an ------- into Wiltshire-Poole Trading Inc.
(A) investigation (B) exploration

7 element
요소

기출 other **elements** of Japan's infrastructure
일본의 사회 기반 시설의 다른 요소들

the basic **elements** of relationships
관계의 기본 요소

> The market research group will consider the design, functionality, and other ------- of the new product.
>
> (A) elements   (B) measurements

8 seating
좌석

기출 but **seating** is limited to 400 people
좌석이 400명으로 제한되어 있지만

a change in the **seating** policy
좌석 정책의 변경

> The food at Bella Bistro has received much praise, but ------- is limited to 15 diners at a time.
>
> (A) seating   (B) permission

9 enhancement
향상, 강화

enhance v. 향상시키다, 강화하다

기출 **enhancement** to the landscape
조경의 향상

> The graphic design consultant believes that ------- to our Web site could significantly boost our online sales.
>
> (A) continuations   (B) enhancements

10 proximity
인접(성), 근접

기출 because of its **proximity** to shopping malls
쇼핑몰들과의 인접성 때문에

Due to its ------- to the Clearmont Convention Center, the Iris Hotel is a popular choice for business travelers.
(A) proximity　　(B) availability

11 observation
관찰, 견해

observe v. 관찰하다, 준수하다
observance n. 준수

기출 **observations** on children's behavior
아이들의 행동에 대한 관찰

Dr. Laing's ------- on the breeding habits of mountain gorillas were published in the latest issue of *Bioscience Monthly*.
(A) observations　　(B) standards

12 admiration
경의, 존경, 감탄

admirable a. 감탄할 만한, 훌륭한

기출 express **admiration** for ~에 대해 경의를 표하다

The baseball players often express ------- for their head coach who has maintained an unbeaten record.
(A) reward　　(B) admiration

13 obligation
의무, 책임

obligate v. ~에게 의무를 지우다

기출 have no **obligation** to do
~할 의무가 없다

acknowledge our **obligation** to do
~할 우리의 책임을 인식하다

Part-time workers have no ------- to attend the monthly company meeting, but it is still strongly recommended.
(A) obligation　　(B) engagement

Week 02　Day 03　Part 5, 6 명사 ④

Week 02　111

14 perspective

- 관점, 전망

  기출 have a unique **perspective** on
  ~에 대한 특이한 관점을 지니다

  King Burger's COO has a unique ------- on the business because he started working at the company as a teenager.

  (A) quality　　　　(B) perspective

15 sequence

- 순서, 배열

  기출 the proper **sequence** of steps
  올바른 조치 순서

  the **sequence** of the day's events
  당일 행사 순서

  The correct ------- of numbers must be entered on the keypad in order to gain access to the building's security office.

  (A) direction　　　　(B) sequence

16 possession

possess v. 소유하다

- 소유물, 재산

  기출 personal **possessions**
  개인 소유물

  return one's **possessions** as quickly as possible
  ~의 재산을 가능한 한 빠르게 돌려주다

  A new modem will be in your ------- within 24 hours, and our technicians will install it free of charge.

  (A) possession　　　　(B) recognition

17 combination

combine v. 통합하다
combined a. 통합된

● 통합, 조합

기출 in **combination** with other preventive measures
다른 예방 조치들과 함께 통합하여

Mario Alvaro's latest business venture is a ------- of a restaurant and a movie theater.
(A) cooperation (B) combination

18 evidence

evident a. 명백한
evidently ad. 명백하게

● 증거

기출 be **evidence** of the growth
성장의 증거이다

provide verifiable **evidence**
증명할 수 있는 증거를 제시하다

Those applying for the position should submit a portfolio so that they can show ------- that they have the necessary skills.
(A) foundation (B) evidence

19 effect

effective a. 효과적인
effectively ad. 효과적으로

● 효력, 효과

기출 come into **effect** (on)
(~에 대해) 효력이 발생하다

in **effect**
효력이 있는, 사실상

Regulations prohibiting the sharing of customer information between different businesses will come into ------- this year.
(A) effect (B) outcome

20 **distribution**

distribute v. 보급하다, 배포하다

- 유통, 보급, 배포

  기출 involved in the manufacturing and **distribution**
  제조와 유통에 관여된

  an energy **distribution** plan
  에너지 보급 계획

  > Alberta Oil is installing new pipelines throughout Canada over the next five years to improve the domestic ------ network.
  >
  > (A) assortment　　　(B) distribution

21 **specification**

specify v. 구체화하다, 명시하다
specified a. 명시된

- 상세 요건, 명세서

  기출 contains the style **specifications** for
  ~에 대한 스타일 상세 요건들을 포함하다

  > Our Web site clearly displays the size and technical ------ for all EZ Electronics kitchen appliances.
  >
  > (A) incidents　　　(B) specifications

22 **restriction**

restrict v. 제한하다

- 제한, 제약

  기출 inform A about the **restriction** imposed on
  ~에 부과된 제한에 대해 A에게 통지하다

  government **restrictions** on the import of
  ~의 수입에 가해진 정부의 제한

  > Trade ------ imposed on the importing of certain foreign goods were put in place to boost the domestic economy.
  >
  > (A) restrictions　　　(B) authorities

23 disruption

disrupt v. 방해하다, 중단시키다
disruptive a. 방해하는, 지장을 주는

● 장애, 중단

기출 a temporary **disruption** in our order system
저희 주문 시스템에 대한 일시적 장애

apologize to its customers for the **disruption** in Internet service
인터넷 서비스에 대한 중단으로 자사 고객들에게 사과하다

> Albion Rail Company apologized to its passengers for the recent ------- in train service caused by track maintenance.
>
> (A) irritation   (B) disruption

24 inspiration

inspire v. 영감을 주다, 자극하다

● 영감, 자극

기출 the **inspiration** for the design
디자인에 대한 영감

> Ronald Ives paints watercolor pictures with ------- from the urban landscape of London.
>
> (A) apprehension   (B) inspiration

25 loyalty

loyal a. 충성스러운

● 충성(도)

기출 build customer **loyalty**
고객 충성도를 형성하다

> To strengthen customer -------, Axon Office Supplies is introducing a membership program with several benefits.
>
> (A) brands   (B) loyalty

26 case

in case that conj. ~경우에 대비하여
in case of prep. ~의 경우

경우, 사례

기출 in the rare case that
~라는 희귀한 경우에

as was the case with
~의 경우에 그랬던 것처럼

As was the ------- with Haitsu Motors' hybrid car, its first fully electric car received excellent reviews all over the world.
(A) reason (B) case

27 motivation

motivate v. 동기를 부여하다

동기 (부여), 의욕

기출 sustain employee motivation
직원 동기 부여를 지속시키다

As the head of our Personnel Department, one of Mr. Hawke's duties is improving worker -------.
(A) motivation (B) consequences

28 enthusiasm

enthusiastic a. 열정적인
enthusiastically ad. 열정적으로
enthusiast n. 애호가, 열성가

열정, 열광

기출 greet guests with enthusiasm
열정으로 손님들을 맞이하다

We'd like to make an excellent first impression on those visiting our restaurant, so please greet all diners with -------.
(A) achievement (B) enthusiasm

29 reliability
reliable a. 믿을 수 있는

- 신뢰도, 신뢰성

기출 emphasize the **reliability** of its products
자사 제품의 신뢰도를 강조하다

In its promotional materials, Zen Full Fiber emphasizes the speed and ------- of its wireless Internet service.
(A) confidence　　　　(B) reliability

30 structure
structural a. 구조적인

- 구조, 시설, 건물

기출 the basic **structure** 기본 구조

To celebrate the founding of the city, the mayor has approved the construction of a commemorative -------.
(A) structure　　　　(B) element

31 convenience
convenient a. 편리한
conveniently ad. 편리하게

- 편의, 편리

기출 for your **convenience**
귀하의 편의를 위해

at your earliest **convenience**
귀하께서 편하신 가장 빠른 시간에

For your -------, we have attached an electronic copy of your invoice to this e-mail.
(A) convenience　　　　(B) usefulness

32 durability
durable a. 내구성이 좋은, 오래 가는

- 내구성

기출 for extra **durability** 추가적인 내구성을 위해

be designed for **durability** 내구성을 위해 고안되다

Many homeowners are opting to have Truegrain hardwood flooring installed because of its -------.
(A) enlargement　　　　(B) durability

33 caution

cautious a. 주의하는
cautiously ad. 주의하여

• 주의

기출 use extreme **caution**
극도로 주의하다

Hotel guests are advised to use ------- when walking through the nearby forest as there are many steep drops.
(A) challenge   (B) caution

34 evaluation

evaluate v. 평가하다

• 평가

기출 request a full **evaluation** of the efficiency of
~의 효율성에 대한 전체적인 평가를 요청하다

sent A samples of products for **evaluation**
평가를 위해 상품들의 견본을 A에게 보내다

The head of the National Aviation Authority requested a thorough ------- of the safety of the new aircraft.
(A) option   (B) evaluation

35 revision

revise v. 수정하다, 개정하다

• 수정, 개정

기출 make the necessary **revisions**
필요한 수정을 하다

Please submit your article to Ken Grimshaw in the editing team in case he wishes to make any additional -------.
(A) revisions   (B) proficiencies

36 comparison

비교, 대조

compare v. 비교하다, 대조하다

기출 a **comparison** of two brands
두 개의 브랜드의 비교

A ------- of Speedy Eats and Go Grub showed that the average delivery time is far less with Speedy Eats.
(A) difference   (B) comparison

37 delegation

대표단

delegate v. 대표로 파견하다, 권한을 위임하다

기출 a **delegation** of officials from the research center
연구 센터에서 온 공무원 대표단

A ------- from the National Athletics Committee will assess the suitability of Clarkson Stadium.
(A) revision   (B) delegation

38 relocation

이전, 재배치

relocate v. 이전하다

기출 after the **relocation**
이전 후에

the pros and cons of **relocation**
이전의 찬반 양론

Following the -------, Sarter Furnishings' headquarters will be situated about 20 kilometers outside New York City.
(A) relocation   (B) residence

39 attention

attentive a. 주의를 기울이는, 배려하는
attentively ad. 주의 깊게

- 주의, 집중

  기출 be brought to one's **attention**
  ~의 주의를 끌다

  immediate **attention**
  즉각적인 집중

  > Editor positions at Guild Publications require an eye for creativity and excellent ------- to detail.
  > (A) demand   (B) attention

40 extension

extend v. (기한을) 연장하다

- (기한) 연장

  기출 be unable to receive the **extension**
  기한 연장을 받을 수 없다

  > The deadline for the sales report is this Friday because we were not granted the ------- we requested.
  > (A) extension   (B) funding

DAILY QUIZ

단어와 그에 알맞은 뜻을 연결해 보세요.

1. extension • • (A) 주의
2. caution • • (B) 내구성
3. durability • • (C) (기한) 연장

빈칸에 알맞은 단어를 선택하세요.

4. at your earliest -------
   귀하께서 편하신 가장 빠른 시간에

5. acknowledge our ------- to do
   ~할 우리의 책임을 인식하다

   (A) case
   (B) investigation
   (C) obligation
   (D) convenience

6. in the rare ------- that
   ~라는 희귀한 경우에

앞서 배운 단어들의 뜻을 생각하면서, 다음 문제를 풀어보세요.

7. The Carmen EXPO Center is a perfect venue for business conventions due to its ------- to several 5-star hotels.

   (A) accomplishment   (B) proximity
   (C) competence   (D) opposition

8. At Prost Publishing Co., we greatly value positive attitudes in our employees, so please try to approach all tasks with -------.

   (A) comparison   (B) allocation
   (C) achievement   (D) enthusiasm

정답 | 1 (C) 2 (A) 3 (B) 4 (D) 5 (C) 6 (A) 7 (B) 8 (D)

 **명사 + 전치사 콜로케이션** Part 5, 6

1 access to

~에 대한 접근(권), ~의 이용(권)

기출 **access to** patient records
환자 기록에 대한 접근

access to the front entrance
정문의 이용

Only full members are granted ------- to the spa and sauna facilities at the swimming pool.
(A) access　　　(B) approval

2 interest in

~에 대한 관심

기출 have **interest in** the new line of
~의 새로운 제품군에 대한 관심을 가지다

Our diners have indicated great ------- in the introduction of a lunchtime buffet.
(A) interest　　　(B) attention

3 adjustment to

~에 대한 조정(사항)

기출 **adjustment to** office supplies
사무용품에 대한 조정(사항)

Please inform Mr. Martin of any ------- to your work availability for the month of December.
(A) adjustments　　　(B) commitments

4 in advance

- 미리

기출 contact A **in advance** A에게 미리 연락하다
be reserved **in advance** 미리 예약되다

Should there be any changes to the ferry schedule, we will contact you in -------.
(A) advance   (B) reply

5 alternative to

- ~에 대한 대안

기출 **alternative to** the name brand
유명 브랜드에 대한 대안

The low-cost, plant-based fiber has proven to be an excellent ------- to traditional clothing materials.
(A) choice   (B) alternative

6 in agreement

- 합의하여, 동의하여

기출 be **in agreement** about the agenda
그 안건에 대해 합의하다

Mr. Hong and Ms. Shipperley are in ------- about the location for this year's company workshop.
(A) agreement   (B) fulfillment

7 approach to

- ~에 대한 접근법

기출 **approach to** resolving problems
문제를 해결하는 것에 대한 접근법

Mr. Traynor's effective ------- to motivating his employees has resulted in a 20 percent increase in productivity.
(A) gathering   (B) approach

8 in conjunction with

- ~와 함께

  기출 be used **in conjunction with** other discounts
  다른 할인과 함께 사용되다

  This voucher may not be used in ------- with any gift certificates or discount codes.
  (A) agreement   (B) conjunction

9 at the request of

- ~의 요청에 따라

  기출 **at the request of** the manager
  부장님의 요청에 따라

  At the ------- of the accounting manager, workers must not use company credit cards for personal expenses.
  (A) necessity   (B) request

10 by means of

- ~을 통해, 사용해서

  기출 **by means of** member referrals
  회원 소개를 통해

  The data on local recreational services was collected primarily by ------- of customer surveys.
  (A) claims   (B) means

11 change in

~의 변경

기출 a **change in** the processing of orders
주문 처리의 변경

changes in editorial staff
편집 직원의 변경

A minor ------- in the company's inventory system will be covered during the meeting on Wednesday morning.
(A) change   (B) return

12 contributions to

~에 대한 공헌

기출 many **contributions to** the local community
지역 사회에 대한 많은 공헌

contribution to public health efforts
공중 보건 활동에 대한 공헌

Mr. Anderson will be recognized by the town's mayor for his valuable ------- to the community.
(A) thoughts   (B) contributions

13 disruption in

~의 중단

기출 recent **disruption in** Internet service
최근 인터넷 서비스의 중단

Galveston Fresh Produce apologized to its customers in Penrith for the recent ------- in its delivery service in the region.
(A) disruption   (B) outbreak

14 expansion into

~로의 확장

기출 recent **expansion into** overseas markets
해외 시장으로의 최근 확장

expansion into the European market
유럽 시장으로의 확장

Due to its recent ------- into European markets, Erasmus Motors has seen its profits almost double.
(A) expansion   (B) qualification

15 confidence in

~에 대한 신뢰

기출 have **confidence in** one's managers
~의 관리자들에 대한 신뢰가 있다

confidence in one's ability to handle local matters
지역 사안을 다룰 능력에 대한 신뢰

Based on the feedback forms that have been submitted, most of our workers have ------- in their branch supervisors.
(A) motivation   (B) confidence

16 improvements to

~에 대한 개선(사항)

기출 recommend **improvements to** the employee manual
직원 안내서에 대한 개선을 권고하다

The interior designer recommended some ------- to the office space we recently purchased.
(A) improvements   (B) exchanges

17 in compliance with

• ~을 준수하여

기출 **in compliance with** environmental standards
환경 기준을 준수하여

in compliance with nutritional guidelines
영양학적 지침을 준수하여

All manufacturing processes must be in ------- with government health and safety standards.

(A) arrangement   (B) compliance

18 in error

• 잘못하여, 오류로

기출 if you received the message **in error**
그 메시지를 잘못 받았다면

If you believe you have received this overdue payment notification in -------, please contact our customer accounts team.

(A) mistake   (B) error

19 increase in

• ~의 증가

기출 due to an **increase in** the demand for
~에 대한 수요의 증가로 인해

a 50 percent **increase in** profits
수익의 50퍼센트 증가

Due to an ------- in the cost of packaging materials, Seaman Fine Foods has had no choice but to raise its prices.

(A) increase   (B) effort

20 proximity to

~와의 인접성

기출 because of its **proximity to** the airport
공항과의 인접성 때문에

because of its **proximity to** shopping malls
쇼핑몰들과의 인접성 때문에

Wayfarer Inn is an ideal place to stay for tourists because of its ------- to the train station.
(A) competence   (B) proximity

21 initiative in

~의 주도권

기출 take the **initiative in** solving problems
문제를 해결하는 것의 주도권을 가지다

initiative in supporting the implementation of
~의 시행을 지원하는 것의 주도권

As a branch manager, Ms. Laing must take the ------- in delegating office tasks.
(A) initiative   (B) advice

22 investigation into

~에 대한 조사

기출 begin **investigation into** using alternative components
대체 부품을 사용하는 것에 대한 조사를 시작하다

Board members at Crick Software have begun ------- into merging with a local mobile application developer.
(A) investigations   (B) modifications

23 modifications to
~에 대한 변경(사항)

기출 **modifications to** the banquet menus
연회 메뉴에 대한 변경

Any ------- to the tour itinerary will be posted on our Web site immediately.

(A) reactions (B) modifications

24 persistence in
~에 있어서의 인내, 고집

기출 require **persistence in** the face of obstacles
장애물의 직면에 있어서의 인내를 요구하다

The founder's ------- in the face of financial problems eventually helped him to establish a successful textile company.

(A) frequency (B) persistence

25 revisions to
~에 대한 개정(사항), 수정(사항)

기출 all **revisions to** the books
그 책들에 대한 모든 개정사항

revisions to the rental agreement
대여 계약서에 대한 수정사항

The clients have asked for ------- to the blueprints for the entertainment complex on South Road.

(A) revisions (B) drawings

26 in response to

~에 대한 응답으로

기출 **in response to** complaints from customers
고객들로부터의 불만에 대한 응답으로

in response to increased competition
증가된 경쟁에 대한 응답으로

In ------- to complaints from our gym members, we have decided to offer a wider range of fitness classes.
(A) effort   (B) response

27 feedback on

~에 대한 피드백, 의견

기출 **feedback on** the new Web site
새로운 웹 사이트에 대한 피드백

feedback on the recent conference
최근 컨퍼런스에 대한 의견

The organizers of the Summer Solstice music festival are seeking ------- on the amenities provided at the event.
(A) quality   (B) feedback

28 in storage

입고 중인, 보관 중인

기출 keep 2 million kilograms of steel **in storage**
철근 2백만 킬로의 입고를 유지하다

During the transition to our new offices in Baileyville, several pieces of equipment will be held in -------.
(A) delivery   (B) storage

29 requirement for

~에 대한 필수요건

기출 a key **requirement for** businesses
사업에 대한 중요한 필수요건

meet the **requirement for** the position
그 직책에 대한 필수요건을 충족하다

An important ------- for those seeking employment in sales is the ability to communicate effectively.

(A) requirement   (B) impact

30 connection with

~와의 연결(성)

기출 **connection with** audience members
청중들과의 연결성

Actor Dan Hargraves enjoys attending conventions as it gives him a chance to feel a ------- with his fans.

(A) connection   (B) observation

31 in recognition of

~을 인정하는

기출 **in recognition of** his outstanding service
그의 뛰어난 서비스를 인정하는

in recognition of her contribution to
~에 대한 그녀의 공헌을 인정하는

Professor Wyatt received the Stanton Award in ------- of his remarkable contribution to the field of education.

(A) recognition   (B) suggestion

32 search on

- ~에 대한 조사

  기출 conduct a **search on** ~에 대한 조사를 실시하다

  Ms. Varney will conduct a ------- on the most ideal locations for her new cosmetics store.
  (A) search　　　　(B) decision

33 in keeping with

- ~을 준수하여

  기출 **in keeping with** company policy
  회사 정책을 준수하여

  In ------- with government noise regulation guidelines, work on the construction site must stop at 5 PM.
  (A) keeping　　　　(B) showing

34 with care

- 주의 깊게, 신중히

  기출 must be handled **with care**
  반드시 주의 깊게 다뤄져야 하다

  The cleaning products may irritate your skin and must therefore be handled with -------.
  (A) maintenance　　(B) care

35 under the supervision of

- ~의 감독 하에, 관리 하에

  기출 **under the supervision of** Dr. Aileen
  에일린 박사의 감독 하에

  As a result of Ms. Corr's absence, the HR department has been under the ------- of Max Bayliss for the past two months.
  (A) sight　　　　(B) supervision

36 in preparation for

~에 대비하여

기출 **in preparation for** the installation of
~의 설치에 대비하여

in preparation for the upcoming inspection
곧 있을 점검에 대비하여

In ------- for the upcoming business awards ceremony, Mr. Edwards has been practicing his speech.

(A) presentation　　(B) preparation

37 under the terms of

~의 조건 하에서

기출 **under the terms of** this agreement
이 계약의 조건 하에서

Under the ------- of this agreement, you must notify us at least three days in advance if you wish to cancel your subscription.

(A) words　　(B) terms

38 decline in

~의 감소

기출 **decline in** revenue 수익의 감소
decline in its stock price 주가의 감소
decline in sales of ~의 매출의 감소

Seraphim Corporation's decision to cancel its advertising campaign led to a ------- in its overall profits.

(A) market　　(B) decline

39 in jeopardy
● 위험에 처한

기출 put the contract **in jeopardy**
계약을 위험에 처하게 하다

> A failure to agree on the new location of the company headquarters could put the proposed business merger in -------.
>
> (A) jeopardy (B) exposure

40 with enthusiasm
● 열정으로

기출 greet all guests **with enthusiasm**
열정으로 모든 투숙객들을 맞이하다

> At Daytona Beach Resort, front desk staff are encouraged to greet all guests with -------.
>
> (A) achievement (B) enthusiasm

DAILY QUIZ

콜로케이션과 그에 알맞은 뜻을 연결해 보세요.

1 interest in • • (A) ~에 대한 관심

2 in conjunction with • • (B) ~에 대비하여

3 in preparation for • • (C) ~와 함께

빈칸에 알맞은 단어를 선택하세요.

4 in ------- with environmental standards
   환경 기준을 준수하여

5 in ------- to complaints from customers
   고객들로부터의 불만에 대한 응답으로

(A) response
(B) requirement
(C) compliance
(D) decline

6 meet the ------- for the position
   그 직책에 대한 필수요건을 충족하다

앞서 배운 콜로케이션들의 뜻을 생각하면서, 다음 문제를 풀어보세요.

7 The supermarket's own brand of laundry detergent is an affordable ------- to the leading products on the market.

   (A) range   (B) exchange
   (C) alternative   (D) choice

8 Considering its ------- to the airport and bus terminal, Canton Exhibition Center is the ideal venue for the International Trade Expo.

   (A) direction   (B) proximity
   (C) opposition   (D) sequence

정답 1 (A) 2 (C) 3 (B) 4 (C) 5 (A) 6 (B) 7 (C) 8 (B)

Day 05 기출 동의어 ❷ Part 7

1 vital

❶ 필수적인, 매우 중요한
→ **essential**

❷ 활력이 넘치는
→ **dynamic**

> The development of renewable energy technologies has played a **vital** role in reducing our dependence on fossil fuels.
> (A) essential   (B) dynamic

재생 가능 에너지 기술의 개발은 화석 연료에 대한 의존도를 줄이는 데 중요한 역할을 했습니다.

2 distinction

❶ 명성, 탁월함
→ **reputation**

❷ 다름, 차이, 대조
→ **difference**

> The company gained a global **distinction** for its innovative product, revolutionizing the food industry and attracting investors from around the world.
> (A) reputation   (B) difference

그 기업은 혁신적인 제품으로 세계적인 명성을 얻었는데, 이 제품이 식품 업계를 혁신시키고 세계 곳곳으로부터 투자자를 유치했습니다.

3 carry

❶ (물건을) 재고로 가지고 있다, 취급하다
→ **keep in stock**

❷ 이동시키다
→ **transport**

> I've checked every grocery store in town, but Holt's Ice Cream seems to only be **carried** by Foodland.
> (A) kept in stock   (B) transported

제가 도시에 있는 모든 식료품점을 확인해 봤지만, 홀트 아이스크림은 오직 푸드랜드에서만 취급되고 있는 것 같습니다.

4 just

❶ 정말, 딱
→ **exactly, quite**

❷ 오직, 단지
→ **only**

❸ 이제 막, 방금
→ **recently**

The new bookstore, filled with an extensive collection of unique and antique books, **just** opened on the second floor.

(A) exactly   (B) recently

독특하고 고풍스러운 서적들로 가득한 새 서점이 2층에 이제 막 문을 열었습니다.

5 as

❶ ~처럼
→ **like**

❷ ~동안
→ **while**

❸ ~ 때문에
→ **because**

The workers weave the blankets by hand **as** the company wants to maintain the traditional authenticity of its products.

(A) while   (B) because

직원들은 수작업으로 담요를 짜서 만드는데, 회사가 자사의 제품에 대해 전통적인 방식의 진정성을 유지하고 싶어 하기 때문입니다.

6 credit

❶ (지불해야 할) 돈
→ **money**

❷ 인정, 칭찬
→ **recognition, praise**

Mr. Reynolds deserves all the **credit** for helping us meet the deadline; he put in a lot of extra hours over the past couple of weeks.

(A) money   (B) recognition

레이놀드 씨는 우리가 마감기한을 지킬 수 있도록 도와주신 것에 대해 모든 인정을 받을 자격이 있습니다; 그분은 지난 몇 주 동안 많은 추가 시간을 쏟았습니다.

7 extend

❶ 연장하다, 늘리다
  → prolong
❷ (사업·영향력을) 확대하다
  → increase
❸ 주다, 베풀다
  → offer

> First of all, I would like to **extend** a welcome to our guests from Wilson Manufacturing, who will soon be working closely with us on several new projects.
> (A) prolong   (B) offer

우선, 저는 윌슨 매뉴팩처링 사에서 오신 저희 손님들께 환영의 인사를 전해 드리고자 하며, 이분들은 곧 여러 새로운 프로젝트에 대해 저희와 긴밀히 작업하시게 될 예정입니다.

8 mark

❶ 표시하다
  → sign
❷ 기념하다
  → celebrate

> Avoid Washington Avenue tomorrow morning since there will be a parade to **mark** the 150th anniversary of the town's foundation.
> (A) sign   (B) celebrate

도시 설립 150주년을 기념하는 퍼레이드가 있을 예정이므로 내일 아침엔 워싱턴 애비뉴를 피하도록 하세요.

9 figure

❶ 인물
  → person
❷ 형체
  → shape
❸ 액수
  → amount

> After a long period of poor sales, Treasure Hotels & Resorts finally released **figures** showing a budget surplus for the last quarter.
> (A) shapes   (B) amounts

오랜 기간의 매출 부진 끝에, 트레저 호텔 앤 리조트는 지난 분기에 마침내 흑자를 보여주는 수치를 발표했습니다.

10 term

❶ 기간
→ **duration**

❷ 조건
→ **condition**

The first **term** of the online business course will last from February to May, with a final exam taking place in the last month.

(A) duration (B) condition

온라인 비즈니스 과정의 첫 번째 학기는 2월부터 5월까지 지속될 것이며, 마지막 달에 기말고사가 실시됩니다.

11 property

❶ 소유물
→ **possession**

❷ 특성
→ **characteristic**

❸ 부지, 구내
→ **location**

Due to a high volume of complaints, pets are no longer allowed at this **property**.

(A) characteristic (B) location

아주 많은 불만 사항들로 인해, 이 건물에서는 애완 동물을 기르는 것이 더 이상 허용되지 않습니다.

12 step

❶ 조치
→ **action**

❷ 발자국
→ **footprint**

❸ 단계
→ **degree**

In response to the recent increase in cyber threats, the IT department will take the necessary **steps** to prevent unauthorized access to sensitive data.

(A) action (B) degree

최근 사이버 위협이 증가하는 것에 대한 대응으로, IT 부서는 민감한 데이터에 대한 무단 접근을 방지하기 위해 필요한 조치를 취할 것입니다.

13 prospect

❶ 기회, 가능성
→ **opportunity**

❷ 조망, 전망
→ **view**, **scene**

The internship at Rilke Technologies leads its participants to an array of exciting career **prospects**.
(A) opportunities (B) views

릴케 테크놀로지 사의 인턴 프로그램은 참가자들을 여러 흥미로운 채용 기회로 안내합니다.

14 outstanding

❶ 우월한, 뛰어난
→ **superior**, **exceptional**, **excellent**

❷ 미지불의
→ **not yet paid**, **unresolved**

Grizzlebee's Diner is a nationwide franchise well known for its **outstanding** service and fantastic food.
(A) excellent (B) unresolved

그리즐비 다이너는 뛰어난 서비스와 환상적인 음식으로 잘 알려진, 전국적인 규모의 프랜차이즈 회사입니다.

15 bear

❶ 견디다
→ **endure**

❷ 가지고 있다
→ **carry**

The banners hanging around the basketball stadium **bear** the names and logos of the teams in the eastern division.
(A) endure (B) carry

농구 경기장 주변에 걸려 있는 현수막들은 동부 지구에 속한 팀들의 명칭과 로고들을 포함하고 있습니다.

16 command

❶ 정통, 능력, 구사력
→ **mastery**

❷ 지시
→ **instruction**

Whoever we elect to oversee operations at the Kyoto facility will need to have a strong **command** of the Japanese language.
(A) mastery　　　(B) instruction

교토의 시설물 운영을 감독하도록 우리가 선정하는 사람은 누구든지 일본어에 능통한 실력을 지니고 있어야 할 것입니다.

17 approach

❶ 방식
→ **method, manner, way**

❷ 진입로
→ **entrance**

Five consecutive months of low sales made it obvious that the marketing team needed to adopt a different **approach**.
(A) method　　　(B) entrance

5개월 연속으로 이어진 저조한 매출로 인해 마케팅 팀이 다른 접근 방법을 취할 필요가 있었다는 점이 분명해졌습니다.

18 secure

❶ 보호하다
→ **protect**

❷ (힘들게) 얻어 내다
→ **obtain**

❸ 고정시키다
→ **fasten**

Secure this group identification tag to your luggage before checking it in at the counter.
(A) protect　　　(B) fasten

카운터에서 체크인하시기 전에 여러분의 수하물에 이 단체 인식표를 고정시켜 두시기 바랍니다.

19 learn

❶ 배우다
→ **study**

❷ 알게 되다
→ **find out**

Siwon Telecom customers will be delighted to **learn** about our latest reduced rates for international calls.
(A) study　　　(B) find out

시원 텔레콤 고객들이 최근 인하된 자사의 국제 전화 요금에 대해 알게 되면 기뻐할 것입니다.

20 trace

❶ 베끼다, 모사하다
→ **copy**

❷ 자취를 따라가다
→ **follow**

> *The President's Shadow* is a fascinating work of nonfiction that **traces** the early days of the United States Secret Service.
> (A) copies (B) follows

<대통령의 그림자>는 미국 비밀 수사국의 초창기를 뒤따라가보는, 매력적인 논픽션 작품입니다.

21 value

❶ 평가하다
→ **estimate**

❷ 소중하게 여기다
→ **appreciate**

> Fans of folk music who **value** catchy melodies and honest lyrics should give Joe Kell's newest album a listen.
> (A) estimate (B) appreciate

귀에 잘 들어오는 멜로디와 솔직한 가사를 중요하게 여기는 포크 음악 팬들은 조 켈 씨의 최신 앨범을 한번 들어봐야 합니다.

22 clear

❶ 밝은
→ **bright**

❷ 확실한, 분명한
→ **obvious**

> There is a **clear** need for a new type of battery that can power the next generation of portable electronic devices.
> (A) bright (B) obvious

차세대 휴대용 전자 기기에 동력을 공급할 수 있는 새로운 종류의 배터리에 대해 분명한 필요성이 있습니다.

23 recognize

❶ (사물이나 사람을) 알아보다
→ **identify**

❷ 공로를 인정하다, 예우하다
→ **honor**

❸ 인정하다, 받아들이다
→ **acknowledge, accept**

> This award is designed to **recognize** employees who provide exceptional service to our clients.
> (A) identify (B) honor

이 상은 우리 고객들에게 뛰어난 서비스를 제공한 직원들의 공로를 인정하기 위해 만들어졌습니다.

24 cover

❶ 보도하다, 취재하다, 주제로 다루다
→ **report on, talk about, include**

❷ 덮다, 씌우다
→ **spread over, wrap**

❸ ~에 대한 돈을 충당하다
→ **pay for**

❹ (보험, 품질 보증서 등)으로 보장하다
→ **insure, protect**

> All meals will be <u>covered</u> by the company, but transportation will need to be figured out individually.
> (A) protected (B) paid
>
> 모든 식사는 회사에서 비용을 부담할 것이지만 교통편은 개인적으로 해결해야 할 것입니다.

25 balance

❶ 균형, 안정
→ **stability**

❷ 잔액
→ **remainder, remaining amount**

> To avoid monthly fees, a minimum <u>balance</u> of $500 must be kept in the account.
> (A) stability (B) remainder
>
> 월간 요금을 피하시려면, 계좌에 최소 500달러의 잔액이 있어야 합니다.

26 meet

❶ 만나다
→ **get together**

❷ (요건을) 충족시키다
→ **fulfill, satisfy**

> Dolson Chemicals spent millions of dollars renovating its factories in order to <u>meet</u> the requirements of the new environmental protection policies.
> (A) get together (B) satisfy
>
> 돌슨 케미컬 사는 새로운 환경 보호 정책의 요건들을 충족시키기 위해 자사의 공장들을 개조하는 데 수백만 달러를 소비했습니다.

27 shape

❶ 형체
→ **figure**

❷ 상태
→ **condition**

> After you return the equipment, an associate will check that it's in good **shape** before refunding your deposit.
> (A) figure   (B) condition
>
> 장비를 반납하신 후에는, 예치금을 환불해 드리기 전에 직원 한 명이 그 장비의 상태가 좋은지 확인해 볼 것입니다.

28 issue

❶ 발부하다, 지급하다
→ **distribute**

❷ 공표하다, 보도하다
→ **report**

❸ 발행하다
→ **publish**

> New parking passes will be **issued** to all company employees before the end of the month.
> (A) distributed   (B) reported
>
> 이달 말이 되기 전에 회사의 전 직원에게 새로운 주차 출입증이 발급될 것입니다.

29 condition

❶ 환경, 상황
→ **circumstances**

❷ 필요 조건
→ **requirement**

> The bus trip to Cleveland could take up to five hours, depending on traffic **conditions**.
> (A) circumstances   (B) requirements
>
> 클리블랜드로 가는 버스 여행은 교통 상황에 따라 최대 5시간까지 걸릴 수 있습니다.

30 turn

❶ 회전하다
→ **rotate**

❷ 바꾸다
→ **transform**

> The planned renovations will **turn** the vacant office space on the third floor into a small auditorium.
> (A) rotate   (B) transform
>
> 계획된 개조 공사는 3층에 비어 있는 사무실 공간을 작은 강당으로 바꿀 것입니다.

DAILY QUIZ

밑줄 친 단어와 가장 가까운 의미를 지닌 것을 고르세요.

1
> The magazine will **cover** the artist's latest exhibition in its next issue, featuring an exclusive interview as well. Readers can also look forward to a visually stunning showcase of the exhibition through vivid photographs and detailed commentary.

(A) include
(B) protect
(C) wrap
(D) insure

2
> We make washers that are not only affordable and practical, but they also **meet** the energy efficiency standards for home appliances set by The Energy Policy and Conservation Act.

(A) touch
(B) satisfy
(C) please
(D) pay

3
> Thank you for choosing our services for your landscaping needs. We **value** your business and are committed to delivering outstanding results that will exceed your expectations.

(A) estimate
(B) appreciate
(C) increase
(D) know

/ Week /
02   실전 TEST

MP3 바로듣기

강의 바로보기

LISTENING

● Part 1

1.

2.

3.

4.

READING

Part 5

5. The cleaning robot is still in the prototype ------- and is not ready to be exhibited at this month's technology convention.

    (A) portion
    (B) degree
    (C) stage
    (D) compartment

6. National safety ------- require that all construction workers wear protective helmets inside building sites.

    (A) factors
    (B) subjects
    (C) regulations
    (D) processes

7. The results of the study showed that very few Epping residents have ------- in their local council members.

    (A) honesty
    (B) strength
    (C) motivation
    (D) confidence

8. Ms. Jensen, CEO of Walgrens Inc., is responsible for approving any ------- to the company's work policies.

    (A) turns
    (B) revisions
    (C) shapes
    (D) choices

9. When the Stockholm ------- visits our production facility, Mr. Martinez will show them how we manufacture our automobiles.

    (A) deviation
    (B) precision
    (C) delegation
    (D) translation

10. The director's latest movie uses some fundamental ------- of classic American films from the 1950s.

    (A) exercises
    (B) elements
    (C) similarities
    (D) awards

11. At the ------- of the prospective investors from China, the tour of the manufacturing plant was postponed until the following month.

    (A) effect
    (B) request
    (C) certainty
    (D) necessity

12. The owner of Iced Treats is waiting for ------- on its latest flavor of frozen yogurt.

    (A) quality
    (B) feedback
    (C) statement
    (D) conduct

Part 6

Questions 13-16 refer to the following memo.

To: All Security Personnel
Date: August 16
RE: New Security Measures

As many of you are already aware, we have recently suffered a series of security breaches. While most didn't lead to any serious problems, the last incident almost cost us blueprints **13.** ------- several million dollars. Fortunately, we were able to recover them before they fell into the hands of our competitors. **14.** -------.

First of all, you must now scan the ID cards of everyone coming into the facility. There will be no **15.** -------. This is true even for our highest-ranking employees. Also, all computers must be checked to ensure that they have the proper security software installed. Finally, after closing time, security must check the entire facility to make sure no one is staying late without **16.** ------- permission.

Thank you in advance for your compliance.

Greg Davidson, Chief Security Officer

---

13. (A) worth
 (B) expensive
 (C) valued
 (D) priced

14. (A) It will be difficult to replace these documents.
 (B) Therefore, we are implementing a new set of security policies.
 (C) So, please think carefully before sharing information.
 (D) Thank you for your attention on this serious matter.

15. (A) submissions
 (B) exceptions
 (C) transactions
 (D) correlations

16. (A) write
 (B) writing
 (C) wrote
 (D) written

Part 7

Questions 17-18 refer to the following article.

Argo Solutions Reaches Target

Detroit (September 7) – Argo Solutions has achieved its target of establishing computer programming workshops for those hoping to learn skills required for jobs in the technology sector. Argo specializes in creating business spreadsheet and database programs.

With the financial assistance of local governments in Detroit, Chicago, and St. Louis, several companies have set up various professional development workshops to provide opportunities for individuals to learn useful new skills. In the case of Argo Solutions, its workshops are held every Monday at its headquarters in Detroit.

"According to the terms set out by the providers of the funding, we had to provide a comprehensive learning experience that runs regularly throughout the year," said Argo Solutions CEO Leon Dolenz. "We are proud of the workshops that we now offer, which are led by some of our most experienced and skilled programmers."

In addition to joining the education initiative, the company is planning to hire around 100 new workers at its headquarters later this year, as demand for the company's products is rising sharply.

17. What does Argo Solutions produce?

(A) Software for business use
(B) University textbooks
(C) Laptops for local schools
(D) Market research reports

18. The word "terms" in paragraph 3, line 1, is closest in meaning to

(A) ideas
(B) durations
(C) labels
(D) conditions

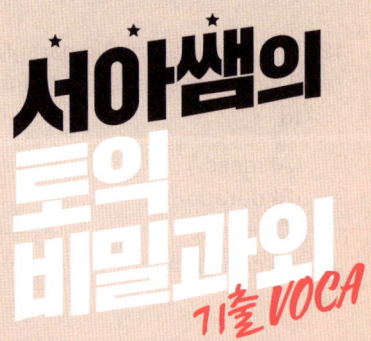

Week 03

Contents	Page	Date	Check
Day 01　`Part 2~4` LC가 잘 들리는 어휘 ①	152	월　일	☐
Day 02　`Part 5, 6` 동사 ①	166	월　일	☐
Day 03　`Part 5, 6` 동사 ②	180	월　일	☐
Day 04　`Part 5, 6` 동사 + 명사 콜로케이션	194	월　일	☐
Day 05　`Part 7` 기출 동의어 ③	208	월　일	☐
Week 03 실전 TEST	218	월　일	☐

Day 01 LC가 잘 들리는 어휘 ❶ Part 2~4

QR코드 하나를 가리고 찍으면 편해요!

MP3 바로듣기 / 강의 바로보기

1 budget

● n. 예산

W: Greg, could you update me on our finances?
M: We are still operating well within our **budget**.

여: 그렉, 우리의 재정 상황을 알려주시겠어요?
남: 우리는 여전히 예산 내에서 잘 운영되고 있습니다.

2 assignment

● n. 과업, 과제, 임무

W: Who's writing the product development proposal?
M: That **assignment** hasn't been officially given out.

여: 제품 개발 제안서를 누가 쓰고 있나요?
남: 그 업무는 아직 공식적으로 할당되지 않았어요.

3 be assigned to + 동사원형

● ~하도록 맡겨지다, 할당되다

W: Who'll **be assigned to lead** the marketing team?
M: The management is deciding that now.

여: 누가 마케팅 팀을 이끄는 업무를 맡게 될까요?
남: 경영진이 지금 그걸 결정하고 있어요.

> **만점 TIP**
> • 관련 기출
>   「be assigned to + 사람」 ~에게 할당되다
>   assign A to B A를 B에게 할당하다

4 behind schedule
● 일정에 뒤처진

W: We're running **behind schedule** and need to make some adjustments to meet the deadline.
M: Hmm, then I'll assign a few tasks to our intern Jaime so that the workload is spread out between us.

여: 저희가 일정에 뒤처지고 있어서 기한을 맞추기 위해서는 조정이 필요합니다.
남: 음, 그럼 인턴사원 제이미에게 몇 가지 일을 맡겨서 업무량이 분산될 수 있도록 하겠습니다.

> **만점 TIP**
>
> • 관련 기출
>   ahead of schedule 일정보다 앞서서

5 have difficulty -ing
● ~하는 데 어려움을 겪다

W: I'm **having difficulty replacing** the ink cartridge in the printer. Can you help me out?
M: Sure thing. I'll be there shortly.

여: 제가 프린터의 잉크 카트리지를 교체하는 데 어려움을 겪고 있어요. 도와주실 수 있나요?
남: 물론이죠. 금방 가겠습니다.

> **만점 TIP**
>
> • 기출 Paraphrasing
>   have difficulty -ing → have a problem[trouble] -ing
>   (~하는 데 문제가 있다)

6 commute
● n. 통근
v. 통근하다

W: How long is your **commute** to work?
M: Only about 20 minutes by bus.

여: 통근 시간이 얼마나 걸리나요?
남: 버스로 약 20분 정도밖에 안 걸립니다.

7 be good at
● ~에 능통하다, ~을 잘 하다

W: I need some visual materials to go along with my sales presentation tomorrow.
M: Thomas **is good at** designing slideshows.
여: 내일 영업 발표 때 같이 사용할 시각 자료가 필요해요.
남: 토마스가 슬라이드쇼 디자인을 잘 합니다.

만점 TIP

• 기출 Paraphrasing
be good at → be proficient[skilled] at, be familiar with (~에 능통하다)

8 not until + 일시
● ~까지는 아니다, ~은 되어야 하다

W: Hi, I just saw that Parking Lot C is closed. When will it reopen?
M: Unfortunately, **not until next month**.
여: 안녕하세요, 방금 C 주차장이 폐쇄되었다는 걸 봤습니다. 언제 다시 열리나요?
남: 유감스럽게도, 다음 달은 되어야 합니다.

만점 TIP

• 관련 기출
「not A until + 일시」 ~은 되어야 A하다
I won't have time until tomorrow.
난 내일은 되어야 시간이 날 거야.

9 be scheduled for + 일시
● ~로 예정되어 있다

W: Have you had your job interview yet?
M: No, it'**s scheduled for Friday**.
여: 혹시 면접 보셨나요?
남: 아니요, 금요일로 예정되어 있습니다.

만점 TIP

• 관련 기출
「schedule A for + 일시」 A하는 일정을 ~로 잡다
be scheduled to do ~할 예정이다

10 appointment

n. 약속, 예약

W: Could I schedule my **appointment** with Dr. Roy for Friday?
M: Sorry, he's busy that day.

여: 로이 박사님과의 진료 예약을 금요일로 잡을 수 있을까요?
남: 죄송하지만, 박사님은 그날 바쁘세요.

만점 TIP

• 관련 기출

doctor's appointment 진료 예약
dentist[dental] appointment 치과 예약
lunch appointment 점심 약속
make an appointment 만날 약속을 하다
make an appointment with a doctor 진료 예약을 하다

11 due + 일시

~가 지불 기한인, ~이 마감 기한인

W: This assignment is **due next week**.
M: I'll get started right away.

여: 이 과제는 다음 주가 마감입니다.
남: 바로 시작하겠습니다.

12 be due to + 동사원형

~할 예정이다

W: When's the safety inspector **due to visit** our factory?
M: Wednesday, at the latest.

여: 우리 공장에 안전 점검관이 언제 방문할 예정입니까?
남: 늦어도 수요일입니다.

13 come up with

- ~을 생각해 내다, 떠올리다

W: Our current sales approach isn't yielding the results we want. We need to **come up with** a new strategy.
M: I agree. Let's set up a team meeting to discuss it further.

여: 우리의 현재 영업 방식은 우리가 원하는 결과를 내지 못하고 있어요. 새로운 전략을 생각해 낼 필요가 있어요.
남: 동의합니다. 팀 회의를 잡아서 그것에 대해 더 논의해 봅시다.

14 be done

- 마치다, 끝내다

W: Have you finished designing the book cover?
M: Not yet, but it's almost **done**.

여: 책 표지 디자인 끝내셨어요?
남: 아직이요, 하지만 거의 다 되었어요.

> **만점 TIP**
> • 관련 기출
>   get A done A를 하다, A를 마치다

15 troubleshoot

- v. (컴퓨터의) 문제를 해결하다

W: The computer in the conference room isn't working. Could you come and **troubleshoot** the problem?
M: I'll be right there.

여: 회의실에 있는 컴퓨터가 작동하지 않습니다. 오셔서 문제를 해결해 주실 수 있나요?
남: 곧 가겠습니다.

16 figure out

● 알아내다, 파악하다

W: The garden plants look unhealthy.
M: I'll examine the irrigation system and try to **figure out** what the problem is.

여: 정원 식물들이 건강하지 않아 보입니다.
남: 관개 시스템을 조사해서 어떤 문제가 있는지 알아내겠습니다.

만점 TIP

• 관련 기출

  find out ~을 발견하다, 알아내다

17 fundraiser

● n. 모금 행사

W: Would you like to purchase these limited-edition hats with your admission tickets? Our zoo is currently holding a **fundraiser** to help the local Animal Welfare Institute.
M: Oh, sure. I'll take two.

여: 입장권과 함께 이 한정판 모자를 구매하시겠어요? 저희 동물원에서는 현재 지역 동물복지 기관을 돕기 위한 모금 행사를 진행하고 있습니다.
남: 아, 그럼요. 두 개 살게요.

18 travel arrangements

● 여행 준비

W: How are your **travel arrangements** going for your vacation to Maui next month?
M: I already booked a room at a beachside resort, and I plan to rent a car to get around the island, too.

여: 다음 달 마우이로 떠나는 휴가 여행 준비는 어떻게 되어 가나요?
남: 이미 해변 리조트에 방을 예약했고, 차를 빌려서 섬을 돌아다닐 계획입니다.

만점 TIP

• 숙소 예약, 교통편 마련 등의 일을 통틀어 travel arrangements라고 합니다.

19 head

● v. ~을 이끌다, 책임지다

> W: Who is **heading** the committee for the renovation?
> M: Mr. Han is in charge.
> 여: 누가 보수작업 위원회를 이끌고 있나요?
> 남: 한 씨가 담당합니다.

만점 TIP
• 관련 기출
  department head 부서장
  ☞ head가 명사로 쓰이면 '우두머리, 장'이라는 뜻입니다.

20 measure

measurement n. 측정, 치수

● v. ~의 치수를 재다, 측정하다

> W: Is this sofa the right size for the living room?
> M: I **measured** it twice.
> 여: 이 소파가 거실에 맞는 사이즈인가요?
> 남: 제가 두 번 쟀어요.

만점 TIP
• 관련 기출
  take some measurements 치수를 재다

21 be willing to + 동사원형

● 기꺼이 ~하다

> W: Would you **be willing to give** the keynote speech at the conference?
> M: Yes, I'd be happy to.
> 여: 학회에서 기조 연설을 해 주시겠어요?
> 남: 네, 그럼요.

22 alternative

- n. 대안
- a. 대안의, 대체하는

> W: With winter approaching, have you considered any indoor activities as an **alternative** to jogging?
> M: Yes, I'm thinking about joining a yoga class.
>
> 여: 겨울이 다가오는데, 조깅에 대한 대안으로 실내 활동을 고려해 보셨나요?
> 남: 네, 저는 요가 수업을 들을까 생각 중입니다.
>
> W: We can't use the meeting room right now because a different team is already in there. Do you have any **alternative** ideas?
> M: How about we go to the tenth floor café area?
>
> 여: 이미 다른 팀이 들어가 있어서 회의실을 이용할 수가 없습니다. 다른 대안이 없을까요?
> 남: 10층 카페 구역으로 가는 건 어떨까요?

만점 TIP

- 관련 기출

propose[offer] an alternative 대안을 제시하다
take an alternative[alternate] route 다른 길로 가다
alternative energy 대체 에너지

23 performance

- n. 업무 성과

> M: You deserve the promotion. You consistently receive outstanding **performance** reviews from other staff members.
> W: Thank you for your kind words.
>
> 남: 당신은 승진할 자격이 있어요. 다른 직원들로부터 꾸준히 우수한 성과 평가를 받고 있잖아요.
> 여: 친절한 말씀 감사합니다.

만점 TIP

- 사람에 대해 쓰이면 '성과', 기기에 대해 쓰이면 '성능'이라는 뜻이 됩니다. 더불어, '공연'이라는 뜻으로도 쓰인다는 것을 알아 두세요.

24 be supposed to + 동사원형

~하기로 되어 있다

W: How is the production schedule looking, Beatrice?
M: We **were supposed to start** filming tomorrow, but we're still waiting on some camera equipment to come in, so we might have to postpone it.

여: 베아트리스, 제작 일정이 어떻게 되어 가나요?
남: 내일부터 촬영을 시작하기로 했는데, 아직도 카메라 장비가 들어오기를 기다리고 있어서 미뤄야 할 것 같아요.

25 reach out to + 사람

~에게 연락하다

W: I **reached out to** the illustrator about creating an album cover design for us, but I haven't heard back yet.
M: Let's give her a few more days.

여: 일러스트 작가에게 앨범 커버 디자인 제작에 관련해 연락을 했는데, 아직 아무 연락이 없네요.
남: 며칠만 더 시간을 줍시다.

26 see if
see whether

~인지 알아보다

W: Wasn't Paul going to join us for lunch?
M: Yes, I'll **see if** he's ready.

여: 폴이 우리와 점심을 같이 하는 거 아니었나요?
남: 맞아요, 그가 준비 되었는지 알아볼게요.

27 cater

- v. 업체를 통해 (행사 등에) 음식을 공급하다

  W: Instead of eating at a restaurant for our team dinner, why don't we rent out a space for the evening and **cater** some food?
  M: That's a good idea!

  여: 회식 때 식당에서 저녁을 먹지 말고 밤에 공간을 빌려 출장 음식 공급업체에 시키는 게 어때요?
  남: 그거 좋은 생각이군요!

  만점 TIP
  - 관련 기출
    cater the event 행사에 음식을 공급하다
    catering (행사·연회 등을 대상으로 하는) 음식 공급
    caterer 출장 음식 공급 업체

28 be about to + 동사원형

- 막 ~하려던 참이다

  W: Do you mind reviewing this document for me?
  M: I **was** just **about to head** home.

  여: 이 문서 좀 검토해 주시겠어요?
  남: 지금 막 집에 가려던 참이었어요.

  만점 TIP
  - head는 '~로 향하다'라는 뜻의 동사로도 쓰입니다.
    I'm heading to the airport. 나는 공항으로 가는 중이야.

29 be concerned that

- ~에 대해 걱정하다

  W: Should we take a taxi or ride the bus to the conference?
  M: I'**m concerned that** if we take the bus, we might be late.

  여: 회의장까지 택시를 타고 갈까요, 아니면 버스를 타고 갈까요?
  남: 버스를 타면 늦을 것 같아서 걱정입니다.

30 **go ahead with** ● ~을 진행시키다

> W: Have we received all the summer clothing inventory for sale? I'm wondering if it's okay to begin planning our store layout.
> M: Yes, we have all the new merchandise, so you can **go ahead with** the setup.
>
> 여: 우리가 세일용 여름 의류 제품 재고품을 다 받았나요? 매장 배치 계획을 세워도 될지 궁금해서요.
> 남: 네, 신제품이 다 준비되어 있으니 배치를 진행하시면 됩니다.

만점 TIP
- 관련 기출
  proceed with ~을 진행시키다

---

31 **That's a relief.** ● 그거 다행이네요.

> W: I was able to submit our finalized project proposal before the deadline.
> M: **That's a relief.** I thought it would take us much longer!
>
> 여: 마감기한 전에 최종 프로젝트 제안서를 제출할 수 있었습니다.
> 남: 그거 다행이네요. 시간이 훨씬 더 걸릴 줄 알았는데요!

---

32 **reception desk** ● 접수처, 안내 데스크(= front desk)

> W: Can I get a map of the hotel's facilities at the **reception desk**?
> M: Of course you can. Just ask the receptionist.
>
> 여: 안내 데스크에서 호텔 시설 지도를 얻을 수 있나요?
> 남: 물론이죠. 안내 직원에게 요청하시면 됩니다.

만점 TIP
- receptionist(안내 데스크 직원)도 LC에 매우 자주 등장하는 어휘이므로 함께 알아 두세요.

33 I'm afraid

● (부정적인 내용을 말할 때) ~인 것 같아요

> W: I was considering cutting costs by reducing our marketing budget.
> M: **I'm afraid** that's not going to work. Our marketing efforts are crucial for maintaining our customer base.
>
> 여: 마케팅 예산을 줄여서 비용을 절감하는 것을 고려하고 있었습니다.
> 남: 그건 안 될 것 같습니다. 고객 기반을 유지하기 위해서는 마케팅 활동이 매우 중요합니다.

만점 TIP
• 관련 기출
I'm afraid not. 유감스럽지만 그럴 수 없을 것 같아요.

34 down the hall/ street

● 복도/길 저쪽에

> W: Where can I find the closest pharmacy?
> M: A new one just opened **down the street** from here.
>
> 여: 가장 가까운 약국은 어디에서 찾을 수 있나요?
> 남: 여기서 길 저쪽에 새로운 곳이 막 문을 열었어요.

35 leave for the day

● 퇴근하다

> W: When does the cleaning staff **leave for the day**?
> M: They typically finish at around 6 PM.
>
> 여: 청소부원들은 언제 퇴근하나요?
> 남: 보통 오후 6시쯤에 끝납니다.

36 I wish I could.

● 그럴 수 있으면 좋겠네요.

> W: I need to assemble 50 boxes today. Could you perhaps help me out?
> M: **I wish I could**, but I'm a bit busy right now.
>
> 여: 오늘 50박스를 조립해야 해요. 혹시 도와주실 수 있나요?
> 남: 저도 그러고 싶지만, 지금 좀 바빠요.

37 That makes sense.

- 말이 되네요. 이치에 맞네요.

  W: The outdoor workshop got postponed to next Thursday.
  M: **That makes sense.** I heard a storm is going to pass through tomorrow.

  여: 야외 워크숍이 다음 주 목요일로 연기되었습니다.
  남: 그럴 만도 해요. 내일 폭풍이 지나간다고 하던데요.

38 It depends on + 명사

- ~에 따라 다르다

  W: How soon can we initiate the research project?
  M: Well, **it depends on** the availability of government funding. The anticipated cost estimate may be too high.

  여: 연구 프로젝트를 얼마나 빨리 시작할 수 있을까요?
  남: 글쎄요, 정부 지원금의 이용 가능성에 따라 달라요. 예상되는 비용이 너무 클 수도 있어서요.

39 be up to + 사람

- ~에게 달려 있다

  W: I've heard rumors about the company's expansion plans. Any idea when we'll get a confirmation?
  M: It'll **be up to** board members to decide. They're meeting next week to discuss it further.

  여: 회사 확장 계획에 대한 소문을 들었습니다. 언제쯤 확정될까요?
  남: 결정은 이사회 구성원들에게 달려 있습니다. 다음 주에 회의를 해서 더 논의할 예정이라고 합니다.

40 buy one, get one free

- 1+1, 하나를 사면 하나를 더 주는 판매 방식

  W: Hi, are these granola bars **buy one, get one free**?
  M: Yes! If you buy one box of any flavor, you can get another one for free.

  여: 안녕하세요, 이 그래놀라 바는 원 플러스 원인가요?
  남: 네! 어떤 맛이든 한 박스를 구매하시면 무료로 한 박스 더 드립니다.

DAILY QUIZ

단어와 그에 알맞은 뜻을 연결해 보세요.

1 fundraiser •   • (A) 통근

2 commute   •   • (B) 모금 행사

3 alternative •   • (C) 대안

빈칸에 알맞은 단어를 선택하세요.

4 Who'll be ------- to lead the marketing team?
   누가 마케팅 팀을 이끄는 업무를 맡게 될까요?

5 I'm ------- that if we take the bus, we might be late.
   버스를 타면 늦을 것 같아서 걱정입니다.

   (A) willing
   (B) assigned
   (C) concerned
   (D) due

6 This assignment is ------- next week.
   이 과제는 다음 주가 마감입니다.

음원을 듣고 질문에 어울리는 응답을 고르세요. 🎧

7 (A)   (B)   (C)

8 (A)   (B)   (C)

정답 | 1 (B) 2 (A) 3 (C) 4 (B) 5 (C) 6 (D) 7 (A) 8 (C)

Day 02 동사 ❶ Part 5, 6

1 require
required a. 필수의
requirement n. 요구 조건, 필수 요건

● 요구하다, 필요로 하다

[기출] be **required** to attend
참석하는 것이 요구되다

be **required** for online orders
온라인 주문을 위해 필요하다

> Employees are ------- to submit travel expense reports for business trips.
> (A) acquired (B) required

2 submit
submission n. 제출(물)

● 제출하다

[기출] **submit** an application to ~에게 지원서를 제출하다
be **submitted** by mail 우편으로 제출되다

> If you are interested in joining Colleen Cosmetics, please ------- your résumé to the company's head office.
> (A) submit (B) propose

3 include
including prep. ~을 포함하여
inclusive a. 포함된, 포괄적인

● 포함하다

[기출] **include** a service agreement
서비스 계약을 포함하다

include one's account number
계좌번호를 포함하다

> Please be sure to ------- your e-mail address when registering for the upcoming technology convention.
> (A) include (B) extend

4 approve · 승인하다

approval n. 승인

기출 **approve** a plan to do
~하려는 계획을 승인하다

be **approved** by the HR department
인사부에 의해 승인되다

Renovation of the hotel's reception area will begin once the owner has ------- the design.
(A) persuaded (B) approved

5 announce · 발표하다, 알리다

announcement n. 발표, 공지

기출 **announce** that ~라고 발표하다

announce the appointment of ~의 임명을 알리다

Company founder Tim Jeffries is going to ------- his decision to retire during the year-end banquet.
(A) interfere (B) announce

6 ensure · 보장하다, 확실히 하다

기출 to **ensure** that ~라는 것을 보장하기 위해

Please ------- that all labels are printed correctly.
(A) ensure (B) apply

7 expect · 기대하다, 예상하다

expected a. 예상되는
expectation n. 기대, 예상

기출 be **expected** to increase
증가할 것으로 기대되다

do not **expect** any problems with
~에 어떠한 문제가 있을 것이라고 예상하지 못하다

Because of the hot and sunny weather, this weekend's beach party is ------- to be busy.
(A) completed (B) expected

8 deliver

delivery n. 배송, 전달

● 배송하다, 전달하다

기출 **deliver** one's parcel on time
소포를 제시간에 배송하다

deliver the invitation in person
초대장을 직접 전달하다

Customers can track their package on the Web site and see the approximate time that the driver will ------- the package.
(A) deliver　　　(B) observe

9 expand

expansion n. 확대, 확장
expanded a. 넓어진, 확장된

● 확대하다, 확장하다

기출 **expand** its delivery service into
~에까지 배송 서비스를 확대하다

expand its customer base
자사의 고객층을 확장하다

Next year, Allenby Cereals Inc. will ------- its product range in order to attract more customers.
(A) select　　　(B) expand

10 improve

improvement n. 향상, 개선

● 향상시키다, 개선시키다

기출 **improve** an applicant's chances of being hired
지원자의 고용될 기회를 향상시키다

improve the way we serve you
귀하에게 서비스를 제공하는 방식을 개선시키다

Having a qualification in marketing ------- an applicant's chances of being offered a job at our company.
(A) performs　　　(B) improves

11 **respond**

response n. 응답, 대응
responsive a. 반응하는

- 응답하다, 대응하다(to)

  기출 **respond** to all inquiries concerning
  ~에 관한 모든 질의에 응답하다

  respond to all customer complaints
  모든 고객 불만에 대응하다

  During the afternoon, the CS Manager often ------- to customer complaints by phone or by e-mail.
  (A) responds　　　(B) applies

12 **participate**

participating a. 참가하는
participant n. 참가자

- 참가하다

  기출 **participate** in the charity event
  자선 행사에 참가하다

  be invited to **participate**
  참가하도록 요청받다

  Over five thousand shoppers were asked to ------- in a short customer survey at Redmond Department Store last month.
  (A) write　　　(B) participate

13 **recommend**

recommendation n. 추천, 권고

- (사람을) 추천하다, (~하도록) 권고하다

  기출 **recommend** A as a candidate
  A를 후보자로 추천하다

  recommend that all customers change their passwords
  모든 고객들에게 비밀번호를 바꾸도록 권고하다

  Ezerman Inc. board members ------- Ms. Farley for the promotion to the management team.
  (A) settled　　　(B) recommended

14 retain

- 보관하다, 유지하다

  기출 **retain** the receipt for one's records
  기록용으로 영수증을 보관하다

  retain a copy of all sales documents
  모든 판매 자료 사본을 보관하다

  > The new company will ------- most of the previous company's branding and promotional materials.
  >
  > (A) retain　　　　(B) practice

15 vary

variety n. 다양성
various a. 다양한

- 다르다, 다양하다

  기출 **vary** slightly
  약간 다르다

  vary according to
  ~에 따라 다양하다

  > Customer opinions about Village Fashion's new clothing line ------- greatly among different age groups.
  >
  > (A) vary　　　　(B) allow

16 operate

operation n. 운영, 작동
operational a. 가동 중인

- 운영되다, 운영하다, 작동하다

  기출 **operate** under the name of
  ~라는 이름으로 운영되다

  operate seven other plants
  7개의 다른 공장들을 운영하다

  > The fast food company currently ------- over 250 restaurants in locations throughout North America.
  >
  > (A) serves　　　　(B) operates

17 distribute

distributor n. 유통업체
distribution n. 배포, 유통, 분배

● 배포하다, 유통하다, 분배하다

기출 **distribute** the meeting materials
회의 자료를 배포하다

will be **distributed** to all employees
모든 직원들에게 분배될 것이다

Ms. Jameson asked us to ------- the flyers to shoppers in Westfield Mall.
(A) distribute   (B) relate

18 anticipate

anticipation n. 예상, 기대
anticipated a. 기대하던

● 예상하다, 기대하다

기출 mistakenly **anticipate**
잘못 예상하다

anticipate any supply shortage
어떠한 공급 부족이라도 발생할 것을 예상하다

The retirement of the CEO is ------- to be announced at a press briefing tomorrow.
(A) anticipated   (B) processed

19 assist

assistance n. 지원, 보조

● 돕다, 보조하다

기출 **assist** A to develop the necessary skills
A가 필수적인 기술들을 발전시키도록 돕다

assist A in managing accounts
A가 계좌를 관리하는 것을 보조하다

Greenchip Investment ------- entrepreneurs in starting up small businesses in the technology industry.
(A) assists   (B) attracts

20 install

installation n. 설치
installment n. 분할 (납부)

- 설치하다

  기출 **install** solar panels
  태양 전지판을 설치하다

  will be **installed** automatically
  자동으로 설치될 것이다

  > The stage at the concert hall was built two months ago, but the venue manager ------- the sound system only yesterday.
  > (A) installed (B) entered

21 consult

consultation n. 상담, 참조
consultant n. 상담가, 자문 위원

- (사람에) 상담하다, (자료를) 참조하다

  기출 **consult** with A
  A와 상담하다

  consult the manual
  설명서를 참조하다

  > Please ------- Ms. Anderson's e-mail dated January 8 to check the date and time of your performance review.
  > (A) inquire (B) consult

22 advise

advice n. 조언
advisor n. 고문
advisory a. 자문의

- 권고하다, (정식으로) 알리다, 조언하다

  기출 be **advised** to check that
  ~라는 것을 확인하도록 권고되다

  advise A of the changes
  A에게 변경 사항에 대해 알리다

  > International travelers are ------- to arrive at the airport at least 3 hours before their departure time.
  > (A) advised (B) criticized

23 rely

- 의존하다(on, upon)

  기출 **rely** on outside consultants
  외부 상담가들에 의존하다

  rely upon team leaders
  팀 리더들에 의존하다

  > In the past, we ------- branch managers to provide health and safety training to employees.
  > (A) relied on   (B) stated that

24 obtain

- 얻다, 획득하다

  기출 **obtain** a free quote
  무료 견적을 얻다

  obtain a commercial driver's license
  사업용 운전 면허를 획득하다

  > King Taco workers can ------- replacements for work uniforms by visiting the personnel office.
  > (A) obtain   (B) apply

25 replace

replacement n. 교체, 후임

- (사물을) 교체하다, (사람을) 대체하다

  기출 **replace** our current e-mail system
  우리의 현 이메일 시스템을 교체하다

  need to be **replaced** because
  ~ 때문에 교체되어야 하다

  > A spokesperson for Maitland Engineering stated that Barbara Smalling will ------- Craig Stevens as the HR director.
  > (A) replace   (B) connect

26 **revise**

revision n. 수정, 개정
revised a. 수정된, 개정된

● 수정하다, 개정하다

기출 be asked to **revise** the report
보고서를 수정하도록 요청받다

revise the dress code
복장 규정을 개정하다

The COO has recently decided to ------- the company's returns and exchanges policy.
(A) refer   (B) revise

27 **notify**

notification n. 알림, 통지

● 알리다, 통지하다

기출 **notify** the catering coordinator
케이터링 담당자에게 알리다

will **notify** you as soon as your item is ready
귀하의 물건이 준비되는 대로 통지할 것이다

Please ------- Ms. Richards that her reservation of the third floor meeting room has been approved.
(A) present   (B) notify

28 **seek**

● ~을 찾다, 구하다

기출 **seek** experienced and motivated managers
경험 많고 의욕적인 관리자들을 찾다

seek advice about the regulation
규제에 대해 조언을 구하다

In order to compete with rival firms, Estro Inc. must ------- new ways to target customers in the 25-35 age range.
(A) seek   (B) focus

29 establish

established a. 자리를 확고히 잡은, 인정받는
establishment n. 설립, 기관

- 설립하다, 확립하다

  기출 **establish** a new office in Japan
  일본에 새로운 사무실을 설립하다

  Having just ------- a new branch office in Milan, Romeo Fashion hopes to make a big impact in the European market.
  (A) established   (B) enforced

30 recognize

recognizable a. 알아볼 수 있는
recognition n. 인정, 인지, 표창

- (공로 등을, 사실임을) 인정하다, 인지하다

  기출 **recognize** innovation in the field of
  ~의 분야에서의 혁신을 인정하다

  be frequently **recognized** as a company that
  ~인 회사로서 자주 인지되다

  Mr. Drake will be ------- for his innovative designs when he is awarded the prestigious award later this month.
  (A) recognized   (B) permitted

31 determine

determination n. 결정, 결심
determined a. 확고한

- 확정하다, 결정하다, 알아내다

  기출 **determine** that all problems were solved
  모든 문제가 해결되었음을 확정하다

  determine the appropriate size for
  ~을 위한 적절한 크기를 알아내다

  Engineers are still trying to ------- the most efficient way to strengthen the foundations of Selway Bridge.
  (A) resolve   (B) determine

32 fill

- 채우다

  기출 will be **filled** by the shipping department
  운송부에 의해 채워질 것이다

  Centracorp has four open technical support positions that we hope to ------- by the end of the month.
  (A) fill   (B) inform

33 attract

attraction n. 매력, 명소

- 끌어들이다

  기출 **attract** large crowds
  큰 규모의 관중을 끌어들이다

  attract tourists to the city
  관광객들을 그 도시로 끌어들이다

  With the temperatures soaring this week, many local stores are offering free refreshments to ------- shoppers.
  (A) attract   (B) await

34 predict

predictable a. 예측할 수 있는
prediction n. 예측, 예언

- 예측하다, 예상하다

  기출 **predict** an increase in
  ~의 증가를 예측하다

  Property market experts ------- that house prices in major cities will continue to rise over the next five years.
  (A) represent   (B) predict

35 implement

implementation n. 시행, 실행

- 시행하다, 실행하다

  기출 **implement** a new policy
  새로운 정책을 시행하다

  implement a recycling program
  재활용 프로그램을 실행하다

  The new protocols were ------- to ensure the safe disposal of waste from Markton Production's manufacturing plant.

  (A) implemented　　(B) occupied

36 assign

assignment n. 배정, 과제

- 배정하다, 할당하다

  기출 be **assigned** accounts to manage
  관리할 계정들을 배정받다

  New recruits undergo a three-month training and probation period before they are ------- full-time positions.

  (A) assigned　　(B) received

37 arrange

arrangement n. 준비, 약속

- 준비하다, 계획하다

  기출 **arrange** transportation
  교통편을 준비하다

  be **arranged** for A
  A를 위해 계획되다

  Ms. Kowalski will ------- for Mr. Timmins to tour the new production facility early next month.

  (A) arrange　　(B) identify

38 exceed

exceedingly ad. 극도로
excess n. 초과, 과잉
excessive a. 과도한

● (한도를) 초과하다, (양을) 넘다

> 기출 **exceed** the weight limit
> 무게 제한을 초과하다
>
> **exceed** one's expectations
> 기대치를 넘어서다

The Burwell MX5 sports car ------- 300 kilometers per hour and demonstrated exceptionally efficient gas mileage.
(A) processed　　　(B) exceeded

39 postpone

● 연기하다

> 기출 be **postponed** until December 15
> 12월 15일까지 연기되다
>
> **postpone** the fundraising campaign
> 모금 캠페인을 연기하다

Due to certain design flaws, the release of our new product has been ------- until June 30.
(A) postponed　　　(B) confirmed

40 acquire

acquired a. 습득한, 후천적인
acquisition n. 인수

● (기업을) 인수하다, 획득하다

> 기출 recently **acquired** a company
> 최근에 회사를 인수했다
>
> **acquire** enough points
> 충분한 포인트를 획득하다

Allen Health Foods Inc. recently ------- three warehouses as part of its efforts to expand its distribution network.
(A) acquired　　　(B) borrowed

DAILY QUIZ

단어와 그에 알맞은 뜻을 연결해 보세요.

1. expand • • (A) (사람에) 상담하다, (자료를) 참조하다
2. consult • • (B) 확대하다, 확장하다
3. assign • • (C) 배정하다, 할당하다

빈칸에 알맞은 단어를 선택하세요.

4. ------- a plan to do
   ~하려는 계획을 승인하다

5. ------- innovation in the field of
   ~의 분야에서의 혁신을 인정하다

6. ------- a new policy
   새로운 정책을 시행하다

(A) recognize
(B) implement
(C) notify
(D) approve

앞서 배운 단어들의 뜻을 생각하면서, 다음 문제를 풀어보세요.

7. To ------- customer satisfaction, Miliano Department Store provides refunds and exchanges for any products purchased up to 30 days ago.

   (A) appraise   (B) grant
   (C) confirm   (D) ensure

8. If you are satisfied with the terms, sign both copies of the employment contract and ------- one of them to Mr. Ogilvie.

   (A) reach   (B) submit
   (C) yield   (D) alert

정답 1 (B) 2 (A) 3 (C) 4 (D) 5 (A) 6 (B) 7 (D) 8 (B)

Day 03 동사 ❷ Part 5, 6

1 affect
● ~에 영향을 미치다

> [기출] will **affect** the sales of the vendors
> 판매사의 매출에 영향을 미칠 것이다

If your can of NutriKind Vegetable Juice is not shaken vigorously, it may ------- the taste of the beverage.
(A) affect　　　　(B) assemble

2 accommodate
accommodation n. 숙박

● (요구, 조건 등을) 충족하다, (행사, 사람 등을) 수용하다

> [기출] **accommodate** the increasing demand
> 늘어나는 수요를 충족하다
>
> **accommodate** parties of more than ten people
> 10명 이상의 단체를 수용하다

BTX Motors is developing hybrid vehicles to ------- the growing demand for vehicles with low energy consumption.
(A) accommodate　　(B) experience

3 prevent
prevention n. 예방
preventive a. 예방의, 예방을 위한

● 예방하다, 막다

> [기출] **prevent** damage in shipping
> 배송 중 손상을 예방하다
>
> **prevent** A from -ing
> A가 ~하는 것을 막다

Supervisors should ------- employees from taking excessively long breaks unless it is deemed necessary.
(A) realize　　　　(B) prevent

4 attribute

- ~의 원인, 탓으로 돌리다

  기출 **attribute** A to B
  A의 원인을 B로 돌리다

  be **attributed** to fierce competition
  치열한 경쟁 탓으로 돌려지다

  > The advertising team at Jaguar Shoes ------- the low sales numbers to the sales division's lack of effort.
  >
  > (A) suggests (B) attributes

5 donate

donation n. 기부
donor n. 기부자

- 기부하다

  기출 **donate** A to B
  A를 B에게 기부하다

  > The director of *The Lone Ghost* has announced that he will ------- 20% of his earnings from the movie to low-income families.
  >
  > (A) consume (B) donate

6 perform

performance n. 실행, 성과, 공연

- 수행하다, 실행하다

  기출 **perform** mandatory maintenance
  의무적인 유지보수 작업을 수행하다

  > Our computer specialists are ready to ------- a variety of upgrades to keep our customers' machines operating optimally.
  >
  > (A) perceive (B) perform

7 **coordinate**

coordination n. 조정, 조화

● 조정하다, 잘 어울리다

기출 **coordinate** the activities of several departments
여러 부서들의 활동을 조정하다

In his current role, Mr. Hooper is responsible for ------- the projects of several departments.
(A) coordinating　　　(B) intending

8 **adjust**

adjustment n. 조절, 조정
adjustable a. 조절할 수 있는

● 조절하다, 조정하다

기출 **adjust** the height
높이를 조절하다

arrange for the deadline to be **adjusted**
마감일이 조정되도록 준비하다

In some circumstances, the front desk staff may be able to arrange for the check-out time to be -------.
(A) reached　　　(B) adjusted

9 **resolve**

resolution n. 해결

● 해결하다

기출 identify and **resolve** problems
문제를 찾아 해결하다

resolve customer problems
고객 문제를 해결하다

Ms. Kim's duties include responding to and ------- complaints from customers.
(A) introducing　　　(B) resolving

10 acknowledge

acknowledgement n. 시인, 인정

• 수령을 확인하다, 인정하다

기출 **acknowledge** receipt of the document
문서의 수령을 확인하다

I am writing this e-mail to ------- receipt of your application for the position.
(A) acknowledge (B) suggest

11 enhance

enhancement n. 향상, 강화

• 향상시키다, 강화하다

기출 **enhance** the guest experience
투숙객의 경험을 향상시키다

enhance the landscape
조경을 강화하다

Lumoflow Technology's Super Bright Lighting is guaranteed to ------- any workspace.
(A) enhance (B) illustrate

12 negotiate

negotiation n. 협상, 협의

• 협상하다, 협의하다

기출 be willing to **negotiate** 기꺼이 협상하다

negotiate with the owner 소유자와 협의하다

As the manager of the personnel department, Mr. Mackey will recruit new staff and ------- salaries with them.
(A) negotiate (B) assign

13 certify

certified a. 인증 받은, 공인된
certificate n. 인증서, 자격증
certification n. 인증, 증명

• 인증하다, 보증하다

기출 **certify** that all specifications are met
모든 사양을 충족하는 것을 인증하다

After safety inspectors ------- that all requirements are met, the factory will begin production.
(A) certify (B) associate

14 **demonstrate**

demonstration n. 시연, 입증

● 시연하다, 입증하다

기출 **demonstrate** how to use the program
그 프로그램을 사용하는 방법을 시연하다

demonstrate one's commitment
~의 헌신을 입증하다

> Flight attendants must be able to ------- how to put on a life vest correctly.
>
> (A) implement   (B) demonstrate

15 **collaborate**

collaborative a. 협력하는
collaboratively ad. 협력하여

● 협력하다

기출 **collaborate** with
~와 협력하다

collaborate on a study
한 연구에 대해 협력하다

> Mr. Teale hopes to ------- more frequently with Ms. Easton now that their offices are located on the same floor.
>
> (A) establish   (B) collaborate

16 **finalize**

finalized a. 마무리된, 완결된

● 마무리하다

기출 **finalize** the details of
~의 세부사항들을 마무리하다

finalize the decision
결정을 마무리하다

> Ms. Hogg still has to ------- several details for the year-end party, such as the dinner menu and the entertainment.
>
> (A) finalize   (B) treat

17 assess

assessment n. 평가

● 평가하다

기출 **assess** the problems 문제들을 평가하다
assess one's progress ~의 진척도를 평가하다

The city of Lornten will send out plumbers to ------- the water supply problems that residents are experiencing.
(A) assess (B) distribute

18 surpass

● 능가하다, 뛰어넘다

기출 **surpass** one's sales goals ~의 매출 목표를 능가하다

The number of new subscribers this year has ------- the number projected back in January.
(A) preceded (B) surpassed

19 prohibit

prohibition n. 금지

● 금지하다

기출 **prohibit** parking on the street
거리에서의 주차를 금지하다

be **prohibited** throughout
~ 전역에서 금지되다

Visitors are reminded that flash photography is strictly ------- throughout the art gallery.
(A) prohibited (B) bothered

20 contain

● 포함하다

기출 **contain** information on ~에 대한 정보를 포함하다

Account passwords should not ------- easily guessable information such as birthdates.
(A) differ (B) contain

21 coincide

- 시점이 겹치다(with)

  기출 **coincide** with Mr. Smith's business trip
  스미스 씨의 출장과 시점이 겹치다

  coincide with the fair
  박람회와 시점이 겹치다

  > The Chicago conference date conveniently ------- with Mr. Wilmore's meeting with a client in the city.
  >
  > (A) collaborates　　(B) coincides

22 strive

- 노력하다

  기출 **strive** to maintain its position in the market
  시장에서 그 위치를 유지하도록 노력하다

  strive to recognize the achievement of
  ~의 성과를 인지하도록 노력하다

  > Ms. Quincy always ------- to motivate her workers to meet their sales targets.
  >
  > (A) strives　　(B) states

23 reveal

- 공개하다, 발표하다, (연구, 조사가) 결과를 보여주다

  기출 **reveal** the plan for
  ~을 위한 계획을 공개하다

  reveal a strong preference for SUVs over sedans
  세단보다 SUV에 대한 강력한 선호를 보여주다

  > A recent study ------- that people who eat breakfast regularly tend to be healthier than those who skip breakfast.
  >
  > (A) admits　　(B) reveals

24 represent

representative n. 직원, 대표

- 대표하다, 대변하다, 나타내다

  기출 will **represent** the company in Canada
  캐나다에서 회사를 대표할 것이다

  represent a significant advance over
  ~에 비해 중대한 발전을 나타내다

  > Scientist Jill Goldstein will ------- Rapido Corporation at the environmental conference next week.
  > (A) represent   (B) compete

25 argue

argument n. 주장, 논리
arguably ad. 거의 틀림없이

- 주장하다

  기출 Some critics **argue** that ~.
  몇몇 비평가들은 ~라고 주장한다.

  > Some analysts ------- that the company's plan to expand into the automobile industry will fail.
  > (A) cite   (B) argue

26 patronize

patron n. (단골) 손님
patronage n. 단골 거래, 애용

- 단골로 이용하다

  기출 be likely to **patronize** stores with
  ~을 가진 매장들을 단골로 이용할 것 같다

  > Market research indicates that customers are more likely to ------- stores that sell reliable products at reasonable prices.
  > (A) verbalize   (B) patronize

27 **recover**

recovery n. 회복, 복구

● 회복하다, 복구하다

기출 fully **recover** from the economic difficulties
경기 불황에서 완전히 회복하다

The extent to which the firm has ------- from its financial difficulties will become clear over the next few weeks.
(A) endured　　　　(B) recovered

28 **evolve**

evolution n. 진화

● 발전하다, 진화하다

기출 **evolve** from a small local band
지역의 작은 밴드에서 발전하다

evolve beyond the traditional role
전통적인 역할을 넘어 진화하다

The city has ------- beyond its traditional role as a stopover location into a major tourist destination.
(A) focused　　　　(B) evolved

29 **utilize**

utilization n. 이용, 활용

● 이용하다, 활용하다

기출 be **utilized** throughout the process
과정 전반에 걸쳐 이용되다

Robot technology has been ------- in various sectors, such as the manufacturing and medical industries.
(A) utilized　　　　(B) assembled

30 prolong
prolonged a. 장기적인, 오랜

● (기한을) 연장하다

기출 undergo regular maintenance to **prolong** the life of the vehicle
차량의 수명을 연장하기 위해 정기적인 유지보수를 받다

> The device should always be turned off when not in use to ------- the life of battery.
> (A) enlarge (B) prolong

31 alleviate
alleviation n. 경감, 완화

● 경감하다, 완화하다

기출 do little to **alleviate** concerns about
~에 대한 우려를 경감하는 데 거의 도움이 되지 않다

in an effort to **alleviate** congestion
혼잡을 완화하려는 노력의 일환으로

> The slight decrease in traffic congestion has done little to ------- concerns about the city's transportation systems.
> (A) confiscate (B) alleviate

32 place
placement n. 배치

● 배치하다, 놓다

기출 must be **placed** by March 18
3월 18일까지 배치되어야 하다

> Please note that used batteries should be ------- in a clear plastic bag and left next to the recycle bin.
> (A) declined (B) placed

33 account

accounting n. 회계(학)
accountant n. 회계사
accountable a. 책임이 있는

• 설명하다(for)

기출 **account** for the increase in
~에서의 증가를 설명하다

The freezing temperatures ------- for the low turnout at today's outdoor music festival.
(A) account　　　　(B) state

34 inform

information n. 정보
informative a. 유익한

• ~에게 알리다, 통지하다

기출 **inform** the building manager that
건물 관리인에게 ~라고 알리다

Please ------- the accounting department of your working hours before the end of the week.
(A) inform　　　　(B) invite

35 undergo

• 겪다, 경험하다

기출 **undergo** renovations 보수공사를 겪다
　　　undergo a full review 완전한 검토를 경험하다

Daisy Restaurant will be ------- extensive remodeling as it seeks to attract more diners.
(A) dealing　　　　(B) undergoing

36 enlarge

• 확장하다

기출 a plan to **enlarge** the sales division
영업부를 확장하는 계획

The CEO recently announced a proposal to ------- the company's human resources department.
(A) enlarge　　　　(B) declare

37 remain

remaining a. 남아 있는
remainder n. 나머지

- **(~인 상태를) 유지하다, 남다**

  기출 **remain** the same
  같은 상태를 유지하다

  remain the top holiday destination
  최고 휴양지의 입지를 유지하다

  Despite the considerable growth in sales this quarter, Magenta Electronics' profits have ------- the same.
  (A) raised   (B) remained

38 appoint

appointed a. 임명된, 예정된
appointment n. 임명, 약속

- **임명하다**

  기출 **appoint** a new financial manager
  신임 재무부장을 임명하다

  be **appointed** as
  ~로 임명되다

  The board of directors has ------- Mr. Lewinson as the new Chief Operations Officer, replacing retiring Mr. Simons.
  (A) invested   (B) appointed

39 encourage

encouragement n. 격려, 권고

- **격려하다, 권고하다, 촉진하다**

  기출 **encourage** employees to submit ideas
  직원들에게 아이디어를 제출하도록 격려하다

  encourage a healthy lifestyle
  건강한 생활방식을 권고하다

  To ensure a spot at the training workshop, we ------- interested individuals to register by Friday, April 16.
  (A) encourage   (B) provide

40 monitor

monitoring n. 관찰, 감시

- 관찰하다, 감시하다

  기출 **monitor** the temperature
  기온을 관찰하다

  monitor unplanned expenditures
  계획에 없던 지출을 감시하다

  FitTek Inc. has developed a new range of smartwatches that can ------- the heart rate and blood pressure of wearers.
  (A) monitor   (B) reserve

DAILY QUIZ

단어와 그에 알맞은 뜻을 연결해 보세요.

1. adjust • • (A) 임명하다
2. appoint • • (B) 대표하다, 대변하다, 나타내다
3. represent • • (C) 조절하다, 조정하다

빈칸에 알맞은 단어를 선택하세요.

4. ------- the guest experience
   투숙객의 경험을 향상시키다

5. ------- that all specifications are met
   모든 사양을 충족하는 것을 인증하다

   (A) argue
   (B) certify
   (C) enhance
   (D) finalize

6. ------- the details of
   ~의 세부사항들을 마무리하다

앞서 배운 단어들의 뜻을 생각하면서, 다음 문제를 풀어보세요.

7. RJT Entertainment will relocate the Summer Sizzle Music Festival to Lawson Park to ------- the event's rise in popularity.

   (A) allocate
   (B) provide
   (C) incapacitate
   (D) accommodate

8. The state's transportation department has the right to ------- cycling in local parks.

   (A) prohibit
   (B) ride
   (C) bother
   (D) avoid

정답 1 (C) 2 (A) 3 (B) 4 (C) 5 (B) 6 (D) 7 (D) 8 (A)

Day 04 동사 + 명사 콜로케이션 Part 5, 6

 MP3 바로듣기
 강의 바로보기

1 meet the expectations
● 기대를 충족하다

기출 **meet** the needs of
~의 필요를 충족하다

meet the qualifications
자격요건을 충족하다

Despite an extensive marketing campaign, sales of the new Elba mobile phone did not ------- consumers' expectations.

(A) meet　　　　　(B) seem

2 institute a policy
● 정책을 도입하다

기출 **institute** a minimum fee for delivery
배달에 대한 최소 요금을 도입하다

Trinket Corporation has ------- a policy that provides financial incentives to boost worker morale in its offices.

(A) instituted　　　(B) proved

3 reduce expenses
● 비용을 줄이다

기출 **reduce** erosion 침식을 줄이다

reduce the volume of ~의 분량을 줄이다

SJ Electronics has ------- expenses by 30 percent after upgrading its fleet of vehicles.

(A) examined　　　(B) reduced

4 **lead a seminar** · 세미나를 이끌다

> 기출 **lead** a tour of ~의 견학을 이끌다
> **lead** the company 회사를 이끌다

Bob Mitchell, the call center manager, will ------- a seminar on customer service next Wednesday.
(A) lead   (B) charge

5 **indicate a preference** · 선호도를 나타내다, 표시하다

> 기출 **indicate** a need to do ~할 필요성을 나타내다
> **indicate** one's height ~의 키를 표시하다

The comments on the feedback forms ------- a high preference for vegan-friendly dishes on our menus.
(A) advise   (B) indicate

6 **extend an offer** · 제안하다

> 기출 **extend** the service contract 서비스 계약을 연장하다
> **extend** the warranty 보증기간을 연장하다

The company founder ------- an offer to all shareholders to take a tour of the new factory.
(A) extended   (B) assigned

7 **reject a proposal** · 제안을 거절하다

> 기출 **reject** the claim 주장을 거절하다
> **reject** a plan 계획을 거절하다

Because of the large number of advance ticket sales, Ms. Potter ------- a proposal to postpone the music festival.
(A) inquired   (B) rejected

8 attend the training session

- 교육 시간에 참석하다

  기출 **attend** the meeting
  회의에 참석하다

  attend development seminars
  개발 세미나에 참석하다

  > All new recruits must ------- the training session before reporting to their respective department managers.
  >
  > (A) attend　　　　(B) invite

9 accept applications

- 지원서를 받다

  기출 **accept** telephone cards 전화 카드를 받다

  accept assistance 도움을 받다

  accept bids 입찰을 받다

  > Biosense Inc. is now ------- applications for the research scientist position at its laboratory.
  >
  > (A) accepting　　　(B) running

10 renew an agreement

- 약정을 갱신하다

  기출 **renew** a contract
  계약을 갱신하다

  renew your membership
  귀하의 회원권을 갱신하다

  renew your subscription
  귀하의 구독을 갱신하다

  > Mizeno Graphic Design has decided to ------- an agreement with Rocco Corporate Catering.
  >
  > (A) proceed　　　(B) renew

11 confirm an appointment

- 예약을 확정하다

  [기출] **confirm** a patient's prescription
  환자의 처방을 확정하다

  confirm receipt of the invoice
  송장의 수령을 확정하다

  > Please ------- your appointment by phone or e-mail before arriving at Riddick Health Clinic.
  > (A) confirm　　　(B) remind

12 undergo restructuring

- 구조조정을 하다

  [기출] **undergo** a committee review 위원회 검토를 하다

  undergo renovations 보수공사를 하다

  > Ealing Publishing Co. will ------- restructuring in order to improve its productivity.
  > (A) resupply　　　(B) undergo

13 improve a chance

- 기회를 향상시키다

  [기출] **improve** sales results 영업 결과를 향상시키다

  improve work conditions 근무 조건을 개선하다

  > Being fluent in at least two languages ------- the chances of being hired by Royston Travel Agency.
  > (A) improves　　　(B) achieves

14 deserve high-quality service

- 높은 품질의 서비스를 받을 자격이 있다

  [기출] **deserve** a promotion 승진할 자격이 있다

  > Whether flying in economy or first class, Alpine Airlines passengers ------- high-quality service.
  > (A) satisfy　　　(B) deserve

15 review the manuals

● 설명서를 검토하다

기출 **review** the enclosed instructions
동봉된 설명서를 검토하다

review proposals
제안서를 검토하다

To avoid any confusion, all users should ------- the manuals before they start the program.

(A) decide　　　　　(B) review

16 express appreciation

● 감사를 표하다

기출 **express** concern
우려를 표하다

express interest
관심을 표하다

At the charity fundraising event, several organization members ------- their appreciation for Mr. Donaldson's generous donation.

(A) expressed　　　　(B) thanked

17 resolve problems

● 문제를 해결하다

기출 **resolve** scheduling conflicts
일정 충돌을 해결하다

resolve the matter
사안을 해결하다

The customer service team at Spritz Department Store are trained to ------- problems promptly and efficiently.

(A) set　　　　　　(B) resolve

18 demonstrate the capability

- 능력을 보여주다

  기출 **demonstrate** the method of
  ~의 방법을 보여주다

  demonstrate its commitment to
  ~에의 헌신을 보여주다

  > Engineers from Dayatsu Motors will ------- the capabilities of their new luxury sedan at the upcoming International Auto Show.
  >
  > (A) tolerate (B) demonstrate

19 sign an agreement

- 약정에 서명하다

  기출 **sign** a 12-month lease
  12개월 임대계약에 서명하다

  sign an employment contract
  고용계약에 서명하다

  > Next Thursday, the chief operating officers of both firms will ------- an agreement about the joint venture.
  >
  > (A) inform (B) sign

20 expedite the process

- 처리를 신속하게 하다

  기출 **expedite** Mr. Yoon's order
  윤 씨의 주문을 신속하게 처리하다

  > To ------- the process, simply click on express shipping on the checkout Web page.
  >
  > (A) expedite (B) acquire

21 address the issue

문제를 다루다

기출 **address** concerns about budget proposals
예산안에 대한 우려를 다루다

address customer requests
고객 요청사항을 처리하다

> Mr. Barnes will make himself available between 1 PM and 4 PM today to ------- the issue regarding the new wage structure.
> (A) address　　　(B) allow

22 use electronic devices

전자기기를 사용하다

기출 **use** vacation days
휴가를 사용하다

use the alternate route
대체 경로를 이용하다

> The number of restaurants which ------- electronic devices for taking orders is increasing.
> (A) use　　　(B) show

23 authorize payment

지불을 허가하다

기출 **authorize** the final budget
최종 예산안을 허가하다

authorize improvements to
~의 개선을 허가하다

> The branch manager will ------- the payment once the necessary documentation is submitted and reviewed.
> (A) remind　　　(B) authorize

24 observe safety regulations

- 안전 규정을 준수하다

  기출 **observe** the safety instructions
  안전 지시를 준수하다

  > Please ------- safety regulations when operating the new assembly line machinery to ensure a secure work environment.
  >
  > (A) observe   (B) comply

25 assume the title of

- ~의 직함을 달다

  기출 **assume** responsibility for organizing seminars
  세미나를 기획하는 것에 대한 책임을 떠맡다

  assume the ownership of
  ~의 소유권을 취하다

  > Ms. Tebbitt will ------- the title of marketing director after Mr. Lomas retires in September.
  >
  > (A) assume   (B) become

26 earn a reputation

- 평판을 얻다

  기출 **earn** the admiration of
  ~의 존경을 받다

  earn a degree
  학위를 받다

  earn a bonus
  보너스를 얻다

  > Soleil Beach Resort ------- a reputation largely due to the wealth of activities and amenities it offers.
  >
  > (A) earned   (B) treated

27 settle a dispute

- 분쟁을 해결하다

  기출 **settle** a disagreement
  의견 차이를 해결하다

  settle the account
  거래를 청산하다

  Ms. Jones ------- a dispute with her coworker after he agreed to revise the project timeline.

  (A) suggested　　　(B) settled

28 accelerate production

- 생산을 가속화하다

  기출 **accelerate** the hiring process
  채용 과정을 가속화하다

  accelerate the completion of
  ~의 완성을 촉진하다

  Workshop attendees will learn how to ------- the production of electronic components using advanced manufacturing methods.

  (A) accelerate　　　(B) notify

29 enforce dress code

- 복장 규정을 시행하다

  기출 **enforce** strict parking rules
  엄격한 주차 규정을 시행하다

  enforce a one-hour lunch policy
  1시간 점심시간 정책을 시행하다

  Repcon Corporation ------- a dress code to maintain a professional appearance among its employees.

  (A) obeys　　　(B) enforces

30 hold employment sessions

● 채용 설명회를 개최하다

기출 **hold** a career fair
취업 박람회를 개최하다

hold management meetings
경영진 회의를 개최하다

During the summer, Benning Enterprises ------- employment sessions to engage with potential candidates and answer their questions.

(A) holds (B) waits

31 announce changes

● 변화를 알리다, 변경사항을 발표하다

기출 **announce** the planned expansion
계획된 확장을 알리다

announce the appointment of
~의 임명을 발표하다

The marketing department plans to ------- changes to the company's online advertising strategy.

(A) announce (B) involve

32 submit requests

● 요청사항을 제출하다

기출 **submit** an energy-efficient design
에너지 효율적인 디자인을 제출하다

submit necessary documents
필요한 서류들을 제출하다

Apartment building tenants must ------- requests for private parking spaces by January 31.

(A) apply (B) submit

33 seek candidates
후보자를 찾다

기출 **seek** experienced guides
경험이 많은 가이드들을 찾다

seek advice about the regulation
규제에 대한 조언을 구하다

We are ------- candidates for the sales representatives role who are equally comfortable speaking with customers over the phone as they are in person.

(A) seeking　　　　(B) urging

34 order office supplies
사무용품을 주문하다

기출 regularly **order** new stocks
주기적으로 새로운 재고품을 주문하다

order the replacement parts
대체 부속품을 주문하다

Mr. Duvall will check the inventory before he ------- more office supplies.

(A) contains　　　　(B) orders

35 boost productivity
생산성을 증진시키다

기출 **boost** Elex Motors' profits
엘렉스 모터스 사의 수익을 증진시키다

boost sales figures
매출을 신장시키다

To ------- productivity, Corona Landscaping intends to upgrade its equipment and offer flexible working hours.

(A) distribute　　　　(B) boost

36 assist firms

- 회사를 돕다

  기출 **assist** the efforts of aid organizations
  지원 기관들의 활동을 돕다

  assist technical research
  기술 연구를 돕다

  First Recruitment ------- firms in hiring skilled workers to fill a wide variety of roles.

  (A) assists　　　　(B) allows

37 offer discounts

- 할인을 제공하다

  기출 **offer** a complete program
  완성된 프로그램을 제공하다

  offer a wide range of banking services
  다양한 은행 서비스를 제공하다

  Greenway Supermarket ------- discounts on a large range of products on the last Sunday of every month.

  (A) buys　　　　(B) offers

38 include the account number

- 계좌번호를 포함하다

  기출 **include** a service agreement
  서비스 계약을 포함하다

  include the signed claim form
  서명된 배상 청구서를 포함하다

  Please be sure to ------- your account number whenever you contact customer support at Hitchens Bank.

  (A) include　　　　(B) address

39 receive a promotion

- 승진하다

  기출 **receive** an award
  상을 받다

  receive the updated files
  업데이트된 파일을 받다

  Mr. Royce ------- a promotion because of his outstanding achievements in the last quarter.

  (A) received　　　(B) raised

40 take brochures

- 안내 책자를 가져가다

  기출 **take** a walk
  산책하다, 걷다

  take a different route
  다른 길로 가다

  take thirty minutes
  30분이 걸리다

  Tour group members should ------- their brochures with them whenever they leave the bus.

  (A) turn　　　(B) take

DAILY QUIZ

콜로케이션과 그에 알맞은 뜻을 연결해 보세요.

1. extend an offer • • (A) 예약을 확정하다
2. accept applications • • (B) 제안하다
3. confirm an appointment • • (C) 지원서를 받다

빈칸에 알맞은 단어를 선택하세요.

4. ------- concern
   우려를 표하다

5. ------- a 12-month lease
   12개월 임대계약에 서명하다

   (A) observe
   (B) assume
   (C) express
   (D) sign

6. ------- the safety instructions
   안전 지시를 준수하다

앞서 배운 콜로케이션들의 뜻을 생각하면서, 다음 문제를 풀어보세요.

7. Not being late for work ------- an intern's chances of being offered a full-time position with Adler Legal.

   (A) accomplishes   (B) verifies
   (C) performs   (D) improves

8. Because of potential commuting difficulties, Mr. Morgan ------- the proposals to relocate the company's headquarters to the suburbs.

   (A) observed   (B) rejected
   (C) proved   (D) worked

정답 1 (B) 2 (C) 3 (A) 4 (C) 5 (D) 6 (A) 7 (D) 8 (B)

Day 05 기출 동의어 ❸ Part 7

1 direct

❶ 특정인에게/장소에 보내다
→ **address, send**

❷ 지시하다, 이끌다
→ **instruct, guide, supervise**

> Please **direct** any questions or concerns you may have about our products, services, or policies to our customer support team, who are available to assist you promptly.
>
> (A) address   (B) supervise

저희의 제품, 서비스 혹은 정책에 관해 질문이나 우려 사항이 있으실 경우, 여러분을 즉시 도울 수 있는 저희 고객 지원팀에 보내주세요.

2 slot

❶ 구멍, 틈
→ **hole, crack**

❷ 빈 자리, 빈 시간
→ **opening**

> There are no more available **slots** left for that workshop on Tuesday, so I'll have to register you for the one on Wednesday instead.
>
> (A) holes   (B) openings

화요일에 열리는 그 워크샵에는 더 이상 가능한 자리가 없어서, 대신 수요일에 있는 워크샵에 등록해 드리겠습니다.

3 appeal

❶ 간청하다
→ **ask, request, beg**

❷ 마음을 사로잡다
→ **attract**

> Our hotel offers amenities that will **appeal** to guests of all ages, no matter where you are visiting from.
>
> (A) request   (B) attract

저희 호텔은 어디서 방문하시는지에 관계없이 모든 연령대의 투숙객들의 마음을 사로잡을 편의시설을 제공합니다.

4 perform

❶ 공연하다
→ **play, be on stage**

❷ 수행하다
→ **carry out, complete, fulfill, conduct**

❸ 기능하다, 작동하다
→ **work, function**

We were able to gather participants, **perform** the laboratory experiments, and produce insightful results within a week.

(A) play　　　　　(B) carry out

저희는 참가자들을 모집하고, 실험실 실험을 수행하고, 그리고 통찰력 있는 결과를 만들어 내는 것을 일주일 이내에 할 수 있었습니다.

5 resolution

❶ 해상도
→ **level of detail**

❷ 해결
→ **settlement**

❸ 결심
→ **decision, intention**

To meet the demands of professional photographers, the new camera model boasts a special feature designed to enhance the **resolution** of captured images.

(A) level of detail　　(B) decision

전문 사진작가들의 요구를 충족시키기 위해, 새로운 카메라 모델은 캡처된 이미지의 해상도를 향상시키도록 설계된 특별한 기능을 자랑합니다.

6 solid

❶ 단단한, 굳은
→ **hard, firm**

❷ 시간상 꼬박 계속되는
→ **constant**

❸ 확실한, 믿을 수 있는
→ **thorough, well-grounded, reliable**

Harry sent me a **solid** business plan yesterday regarding our project launch. I think you'll be impressed by its quality, so I have attached it to this e-mail for your reference.

(A) constant　　　(B) thorough

해리 씨가 우리의 프로젝트 개시에 관해 믿을 수 있는 사업 계획을 어제 저에게 보내주었습니다. 당신이 그 우수함에 깊은 인상을 받을 것이라 생각해, 참고하실 수 있도록 그것을 이 이메일에 첨부했습니다.

7 occupy

❶ 공간을 차지하다
→ **take up**, **fill**

❷ 바쁘게 하다, 시간을 차지하다
→ **keep busy**

❸ 마음을 사로잡다
→ **engage**, **capture**

> Although the majority of our space is **occupied** by long-term leases, we do offer a small selection of seasonal contracts with a minimum duration of three months.
> (A) filled   (B) kept busy
>
> 비록 저희 공간의 대부분은 장기 임대로 채워져 있지만, 최소 3개월 기간의 계절 계약도 일부 제공하고 있습니다.

8 program

❶ 방송
→ **show**, **broadcast**

❷ 계획
→ **plan**

❸ (콘서트, 연극 등) 시간표, 일정 등을 담은 책자
→ **schedule**, **timetable**

> If you'd like, we can create a customized exercise **program** that caters to your fitness goals. Here at Aries Health & Fitness, we even have a nutritionist on site that can provide dietary advice and consultation.
> (A) broadcast   (B) plan
>
> 원하신다면, 저희는 귀하의 운동 목표들을 충족시킬 맞춤형 운동 프로그램을 만들 수 있습니다. 이곳 에리즈 헬스 앤 피트니스에는, 식단 조언과 상담을 제공할 수 있는 영양사도 현장에 있습니다.

9 instrumental

❶ 악기의
→ **musical**

❷ 기구의, 기계의
→ **mechanical**

❸ 도움이 되는, 중요한
→ **helpful**, **essential**

> Our monthly team-building seminars have been an **instrumental** part of our company's culture because they help build trust among employees.
> (A) mechanical   (B) essential
>
> 우리의 월별 팀 빌딩 세미나는 우리 회사 문화의 중요한 부분인데, 직원들 사이에 신뢰를 구축하는 데 도움이 되기 때문입니다.

10 status

① 지위, 명망
→ **high rank**

② 상황, 상태
→ **condition**

Is there a way for me to check the shipping **status** of my package? I could not find any information on your Web site.

(A) high rank (B) condition

제 소포의 배송 상태를 확인할 수 있는 방법이 있을까요? 귀하의 웹 사이트에서는 어떤 정보도 찾을 수가 없습니다.

11 regular

① 정기적인, 규칙적인
→ **periodic, habitual**

② 일정한, 균일한
→ **even, unchanging**

③ 일상적인, 평소의
→ **usual, normal**

As a security measure, the system automatically prompts users to reset their password on a **regular** basis.

(A) periodic (B) unchanging

보안 조치의 일환으로, 그 시스템은 자동으로 이용자들이 정기적으로 그들의 비밀번호를 재설정하도록 유도합니다.

12 anticipate

① 예상하다
→ **expect**

② 고대하다
→ **look forward to**

I **anticipate** that over 100 people will attend the event, so we'll need to make sure to provide enough chairs for everyone.

(A) expect (B) look forward to

저는 100명 이상의 인원이 그 행사에 참석할 것으로 예상하므로, 우리는 모두에게 충분한 의자가 제공되도록 확실히 할 필요가 있습니다.

13 assume

① 맡다, 떠맡다
→ **undertake, accept, take on**

② 추정하다
→ **think, suppose**

Having demonstrated expertise in financial management, Michael has now **assumed** the position of CFO, ensuring the company's financial stability.

(A) undertaken (B) thought

재무관리에서의 전문성을 입증한 마이클 씨는 이제 회사의 재정 안정성을 보증할 재무 담당 최고 책임자 직책을 맡게 되었습니다.

14 capture

❶ 점유하다, 차지하다
→ **gain, occupy**

❷ (감정이나 분위기를) 포착하다, 담아내다
→ **express, represent**

❸ 마음을 사로잡다
→ **attract**

> This sales report does not **capture** the full extent of our business's potential, but I hope that it offers helpful reference to how we operate.
> (A) gain (B) represent

이 매출 보고서가 우리 사업의 잠재성 전체를 담아내진 않지만, 우리가 어떻게 영업하는지에 대해 유용한 참고 자료를 제공하길 바랍니다.

15 plus

❶ 추가
→ **addition**

❷ 이점, 좋은 점
→ **benefit**

> I believe that being a bilingual speaker is a **plus**, so I felt that my qualifications make me more than eligible for this position.
> (A) addition (B) benefit

저는 2개 국어 가능자라는 것이 이점이라고 생각해서, 제 자질들이 이 직책에 저를 매우 적합하게 만든다고 생각했습니다.

16 fashion

❶ 스타일, 외양
→ **style, look**

❷ 유행
→ **vogue, trend**

❸ 방식, 방법
→ **manner**

> Please make sure that guests are lined up in an orderly **fashion** while waiting to enter the theater. We don't want anyone to get hurt.
> (A) trend (B) manner

손님들이 극장에 들어가기 위해 기다리는 동안 질서 있는 방식으로 줄을 서도록 해 주시기 바랍니다. 저희는 누구도 다치는 것을 원하지 않습니다.

17 conclude

❶ 결론을 내리다
→ **decide, believe**

❷ 끝나다, 마치다
→ **finish**

I expect the meeting to **conclude** before noon, since the chairman has an important lunch to attend.

(A) decide   (B) finish

의장님께서 참석하실 중요한 점심 식사가 있기 때문에, 저는 이 회의가 정오 전에는 끝날 것으로 예상합니다.

18 fit

❶ (일자리에) 적합하다, 어울리다
→ **match**

❷ 조정하여 맞추다, 끼우다
→ **adjust, lay, put in place**

❸ 의복 등이 꼭 맞다, 잘 어울리다
→ **be the right size**

Upon reviewing her résumé and background, it appears that her interests seem to **fit** our company's goals perfectly.

(A) match   (B) adjust

그녀의 이력서와 배경을 검토해보니, 그녀의 관심사가 우리 회사의 목표와 완벽하게 어울리는 것 같습니다.

19 serve

❶ 시중을 들다
→ **attend to**

❷ 음식을 제공하다
→ **cater, provide food**

❸ 일하다, 기능하다
→ **work, function**

The new community center is not only a space for cultural events but also aims at **serving** as a place for employment opportunities through various skill development programs.

(A) attending to   (B) functioning

새 지역 주민센터는 문화 행사를 위한 공간일 뿐만 아니라 다양한 역량 개발 프로그램을 통해 고용 기회를 얻기 위한 공간으로 기능하는 것도 목표로 합니다.

20 realize

❶ 현실화하다, 이루다
➜ **achieve**

❷ 깨닫다
➜ **comprehend**

> I did not **realize** the importance of one's body language when giving a presentation. I will make sure to do a better job next time.
> (A) achieve   (B) comprehend

저는 발표할 때의 보디랭귀지의 중요성을 깨닫지 못했어요. 다음번에는 좀 더 잘할 수 있도록 하겠습니다.

21 convey

❶ 나르다, 옮기다
➜ **transport, carry**

❷ (생각·감정을) 전달하다
➜ **communicate, relay, pass on**

> In order to ensure smooth project execution, it is crucial for a project manager to **convey** expectations clearly to team members.
> (A) transport   (B) communicate

원만한 프로젝트 수행을 보장하기 위해서는 프로젝트 책임자가 팀원들에게 기대하는 것을 명확하게 전달하는 것이 매우 중요합니다.

22 modest

❶ 겸손한
➜ **humble, shy**

❷ 그다지 대단하지 않은, 보통의
➜ **small, ordinary, simple**

> I only have a **modest** amount of knowledge on the subject, so I believe it would be best to contact Ms. Jones, our accountant.
> (A) shy   (B) small

저는 그 주제에 관해 보통 수준의 지식만을 가지고 있어서, 저희의 회계사인 존스 씨에게 연락하는 것이 가장 좋을 것이라고 생각합니다.

23 drop

❶ 떨어지다, 떨어뜨리다
➜ **fall**

❷ 낮추다, 약해지다
➜ **lower**

❸ 그만 두다
➜ **quit**

> Due to unforeseen financial constraints, Peter had no choice but to **drop** the class before the tuition refund deadline.
> (A) fall   (B) quit

예상하지 못한 재정적인 제약으로 인해, 피터 씨는 수업료 환불 마감기한 전에 수업을 그만둘 수밖에 없었습니다.

24 deliver

❶ 배달하다
→ bring, send, transport

❷ 제공하다
→ provide

We **deliver** a wide range of laundry services to fit your various needs. Furthermore, no membership is needed to use our machines.
(A) send   (B) provide

저희는 여러분의 여러 필요사항을 충족하기 위해 다양한 세탁 서비스를 제공합니다. 게다가, 저희 기계를 사용하는 데 회원가입이 필요하지 않습니다.

25 put aside

❶ 무시하다, 제쳐놓다
→ ignore

❷ 나중에 쓰도록 따로 두다
→ save up

The lost and found box at the office is filled with various items that are frequently **put aside** or misplaced by forgetful employees.
(A) ignored   (B) saved up

사무실에 있는 분실물 보관함은 건망증이 있는 직원들에 의해 자주 제쳐지거나 제자리에 놓이지 않은 다양한 물품들로 채워져 있습니다.

26 redeem

❶ 상환하다, 변제하다
→ pay

❷ ~을 …로 바꾸다, 교환하다
→ trade in

❸ 보완하다, 상쇄하다
→ compensate for

Each time you accrue 1000 points, you can **redeem** the points for valuable discounts on your next purchase.
(A) compensate for   (B) trade in

여러분이 1000 포인트를 모을 때마다, 그 포인트를 다음 구입에 적용할 가치 있는 할인으로 바꿀 수 있습니다.

27 apply

❶ 신청하다, 지원하다 (for)
→ put in, ask for

❷ 쓰다, 적용하다 (to)
→ use, exercise, employ

Please make sure that the format I have outlined above is **applied** to all future reports. Otherwise, there might be a lack of consistency going forward.
(A) asked for   (B) used

제가 위에 개요를 서술한 이 형식이 향후 모든 보고서들에 적용될 수 있도록 해주시기 바랍니다. 그렇지 않으면, 앞으로 일관성이 부족해질 수도 있습니다.

Week 03 | Day 05 | Part 7 기출 동의어 ③

28 allow

❶ 허락하다, 허용하다
→ **give permission**

❷ 가능하게 하다
→ **make possible**

> The newly installed, indoor heated pool at the community center <u>allows</u> for swimming all year, making it a perfect spot to relax regardless of the weather outside.
>
> (A) gives permission　(B) makes possible

지역 복지관에 새로 설치된 실내 온수 수영장은 일년 내내 수영을 가능하게 하여, 그곳을 외부 날씨와 무관하게 휴식을 취할 수 있는 완벽한 장소로 만듭니다.

29 pose

❶ 위협·문제 등을 제기하다
→ **present**

❷ 자세를 취하다
→ **model**

> Falling debris and unstable structures <u>pose</u> a risk for construction workers. Hard hats should be worn at all times.
>
> (A) present　(B) model

떨어지는 잔해와 불안정한 구조물들이 건설 작업자들에게 위험을 제기하고 있습니다. 항상 안전모를 착용해야 합니다.

30 stage

❶ 공연의 무대
→ **platform**

❷ 단계, 시기
→ **phase, step**

> The first <u>stage</u> of construction has wrapped up well. We are now preparing to build the exterior of the building.
>
> (A) platform　(B) phase

건설 공사의 첫 번째 단계가 잘 마무리되었습니다. 저희는 이제 건물의 외부를 지을 준비를 하고 있습니다.

DAILY **QUIZ**

밑줄 친 단어와 가장 가까운 의미를 지닌 것을 고르세요.

1
> Our team can **perform** computer software installations for you in less than half an hour. Whether you need to set up a new program, update existing software, or troubleshoot installation issues, we have the expertise to get it done efficiently.

(A) entertain (B) function
(C) complete (D) fix

2
> Please check the temperature sensor on the machine at **regular** intervals to prevent it from overheating. If you need help with adjusting its settings, the technician's number is 555-1648.

(A) orderly (B) customary
(C) periodic (D) even

3
> The project was completed in a timely **fashion** with no delays, showcasing the team's efficiency and dedication. This accomplishment not only satisfied the client's expectations but also strengthened the team's reputation for reliability in the industry.

(A) form (B) trend
(C) event (D) manner

정답 1 (C) 2 (C) 3 (D)

/ Week / 03 실전 TEST

LISTENING

• **Part 2**

1. Mark your answer.   (A)   (B)   (C)
2. Mark your answer.   (A)   (B)   (C)
3. Mark your answer.   (A)   (B)   (C)
4. Mark your answer.   (A)   (B)   (C)
5. Mark your answer.   (A)   (B)   (C)
6. Mark your answer.   (A)   (B)   (C)
7. Mark your answer.   (A)   (B)   (C)
8. Mark your answer.   (A)   (B)   (C)
9. Mark your answer.   (A)   (B)   (C)
10. Mark your answer.   (A)   (B)   (C)

READING

Part 5

11. Ms. Bendtner asked us to ------- the promotional flyers to shoppers in Grand Rapids Mall.

    (A) distribute
    (B) relate
    (C) inquire
    (D) continue

12. Mayor Larkin has opposed calls to ------- additional bus stops on Milton Avenue.

    (A) embark
    (B) install
    (C) transport
    (D) invest

13. Astro Gym members can ------- padlocks for their lockers by speaking with a front desk employee.

    (A) obtain
    (B) apply
    (C) develop
    (D) trade

14. If you brought in any unwanted clothing you plan to -------, please place it in the collection bin in the reception area.

    (A) create
    (B) assemble
    (C) donate
    (D) produce

15. Although the owner of the company would like you to start working no later than May 5, he may be willing to ------- if you have a valid reason.

    (A) negotiate
    (B) recommend
    (C) ascertain
    (D) contradict

16. Mr. Alphey will ------- how to update the customer database during the department meeting this afternoon.

    (A) offer
    (B) demonstrate
    (C) attempt
    (D) participate

17. Ergofit International manufactures office equipment and furnishings that ------- a healthy posture.

    (A) anticipate
    (B) encourage
    (C) succeed
    (D) deserve

18. Mitchum Business Solutions ------- its dress code on all members of staff, including part-time workers.

    (A) follows
    (B) limits
    (C) prefers
    (D) enforces

• Part 6

Questions 19-22 refer to the following letter.

Dear Ms. Lockhart,

19. ------- . I understand that we will meet in the dining hall of the Canton Hotel at one o'clock. In attendance will be our Marketing team, which includes Monty Warren and Martha Solomon. Regrettably, Michelle Goldberg will be unable to join us due to a scheduling **20.** -------.

We hope to discuss techniques for improving sales in the upcoming months and are eager to hear your ideas. I know that you have a wealth of experience, and I feel that our team can benefit hugely **21.** ------- your expertise. I am confident that we will be able to identify the strengths and weaknesses of our current strategy and create a plan that will help **22.** ------- our market share.

I look forward to our meeting and future correspondence.

Sincerely,

Samantha Kasten

19. (A) I would like to thank you for arranging my accommodation during my stay.
　 (B) Please proceed with the booking of a room for our upcoming meeting.
　 (C) We have many items to add to our sales meeting agenda.
　 (D) I am writing to confirm the details of our meeting scheduled for this Friday.

20. (A) conflict
　 (B) conflicts
　 (C) conflicting
　 (D) conflicted

21. (A) over
　 (B) from
　 (C) out of
　 (D) as

22. (A) grant
　 (B) suggest
　 (C) improve
　 (D) register

Part 7

Questions 23-24 refer to the following e-mail.

To: ahayat@windfieldhotel.com
From: lhaines@fyrefly.com
Date: April 16
Subject: Reservation #458278
Attachment: Booking_confirmation.docx

Dear Ms. Hayat,

The booking confirmation for our hotel reservation (#458278) arrived today, and it includes a room with multiple queen beds, which we did not reserve. We only need three rooms while we are in Denver for the upcoming conference. I checked my company credit card balance, and it appears that we have been charged for four rooms. I assume you will cancel this part of our reservation, which one of your colleagues must have made in error. However, I'd like to know what must be done in order to remove the wrong charge from the credit card.

Regards,

Lincoln Haines
Fyrefly Corporation

---

23. The word "assume" in paragraph 1, line 5, is closest in meaning to

(A) collect
(B) suppose
(C) handle
(D) accept

24. What information does Mr. Haines request?

(A) How to extend a booking
(B) How to obtain a refund
(C) How to cancel a reservation
(D) How to make a payment

서아쌤의 토익 비밀과외
기출 VOCA

Week 04

Contents		Page	Date	Check
Day 01	Part 2~4 LC가 잘 들리는 어휘 ②	224	월 일	☐
Day 02	Part 5,6 동사 ③	238	월 일	☐
Day 03	Part 5,6 동사 ④	252	월 일	☐
Day 04	Part 5,6 동사 + 전치사 콜로케이션	266	월 일	☐
Day 05	Part 7 기출 동의어 ④	280	월 일	☐
Week 04 실전 TEST		290	월 일	☐

Day 01 LC가 잘 들리는 어휘 ❷ Part 2~4

1 miss

● v. ~을 놓치다

M: What happened at the workshop yesterday?
W: I **missed** it too.

남: 어제 워크숍에서 무슨 일이 있었나요?
여: 저도 거기 못 갔어요.

만점 TIP
• 관련 기출
　miss the deadline 마감일을 못 지키다
• 토익 LC에서 miss는 주로 '~을 놓치다, (회의 등에) 못 가다'의 의미로 나오지만 '~을 그리워하다'라는 뜻도 있습니다.

2 patron

● n. 고객, 후원자

M: Our **patrons** come from all over the world just to try our famous pasta.
W: I can understand why! It's delicious.

남: 우리 고객들은 단지 우리의 유명한 파스타를 맛보기 위해 전 세계에서 옵니다.
여: 왜 그런지 알겠어요! 맛있어요.

만점 TIP
• 일반적인 의미의 고객은 customer라고 하며, 주로 전문적인 서비스를 의뢰한 고객을 client라고 합니다. patron, customer, client 모두 LC에 자주 등장합니다.

3 refrain from -ing

● ~하는 것을 삼가다

M: Please **refrain from speaking** loudly on the phone in the waiting area.
W: Sorry about that. I'll take my call outside.

남: 대기실에서 큰 소리로 통화하는 것은 삼가주시기 바랍니다.
여: 죄송합니다. 전화를 바깥에서 받겠습니다.

4 **bring A with me** • A를 가지고 가다

> M: I'm meeting with the client tomorrow to discuss the project proposal. Do you have the latest version of the document?
> W: Yes, I'll **bring a copy with me** to the meeting.
>
> 남: 내일 고객과 만나 프로젝트 제안서에 대해 논의할 예정입니다. 그 문서의 최신 버전이 있나요?
> 여: 네, 회의할 때 사본을 가지고 가겠습니다.

5 **tenant** • n. 임차인

> M: When did the new **tenant** for Unit 223 say she would move in?
> W: On May 1, I believe. The unit has already been cleaned and is ready to go.
>
> 남: 223호실의 새 임차인이 언제 입주하겠다고 했습니까?
> 여: 아마 5월 1일일 거예요. 그 호실은 이미 청소가 끝났고 사용할 준비가 완료되었습니다.

만점 TIP

• 관련 기출
    landlord 집주인
    resident 거주자, 주민

6 **board of directors** • n. 이사회, 위원회

> M: I hope the **board of directors** considers our proposal seriously.
> W: Yes, let's hope they see the potential benefits.
>
> 남: 이사회에서 우리의 제안서를 진지하게 고려하면 좋겠어요.
> 여: 네, 그들이 잠재적인 이점을 볼 수 있기를 바랍시다.

만점 TIP

• 관련 기출
    board member 이사회 구성원, 이사
    board meeting 이사회 회의

7 have yet to + 동사원형

- 아직 ~하지 않았다

> M: I **have yet to receive** a text from the technician about when he'll stop by to fix our air conditioner.
> W: Should we give him a call?
>
> 남: 기술자로부터 언제 우리 에어컨을 수리하러 들를지에 대한 문자를 아직 받지 못했습니다.
> 여: 그에게 전화를 해야 할까요?

8 attendance

- n. 참석자 수

> M: **Attendance** to today's skills workshop was low, wasn't it?
> W: Yes, many people seem to be away for the holidays.
>
> 남: 오늘 기술 워크숍 참석자 수가 적었죠?
> 여: 네, 많은 분들이 연휴로 자리에 안 계신 것 같습니다.

만점 TIP
- 관련 기출
  well-attended 참석률이 좋은

9 in the middle of

- ~하는 중인

> M: I need to schedule a meeting, but the system seems to be down.
> W: I apologize for the inconvenience. Mr. Yan is **in the middle of** updating our appointment system to improve its speed.
>
> 남: 회의 일정을 잡아야 하는데, 시스템이 다운된 것 같습니다.
> 여: 불편을 끼쳐드려 죄송합니다. 얀 씨가 저희 예약 시스템의 속도를 개선하기 위해 업데이트를 진행 중입니다.

10 call a meeting
- 회의를 소집하다

M: The finance supervisor just **called a meeting** to discuss reallocating surplus funds.
W: Do I need to be there, too?

남: 방금 재무팀장이 여유 자금의 재분배를 논의하기 위해 회의를 소집했습니다.
여: 저도 거기에 있어야 하나요?

11 care to + 동사원형
- ~하고 싶다

M: Would you **care to have** a cup of coffee while you wait?
W: No thanks, I'm actually quite sensitive to caffeine.

남: 기다리시는 동안 커피 한 잔 하고 싶으신가요?
여: 괜찮습니다, 저는 사실 카페인에 꽤 민감해요.

12 disturb
- v. ~을 방해하다

M: Shelly is in an online conference call right now, so you probably shouldn't **disturb** her.
W: Okay, I won't.

남: 셸리는 지금 온라인 전화 회의 중이니 방해하지 않으셔야 할 것 같습니다.
여: 알겠습니다. 방해하지 않을게요.

13 stick with
- ~을 고수하다

M: I heard your team is considering some bold new digital marketing ideas.
W: But the board wants us to **stick with** traditional advertising.

남: 당신 팀에서 과감하고 새로운 디지털 마케팅 아이디어를 검토 중이라고 들었습니다.
여: 하지만 이사회는 우리가 전통적인 광고를 고수하기를 원합니다.

14 just in case

● 만일의 경우를 대비해서

> M: We should probably bring some raincoats with us to the forest expedition **just in case**.
> W: You're right. It could start pouring unexpectedly.
>
> 남: 만일의 경우를 대비해서 숲 탐험에 우비를 좀 가지고 가야겠네요.
> 여: 맞아요. 갑자기 비가 쏟아질 수도 있으니까요.

만점 TIP

• 관련 기출

「in case of + 명사」/「in case + 절」 ~의 경우에 대비해
We should leave soon in case of traffic.
We should leave soon, in case there's traffic.
교통 체증이 있을지도 모르니 곧 나서야 해요.

15 rather than

● ~보다는

> M: Should we book the beachfront location or the city park for the team-building event?
> W: Let's use the city park **rather than** the beachfront. It's more accessible for everyone.
>
> 남: 팀 단합 행사를 위해 해변으로 예약할까요, 시내 공원으로 할까요?
> 여: 해변보다는 시내 공원으로 합시다. 모두에게 접근성이 더 좋잖아요.

16 be named/appointed

● 임명되다, 지명되다

> M: Has the new marketing manager **been named** yet?
> W: I'm hoping it will be Ms. Cohen.
>
> 남: 새로운 마케팅 부장이 임명되었나요?
> 여: 코헨 씨가 되길 바라고 있어요.

만점 TIP

• 관련 기출

name[appoint] A as B A를 B에 임명하다
☞ as는 생략 가능
named + 이름 ~라는 이름의
a woman named Natalie 나탈리라는 이름의 여자

17 vacate

• v. (건물, 공간 등을 다른 사람이 사용할 수 있도록) 비우다

> M: By when were we asked to **vacate** the building?
> W: The end of June at the latest, but we can request an extension if needed.
> 남: 언제까지 건물을 비워달라는 요청을 받았습니까?
> 여: 늦어도 6월 말까지요, 하지만 필요하다면 연장을 요청할 수 있습니다.

18 get A B

• A에게 B를 얻어주다

> M: You can't **get us an earlier flight**, can you?
> W: No, they're fully booked.
> 남: 저희에게 더 이른 비행편을 구해주실 수는 없겠죠?
> 여: 못 해요, 예약이 꽉 찼습니다.

19 place an order

• 주문하다

> M: Hi, I'm calling because I'd like to **place an order** for 1,000 business cards.
> W: Okay. Is there a specific design that you wanted to use for your cards?
> 남: 안녕하세요, 명함 1,000장을 주문하고 싶어서 전화드렸습니다.
> 여: 알겠습니다. 혹시 명함에 사용하고 싶은 특정한 디자인이 있으신가요?

만점 TIP

• 관련 기출

　place a call 전화를 걸다

20 fill an order

- 주문에 맞춰 물품을 공급하다

> M: Hey, did you take care of the request for 100 spiral notebooks and 200 lined-paper notepads?
> W: Yes, I **filled that order** earlier this morning.
> 남: 저, 스프링 공책 100개와 줄 쳐진 메모장 200개 요청은 잘 처리하셨나요?
> 여: 네, 오늘 아침 일찍 주문에 맞춰 물품을 공급했습니다.

21 bring A up

- A(문제나 이슈)를 제기하다

> M: Have you noticed any issues with the office coffee machine lately?
> W: Yes, it's been acting up. I'll **bring it up** at our staff meeting tomorrow.
> 남: 최근에 사무실 커피 머신에 문제가 생긴 것을 알고 계셨나요?
> 여: 네, 계속 작동이 잘 안되었어요. 내일 직원 회의에서 그 문제를 제기할 것입니다.

22 take inventory

- 재고 조사를 하다

> M: Before wrapping up for the day, the most important step is to **take inventory** of all our merchandise.
> W: I should use this checklist over here, right?
> 남: 하루를 마무리하기 전에 가장 중요한 단계는 우리의 모든 상품에 대한 재고 조사를 하는 것입니다.
> 여: 여기 있는 이 체크리스트를 써야 하는 거죠?

23 keep track of

● ~을 추적하다, ~의 정보를 계속 파악하다

M: How do we **keep track of** the shipments we've unloaded?
W: We use a barcode scanning software to log them into our inventory management system.
남: 내린 화물을 어떻게 추적합니까?
여: 저희는 바코드 스캔 소프트웨어를 사용하여 재고 관리 시스템에 기록합니다.

만점 TIP
• track이 동사로 쓰이면 '~을 추적하다'라는 의미입니다.

24 aim to + 동사원형

● ~하는 것을 목표로 하다

M: We're **aiming to finish** painting the walls tomorrow.
W: That sounds great! Thank you for the update.
남: 내일 벽 페인트 칠 작업을 끝내는 걸 목표로 하고 있어요.
여: 아주 잘됐네요! 소식 알려주셔서 감사합니다.

만점 TIP
• 관련 기출
  be aimed at ~을 대상으로 하다, ~을 겨냥하다
  aim n. 목적, 목표

25 shift

● n. 교대 근무

M: Doesn't Jacob usually work the evening **shift**?
W: Someone from the day shift called in sick today.
남: 제이콥 씨는 보통 저녁 근무를 하지 않나요?
여: 낮 근무인 어떤 분이 오늘 아파서 못 나왔거든요.

만점 TIP
• 관련 기출
  work extra shift 추가 근무를 서다
  cover one's shift ~의 근무를 대신 서다

26 claim

- v. ~을 청구하다, 주장하다

  n. 청구[신청], 주장

  > M: I heard there's a new procedure for **claiming** travel expenses.
  > W: Yes. Instead of the paper forms, now we can submit our expenses online.
  >
  > 남: 출장 비용 청구 절차가 새로 생겼다고 들었어요.
  > 여: 네, 종이 양식 대신에, 이제 온라인으로 비용 내역을 제출할 수 있습니다.

  만점 TIP
  - 관련 기출

    baggage claim area (공항의) 수하물 찾는 곳

27 belongings

- n. 소지품, 소유물

  > M: Hey Lisa, congratulations on your promotion! Do you need any help moving your personal **belongings** to your new desk?
  > W: Thanks so much. And, it's alright, I should be able to do it by myself.
  >
  > 남: 리사, 승진 축하해요! 개인 소지품을 새 책상으로 옮기는 데 도움이 필요하신가요?
  > 여: 정말 감사합니다. 그리고 괜찮아요, 저 혼자 할 수 있을 거예요.

28 landscaping

- n. 조경 (작업)

  > M: I'd like to get some **landscaping** done around my house. Can you stop by and give me an estimate?
  > W: Sure. Where is it located?
  >
  > 남: 집 주변에 조경 작업을 좀 하고 싶은데요. 이번 주 중에 들러서 견적을 알려주실 수 있나요?
  > 여: 물론이죠. 어디에 위치해 있나요?

29 loyal

a. 충성스러운, 단골의

M: Is there any way to expedite the shipping of my purchase?
W: Of course, we can arrange that for you. Since you're our **loyal** customer, we'll prioritize your shipment.

남: 제가 구매한 물건의 배송을 신속히 처리할 수 있는 방법이 있을까요?
여: 물론이죠, 조정해 드리겠습니다. 고객님이 저희의 단골고객인 만큼 우선적으로 배송해드리겠습니다.

만점 TIP

• 관련 기출

loyal customer / frequent customer 단골 손님

30 extend the deadline

마감일을 연장하다

M: Beth, this project is going to require more research than I anticipated.
W: Okay, I can **extend the deadline** for you.

남: 베스, 이번 프로젝트는 제가 예상했던 것보다 더 많은 연구가 필요할 것 같습니다.
여: 알겠어요, 기한을 연장해 드릴 수 있습니다.

만점 TIP

• 관련 기출

extend the operation hours 운영 시간을 연장하다

31 set A apart from B

A를 B로부터 구별하다, 눈에 띄게 하다

M: Can you recommend some laptops for remote work?
W: Sure, I recommend the HG X-100 model; what **sets it apart from other brands** is its impressive battery life.

남: 원격 근무용 노트북 컴퓨터를 추천해주시겠어요?
여: 물론이죠, HG X-100 모델을 추천합니다. 그 제품이 다른 브랜드와 차별화되는 점은 인상적인 배터리 수명입니다.

32 corporate

a. 회사의, 기업의

M: I'd like to ask you about your catering service. I'm having a **corporate** party next month, and I'd like to see your price list.
W: Sure, I'd be happy to provide you with information about our services.

남: 케이터링 서비스에 대해 문의드리고 싶습니다. 다음 달에 회사 파티를 하는데요, 귀사의 가격 리스트를 보고 싶어요.
여: 물론이죠, 저희 서비스에 대한 정보를 제공해 드리겠습니다.

만점 TIP

• 관련 기출

corporate event 회사 행사
corporate dinner 회식
corporate discount 기업 할인

33 keep A up to date

A에게 계속 최신 소식을 알려주다 (= keep A updated)

W: How's the project coming along?
M: We've made some progress, but there are a few challenges we're facing. I'll **keep you up to date** on our developments.

여: 프로젝트는 어떻게 되어 가나요?
남: 진척이 좀 있습니다만, 몇 가지 어려움들을 직면하고 있어요. 개발 상황에 대해 계속 최신 소식을 알려드리겠습니다.

만점 TIP

• 관련 기출

keep A informed[posted] A에게 계속 소식을 알려주다

34 highly recommended

- 강력히 추천되는

M: Thanks for meeting with me. Your interior design services came **highly recommended** by a colleague of mine.
W: It's my pleasure. Now, which section of your house do you want to remodel?

남: 만나주셔서 감사합니다. 귀하의 인테리어 디자인 서비스를 제 동료가 강력히 추천했습니다.
여: 천만에요. 그럼, 집의 어느 부분을 리모델링하고 싶으신가요?

35 interview

- v. (면접관이) 면접을 보다, (언론 기관에서) 인터뷰를 하다
  n. 면접, 인터뷰

M: How's your schedule looking this afternoon?
W: I'm **interviewing** new applicants for our software engineer position at 3.

남: 오늘 오후 일정은 어떤가요?
여: 3시에 소프트웨어 엔지니어 자리에 지원한 새로운 지원자들 면접을 볼 겁니다.

만점 TIP

• 관련 기출

conduct an interview 면접을 실시하다

36 accommodate

- v. ~을 수용하다

M: How large is the conference center for the workshop?
W: It can **accommodate** up to 200 people.

남: 워크숍을 위한 컨퍼런스 센터의 규모는 어느 정도입니까?
여: 200명까지 수용 가능합니다.

만점 TIP

• accommodate에는 여러 뜻이 있지만 LC에서는 주로 '~을 수용하다'라는 의미로 등장합니다. 참고로, 명사형 accommodation(숙박)도 자주 나오므로 꼭 알아 두세요.

37 renovate

- v. ~을 개조하다

> M: Are we still planning to **renovate** our office this summer?
> W: Yes, we're going to get all our desks and computers replaced and the walls repainted.
> 남: 여전히 이번 여름에 사무실을 개조할 계획인가요?
> 여: 네, 책상과 컴퓨터를 모두 교체하고 벽도 다시 칠할 예정입니다.

38 capacity

- n. 용량, 수용력, 능력

> M: What's the seating **capacity** of this auditorium?
> W: About 500 people.
> 남: 이 강당의 좌석 수용력은 얼마나 되나요?
> 여: 약 500명입니다.

39 leak

- n. 누수

> M: How should I deal with the **leak** under the sink?
> W: You should call a plumber.
> 남: 싱크대 아래 누수를 어떻게 처리해야 할까요?
> 여: 배관공에게 전화해 보세요.

40 property

- n. 부동산, 건물

> M: This is Marland's Real Estate office.
> W: Hello, I'm interested in seeing the **property** on Olive Avenue that you have listed for sale on your website.
> 남: 말랜드 부동산 사무실입니다.
> 여: 안녕하세요, 웹사이트에 매물로 올려주신 올리브 애비뉴의 부동산을 보고 싶습니다.

만점 TIP

- Part 3에서 아파트에 문제가 발생했을 때 property manager(부동산 관리인)에게 도움을 요청하는 대화가 종종 나옵니다.

DAILY QUIZ

단어와 그에 알맞은 뜻을 연결해 보세요.

1 tenant   •   • (A) 참석자 수

2 shift   •   • (B) 임차인

3 attendance   •   • (C) 교대 근무

빈칸에 알맞은 단어를 선택하세요.

4 I heard the project deadline has been -------.
   프로젝트 마감일이 연장되었다고 들었어요.

5 Has the new sales director been ------- yet?
   새 영업 이사가 지명 되었나요?

(A) disturbed
(B) named
(C) called
(D) extended

6 The CEO ------- a special meeting for 9:00 AM tomorrow.
   CEO가 내일 오전 9시로 특별 회의를 소집했어요.

음원을 듣고 질문에 어울리는 응답을 고르세요.

7 (A)   (B)   (C)

8 (A)   (B)   (C)

Day 02 동사 ❸ Part 5, 6

1 inspect
inspection n. 점검, 검토
inspector n. 조사관

● 점검하다, 검토하다

기출 be thoroughly **inspected** by
~에 의해 철저하게 점검되다

inspect billing statements for extra fees
추가 요금에 대해 청구서를 검토하다

Assembly line managers ------- the products frequently to ensure they meet quality standards.
(A) inspect   (B) perform

2 handle
handling n. 처리, 취급

● 처리하다, 다루다

기출 **handle** all inquiries about
~에 대한 모든 문의사항을 처리하다

will be **handled** by the customer service department
고객 서비스부에 의해 다뤄질 것이다

All inquiries about our new service are ------- swiftly by our customer service representatives.
(A) handled   (B) applied

3 record

● 기록하다

기출 **recorded** one's highest profits in the last quarter
지난 분기에 가장 높은 이익을 기록했다

As a result of decreased demand for wristwatches, Prestige Company ------- its lowest sales ever last year.
(A) proved   (B) recorded

4 intend

intention n. 의도
intentionally ad. 고의로
intended a. 의도된

● ~하려고 생각하다, ~할 예정이다

기출 **intend** to open a factory in
~에 공장을 열 생각이다

be **intended** for employees who
~한 직원들을 대상으로 할 예정이다

Humble Industries reported that it ------- to discontinue production of its line of Nexus Microwaves next year.

(A) intends   (B) invites

5 select

selective a. 까다로운, 선별적인
selection n. 선택 (대상)

● 선택하다, 선정하다

기출 be **selected** for publication
출판 대상으로 선택되다

select a replacement
후임을 선정하다

Mr. Hamato has been ------- to receive the Architect of the Year award at the 7th Annual Architecture Convention.

(A) selected   (B) delivered

6 remove

removal n. 제거
removable a. 제거할 수 있는

● 제거하다

기출 be **removed** from the list
목록에서 제거되다

When ------- the bicycle parts from the packaging, Grind Cycles recommends checking the provided inventory list.

(A) producing   (B) removing

7 supply

supplier n. 공급업체

• 공급하다, 제공하다

기출 **supply** billing software 청구 소프트웨어를 공급하다
supply all the materials 모든 재료를 제공하다

The personnel office will ------- all presenters at the job fair with ID tags that display the individual's name.
(A) train　　　　　　(B) supply

만점 TIP
supply는 '물품'이라는 뜻의 복수명사 supplies로도 출제된다.

8 repair

• 수리하다

기출 **repair** a washing machine 세탁기를 수리하다
need to be **repaired** 수리되어야 하다

Nile's Auto Shop normally ------- damaged vehicles completely within two weeks.
(A) repairs　　　　　(B) installs

만점 TIP
repair는 road repairs(도로 수리)처럼 명사로도 자주 출제된다.

9 delay

• 연기하다, 지연시키다

기출 be **delayed** by a construction project
건설 프로젝트로 인해 연기되다

be significantly **delayed**
상당히 지연되다

The launch of Ronson Digital's latest laptop has been ------- due to extensive flooding at its factory.
(A) included　　　　(B) delayed

만점 TIP
delay는 명사로도 사용될 수 있는데, 가산명사(delays in)와 불가산명사(without delay)로 모두 출제된다.

10 feature

- ~을 특징으로 하다, 특별히 포함하다

  기출 **feature** a variety of events
  다양한 행사들을 특징으로 하다

  feature live music
  라이브 음악을 특별히 포함하다

  This year's Hampton Film Festival will ------- several films made by local independent filmmakers.
  (A) feature　　　　(B) collect

11 address

- (문제를) 다루다, 처리하다

  기출 **address** concerns about the budget proposal
  예산 제안서에 대한 우려를 다루다

  address customer requests
  고객 요청을 처리하다

  To ------- the complaints from local residents, the city council will host a public forum next month.
  (A) prevent　　　　(B) address

12 hire

- 채용하다, 고용하다

  기출 **hire** a new manager
  새로운 부장을 채용하다

  hire extra editors to meet the deadline
  마감일을 맞추기 위해 추가 편집자들을 채용하다

  Spinks Corporation wants to ------- a new graphic designer to improve its promotional materials.
  (A) hire　　　　(B) plan

13 access

accessible a. 접근 가능한, 이용 가능한

- ~에 접근하다, ~을 이용하다

  기출 **access** important overseas markets by
  ~함으로써 중요한 해외 시장에 접근하다

  > Hasting Corporation hopes to ------- European markets with its new line of tablet computers.
  >
  > (A) access (B) proceed

14 resume

- 재개하다, 재개되다

  기출 will **resume** one's duties
  ~의 직무를 재개할 것이다

  will **resume** as soon as possible
  가능한 한 빨리 재개될 것이다

  > Riley Railways' normal train service will ------- as soon as the snowstorm has passed.
  >
  > (A) assemble (B) resume

15 release

- 출시하다, 공개하다

  기출 **release** one's latest product
  신제품을 출시하다

  release one's information to
  ~에게 …의 정보를 공개하다

  > Athletico is about to ------- its new line of running shoes in all major sportswear stores.
  >
  > (A) release (B) develop

16 cause

- 야기하다, 일으키다

  기출 **cause** traffic delays 교통 지연을 야기하다

  > The inclement weather has ------- power disruption throughout 30 percent of the city.
  >
  > (A) caused (B) directed

17 estimate

추정하다, 견적을 내다

기출 **estimate** the number of working hours
근무 시간을 추정하다

By entering your shipping information, Corstin Delivery can ------- the amount of time it will take to deliver your order.

(A) estimate　　　　(B) endure

18 reserve

reservation n. 예약
reserved a. 보류된, 예약된

예약하다, (권리를) 가지다

기출 **reserve** the table for the luncheon
오찬을 위한 테이블을 예약하다

reserve the right to do
~할 권리를 가지다

Visit our Web site to ------- a room or to find out more information about our lodgings.

(A) reserve　　　　(B) decide

19 transfer

(직장, 부서를) 전근하다, 이체하다

기출 **transfer** to the accounting department
회계부로 전근하다

transfer funds to another account
자금을 다른 계좌로 이체하다

Mr. Connolly will be ------- to the Newport branch from the Cardiff branch in August.

(A) placing　　　　(B) transferring

20 conduct

- 수행하다, 실시하다

  기출 **conduct** an inspection
  점검을 수행하다

  conduct a tour of the factory
  공장 견학을 실시하다

  > Mr. Chong and his team will ------- an extensive analysis of the market research data.
  > (A) detain   (B) conduct

21 focus

- 초점을 맞추다, 집중하다

  기출 **focus** on analyzing financial data
  재무 데이터를 분석하는 데 초점을 맞추다

  focus on developing a new material
  새로운 재료를 개발하는 데 집중하다

  > The seminar ------- on developing management skills that can be applied to all kinds of businesses.
  > (A) cooperates   (B) focuses

22 guarantee

- 보장하다, 보증하다

  기출 **guarantee** its delivery time
  배송 시간을 보장하다

  guarantee the privacy of personal information
  개인 정보 보호를 보장하다

  > In order to ------- your place at the marketing workshop, you must register online by April 12.
  > (A) guarantee   (B) expand

23 grant

● 승인하다, 제공하다

기출 **grant** Ms. Higgins a raise
히긴스 씨에게 급여 인상을 승인하다

grant employees more paid leave
직원들에게 더 많은 유급 휴가를 제공하다

This voucher ------- the holder an extra meal of equal value when purchasing a meal at any Joker's Restaurant location.

(A) accepts (B) grants

24 contact

● 연락하다

기출 **contact** Mr. Hamilton in Human Resources
인사팀의 해밀턴 씨에게 연락하다

If you wish to request annual leave, please ------- the HR department on Extension 102.

(A) contact (B) speak

25 exchange

● (같은 종류로) 교환하다

기출 **exchange** one's item for another item
다른 제품으로 ~의 제품을 교환하다

Diners who want to ------- one side dish with a different one should speak to their server.

(A) exchange (B) design

26 launch

● 개시하다, 착수하다

[기출] **launch** an advertising campaign
광고 캠페인을 개시하다

> To make sure its new cell phone is a success, Swipe Electronics will ------- a global marketing campaign.
> (A) launch　　　　(B) pass

27 decline

declining a. 쇠퇴하는, 하락하는

● 거절하다, 하락하다

[기출] **decline** applications
지원서를 거절하다

typically **decline** during the winter season
보통 겨울철에 하락하다

> Demand for our range of hot beverages typically ------- during the summer months but recovers starting in October.
> (A) declines　　　(B) delays

28 share

● (물건, 의견을) 공유하다, 나누다

[기출] **share** the results of the poll
여론조사의 결과를 공유하다

share any concerns
어떠한 우려라도 나누다

> The CEO will ------- his plans for the company's continued growth at this week's board meeting.
> (A) split　　　　(B) share

29 limit

limited a. 제한된, 한정된
limitation n. 한계

- 제한하다

  기출 **limit** one's presentation to 시간
  발표 시간을 ~로 제한하다

  > In order to complete the order on time, we have no choice but to ------- employee lunch breaks to thirty minutes this week.
  >
  > (A) limit　　　　　(B) separate

30 outline

- 요약하다, 간략하게 서술하다

  기출 **outline** the strengths of
  ~의 강점을 요약하다

  outline the basic responsibilities of
  ~의 기본 의무를 간략하게 서술하다

  > The memo distributed by Mr. Finnegan ------- the company's new marketing strategy and sales targets.
  >
  > (A) outlines　　　　(B) instructs

31 influence

- 영향을 미치다, 영향을 주다

  기출 **influence** consumer spending
  소비자 지출에 영향을 미치다

  be **influenced** by
  ~에 영향을 받다

  > The mayor of Chester believes that the construction of the new amusement park will positively ------- local tourism.
  >
  > (A) influence　　　(B) exchange

32 promise

- 약속하다

  기출 **promise** to reduce taxes
  세금을 줄이는 것을 약속하다

  > The hiring committee decided to offer Mr. Reynolds the position of financial manager because he ------- to reduce annual expenditure.
  > (A) followed   (B) promised

33 encounter

- (우연히) 마주치다, 접하다

  기출 **encounter** A abroad
  해외에서 A를 우연히 마주치다

  encounter problems with products
  제품에 대한 문제를 접하다

  > Users who ------- issues with our anti-virus software are advised to refer to the troubleshooting guide.
  > (A) inform   (B) encounter

34 substitute

- 대체하다, 대신하다

  기출 **substitute** honey for sugar
  설탕을 꿀로 대체하다

  Pork may be **substituted** for beef.
  소고기가 돼지고기로 대체될 수 있습니다.

  > If you would prefer to reduce the calories of the recipe, you may ------- cream with low-fat yogurt.
  > (A) substitute   (B) classify

35 last

lasting a. 지속적인, 오래 남는

- (기능이) 지속되다

  기출 **last** longer than those of competitors
  경쟁사들의 제품보다 더 오래 지속되다

> All electrical components in the running machine are guaranteed to ------- for at least three years.
> (A) retain (B) last

36 present

- 제시하다, (선물, 상을) 받다

  기출 **present** one's card at the main entrance
  정문 입구에서 카드를 제시하다

  be **presented** with an award
  상을 받다

> To gain access to the research laboratory, you must ------- your security pass to the guard at the entrance.
> (A) place (B) present

37 express

expression n. 표현

- (감정을) 표현하다, 표하다

  기출 **express** one's interest in
  ~에 대한 관심을 표현하다

  express full support for
  ~에 대한 전폭적 지지를 표하다

> Mr. Darling has ------- his support for the construction of a new manufacturing plant on the outskirts of Detroit.
> (A) expressed (B) focused

38 double

- 두 배가 되다

  기출 have nearly **doubled** in the last decade
  지난 10년간 거의 두 배가 되었다

  After ProVision's new game consoles sold out in stores, the price of the product almost ------- in online markets.

  (A) predicted (B) doubled

39 deliberate

deliberately ad. 신중하게

- 숙고하다, 신중히 생각하다

  기출 **deliberated** for more than 6 hours before
  ~하기 전에 6시간 이상 숙고했다

  Members of the judging panel ------- for two hours before announcing the winners of this year's UK Gymnastics Competition.

  (A) deliberated (B) mediated

40 welcome

- 환영하다, 맞이하다

  기출 **welcome** the new director
  신임 이사를 환영하다

  welcome tour groups on Saturdays
  토요일마다 단체 견학을 맞이하다

  The Franklin Science Museum ------- visitors seven days a week, from 10 AM to 8 PM.

  (A) welcomes (B) introduces

DAILY QUIZ

단어와 그에 알맞은 뜻을 연결해 보세요.

1. inspect • • (A) 승인하다, 제공하다
2. release • • (B) 점검하다, 검토하다
3. grant • • (C) 출시하다, 공개하다

빈칸에 알맞은 단어를 선택하세요.

4. ------- to open a factory in
   ~에 공장을 열 생각이다

5. ------- a variety of events
   다양한 행사들을 특징으로 하다

6. ------- customer requests
   고객 요청을 처리하다

(A) intend
(B) address
(C) delay
(D) feature

앞서 배운 단어들의 뜻을 생각하면서, 다음 문제를 풀어보세요.

7. Unless the event organizer can ------- an alternative venue, the Melody Music Festival may not be held this year.

   (A) distribute (B) select
   (C) perform   (D) withdraw

8. Because Presidio Events Company ------- its rates, we were able to organize the fundraiser within our proposed budget.

   (A) guarantees (B) advises
   (C) requires   (D) delays

정답 1 (B) 2 (C) 3 (A) 4 (A) 5 (D) 6 (B) 7 (B) 8 (A)

Day 03 동사 ❹ Part 5, 6

1 refund

refundable a. 환불 가능한

● 환불해주다

기출 have all charges **refunded**
모든 요금을 환불 받다

The cost of Mr. Black's plane ticket was ------- to him as the flight was overbooked.
(A) changed　　　(B) refunded

2 charge

● (요금을) 청구하다, 충전하다

기출 **charge** fees for all vehicles
모든 차량에 대해 요금을 청구하다

charge laptops and mobile phones
노트북과 휴대전화를 충전하다

The convention center ------- parking fees for all vehicles between the hours of 9 AM and 6 PM.
(A) charges　　　(B) measures

3 recruit

recruiting n. 채용

● 채용하다

기출 **recruit** additional customer service representatives
추가 고객 서비스 직원들을 채용하다

To ensure that the store's grand opening is a success, we plan to ------- an experienced event organizer.
(A) recruit　　　(B) complete

4 display

- 보여주다, 진열하다

  기출 **display** a parking permit
  주차 허가증을 보여주다

  > Vendors should noticeably ------- both their business name and their vending permit on their stall or booth.
  > (A) state　　　　　(B) display

5 exhibit

exhibition n. 전시회

- 전시하다

  기출 artists interested in **exhibiting** their work
  자신들의 작품을 전시하는 데 관심이 있는 예술가들

  > Anyone interested in ------- their work at the Harmony Festival Gallery in the community center should contact Ms. Hughes.
  > (A) acquiring　　　　(B) exhibiting

  만점 TIP
  • exhibit은 명사로도 사용할 수 있지만, 명사의 의미일 때는 주로 exhibition으로 출제된다.

6 issue

- 발행하다, 발부하다

  기출 **issue** building permits
  건축 허가증을 발행하다

  issue a summary with a list of recommendations
  추천서 목록과 함께 요약본을 발부하다

  > Your membership card for Stanton Library has been ------- and should arrive within three days.
  > (A) included　　　　(B) issued

  만점 TIP
  • issue가 명사로 사용되는 경우, '(잡지의) 호' 또는 '(사회) 문제' 등 동사와는 전혀 다른 뜻으로 사용된다.

7 gain

● 얻다, 늘리다

기출 **gain** the necessary experience
필요한 경험을 얻다

gain 4,000 jobs in the technology industry
기술 업계에서 4,000개의 일자리를 늘리다

It has been shown that our seminars help entry-level employees to ------- confidence.

(A) complete   (B) gain

8 renovate

renovation n. 개조, 보수

● 개조하다, 보수하다

기출 be fully **renovated** into a sports arena
스포츠 경기장으로 완전히 개조되다

renovate houses and flats
주택과 아파트를 보수하다

Known for its outstanding designs and reliable workforce, Garmond Interiors ------- both residential and business properties.

(A) insures   (B) renovates

9 find

findings n. 발견물, 조사 결과

● 확인하다, 찾다

기출 **find** enclosed one's membership card
동봉된 회원 카드를 확인하다

find the way around the convention center
컨벤션 센터 주변의 길을 찾다

Please ------- enclosed a gift voucher that can be exchanged for a free dessert at any Roma Pasta location.

(A) look   (B) find

10 allow

allowance n. 허용

- ~하게 해주다, 허용하다

  기출 **allow** users to automate repetitive tasks
  사용자들이 반복 업무를 자동화할 수 있게 해주다

  allow customers to upgrade from A to B
  고객들이 A에서 B로 업그레이드하게 허용하다

  > Mobile Mail ------- smartphone users to check up to ten different e-mail accounts using just one application.
  > (A) allows　　　　(B) accepts

11 proceed

- 진행하다, 나아가다

  기출 if you would like to **proceed**
  진행하고 싶으시다면

  proceed with development
  발전해 나가다

  > Although there have been some reports of minor faults, Henley Technologies will ------- with the release of its new line of refrigerators.
  > (A) proceed　　　(B) treat

12 cancel

cancellation n. 취소

- 취소하다

  기출 **cancel** one's subscription to
  ~의 정기구독을 취소하다

  cancel one's conference call
  전화회의를 취소하다

  > If you would like to ------- your membership at Sierra Gym, please e-mail our customer support team.
  > (A) cancel　　　　(B) offer

13 protect

protective a. 보호하는

- 보호하다

  기출 **protect** the company's property
  회사의 자산을 보호하다

  protect your home
  귀하의 자택을 보호하다

  Carter Health Clinic requires all workers to sign an agreement in order to ------- the privacy of its patients.
  (A) prevent　　　　(B) protect

14 remind

reminder n. 상기시키는 것

- 상기시키다

  기출 I want to **remind** you that ~.
  ~라는 점을 상기시켜 드리고 싶습니다.

  remind all visitors to be in the lobby
  모든 방문객들이 로비에 있도록 상기시키다

  To avoid any thefts or accidents, the apartment building manager ------- all tenants not to leave personal items in the corridors.
  (A) reminded　　　　(B) memorized

15 explain

explanation n. 설명

- 설명하다

  기출 **explain** our proposal to customers
  고객들에게 우리의 제안을 설명하다

  Ms. Evers will ------- the new shift scheduling procedure to the heads of each department.
  (A) decide　　　　(B) explain

16 celebrate

celebratory a. 기념하는

- 기념하다

기출 **celebrate** the 20th anniversary of
~의 20주년을 기념하다

> On July 29, Ms. Elba will ------- her twentieth anniversary as the CEO of Muntero Pharmaceuticals.
> (A) join (B) celebrate

17 hesitate

hesitant a. 주저하는, 망설이는
hesitation n. 주저함, 망설임

- 주저하다, 망설이다

기출 Do not **hesitate** to contact me.
제게 연락하는 것을 주저하지 마십시오.

> If you require assistance with setting up your device, please do not ------- to call our tech support team.
> (A) hesitate (B) qualify

18 describe

description n. 묘사, 설명

- 묘사하다, 설명하다

기출 clearly **describe** the missing item
분실물을 명확하게 묘사하다

> At the shareholder meeting, Mr. Peng ------- the company's goals and expansion plans for the coming year.
> (A) described (B) persisted

19 depart

departure n. 출발

- 출발하다, 떠나다

  기출 **depart** from each station every 10 minutes
  매 10분마다 각 역을 출발하다

  be scheduled to **depart** at 11:00 AM
  오전 11시에 떠날 예정이다

  > A shuttle bus ------- every thirty minutes from the airport and stops at the Maxi Hotel and the Evercrest Inn.
  > (A) exports (B) departs

20 occupy

- (장소를) 사용하다, 점유하다

  기출 **occupy** the top floor of the building
  건물의 최고층을 사용하다

  > Based on the first draft of the blueprint, Arcadia Cinema will ------- the entire top floor of the shopping mall.
  > (A) sell (B) occupy

21 oversee

- 감독하다

  기출 **oversee** all aspects of the remodeling project
  리모델링 프로젝트의 모든 면을 감독하다

  > Mr. Rodrigo has been asked to ------- all aspects of the employee orientation program.
  > (A) contend (B) oversee

22 enable

- ~할 수 있게 하다

  기출 **enable** people to be more efficient
  사람들을 더 효율적이게 하다

  The improved assembly line technology would ------- the manufacturing plant to triple its production rate.
  (A) enable   (B) prefer

23 enroll

enrollment n. 등록(자 수)

- 등록하다(in)

  기출 **enroll** in the sales seminar
  영업 세미나에 등록하다

  All Minturn Inc. employees can ------- in the advanced sales workshop free of charge.
  (A) enroll   (B) apply

24 add

addition n. 추가
additional a. 추가의
additionally ad. 게다가

- 추가하다, (말을) 덧붙이다

  기출 be **added** 추가되다
  　　　add that ~라고 덧붙이다

  In her closing statement, the new CEO ------- that she is looking forward to taking on new challenges.
  (A) provided   (B) added

25 relocate

relocation n. 이전, 이사

- 이전하다, 이사하다

  기출 **relocate** the plants' main base of operation
  공장 운영의 주된 근거지를 이전하다

  Mr. Houston outlined numerous benefits of ------- the company's headquarters to Des Moines.
  (A) acquiring   (B) relocating

26 restore

restoration n. 복구, 복원

- 복구하다, 복원하다

  기출 **restore** the historic building to its former glory
  역사적 건물을 이전의 영화로운 상태로 복구하다

  be **restored** to its original style by the city
  시에 의해 원래 양식으로 복원되다

  > A renowned architectural firm has been contracted to ------- the 150-year-old Richmond Theater to its original condition.
  > (A) restore   (B) replace

27 mandate

- 의무화하다

  기출 **mandate** all workers to wear hard hats
  모든 근로자들이 안전모를 착용하는 것을 의무화하다

  > To reduce the risk of computer viruses, new policies ------- all workers to keep anti-virus software installed.
  > (A) organize   (B) mandate

28 differ

different a. 다른
difference n. 차이

- 다르다

  기출 **differ** based on the weekly promotion
  주간 홍보에 따라 다르다

  differ in their opinions of
  ~에 대한 의견이 다르다

  > Salaries will ------- based on expertise and experience.
  > (A) differ   (B) calculate

29 maintain

maintenance n. 유지보수

● 유지하다

기출 **maintain** the current staffing level
현재 직원 수준을 유지하다

Pall Valley Beverages has ------- a strong customer base and plans to expand overseas next year.
(A) afforded (B) maintained

30 possess

possession n. 소유(물)

● 소유하다, 보유하다

기출 **possess** a valid driver's license
유효한 운전면허증을 소유하다

possess at least three years of experience
적어도 3년의 경력을 보유하다

Successful candidates should ------- at least four years of experience and expertise in human resources.
(A) occupy (B) possess

31 preserve

preservation n. 보존, 보호

● 보존하다, 보호하다

기출 **preserve** its original features
원래의 특성들을 보존하다

to **preserve** the historic city hall
역사적인 시청 건물을 보호하기 위해

The city council promised that the old theater will be ------- even though several adjacent buildings are scheduled for demolition.
(A) preserved (B) specialized

32 discontinue

discontinued a. 단종된

- (서비스, 제품 생산을) 중단하다

  기출 **discontinue** its operations
  운영을 중단하다

  Our model has been **discontinued**.
  저희 모델은 생산이 중단되었습니다.

  Apex Sportswear is downsizing and will be ------- its least popular ranges of clothing.
  (A) unfolding　　(B) discontinuing

33 emphasize

emphasis n. 강조

- 강조하다

  기출 **emphasize** the needs of
  ~의 필요를 강조하다

  emphasize its fuel efficiency
  연료 효율을 강조하다

  The founder of the technology company has ------- the importance of providing excellent customer service.
  (A) emphasized　　(B) demanded

34 analyze

analysis n. 분석

- 분석하다

  기출 **analyze** all project details
  모든 프로젝트 세부사항을 분석하다

  analyze the consumer survey
  소비자 설문조사를 분석하다

  The mechanical problems should be further ------- before any work on the production line is resumed.
  (A) conducted　　(B) analyzed

35 restrict

restriction n. 제한

- 제한하다

  기출 **restrict** the availability of parking in the downtown area
  시내 지역에서 주차장 이용을 제한하다

  Parking is ------- on many of the streets surrounding Belmont Fire Station.
  (A) restricted   (B) enhanced

36 commend

- 칭찬하다, 추천하다

  기출 be **commended** by one's supervisor for
  ~에 대해 상사에게 칭찬받다

  be **commended** by local authorities for
  지역 당국으로부터 ~에 대해 추천받다

  Ms. Finnigan has been ------- by the city council for raising over ten thousand dollars for local charities.
  (A) proposed   (B) commended

37 endorse

endorsement n. 홍보, 지지

- (유명인이 제품, 기업 등을) 홍보하다, 지지하다

  기출 **endorse** eco-friendly transportation routes
  친환경적인 교통 경로를 홍보하다

  agree to **endorse** the new makeup line
  새로운 메이크업 제품군을 홍보하는 것에 동의하다

  Famous baseball player Johnny Redmond has agreed to ------- our sportswear.
  (A) appeal   (B) endorse

38 distinguish

- 구분 짓다, 구분하다

  기출 **distinguish** oneself by -ing
  ~함으로써 자신을 구분 짓다

  can be **distinguished** by their labels
  그들의 상표로 구분될 수 있다

  Our healthy food products can be easily ------- by their green "government-certified" labels.
  (A) distinguished　　(B) corrected

39 evaluate

evaluation n. 평가(서)

- 평가하다

  기출 **evaluate** Ms. Monroe as a candidate
  먼로 씨를 후보자로서 평가하다

  be **evaluated** quarterly
  분기별로 평가되다

  In order for us to ------- Mr. Kane as a potential collaborator, we asked him to submit a portfolio of his previous photography work.
  (A) evaluate　　(B) persuade

40 refrain

- 삼가다, 자제하다

  기출 **refrain** from talking to other people
  다른 사람들에게 말하는 것을 삼가다

  We ask that passengers ------- from leaving their seats while the plane is taking off.
  (A) refrain　　(B) prohibit

DAILY QUIZ

단어와 그에 알맞은 뜻을 연결해 보세요.

1. relocate • • (A) 유지하다
2. maintain • • (B) 이전하다, 이사하다
3. restrict • • (C) 제한하다

빈칸에 알맞은 단어를 선택하세요.

4. ------- fees for all vehicles
모든 차량에 대해 요금을 청구하다

5. ------- one's subscription to
~의 정기구독을 취소하다

(A) cancel
(B) charge
(C) display
(D) enroll

6. ------- in the sales seminar
영업 세미나에 등록하다

앞서 배운 단어들의 뜻을 생각하면서, 다음 문제를 풀어보세요.

7. Ms. Crawford hired a highly regarded accountant to ------- all financial matters affecting her company.

　(A) accumulate　　(B) demand
　(C) oversee　　　 (D) participate

8. Tomorrow's seminar will help sales representatives ------- their ability to identify, approach, and engage with potential customers.

　(A) succeed　　(B) prefer
　(C) announce　 (D) evaluate

정답 1 (B) 2 (A) 3 (C) 4 (B) 5 (A) 6 (D) 7 (C) 8 (D)

Day 04 동사 + 전치사 콜로케이션 Part 5, 6

1 evolve from

● ~로부터 진화하다, 발전하다

기출 **evolve from** a mobile app developer
모바일 어플 개발회사로부터 진화하다

Over the past few years, the Redhill neighborhood has ------- from a quiet residential district into a popular shopping area.

(A) evolved   (B) elaborated

2 respond to

● ~에 응답하다

기출 **respond to** rising demand
증가하는 수요에 응답하다

respond to reporters' questions
기자들의 질문에 응답하다

At tenant association meetings, the organization's president often ------- to members' questions about rental rates.

(A) applies   (B) responds

3 look for

● ~을 찾다

기출 **look for** a new shipping company
새로운 운송 회사를 찾다

look for ways to reduce greenhouse gas emissions
온실가스 배출을 줄이기 위한 방법들을 찾다

The COO of Guelph Manufacturing is ------- for ways to make the production process more efficient.

(A) looking   (B) seeing

4 reply to

• ~에 답장하다

기출 Please **reply to** this e-mail by Friday.
금요일까지 이 이메일에 답장해주십시오.

Please **reply to** this letter at your convenience.
편하실 때 이 편지에 답장해주십시오.

Please ------- to this text message if you wish to change your appointment time for the dental surgery.

(A) confirm   (B) reply

5 register for

• ~에 등록하다

기출 **register for** the guided tour
가이드 투어에 등록하다

register for the conference
컨퍼런스에 등록하다

If no one ------- for the workshop, it will be canceled without prior notice.

(A) registers   (B) approves

6 participate in

• ~에 참가하다

기출 **participate in** all the activities
모든 활동에 참가하다

participate in the upcoming seminar
곧 있을 세미나에 참가하다

Local residents who wish to ------- in the upcoming town forum should register on the city council Web site.

(A) participate   (B) attend

7 expand into

● ~으로 확장하다

기출 **expand into** the Wellington region
웰링턴 지역으로 확장하다

consider **expanding into** overseas markets
해외 시장으로 확장하는 것을 고려하다

British sportswear company Salway Inc. announced in a press release that it is planning to expand ------- North America.
(A) into　　　　　　(B) around

8 result in

● ~라는 결과를 낳다, (결과적으로) ~을 야기하다

기출 **result in** a higher-quality product
더 높은 품질의 상품이라는 결과를 낳다

result in a 30 percent increase
30퍼센트 증가를 야기하다

The more cost-effective product packaging will ------- in reduced product prices.
(A) result　　　　　(B) complete

9 focus on

● ~에 주력하다, 초점을 맞추다

기출 **focus on** our most recent policy updates
가장 최근의 정책 업데이트에 주력하다

focus on serving small businesses
소규모 업체들에게 서비스를 제공하는 데 초점을 맞추다

The seminar ------- on building strong work relationships between employees and customers.
(A) cooperates　　　(B) focuses

10 enroll in

- ~에 등록하다

  기출 **enroll in** the technology courses
  기술 강좌에 등록하다

  enroll in the employee mentoring program
  직원 멘토링 프로그램에 등록하다

  Management requires all workers who have not attained the Level 1 safety certificate to ------- in the health and safety workshop.

  (A) enroll   (B) attend

11 refer to

- ~을 참조하다

  기출 **refer to** the fourth page of the agreement
  계약서의 네 번째 페이지를 참조하다

  Please **refer to** your employee guide.
  귀하의 직원 안내서를 참조하십시오.

  For a list of licensed Mago Software vendors, please ------- to Page 10 of the user manual.

  (A) refer   (B) adapt

12 appear on

- ~에 나타나다, 나오다

  기출 **appear on** the billing statement
  청구서에 나타나다

  appear on a special broadcast
  특별 방송에 나오다

  Sam Singh, the founder of the social media platform, ------- on a two-hour episode of Joe Fagan's popular podcast.

  (A) appeared   (B) seemed

13 consult with

- ~와 협의하다, 의논하다

  기출 **consult with** Mr. Bingham 빙햄 씨와 협의하다
  consult with an engineer 기술자와 의논하다

  If you need to ------- with Mr. Kitson, please make an appointment with his personal assistant.
  (A) arrange　　　　(B) consult

14 come with

- ~이 딸려 오다

  기출 **come with** a standard one-year warranty
  표준 1년 보증서가 딸려 오다

  Each Lumos flashlight ------- with a 2-year warranty covering any manufacturer defects.
  (A) includes　　　　(B) comes

15 emerge as

- ~로 떠오르다, 등장하다

  기출 **emerge as** one of the most famous stars
  가장 유명한 스타들 중 한 명으로 떠오르다

  Fiona Middleton has ------- as the most likely candidate to take over for Mr. Stillman as CEO.
  (A) appointed　　　　(B) emerged

16 merge with

- ~와 합병하다, 합치다

  기출 will **merge with** another software company
  또 다른 소프트웨어 회사와 합병할 것이다

  Corsair Courier Services will ------- with Reliant Shipping early next year.
  (A) attract　　　　(B) merge

17 comply with

~을 지키다, 따르다

기출 **comply with** the firm's new policy
회사의 새로운 정책을 지키다

comply with safety regulations
안전 규정을 따르다

All appliances in our kitchens must ------- with the common safety standards of the restaurant industry.
(A) associate   (B) comply

18 consist of

~으로 구성되다

기출 **consist of** community leaders
지역사회 지도자들로 구성되다

consist of paintings and sculptures
그림과 조각품들로 구성되다

Halo Charitable Foundation ------- of more than 25,000 members based all over the world.
(A) spreads   (B) consists

19 coincide with

~와 겹치다, 일치하다

기출 will **coincide with** the summer holidays
여름 휴가와 겹칠 것이다

coincide with Ms. Emily's business trip
에밀리 씨의 출장 일자와 일치하다

The launch of Sunsport's new range of T-shirts and swimwear will ------- with the summer holidays.
(A) produce   (B) coincide

20 conform to

• ~에 따르다, 순응하다

기출 **conform to** company standards
회사 기준에 따르다

Please ensure that your article's length and format ------- to the guidelines in the writing manual.
(A) conform (B) attach

21 communicate with

• ~와 (의사)소통하다

기출 **communicate with** family
가족과 소통하다

communicate with other bidders
다른 입찰자들과 소통하다

Mobile messaging applications enable users to ------- easily with family and friends.
(A) communicate (B) state

22 concentrate on

• ~에 집중하다

기출 **concentrate on** the importance of customer service
고객 서비스의 중요성에 집중하다

The documentary will ------- on uncovering the reasons why the technology corporation went bankrupt.
(A) concentrate (B) study

23 proceed with

- ~을 진행하다, 계속하다

  기출 **proceed with** development
  개발을 진행하다

  will **proceed with** negotiations cautiously
  신중하게 협상을 계속할 것이다

  Although several faults were noted during the testing phase, it is crucial for us to ------- with the product launch schedule.

  (A) proceed　　　　(B) treat

24 revert to

- ~로 되돌아가다

  기출 **revert to** their original systems
  원래 시스템으로 되돌아가다

  After keeping the clothing store open until 7 PM for a few weeks, the owner decided to ------- to the original business hours.

  (A) recover　　　　(B) revert

25 collaborate with

- ~와 협동하다, 협력하다

  기출 **collaborate with** each other
  서로 협동하다

  collaborate with marketing specialists
  마케팅 전문가와 협력하다

  The director of the movie ------- with Dr. Marjorie Irvine to ensure that all medical scenes were portrayed accurately.

  (A) provided　　　　(B) collaborated

26 **specialize in**

● ~을 전문으로 하다

기출 **specialize in** machinery manufacturing
기계 제작을 전문으로 하다

specialize in the beverage industry
음료 산업을 전문으로 하다

> Attica Prints, one of the newest stores in Ascot Shopping Mall, ------- in converting photographs into posters or printed canvases.
>
> (A) specializes　　　(B) identifies

27 **compete against**

● ~와 경쟁하다

기출 **compete against** other construction firms
다른 건축 회사들과 경쟁하다

> Before he can progress to the interview stage for the position, Mr. Raglan must first ------- against several other experienced applicants.
>
> (A) compete　　　(B) associate

28 **lead to**

● ~로 이어지다

기출 **lead to** an increase in parking fees
주차 요금에서의 증가로 이어지다

lead to a permanent position
정규직으로 이어지다

> The Mayor of Corben has insisted that hosting the music festival will not ------- to an increase in litter.
>
> (A) lead　　　(B) intend

29 look into

● ~을 조사하다, 주의깊게 살피다

기출 promise to **look into** the matter
그 사안을 조사하기로 약속하다

Mr. Holden believes that the accounting department should ------- hiring an additional intern.
(A) use up   (B) look into

30 refrain from

● ~을 자제하다, 삼가다

기출 **refrain from** talking to the people
사람들에게 이야기하는 것을 자제하다

refrain from using mobile devices
휴대기기를 사용하는 것을 삼가다

Please ------- from feeding the animals when visiting Oakview City Farm.
(A) refrain   (B) differ

31 work on

● ~에 대해 작업하다, ~로 일하다

기출 **work on** the Cambridge bridge
캠브리지 다리에 대해 작업하다

work on the rotating shifts
교대 근무로 일하다

Staff members at Kathy's 24-Hour Diner ------- on rotating shifts and receive bonus pay between 10 PM and 6 AM.
(A) work   (B) employ

32 adhere to

- ~을 고수하다, ~에 (들러)붙다

  기출 **adhere to** the regulations stated in the manual
  안내서에 명시된 규정을 고수하다

  adhere to the surface made of other materials
  다른 재질로 만들어진 표면에 붙다

  > Press the suction cup of the camera firmly against the glass to ensure that it ------- to the vehicle's windshield.
  > (A) adheres   (B) polishes

33 meet with

- ~와 만나다

  기출 **meet with** clients who have appointments
  약속을 한 고객들과 만나다

  meet with supervisors frequently
  상사들과 자주 만나다

  > Ms. Lawson usually ------- only with clients based in the local area, but she has agreed to travel to Los Angeles to speak with Mr. Jenner.
  > (A) fits   (B) meets

34 depart from

- ~에서 출발하다, 떠나다

  기출 will **depart from** gate 47
  47번 게이트에서 출발할 것이다

  > Before ------- from the baseball stadium, kindly place your trash in the bins provided.
  > (A) departing   (B) surrounding

35 rely on

● ~에 의존하다

기출 **rely on** outside consultants
외부 상담가들에 의존하다

rely on online product ratings
온라인 상품 평가에 의존하다

> The launch of Mr. Anderson's new company will ------- on the financial backing of several investors.
>
> (A) interfere (B) rely

36 search for

● ~을 찾다

기출 **search for** qualified candidates
자격을 갖춘 지원자들을 찾다

search for specific phrases in an article
한 기사에서 특정 문구들을 찾다

> *The Bedford Times* has hired a recruitment firm to ------- for skilled college graduates seeking a career in journalism.
>
> (A) search (B) replace

37 benefit from

● ~에서 이익을 얻다

기출 **benefit from** the increasing competition
증가하는 경쟁에서 이익을 얻다

benefit from the new data analysis program
새로운 데이터 분석 프로그램에서 이익을 얻다

> Rosalita Coffee Shop ------- from its close proximity to Adelaide University.
>
> (A) explores (B) benefits

38 serve as

● ~로서 근무하다

기출 **serve as** the temporary replacement
임시 후임으로서 근무하다

be appointed to **serve as** the director
이사로서 근무하도록 임명되다

> Andy Chen has been asked to ------- as the temporary branch manager while Ms. Pettigrew is on maternity leave.
>
> (A) recognize   (B) serve

39 appeal to

● ~에게 호소하다, 매력적으로 다가가다

기출 **appeal to** readers under the age of 19
19세 미만의 독자들에게 호소하다

appeal to different types of customers
다른 유형의 고객들에게 매력적으로 다가가다

> Lilypad Bistro has introduced a selection of vegetarian dishes to ------- an even broader customer base.
>
> (A) call out   (B) appeal to

40 invest in

● ~에 투자하다

기출 **invest in** renewable energy
재생 에너지에 투자하다

invest in areas of promising research
전망이 있는 연구 분야에 투자하다

> After consulting with his financial advisor, Mr. Hartmann decided to invest ------- a promising new technology company.
>
> (A) about   (B) in

DAILY QUIZ

콜로케이션과 그에 알맞은 뜻을 연결해 보세요.

1 consist of • • (A) ~에 집중하다
2 concentrate on • • (B) ~을 전문으로 하다
3 specialize in • • (C) ~으로 구성되다

빈칸에 알맞은 단어를 선택하세요.

4 Please ------- to this e-mail by Friday.
   금요일까지 이 이메일에 답장해주십시오.

5 ------- in the technology courses
   기술 강좌에 등록하다

(A) comply
(B) enroll
(C) reply
(D) adhere

6 ------- with the firm's new policy
   회사의 새로운 정책을 지키다

앞서 배운 콜로케이션들의 뜻을 생각하면서, 다음 문제를 풀어보세요.

7 The Mayfair Walnut Wardrobe does not come pre-assembled, so please ------- to the assembly instructions included.

   (A) refer   (B) adapt
   (C) present   (D) follow

8 The last ferry to Skinner Island will ------- from the harbor at 4 in the afternoon.

   (A) welcome   (B) depart
   (C) withdraw   (D) attend

정답 1 (C) 2 (A) 3 (B) 4 (C) 5 (B) 6 (A) 7 (A) 8 (B)

Day 05 기출 동의어 ④ Part 7

1 depress

❶ 떨어뜨리다, 하락시키다
→ **reduce, lower**

❷ 우울하게 하다
→ **make unhappy, sadden**

> The announcement of a new technology upgrade would **depress** sales of the current model as customers wait for the improved version.
>
> (A) reduce (B) sadden

소비자들이 개선된 버전을 기다리기 때문에 새로운 기술 업그레이드 소식은 현재 모델의 매출을 떨어뜨릴 것입니다.

2 illustrate

❶ 삽화를 쓰다
→ **add pictures, decorate**

❷ 분명히 보여주다
→ **represent, show, demonstrate**

> Please write a short response about a time you faced a challenge and how you overcame it. Do your best to use an example that **illustrates** your character.
>
> (A) decorates (B) represents

당신이 어려움을 직면했던 때와, 어떻게 그것을 극복했는지에 관해 짧은 답변을 작성해 주세요. 당신의 성격을 분명히 보여주는 예시를 사용할 수 있도록 최선을 다해 주시기 바랍니다.

3 serious

❶ 심각한
→ **severe, critical**

❷ 진심인, 진지한
→ **earnest**

> The law firm is known for providing exceptional legal services, staffed by a team of **serious** and highly qualified attorneys.
>
> (A) severe (B) earnest

그 법률 회사는 진지하고 우수한 자격을 갖춘 변호사 팀을 갖추고 있어, 탁월한 법률 서비스를 제공하는 것으로 알려져 있습니다.

4 hit

❶ 타격
→ **impact**

❷ 성공
→ **success**

> Immediately after its release, Murphy Band's debut song was a <u>hit</u> and reached the number one spot on various music charts.
>
> (A) impact   (B) success

발매와 동시에, 머피 밴드의 데뷔곡은 성공했고, 다수의 음악 차트에서 1위 자리에 이르렀습니다.

5 practice

❶ 관행
→ **regular action, custom, habit**

❷ 훈련, 연습
→ **training, exercise**

❸ (의료, 법률 등의) 직업 활동
→ **professional business**

> In today's market, offering personalized shopping recommendations based on customer browsing history has become a common <u>practice</u> among e-commerce companies.
>
> (A) regular action   (B) training

오늘날의 시장에서는, 고객 검색 기록에 근거한 개인화된 쇼핑 추천을 제공하는 것이 전자 상거래 회사들 사이에서 흔한 관행이 되었습니다.

6 commitment

❶ 헌신, 전념
→ **dedication, devotion**

❷ 책임, 책무
→ **responsibility, duty**

> We have taken various initiatives to demonstrate our <u>commitment</u> to environmentally friendly practices, such as reducing single-use plastic consumption and participating in community clean-up events.
>
> (A) dedication   (B) responsibility

저희는 친환경적 관행에 대한 헌신을 증명하기 위해 일회용 플라스틱 소비 줄이기와 지역사회 환경미화 행사에 참여하기와 같이 다양한 계획을 실행했습니다.

7 saturate

❶ 흠뻑 적시다
→ **soak**

❷ 포화 상태로 만들다
→ **fill, oversupply**

> When applying the cleaning solution, ensure that the fabric is not completely <u>saturated</u> to prevent potential damage.
> (A) soaked (B) filled

세척액을 바를 때는, 손상 가능성을 방지하기 위해 천이 완전히 흠뻑 젖지 않도록 유의해야 합니다.

8 impression

❶ 인상, 느낌
→ **idea**

❷ 눌렀을 때 나는 자국
→ **mark**

> I get the <u>impression</u> that the clients from Pronto Motors were expecting a more original concept for their commercial.
> (A) idea (B) mark

저는 프론토 모터스 측의 고객들이 그들의 광고에 대해 더 창의적인 컨셉을 기대하고 있었다는 인상을 받았습니다.

9 spot

❶ 얼룩, 반점
→ **mark, dot**

❷ 장소, 자리, 곳
→ **place**

> With its breathtaking views and tranquil surroundings, it's hard to find a better <u>spot</u> for a relaxing weekend getaway.
> (A) dot (B) place

숨이 막히도록 아름다운 경치와 고요한 주변환경이 있어서, 편안한 주말 휴가를 보내기에 더 나은 장소를 찾기는 어렵습니다.

10 beyond

❶ ~보다 뛰어난
→ **superior to**

❷ (범위·한도) ~을 넘어, ~할 수 없는
→ **outside the reach of**

> The extent of the water damage was so severe that your phone was <u>beyond</u> repair.
> (A) superior to (B) outside the reach of

침수 피해의 정도가 너무 심각해서 귀하의 휴대폰은 수리할 수 없었습니다.

11 roll out

❶ 출시하다, 내놓다
→ **introduce**

❷ 펼치다
→ **spread, flatten**

> The company plans to **roll out** an entirely new model of the vehicle by the end of next year.
> (A) introduce   (B) spread
>
> 그 회사는 내년 말까지 완전히 새로운 차량 모델을 출시할 계획입니다.

12 consider

❶ 고려하다, 생각하다
→ **think about**

❷ ~라고 여기다
→ **regard, view**

> If you enjoyed your dining experience with us, please **consider** writing a review to share your feedback with others.
> (A) think about   (B) regard
>
> 저희와의 식사 경험에 만족하셨다면, 귀하의 의견을 다른 사람들과 나눌 수 있도록 후기를 작성하는 것을 고려해 주세요.

13 establish

❶ 설립하다
→ **found**

❷ 입증하다
→ **prove, confirm**

> Our company was **established** in 1921, with just a team of three engineers, one designer, and one business manager.
> (A) founded   (B) proved
>
> 저희 회사는 1921년에 설립되었으며, 엔지니어 세 명, 디자이너 한 명, 그리고 영업 부장 한 명으로 이루어진 단 한 개의 팀으로 되어 있습니다.

14 retain

❶ 유지하다, 보유하다
→ **keep**

❷ 기억하다
→ **remember**

> Our flasks include a special coating that helps **retain** the temperature of your beverage, hot or cold.
> (A) keep   (B) remember
>
> 저희 물병 제품들은 따뜻하거나 차가운 음료의 온도를 유지하는 데 도움을 주는 특별한 코팅을 포함하고 있습니다.

15 welcome

❶ 환영하다, 맞이하다
→ **greet**

❷ 기꺼이 받아들이다
→ **accept**

> As a non-profit organization, we rely on the generosity of individuals like you, and we **welcome** donations to continue our important work.
>
> (A) greet   (B) accept

비영리 단체로서, 저희는 귀하와 같은 개인들의 관대함이 필요하며, 중요한 일을 계속할 수 있는 기부도 기꺼이 받습니다.

16 boom

❶ 쿵 하는 소리
→ **a loud sound, thunder**

❷ 호황, 갑작스런 인기
→ **growth, increase**

> The town's economic **boom** continues, creating new jobs and boosting local markets.
>
> (A) sound   (B) growth

마을의 경제 호황이 계속되어, 새로운 일자리를 창출하고 지역 시장을 활성화하고 있습니다.

17 point

❶ 요점
→ **main idea**

❷ 의도, 의미
→ **purpose**

❸ 요소, 항목, 세부
→ **detail**

❹ 시점
→ **moment**

❺ 특정 장소
→ **place**

> As you know, our city is best known for having many ports that act as convenient **points** of arrival and departure for fishermen.
>
> (A) purposes   (B) places

여러분도 아시다시피, 우리 도시는 어부들에게 도착과 출발이 편리한 장소의 역할을 하는 항구들이 많은 것으로 잘 알려져 있습니다.

18 pass

❶ 지나가다, 이동하다
→ **go, proceed**

❷ 시간이 흐르다
→ **elapse**

❸ 건네다
→ **hand, give**

Several months need to **pass** before we can renew our construction permit again.
(A) give (B) elapse

여러 달이 지나야 건설 허가증을 다시 갱신할 수 있습니다.

19 address

❶ 응대하다, 해결하다
→ **respond to**

❷ 연설하다, 말하다
→ **talk to, give a speech to**

❸ 보내다, 전달하다
→ **send, direct**

Action Telecom is striving to improve service by actively **addressing** customers' concerns.
(A) responding to (B) sending

액션 텔레콤은 고객들의 우려를 적극적으로 해결함으로써 서비스를 개선하고자 노력하고 있습니다.

20 project

❶ 계획하다, 기획하다
→ **plan**

❷ 예상하다, 추정하다
→ **calculate, estimate**

❸ (빛이나 소리를) 전달하다
→ **transmit**

Our high-end audio system allows for actors' voices to be **projected** clearly to all members of the audience, regardless of where their seat is located in the theater.
(A) planned (B) transmitted

저희의 고급 오디오 시스템은 관객들의 자리가 극장 어디에 있든지 관계없이, 배우의 목소리가 모든 관객들에게 또렷하게 전달될 수 있게 합니다.

21 original

❶ 원래의, 처음의
→ **initial**

❷ 독특한, 창의적인
→ **unique**, **creative**

Please make sure to return the product in its **original** packaging to ensure a smooth return process.
(A) initial   (B) creative

원활한 반환 과정이 될 수 있도록 제품을 원래의 포장에 반납해 주시기 바랍니다.

22 gain

❶ 얻다, 획득하다
→ **obtain**

❷ 늘리다, 늘다
→ **increase**

The access card provided can be used to **gain** entry to the building during non-business hours.
(A) obtain   (B) increase

제공된 출입 카드는 영업시간 외의 시간에 건물 출입 권한을 얻는 데 사용될 수 있습니다.

23 facility

❶ 시설
→ **establishment**

❷ 능력
→ **capacity**

Most of the first day of training will be spent touring the manufacturing **facility** and the surrounding grounds.
(A) establishment   (B) capacity

교육 첫날의 대부분은 제조 시설과 주변 장소들을 견학하는 데 사용될 것입니다.

24 design

❶ 만들다, 고안하다
→ **create**

❷ 도안을 그리다
→ **draw**, **sketch**

The conference will feature a keynote speaker who will discuss how to **design** challenging and effective classes that cater to diverse learning styles.
(A) create   (B) draw

그 컨퍼런스는 다양한 학습 유형에 맞는, 도전적이고 효과적인 수업을 고안하는 방법에 관해 이야기할 기조 연설자를 특별히 포함할 것입니다.

25 opening

❶ 개장, 개점
→ **launch**

❷ 공석
→ **vacancy**

The mayor attended the ribbon-cutting ceremony to celebrate the **opening** of a new French restaurant, highlighting the city's growing culinary diversity.
(A) launch   (B) vacancy

그 시장은 새로운 프랑스 레스토랑의 개업을 축하하기 위한 리본 커팅식에 참석하여 도시의 점점 커지고 있는 요리의 다양성을 강조했습니다.

26 fine

❶ 숙련된, 솜씨 좋은
→ **skillful**

❷ 기분 좋은, 컨디션이 좋은
→ **agreeable**

Our master crafters do exceptionally **fine** work, creating furniture pieces that blend artistry and functionality.
(A) skillful   (B) agreeable

저희의 장인들은 대단히 솜씨 좋은 작업을 수행하여, 예술성과 기능성이 조화를 이루는 가구 작품을 만듭니다.

27 standing

❶ 지위, 위치, 평판
→ **status**

❷ 지속 기간
→ **duration**

The addition of new luxury resorts and a diverse range of recreational activities will further strengthen its **standing** as a growing vacation destination.
(A) status   (B) duration

새로운 호화 리조트들과 다양한 범위의 여가 활동이 추가로 생겨나서, 떠오르는 휴가지로서의 그곳의 평판이 더욱 강화될 것입니다.

28 pick up

❶ 가져가다
→ **get, collect, obtain**

❷ 들어올리다, 줍다
→ **lift**

❸ 회복되다, 개선되다
→ **recover**

Kline Pharmacy sends its customers a text message when their prescriptions are ready to be **picked up**.
(A) obtained   (B) recovered

클라인 약국은 고객들의 처방된 약이 가져갈 수 있도록 준비되면 그들에게 문자 메시지를 발송합니다.

29 temper

❶ 완화시키다
→ moderate

❷ 단련시키다, 강하게 하다
→ harden, strengthen

Applying sunscreen daily can **temper** the effects of sun exposure, reducing the risk of skin damage.
(A) moderate (B) strengthen

자외선 차단제를 매일 바르면 햇빛 노출로 인한 영향을 완화하여 피부 손상의 위험을 줄일 수 있습니다.

30 work out

❶ 운동하다
→ exercise

❷ 해결하다
→ resolve

We need to schedule a meeting to **work out** the details of the upcoming project launch.
(A) exercise (B) resolve

다가오는 프로젝트 출시의 세부사항을 해결할 수 있도록 회의 일정을 정해야 합니다.

DAILY QUIZ

밑줄 친 단어와 가장 가까운 의미를 지닌 것을 고르세요.

1

> Many companies are now adopting environmentally friendly **practices**, such as implementing energy-efficient technologies, reducing single-use plastics, and incorporating recycling programs into their operations.

(A) exercises
(B) regular actions
(C) preparations
(D) professions

2

> Rest assured, our customer support team will **address** your concerns about the recent service disruption and work to provide a swift resolution to minimize any inconveniences.

(A) supervise
(B) respond to
(C) send
(D) talk to

3

> The company plans to **roll out** its new line of smartphones next month, generating anticipation among tech enthusiasts eager to experience the latest advancements in mobile technology.

(A) spread
(B) remove
(C) draw
(D) introduce

정답 1 (B) 2 (B) 3 (D)

/ Week / 04 실전 TEST

LISTENING

• Part 2

1. Mark your answer.   (A) (B) (C)
2. Mark your answer.   (A) (B) (C)
3. Mark your answer.   (A) (B) (C)
4. Mark your answer.   (A) (B) (C)
5. Mark your answer.   (A) (B) (C)
6. Mark your answer.   (A) (B) (C)
7. Mark your answer.   (A) (B) (C)
8. Mark your answer.   (A) (B) (C)
9. Mark your answer.   (A) (B) (C)
10. Mark your answer. (A) (B) (C)

READING

Part 5

11. Midlands Bank hopes to ------- an experienced Web designer for its online banking team.

    (A) plan
    (B) enter
    (C) hire
    (D) lead

12. For specific details about the upcoming company trip, please ------- Mr. Langmore in the administration office.

    (A) appeal
    (B) identify
    (C) contact
    (D) register

13. Riverside Department Store customers who want to ------- their purchase for another item must present a valid receipt.

    (A) exchange
    (B) design
    (C) wear
    (D) display

14. In order to meet demand over the holiday season, Heron Department Store will need to ------- additional sales assistants.

    (A) apply
    (B) conclude
    (C) recruit
    (D) perform

15. The marketing materials for the new Holbrook Group hotel ------- its affordability and convenient location.

    (A) position
    (B) emphasize
    (C) influence
    (D) accessorize

16. Mayford Energy Inc. is currently seeking a marketing consultant to ------- consumer survey results.

    (A) decline
    (B) analyze
    (C) advise
    (D) conduct

17. All Zazzo Electronics appliances ------- with a 2-year warranty covering repairs and replacements for all parts.

    (A) come
    (B) produce
    (C) change
    (D) hold

18. Wonderworld Theme Park visitors are reminded to ------- from using mobile phones while enjoying the park's rides.

    (A) refrain
    (B) forbid
    (C) retreat
    (D) hesitate

• **Part 6**

Questions 19-22 refer to the following excerpt from a brochure.

Animal Defense Foundation

The goal of the Animal Defense Foundation is to ensure that no local wildlife is wrongfully harmed through illegal hunting. We **19.** ------- patrol the woodland areas and streams in Berkshire County. **20.** -------. We then report their presence to the local authorities.

21. ------- a locally founded group, the Animal Defense Foundation depends on the assistance of local residents. We need your support to **22.** ------- our local wildlife. If you believe that illegal hunting may be occurring in your area, please contact us at 555-3878.

---

19. (A) continue
(B) continuous
(C) continued
(D) continuously

20. (A) A water conservation law has been passed recently.
(B) Finally, we offer environmental education opportunities.
(C) This enables us to stop hunters from entering the area.
(D) Our organization is dedicated to public health in the region.

21. (A) As
(B) At
(C) Through
(D) Including

22. (A) control
(B) protect
(C) obtain
(D) deliver

Part 7

Questions 23-24 refer to the following e-mail.

To: Paul Sullivan <psullivan@htchemicals.com>
From: Ernie Hobbs <ehobbs@htchemicals.com>
Subject: RE: Lost key
Date: April 23

Hi Paul,

I am sorry that you are having such trouble getting supplies. I always have a key, since I have the master key to all the rooms and offices in our building. I have now placed a back-up key in the drawer of the receptionist's desk, so your assistant can pick up anything she needs at any time today.

We lock the supply room mainly because the late-night janitorial service staff had been taking things, not employees. I did not realize that locking the room would cause a problem for people in the course of their job.

Would you like me to get a copy of the key made for each manager so that they can take care of their own needs? Or perhaps I should open the room each morning and lock it up again at the end of the day, keeping it open all day.

Regards,

Ernie

---

23. How has Ernie solved the problem?

(A) He gave each supervisor a key.
(B) He found a new janitorial service.
(C) He personally distributed supplies.
(D) He put a key in the receptionist's desk.

24. The word "pick up" in paragraph 1, line 4, is closest in meaning to

(A) meet
(B) harvest
(C) get
(D) deliver

Week 05

Contents	Page	Date	Check
Day 01 `Part 2~4` LC가 잘 들리는 어휘 ③	296	월 일	☐
Day 02 `Part 5,6` 형용사 ①	310	월 일	☐
Day 03 `Part 5,6` 형용사 ②	324	월 일	☐
Day 04 `Part 5,6` 형용사 + 명사 콜로케이션	338	월 일	☐
Day 05 `Part 7` 독해가 쉬워지는 어휘 ①	352	월 일	☐
Week 05 실전 TEST	364	월 일	☐

Day 01 LC가 잘 들리는 어휘 ❸ Part 2~4

1 be held

● 열리다, 개최되다

W: Where will the technology trade show **be held** this year?
M: In Orlando, Florida.
여: 올해 기술 박람회는 어디에서 열리나요?
남: 플로리다 주의 올랜도에서 열립니다.

만점 TIP

• 관련 기출
　hold an event   행사를 개최하다
　hold a meeting   회의를 열다

2 pursue

● v. ~을 추구하다, ~을 해 나가다

W: Why did you **pursue** a career in music?
M: Because I have a talent for it.
여: 왜 음악 계통의 일을 택해 하셨나요?
남: 거기에 재능이 있어서요.

3 representative

● n. 직원, 대표자

W: As a sales **representative**, you'll be working with a diverse range of customers.
M: That's what I'm most looking forward to. I enjoy interacting with new people!
여: 영업 직원으로서, 귀하는 다양한 고객들과 일하게 될 겁니다.
남: 그게 바로 제가 가장 기대하는 것이에요. 저는 새로운 사람들과 교류하는 것을 즐깁니다!

4 merger

• n. 합병

W: Our company **merger** with Rudolph Technical Solutions is going to create a lot of changes to our working environment, won't it?
M: Yes. I heard we might even be relocating to a new office in St. Louis.

여: 우리 회사가 루돌프 테크니컬 솔루션즈 사와 합병하게 되면 업무 환경에 많은 변화가 생기겠죠?
남: 네. 세인트 루이스에 있는 새 사무실로 옮길지도 모른다고 들었어요.

만점 TIP

• 관련 기출
  mergers and acquisitions 기업 인수 합병(M&A)
  be merged with ~와 합병되다
  acquire ~을 인수하다

5 rate

• n. 요금

W: What's the parking **rate** at Eastfield Mall?
M: According to their website, it costs 3 dollars per hour.

여: 이스트필드 몰의 주차 요금은 얼마입니까?
남: 그들의 웹사이트에 의하면, 한 시간당 3달러입니다.

만점 TIP

• 관련 기출
  fee / charge 요금, 수수료

6 vicinity

• n. 인근

W: Where should we have our company dinner after the seminar?
M: Let's search up what's in the **vicinity** of the conference center.

여: 세미나 끝나고 회식 장소는 어디로 할까요?
남: 회의장 인근에 뭐가 있는지 찾아봅시다.

7 feature

- ① n. 특색, 특징
- ② n. 특집
- ③ v. ~을 특별히 포함하다, 특징으로 삼다

> W: Good morning. I'm looking for a new computer.
> M: Okay. What **features** are you looking for?
> 여: 좋은 아침입니다. 저는 새 컴퓨터를 찾고 있어요.
> 남: 알겠습니다. 어떤 특징을 찾고 계십니까?
>
> W: I found out that our favorite restaurant was **featured** in a news article.
> M: That's great! What did they say about it?
> 여: 뉴스 기사에 저희가 제일 좋아하는 식당이 특집으로 실렸다는 것을 알게 되었어요.
> 남: 잘됐네요! 뭐라고 하던가요?

만점 TIP

- 관련 기출
  feature article (신문이나 잡지의) 인기 기사
  special feature 특별한 특징
  featured exhibit 특별 전시
  featured speaker[guest] 특별 연사[손님]

8 outdated

- a. 구식의

> W: Why are you installing new security cameras?
> M: Because our current cameras are **outdated**.
> 여: 왜 새 보안 카메라를 설치하세요?
> 남: 현재 카메라가 구식이어서요.

9 review

- n. 후기, 평

> W: How have customer **reviews** been for our new line of silicon kitchen utensils?
> M: They've been mostly positive.
> 여: 새로운 실리콘 주방용품 제품군에 대한 고객 평가가 어떻습니까?
> 남: 긍정적인 반응이 대부분입니다.

10 stand out

- 눈에 띄다

W: A new logo might help our business **stand out** more.
M: I agree. Our current logo is quite outdated.
여: 새 로고가 우리 회사를 더 눈에 띄게 하는 데 도움이 될 것 같아요.
남: 맞아요. 현재 로고는 많이 구식이죠.

11 operate

- v. ~을 작동시키다, 운영하다

W: I don't know how to **operate** this coffee machine.
M: I've never used it, either. Maybe there are instructions on the side.
여: 이 커피 머신 작동법을 모르겠어요.
남: 저도 사용해 본 적 없어요. 측면에 사용 설명서가 있을 지도 몰라요.

12 on short notice

- 예고 없이, 촉박하게

W: Sorry for letting you know **on** such **short notice**, but I'll need you to send me the sales report before the end of today.
M: No problem, I'll send the report today.
여: 이렇게 급하게 알려드려서 죄송합니다만, 오늘 내로 매출 보고서를 보내주셔야겠습니다.
남: 문제 없어요, 보고서를 오늘 보내드리겠습니다.

13 apparently

- ad. 듣자 하니, 명백히

W: Any updates on our competitors?
M: **Apparently**, Big Star Electronics' latest reading tablet has received poor customer reviews.
여: 경쟁사에 대한 최신 정보가 있나요?
남: 듣자 하니, 최근 출시된 빅스타 전자의 독서용 태블릿은 고객들의 평가가 좋지 않은 것 같습니다.

14 refundable

a. 환불 가능한

W: I purchased two tickets for a flight to Dubai this November, but I want to cancel them.
M: Okay. I see that you selected flexible tickets, so your purchase should be fully **refundable**. How would you like to receive your payment back?

여: 이번 11월에 두바이로 가는 비행기 표를 두 장 구매했는데, 취소하고 싶습니다.
남: 알겠습니다. 변경 가능한 항공권을 선택하셨기 때문에 전액 환불이 가능할 것 같습니다. 결제금은 어떻게 돌려받으시겠어요?

만점 TIP

• 관련 기출
  full refund 전액 환불
  partial refund 부분 환불

15 prescription

n. 처방, 처방전, 처방된 약

W: I'm here to pick up some cold medicine that was prescribed to me by my doctor.
M: May I see your **prescription**, please?

여: 의사에게 처방 받은 감기약을 받으러 왔습니다.
남: 처방전을 볼 수 있을까요?

만점 TIP

• 관련 기출
  fill a prescription 처방전대로 약을 조제하다
  pick up one's prescription 처방된 약을 찾아가다

16 be aware + that절
be aware of + 명사

~을 알고 있다

W: Please **be aware that** our library closes early on weekends.
M: Okay, I'll make a note of it on my calendar.

여: 저희 도서관이 주말엔 일찍 닫는다는 걸 알아 두세요.
남: 알겠습니다, 달력에 적어 둘게요.

17 lease

- v. 임대하다, 임차하다
- n. 임대, 임대차 계약

> W: There's a lovely apartment available for rent on Main Street.
> M: Great! My current **lease** is about to expire, so I'll definitely consider it.
>
> 여: 메인 스트리트에 임대할 수 있는 아파트가 좋은 게 하나 있습니다.
> 남: 잘됐네요! 제 현재 임대차 계약이 곧 만료되어서, 그걸 꼭 고려해 봐야겠어요.
>
> W: What a nice office! Are you **leasing** this space?
> M: Yes. I signed a two-year contract.
>
> 여: 사무실이 참 좋네요! 이 공간을 임대하시는 건가요?
> 남: 네. 2년 계약을 했습니다.

만점 TIP

- 관련 기출
  long-term lease 장기 임대
  lease agreement 임대 계약(서)

18 get to + 장소

- ~에 도착하다

> W: How long does it take to **get to Ann Arbor** from here?
> M: If you take the express train, only about one hour.
>
> 여: 여기서 앤 아버까지 얼마나 걸립니까?
> 남: 급행 열차를 타면 한 시간 정도밖에 안 걸립니다.

19 keep up with

- ~을 뒤처지지 않고 따라가다

> W: How are you able to **keep up with** your meetings and appointments? You seem so busy all the time.
> M: I use a calendar app to help me keep track of everything.
>
> 여: 회의나 약속을 어떻게 잘 따라가시는 거죠? 항상 바쁘신 것 같은데.
> 남: 달력 앱을 사용해서 모든 것을 놓치지 않게 도움을 받고 있어요.

20 draft

- n. 원고, 초안

v. 원고를 작성하다

> W: When can I see the final **draft** of the project proposal?
> M: I'm aiming to have it ready for your review by tomorrow morning.
> 여: 프로젝트 제안서의 최종 원고를 언제 볼 수 있을까요?
> 남: 내일 오전까지 검토하실 수 있게 준비할 것을 목표로 하고 있어요.

21 ideal

- a. 이상적인, 가장 알맞은, 완벽한

> W: What do you think of the apartment?
> M: Its location is **ideal** for us working downtown.
> 여: 그 아파트에 대해 어떻게 생각해요?
> 남: 위치가 시내에서 근무하는 우리에게 이상적이에요.

22 set up

- ~을 설치하다, 세팅하다

> W: Could you **set up** the chairs for the afternoon meeting?
> M: Sure, I'd be happy to.
> 여: 오후 회의를 위해 의자들을 세팅해 주겠어요?
> 남: 그럼요, 기꺼이요.

23 **contractor**

n. 계약자, 도급업자

W: Can we ask our IT worker to fix the electrical wiring issues?
M: No, that's out of his scope of expertise. We'll have to hire a **contractor**.
여: IT 담당자에게 전기 배선 문제를 해결해 달라고 요청할 수 있을까요?
남: 아니요, 그건 그분의 전문 지식 범위를 벗어난 거예요. 우리가 도급업자를 고용해야 할 겁니다.

24 **bill**

n. 고지서, 청구서
v. ~에게 청구하다

W: I don't understand why my water **bill** for this month is so high!
M: Have you checked your lawn sprinklers? Many residents tend to leave them on for too long.
여: 이번 달 수도 요금이 왜 이렇게 많이 나왔는지 이해가 안 가요!
남: 잔디 스프링클러를 확인해보셨나요? 많은 주민들이 그것을 너무 오래 켜두는 경향이 있습니다.

W: This is the customer call center for Horizon Mobile. How can I help you?
M: Hi, I was **billed** an extra item for my mobile service last month, but I don't know why.
여: 호라이즌 모바일의 고객 콜센터입니다. 무엇을 도와드릴까요?
남: 안녕하세요, 지난달에 모바일 서비스에 대해 추가 요금을 청구받았는데, 이유를 모르겠습니다.

만점 TIP

• 관련 기출
billing error 청구 오류
billing records 청구 기록
billing address 청구지 주소

25 projections

n. 추정, 예상

W: How are our cost **projections** looking for next quarter?
M: We should be able to stay well within budget as long as the price of raw materials does not increase.
여: 다음 분기 비용 전망은 어떻습니까?
남: 원자재 가격이 오르지 않는 한 예산 내에서 잘 머무를 수 있을 겁니다.

만점 TIP
• 관련 기출
  sales projections 매출 추정치

26 flyer

n. (광고용) 전단

W: My printing company specializes in making paper advertisements, like posters, banners, and **flyers**.
M: I've seen your designs, and they look wonderful.
여: 저희 인쇄소는 포스터, 현수막, 전단 같은 종이 광고를 만드는 것을 전문으로 합니다.
남: 당신의 디자인을 봤는데, 정말 멋지더라고요.

27 subscription

n. 구독

W: If I renew my **subscription** with your magazine for another year, can I get a discount?
M: I'm sorry, only new subscribers can receive a reduced rate.
여: 귀사의 잡지를 1년 더 구독하면 할인을 받을 수 있나요?
남: 죄송합니다, 신규 가입자만 할인 혜택을 받을 수 있습니다.

만점 TIP
• 관련 기출
  「subscribe to + 대상」 ~을 구독하다
  subscriber 구독자

28 run out

- ~을 다 쓰다, ~이 다 떨어지다

> W: Why haven't you finished printing the documents?
> M: We **ran out** of ink, so I've ordered more and it should be here soon.
> 여: 왜 문서 인쇄를 끝내지 않았죠?
> 남: 잉크가 떨어져서 더 주문했고, 곧 올 겁니다.

29 transfer

- n. 전근, 이동
- v. 전근하다, 이동하다

> W: What is your long-term goal if you were to work at our banking firm?
> M: Eventually, I want to **transfer** to an overseas branch and be an international representative for this company.
> 여: 우리 은행에서 일하게 된다면 장기적인 목표는 무엇입니까?
> 남: 궁극적으로, 저는 해외 지사로 전근하여 이 회사의 국제 대표가 되고 싶습니다.

만점 TIP

• 관련 기출

transfer money to 돈을 ~로 보내다
☞ transfer는 '(돈을) 보내다, 송금하다'라는 뜻으로도 잘 나옵니다.

30 no later than + 일시

- 늦어도 ~까지

> W: By when do I need to submit the travel receipts from last week's business trip again?
> M: **No later than this Thursday**.
> 여: 지난주 출장 영수증은 언제까지 다시 제출하면 되나요?
> 남: 늦어도 이번 주 목요일까지입니다.

만점 TIP

• 관련 기출

by Thursday at the lastest 늦어도 목요일까지
☞ 같은 의미인 「by + 일시 + at the latest」도 함께 알아두세요.

31 make sure

- 반드시 ~하도록 하다 (= ensure)

> W: I think the table decorations look good and are all set now.
> M: Let's double-check the tableware to **make sure** nothing is missing.
>
> 여: 테이블 장식도 보기 좋고 이제 다 준비된 것 같아요.
> 남: 식기류를 다시 한번 점검해보고 누락된 부분이 없도록 합시다.

32 store

- v. ~을 보관하다

> W: Where can I **store** these flyers until the opening event?
> M: In the closet over there.
>
> 여: 개점 행사 때까지 이 전단들을 어디에 보관할까요?
> 남: 저쪽에 있는 벽장에요.

33 make it

- 참석하다, 해내다, 시간에 맞게 가다

> W: Where's the marketing seminar being held?
> M: Oh, I didn't think you could **make it**.
>
> 여: 마케팅 세미나가 어디에서 열리죠?
> 남: 오, 당신이 참석할 수 있을 거라고 생각 못했어요.

34 discontinue

- v. ~을 단종시키다, 중단하다

> W: Hi, do you have this dishware set in stock?
> M: Unfortunately, that design got **discontinued** a few months ago.
>
> 여: 안녕하세요, 혹시 이 식기 세트 재고가 있나요?
> 남: 안타깝게도 그 디자인은 몇 달 전에 단종되었습니다.

35 warranty

- n. 제품의 품질 보증(서)

  W: Does this printer come with a lifetime **warranty**?
  M: Yes. If it needs to be repaired for whatever reason, we can do that for you free of charge.

  여: 이 프린터는 평생 보증이 제공되나요?
  남: 네, 어떤 이유로든 수리가 필요하시면 무료로 해드릴 수 있습니다.

  > **만점 TIP**
  >
  > • '제품에 ~이 딸려 나오다'라는 뜻의 표현을 알아 두세요.
  >   This watch comes with an extra battery.
  >   이 손목시계는 추가 배터리가 딸려 나옵니다.

36 promote

- ① v. 승진시키다
- ② v. ~을 조장하다, 촉진하다
- ③ v. ~을 홍보하다

  W: Did you hear the news? Hong-joo got **promoted** and moved up into management.
  M: Really? She totally deserves it since she's always so diligent in her work.

  여: 그 소식 들었어요? 홍주 씨가 승진해서 경영진으로 올라갔어요.
  남: 정말요? 그녀는 항상 일에 부지런하기 때문에 충분히 그럴 자격이 있어요.

  W: What can we do to **promote** worker productivity?
  M: One effective approach could be to provide regular training and skill development opportunities.

  여: 직원 생산성을 촉진하려면 무엇을 할 수 있을까요?
  남: 정기적인 교육과 기술 개발 기회를 제공하는 것이 한 가지 효과적인 접근법이 될 수 있어요.

  W: We need new ideas on how to **promote** our business.
  M: How about running a limited-time discount?

  여: 사업을 어떻게 홍보할 것인지에 대한 새로운 아이디어가 필요합니다.
  남: 한시적 할인 행사를 운영하면 어떨까요?

37 be public
- 공개되다

W: What's the latest news about the upcoming merger?
M: The information **isn't public** yet.

여: 곧 있을 합병에 대해 최신 뉴스가 있습니까?
남: 아직 정보가 공개되지 않았어요.

> **만점 TIP**
> • 관련 기출
>   the public 일반 사람들, 대중

38 business card
- 명함

W: Do you know how to contact me if you need further assistance?
M: Certainly, I have your **business card**.

남: 도움이 더 필요하실 경우 제게 연락할 방법을 아세요?
여: 그럼요, 당신의 명함을 갖고 있어요.

39 fill in for
- ~을 대신하다

W: Are you available on Wednesday afternoon? I need someone to **fill in for** me that day.
M: Let me check my calendar.

여: 수요일 오후에 시간 되세요? 그날 저를 대신해 줄 사람이 필요해요.
남: 제 달력을 확인해 볼게요.

40 cut back on
- ~을 줄이다

W: Don't you usually add vanilla syrup to your coffee?
M: Yes, but my doctor told me that I should **cut back on** sugar.

여: 보통 커피에 바닐라 시럽을 넣지 않나요?
남: 네, 그런데 의사 선생님께서 제가 설탕을 줄여야 한다고 하셨어요.

DAILY QUIZ

단어와 그에 알맞은 뜻을 연결해 보세요.

1. merger • • (A) 구독
2. lease • • (B) 합병
3. subscription • • (C) 임대차 계약

빈칸에 알맞은 단어를 선택하세요.

4. I'm not feeling well today. Can you ------- me during the afternoon meeting?
   제가 오늘 몸이 좋지 않네요. 저 대신 오후 회의에 가 주실 수 있으세요?

5. Please ------- you turn off the lights when you leave the meeting room.
   회의실을 나갈 때 반드시 전등을 끄도록 하세요.

(A) get to
(B) keep up with
(C) make sure
(D) fill in for

6. Do you know how to ------- the convention center?
   컨벤션 센터로 가는 길을 아십니까?

음원을 듣고 질문에 어울리는 응답을 고르세요.

7. (A) (B) (C)

8. (A) (B) (C)

정답 1 (B) 2 (C) 3 (A) 4 (D) 5 (C) 6 (A) 7 (A) 8 (B)

Week 05 309

Day 02 형용사 ❶ Part 5, 6

1 available

시간이 나는, 이용할 수 있는, 구할 수 있는

[기출] be **available** to work weekends
주말에 일할 시간이 나다

be **available** between 9 AM and 6 PM
오전 9시와 오후 6시 사이에 이용할 수 있다

> Three afternoon time slots are ------- for anyone who wishes to take a boat tour along the River Tyne.
> (A) available   (B) necessary

2 local

지역의, 현지의

[기출] **local** greenhouse
지역 온실

use grains only from **local** farms
현지 농장에서 재배한 곡물만 사용하다

> The weekly farmers' market gives residents a chance to buy fresh produce from ------- farmers at low prices.
> (A) casual   (B) local

3 recent

최근의

[기출] **recent** policy updates 최근 정책 업데이트
the **recent** merger with ~와의 최근 합병

> Meta Moon Chronicles is the most ------- recipient of the Video Game of the Year award.
> (A) late   (B) recent

4 **due** • ~하기로 예정된, 기한이 만료되는, 지불 기한인

　기출　be **due** back to the library
　　　도서관으로 돌아오기로 예정되어 있다

　　　be **due** two weeks from the checkout date
　　　대출일로부터 2주 후에 반납 기한이 만료되다

> The amount stated on your electricity bill is ------- no later than June 14.
> (A) due　　　　　(B) active

5 **subject** • ~에 영향을 받는, ~하기 쉬운

　기출　be **subject** to additional charges
　　　추가 요금에 영향을 받을 수 있다

　　　be **subject** to change without notice
　　　공지 없이 변경될 수 있다

> All ferry departure times are ------- to change in accordance with weather conditions.
> (A) general　　　　　(B) subject

6 **designed** • 고안된

design v. 고안하다, 디자인하다

　기출　food **designed** to do
　　　~하기 위해 고안된 음식

　　　be specifically **designed** for
　　　~을 위해 특별히 고안되다

> Ergo Solutions manufactures office desks and chairs ------- to improve posture and blood circulation.
> (A) designed　　　　　(B) progressed

7 successful

success n. 성공(작)
successfully ad. 성공적으로
succeed v. 성공하다, ~의 뒤를 잇다

• 성공적인

기출 make our products **successful**
우리의 제품들을 성공적으로 만들다

good ideas for **successful** writing
성공적인 글쓰기를 위한 좋은 아이디어들

The Turning of the Leaves is author Richard Dean's most ------- novel yet.

(A) successful　　　(B) wealthy

8 additional

add v. 추가하다
addition n. 추가 (인원), 추가하는 것
additionally ad. 추가적으로, 게다가

• 추가적인

기출 if you need **additional** information
추가 정보가 필요하다면

take the following **additional** steps
다음 추가 조치를 취하다

Over the coming months, the accountant hopes to find ------- ways to reduce our business expenses.

(A) additional　　　(B) approximate

9 pleased

pleasure n. 즐거움
pleasant a. 쾌적한
please v. ~을 즐겁게 하다
pleasing a. 기쁨을 주는

• 기쁜, 즐거운

기출 be **pleased** to offer a new service
새로운 서비스를 제공하게 되어 기쁘다

be **pleased** to announce that
~라는 것을 알리게 되어 기쁘다

Local residents were ------- to hear that the city council listened to their concerns regarding the construction proposal.

(A) pleased　　　(B) settled

10 current

currently ad. 현재

- 현행의, 현재의

  기출 follow the **current** regulations
  현행 규정을 따르다

  obtain the **current** schedule
  현재의 일정표를 얻다

  Several dishes on our ------- menu are likely to be discontinued based on feedback from our diners.
  (A) consistent   (B) current

11 based

basis n. 기반, 기초, 토대

- ~에 기반한(on), 본사를 둔(in)

  기출 **based** on our review of
  ~의 후기에 기반한

  based in Wellington
  웰링턴에 본사를 둔

  Next month, Mr. Senna will join a technology company ------- in San Francisco.
  (A) based   (B) approved

12 interested

interesting a. 흥미로운

- 관심이 있는

  기출 be **interested** in receiving the training
  교육을 받는 데 관심이 있다

  interested in the sales job
  영업 직무에 관심이 있는

  Gym members who are ------- in attending our new yoga classes may sign up on our Web site.
  (A) interested   (B) advanced

13 possible

possibility n. 가능성
possibly ad. 아마도

• 가능한

기출 make A **possible** in some areas
일부 지역에서 A를 가능하게 하다

possible through brilliant marketing
훌륭한 마케팅을 통해 가능한

> Mr. Brown intends to start up his business in any way -------, even if he needs to take out a sizable bank loan.
> (A) possible　　　(B) valuable

14 limited

limit n. 제한, 한도
limitation n. 제약, 한계
unlimited a. 한도가 없는, 무제한의

• 제한된, 한정된

기출 for a **limited** time only 제한된 시간 동안만

as seating is **limited** 좌석 수가 한정되어 있으므로

> Half-price tickets for Honeydew Amusement Park are available for a ------- time only.
> (A) limited　　　(B) speedy

15 main

mainly ad. 주로

• 주요한

기출 the **main** selling point for ~에 대한 주요한 장점

> The emergence of artificial intelligence is the ------- theme of the current art exhibition at AX Gallery.
> (A) high　　　(B) main

16 necessary

necessitate v. 필요하게 만들다
necessarily ad. 반드시

• 필수적인, 필요한

기출 The online store was becoming **necessary**.
온라인 매장이 필수적인 것으로 되었다.

> Please ensure that you include all ------- documents when submitting your application for a construction permit.
> (A) necessary　　　(B) apparent

17 previous

이전의

기출 ignore the **previous** message
이전 메시지를 무시하다

on the basis of **previous** purchases
이전 구매에 기반하여

> This year's music festival will feature 45 more performers than the ------- one did.
> (A) adjacent (B) previous

18 popular

popularity n. 인기

인기 있는

기출 **popular** among tourists
관광객들 사이에서 인기 있는

the most **popular** ever
여지껏 가장 인기 있는

> Our new range of sports shoes is becoming increasingly ------- with teenagers.
> (A) popular (B) numerous

19 effective

effectively ad. 효과적으로
effect n. 영향
effectiveness n. 효과(성)

효과적인, 시행되는

기출 highly **effective** measures to reduce costs
비용을 줄일 매우 효과적인 조치들

effective October 4
10월 4일부터 시행되는

> According to a recent article in *Business Weekly*, one of the most ------- marketing strategies is social media advertising.
> (A) effective (B) successive

20 leading

leader n. 지도자, 리더
lead v. 초래하다(to), 이끌다

● 선도적인, 주도적인

기출 become a **leading** manufacturer
선도적인 제조사가 되다

a **leading** supplier
선도적인 공급업체

> Since its founding ten years ago, Ebbon Manufacturing has become a ------- producer of microchips.
> (A) leading   (B) continuing

21 upcoming

● 다가오는, 곧 있을

기출 questions about the **upcoming** installation
다가오는 설치 작업에 대한 질문들

do research for one's **upcoming** novel
곧 나올 소설에 대한 조사를 하다

> Ms. Gellatly plans to hire more part-time workers to deal with demand during the ------- festive shopping period.
> (A) upcoming   (B) potential

22 convenient

convenience n. 편리, 편의
conveniently ad. 편리하게

● 편리한, 편한

기출 offer **convenient** customer service hours
편리한 고객 서비스 시간을 제공하다

time that would be **convenient** for all
모두에게 편할 시간

> The Almond Hotel is in an extremely ------- location for those planning to attend an event at the conference center.
> (A) competent   (B) convenient

23 accessible

- 접근 가능한, 이용 가능한

  [기출] easily **accessible** by bus
  버스로 쉽게 접근 가능한

  accessible only to customers with identification
  신분증을 가진 고객들만 이용 가능한

  > Conference notes and presentation slides will be ------- on our Web site following the event.
  > (A) accessible   (B) responsible

24 various

vary v. 다양하다, 변하다
variation n. 변화
variable a. 변하기 쉬운, 가변적인

- 다양한

  [기출] offer tenants **various** conveniences
  세입자들에게 다양한 편의시설을 제공하다

  various health-care services
  다양한 의료 복지 서비스

  > Tents manufactured by Ventron come in ------- colors and sizes.
  > (A) various   (B) relative

25 residential

residence n. 집, 주택
resident n. (거)주민
reside v. 거주하다

- 주거의

  [기출] include some **residential** services
  몇몇 주거 서비스를 포함하다

  traditionally known as a **residential** area
  전통적으로 주거 지역으로 알려진

  > Ashcroft City Council plans to convert the land behind the bus station into a ------- district containing 85 houses.
  > (A) habitual   (B) residential

26 acceptable

- 받아들일 수 있는, 괜찮은, 만족스러운

  기출 other **acceptable** forms of payment
  받아들여질 수 있는 다른 지불 유형들

  Please let me know whether the new date is **acceptable**.
  새로운 날짜가 괜찮은지 저에게 알려주시기 바랍니다.

  > Please ensure that the interview date and time are ------- and contact us if you wish to make any changes.
  > (A) capable   (B) acceptable

27 vulnerable

vulnerability n. 취약점

- 취약한, 무방비인

  기출 be more **vulnerable** to damage
  훼손에 더 취약하다

  be **vulnerable** to changes
  변화에 무방비이다

  > Our patio furniture is ------- to mold if it is not maintained properly using appropriate protective varnish.
  > (A) delicate   (B) vulnerable

28 timely

- 때에 알맞은, 신속한

  기출 in a **timely** manner
  제때에

  > In accordance with company policy, you must submit requests for vacation leave to your manager in a ------- manner.
  > (A) timely   (B) near

29 inaccurate

● 잘못된, 부정확한

기출 find **inaccurate** details
잘못된 세부사항을 발견하다

inaccurate information on labels
라벨에 있는 부정확한 정보

> An error on the Euro Rail Web site resulted in the posting of ------- departure times for several trains.
> (A) inaccurate (B) intensive

30 desired

desire v. 바라다, 요구하다

● 원하는, 바람직한

기출 have the **desired** effect on
~에 대해 원하는 효과를 가지다

> Use the remote control to set the water to your ------- temperature before getting into the hot tub.
> (A) organized (B) desired

31 reliable

reliably ad. 확실히
reliability n. 믿음직함, 신뢰도

● 믿을 만한, 신뢰할 수 있는

기출 offer **reliable** transportation
믿을 만한 교통편을 제공하다

provide **reliable** products at an affordable price
알맞은 가격으로 신뢰할 수 있는 제품을 제공하다

> Most local residents agree that the subway system is the most ------- form of public transportation in the city.
> (A) skilled (B) reliable

32 efficient

efficiency n. 효율(성)
efficiently ad. 효율적으로

- 효율적인

  기출 designed to be more **efficient**
  더욱 효율적이기 위해 고안된

  be more **efficient** for workers
  근로자들에게 더 효율적이다

  > The HR manager has created an ------- system that allows employees to request annual leave days through the Intranet.
  > (A) eager   (B) efficient

33 unable

- ~할 수 없는

  기출 be **unable** to attend the meeting
  회의에 참석할 수 없다

  be **unable** to offer you a contract
  귀하에게 계약을 제안할 수 없다

  > Employees who are ------- to attend the training workshop will receive the presentation slides by e-mail.
  > (A) absent   (B) unable

34 related

related to prep. ~와 관련된

- 관련된

  기출 have **related** work experience
  관련된 근무 경력을 가지다

  other **related** paperwork
  다른 관련된 서류 작업

  > Applicants for the laboratory manager position must have a degree in biotechnology or a ------- area of study.
  > (A) related   (B) prepared

35 eligible

eligibility n. 적임, 적격

- 자격이 있는

  기출 be **eligible** for renewal
  갱신의 자격이 있다

  be **eligible** to apply for the manager position
  관리자 직책에 지원할 자격이 있다

  Factory workers who work after 7 PM are ------- for the overtime pay.
  (A) compatible   (B) eligible

36 initial

initially ad. 초기에, 처음에

- 초기의, 처음의

  기출 the **initial** findings
  초기 발견 내용

  the **initial** shipment of books
  도서에 대한 일차 발송

  The company expects to cover the ------- start-up costs within 6 months of operation.
  (A) forward   (B) initial

37 satisfied

satisfaction n. 만족

- 만족하는

  기출 be completely **satisfied** with the purchase
  구매품에 완전히 만족하다

  reviews from **satisfied** customers
  만족한 고객들의 후기들

  If you are not completely ------- with your purchase, you may return it for a refund within ten days.
  (A) acquainted   (B) satisfied

38 expensive

expense n. 비용

• 비싼

기출 the need for **expensive** repairs
비싼 수리의 필요성

offer a less **expensive** alternative
덜 비싼 대안을 제공하다

> Although enrolling employees in training courses is ------- , the CEO believes it will benefit the company overall.
>
> (A) cautious   (B) expensive

39 sufficient

sufficiently ad. 충분히

• 충분한

기출 produce **sufficient** electricity
충분한 전기를 생산하다

sufficient time to address mistakes
실수를 처리할 충분한 시간

> According to the real estate agent, the office building has ------- space for at least 150 employees.
>
> (A) sufficient   (B) frequent

40 beneficial

beneficially ad. 유익하게
benefit n. 이점, 혜택

• 이로운, 유익한

기출 **beneficial** to the community
지역사회에 이로운

beneficial in several ways
여러 방면으로 유익한

> The new employee incentive scheme has had a highly ------- effect on overall staff productivity.
>
> (A) abundant   (B) beneficial

DAILY QUIZ

단어와 그에 알맞은 뜻을 연결해 보세요.

1 based   • (A) 다가오는, 곧 있을
2 upcoming   • (B) 최근의
3 recent   • (C) ~에 기반한, ~에 본사를 둔

빈칸에 알맞은 단어를 선택하세요.

4 offer ------- transportation
   믿을 만한 교통편을 제공하다

5 as seating is -------
   좌석 수가 한정되어 있으므로

(A) satisfied
(B) additional
(C) reliable
(D) limited

6 take the following ------- steps
   다음 추가 조치를 취하다

앞서 배운 단어들의 뜻을 생각하면서, 다음 문제를 풀어보세요.

7 The pedestrian footbridge near Milton High School is not ------- because of dangerous black ice.

   (A) raised   (B) accessible
   (C) critical   (D) profitable

8 The proposed design of the waterfront area is ------- to view online on the City Hall Web site.

   (A) available   (B) frequent
   (C) considerable   (D) helpful

정답 1 (C) 2 (A) 3 (B) 4 (C) 5 (D) 6 (B) 7 (B) 8 (A)

Day 03 형용사 ❷ Part 5, 6

 MP3 바로듣기  강의 바로보기

1 confidential
confidentiality n. 기밀성

● 기밀의

기출 all **confidential** documents 모든 기밀 문서들
remain **confidential** 기밀인 상태로 남아 있다

Health clinic employees must keep all patient information ------- in accordance with the clinic's policy.
(A) confidential (B) mandatory

2 damaged
damage v. 손상시키다
n. 손상

● 손상된

기출 ship the **damaged** item 손상된 상품을 배송하다
damaged in transit 운송 중에 손상된

The shipment of coffee mugs arrived ------- due to the items being improperly packaged.
(A) assembled (B) damaged

3 valid
validate v. 유효하게 하다, 입증하다
validation n. 유효성

● 유효한

기출 present a **valid** identification card
유효한 신분증을 제시하다
be **valid** for two years
2년 동안 유효하다

Vehicles may only be parked in the east parking lot if a ------- parking permit is clearly displayed.
(A) valid (B) direct

4 likely

가망 있는, ~할 것 같은

기출 **likely** winner of next week's election
다음 주 선거에서의 가망 있는 당선자

be **likely** to differ among departments
부서마다 다를 것 같다

Mr. Venson believes that guests are ------- to approve of the changes to the room service menu.
(A) firstly (B) likely

5 positive

positively ad. 긍정적으로

긍정적인

기출 receive **positive** responses from readers
독자들로부터 긍정적인 반응을 받다

positive comments from customers
고객들로부터의 긍정적인 논평

The new movie starring James Metcalfe has received generally ------- reviews from the majority of critics.
(A) certain (B) positive

6 appropriate

appropriately ad. 적절하게

적절한, 적합한

기출 must wear the **appropriate** safety gear
반드시 적절한 안전 장비를 착용하다

recommend an **appropriate** system
적합한 시스템을 추천하다

All those joining the company hike this weekend are reminded to wear ------- footwear and sunscreen.
(A) appropriate (B) cautious

7 affordable

afford v. (경제적, 시간적) 여유가 있다
affordably ad. 감당할 수 있게
affordability n. 감당할 수 있는 비용

- (가격이) 적당한, 알맞은

  기출 become **affordable** for most people
  대부분의 사람들에게 가격이 적당해지다

  offer customers **affordable** holiday packages
  고객들에게 가격이 적당한 휴일 패키지 여행을 제공하다

  > Due to the introduction of various basic models, mobile phones have finally become ------- for almost everyone.
  > (A) comparable　　　(B) affordable

8 impressive

impress v. 깊은 인상을 주다
impression n. 인상, 감명
impressively ad. 인상 깊게

- 인상 깊은, 인상적인

  기출 **impressive** economic growth in the region
  지역에서의 인상 깊은 경제 성장

  > Corona Coffee Shop has an ------- range of pastries and sandwiches.
  > (A) impressive　　　(B) favorite

9 notable

note v. 주목하다
notably ad. 현저하게, 뚜렷하게

- 유명한, 주목할 만한

  기출 **notable** economist
  유명한 경제학자

  be **notable** for its extensive use
  광범위한 사용으로 주목할 만하다

  > The judging panel at the independent film festival will include several ------- directors and actors.
  > (A) notable　　　(B) customary

10 brief

briefly ad. 짧게, 간단히

- 잠깐의, 간단한

  기출 a **brief** absence
  잠깐의 부재

  write a **brief** report on the research
  연구에 대한 간단한 보고서를 쓰다

  The training workshop will stop for a ------- refreshment break at 2:30 PM.
  (A) recent   (B) brief

11 unique

- 독특한, 특이한

  기출 develop a **unique** process for
  ~하기 위한 독특한 공정을 개발하다

  launch a **unique** online service
  특이한 온라인 서비스를 출시하다

  Aero Technologies is known for developing ------- mobile applications that are used all over the world.
  (A) unique   (B) skilled

12 accurate

accuracy n. 정확도
accurately ad. 정확하게

- 정확한

  기출 contain an **accurate** description
  정확한 설명을 포함하다

  The national park's Web site provides ------- information regarding the length and difficulty of hiking trails.
  (A) gradual   (B) accurate

13 confident

confidence n. 자신(감), 신뢰

- 확신하는, 자신 있는

  기출 be **confident** that ~라는 것을 확신하다

  The city council remains ------- that the street parade will take place as planned despite bad weather.
  (A) confident   (B) obvious

14 skilled

skill n. 기술

- 능숙한, 숙련된

  기출 especially **skilled** at negotiation
  협상에 특히 능숙한

  Boreham Corporation intends to recruit over 250 ------- workers for its new factory in Exeter.
  (A) raised   (B) skilled

15 aware

awareness n. 의식

- (내용을) 알고 있는, (사실에) 유의하는

  기출 make people more **aware** of the brand
  사람들이 그 브랜드에 대해 더 많이 알도록 만들다

  Please be **aware** that ~.
  ~라는 것에 유의하시기 바랍니다.

  Members of Hinckley Library need to be ------- that there is a charge for overdue books.
  (A) aware   (B) known

16 ongoing

- 계속되는, (현재) 진행 중인

  기출 as a result of **ongoing** problems
  계속되는 문제들의 결과로서

  Sirius Telecom wishes to apologize for the ------- disruption to your broadband service.
  (A) ongoing   (B) limited

17 rising

rise v. 상승하다, 증가하다
n. 상승, 증가

● 상승하는, 증가하는

기출 **rising** demand for sportswear
상승하는 스포츠 의류에 대한 수요

due to **rising** production costs
증가하는 생산비로 인해

Market experts have noticed ------- demand for affordable television streaming services.
(A) profitable   (B) rising

18 complimentary

● 무료의

기출 attach **complimentary** dinner coupons
무료 저녁식사 쿠폰을 첨부하다

All convention attendees have access to ------- transportation from a variety of downtown hotels.
(A) complimentary   (B) subsequent

19 internal

internally ad. 내부적으로

● 내부의

기출 **internal** inquiry
내부 문의

consider **internal** applicants
내부 지원자들을 고려하다

The management positions will be filled through ------- recruitment rather than posting the vacancies online.
(A) internal   (B) preferable

20 comfortable

comfortably ad. 편안하게

- 편안한

  기출 be more **comfortable** than the old one
  예전의 것보다 더 편안한

  more **comfortable** for patients
  환자들을 위해 더욱 편안한

  > The lobby of the Regent Hotel contains several ------ sofas and armchairs for guests.
  > (A) cautious　　　(B) comfortable

21 eager

eagerly ad. 열망하여, 열심히

- 간절히 바라는, 열망하는

  기출 **eager** to expand its business in South America
  남미에서의 사업을 확장하는 것을 간절히 바라는

  be **eager** to form business relationships
  사업적 관계를 형성하기를 열망하다

  > Jeff Brightman is an experienced music video director ------ to direct his first full motion picture.
  > (A) eager　　　(B) relative

22 essential

essentially ad. 필수적으로

- 필수적인

  기출 be **essential** for maintaining steady production
  꾸준한 생산량을 유지하기 위해 필수적이다

  It is **essential** that~. ~라는 점은 필수적이다.

  > A professional, well-designed Web site is ------ for any business to become successful.
  > (A) essential　　　(B) initial

23 familiar

familiarize v. 익숙하게 하다

• 익숙한, 친숙한

기출 become **familiar** with the details
세부사항에 익숙해지다

be **familiar** with the city's transportation
도시의 교통편에 익숙해지다

> Mr. Ruiz will continue conducting weekly training workshops until all staff are ------- with the new database system.
> (A) typical (B) familiar

24 knowledgeable

knowledge n. 지식

• 박식한

기출 be **knowledgeable** about art
미술에 대해 박식하다

be **knowledgeable** in one's field
~의 분야에서 박식하다

> The wait staff at Jumba Restaurant are extremely ------- about local ingredients and wine.
> (A) knowledgeable (B) distinctive

25 steady

steadily ad. 꾸준히

• 꾸준한

기출 remain **steady** over the past four quarters
지난 4분기 동안 꾸준한 상태이다

maintain **steady** sales
꾸준한 매출을 유지하다

> Property market experts have noted a ------- increase in house prices in Glen Valley and the surrounding area.
> (A) steady (B) sturdy

26 unexpected

- 예상치 못한

unexpectedly ad. 예상치 못하게

기출 receive an **unexpected** bonus
예상치 못한 보너스를 받다

due to the **unexpected** delay
예상치 못한 지연으로 인해

> Due to ------- travel delays, the Japanese clients will not arrive at the factory until 4 PM.
>
> (A) unexpected   (B) indefinite

27 superior

- 우수한

superiority n. 우수, 우월성

기출 one's **superior** analytical skills
~의 우수한 분석 능력

make A **superior** to other leading brands
다른 선도적인 브랜드들보다 A를 우수하게 만들다

> Tiara Catering is known for its ------- menus and excellent customer service.
>
> (A) superior   (B) absolute

28 equal

- 동등한(to)

equally ad. 동등하게

기출 be nearly **equal** to
~와 거의 동등하다

> The annual profits of our Everley branch have finally become ------- to those of our flagship store.
>
> (A) equal   (B) high

29 comparable

compare v. 비교하다
comparison n. 비교

● 비교할 만한

기출 **comparable** quality on the market
시장에서 비교할 만한 품질

The new mobile phones launched by Salazar and Indigo offer ------- features and value for money.
(A) comparable   (B) separate

30 functional

function v. 기능하다
n. 기능

● 작동하는, 가동 중인

기출 remain **functional**
작동하는 상태이다

appear to be **functional**
가동 중인 것으로 보인다

The CEO expects the manufacturing plant to be fully ------- by April 20.
(A) functional   (B) appropriate

31 proposed

propose v. 제안하다
proposal n. 제안(서)

● 제안된

기출 **proposed** renovation project
제안된 보수공사 프로젝트

near the **proposed** site of a new shop
새로운 매장의 제안된 부지 근처에

The client is satisfied with the architect's ------- changes to the airport blueprint.
(A) obliged   (B) proposed

32 **dependent**

dependently ad. 의존적으로

- 의존하는

기출 be **dependent** on the inspection results
검사 결과에 의존하다

> The destination for the staff excursion is heavily ------- on the budget allocated by the finance manager.
> (A) subsequent　　　(B) dependent

33 **exceptional**

exception n. 예외
exceptionally ad. 예외적인 경우에만, 유난히

- 우수한, 특출난, 예외적인

기출 show **exceptional** performance
우수한 성과를 보여주다

win awards for one's **exceptional** work
~의 특출난 작업으로 상을 타다

> Employees who show ------- work ethic and productivity are rewarded with an annual bonus.
> (A) exceptional　　　(B) eventual

34 **apparent**

apparently ad. 명백히

- 명백한

기출 become **apparent** that ~라는 것이 명백해지다

> There is no ------- difference between the two candidates.
> (A) apparent　　　(B) current

35 **seasonal**

- 계절의, 계절적인

기출 include **seasonal** fruits 계절 과일을 포함하다

> Fifty part-time employees have been hired in our branches to help us cope with ------- demand throughout December.
> (A) seasonal　　　(B) equal

36 durable

- 내구성이 좋은, 오래 견디는

  [기출] **durable** material
  내구성이 좋은 자재

  > The Ridgeback Trail shoes are suitable for long hikes thanks to their ------- soles.
  > (A) consumable　　(B) durable

37 relevant

relevance n. 관련성

- 관련된

  [기출] at least two years of **relevant** work experience
  적어도 2년의 관련 근무 경력

  be accompanied by **relevant** receipts
  관련 영수증을 첨부하다

  > A series of training workshops -------- to our employees' job duties will be held during January.
  > (A) competent　　(B) relevant

38 vacant

vacancy n. 공석, (채용 중인) 일자리

- 비어 있는

  [기출] purchase a **vacant** store
  비어 있는 상점을 매입하다

  > The Sidmouth Concert Center hopes to expand its parking capacity by purchasing the ------- land behind the venue.
  > (A) busy　　(B) vacant

39 casual

- 편안한, 우연한

  기출 take a **casual** walk
  편안한 산책을 하다

  As part of the new office policy, staff may wear ------- clothing on the last Friday of each month.
  (A) casual   (B) loose

40 prospective

prospect n. 전망

- 잠재적인, 가망이 있는

  기출 **Prospective** employees must possess ~.
  잠재적인 직원들은 반드시 ~을 갖춰야 한다.

  Before joining the badminton club, each ------- member must first attend a practice session.
  (A) evident   (B) prospective

DAILY QUIZ

단어와 그에 알맞은 뜻을 연결해 보세요.

1 internal   •   • (A) 기밀의

2 confidential   •   • (B) 내부의

3 equal   •   • (C) 동등한

빈칸에 알맞은 단어를 선택하세요.

4 attach ------- dinner coupons
   무료 저녁식사 쿠폰을 첨부하다

5 become ------- for most people
   대부분의 사람들에게 가격이 적당해지다

6 ------- renovation project
   제안된 보수공사 프로젝트

(A) affordable
(B) proposed
(C) vacant
(D) complimentary

앞서 배운 단어들의 뜻을 생각하면서, 다음 문제를 풀어보세요.

7 As a world-famous director, Mr. Lloyd has been widely recognized for his -------- contributions to theater.

   (A) severe   (B) established
   (C) abnormal   (D) exceptional

8 To park a vehicle in the South Street parking lot, individuals must display a ------- country club membership card.

   (A) valid   (B) direct
   (C) gradual   (D) prolific

정답 1 (B) 2 (A) 3 (C) 4 (D) 5 (A) 6 (B) 7 (D) 8 (A)

Day 04 형용사 + 명사 콜로케이션 Part 5, 6

1 personal reason

● 개인 사유

기출 **personal** information 개인 정보
personal belongings 개인 물품

Employees are not allowed to use company property for ------- reasons.
(A) unlimited   (B) personal

2 excessive amount

● 과도한 양

기출 **excessive** waste of raw materials
과도한 원자재 쓰레기

excessive inventory
과잉 재고

Most drivers are not interested in Vorcon Motors' SUVs because of the ------- amount of gasoline they consume.
(A) exciting   (B) excessive

3 full capacity

● 최고 성능, 전면 가동, 최대 수용 인원

기출 seating **capacity** 좌석 수용력
manufacturing **capacity** 제조 성능

Many of the riverside hotels are expected to operate at full ------- during the peak tourist season this year.
(A) capacity   (B) price

4 **fresh vegetables** • 신선한 채소

　기출　**fresh** meals
　신선한 식사

> Logan Farm is proud of providing the ------- vegetables to our customers.
>
> (A) clearest　　　(B) freshest

5 **scenic view** • 아름다운 경치

　기출　**scenic** coastal route
　경치가 좋은 해안로

> Mr. Glonting prefers to take the train for business trips as he enjoys the ------- views of the countryside.
>
> (A) recent　　　(B) scenic

6 **substantial contribution** • 상당한 기여

　기출　**substantial** number
　상당 수

　　　substantial changes
　상당한 변화

　　　substantial donations
　상당한 기부(금)

> Mr. Oliver Hardy has made a ------- contribution to the company and fully deserves his recent promotion.
>
> (A) mutual　　　(B) substantial

만점 TIP
- 형용사 substantial은 large, considerable, significant 등과 바꾸어 쓸 수 있다.

7 numerous activities

● 수많은 활동들

[기출] **numerous** supplies 수많은 공급업체들
numerous copies 수많은 사본들

> Our summer package offers ------- outdoor activities for businesses and organizations.
> (A) capable　　　　　(B) numerous

만점 TIP
• 형용사 numerous는 수가 강조되는 복수명사를 수식한다.

8 extensive changes

● 폭넓은 변화

[기출] **extensive** experience 폭넓은 경험
extensive knowledge 폭넓은 지식
extensive analysis 폭넓은 분석

> Manley Industries will make ------- changes to its production practices to increase efficiency.
> (A) extensive　　　　　(B) accurate

만점 TIP
• 형용사 extensive는 large, wide, comprehensive 등과 바꾸어 사용할 수 있다.

9 exclusive access

● 독점적인 이용(권)

[기출] **exclusive** interview 독점 인터뷰
exclusive property 독점적인 자산

> Ray Jones Gym members get ------- access to a wide range of fitness classes led by experienced instructors.
> (A) exclusive　　　　　(B) creative

10 extended warranties

- 연장된 품질 보증 기간

  기출 **extended** hours
  연장된 영업 시간

  extended deadline
  연장된 마감기한

  extended vacation time
  연장된 휴가 기간

  AK Electronics has decided to offer ------- warranties to its customers with no additional fees.
  (A) extended　　　(B) defective

11 major investment

- 중대한 투자, 규모가 큰 투자금

  기출 a **major** portion of ~의 (절반 이상) 대부분

  major exporter 주요 수출업자

  The development of infrastructure requires ------- investment, both in terms of financial resources and dedicated personnel.
  (A) major　　　(B) social

  만점 TIP
  - 형용사 major가 기업이나 사람 앞에 쓰이면 '중요한, 주요한'의 의미이고, 행위나 사물 앞에 쓰이면 '(규모가) 큰'이라는 뜻이다.

12 valuable suggestion

- 귀중한 제안

  기출 **valuable** information 귀중한 정보

  valuable insight 귀중한 통찰력

  The S&B Retailer Group is seeking ------- suggestions about improving customer satisfaction and loyalty.
  (A) recent　　　(B) valuable

13 completed job application

● 완성된 입사 지원서

[기출] **completed** form 완성된 양식
completed documents 완성된 문서

> Please submit your ------- job application to the human resources office by e-mail by August 15.
> (A) delayed (B) completed

14 advanced technology

● 고급 기술

[기출] **advanced** skill
고급 기술

advanced college degrees
고급 대학 학위

advanced user
상급 사용자

> Rogan Logistics recently adopted ------- technology to track its shipments in real time.
> (A) numerous (B) advanced

15 prior authorization

● 사전 허가

[기출] **prior** approval 사전 승인
prior experience 이전 경력

> Employees must obtain ------- authorization before sharing any information about their work on social media.
> (A) prior (B) calm

16 experienced technical workers

- 숙련된 기술자들, 경험이 많은 기술직 직원들

  기출 **experienced** graphic designers
  숙련된 그래픽 디자이너들

  experienced managers
  경험이 많은 관리자들

  > We are currently hiring several highly ------- technical workers who will work in our branch offices.
  >
  > (A) remaining (B) experienced

17 routine inspection

- 정기 점검

  기출 **routine** maintenance checks 정기적인 유지보수 점검
  routine practice 주기적인 관행
  routine tasks 일상적인 업무

  > The department of workplace safety will conduct a ------- inspection of our machinery at Olsen Manufacturing.
  >
  > (A) routine (B) opposed

18 a wide selection of

- 아주 다양한

  기출 a **wide** variety of
  아주 다양한

  a **wide** range of
  아주 다양한

  > Blue Skyline provides a ------- selection of sporting goods, such as athletic footwear and football jerseys.
  >
  > (A) various (B) wide

  만점 TIP
  - 형용사 wide가 '다양한, 많은'의 뜻을 가질 때는 broad로 바꾸어 쓸 수도 있다.

19 updated training schedule

최신 교육 일정

기출 **updated** version
최신 개정판

updated employee manual
최신 직원 안내서

> The ------- training schedule has been reposted on the company Web site due to a scheduling conflict.
> (A) excited　　　　(B) updated

20 limited access

제한된 접근 권한

기출 for a **limited** (period of) time
제한된 시간 동안

limited seating
한정된 좌석 수

limited supplies
한정된 공급품

> Temporary employees are only granted ------- access to the confidential customer database.
> (A) limited　　　　(B) similar

21 supplemental information

보충 정보

기출 **supplemental** documentation 보충 서류

> Please refer to the ------- information provided in the appendix for further details on the agreement.
> (A) supplemental　　　(B) potential

만점 TIP
형용사 supplemental이 '보충의, 추가적인'의 뜻으로 사용될 때 supplementary로 바꾸어 사용되기도 한다.

22 public meeting

- 공청회, 공개 회의

  기출 **public** comment
  대중적인 의견

  > Millhaven City Council will hold a ------- meeting to give residents a chance to share their opinions.
  > (A) future　　　　　(B) public

23 high standards

- 높은 기준들

  기출 **high** quality 높은 품질
  　　　high price 높은 가격
  　　　high priorities 높은 우선순위

  > The company handbook outlines the high ------- that the employees are expected to meet every day.
  > (A) recommendations　(B) standards

24 exemplary performance

- 모범적인 성과, 본보기가 될 만한 성과

  기출 **exemplary** leadership
  모범적인 지도력

  > Dominique Sato was honored with the Employee of the Year award for her ------- performance on the job.
  > (A) exemplary　　　(B) dependent

25 dedicated employee

- 헌신적인 직원

  기출 a **dedicated** sales team 헌신적인 영업팀

  The Diamond Group's ------- employees recorded their highest sales last week.
  (A) dedicated   (B) introduced

  만점 TIP
  형용사 dedicated가 기업이나 활동을 나타내는 명사를 수식할 때는 '(~ 분야/활동에) 전념하는'으로 해석하고, 회사의 구성원을 수식할 때는 '(조직에) 헌신하는'으로 해석한다.

26 comprehensive warranty

- 종합적인 제품 보증

  기출 **comprehensive** directory
  종합적인 안내 책자

  comprehensive care
  포괄적인 관심

  comprehensive study
  포괄적인 연구

  Our new plan includes a ------- warranty that covers damage to both your computer and your monitor.
  (A) comprehensive   (B) knowledgeable

27 prestigious award

- 명망 있는 상

  기출 **prestigious** medal 명망 있는 훈장

  Ms. Gomez has received the ------- International Writers Award for her extraordinary contribution to the art of storytelling.
  (A) vigorous   (B) prestigious

28 heavy call volumes

- 과도한 통화량

  기출 **heavy** usage
  과도한 사용량

  heavy rain
  폭우

  Due to ------- call volumes at our customer service center, you may need to wait to speak with an operator.
  (A) heavy   (B) lengthy

29 coming year

- 다음 해, 내년

  기출 in the **coming** month 다음 달에

  The main aim of tomorrow's staff meeting is to set up our sales targets for the ------- year.
  (A) occurring   (B) coming

30 rapid changes

- 빠른 변화

  기출 **rapid** growth
  빠른 성장

  rapid evolution
  빠른 진화

  Mr. Larry Wilkins is expected to be honored for making ------- changes to our manufacturing processes.
  (A) eager   (B) rapid

Week 05 347

31 innovative design

● 혁신적인 디자인

기출 **innovative** television commercials
혁신적인 TV 광고

innovative cost-cutting measure
혁신적인 비용 절약 조치

innovative approach
혁신적인 접근

> Sweet Sounds Inc.'s research team was recognized for the ------- design of the car stereo system it developed.
> (A) innovative　　　(B) various

32 lasting impact

● 지속적인 영향

기출 **lasting** effect 지속적인 효과

lasting impression 오래가는 인상

> The Internet is considered to be the greatest invention that has had a ------- impact on the spread of knowledge.
> (A) private　　　(B) lasting

33 outstanding contribution

● 뛰어난 기여

기출 **outstanding** work 뛰어난 작업(물)

outstanding service 훌륭한 서비스

outstanding effort 훌륭한 노력

> Dr. Roy Benson has received the award for his ------- contribution to the development of a new engine.
> (A) approaching　　　(B) outstanding

만점 TIP
형용사 outstanding은 주로 공헌 또는 업적을 나타내는 명사를 수식하는데, 이때 exceptional, impressive, superb 등의 단어와 바꾸어 쓸 수 있다.

34 qualified applicant

• 자격을 갖춘 지원자

기출 **qualified** graphic artist
자격을 갖춘 그래픽 예술가

All ------- candidates for the production manager position should submit their résumés by October 15.
(A) qualified　　　　(B) beneficial

35 detailed information

• 상세 정보

기출 **detailed** descriptions
상세한 설명

detailed reviews
상세한 후기

detailed manual
상세한 사용설명서

------- information about the actors participating in the theatrical performance is included in the pamphlet.
(A) Detailed　　　　(B) Experienced

36 reasonable prices

• 합리적인 가격

기출 **reasonable** rates 합리적인 요금

a **reasonable** amount of time 적절한 시간

Our goal is to offer products and services of the highest quality at the most ------- prices.
(A) valuable　　　　(B) reasonable

만점 TIP
형용사 reasonable은 지불하는 사람의 능력에 따라 그 수준이 달라지지만, 비슷한 의미를 가진 affordable은 누구라도 지불할 만큼 저렴한 것을 나타낸다.

37 competitive salaries

● 경쟁력 있는 급여

기출 **competitive** compensation 경쟁력 있는 보상
　　　　competitive rates 경쟁력 있는 요금
　　　　competitive advantage 경쟁력 있는 장점

Smart Eats offers ------- salaries to those who have previously worked in food distribution.
(A) competitive　　　(B) protective

38 defective merchandise

● 결함 있는 상품

기출 **defective** item 결함 있는 상품
　　　　defective garment 결함 있는 의류

All our new products come with a two-year warranty, and we will replace any ------- merchandise at no extra cost.
(A) defective　　　(B) expensive

39 enclosed contract

● 동봉된 계약서

기출 **enclosed** order slip 동봉된 주문서

Please read the ------- contract very carefully before you sign it to avoid any misunderstandings.
(A) enclosed　　　(B) surrounding

40 final phase

● 최종 단계

기출 the first **phase** 첫 단계

In the final ------- of market research testing, patients preferred the wooden game pieces to the plastic ones.
(A) opinion　　　(B) phase

> **만점 TIP**
> • 명사 phase가 들어갈 자리에 stage를 사용하기도 한다.

DAILY QUIZ

콜로케이션과 그에 알맞은 뜻을 연결해 보세요.

1. final phase • • (A) 과도한 양
2. extended warranties • • (B) 연장된 품질 보증 기간
3. excessive amount • • (C) 최종 단계

빈칸에 알맞은 단어를 선택하세요.

4. ------- coastal route
   경치가 좋은 해안로

5. ------- usage
   과도한 사용량

6. ------- effect
   지속적인 효과

(A) lasting
(B) enclosed
(C) heavy
(D) scenic

앞서 배운 콜로케이션들의 뜻을 생각하면서, 다음 문제를 풀어보세요.

7. Subscribers to the magazine get ------- access to events, such as live performances at Eastley Music Hall.

   (A) exclusive   (B) unknown
   (C) creative   (D) previous

8. Brittany Food was awarded a catering contract with Logan Hall Conference Center because it is known for offering quality service at a ------- price.

   (A) brief   (B) reasonable
   (C) limited   (D) sudden

정답 1 (C) 2 (B) 3 (A) 4 (D) 5 (C) 6 (A) 7 (A) 8 (B)

Day 05 독해가 쉬워지는 어휘 ❶ Part 7

 MP3 바로듣기  강의 바로보기

1 allocate
allocation n. 할당

● v. ~을 할당하다, 배분하다

> Our company understands the importance of staying competitive, so we've decided to double the budget **allocated** to research and development.
> 저희 회사는 경쟁력을 유지하는 것의 중요성을 잘 알고 있기에, 연구 및 개발에 할당되는 예산을 두 배로 늘리기로 결정하였습니다.

2 invest
investment n. 투자
investor n. 투자자

● v. 투자하다

> The company's expansion plan included **investing** in real estate to establish a strong presence in key markets.
> 회사의 확장 계획은 주요 시장에서 강력한 입지를 구축하기 위해 부동산에 투자하는 것을 포함했습니다.

3 prioritize
priority n. 우선 사항

● v. 우선순위를 매기다, ~을 우선적으로 처리하다

> When managing multiple commitments, it's crucial to **prioritize** and allocate time wisely.
> 여러 일들을 처리할 때에는, 우선순위를 정하고 시간을 현명하게 배분하는 것이 매우 중요합니다.

4 regularly
regular a. 규칙적인, 정기적인

● ad. 규칙적으로, 정기적으로

> We meet **regularly** to hold brainstorming sessions aimed at generating innovative ideas.
> 우리는 정기적으로 만나 혁신적인 아이디어를 창출하기 위한 브레인스토밍 회의를 개최합니다.

5 offset

• v. ~을 상쇄하다, 충당하다

> The factory workers had to work overtime to **offset** the production shortfall caused by the unexpected machine breakdown.
>
> 공장 직원들은 예상치 못한 기계 고장으로 인한 생산량 부족을 상쇄하기 위해 초과 근무를 해야 했습니다.

6 as often as needed

• 필요할 때마다

> The project timeline can be adjusted **as often as needed** to accommodate any changes or unexpected challenges.
>
> 프로젝트 일정은 변경 사항이나 예상치 못한 문제 상황에 맞추기 위해 필요할 때마다 조정될 수 있습니다.

만점 TIP
• 기출 Paraphrasing
  as often as needed → whenever necessary

7 press release

• 보도 자료

> In a **press release** issued today, Triton Chemical announced that it aims to acquire GreenTech Innovations next month.
>
> 오늘 발표된 보도자료에서, 트라이톤 케미컬 사는 다음 달에 그린테크 이노베이션즈 사를 인수하는 것을 목표로 한다고 발표했습니다.

만점 TIP
• 관련 기출
  press conference 기자 회견

8 funding

fund n. 자금, 돈
　　 v. 자금을 대다

● n. 자금, 재정 지원

> The budget allocation for the upcoming project includes an increase in **funding** for state-of-the-art equipment.
>
> 이번 프로젝트의 예산 배정은 최첨단 장비에 대한 재정 지원을 늘린 것을 포함합니다.

9 loan

● n. 대출

> Before finalizing the **loan** application, make sure to review all the terms and conditions outlined by the lender.
>
> 대출 신청을 마무리하기 전에, 대출기관이 약술한 모든 약관을 검토하십시오.

10 proceed with

● ~을 진행하다, 계속해서 하다

> The legal team has reviewed the contract, and they have advised us that it's safe to **proceed with** the partnership.
>
> 법무팀이 계약서를 검토했고, 협력 계약을 진행하는 것이 안전하다고 조언했습니다.

만점 TIP

- 관련 기출
  proceed to ~로 나아가다, 이동하다
  proceeds 이익금, 수익금

11 take A into account

● A를 계산에 넣다, 고려[참작]하다

> When making financial decisions, it's wise to **take** potential risks **into account** to protect your investments.
>
> 재정적인 결정을 내릴 때에는, 투자금을 지키기 위해 잠재적 위험을 고려하는 것이 현명합니다.

12 follow up on

~에 대해 후속 조치를 하다, ~을 끝까지 챙기다

After the initial meeting, I will **follow up on** the progress of the project to ensure everything is on track.

첫 회의가 끝난 후에, 모든 것이 제대로 잘 진행될 수 있도록 프로젝트 진행 상황을 끝까지 챙기도록 하겠습니다.

13 outsource

outsourcing n. 아웃소싱, 외주

v. ~을 외부에 위탁하다

To meet the tight deadline, the work has been **outsourced** to a local freelance team with expertise in web design.

빠듯한 마감일을 맞추기 위해, 웹 디자인에 전문 지식을 갖춘 현지 프리랜서 팀에 작업을 위탁했습니다.

14 founder

n. 창립자, 설립자

Mark, the **founder** and CEO, started the business with a small team and has since turned it into a global industry leader.

창업자이자 CEO인 마크는 작은 팀으로 사업을 시작했고 이후 그것을 세계적인 업계 선두주자로 변화시켰습니다.

만점 TIP
• 관련 기출
'설립하다'라는 뜻의 동사는 found로서, 이때 동사변화는 found-founded-founded와 같습니다.

15 protocol

n. 규약, 실시 요강, 프로토콜

Safety **protocols** at the Blue Garden restaurant chain were modified in order to comply with the new public health guidelines.

블루 가든 레스토랑 체인의 안전 규약은 새 공중 보건 지침을 준수하기 위해 수정되었습니다.

16 joint

jointly ad. 합동으로

a. 공동의, 합동의

The CEOs of the two companies delivered a **joint** presentation to announce their strategic partnership and future plans.

양사 CEO들은 전략적 파트너십과 향후 계획을 알리기 위해 합동 발표를 했습니다.

만점 TIP

• 관련 기출

collaborative 공동의
collaborate on ~을 공동 작업하다
cooperate with ~와 협력하다

17 as of + 일시

~부로, ~부터

As of May 1, the policy requiring employees to use the designated parking area will be implemented to improve parking management.

5월 1일부터 주차 관리 개선을 위해 직원들이 지정된 주차 구역을 의무적으로 사용하도록 하는 정책이 시행될 것입니다.

만점 TIP

• 관련 기출

= beginning + 일시, starting + 일시, effective from + 일시

18 up-to-date

a. 최신의

It's important to keep your software **up-to-date** to ensure optimal performance.

최적의 성능을 보장하기 위해서는 소프트웨어를 최신 상태로 유지하는 것이 중요합니다.

19 within budget

예산 범위 내에서

Despite unexpected challenges, the construction project was finished on time and **within budget**.

예상치 못한 어려움에도 불구하고, 건설 프로젝트는 제때에 예산 범위 내에서 완료되었습니다.

만점 TIP
• 관련 기출
  beyond budget 예산을 초과하여
  exceed the budget 예산을 초과하다

20 subcontract

v. ~을 하도급 주다, 하청 주다

The construction company decided to **subcontract** the electrical work to a contractor with expertise in wiring and installations.

그 건설사는 전기공사를 배선과 설비에 전문성을 갖춘 업자에게 하청을 주기로 했습니다.

만점 TIP
• 관련 기출
  contractor 계약자, 도급업자

21 renew a contract

계약을 갱신하다

The company decided to **renew the contract** with their supplier for another year to maintain a steady supply of raw materials.

그 회사는 원료의 안정적인 공급을 유지하기 위해 공급업체와 1년 더 계약을 갱신하기로 결정했습니다.

만점 TIP
• 관련 기출
  supplier 공급업자

22 streamline

• v. ~을 간소화[능률화]하다

> The airline introduced self-check-in kiosks to **streamline** the check-in process and reduce waiting time for passengers.
>
> 그 항공사는 체크인 절차를 간소화하고 승객들의 대기 시간을 줄이기 위해 셀프 체크인 키오스크를 도입했습니다.

만점 TIP
- 기출 Paraphrasing
   streamline → simplify (간소화하다)

23 in effect

• 이행[발효] 중인, 시행 중인

> As of January 1, the new regulations will be **in effect**, impacting how businesses handle customer data.
>
> 1월 1일부터, 새로운 규제가 시행되어 기업들이 고객 데이터를 처리하는 방식에 영향을 줄 것입니다.

만점 TIP
- 관련 기출
   come into effect 효력이 발생하다

24 stipulate

stipulation n. 규정
stipulated a. 약정한

• v. ~을 규정하다, 명시하다

> The law **stipulates** that employers must provide a safe working environment for their employees.
>
> 이 법은 고용주가 고용인들에게 안전한 근무 환경을 제공해야 한다고 규정하고 있습니다.

25 adopt

adoption n. 채택, 선정
adopted a. 채택된

• v. ~을 도입하다, 채택하다

> Since **adopting** chemical-free farming methods last year, Trickle Creek Orchard has almost doubled its profit margin.
>
> 지난해 화학성분이 없는 농업 방식을 채택한 이후, 트리클 크리크 과수원은 이윤 폭이 거의 두 배로 뛰었습니다.

26 provided (that)

- 만약 ~이라면, ~이라는 조건하에

  Employees of ACE Inc. will receive a salary increase next year **provided that** their performance meets the established targets.

  에이스 사의 직원들은 그들의 성과가 정해진 목표를 달성한다면 내년에 급여 인상을 받게 될 것입니다.

27 capital

- n. 자본금, 자금

  The office will be renovated next year provided that the **capital** budget proposal is approved.

  사무실은 자본예산안이 승인된다면 내년에 보수될 것입니다.

28 strengthen

strength n. 강점

- v. ~을 강화하다

  To **strengthen** relations between the divisions, the company is implementing a series of team-building workshops.

  부서 간의 관계를 강화하기 위해, 회사는 일련의 팀 구성 워크숍을 시행하고 있습니다.

29 unveil

unveiling n. 제막식, 첫 공개

- v. ~을 공개하다, 발표하다

  We will **unveil** at least four new products to the public during the upcoming product launch event.

  곧 있을 제품 출시 행사에서는 최소 네 개의 신제품을 대중에 공개할 예정입니다.

30 input

- n. 조언, 투입, 입력
- v. 입력하다

> Your **input** is crucial to us, so please take a moment to provide your feedback on our new product design.
> 귀하의 조언은 저희에게 매우 중요하므로, 잠시 시간을 내어 저희 신제품 디자인에 대해 의견을 주시기 바랍니다.

만점 TIP
- 기출 Paraphrasing
  input → advice (조언)

31 status

- n. (진행 과정상의) 상황

> You can easily check the **status** of your order by entering your order number on our website.
> 당사 웹사이트에서 주문번호를 입력하시면 주문 상황을 쉽게 확인하실 수 있습니다.

32 media outlet

- 언론 매체, 매스컴

> *Finance Daily* was the first **media outlet** to report on the proposed merger between Triton Chemicals and GreenTech Innovations.
> <파이낸스 데일리> 지는 트라이톤 케미컬 사와 그린테크 이노베이션즈 사 간의 합병 제안을 보도한 최초의 언론 매체였습니다.

33 repayment

- n. 반환(금), 상환

> It's important to stick to your budget to ensure timely **repayment** of your credit card debt.
> 신용카드 빚을 제때 갚기 위해서는 자금 계획을 지키는 것이 중요합니다.

34 export

- v. 수출하다
- n. 수출

> SM Corporation **exports** a variety of electronic components and devices to 25 countries around the world.
>
> SM 사는 전 세계 25개국에 다양한 전자부품과 기기를 수출합니다.

만점 TIP

- 관련 기출
  - import 수입하다
  - commerce 무역, 상업
  - trade 무역

35 economize

- v. 절약하다, 아끼다

> The company had to make tough decisions to **economize** during the economic downturn, including layoffs and budget cuts.
>
> 그 회사는 경기 침체 기간 동안 절약하기 위해 어려운 결정을 내려야 했는데, 이는 해고와 예산 삭감을 포함합니다.

만점 TIP

- 기출 Paraphrasing
  - economize → save money

36 compelling

compel v. ~을 강요[강제]하다

- a. 설득력 있는; 강제적인

> The sales presentation included a **compelling** argument for why their product was the best in the market.
>
> 영업 발표에는 그들의 제품이 시장에서 가장 우수한 이유에 대한 설득력 있는 주장이 포함되었습니다.

37 emerging

emerge v. 나오다, 드러나다

- a. 떠오르는, 최근 생겨난

> The **emerging** trends in technology suggest that artificial intelligence will play a significant role in the future of many industries.
>
> 기술 업계의 최근 추세는 인공지능이 많은 산업의 미래에 중요한 역할을 할 것임을 시사합니다.

38 switch

- v. ~로 전환하다, 바꾸다 (to)
- n. 전환

> **Switching** to a vegetarian diet has numerous health benefits, including reduced risk of heart disease and improved digestion.
>
> 채식주의 식단으로 바꾸는 것은 심장병의 위험 감소와 소화 개선을 포함하여 많은 건강상의 이점을 가지고 있습니다.

39 pilot test

- n. 시범 테스트

> Before launching the new software, we conducted a **pilot test** with a small group of users to gather feedback.
>
> 신규 소프트웨어를 출시하기 전에, 피드백을 수집하기 위해 소규모 사용자 그룹을 대상으로 시범 테스트를 실시하였습니다.

40 refurbishment

refurbish v. ~을 새로 꾸미다[재단장하다]

- n. 개조, 재단장

> The shopping mall's **refurbishment** included renovating storefronts, adding new lighting, and upgrading the food court.
>
> 쇼핑몰의 재단장에는 매장 전면 개조, 조명 추가, 그리고 푸드코트 업그레이드가 포함됐습니다.

DAILY QUIZ

단어와 그에 알맞은 뜻을 연결해 보세요.

1 up-to-date   •   • (A) 공동의, 합동의

2 emerging   •   • (B) 최신의

3 compelling   •   • (C) 설득력 있는

4 joint   •   • (D) 떠오르는, 최근 생겨난

빈칸에 알맞은 단어를 선택하세요.

5 I'm writing to ask you to ------- additional budget resources for the Marketing Department.
   마케팅 부서에 추가 예산 자원을 할당해 주시기를 요청하고자 이 편지를 씁니다.

6 Employees were provided with a generous travel allowance to ------- various travel expenses.
   직원들은 각종 여행 경비를 충당하도록 넉넉한 여행 수당을 지급받았습니다.

   (A) streamline
   (B) allocate
   (C) offset
   (D) proceed

7 The human resources department announced that it will ------- the procedure for submitting vacation request forms.
   인사부는 휴가신청서 제출 절차를 간소화하겠다고 발표했습니다.

8 Once you have picked up your tickets, please ------- to the boarding gate for departure.
   티켓을 수령하셨으면, 출발을 위해 탑승 게이트로 가시기 바랍니다.

정답 | 1 (B) 2 (D) 3 (C) 4 (A) 5 (B) 6 (C) 7 (A) 8 (D)

/ Week / 05 실전 TEST

 MP3 바로듣기
 강의 바로보기

LISTENING

• Part 2

1. Mark your answer.   (A)   (B)   (C)
2. Mark your answer.   (A)   (B)   (C)
3. Mark your answer.   (A)   (B)   (C)
4. Mark your answer.   (A)   (B)   (C)
5. Mark your answer.   (A)   (B)   (C)
6. Mark your answer.   (A)   (B)   (C)
7. Mark your answer.   (A)   (B)   (C)
8. Mark your answer.   (A)   (B)   (C)
9. Mark your answer.   (A)   (B)   (C)
10. Mark your answer.   (A)   (B)   (C)

READING

Part 5

11. The Moonveil Hotel offers guests ------- amenities including free Wi-Fi service and a 24-hour business center.

(A) descriptive
(B) instructed
(C) various
(D) alert

12. The decision to switch to a more affordable supplier is having the ------- impact on our monthly expenses.

(A) eventful
(B) desired
(C) diligent
(D) experienced

13. Environmental groups hope that the mayor allocates ------- funding for clean-up efforts at the Tusker River site.

(A) competent
(B) intentional
(C) sufficient
(D) dependent

14. Because the dining table appeared ------- upon delivery, Mr. Kang demanded that the items be picked up.

(A) damaged
(B) organized
(C) assembled
(D) unopened

15. To accommodate all gym members, Star Fitness has added new yoga classes ------- for all fitness levels.

(A) appropriate
(B) adjacent
(C) mutual
(D) cautious

16. The number of visitors has stayed ------- throughout the museum's recent period of renovation.

(A) frequent
(B) distinct
(C) proper
(D) steady

17. The ------- information in the welcome pack can help new staff to settle into our company's work environment more easily.

(A) arbitrary
(B) supplemental
(C) superfluous
(D) potential

18. Elizabeth Barker was presented with a ------- award for her critically acclaimed novel, *A Summer Affair*.

(A) prestigious
(B) repetitive
(C) prolific
(D) laborious

Part 6

Questions 19-22 refer to the following article.

Los Angeles, April 23– Local station JSV Television has lost millions so far this year with a record second quarter loss of $22 million and could even face bankruptcy by the end of the year. The downturn in revenue can be **19.** ------- to the global decline of media companies and a difficult economic environment.

20. -------. This move into print media is worrying some shareholders who voiced their opposition to the purchase at a recent meeting.

JSV Television is the largest privately owned television station in the state of California and has become one of the **21.** ------- companies in the industry ever since its **22.** ------- by Harry Smithson in 1964. The company currently employs 6,800 staff.

19. (A) attributed
(B) contributed
(C) committed
(D) applied

20. (A) Industry analysts predict that the sluggish economy will soon recover.
(B) Despite the drop in earnings, JSV Television recently acquired a daily newspaper.
(C) Media companies need to find ways to adapt to how people consume media.
(D) It saw many customers drop their service in favor of cheaper plans.

21. (A) leading
(B) accustomed
(C) originated
(D) moving

22. (A) founding
(B) found
(C) founder
(D) founded

Part 7

Questions 23-24 refer to the following letter.

Mr. Fulci,

I am contacting you to follow up on the discussion we had at the convention last Tuesday. As I mentioned, I am the founder of a mobile application development company called Leisuresoft and seeking those willing to invest in my business.

Provided that we secure adequate investment, we will prioritize our event ticketing application called EazyTix. The status of this project is currently 30 percent complete. We subcontracted the programming to Horizon IT Solutions to complete the first phase of the project within budget. Our board members have unanimously agreed to renew the contract with Horizon for the final phase of programming.

If you are interested in investing in our company, your funds would be allocated primarily for marketing EasyTix. We would regularly provide up-to-date reports on our projects, and you can anticipate repayment of your initial investment, plus dividends, within two years.

I hope to hear from you soon regarding this exciting opportunity.

Regards,

Kyle Glass
Founder and President, Leisuresoft Inc.

23. What is the main purpose of the letter?

   (A) To offer Mr. Fulci a job
   (B) To finalize a company merger
   (C) To celebrate the success of a project
   (D) To seek financial assistance

24. What is true about Leisuresoft Inc.?

   (A) It developed a successful fitness application.
   (B) It has been working on a project without overspending.
   (C) It has collaborated with Mr. Fulci in the past.
   (D) It will be representing at the upcoming convention.

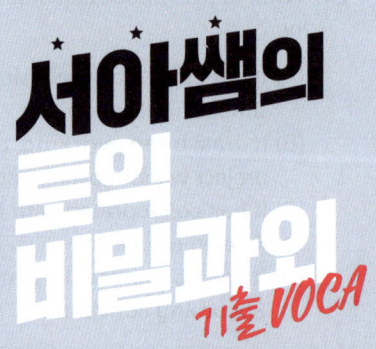

Week 06

Contents		Page	Date	Check
Day 01	Part 3, 4 기출 패러프레이징 ①	370	월 일	☐
Day 02	Part 5, 6 형용사 ③	384	월 일	☐
Day 03	Part 5, 6 형용사 ④	398	월 일	☐
Day 04	Part 5, 6 형용사 + 전치사 콜로케이션	412	월 일	☐
Day 05	Part 7 독해가 쉬워지는 어휘 ②	426	월 일	☐
Week 06 실전 TEST		438	월 일	☐

 **기출 패러프레이징 ❶** Part 3, 4

QR코드 하나를 가리고 찍으면 편해요!

MP3 바로듣기 　 강의 바로보기

---

1 contact

- talk to / speak to
  ~에게 말하다
- call / give A a call
  (A에게) 전화하다
- e-mail / send an e-mail
  이메일을 보내다

● ~에게 연락하다

M: I'll **send out an e-mail** to the staff and see what they think about the new schedule.
직원들에게 이메일을 보내서 그들이 새 일정에 대해 어떻게 생각하는지 알아보겠습니다.

Q. 무엇을 할 것인가?
→ **Contact** some employees

> 만점 TIP
> - phone number, e-mail address, fax number, mailing address 등을 통칭하여 contact information(연락처)이라고 합니다.

---

2 public transportation

- bus, taxi, subway

● 대중교통

W: I was thinking I should take the **bus or subway**. That way, I won't have to worry about parking.
버스나 지하철을 타야 할까 생각 중이었어요. 그럼 주차 걱정을 할 필요가 없으니까요.

Q. 무엇을 할 것인가?
→ Use **public transportation**

> 만점 TIP
> - 상위어 Paraphrasing
>   paper, ink cartridges, pens → office supplies (사무용품)

---

3 launch

- introduce 소개하다
- release 출시하다
- put A on the market
  A를 시장에 내놓다

● (상품 등을) 출시하다

M: We'll be **launching** a new medication within the year. 올해 안에 신약을 출시할 예정입니다.

Q. 올해 무슨 일이 있을 것인가?
→ A new product will be **introduced[released]**.

4 relocate

- move 옮기다, 이사하다
- transfer 옮기다, 이동하다

● (~을) 옮기다, 이전하다

W: Last month, we **moved** our office to a more strategic location in the heart of the city.

지난달에 저희는 시내 중심부에 있는 보다 전략적인 위치로 사무실을 이전하였습니다.

Q. 지난달에 어떤 일이 있었는가?
→ An office **was relocated**.

5 call A back

- return a call 답신 전화를 하다
- get back to A
  A에게 다시 연락을 주다

● A에게 답신 전화를 하다

M: We need to discuss the upcoming project deadline. Please **call me back** as soon as you receive this message.

곧 있을 프로젝트 마감일에 대해 논의해야 합니다. 이 메시지를 받는 대로 제게 다시 전화 주세요.

Q. 청자에게 무엇을 요청하는가? → **Return a call**

6 postpone

- put off, delay 미루다

● ~을 미루다, 연기하다

W: There was a thunderstorm approaching, so my departure **was postponed** by two hours.

폭풍우가 다가오고 있어서, 제 출발이 2시간 지연되었습니다.

Q. 무슨 문제가 있는가? → A flight **was delayed**.

7 expire

- no longer valid[good]
  더 이상 효력이 없는

● 만료되다

M: I'm sorry, but I can't process this voucher. It **expired** last week.

죄송하지만, 이 상품권을 처리해드릴 수 없습니다. 지난주에 만료되었습니다.

Q. 무슨 문제가 있는가?
→ A voucher is **no longer valid**.

8 estimate

- quote 견적가
- how much it will cost 비용이 얼마가 될지

• 견적, 견적서

W: I received some **quotes** from a few local caterers. Our budget is pretty tight, so I'm leaning toward Culinary Canvas Catering.

몇몇 지역 출장연회업체들로부터 견적을 받았습니다. 저희 예산이 꽤 빠듯해서, 저는 큘리너리 캔버스 캐이터링 쪽으로 마음이 기울고 있습니다.

Q. 무엇을 받았는가?
→ Some price **estimates**

만점 TIP
- 관련 기출
  cost estimate 비용 견적
  price estimate 가격 견적

9 submit

- hand in 제출하다

• ~을 제출하다

M: I finished all the data analysis, but still need to put together my findings. I'll **hand in** the report tomorrow morning.

모든 데이터 분석을 마쳤습니다만, 아직 제가 알아낸 사실들을 취합해야 합니다. 보고서를 내일 오전에 제출할 것입니다.

Q. 내일 오전에 무엇을 할 것인가?
→ **Submit** a report

10 acquire

- buy, purchase 매수하다
- take over 인계받다
- merge 합병시키다

• (기업을) 인수하다

W: I spoke with a representative from KU Corporation, and it turns out they're interested in **buying** my business.

제가 KU 코퍼레이션의 대표와 이야기를 나누었는데요, 그들이 저희 회사를 인수하는 것에 관심 있어 하는 것 같습니다.

Q. KU Corporation이 관심을 보이는 것은?
→ **Acquiring** a business

11 annual

- yearly, annually, once a year, every year 매년

매년의

M: Thanks again for planning Friday's **annual** banquet for our museum's supporters.

박물관 후원자들을 위한 금요일의 연례 만찬회를 기획해 주셔서 다시 한 번 감사해요.

Q. 무엇에 대해 얘기하고 있는가?
→ A **yearly** dinner

만점 TIP
- 관련 기출
  daily (매일의), weekly (매주의), monthly (매월의), quarterly (분기별의)

12 coworker

- colleague 동료
- associate, staff, employee 직원
- 사람 이름 in[from] 부서명

(직장) 동료

W: I'll check with **Ms. Bishop in our legal department**.

법무팀의 비숍 씨에게 확인을 해보겠습니다.

Q. 무엇을 하겠다고 하는가?
→ Contact a **colleague**

13 handle

- take care of, deal with, manage 처리하다

~을 처리하다, 다루다

M: I'm confident that we can **take care of** all your travel needs, from booking flights and accommodations to arranging ground transportation.

저희는 항공권 및 숙소 예약부터 지상 교통편 마련까지 귀하의 모든 여행 관련 필요사항을 다 처리해드릴 자신이 있습니다.

Q. 무엇을 전문으로 하는 곳인가?
→ **Handling** travel arrangements

14 clothing

- attire, apparel, garment, outfits, wear, dress
  옷, 의복

● 옷, 의류

W: There's a lot of interest in our new line of women's summer **dresses**. It looks like demand will be high, so we'd better increase production to be sure we have a supply of all **garment** sizes.

여성용 여름 원피스 신제품 라인에 많은 관심이 쏠리고 있어요. 수요가 높을 것으로 보이니 모든 의복 사이즈를 공급할 수 있도록 생산량을 늘리는 게 좋을 것 같아요.

Q. 어떤 업체인가?
→ A **clothing** company

15 set aside

- put aside, put on hold, hold, keep, reserve
  (물건 등을) 따로 맡아 두다

● (물건을) 따로 맡아 두다

M: I won't be able to come in until tomorrow evening. Would it be possible to **put** the shirt **on hold** so that someone else doesn't buy it before I get there?

제가 내일 저녁까진 갈 수 없을 것 같습니다. 제가 가기 전에 다른 사람이 사가지 않도록 셔츠를 따로 맡아 주실 수 있을까요?

Q. 무엇을 부탁하는가?
→ **Set aside** an item

16 break down

- out of order, broken
  고장 난
- malfunction
  제대로 작동하지 않다
- stop working 작동을 멈추다
- is not working properly, is acting up
  제대로 작동하지 않고 있다

● 고장 나다

W: The elevator **broke down** last week, and it is still **out of order**, so we'll have to take the stairs.

엘리베이터가 지난주에 고장나서 아직까지 안 되고 있어요. 그래서 계단을 이용해야 할 거예요.

Q. 무엇이 문제인가?
→ An elevator **stopped working**.

만점 TIP

● 관련 기출
faulty 고장난
defective 결함이 있는
damaged 파손된

17 sold out

- out of stock, not in stock
  재고가 없는
- not available
  이용[구매]할 수 없는

다 팔린, 매진된

M: We do **not** have any seats **available** on any flights to Jeju tomorrow. It's a holiday weekend, so many people are traveling. Would you like to reserve a ticket for the following day?

내일 이용 가능한 제주행 항공편이 하나도 없어요. 공휴일이 낀 주말이어서 많은 사람들이 여행을 하나봐요. 다음 날 항공권으로 예약하시겠습니까?

Q. 무엇이 문제인가?
→ Some tickets are **sold out**.

18 oversee

- supervise, manage
  관리 감독하다

~을 관리 감독하다

W: We're planning to open more retail stores in Asian countries nearby. So, we're looking for someone to **oversee** operations at the new stores.

저희는 인근 아시아 국가에 더 많은 소매점을 열 계획입니다. 그래서 신규 매장 운영을 관리 감독할 사람을 찾고 있습니다.

Q. 새 직책의 직무는 무엇인가?
→ **Managing** multiple stores

만점 TIP

- 관련 기출
  supervisor / manager 관리자, 감독관

19 inclement weather

- poor[bad, severe] weather 나쁜 날씨
- heavy rain(폭우), storm(폭풍), snowstorm(눈보라), thunderstorm(뇌우)

악천후

M: Attention all passengers on Flight WA15. Due to the approaching **snowstorm**, this flight has been canceled. We are very sorry for the inconvenience.

WA15편에 탑승하신 모든 승객 여러분께 알립니다. 눈보라가 다가와서 이 항공편이 취소되었습니다. 불편을 끼쳐드려 대단히 죄송합니다.

Q. 무엇이 문제인가?
→ **Inclement weather**

20 refreshments

- food and beverages
  식음료
- snacks and drinks
  간식과 음료

● 다과

W: I hope you stay after the meeting and have some **snacks and drinks** that will be provided in the room next door.
회의가 끝난 후에도 계속 머무시며 옆방에서 제공될 다과를 드시길 바랍니다.

Q. 어떤 일이 있을 것인가?
→ **Refreshments** will be served.

21 renovation

- remodeling 리모델링
- improvement 향상, 개선
- repair work 수리 작업

● 보수공사

M: Ms. Parker is going to talk about her current project – the **renovation** of a large apartment complex on the east side of town.
파커 씨는 현행 프로젝트인 마을 동쪽에 있는 대규모 아파트 단지의 보수공사에 대해 이야기할 예정입니다.

Q. 파커 씨는 무엇에 대해 이야기할 것인가?
→ A **remodeling** project

22 take part in

- attend, participate in
  참가하다

● ~에 참가하다

W: If you're interested in **participating in** this program, please send an e-mail to Angela Ingram.
이 프로그램에 참여하고 싶으시면, 안젤라 잉그램에게 이메일을 보내주시기 바랍니다.

Q. 왜 안젤라 잉그램에게 이메일을 보내는가?
→ To **take part in** a program

23 rule

- regulations, policy
  규정, 방침
- guideline 가이드라인, 지침
- standard 기준

● 규칙

M: I've received some feedback from our employees about the new **guidelines** for contacting the technical help staff, and most are not very happy with it.

직원들로부터 기술 지원팀 직원에게 연락하는 것에 대한 새 지침에 관해 피드백을 받았는데, 대부분이 이를 마음에 들어하지 않고 있습니다.

Q. 무엇에 대해 얘기하고 있는가?
→ A **policy** for getting technical help

24 cancel

- withdraw, call off
  취소하다, 철회하다

● ~을 취소하다

W: I just read the e-mail that said today's department luncheon has been **called off**. Do you know why?

오늘 부서 오찬이 취소되었다는 메일을 방금 읽었습니다. 이유를 아시나요?

Q. 왜 이메일을 받았는가?
→ An event has been **canceled**.

25 contract

- agreement 합의, 협약

● 계약(서)

M: Here's your copy of the rental **contract** for your new apartment. I've made a note that you're moving in on Tuesday.

여기 새 아파트 임대 계약서 사본입니다. 화요일에 이사오신다고 적어두었습니다.

Q. 무엇을 건네주는가?
→ A rental **agreement**

26 event

- function, occasion 행사
- concert(콘서트), grand opening(개장), company dinner(회식), trade show(무역박람회), job fair(직업박람회) 등

● 행사

W: It looks like there's a problem with the funds for the **company dinner**. I just found out that we're going to have to reduce our expenses by 15 percent.

회식 자금에 문제가 있는 것 같아요. 경비를 15% 줄여야 한다는 걸 방금 알았어요.

Q. 무엇에 대해 얘기하는가?
→ Reducing the cost of an **event**

27 sufficient

- adequate 충분한, 적절한
- enough 충분한

● 충분한

M: Our department's budget is not large **enough** to cover a major renovation project right now.

우리 부서의 예산이 당장 주요 보수 공사를 감당하기에는 충분하지 않습니다.

Q. 무슨 문제가 있는가?
→ A budget is not **sufficient**.

만점 TIP
- 토익에 자주 나오는 '예산이 충분하지 않다' 표현
  A budget has been reduced. 예산이 줄었다.
  A budget is tight. 예산이 빠듯하다.
  a limited budget 제한된 예산

28 run short of[on]

- shortage 부족
- lack v. 부족하다 n. 부족

● ~이 부족하다

W: It seems like we're **running short of** printer paper and ink cartridges.

프린터 용지와 잉크 카트리지가 부족한 것 같습니다.

Q. 무엇이 문제인가?
→ There is a **lack** of some office supplies.

29 **complimentary**

- free 무료의
- at no cost, at no charge, for free 무료로

● 무료의

M: Because a number of attendees will be staying with us that weekend, we'll be running a **complimentary** shuttle between the hotel and the convention center.

그 주말에 많은 참석자들이 저희 호텔에 머물기 때문에, 저희는 호텔과 컨벤션 센터 사이에 무료 셔틀을 운행할 예정입니다.

Q. 무엇에 대해 얘기하는가?
→ A shuttle service will be provided **for free**.

30 **understaffed**

- shorthanded, shortstaffed 일손이 부족한
- not enough staff 직원이 충분하지 않은

● 일손이 모자란

W: The marketing department is pretty **shorthanded** right now because a few team members are out on vacation.

지금 마케팅 부서는 일부 팀원들이 휴가 중이라 일손이 많이 부족합니다.

Q. 마케팅팀에 대해 뭐라고 하는가?
→ It is currently **understaffed**.

31 **location**

- place, venue, spot, space, site 장소

● 위치, 장소

M: There's been a change in **location** for our charity event tomorrow. Instead of Central Park, it's now going to be at the café down the street.

내일 있을 자선 행사 장소가 바뀌었습니다. 센트럴 파크 대신 길가에 있는 카페에서 열릴 것입니다.

Q. 무슨 내용을 알려주는가?
→ A **venue** has been changed.

만점 TIP

- 행사가 열리는 장소를 주로 venue라고 하는데, Part 3, 4의 선택지에 자주 등장하는 어휘이므로 꼭 알아 두세요.

32 reasonable

- affordable 가격이 적당한

● (가격이) 합리적인

W: Try the SavorySpoon Bistro. It's a bit far from our office, but it is well worth the trip. They have very **affordable** prices.

세이버리스푼 비스트로에 가보세요. 사무실에서 조금 멀긴 하지만 충분히 갈 만한 가치가 있어요. 가격이 아주 합리적이에요.

Q. 왜 SavorySpoon Bistro를 추천하는가?
→ Their prices are **reasonable**.

33 reimburse

- pay back 돈을 돌려주다
- compensate 보상을 해주다

● ~에게 배상해주다, 변제해주다

M: I have one question about relocating. Will I be **compensated** for all my moving costs?

이사에 대해 한 가지 질문이 있습니다. 이사비는 전부 보상받나요?

Q. 무엇에 대해 문의하는가?
→ A **reimbursement**

34 promote

- advertise 광고하다

● ~을 홍보하다

W: I'm calling about an idea to **promote** your new restaurant. Why don't we film a television commercial right there on site?

당신의 새 식당을 홍보할 아이디어 때문에 전화 드렸습니다. 바로 그곳 현장에서 텔레비전 광고를 촬영해 보는 것은 어떨까요?

Q. 무엇에 대해 얘기하는가?
→ How to **advertise** a business

35 revise

- edit (글을) 수정하다
- make changes, modify, make revisions 수정하다
- correct 바로잡다, 고치다
- update 새로운 내용으로 바꾸다

~을 수정하다, 개정하다

M: I just finished reviewing your first draft of the presentation, and I feel like it needs some **editing**.

당신의 발표 초안 검토를 이제 막 끝냈는데요, 수정이 좀 필요할 것 같습니다.

Q. 무엇을 하라고 하는가?
→ **Revise** a draft

36 sign up for

- register for, enroll in 등록하다

~을 신청하다, ~에 등록하다

W: You can **sign up for** a fun guided tour here. It's a fantastic way to explore the city's landmarks.

여러분은 이곳에서 재미있는 가이드 투어를 신청할 수 있습니다. 도시의 랜드마크를 둘러볼 수 있는 환상적인 방법입니다.

Q. 무엇을 권하는가?
→ **Register for** a guided tour

37 give[offer] a ride

- provide[offer] transportation 교통편을 제공하다

차로 태워주다

M: I heard your car is still in the repair shop. I can **give you a ride** home after work today.

당신의 차가 아직 정비소에 있다고 들었습니다. 제가 오늘 퇴근 후에 집까지 태워다 드릴 수 있습니다.

Q. 무엇을 해주겠다고 하는가?
→ **Provide transportation**

38 detour

- alternate[alternative] route, bypass 대체로, 우회로
- different road 다른 도로

• 우회로

W: Because of road repairs, Exit 4B on Emmerson Highway is closed. To avoid the affected area, drivers are advised to take a **detour** using local roads.

도로 보수 공사로 인해 에머슨 고속도로 4B번 출구가 폐쇄되어 있습니다. 해당 구역을 피하기 위해, 운전자들께서는 지방 도로를 이용하여 우회하시기 바랍니다.

Q. 무엇을 권하는가?
→ Taking an **alternate route**

39 traffic congestion

- stuck in traffic 교통 체증에 갇힌
- backed up 교통이 막히는
- traffic jam 교통 체증
- traffic is slow 길이 막히다

• 교통 체증

M: I'm sorry I'm late to work. **Traffic was really slow** this morning because of the rain.

회사에 늦어서 죄송합니다. 오늘 아침에 비가 와서 정말 길이 막혔어요.

Q. 남자는 무엇 때문에 늦었는가?
→ **Traffic congestion**
→ He was **stuck in traffic**.

40 state-of-the art

- cutting-edge 최신식의

• 최첨단의, 최신식의

W: The reason our customers keep coming back to our business is our **state-of-the-art** facilities.

고객들이 계속해서 우리 업체를 다시 찾는 이유는 우리의 최첨단 시설 때문입니다.

Q. 고객들이 업체에 대해 무엇을 좋아하는가?
→ It has **cutting-edge** facilities.

DAILY QUIZ

🎧 질문을 읽고 음원을 들은 뒤, 정답을 골라보세요.

1 What is the problem?

(A) Some items are missing.
(B) Some products are out of stock.

M: I'm sorry, we don't have any oak tables available now. We'll get a new shipment next week.
W: Is the floor model available?
M: Let me check with my manager.

2 What does the woman suggest the man do?

(A) Contact a colleague
(B) Report to his supervisor

M: I need to set up the automatic deposit for my paycheck, but I'm not sure how to do it.
W: You should talk to Samantha in Payroll. She can give you some instructions.
M: Okay. I'll go and see her after lunch.

3 What is the speaker calling about?

(A) A project delay
(B) A broken appliance

W: Hello, this is Jane Doe calling from apartment 4B on 23 Maple Street. I am calling because my refrigerator is not functioning properly, and it requires immediate attention. Please send a repair person as soon as possible to address the issue.

정답 1 (B) 2 (A) 3 (B)

1 considerable

considerably ad. 상당히

● 상당한

기출 put in **considerable** effort
상당한 노력을 쏟다

expect a **considerable** upturn
상당한 호전을 예상하다

The repair of the damaged cathedral roof will require ------- time and expense.
(A) proficient   (B) considerable

2 sensitive

sense n. 감각
     v. 감지하다, 느끼다
sensitivity n. 민감함, 예민함

● 민감한, 예민한

기출 due to the **sensitive** nature of
~의 민감한 특성으로 인해

sensitive client information
민감한 고객 정보

Ms. Henley instructs office workers to store all documents containing ------- information in the safe.
(A) appropriate   (B) sensitive

3 adequate

adequately ad. 충분히, 적절히

● 충분한, 적절한

기출 ensure **adequate** space for attendees
참석자들을 위해 충분한 공간을 보장하다

find one's qualifications **adequate**
~의 자격사항이 적절하다고 생각하다

The private dining room at Percival Bistro provides ------- space for parties of up to 20 individuals.
(A) competent   (B) adequate

4 diverse

- 다양한

  기출 a **diverse** line of products
  다양한 제품군

  the use of more **diverse** energy sources
  더 다양한 에너지 자원의 사용

  Starlit Enterprises employs a ------- workforce featuring people of various nationalities and backgrounds.

  (A) contrary　　　　(B) diverse

5 fragile

- 깨지기 쉬운, 연약한

  기출 handle **fragile** items with utmost care
  극도의 주의를 기울여 깨지기 쉬운 상품들을 다루다

  We use special packing materials to ensure ------- items are not damaged during shipping.

  (A) cautious　　　　(B) fragile

6 promising

- 유력한, 전망이 좋은

  기출 **promising** location for investors
  투자자들을 위한 유력한 장소

  We have received a lot of ------- feedback from members regarding our new fitness classes.

  (A) promising　　　　(B) profitable

7 reluctant

reluctantly ad. 꺼려하여, 마지못해

• 꺼려하는

기출 be **reluctant** to purchase a new model
새로운 모델을 구매하는 것을 꺼려하다

> Although the auction attracted a large number of attendees, most were ------- to place any bids.
> (A) uncertain　　　(B) reluctant

8 practical

• 실용적인

기출 innovative yet **practical** 혁신적이지만 실용적인

> Trion Consulting specializes in providing clients with innovative yet ------- solutions.
> (A) practical　　　(B) internal

9 urgent

• 긴급한

기출 require **urgent** attention
긴급한 주의를 필요로 하다

contact A for any **urgent** matters
어떠한 긴급한 사안들에 대해 A에게 연락하다

> Even though Ms. Pratt is on annual leave, she may be contacted by phone if you have any ------- issues.
> (A) urgent　　　(B) obedient

10 ambitious

• 야심찬

기출 meet one's **ambitious** goals
야심찬 목표를 달성하다

announce an **ambitious** plan
야심찬 계획을 발표하다

> Mr. Krieger will outline his ------- plan to open twenty new branches of Codmo Burger throughout the UK.
> (A) ambitious　　　(B) envious

11 hopeful

- 희망적인, 기대하는

  기출 be **hopeful** that
  ~라는 점이 희망적이다

  > Every board member is ------- that revenues can double to $2 billion this year.
  > (A) cheerful (B) hopeful

12 unavailable

- 이용할 수 없는, 시간이 없는

  기출 will be **unavailable** to customers
  고객들이 이용할 수 없을 것이다

  currently **unavailable** in the color you requested
  현재 귀하께서 요청하신 색상으로는 이용할 수 없는

  > We regret to inform library members that the private reading rooms will be ------- during the renovation work.
  > (A) unavailable (B) underdeveloped

13 consecutive

- 연속적인

  기출 predict four **consecutive** days of rain
  4일 연속의 비를 예측하다

  win one's sixth **consecutive** international tournament
  6회 연속 국제 경기를 우승하다

  > Matt Rodgers received the Best Songwriter of the Year award for the third ------- year.
  > (A) following (B) consecutive

14 persistent

persistently ad. 끊임없이

- 끊임없이 지속되는, 끈질긴

  기출 remove a **persistent** stain
  끊임없이 지속되는 얼룩을 제거하다

  > Numerous local residents have filed complaints about the ------- noise coming from the nearby construction site.
  > (A) persistent   (B) defective

15 subsequent

subsequently ad. 그 후에, 그 뒤에

- 후속의, 다음의

  기출 **subsequent** events
  후속 행사들

  in the **subsequent** year
  그 다음 해에

  > Few people watched *Circle of Friends* during its first season, but ------- seasons attracted a high number of viewers.
  > (A) timely   (B) subsequent

16 sturdy

sturdily ad. 견고하게

- 견고한

  기출 thanks to **sturdy** construction
  견고한 건축 덕분에

  recommend a **sturdy** bed frame
  견고한 침대 틀을 추천하다

  > To protect your laptop, a ------- carrying case with padding is recommended.
  > (A) intense   (B) sturdy

17 unprecedented

● 전례 없는, 이례적인

기출 an **unprecedented** increase in sales
매출에서의 전례 없는 증가

be **unprecedented** in the history of
~의 역사에서 이례적이다

> Southern Electricity customers have been outraged by the ------- increase in their monthly energy bills.
> (A) impenetrable   (B) unprecedented

18 strategic

strategically ad. 전략적으로
strategy n. 전략

● 전략적인

기출 a **strategic** move to attract more customers
더 많은 고객들을 끌어들이기 위한 전략적인 이동

> Apex Hotel's ------- location near the convention center makes it popular with business travelers.
> (A) strategic   (B) distant

19 harsh

harshly ad. 가혹하게, 혹독하게

● 가혹한, 혹독한

기출 given the **harsh** reviews written by critics
평론가들에 의해 작성된 가혹한 후기를 고려하면

> The new play written by Desmond Akumba received ------- reviews from the majority of theater critics.
> (A) harsh   (B) deep

20 disappointed

- 실망한

  기출 be **disappointed** that
  ~라는 것에 실망하다

  Some employees were left ------- with the outcome of the salary negotiations.
  (A) complicated　　　(B) disappointed

21 inaccessible

- 이용할 수 없는, 접근할 수 없는

  기출 be **inaccessible** starting December 30
  12월 30일부터 이용할 수 없다

  The staff cafeteria will be ------- while the work crew is installing new seating and tables.
  (A) inaccessible　　　(B) improbable

22 overdue

- (기한이) 지난, 연체된

  기출 **overdue** for your annual checkup
  귀하의 연례 검진 기한이 지난

  be **overdue** since last year
  작년 이후로 연체되다

  Starting next month, all ------- bill payments will be subject to a ten percent administration fee.
  (A) overdue　　　(B) worthy

23 superb

- 최상의

  기출 **superb** customer service
  최상의 고객 서비스

  impress the audience with one's **superb** technique
  최상의 기술로 청중에게 깊은 인상을 남기다

  > Marcus Toft received an award for his ------- performance in the television show *Elden Oaks*.
  > (A) superb   (B) evasive

24 convincing

convince v. 설득하다

- 설득력 있는

  기출 be so **convincing** that
  매우 설득력 있어서 ~하다

  > The athletics committee made a highly ------- argument to have the event held in Los Angeles.
  > (A) convincing   (B) verified

25 versatile

versatility n. 다재다능

- 다재다능한, 다용도의, 다양한 기능을 지닌

  기출 be **versatile** enough to do
  ~하기에 충분히 다재다능하다

  versatile furniture
  다용도 가구

  > Quartet's new digital camera is ------- enough to be used in a wide variety of environments.
  > (A) versatile   (B) financial

26 incorrect

incorrectly ad. 정확하지 않게

- 정확하지 않은

  기출 if your billing statement is **incorrect**
  귀하의 대금 청구서가 정확하지 않다면

  If any of the details on the application form are --------, you will not be issued a vendor permit for the event.

  (A) imperative　　　(B) incorrect

27 mandatory

mandate v. 의무화하다

- 의무적인

  기출 **mandatory** safety training
  의무적인 안전 교육

  take a **mandatory** break
  의무적인 휴식을 갖다

  Employees are reminded that it is ------- to attend the weekly branch meeting at 8:45 AM on Mondays.

  (A) mandatory　　　(B) probable

28 optimistic

- 낙관적인

  기출 be **optimistic** about
  ~에 대해 낙관적이다

  optimistic quarterly projections
  낙관적인 분기별 예상치

  The board members are ------- about the profitability of the new manufacturing plant.

  (A) optimistic　　　(B) ample

29 perishable

perish v. 상하다, 부패하다

- 상하기 쉬운

  기출 **perishable** products
  상하기 쉬운 제품들

  > Jonson Refrigeration produces containers designed for the transportation of ------- goods, such as meat and dairy products.
  >
  > (A) coincidental   (B) perishable

30 punctual

punctuality n. 시간 엄수

- 시간을 엄수하는

  기출 try to be **punctual**
  시간을 엄수하도록 노력하다

  > All participants must try to be ------- for the city tour, which will depart from the hotel lobby at precisely 9 AM.
  >
  > (A) punctual   (B) eventual

31 unfavorable

unfavorably ad. 불리하게

- 좋지 않은, 호의적이지 않은

  기출 due to **unfavorable** weather conditions
  좋지 않은 기상 조건 때문에

  due to **unfavorable** conditions in the market
  시장에서의 좋지 않은 상황 때문에

  > The launch of the new cell phone model has been delayed in light of the ------- feedback from product testers.
  >
  > (A) unfavorable   (B) functional

32 delicate

- 다루기 힘든, 정교한

  기출 **delicate** contract negotiations
  다루기 힘든 계약 협상

  > Ms. Sharpe is experienced in handling ------- matters involving dissatisfied customers.
  > (A) delicate   (B) talented

33 dependable

depend v. 의존하다
dependent a. 의존적인

- 믿을 만한, 의존할 만한

  기출 become **dependable** 믿을 만해지다

  > Since joining the firm six months ago, Mr. Lopez has proven himself to be a ------- member of the sales team.
  > (A) customized   (B) dependable

34 manageable

manage v. 관리하다

- 관리하기 쉬운, 다루기 쉬운

  기출 The project will be **manageable**.
  그 프로젝트는 관리하기 쉬울 것이다.

  > Day trips to Bird Peak Waterfall are easily ------- thanks to the hotel's regular shuttle bus service.
  > (A) manageable   (B) challenging

35 memorable

- 기억할 만한

  기출 deliver a **memorable** speech
  기억할 만한 연설을 하다

  > The new interactive exhibits at Walford Science Museum promise to provide a ------- experience for the whole family.
  > (A) memorable   (B) victorious

36 provisional

임시의

기출 be hired on a **provisional** basis
임시로 채용되다

Several employees will be hired on a ------- basis, and some of them will be offered full-time contracts in March.

(A) provisional (B) marginal

37 adverse

adversely ad. 부정적으로, 불리하게

부정적인, 불리한

기출 have an **adverse** effect on
~에 부정적인 영향을 끼치다

The quarterly financial report shows that the new advertising campaign had an ------- effect on sales.

(A) affordable (B) adverse

38 informative

informatively ad. 유익하게

유익한

기출 both **informative** and interesting
둘 다 유익하고 흥미로운

the most **informative** speech
가장 유익한 강연

Guests can pick up ------- pamphlets about local sights from the hotel's reception area.

(A) informative (B) enthusiastic

39 redeemable

- (현금, 상품 등으로) 교환 가능한

  기출 be **redeemable** by the recipient
  수령인에 의해 교환 가능하다

  > Loyalty points and discount codes are ------- on our Web site.
  > (A) redeemable (B) eligible

40 unanimous

unanimously ad. 만장일치로

- 만장일치의

  기출 be **unanimous** in one's decision to do
  ~하는 결정에 있어서 만장일치이다

  > The shareholders reached a ------- decision to relocate the company from California to Texas.
  > (A) numerous (B) unanimous

DAILY QUIZ

단어와 그에 알맞은 뜻을 연결해 보세요.

1. informative • • (A) 유익한
2. considerable • • (B) 기억할 만한
3. memorable • • (C) 상당한

빈칸에 알맞은 단어를 선택하세요.

4. ------- quarterly projections
   낙관적인 분기별 예상치

5. a ------- line of products
   다양한 제품군

(A) diverse
(B) overdue
(C) optimistic
(D) redeemable

6. ------- for your annual checkup
   귀하의 연례 검진 기한이 지난

앞서 배운 단어들의 뜻을 생각하면서, 다음 문제를 풀어보세요.

7. Of all the potential banquet locations, The Maple Lounge appears to be the only one ------- for our needs.

   (A) popular (B) tentative
   (C) extensive (D) adequate

8. Technical issues that require ------- attention should be addressed before any other relatively minor problems.

   (A) near (B) fluent
   (C) absent (D) urgent

정답 1 (A) 2 (C) 3 (B) 4 (C) 5 (A) 6 (B) 7 (D) 8 (D)

Day 03 형용사 ❹ Part 5, 6

1 attentive
attentively ad. 주의하여

● 주의를 기울이는

기출 stay **attentive** to
~에 계속 주의를 기울이다

Many online reviews note how ------- the wait staff at the restaurant are to diners' needs.
(A) available   (B) attentive

2 imperative

● 필수적인

기출 it is **imperative** that
~하는 것이 필수적이다

It is ------- that you give at least 30 days of notice prior to the termination of the employment contract.
(A) imperative   (B) willing

3 marked
markedly ad. 뚜렷하게

● 뚜렷한

기출 show a **marked** improvement
뚜렷한 개선을 보여주다

Mr. Bridges has noticed ------- improvement in staff productivity since the remodeling of the office space.
(A) respective   (B) marked

4 **proud**

- 자랑스러운

  기출 be **proud** to present artists who
  ~한 예술가들을 소개하게 되어 자랑스럽다

  > Ms. Winters was the ------- recipient of this year's Young Writer of the Year award.
  > (A) proud　　　　(B) general

5 **distinct**

distinctive a. 독특한
distinctively ad. 독특하게

- 뚜렷한, 뚜렷이 구별되는

  기출 if the sound is not **distinct**
  만약 소리가 뚜렷하지 않다면

  > Dawson National Park has added ------- trail markers to ensure that hikers do not get lost.
  > (A) perceptive　　　(B) distinct

6 **immense**

immensely ad. 엄청나게

- 엄청난 (양의), 방대한 (크기의)

  기출 **immense** collection of reviews
  엄청난 양의 후기 모음

  feature an **immense** lobby
  방대한 크기의 로비를 특징으로 하다

  > Flix Star, a new movie streaming platform, boasts an ------- catalog of more than 10,000 films.
  > (A) impending　　　(B) immense

7 costly

cost n. 비용

- 비용이 많이 드는

  기출 protect your system from **costly** breakdowns
  비용이 많이 드는 고장으로부터 귀하의 시스템을 보호하다

  > It is advisable to follow the cleaning guidelines for the air conditioning system in order to prevent ------- malfunctions.
  >
  > (A) costly　　　　(B) clear

8 sizable

- (크기, 액수가) 상당한

  기출 create a **sizable** demand for
  ~에 대한 상당한 수요를 만들다

  > The CEO privately thanked Mr. Hogg for his ------- donation at last week's charity fundraiser.
  >
  > (A) sizable　　　　(B) durable

9 unfamiliar

- 익숙하지 않은

  기출 be **unfamiliar** with
  ~에 익숙하지 않다

  engineers **unfamiliar** with the program
  그 프로그램에 익숙하지 않은 기술자들

  > Workers who are still ------- with the new database system are invited to attend a workshop at 2 PM tomorrow.
  >
  > (A) difficult　　　　(B) unfamiliar

10 demanding

demand n. 요구

- 힘든, 까다로운

  [기출] much too **demanding** for A
  A에게 매우 힘든

  The walking trail to the summit of Grouse Mountain is not particularly ------- and is suitable for people of all ages.
  (A) uneasy   (B) demanding

11 tentative

tentatively ad. 잠정적으로, 임시로

- 잠정적인, 임시의

  [기출] discuss a **tentative** agreement with
  ~와 잠정적인 협정을 논의하다

  a **tentative** schedule of events
  행사의 임시 일정

  November 10 has been chosen as the ------- date for the grand opening of Summerville Shopping Mall.
  (A) tentative   (B) hesitant

12 renowned

- 유명한

  [기출] **renowned** sculptor
  유명한 조각가

  renowned for its architectural beauty
  건축미로 유명한

  The keynote speaker for the International Finance Convention will be the ------- businessman, Alan Kane.
  (A) eligible   (B) renowned

13 repetitive

repeat v. 반복하다

- 반복적인

  [기출] **repetitive** work 반복적인 작업

  Several factory workers have complained of muscle pain resulting from the ------- nature of the jobs they must perform.
  (A) repetitive　　　(B) former

14 encouraging

encourage v. 격려하다

- 희망적인, 고무적인

  [기출] indicate an **encouraging** trend
  희망적인 경향을 보여주다

  The high number of advanced orders placed for our new car has been very ------- so far.
  (A) encouraging　　　(B) available

15 desirable

desire n. 바람, 열망

- 바람직한, 매력적인

  [기출] be constructed on the most **desirable** land
  가장 매력적인 땅에 건설되다

  Green Hills has become a highly ------- neighborhood for families thanks to its excellent parks and schools.
  (A) attainable　　　(B) desirable

16 compatible

- 호환되는(with)

  [기출] be **compatible** with the system
  그 시스템과 호환되다

  Before downloading the file, employees should make sure its format is ------- with their mobile devices.
  (A) compatible　　　(B) amenable

17 full

fully ad. 전적으로, 완전히

- 최대의, 전체의, 완전한

  기출 operate at **full** capacity
  최대 수용력으로 운영되다

  > The mayor aims to use the ------- extent of his influence to ensure the city is chosen to host the athletics event.
  >
  > (A) full　　　　　　(B) most

18 helpful

help v. 돕다

- 유용한, 도움이 되는

  기출 especially **helpful**
  특히 유용한

  it is **helpful** to do
  ~하는 것이 도움이 되다

  > Our Web site includes several ------- tips to make sure your visit to Turtle Island goes smoothly.
  >
  > (A) helpful　　　　(B) capable

19 temporary

temporarily ad. 임시로, 일시적으로

- 임시의, 일시적인

  기출 serve as a **temporary** replacement for
  ~의 임시 후임으로 일하다

  a **temporary** solution to do
  ~하기 위한 임시 해결책

  > Upon registering as a member on our Web site, you will be given a ------- password that you should change.
  >
  > (A) comparable　　(B) temporary

20 remarkable

remarkably ad. 현저히

- 주목할 만한, 눈에 띄는

  기출 result in a **remarkable** 40% rise in sales
  매출에서 주목할 만한 40퍼센트 상승의 결과를 낳다

Since Mr. Glenn joined Mitchum Enterprises, the company has seen a ------- 30 percent decrease in annual expenditure.
(A) remarkable　　　(B) receptive

21 protective

protect v. 보호하다
protection n. 보호

- 보호하는

  기출 as a **protective** measure for the company
  회사를 위한 보호 조치로

All factory workers are required to wear ------- masks and gloves when operating dangerous machinery.
(A) protective　　　(B) settled

22 lengthy

- 긴, 오랜

  기출 it is too **lengthy** for
  ~에게 너무 길다

The hiring committee eventually decided to offer a contract to Helen Jones after ------- deliberation.
(A) lengthy　　　(B) wide

23 challenging

challenge n. 도전, 난제

• 힘든, 도전적인

기출 **challenging** project
힘든 프로젝트

fulfill the demands of one's **challenging** role as CEO
대표이사라는 힘든 역할의 책무를 완수하다

Adjusting to a new environment can be -------, so please do not hesitate to ask me if you need any help.

(A) interesting　　　(B) challenging

24 operational

operate v. 작동하다, 가동하다, 운영하다
operation n. 작동, 가동, 운영

• 작동하는, 가동되는, 운영되는

기출 when the module is **operational**
그 모듈이 작동할 때

should be **operational** by June 4
6월 4일까지 가동되어야 한다

Several new Patson Metro Transit bus routes will become ------- in September.

(A) ended　　　(B) operational

25 updated

update v. 최신 정보로 교체하다, 갱신하다
n. 최신 정보, 갱신

• 최신의, 갱신된

기출 the **updated** training schedule
최신 교육 일정

need to be **updated** immediately
즉시 갱신될 필요가 있다

The ------- edition of author Stephen Laing's most popular novel will include a foreword by his editor.

(A) numerous　　　(B) updated

26 attached

- 첨부된

  기출 The **attached** file contains ~.
  첨부된 파일은 ~을 포함하고 있다.

  All factory workers should follow the ------- safety guidelines at all times.
  (A) attached   (B) direct

27 interactive

interact v. 상호작용하다
interaction n. 상호작용

- 상호작용하는, 쌍방의

  기출 offer **interactive** features
  상호작용하는 특징들을 제공하다

  The Fornley Science Museum has many ------- exhibits that visitors of all ages will find interesting.
  (A) conclusive   (B) interactive

28 overwhelming

overwhelmingly ad. 압도적으로

- 압도적인

  기출 The number of survey responses has been **overwhelming**.
  설문조사 응답의 수가 압도적이었다.

  Our e-mail service users are always complaining that the volume of spam e-mail they receive in a day has become -------.
  (A) reduced   (B) overwhelming

29 accomplished

accomplish v. 성취하다
accomplishment n. 성취, 업적

● 뛰어난

기출 the most **accomplished** authors
가장 뛰어난 작가들

This month's concert series will feature many of the world's most ------- musicians.
(A) remaining   (B) accomplished

30 designated

designate v. 지정하다
designation n. 지정

● 지정된

기출 only in the **designated** space
지정된 공간에서만

During the repaving process, only ------- zones in the employee parking lot will be available for use.
(A) designated   (B) advanced

31 equipped

equip v. (시설, 장비 등을) 갖추다
equipment n. 기구, 장비

● (시설, 장비 등을) 갖춘

기출 be **equipped** with
~을 갖추다

All Metz Rental vehicles are fully ------- with a top-of-the-range satellite navigation system.
(A) serviced   (B) equipped

32 capable

capability n. 능력, 가능성

● ~ 할 수 있는

기출 be **capable** of causing damage
손상을 일으킬 수 있다

Excessive noise is ------- of causing major disruption in office environments, leading to reduced productivity.
(A) capable   (B) potential

33 economical

economic a. 경제의
economically ad. 경제적으로

- 경제적인, 비용이 낮은

기출 **economical** manufacturing process
경제적인 제조 과정

> Interior designer John Lee is known for his ------- use of floor space.
>
> (A) average (B) economical

34 spacious

- 넓은

기출 offer more **spacious** meeting rooms
더 넓은 회의실을 제공하다

> Subatu Motors is known for producing more ------- automobiles that are suitable for large families.
>
> (A) satisfied (B) spacious

35 fortunate

fortunately ad. 운 좋게, 다행히

- 운이 좋은, 다행인

기출 be **fortunate** to do
~할 만큼 운이 좋다

> We are ------- to have many gifted local musicians here at Franklin Gas Services's 20th anniversary celebration.
>
> (A) fortunate (B) obvious

36 productive

productivity n. 생산성
productively ad. 생산적으로

- 생산적인

  기출 find it **productive**
  생산적인 것을 알게 되다

  remain **productive**
  생산적인 상태를 유지하다

  Troy Manufacturing determined that Ms. Landry's team is the least ------- and requires further training.
  (A) abundant　　　　(B) productive

37 growing

grow v. (크기, 수, 정도가) 늘다, 성장하다
growth n. 성장, 발전

- (크기, 수, 정도가) 증가하는, 성장하는

  기출 due to the **growing** number of
  증가하는 ~의 수로 인해

  To meet the needs of Ellington Inc.'s ------- workforce, the company has approved the construction of a new staff cafeteria.
  (A) growing　　　　(B) concluding

38 similar

similarly ad. 유사하게
similarity n. 유사성

- 유사한, 비슷한

  기출 be **similar** to other models
  다른 모델들과 유사하다

  make a **similar** observation
  비슷한 의견을 말하다

  Although the new Zabu 250 laptop looks ------- to other computers, it is the lightest on the market by far.
  (A) similar　　　　(B) reflected

39 multiple

- 다수의

  기출 travel to **multiple** destinations
  다수의 목적지를 여행하다

  multiple parts
  다수의 부품들

  > Morning Sun Airways is offering discounted flights to ------- destinations for families and groups of five or more people.
  >
  > (A) interested   (B) multiple

40 vital

- 중요한

  기출 it is **vital** that
  ~하는 것이 중요하다

  > The personnel department plays a ------- role in facilitating communication between higher management and employees.
  >
  > (A) vital   (B) poised

DAILY QUIZ

단어와 그에 알맞은 뜻을 연결해 보세요.

1. temporary • • (A) 첨부된
2. attached • • (B) 뚜렷한, 뚜렷이 구별되는
3. distinct • • (C) 임시의, 일시적인

빈칸에 알맞은 단어를 선택하세요.

4. should be ------- by June 4
   6월 4일까지 가동되어야 한다

5. indicate an ------- trend
   희망적인 경향을 보여주다

   (A) remarkable
   (B) operational
   (C) encouraging
   (D) costly

6. result in a ------- 40% rise in sales
   매출에서 주목할 만한 40퍼센트 상승의 결과를 낳다

앞서 배운 단어들의 뜻을 생각하면서, 다음 문제를 풀어보세요.

7. Each manager is assigned a ------- parking space after being hired by Rodden Financial Inc.

   (A) moderated   (B) tolerated
   (C) concerned   (D) designated

8. Even though Mr. Chang is a ------- supervisor, he is still well-liked by most of his employees.

   (A) demanding   (B) compatible
   (C) preferable   (D) collective

정답 1 (C) 2 (A) 3 (B) 4 (B) 5 (C) 6 (A) 7 (D) 8 (A)

Day 04 형용사 + 전치사 콜로케이션 Part 5, 6

1 subject to

● ~의 대상인

기출 be **subject to** modification
수정의 대상이다

be **subject to** additional charges
추가 요금의 대상이다

All requests for holiday leave are ------- to review and depend largely on staff levels.
(A) entitled   (B) subject

2 responsive to

● ~에 대해 빠른 반응을 보이는

기출 be **responsive to** customers
고객들에 대해 빠른 반응을 보이다

be **responsive to** our needs
우리의 요구에 빠른 반응을 보이다

Since assuming the role of HR manager, Ms. Dias has been very ------- to the needs of our workers.
(A) responsive   (B) reluctant

3 identical to

● ~와 동일한

기출 appear **identical to** a natural diamond
천연 다이아몬드와 동일하게 보이다

To most listeners, the cover songs performed by the band sounded ------- to the original versions.
(A) identical   (B) suitable

4 entitled to

• ~의 자격이 있는

기출 be **entitled to** a room upgrade
객실 업그레이드의 자격이 있다

be **entitled to** paid vacation
유급 휴가의 자격이 있다

All Rodeo Burger employees are ------- to a one-hour meal break per shift.

(A) allowed   (B) entitled

5 adequate for

• ~에 충분한, 적당한

기출 be **adequate for** our needs
우리의 요구에 충분하다

be **adequate for** our purposes
우리의 목적에 적당하다

Mr. Ratner believes that the ballroom at the Edgemont Hotel is the only venue ------- for our needs.

(A) cooperative   (B) adequate

6 relevant to

• ~와 관련이 있는

기출 be **relevant to** their jobs
그들의 직무와 관련이 있다

be **relevant to** the shipbuilding industry
조선업과 관련이 있다

During your interview, please try to share only the information that is ------- to the position for which you are applying.

(A) acceptable   (B) relevant

7 devoted to

● ~에 전념하는, 바치는

기출 will be **devoted to** research in the coming year
다가올 연도에 연구에 전념할 것이다

be **devoted to** updating its safety policies
자사의 안전 정책을 업데이트하는 데 전념하다

> The majority of the advertising budget was ------- to developing a series of television commercials.
> (A) devoted　　(B) impressed

8 eligible for

● ~에 대한 자격이 있는

기출 be **eligible for** promotion
승진에 대한 자격이 있다

be **eligible for** a raise
(임금) 인상에 대한 자격이 있다

> To be ------- for the company's Employee of the Year award, you must not have been absent for five days or more.
> (A) comfortable　　(B) eligible

9 attractive to

● ~에게 매력적인

기출 **attractive to** potential customers
잠재 고객들에게 매력적인

> The remodeling work should make Wilmington Hotel's main lobby more ------- to its guests.
> (A) attractive　　(B) thoughtful

10 visible to

- ~의 눈에 보이는

  기출 be **visible to** attendees
  참석자들의 눈에 보이다

  > The display of sunglasses has been set up right beside the cash registers, so it is very ------- to shoppers.
  >
  > (A) visible   (B) eager

11 attentive to

- ~에 집중하는, 주의를 기울이는

  기출 be **attentive to** the needs of the patients
  환자들의 요구에 집중하다

  remain **attentive to** the long-term goals
  장기적인 목표에 주의를 기울이는 상태이다

  > The restaurant owner demands that the wait staff stay ------- to the needs of our diners.
  >
  > (A) related   (B) attentive

12 equivalent to

- ~와 동등한

  기출 be **equivalent to** having certification
  증명서를 가지고 있는 것과 동등하다

  > The installation and maintenance of one robot is ------- to paying the annual salaries of five workers.
  >
  > (A) equivalent   (B) appropriate

13 agreeable to

● ~에 동의하는

기출 appear **agreeable to** the recent changes
최근 변화에 동의하는 것처럼 보이다

During the public forum, most local residents appeared ------- to the proposed demolition of the abandoned theater.

(A) agreeable (B) reliable

14 vulnerable to

● ~에 취약한

기출 be **vulnerable to** changes in the environment
환경의 변화에 취약하다

be **vulnerable to** staining
얼룩에 취약하다

Wood that has not been treated with a protective coating is more ------- to damage from moisture.

(A) concealed (B) vulnerable

15 accountable for

● ~에 대해 책임을 지는

기출 be **accountable for** any costs
어떠한 비용에 대해서도 책임을 지다

hold A **accountable for** their team performances
팀 성과에 대해 A에게 책임을 지우다

When returning undamaged products for a refund, customers will be ------- for any shipping costs.

(A) accountable (B) manageable

16 acceptable to

• ~에게 받아들여질 수 있는

기출 be **acceptable to** the client
의뢰인에게 받아들여질 수 있다

> Before our interior design team makes changes to the office layout, we need to ensure that the design is ------- to the client.
>
> (A) acceptable   (B) probable

17 valid for

• ~ 동안 유효한, ~에 대해 유효한

기출 be **valid for** two years
2년 동안 유효하다

be **valid for** devices purchased before January 17
1월 17일 이전에 구매된 기기에 대해 유효하다

> New members of the country club must apply for a parking permit, which is ------- for six months.
>
> (A) qualified   (B) valid

18 interested in

• ~에 관심이 있는

기출 be **interested in** receiving the training
교육을 받는 데 관심이 있다

be **interested in** investment options
투자 상품들에 관심이 있다

> Hotel guests who are ------- in the tour departing at 9 AM should notify the front desk staff.
>
> (A) skilled   (B) interested

19 based in

~에 본사를 둔

기출 be **based in** Australia
호주에 본사를 두다

be currently **based in** Dubai
현재 두바이에 본사를 두다

Saltire Airways, ------- in Edinburgh, is offering low-cost flights to Amsterdam and Brussels.

(A) based   (B) stayed

20 divided into

~로 분리된

기출 be **divided into** groups based on their income
소득에 기반한 그룹으로 분리되다

be **divided into** three categories
세 개의 유형으로 분리되다

For the role play activity, workshop attendees were ------- into groups based on their field of employment.

(A) divided   (B) evaluated

21 assigned to

~에 할당된, 배정된

기출 be **assigned to** a particular task
특정 업무에 할당되다

be **assigned to** the customer service group
고객 서비스 그룹으로 배정되다

At the orientation session, new recruits will be ------- to specific departments.

(A) assigned   (B) influenced

22 aware of

- ~을 알고 있는

  기출 be **aware of** all the factory's operations
  모든 공장의 운영을 알고 있다

  make people more **aware of** the brand
  사람들이 그 브랜드를 더 많이 알게 만들다

  All assembly line workers are expected to be ------- of the factory's safety regulations.

  (A) aware　　　　(B) serious

23 skilled at

- ~에 능숙한, 숙련된

  기출 be especially **skilled at** contract negotiation
  계약 협상에 특히 능숙하다

  be **skilled at** making delicious cookies
  맛있는 쿠키를 만드는 데 숙련되다

  Mr. Rooney believes that Ms. Appleby is especially ------- at public speaking.

  (A) skilled　　　　(B) willing

24 dependent on

- ~에 의존하고 있는, 달려있는

  기출 find oneself **dependent on** one's coworkers
  동료들에 의존하고 있는 자신을 발견하다

  be **dependent on** the inspection results
  검사 결과에 달려있다

  The decision on whether to make additional modifications to the prototype is ------- on customer feedback.

  (A) dependent　　　　(B) supportive

25 available for

• ~을 위한 시간이 있는, 이용 가능한

> [기출] be **available for** meetings up until 11 AM
> 오전 11시까지 회의를 위한 시간이 있다
>
> be **available for** rental
> 대여로 이용 가능하다

> Mr. Heenan, the new dentist at Dewar Dental Clinic, will be ------- for appointments from 9 AM on Monday.
> (A) grateful (B) available

26 capable of

• ~을 할 수 있는

> [기출] be **capable of** designing skyscrapers
> 고층 건물들을 디자인할 수 있다
>
> be **capable of** improving an organization's efficiency
> 조직의 효율을 향상시킬 수 있다

> Chefs at A1 Restaurant are ------- of customizing dishes to suit any diner's preferences.
> (A) capable (B) knowledgeable

27 beneficial to

• ~에 이로운

> [기출] be **beneficial to** the community
> 지역사회에 이롭다
>
> be **beneficial to** both companies
> 양사에 모두 이롭다

> Although the cost of constructing the entertainment complex is high, city council members agreed that the project will be ------- to the economy.
> (A) financial (B) beneficial

28 applicable toward

~에 적용될 수 있는

기출 be **applicable toward** the purchase of new freezers
새로운 냉동고 구매에 적용될 수 있다

The $50 coupon is ------- toward the membership renewal fee at Hurley Gym.

(A) diverted   (B) applicable

29 familiar with

~에 익숙한

기출 analysts **familiar with** the housing market
주택 시장에 익숙한 분석가들

be not **familiar with** the new software program
새로운 소프트웨어 프로그램에 익숙하지 않다

Many environmental scientists ------- with the Wolong region predict that temperatures will continue to rise over the coming months.

(A) recognizable   (B) familiar

30 skeptical of

~에 회의적인

기출 be **skeptical of** the marketing campaign
마케팅 캠페인에 회의적이다

Mr. Tarrant was ------- of reducing the overtime rate paid to the company's employees, believing that many workers would resign.

(A) skeptical   (B) capable

31 exempt from

• ~에서 면제된

기출 be **exempt from** turning in receipts
영수증을 제출하는 것에서 면제되다

To check whether your vehicle is ------- from the parking fee, please refer to the information board.
(A) replaced   (B) exempt

32 similar to

• ~와 유사한

기출 be **similar to** other models
다른 모델들과 유사하다

be **similar to** the style of existing structures
현존하는 구조물의 스타일과 유사하다

Although the latest edition of the travel guide is ------- to previous versions, it does include an improved map of the city.
(A) similar   (B) likable

33 qualified for

• ~에 대한 자격을 갖춘

기출 be most **qualified for** the position
그 직책에 대해 가장 나은 자격을 갖추다

be well **qualified for** the managerial role
관리자 직책에 대해 충분한 자격을 갖추다

Ms. Chung will conduct a series of interviews this week before selecting the candidate best ------- for the role.
(A) qualified   (B) employed

34 compatible with

~와 호환되는, 어울리는

기출 be **compatible with** most television brands
대부분의 TV 브랜드와 호환되다

be **compatible with** our needs
우리의 요구와 어울리다

Your new Hive home heating hub is ------- with all Hive radiator smart valves.

(A) compatible (B) reflective

35 enthusiastic about

~에 대해 열정적인

기출 be **enthusiastic about** the advertising campaign
광고 캠페인에 대해 열정적이다

The new documentary filmed by Edmond Atherton will particularly appeal to those who are ------- about travel and exploration.

(A) enthusiastic (B) pleasant

36 appreciative of

~에 대해 감사하는

기출 seem **appreciative of** our efforts
우리의 노력에 감사하는 것처럼 보인다

Zanzibar Beach Resort is ------- of your feedback, and we look forward to welcoming you again on your next visit.

(A) decisive (B) appreciative

37 superior to

- ~보다 우수한

  기출 **superior to** other leading brands
  다른 선도적인 브랜드들보다 우수한

  Extra-long battery life and an extremely powerful operating system make the Zio 3 mobile phone ------- to other leading models.
  (A) advanced　　　(B) superior

38 credited with

- ~에 대해 (공로를) 인정받은

  기출 be **credited with** the restoration of the monument
  기념비의 복원에 대해 공로를 인정받다

  Mr. Rollins is ------- with increasing the firm's annual earnings by 20 percent since assuming the role of CFO last year.
  (A) credited　　　(B) agreed

39 selective about

- ~에 대해 까다로운

  기출 be **selective about** which article they publish
  어떤 기사를 출간할지에 대해 까다롭다

  The owners of Ealing Modern Art Gallery are ------- about which artworks they exhibit.
  (A) prominent　　　(B) selective

40 equipped with

- ~을 갖추고 있는

  기출 be **equipped with** many expensive devices
  많은 값비싼 기기들을 갖추고 있다

  All of the chalets at Zell Ski Resort are ------- with a hot tub and a barbecue.
  (A) conducted　　　(B) equipped

DAILY QUIZ

콜로케이션과 그에 알맞은 뜻을 연결해 보세요.

1. enthusiastic about • • (A) ~로 분리된
2. equivalent to • • (B) ~와 동등한
3. divided into • • (C) ~에 대해 열정적인

빈칸에 알맞은 단어를 선택하세요.

4. be currently ------- in Dubai
   현재 두바이에 본사를 두다

5. appear ------- to a natural diamond
   천연 다이아몬드와 동일하게 보이다

   (A) aware
   (B) identical
   (C) exempt
   (D) based

6. be ------- of all the factory's operations
   모든 공장의 운영을 알고 있다

앞서 배운 콜로케이션들의 뜻을 생각하면서, 다음 문제를 풀어보세요.

7. Any hotel guests who are ------- in the morning yoga classes should come to the fitness center at 7 AM.

   (A) skilled   (B) connected
   (C) interested   (D) contained

8. The report based on the recently compiled market research findings only includes details that are ------- to our current projects.

   (A) acceptable   (B) completed
   (C) relevant   (D) certain

정답 1 (C) 2 (B) 3 (A) 4 (D) 5 (B) 6 (A) 7 (C) 8 (C)

Day 05 독해가 쉬워지는 어휘 ❷ Part 7

1 in business

- 영업 중인

> After 20 years **in business**, our store is closing, and we'd like to express our gratitude through our closing sale.
> 20년간 영업한 끝에 저희 매장은 폐점할 예정이며, 폐점 세일 행사를 통해 저희의 감사한 마음을 표하고자 합니다.

만점 TIP

• 기출 Paraphrasing
  close (문을 닫다, 폐업하다) → no longer in business (더 이상 영업하지 않다), go out of business (폐업하다)

2 cater to

- v. ~의 마음에 들다, ~을 만족시키다

> The resort offers a variety of activities, **catering to** guests of all ages and interests.
> 그 리조트는 다양한 활동을 제공하여 모든 연령대와 관심사의 고객들을 만족시키고 있습니다.

만점 TIP

• 기출 Paraphrasing
  cater to → appeal to (~의 마음에 들다)

3 boast

- v. 뽐내다, 자랑하다, 자랑할 만한 ~을 갖고 있다

> The hotel **boasts** breathtaking ocean views from every room, offering guests a remarkable experience.
> 그 호텔은 모든 객실에서 숨막히게 아름다운 바다 전망을 자랑하며, 고객들에게 놀라운 경험을 선사합니다.

4 culinary

a. 요리의

To thrive in the competitive **culinary** market, businesses need to stay updated with the latest food trends and adapt their menus accordingly.

경쟁적인 요리 시장에서 번창하기 위해서, 사업체들은 최신 음식 트렌드를 계속 최신화하고 그에 따라 메뉴를 조정할 필요가 있습니다.

5 disposable

a. 일회용의

Our catering service specializes in eco-friendly events and offers **disposable** utensils made from biodegradable materials.

저희 케이터링 서비스는 환경친화적인 행사를 전문적으로 하고 있으며, 생분해성 물질로 만들어진 일회용품들을 제공합니다.

만점 TIP
- 기출 Paraphrasing
  dispose of ~을 처리하다, 없애다

6 customized

customize v. ~을 주문 제작하다
custom a. 주문 제작한

a. 주문 제작의, 맞춤의

The fitness app provides users with **customized** workout routines based on their fitness levels and goals.

이 피트니스 앱은 사용자의 체력 수준과 목표에 따라 맞춤형 운동 루틴을 제공합니다.

만점 TIP
- 기출 Paraphrasing
  customized → personalized (개인의 필요에 맞춘)

7 proof of purchase

● 구매 증명(서)

Our store's return policy mandates that all items returned must be accompanied by a **proof of purchase**.

저희 매장의 반품 규정은 반품되는 모든 상품에 반드시 구매 증명서를 첨부하는 것을 의무화하고 있습니다.

만점 TIP

• 기출 Paraphrasing
  proof of purchase → receipt (영수증)

8 retailer

retail n. 소매(업)

● n. 소매업자, 소매상, 소매업

The **retailer**'s summer sale attracted a large crowd of shoppers looking for discounts.

그 소매점의 여름 세일은 할인을 원하는 많은 쇼핑객들을 끌어들였습니다.

만점 TIP

• 관련 기출
  wholesaler 도매업자
  distributor 유통업자, 판매대리점
  supplier / provider 공급업자
  vendor 판매업자

9 dietary preference

● 식단 선호 사항

We offer a diverse menu that caters to various needs. Please let us know if you have any specific **dietary preferences** or requirements.

저희는 여러 필요 사항을 만족시키는 다양한 메뉴를 제공하고 있습니다. 특정 식사 선호 사항이나 요청 사항이 있으시면 말씀해 주세요.

10 worth + 명사

• ~을 들일 만한 가치가 있는

> Many customers find that the premium features of this smartphone make it **worth** the money spent.
> 많은 고객들은 이 스마트폰의 프리미엄 기능들이 돈을 들일 가치가 있다고 생각합니다.

11 save + 금액

• (~만큼) 아끼다, 절약하다

> Upgrade your subscription plan now and **save** $50 on your annual membership fee.
> 지금 구독 요금제를 업그레이드하고 연회비를 50달러 절약하세요.

만점 TIP
• 기출 Paraphrasing
  save $50 → a discount (할인)

12 query

• n. 질문, 문의 사항

> The tech support team is available to respond to all **queries** concerning software installation and troubleshooting.
> 기술 지원 팀은 소프트웨어 설치 및 문제 해결과 관련된 모든 문의에 응답할 수 있습니다.

만점 TIP
• 기출 Paraphrasing
  query → question, inquiry (질문, 의문 사항)

13 drawing

• n. 제비뽑기, 추첨

> The grand opening event concluded with the **drawing** of lucky numbers for prizes.
> 그 개점 행사는 경품을 주는 행운의 숫자 추첨으로 끝났습니다.

14 payment arrangements

- 결제 방식, 지불 약정

We offer flexible **payment arrangements** to accommodate various budget constraints and financial situations.
저희는 다양한 예산 제약과 재정 상황에 맞출 수 있는 유연한 지불 방법을 제공합니다.

만점 TIP
- 기출 Paraphrasing
  payment arrangements → payment plans

15 back order

- 밀린 주문, 이월 주문

The tool you were hoping to purchase is on **back order** because of a temporary halt in production.
귀하께서 구매하고 싶어하셨던 공구가 일시적인 생산 중단으로 인해 주문이 밀려 있습니다.

만점 TIP
- 기출 Paraphrasing
  back order → delay (지연)

16 produce

- n. 농산물

The grocery store offers a continuous supply of fresh and organic **produce** throughout the year.
그 식료품점은 연중 내내 신선하고 유기농으로 재배된 농산물을 지속적으로 공급합니다.

만점 TIP
- produce가 동사로 쓰일 경우 '~을 생산하다'라는 뜻이며, 이때의 명사형은 production(생산)입니다.

17 act up
- 말을 안 듣다, 제 기능을 못하다

> The old washing machine has been **acting up** lately, making strange noises during the spin cycle.
> 그 오래된 세탁기는 최근 제 기능을 못하고 있는데, 회전하는 동안 이상한 소리를 냅니다.

18 customer base
- 고객층, 고객 기반

> By introducing a user-friendly mobile app, the bank aims to expand its **customer base** across a younger demographic.
> 그 은행은 사용자 친화적인 모바일 앱을 도입함으로써 젊은 인구층에 걸쳐 고객 기반을 확대하는 것을 목표로 하고 있습니다.

19 compact
- a. 소형의

> Due to their **compact** design, these new laptops are perfect for travelers who need a lightweight yet powerful device.
> 소형의 디자인으로 인해, 이 새로운 노트북들은 가벼우면서도 강력한 장치를 필요로 하는 여행객들에게 안성맞춤입니다.

만점 TIP
- 제품의 특징을 나타내는 빈출 형용사
  durable 튼튼한
  lightweight 가벼운

20 portable
- a. 휴대용의

> This compact camera is not only **portable** but also features advanced settings for professional-quality shots.
> 이 소형 카메라는 휴대용일 뿐만 아니라 전문가 수준의 촬영을 위한 고급 설정 기능도 갖추고 있습니다.

21 synthetic

synthesize v. 합성하다

a. 합성의

The **synthetic** material developed by the research team offers a solution for lightweight, durable, and eco-friendly packaging.
연구팀이 개발한 합성 소재는 가볍고 내구성이 뛰어나며 친환경적인 포장에 대한 해결책을 제공합니다.

22 existing

a. 기존의

We have exciting promotions and exclusive offers available for both new and **existing** customers.
저희는 신규 고객과 기존 고객 모두에게 흥미로운 프로모션과 독점 혜택을 제공합니다.

23 violation

n. 위반

We regret to inform you that your restaurant was in **violation** of the city's Health and Sanitation Code.
귀하의 레스토랑이 시의 보건 및 위생 규정을 위반했다는 사실을 알려 드리게 되어 유감입니다.

만점 TIP
• 관련 기출
in violation of ~을 위반하여

24 reduced

reduce v. ~을 줄이다
reduction n. 축소, 삭감, 감소

a. 할인된, 줄어든

Tickets to the concert will be available at the door, or you can purchase them in advance at **reduced** rates.
콘서트 티켓은 문 앞에서 구매 가능하며, 할인된 가격으로 미리 구매하실 수도 있습니다.

만점 TIP
• 관련 기출
reduction in price 가격 인하

25 urge

- v. ~에게 권고하다, 촉구하다
- n. 충동

> The hotel **urged** customers to provide feedback on their recent stay to help improve their services.
> 호텔 측은 서비스를 개선하기 위해 고객들에게 최근 숙박에 대한 피드백을 제공할 것을 촉구했습니다.

26 component

- n. 구성품, 구성 요소

> To receive a full refund, the product must be returned with all its **components** and in its original packaging.
> 전액 환불을 받기 위해서는 제품이 모든 구성품들과 함께 원래의 포장 상태로 반환되어야 합니다.

27 fall short of

- ~에 못 미치다

> The restaurant's new menu items **fell short of** customers' expectations, leading to a decline in customer satisfaction.
> 식당의 신메뉴가 손님들의 기대에 미치지 못해 손님 만족도가 떨어졌습니다.

28 upon request

- 요청 시에

> Complimentary gift wrapping is offered **upon request** for all purchases.
> 모든 구매품에 대해 요청 시에 무료 선물 포장이 제공됩니다.

29 attend to

● ~을 처리하다

The hotel's concierge will **attend to** special requests you may have during your stay.

호텔 컨시어지가 귀하의 투숙 기간 동안 귀하의 특별 요청 사항을 처리해 드릴 것입니다.

만점 TIP
• 타동사 attend는 '~에 참석하다'라는 뜻입니다.

30 showcase

● v. ~을 선보이다, 소개하다
n. 공개 행사

The upcoming culinary event will **showcase** a diverse array of dishes from around the world.

다가오는 요리 행사는 전 세계의 다양한 요리들을 선보일 것입니다.

31 preview

● n. 시사회

The designer showcased her new collection at the fashion show's exclusive **preview**.

그 디자이너는 패션쇼의 단독 시사회에서 자신의 새로운 컬렉션을 선보였습니다.

만점 TIP
• 관련 기출
  premiere 개봉, 초연, 첫 공연

32 assembly

assemble v. ~을 조립하다

● n. 조립

If you find the **assembly** instructions to be unclear, don't hesitate to reach out to our customer support team for guidance.

조립 설명서가 명확하지 않다고 생각하시면, 주저 말고 저희 고객 지원 팀에 연락하셔서 안내를 받으시기 바랍니다.

33 endorsement

endorse v. ~을 지지하다, 보증하다

- n. 유명인이 광고에 나와서 하는 상품 홍보

The skincare brand gained popularity thanks to a celebrity **endorsement** by a famous actress who raved about their products.

그 스킨케어 브랜드는 자사 제품에 대해 극찬한 유명 여배우의 상품 홍보 덕분에 인기를 얻었습니다.

34 label A with B

- A에 B를 표시한 라벨을 붙이다

The curator **labeled** each piece of artwork **with** the artist's name, title, and year of creation to provide context for visitors.

그 큐레이터는 방문객들에게 맥락을 제공하기 위해 각각의 작품에 작가의 이름, 제목, 그리고 창작 연도를 표시한 라벨을 붙였습니다.

35 testimonial

- n. 추천의 글, 증명서

The website is filled with positive **testimonials** from clients who have benefited from our consulting service.

웹사이트는 저희 컨설팅 서비스의 혜택을 받은 고객들의 긍정적인 추천 글로 가득 차 있습니다.

36 poll

- n. 여론 조사, 설문조사

We conducted a **poll** to gather opinions on the proposed changes to the homepage layout.

저희는 홈페이지 레이아웃 변경안에 대한 의견을 수렴하기 위해 여론 조사를 실시하였습니다.

만점 TIP

- 기출 Paraphrasing
  poll → survey
- 관련 기출
  conduct a poll[survey] 설문 조사를 실시하다

37 deduct

- v. ~을 공제하다

> If you choose to return the product, please note that the shipping charge will be **deducted** from your refund.
> 반품하실 경우 배송비는 환불금액에서 공제된다는 점을 참고 부탁드립니다.

38 energy-efficient

- a. 에너지 효율이 좋은

> The new appliances are designed to be highly **energy-efficient**, reducing your electricity bills.
> 새 가전제품은 에너지 효율이 높도록 설계되어 있어, 귀하의 전기료를 절감시켜 줍니다.

39 household

- a. 가정용의

> All Bay View apartments are equipped with energy-efficient **household** appliances.
> 모든 베이 뷰 아파트에는 에너지 효율이 높은 가전제품이 설치되어 있습니다.

40 gain recognition

- 명성을 얻다

> The fitness app has **gained recognition** for its user-friendly interface and accurate health data tracking.
> 그 피트니스 앱은 사용자 친화적인 인터페이스와 정확한 건강 데이터 추적으로 명성을 얻었습니다.

만점 TIP

- 기출 Paraphrasing

  gain recognition → be recognized (인정받다)

DAILY QUIZ

단어와 그에 알맞은 뜻을 연결해 보세요.

1. testimonial • • (A) 추첨, 뽑기
2. endorsement • • (B) 유명인의 홍보
3. poll • • (C) 여론조사, 설문조사
4. drawing • • (D) 추천의 글

빈칸에 알맞은 단어를 선택하세요.

5. The newly opened restaurant ------- to all tastes, with a menu that includes a wide array of dishes from various international cuisines.
   새롭게 문을 연 그 레스토랑은 다양한 세계 각국의 요리를 포함하는 메뉴를 통해 모든 입맛을 충족시켜 드립니다.

   (A) caters
   (B) boasts
   (C) customized
   (D) reduced

6. Our catering services can be ------- to meet any dietary requirements, ensuring that every guest can enjoy their meal without any concerns.
   저희 케이터링 서비스는 그 어떤 식단 요구 사항도 맞추도록 주문 제작될 수 있으므로 모든 손님이 걱정 없이 식사를 즐길 수 있습니다.

7. The technology store ------- an impressive selection of the latest gadgets, from cutting-edge smartphones to high-performance laptops.
   그 기술 매장에는 최첨단 스마트폰부터 고성능 노트북까지 다양한 최신 기기가 구비되어 있습니다.

8. Some of the major hotels in Hokkaido have ------- room rates as a way of attracting travelers during the off season.
   홋카이도의 일부 주요 호텔들은 비수기 동안 여행객을 유치하기 위해 객실 요금을 인하했습니다.

정답 1 (D) 2 (B) 3 (C) 4 (A) 5 (A) 6 (C) 7 (B) 8 (D)

/ Week /
06 실전 TEST

 MP3 바로듣기
 강의 바로보기

LISTENING

• Part 3

1. What are the speakers discussing?

    (A) A technology conference
    (B) A yearly event
    (C) A product launch
    (D) An employment contract

2. What does the man mention about a caterer?

    (A) It was affordable to reserve.
    (B) There will be many staff on site.
    (C) The food quality is outstanding.
    (D) It will serve unlimited refreshments.

3. What is the woman concerned about?

    (A) Finding a venue
    (B) Meeting a deadline
    (C) Getting stuck in traffic
    (D) Staying within a budget

• Part 4

4. Who are the listeners?

    (A) New interns
    (B) Potential investors
    (C) Research participants
    (D) Security workers

5. What has been revised recently?

    (A) A construction proposal
    (B) A reimbursement policy
    (C) An office floorplan
    (D) Some safety guidelines

6. What will the speaker do next?

    (A) Demonstrate how to use a machine
    (B) Set aside a product for inspection
    (C) Handle a customer inquiry
    (D) Give a tour of a workplace

READING

• Part 5

7. The recently hired sales team manager had the ------- target of attracting 250 new customers in his first month.

   (A) prosperous
   (B) spacious
   (C) qualified
   (D) ambitious

8. Because staff ability and experience are crucial to our firm, an employment background check is ------- for all job applicants.

   (A) liable
   (B) potential
   (C) renewable
   (D) mandatory

9. Hotel guests must be ------- if they intend to board our scheduled airport shuttle bus.

   (A) eventual
   (B) immediate
   (C) punctual
   (D) accessible

10. Douglas Sports Center also has an ------- outdoor sports field that can accommodate several events consecutively.

    (A) alert
    (B) immense
    (C) automatic
    (D) eager

11. A ------- date for this year's jazz festival has been set, but it depends on whether the venue will be renovated in time.

    (A) considerable
    (B) pending
    (C) sudden
    (D) tentative

12. The manufacturing process proposed by Mr. Armitage would result in a ------- decrease in operating costs.

    (A) spacious
    (B) plenty
    (C) sizable
    (D) durable

13. The new interpretation service should make Gary's Private Car Hire more ------- to foreign tourists.

    (A) concerned
    (B) separated
    (C) attractive
    (D) renewed

14. The rooms being renovated on the fourth floor will be ------- for meetings by 9 AM on Monday, January 23.

    (A) grateful
    (B) available
    (C) generous
    (D) relevant

Part 6

Questions 15-18 refer to the following e-mail.

To: Shinsuke Ito <s.Ito@bestapparel.com>
From: Grant Wood <gwood@mbtextiles.com>
Subject: Samples

Dear Mr. Ito,

We welcome the inquiry you made on June 20 and thank you for your interest in our products. Our catalog and some samples are being sent to you today **15.** ------- express mail. Unfortunately, we cannot send you a full range of samples at the present time, but the samples are of the same high quality as the finished products.

16. -------. Mr. Kim, our overseas director, will be in Japan early next month and will be pleased to call on you. He will have a wide range of our products with him, and when you see them, we believe you will agree that the quality of the material and the high standard of craftsmanship will appeal to those who are **17.** ------- about which products they buy.

We very much look forward to **18.** ------- an order from you.

Regards,

Grant Wood

15. (A) with
(B) by
(C) for
(D) in

16. (A) We would like for you to come to our head office.
(B) Our products will be sent out to you tomorrow.
(C) Thank you for sending your feedback on our products.
(D) I have an idea for how you can see our merchandise.

17. (A) preferable
(B) curious
(C) selective
(D) prominent

18. (A) receive
(B) received
(C) be received
(D) receiving

Part 7

Questions 19-20 refer to the following Web page.

---

http://www.heavenlycatering.com/aboutus

| **ABOUT US** | OUR SERVICES | GALLERY | CONTACT | REVIEWS |

Heavenly Catering has been in business for seven years and now boasts an extensive customer base after gaining recognition for our culinary expertise. We offer customized menus upon request, accommodating all dietary preferences and clearly label dishes with stickers displaying the presence of potential allergens. To preview the foods we can provide, we urge you to visit our gallery, which showcases some of our most popular dishes.

In recent years, we have strived to become more environmentally friendly. Although we were never in violation of any governmental standards, we decided to stop using synthetic components and installed energy-efficient kitchen appliances. This approach was also applied to our compact and portable lunchbox range.

If you have a query about our products and services, please contact us! First-time clients can save $50 off their first catering service.

---

19. What is true about Heavenly Catering?

(A) It was founded ten years ago.
(B) It operates in several business locations.
(C) It is currently hiring new staff.
(D) It includes images of food on its Web site.

20. What did Heavenly Catering do to help the environment?

(A) It made a charitable donation.
(B) It changed its delivery service.
(C) It installed new equipment.
(D) It introduced metal cutlery.

서아쌤의
토익
비밀과외
기출 VOCA

Week 07

Contents	Page	Date	Check
Day 01 `Part 3, 4` 기출 패러프레이징 ②	444	월 일	☐
Day 02 `Part 5, 6` 부사 ①	458	월 일	☐
Day 03 `Part 5, 6` 부사 ②	472	월 일	☐
Day 04 `Part 5, 6` 동사 + 부사 콜로케이션	486	월 일	☐
Day 05 `Part 7` 독해가 쉬워지는 어휘 ③	500	월 일	☐
Week 07 실전 TEST	512	월 일	☐

Day 01 기출 패러프레이징 ❷ Part 3, 4

 MP3 바로듣기   강의 바로보기

QR코드 하나를 가리고 찍으면 편해요!

1 book

- make a reservation, reserve 예약하다
- schedule 일정을 잡다

~을 예약하다

M: I'd like to **reserve** two tickets for tonight's city bus tour which departs at 7 PM from the main square.

중앙 광장에서 오후 7시에 출발하는 오늘 밤 시내버스 투어 표 두 장을 예약하고 싶습니다.

Q. 무엇을 하고자 하는가?
→ **Book** a tour

2 missing

- misplaced, lost 없어진
- doesn't include 포함되어 있지 않다
- haven't received 받지 못했다
- can't find[locate] 어디 있는지 모르겠다

행방을 모르는

W: When we converted the client files to digital versions last week, the most recent entries seem to have been **lost**.

지난주에 고객 기록을 디지털 버전으로 변환했을 때, 가장 최근에 입력한 항목들이 없어진 것 같습니다.

Q. 무엇에 대해 얘기하는가?
→ **Missing** information

3 straightforward

- not complicated 복잡하지 않은
- simple 간단한
- easy to follow 따라하기 쉬운

간단한, 쉬운

M: His pasta sauce recipe is quite **straightforward**. Just follow the steps, and you'll have a delicious sauce in no time.

그의 파스타 소스 레시피는 아주 간단합니다. 순서대로 따라가기만 하면 금방 맛있는 소스가 나옵니다.

Q. 레시피에 대해 뭐라고 하는가?
→ It is **easy to follow**.

4 consumer

- customer 고객

● 소비자

W: The biggest trend has been about reducing sugar content. According to a recent **customer** survey, more people want healthier products, but the same great taste.

가장 큰 트렌드는 설탕 함량을 줄이는 것이었습니다. 최근 소비자 조사에 따르면, 더 많은 사람들이 더 건강한, 그러나 똑같이 좋은 맛의 제품을 원합니다.

Q. 무엇에 대해 얘기하고 있는가?
→ A change in **consumer** preferences

5 vendor

- seller 판매자
- supplier, provider 공급업자

● 판매자

M: The **vendor** that we usually order fresh eggs from has increased their prices. We should consider finding another one.

우리가 신선한 계란을 주로 주문하는 판매자가 가격을 올렸습니다. 다른 곳을 찾는 걸 고려해 봐야겠어요.

Q. 무엇을 제안하는가?
→ Hiring a new **supplier**

6 replace

- substitute ~로 대체하다

● ~을 대체하다

W: Tonight's chef special is salmon steak, but unfortunately, we've run out of salmon, so we're **substituting** bass for the fish-of-the-day.

오늘 밤의 셰프 특선은 연어 스테이크입니다만, 아쉽게도 연어가 다 떨어져서 오늘의 생선을 배스로 대체하고 있습니다.

Q. 무엇을 발표하는가?
→ A food item has been **replaced**.

만점 TIP
- 관련 기출
  substitute A for B B를 A로 대체하다, B 대신 A를 사용하다

7 update

- add A to B A를 B에 추가하다

~을 최신 버전으로 바꾸다

M: I'll **add** the new project deadline **to** the calendar to ensure that we stay on track.

새로운 프로젝트 마감일을 달력에 추가해서 저희가 순조롭게 진행할 수 있도록 하겠습니다.

Q. 무엇을 하겠다고 하는가?
→ **Update** a calendar

8 donate

- all proceeds will go toward
  모든 수익금은 ~로 갈 것입니다
- contribute
  기부하다, 기증하다
- financial support
  재정적 지원

~을 기부하다

W: **All** the **proceeds** from the fundraiser **will go toward** Sunshine Children's Hospital.

모금 행사의 모든 수익금은 썬샤인 어린이 병원으로 가게 될 것입니다.

Q. 수익금은 어떻게 될 것인가?
→ They will be **donated** to a hospital.

9 distribute

- hand out, give out
  나눠주다

~을 배부하다, 나눠주다

M: I'm organizing a charity concert at the park, and we're looking for volunteers to help **give out** flyers. Would you be interested in joining us?

공원에서 자선 콘서트를 준비하고 있는데, 전단지를 나눠줄 자원봉사자를 찾고 있습니다. 함께 하실 생각이 있으신가요?

Q. 지원자들은 무엇을 하는가?
→ **Distribute** promotional materials

> **만점 TIP**
>
> - 상위어 Paraphrasing
>
>   brochure, pamphlet, booklet, flyer, leaflet
>   → promotional materials (홍보물)
>
>   books, magazine, newspaper → reading materials (읽을 거리)

10 discount

- reduced rate 할인가
- 50 percent off 50% 할인
- save 50% 50%를 아끼다

• 할인

W: I saw online that you're running a special deal for new members: **30 percent off** the first month's subscription. Can I sign up for that?

온라인에서 보니까 신규 가입자를 위해 첫 달 구독료를 30% 할인해 주는 특가 상품을 제공 중이시네요. 가입할 수 있을까요?

Q. 무엇에 대해 문의하는가?
→ A subscription **discount**

11 locate

- find 찾아내다

• ~의 위치를 찾아내다

M: Have you heard about this new app called EasyPark? It helps you **find** parking spaces more easily.

이지파크라는 이 새로운 앱에 대해 들어본 적이 있나요? 이 앱은 주차 공간의 위치를 더 쉽게 찾을 수 있도록 도와줍니다.

Q. 앱이 무엇을 하는 데 도움이 되는가?
→ **Locate** available parking spaces

12 initiative

- plan 계획

• 계획

W: Next month, we're launching a new **initiative** within our company. It focuses on implementing environmentally friendly practices across all our operations.

다음 달에 회사 내에서 새로운 계획을 시작합니다. 그것은 전 운영에 걸쳐 환경 친화적인 관행을 실시하는 데 중점을 두고 있습니다.

Q. 다음 달에 무엇이 시작되는가?
→ An eco-friendly **plan**

13 manufacturing facility

- factory, plant 공장

● 제조 시설

M: I'm going to their **manufacturing facility** this afternoon to inspect the quality control processes and address any production issues.

오늘 오후에 제조 시설에 가서 품질 관리 과정을 검사하고 생산 관련 문제를 처리할 것입니다.

Q: 오후에 무엇을 할 것인가?
→ Visit a **factory**

14 fill out

- complete 작성하다

● ~을 작성하다

W: I'll e-mail the link to the online registration form. If you'd like to sign up for our membership, please **fill out** the form by the end of this week.

온라인 등록 양식 링크를 이메일로 보내드리겠습니다. 회원 가입을 원하시면 이번 주 말까지 양식을 작성해주세요.

Q. 등록하려면 어떻게 하는가?
→ **Complete** a form

15 feedback

- opinion, thoughts 의견, 생각
- suggestion 제안
- what you think 어떻게 생각하는지
- input 조언

● 피드백, 의견

M: Please share your **opinions** with us so we can improve the design for the cover page.

표지 디자인을 개선할 수 있도록 의견을 공유해 주시기 바랍니다.

Q. 무엇을 요청하는가?
→ Some **feedback**

16 authorize

- approve, give approval
  승인하다

● ~을 승인하다

W: As supervisor, I'll **approve** your travel expense claims once you submit the necessary documentation and receipts.

관리자로서, 필요한 서류와 영수증을 제출하시면 출장 경비 청구를 승인해드리겠습니다.

Q. 무엇을 해주겠다고 하는가?
→ **Authorize** some reimbursements

17 manager

- supervisor
  관리자, 감독관, 상사

● 매니저, 관리자

M: Let me call my **manager**. She'll have to authorize the transaction so I can process the refund.

저희 매니저님께 전화해볼게요. 제가 환불을 진행해 드릴 수 있으려면 매니저님께서 처리를 승인해주셔야 해요.

Q. 무엇을 할 것인가?
→ Call a **supervisor**

18 government official

- mayor 시장
- city council member
  시의회 의원

● 정부 관리

W: We plan to collaborate with the **mayor** and **city council** to increase the number of bicycle lanes throughout the city streets.

도시 거리 곳곳에 자전거 전용도로 수를 늘리기 위해 시장 및 시의회와 협력할 계획입니다.

Q. 누구와 협력할 것인가?
→ **Government officials**

19 workshop

- training session 교육, 연수

● 워크숍, 교육

M: Thanks for attending this food safety **workshop**. Today, you'll learn how to handle food safely and prevent potential hazards.

식품 안전 워크숍에 참석해 주셔서 감사합니다. 오늘은 음식을 안전하게 다루는 방법과 잠재적인 위험을 방지하는 방법을 배울 것입니다.

Q. 무엇이 열리고 있는가?
→ A **training session**

20 popular

- hit, success 성공
- many people signed up 많은 사람들이 신청했다
- well received 호평을 받은

● 인기 있는

W: The workshop on health and wellness was a huge **hit**; **a lot of people signed up**, and it was very **well received** by the employees.

건강에 대한 그 워크숍은 큰 성공을 거두었습니다. 많은 사람들이 신청했고, 직원들에게 호평을 받았습니다.

Q. 워크숍에 대해 뭐라고 하는가?
→ It was very **popular**.

21 review

- look over 검토하다
- take a look at 한번 보다

● ~을 검토하다

M: Why don't you **look over** the results of the survey we distributed to customers last week?

지난주에 우리가 고객들에게 배포한 설문조사 결과를 검토해 보시는 것이 어떨까요?

Q. 무엇을 제안하는가?
→ **Review** some survey results

22 **directions to**

- how to get to ~로 가는 길

~로 가는 길안내

W: The Highbright Building is less than a 10-minute walk from here. Let me show you **how to get there**.

하이브라이트 빌딩은 여기서 걸어서 10분도 안 걸립니다. 제가 가는 길을 알려드리겠습니다.

Q. 무엇을 해주겠다고 하는가?
→ Provide **directions**

23 **work overtime**

- work extra hours 잔업을 하다
- stay late at work 늦게까지 일하다

초과 근무를 하다

M: Management appreciates that your team **stayed late at work** last week. You all did a great job to complete the rush order.

경영진은 지난주 귀하의 팀이 야근한 것에 대해 감사하고 있습니다. 다들 급한 주문 건을 완료하느라 수고 많으셨습니다.

Q. 무엇에 대해 감사하는가?
→ **Working overtime**

24 **socialize with**

- interact with 상호작용을 하다, 교류하다

~와 교류하다, 사귀다

W: Why don't you sign up for the company sports day? It's a good way to **interact with** coworkers outside of work.

회사 운동회에 등록해 보는 건 어때요? 직장 밖에서 동료들과 교류하는 좋은 방법이에요.

Q. 왜 행사에 참가하라고 권하는가?
→ To **socialize with** coworkers

25 competition
- contest 대회, 시합
- race 경주

● 경연 대회, 시합

M: The library will be holding a children's poster **competition** next month, and the city mayor will be the judge.

도서관은 다음 달 어린이 포스터 대회를 열 예정인데, 시장님께서 심사를 맡으실 것입니다.

Q. 다음 달에 무엇이 열릴 것인가?
→ A poster **contest**

26 coupon
- voucher 바우처, 할인권, 쿠폰
- gift certificate 상품권

● 쿠폰, 할인권

W: This flight is overbooked. If you're alright with departing at 10 PM tonight, I can give you a **coupon** for 200 euros off a future flight.

이 항공편은 초과 예약되었습니다. 오늘 밤 10시에 출발해도 괜찮으시다면, 추후 항공편에서 200유로를 할인받을 수 있는 쿠폰을 드릴 수 있습니다.

Q. 무엇을 제시하는가?
→ A discount **voucher**

27 workstation
- desk 책상

● 업무 공간, 작업대

M: Upon request, we can replace your current **desk** with a new one. Simply e-mail the Human Resources department and let them know.

요청하시면 현재 책상을 새 것으로 교체해 드릴 수 있습니다. 인사부에 이메일을 보내 알려주시기만 하면 됩니다.

Q. 무엇을 발표하는가?
→ A **workstation** upgrade

28 dimension

- measurements 치수
- size 크기

● 측정값, 사이즈

W: I can't provide you with a final cost estimate without the exact **dimensions** of each room. Can you please call me back with this information?

각 방의 정확한 사이즈 없이는 최종적인 비용 견적을 드릴 수 없습니다. 해당 정보를 가지고 다시 전화해 주시겠습니까?

Q. 무엇을 요청하는가?
→ Some room **measurements**

29 expand

- open additional stores
  추가로 매장을 열다

● (사업 등을) 확장하다

M: My goal is to **open additional stores** in the future, hopefully within the next 5 years. I think my business has great potential.

제 목표는 앞으로 5년 안에 추가로 매장들을 여는 것입니다. 저는 제 사업이 큰 잠재력을 가지고 있다고 생각합니다.

Q. 5년 안에 무엇을 하겠다고 하는가?
→ **Expand** his business

30 examine

- inspect 검사하다

● ~을 자세히 살펴보다

W: In that case, can you **inspect** the welding machine right now? Our in-house technician is off for the day.

그럼 지금 바로 용접기를 검사해주실 수 있나요? 사내 기술자가 오늘 휴무입니다.

Q. 무엇을 해달라고 하는가?
→ **Examine** some equipment

31 collect

- get 얻다
- gather 모으다

● ~을 수집하다, 모으다

M: I'd like to hold a team meeting to **get** everyone's thoughts about how things went and what we can improve with our next project.

저는 팀 미팅을 개최하여 어떻게 일이 진행되었는지, 다음 프로젝트에서 개선할 수 있는 것이 무엇인지에 대해 모두의 의견을 얻고자 합니다.

Q. 왜 팀회의를 열고자 하는가?
→ To **collect** feedback

32 inaccurate

- wrong, incorrect
  틀린, 잘못된

● 부정확한

W: I believe I've been billed **incorrectly**. I just moved in two days ago, so I wasn't the one using the water in this apartment unit last week.

요금이 잘못 청구된 것 같아요. 저는 이틀 전에 이사를 와서, 지난주까지 이 아파트에서 물을 사용한 사람은 제가 아니에요.

Q. 무엇에 대해 말하는가?
→ An **inaccurate** charge

33 survey

- questionnaire, poll
  설문조사

● 설문조사

M: I finished analyzing the data from the employee **questionnaire**. Overall, the results indicate that staff are satisfied with the office's new open layout.

직원 설문조사 자료 분석을 마쳤습니다. 전체적으로 사무실의 새로운 개방 설계에 대한 직원들의 만족도가 높았습니다.

Q. 무엇에 대해 이야기하는가?
→ **Survey** results

만점 TIP

- 관련 기출
  conduct a survey[poll] 설문조사를 실시하다

34 professional

- expert, specialist 전문가

● 전문가

W: For today's conference, we've invited **experts** from the medical industry to speak about the emergence of artificial intelligence in healthcare.

오늘 컨퍼런스를 위해, 의료계 전문가들을 초청해 의료 분야의 인공지능 출현에 대해 강연해주시도록 하였습니다.

Q. 누가 행사에 초청되었는가?
→ Medical **professionals**

35 abroad

- overseas 해외의, 해외로, 해외에서

● 해외에(서), 해외로

M: During my time **abroad**, I've learned so many new skills and made many new friends. It has been a truly rewarding experience.

해외에 있는 동안 많은 새로운 기술들을 배우고 새로운 친구들을 많이 사귀었습니다. 정말 보람 있는 경험이었습니다.

Q. 무엇이 보람 있었다고 하는가?
→ Spending time **overseas**

36 renowned

- famous, well-known, noted, distinguished 유명한
- have a reputation, be widely known 잘 알려져 있다

● 유명한

W: Daron Goddard is a **renowned** entrepreneur with decades of experience in the tech industry. Why don't we consult with him?

대런 고다드 씨는 기술 산업에서 수십 년의 경험을 보유한 유명한 기업가입니다. 그와 상의해 보는 게 어때요?

Q. 누구에게 상의해보라고 하는가?
→ A **well-known** businessman

37 journalist
- reporter 기자
- my article for the newspaper
  신문에 싣기 위해 쓴 기사

● 언론인

M: My fellow **reporter** and I are from *Bay Area Times*, and we wanted to ask you a few questions about the new city construction initiative.
저와 동료 기자는 <베이 에리어 타임즈> 신문에서 나왔는데요, 신도시 건설 계획에 대해 몇 가지 질문을 드리고자 합니다.

Q. 남자의 직업은? ➜ **Journalist**

38 business hours
- open at ~, close at ~
  ~시에 개장하고 ~시에 폐점합니다
- hours of operation
  운영[영업] 시간

● 영업 시간

W: Instead of 5 PM, we will now be **closing at** 7, so be sure to make a note of that.
오후 5시 대신, 이제 7시에 문을 닫을 예정이오니, 꼭 메모해두시기 바랍니다.

Q. 무엇을 할 것인가? ➜ Extend some **business hours**

39 carpool
- drive together, share a car, share rides with
  함께 차를 타다

● 차를 함께 타다

M: I heard you have a similar commute to work. Would you be interested in **carpooling** together?
출퇴근 길이 비슷하시다고 들었어요. 같이 차를 타시겠어요?

Q. 무엇을 제안하는가? ➜ **Drive** to work **together**

40 commemorate
- celebrate 축하하다

● ~을 기념하다

W: I am truly honored to welcome you to this banquet to **celebrate** our 10th anniversary.
저희 창립 10주년을 축하하기 위한 만찬에 여러분을 모시게 되어 진심으로 영광입니다.

Q. 왜 모여 있는가?
➜ To **commemorate** a special day

DAILY QUIZ

🎧 질문을 읽고 음원을 들은 뒤, 정답을 골라보세요.

1 Where do the speakers most likely work?

(A) At a manufacturing facility
(B) At a grocery store

M: Hey Candace, production levels of our hand soaps at our factory have increased a lot this past week, so our supply of dispenser bottles is already getting low. Can you place an order for more bottles?
W: Sure, but which supplier should I contact?
M: Let's go with the provider that we used last time. They were very efficient.

2 Why is the man speaking to the woman?

(A) To reserve a train ticket
(B) To ask for directions

M: Excuse me, do you know how to get to the nearest subway station?
W: I sure do. See that bank over there? If you walk toward the bank and then turn left at the intersection, Seven Seas Station will be about three blocks further down.

3 What does the speaker say the listener will receive?

(A) A restaurant coupon
(B) A movie theater voucher

W: Hello, this is Su-min calling from Franklin Library. I'm happy to notify you that you have been chosen as the winner of our annual book review contest! Congratulations! You can pick up your prize, which is a gift certificate that is valid at any local cinema, if you stop by our library during our hours of operation.

정답 1 (A) 2 (B) 3 (B)

Day 02 부사 ❶ Part 5, 6

1 instead

● 대신(에)

> 기출 choose **instead** to focus on
> 대신 ~에 집중하기로 결정하다
>
> will be shown on Friday **instead**
> 대신 금요일에 상영될 것이다

> While Mr. Graves is on annual leave, the weekly work schedules will be created by Ms. Jones -------.
> (A) instead (B) likewise

2 therefore

● 그러므로, 따라서

> 기출 have more functions, **therefore** increasing the cost
> 더 많은 기능이 있으므로 비용을 증가시키다
>
> The deadline has been moved forward, and **therefore**, we need more staff.
> 마감일이 앞으로 당겨졌으며, 따라서 우리는 더 많은 직원이 필요하다.

> Jeffrey has already exceeded his monthly sales target. -------, he will be awarded a bonus.
> (A) Therefore (B) Otherwise

3 then

● 그리고 나서

> 기출 be first categorized by subject and **then** alphabetized
> 먼저 주제별로 분류되고 나서 알파벳 순으로 정렬되다

> Mr. Peele booked a venue for the fundraising event. He ------- created invitations to be sent to guests.
> (A) since (B) then

4 currently
현재

current a. 현재의

- 기출 **be currently seeking volunteers**
  현재 자원봉사자들을 구하는 중이다
- **be currently understaffed**
  현재 인원이 부족하다

> We plan to expand our distribution network before the end of this year. -------, we only deliver to customers based within Detroit.
>
> (A) Currently (B) Significantly

5 accordingly
그에 맞춰, (상황에) 따라서

according to prep. ~에 따르면

- 기출 **The bonus will be awarded accordingly.**
  보너스가 그에 맞춰 주어질 것이다.
- **The number of staff will be adjusted accordingly.**
  직원의 수가 상황에 따라서 조정될 것이다.

> Once a decision has been made regarding the changing of our restaurant's name, our menus will be changed -------.
>
> (A) accordingly (B) typically

만점 TIP
주로 Part 6에서 결과를 나타내는 내용을 이끄는 접속부사로 출제된다.

6 increasingly
점점 더

increasing a. 증가하는
increased a. 증가된
increase v. 증가시키다, 증가하다
　　　　 n. 증가

- 기출 **become increasingly concerned about**
  ~에 대해 점점 더 우려하게 되다
- **offset increasingly high energy costs**
  점점 더 높은 에너지 비용을 상쇄하다

> Musician Bill Maddison's songs became ------- popular after being featured in an award-winning television series.
>
> (A) increasingly (B) equally

Week 07 459

7 safely

safe a. 안전한
safety n. 안전

- 안전하게

  기출 access one's account **safely**
  ~의 계좌에 안전하게 접근하다

  lose weight **safely** through exercise
  운동을 통해 안전하게 체중을 줄이다

  All attendees at this year's music festival are reminded to behave ------- and responsibly.
  (A) safely (B) lively

8 financially

finance v. 재정을 조달하다
financial a. 재정의

- 재정적으로

  기출 do well **financially**
  재정적으로 잘하고 있다

  The lead architect has indicated that adding more structures to the shopping mall blueprint is not ------- feasible.
  (A) promptly (B) financially

9 already

- 이미, 벌써

  기출 have **already** turned in a registration form
  이미 등록서를 제출했다

  have **already** been installed
  벌써 설치되었다

  Mr. Shandwick found new ways to increase revenue at his ------- profitable business.
  (A) even (B) already

10 easily

easy a. 쉬운
ease n. 쉬움

● 쉽게

기출 can **easily** enroll online
온라인으로 쉽게 등록할 수 있다

accommodate tour groups **easily**
여행 단체들을 쉽게 수용하다

Tourists can ------- visit several attractions by joining the city's bus tours.

(A) easily   (B) lately

11 finally

final a. 마지막의, 최종의
finalize v. 마무리 짓다

● 마침내

기출 be **finally** accepted by the management
경영진에 의해 마침내 수락되다

be **finally** able to complete the report
마침내 보고서를 완료할 수 있다

After two months of negotiations, Archer Construction Inc. ------- won the contract to build the new international airport.

(A) finally   (B) totally

12 largely

large a. 커다란, (양이) 많은

● 주로, 대체로

기출 **largely** from one's experiences
주로 ~의 경험에서 온

The postponement of the city's annual film festival was due ------- to the proposed event site failing a safety inspection.

(A) ideally   (B) largely

만점 TIP
주로 be동사와 p.p./형용사 사이, 또는 부사구 앞 자리에서 품사 문제로 출제된다.

13 continually

continuous a. 계속되는

• 계속해서

기출 **continually** deliver superior service
우수한 서비스를 계속해서 내놓다

> In order to maximize production efficiency, the factory manager must ------- motivate the workers on the assembly line.
> (A) continually (B) finely

14 shortly

short a. 짧은
shorten v. 짧게 하다, 단축하다

• 곧

기출 be expected to reopen **shortly**
곧 다시 문을 열 것으로 예상되다

will be finished **shortly**
곧 끝날 것이다

> The issue with the faulty security cameras will be attended to ------- after we repair the third floor elevator.
> (A) nearly (B) shortly

15 almost

• 거의

기출 after **almost** 5 years of renovation
거의 5년의 보수공사 이후에

can do **almost** anything
거의 모든 것을 할 수 있다

> Thanks to the addition of our new roller coaster, our ticket sales have ------- tripled compared with last summer.
> (A) closely (B) almost

16 recently

recent a. 최근의

● 최근(에)

기출 **recently** became a permanent employee
최근 정규 직원이 되었다

has **recently** been awarded a contract
최근 계약을 따냈다

Vesuvius Software Company has ------- relocated to the industrial park on the outskirts of town.
(A) recently   (B) fairly

17 immediately

immediate a. 즉각적인

● 즉시

기출 in order to activate your membership **immediately**
회원권을 즉시 활성화시키기 위해

immediately after the items went on sale
물건들이 할인된 직후에

All factory visitors are required to put on safety equipment ------- upon arrival.
(A) immediately   (B) periodically

18 otherwise

● 다르게, 그렇지 않으면

기출 unless **otherwise** instructed
다르게 지시되어 있지 않다면

Please return the book by September 5. **Otherwise**, you'll be charged a late fee.
9월 5일까지 도서를 반납하세요. 그렇지 않으면, 귀하께 연체료가 부과될 것입니다.

Our range of delicious sauces can turn an ------- ordinary meal into a memorable dining experience.
(A) instead   (B) otherwise

만점 TIP
- otherwise는 Part 5에서는 주로 '다르게'라는 뜻으로, Part 6에서는 '그렇지 않으면'의 뜻 접속부사로 사용된다.

19 frequently

● 자주, 빈번하게

기출 **frequently** hold the meeting
자주 회의를 개최하다

be updated **frequently**
빈번하게 업데이트되다

All shelves at Greenway Supermarket are restocked ------- to ensure that customers can always find the items they need.
(A) frequently   (B) previously

20 usually

usual a. 보통의, 일상의

● 보통, 대개

기출 **usually** arrive at the office at 10 AM
보통 오전 10시에 사무실에 도착하다

be **usually** delayed
대개 지연되다

Game schedules and results are ------- posted on the baseball team's Web site.
(A) usually   (B) slightly

21 ahead

● 미리, 앞에

기출 plan **ahead**
미리 계획하다

be advised to call **ahead**
미리 전화하는 것을 권고하다

Temperatures in the coastal areas are anticipated to drop in the weeks -------.
(A) upon   (B) ahead

22 clearly

분명히, 명확하게

기출 in a **clearly** visible way
분명히 보일 수 있는 방식으로

clearly state that
~라는 것을 명확하게 언급하다

Demand for Zola smartphones has ------- decreased since the design of the device was changed last year.

(A) exactly   (B) clearly

23 initially

처음에, 초기에

기출 **initially** be not familiar with the new program
처음에 새로운 프로그램에 익숙하지 않다

must **initially** pay all fees
초기에 모든 요금을 지불해야 하다

New workers at Southern Chicken are ------- provided with two work uniforms, but an additional one is available upon request.

(A) initially   (B) shortly

24 specifically

specify v. (구체적으로) 명시하다
specific a. 구체적인, 특정한

특히, 구체적으로

기출 **specifically** designed for
특히 ~을 위해 고안된

Specifically, your main duty is to manage the work crew.
구체적으로, 귀하의 주 직무는 작업반을 관리하는 것입니다.

The grand opening of Funland Toystore was scheduled ------- to take place on the first day of the school holidays.

(A) specifically   (B) relatively

25 **consistently**

consistent a. 일관성 있는

● 일관성 있게, 지속적으로

기출 be promoted for one's **consistently** outstanding contributions
일관성 있게 뛰어난 기여로 승진되다

be **consistently** late in shipping the order
지속적으로 주문건을 배송하는 데 늦다

Ms. Grainger was recognized at the annual awards ceremony for her ------- outstanding sales performance.

(A) consistently   (B) potentially

26 **intentionally**

intend v. 의도하다
intention n. 의도, 고의
intentional a. 의도적인, 고의적인

● 의도적으로, 고의로

기출 be **intentionally** designed for
의도적으로 ~을 위해 고안되다

intentionally make the battery run out
고의로 배터리를 닳게 만들다

The display of new winter jackets has been ------- assembled near the entrance to attract customer interest.

(A) intentionally   (B) extremely

27 **briefly**

brief a. 간결한, 잠시의

● 간단히, 잠깐

기출 **briefly** review the agenda
안건을 간단히 검토하다

be **briefly** delayed due to a minor problem
사소한 문제로 인해 잠깐 지연되다

The director spoke to the audience only ------- before leaving the film premiere.

(A) briefly   (B) correctly

28 probably

아마도

[기출] **probably** due to a system malfunction
아마도 시스템 장애로 인해

will **probably** take at least five business days
아마도 적어도 영업일 5일이 걸릴 것이다

Property market experts believe that house prices will ------- rise significantly over the next five years.

(A) previously   (B) probably

29 slightly

slight a. 약간의

약간

[기출] rise **slightly** again
다시 약간 상승하다

The CEO has suggested using a ------- cheaper packaging material in order to reduce expenses.

(A) slightly   (B) highly

30 formerly

former a. 이전의, 전직 ~인

~ 출신인, 이전에는

[기출] **formerly** a graphic artist
그래픽 예술가 출신인

be **formerly** a residential area
이전에는 주택가였다

Edward Johnson, ------- the president of Jacoby Corporation, has announced the launch of his new technology company.

(A) formerly   (B) frequently

Week 07   467

31 alternatively

- 그렇지 않으면, 대신

기출 You may use the free shuttle service from the hotel. **Alternatively**, you can take a taxi.
귀하께서는 호텔에서 무료 셔틀 서비스를 이용하실 수 있습니다. 그렇지 않으면, 택시를 이용하셔도 됩니다.

Please print out your train ticket and present it to an agent at the station. -------, you may show an electronic version.
(A) Consequently　　　(B) Alternatively

만점 TIP
주로 Part 6에서 대안을 이끄는 접속부사로 출제된다.

32 primarily

primary a. 주요한

- 주로

기출 be **primarily** responsible for quality control
주로 품질 관리를 맡고 있다

work **primarily** on
주로 ~에 대한 일을 하다

Since the company was founded last month, Vornicon Inc. has received many orders, ------- from firms based in South Korea.
(A) primarily　　　(B) closely

33 cautiously

caution n. 조심, 주의
cautious a. 조심스러운, 신중한

- 조심스럽게, 신중히

기출 as **cautiously** as possible
가능한 한 조심스럽게

cautiously predict a merger between
~ 간의 합병을 신중히 예측하다

Hikers are advised to ------- walk along the ridge trail, which has steep cliffs on either side.
(A) cautiously　　　(B) tightly

34 ideally

ideal a. 이상적인

- 이상적으로

  기출 will **ideally** be completed by next Friday
  다음 주 금요일까지 완료되면 이상적일 것이다

  Mr. Harmon will ------- hire at least ten new sales representatives to help the company deal with the increased demand in manpower.
  (A) ideally   (B) relatively

35 skillfully

- 능숙하게

  기출 how **skillfully** he designed the clothing line
  그가 의류 제품군을 얼마나 능숙하게 디자인하는지

  Greta Moffat is known for ------- crafting handmade furniture from recycled wood.
  (A) likely   (B) skillfully

36 perfectly

perfect a. 완벽한
perfection n. 완벽

- 완벽하게

  기출 be **perfectly** suited for ~에 완벽하게 어울리다

  The new car manufactured by Mazdar Motors is ------- suited for medium-sized families who enjoy going on long road trips.
  (A) gradually   (B) perfectly

37 simply

simple a. 간단한

- 그저, 간단히

  기출 **simply** highlight the item
  그저 그 제품을 강조하다

  simply arrange the flowers
  간단히 꽃들을 배치하다

  To assemble your new Fitmaster treadmill, ------- follow the instructions in the user manual.
  (A) simply   (B) mostly

38 particularly

particular a. 특정한

● 특히

기출 a **particularly** busy day
특히 바쁜 날

even in **particularly** stressful situations
심지어 특히 스트레스가 심한 상황에서도

> Gilman Department Store will remain open until 10 PM on December 24 as this is usually a ------- busy shopping day.
> (A) particularly　　　(B) readily

39 precisely

precise a. 정확한
precision n. 정확

● 정확히

기출 **precisely** to ensure stability of
~의 안정성을 정확히 보장하기 위해

> The opening ceremony of the sports competition will begin at ------- 7 PM this Friday.
> (A) precisely　　　(B) definitely

40 likewise

● 마찬가지로

기출 As his predecessor did, the new CEO **likewise** places top priority on finding a reliable alternative energy source.
전임자가 그랬듯이, 신임 대표이사도 마찬가지로 신뢰할 만한 대체 에너지원을 찾는 것을 최우선 과제로 삼고 있다.

> As with our main branch in Los Angeles, our new clothing store in San Francisco ------- customizes garments at the request of customers.
> (A) likewise　　　(B) meanwhile

만점
- 주로 Part 6에서 앞의 내용과 유사한 내용을 이끄는 접속부사로 출제된다.

DAILY QUIZ

단어와 그에 알맞은 뜻을 연결해 보세요.

1 otherwise • • (A) 처음에, 초기에

2 initially • • (B) 이미, 벌써

3 already • • (C) 다르게, 그렇지 않으면

빈칸에 알맞은 단어를 선택하세요.

4 ------- predict a merger between
~ 간의 합병을 신중히 예측하다

5 be ------- understaffed
현재 인원이 부족하다

(A) shortly
(B) largely
(C) currently
(D) cautiously

6 be expected to reopen -------
곧 다시 문을 열 것으로 예상되다

앞서 배운 단어들의 뜻을 생각하면서, 다음 문제를 풀어보세요.

7 Ryzen Electronics ------- relocated to a new headquarters in downtown Los Angeles.

(A) severely   (B) usually
(C) recently   (D) exactly

8 Audiences responded positively to the test screening of *Galaxy One*, which means the movie will ------- require no further shots or edits.

(A) therefore   (B) often
(C) ever   (D) rather

정답 1 (C) 2 (A) 3 (B) 4 (D) 5 (C) 6 (A) 7 (C) 8 (A)

Day 03 부사 ❷ Part 5, 6

1 exclusively
exclusive a. 독점적인

● 독점적으로

기출 deal almost **exclusively** with
거의 독점적으로 ~와 거래하다

be available **exclusively** on Channel 5
5번 채널에서 독점적으로 볼 수 있다

The upcoming seminar on artificial intelligence is open ------- to members of the Feeney Technology Institute.

(A) exclusively   (B) approximately

2 unfortunately

● 안타깝게도, 아쉽게도

기출 **Unfortunately**, the shipment is missing an item.
안타깝게도, 배송에서 물품이 하나 빠져 있습니다.

-------, the museum's main exhibition hall will be closed to visitors until March 1.

(A) Unfortunately   (B) Precisely

3 rarely
rare a. 드문, 희귀한

● 드물게

기출 **rarely** raise their price
드물게 가격을 인상하다

be **rarely** used by our employees
우리 직원들에 의해 드물게 사용되다

Mr. Edwards prefers to commute by bicycle and ------- uses public transportation or his own car.

(A) readily   (B) rarely

4 **fully** 완전히, 최대로

full a. 완전한, 최대의

- 완전히, 최대로

  기출 will be **fully** recyclable
  완전히 재활용 가능할 것이다

  > The airline ticket is -------- refundable, provided a cancellation request is made at least two weeks prior to the departure date.
  >
  > (A) initially (B) fully

5 **separately**

separate a. 분리된, 별도의

- 따로, 별도로

  기출 be sold **separately**
  따로 판매되다

  > Due to the size of your purchased items, two packages will be delivered ------- to your address on March 5.
  >
  > (A) suddenly (B) separately

6 **necessarily**

- 반드시

  기출 not **necessarily** imply endorsement from
  반드시 ~의 지지를 의미하는 것은 아니다

  not **necessarily** purchase it again
  반드시 그것을 다시 구매해야 하는 것은 아니다

  > Comments posted by users on our online forum do not -------- reflect the views of our organization.
  >
  > (A) necessarily (B) importantly

7 **correctly**

correct a. 정확한

- 정확하게

  기출 **correctly** record the delivery address
  배송 주소를 정확하게 기록하다

  > Please get in touch with the real estate agent to check that we ------- listed the asking price for the property.
  >
  > (A) frequently (B) correctly

Week 07 | Day 03 | Part 5, 6 부사 ②

8 heavily

- 대단히, 심하게, 아주 많이

  [기출] have invested **heavily** in
  ~에 대단히 투자해왔다

  be **heavily** influenced by
  ~에 의해 심하게 영향받다

  be **heavily** discounted until
  ~할 때까지 아주 많이 할인하다

  > Travel to the Muskoka region is not advised because it is expected to snow ------- for the next few days.
  > (A) heavily　　　(B) shortly

9 mutually

mutual a. 상호의

- 상호, 서로

  [기출] **mutually** beneficial relationship
  상호 이로운 관계

  develop **mutually** productive interactions
  서로 생산적인 상호작용을 발전시키다

  > The business arrangement between Seema Health Foods and Flow Shipping will be ------- beneficial.
  > (A) mutually　　　(B) wishfully

10 fairly

fair a. 공정한

- 상당히, 꽤, 공정하게

  [기출] win the election **fairly** easily
  상당히 쉽게 선거를 이기다

  > Sales of the Ryzen 4 smartphone have remained ------- steady despite numerous reports of battery issues.
  > (A) fairly　　　(B) roughly

11 eventually

eventual a. 궁극적인

• 마침내, 결국

기출 will be **eventually** promoted
마침내 승진될 것이다

eventually earn a degree in
결국 ~에서의 학위를 받다

> Provided that Mario Pizza's monthly revenue continues to rise, the business will ------- become profitable.
>
> (A) already   (B) eventually

12 unusually

unusual a. 드문

• 대단히, 드물게

기출 identify an **unusually** large money withdrawal
대단히 큰 돈의 인출을 확인하다

unusually cold weather
드물게 추운 날씨

> Due to the ------- high temperatures this summer, the company has installed air conditioning in its offices.
>
> (A) unusually   (B) easily

13 unexpectedly

unexpected a. 예기치 않은, 뜻밖의

• 예기치 않게, 뜻밖에

기출 **unexpectedly** announce that
~라는 것을 예기치 않게 발표하다

cause schedules to change **unexpectedly**
뜻밖에 일정을 변경하도록 하다

> The train to Manchester was ------- delayed due to a mechanical fault.
>
> (A) unexpectedly   (B) attentively

Week 07 | Day 03 | Part 5, 6 부사 ②

14 alike

- 똑같이, 모두

  기출 adults and children **alike**
  성인과 어린이 똑같이

  older and newer models **alike**
  오래된 모델과 새로운 모델들 모두

  > The Palm Springs resort has an extensive range of amenities, making it the perfect choice for families and solo travelers -------.
  >
  > (A) only   (B) alike

15 altogether

- 완전히, 한꺼번에

  기출 eliminate the rules **altogether**
  규정들을 완전히 없애다

  > The owner of Belmont Bistro has decided to remove the squid dish ------- after receiving feedback from numerous dissatisfied customers.
  >
  > (A) altogether   (B) beyond

16 routinely

routine a. 정기적인, 일상적인

- 정기적으로, 일상적으로

  기출 **routinely** give hotel recommendations
  정기적으로 호텔 추천 정보를 주다

  be cleaned **routinely**
  정기적으로 청소되다

  > All communal areas in the apartment building are ------- cleaned by a skilled maintenance team twice per day.
  >
  > (A) routinely   (B) vastly

17 additionally

addition n. 추가
additional a. 추가적인

• 추가적으로, 게다가

기출 Passengers should present their tickets at the counter. **Additionally**, they must show their identification at security.
탑승객들은 카운터에서 티켓을 제시해야 합니다. 추가적으로, 보안검색대에서 신분증을 보여주셔야 합니다.

Sign up for a membership to receive a 5 percent discount on all purchases. -------, becoming a member grants you free shipping on online orders.
(A) Additionally   (B) However

18 subsequently

subsequent a. 다음의

• 그 후에, 그 다음에

기출 **subsequently** gain a share of the market
그 후에 시장의 점유권을 얻다

be **subsequently** implemented by
그 다음에 ~에 의해 시행되다

Ms. Vardy impressed the board members during her interview and was ------- offered the position of CFO.
(A) highly   (B) subsequently

19 customarily

• 관례상

기출 **customarily** visit the international offices
관례상 해외 지사들을 방문하다

customarily receive a 15 percent discount on
~에 대해서 관례상 15퍼센트 할인을 받다

Guests checking in to a deluxe suite at The Pecan Hotel ------- receive a bottle of sparkling wine and a bowl of fruit.
(A) customarily   (B) perfectly

20 apparently 명백하게

apparent a. 명백한

기출 be **apparently** interested in
명백하게 ~에 관심을 가지고 있다

> Based on the feedback we have received, customers ------- like the new layout of our Web site.
> (A) apparently　　　(B) briefly

만점 TIP
주로 Part 6에서 사실성을 강조하는 내용을 이끄는 접속부사로 사용된다.

21 solely 오로지, 단독으로

기출 advertise **solely** in print
오로지 인쇄물로만 광고하다

rely **solely** on
~에 단독으로 의존하다

> Having very little experience in sales, Ms. Atkinson relied ------- on her knowledge of the company's product ranges to impress the interviewer.
> (A) formally　　　(B) solely

22 traditionally 전통적으로

traditional a. 전통적인

기출 be **traditionally** given to
~에 전통적으로 수여되다

have **traditionally** alternated between
전통적으로 ~ 사이를 번갈아 가다

> The annual Blueford Arts Festival is ------- held on the last weekend of September.
> (A) traditionally　　　(B) positively

23 adequately

adequate a. 적절한, 충분한

- 제대로, 충분히

  기출 **adequately** address concerns
  우려 사항들을 제대로 처리하다

  > The private dining room at Verona Restaurant will ------ meet our needs as the venue for the company banquet.
  > (A) adequately   (B) succinctly

24 quietly

quiet a. 조용한

- 조용하게

  기출 speak as **quietly** as possible
  가능한 한 조용하게 말하다

  > If you wish to exit the auditorium during the seminar, please do so as ------ as possible.
  > (A) quietly   (B) slightly

25 explicitly

explicit a. 명확한

- 명확하게

  기출 Our warranty **explicitly** states that ~.
  저희 보증서는 ~라고 명확하게 명시하고 있습니다.

  be **explicitly** outlined
  명확하게 개요로 설명되다

  > Our policy regarding returns and refunds is ------ detailed on our Web site.
  > (A) explicitly   (B) eventually

Week 07 | Day 03 | Part 5, 6 부사 ②

26 generally

● 일반적으로

기출 **generally** available year-round
일반적으로 1년 내내 구매 가능한

generally take one day to process
~을 처리하는 데 일반적으로 하루가 걸리다

All orders placed through our Web site are ------- delivered within 48 hours of purchase.

(A) generally   (B) lightly

27 moderately

moderate a. 적당한

● 적당히, 어느 정도

기출 be **moderately** successful at first
처음에는 적당히 성공적이었다

have been only **moderately** successful in
~에 있어서 어느 정도 성공했을 뿐이다

Despite an extensive advertising campaign, the new game console has proven to be only ------- successful.

(A) moderately   (B) evenly

28 provisionally

● 임시로, 조건부로

기출 be **provisionally** appointed to serve as
임시로 ~로 근무하도록 임명되다

provisionally accept the job offer
조건부로 일자리 제안을 수락하다

Simon Eggers has been ------- appointed as the leader of the new product development team.

(A) provisionally   (B) comparably

29 equally

equal a. 똑같은, 동등한

● 똑같이, 동등하게

기출 be **equally** important to
~에게 똑같이 중요하다

be **equally** suitable for
동등하게 ~에 적합하다

> Strong leadership and a skilled workforce are ------- necessary in order for a business to be successful.
>
> (A) promptly   (B) equally

30 exactly

exact a. 정확한

● 정확히

기출 **exactly** what you are seeking
정확히 귀하께서 찾는 것

do not know **exactly** why
~한 이유를 정확히 알지 못하다

> The new play currently showing at Garfield Theater runs for ------- two hours.
>
> (A) exactly   (B) timely

31 especially

● 특히

기출 would be **especially** helpful in
~에서 특히 유용할 것이다

especially in the field of marketing
특히 마케팅 분야에서

> Remote work is becoming increasingly common in several industries, ------- those focused on customer service and support.
>
> (A) especially   (B) hardly

32 presently

present a. 현재의

- 현재

  [기출] be **presently** conducting a survey
  현재 설문조사를 실시하고 있다

  be **presently** accepting proposals for
  현재 ~에 대한 제안을 받고 있다

  > A stage is ------- under construction in Davis Plaza in preparation for the city's annual festival.
  > (A) presently (B) enormously

  만점 TIP
  주로 현재진행시제와 함께 출제된다.

33 definitely

definite a. 분명한

- 분명(히)

  [기출] will **definitely** reach their goal
  분명히 목표를 달성할 것이다

  be **definitely** the best part of the book
  분명 그 책의 가장 좋았던 부분이다

  > After canceling some appointments in her schedule, Ms. Jones will ------- be able to attend the shareholder meeting.
  > (A) usually (B) definitely

34 extremely

extreme a. 극도의

- 몹시, 극도로

  [기출] be **extremely** pleased to have won the award
  수상하게 되어 몹시 기쁘다

  > Mr. Allenby is ------- pleased with the landscaping work carried out by Perfect Gardens.
  > (A) extremely (B) remotely

35 furthermore

게다가, 또한

기출 Our financial specialists provide consulting services for small businesses. **Furthermore**, our online services provide flexibility for our customers.
저희 금융 전문가들은 소규모 기업체들에게 컨설팅 서비스를 제공합니다. 게다가, 저희의 온라인 서비스는 고객들에게 유연성을 제공하고 있습니다.

The new expressway provides a faster route between the airport and the downtown area. -------, it significantly reduces traffic congestion on local roads.

(A) Furthermore   (B) However

만점 TIP
- Part 6에서 앞에 제시된 것과 유사한 내용을 추가하는 접속부사로 출제된다.

36 completely

완전히

complete a. 완전한
　　　　 v. 완성하다
completion n. 완성

기출 be **completely** free of charge
완전히 무료이다

be not **completely** reviewed until August
8월이 되어서야 완전히 검토되다

Beach towels are provided to all hotel guests ------- free of charge.

(A) completely   (B) occasionally

37 soon

곧, 조만간

기출 will be joining us **soon**
곧 입사할 것이다

be expected to meet **soon**
조만간 만날 것으로 예상되다

Please direct any questions about the revised policy to the HR manager who will be contacting you -------.

(A) yet   (B) soon

38 properly

proper a. 제대로 된, 올바른

- 제대로, 올바르게

  기출 must be disposed of **properly**
  반드시 제대로 폐기되어야 하다

  be **properly** installed
  올바르게 설치되다

  > Assuming the air conditioning unit is ------- maintained, it should function effectively for at least 25 years.
  > (A) properly (B) originally

39 occasionally

occasional a. 가끔의, 때때로의

- 가끔, 때때로

  기출 **occasionally** lower their price
  가끔 가격을 내리다

  occasionally enter into agreement with
  때때로 ~와 합의를 이루다

  > The fourth floor conference room is normally used for important client meetings, although it is ------- used for staff orientations.
  > (A) marginally (B) occasionally

40 markedly

marked a. 눈에 띄는, 현저한

- 눈에 띄게, 현저하게

  기출 become **markedly** better
  눈에 띄게 더 나아지다

  markedly successful
  현저하게 성공적인

  > Customers have complained that the color of our new sofa is ------- different compared with the images on our Web site.
  > (A) markedly (B) chiefly

DAILY QUIZ

단어와 그에 알맞은 뜻을 연결해 보세요.

1 separately • • (A) 전통적으로

2 extremely • • (B) 따로, 별도로

3 traditionally • • (C) 몹시, 극도로

빈칸에 알맞은 단어를 선택하세요.

4 ------- visit the international offices
관례상 해외 지사들을 방문하다

5 ------- record the delivery address
배송 주소를 정확하게 기록하다

(A) correctly
(B) exclusively
(C) customarily
(D) necessarily

6 deal almost ------- with
거의 독점적으로 ~와 거래하다

앞서 배운 단어들의 뜻을 생각하면서, 다음 문제를 풀어보세요.

7 The record company has collected the final recordings of the late singer and will ------- release them as a full album.

(A) so
(B) well
(C) recently
(D) soon

8 The end of several trade agreements in the Middle East may cause gas prices to rise ------- this year.

(A) commonly
(B) unexpectedly
(C) apparently
(D) nearly

정답 1 (B) 2 (C) 3 (A) 4 (C) 5 (A) 6 (B) 7 (D) 8 (B)

Day 04 동사 + 부사 콜로케이션 Part 5, 6

1 proudly feature
● 자랑스럽게도 ~을 특별히 포함하다

기출 **proudly** unveil
자랑스럽게 ~을 공개하다

proudly carry
자랑스럽게 ~을 취급하다

The Seoul Music Festival will ------- feature many emerging singers this year.

(A) greatly　　　　(B) proudly

2 be produced locally
● 지역에서 생산되다

기출 buy vegetables **locally**
채소를 지역에서 구매하다

Mary's Bakery is proud to use fresh ingredients that are produced -------.

(A) originally　　　　(B) locally

3 proceed directly to
● ~로 곧장 가다

기출 send A **directly** to
A를 ~에게 곧장 전송하다

be shipped **directly** from our warehouse
우리 창고에서 곧장 발송되다

Once you arrive at the main gate of our building, please proceed ------- to the security desk.

(A) directly　　　　(B) closely

4 respond promptly to

● ~에 즉시 반응하다

기출 register **promptly**
즉시 등록하다

be submitted **promptly**
즉시 제출되다

> Customer care associates must respond ------- to all the concerns of customers and resolve any issues with care.
> (A) generally (B) promptly

5 previously unavailable

● 전에는 이용할 수 없었던

기출 **previously** offered to
전에는 ~에게 제공되었던

previously worked in
전에는 ~에서 일했던

> Food delivery services by drones, ------- unavailable due to government regulations, are now gaining in popularity.
> (A) previously (B) currently

만점 TIP
• 부사 previously는 Part 6에서 접속부사로도 자주 출제된다.

6 travel quickly

● 빠르게 이동하다

기출 proceed **quickly** 빠르게 진행되다
quickly sell out 빠르게 매진되다
move **quickly** 빠르게 이동하다

> Now that we have added more express lines, commuters can travel ------- to their destinations.
> (A) quickly (B) shortly

7 carefully inspect
신중하게 검사하다

기출 examine A carefully
A를 신중하게 검사하다

carefully remove
신중하게 제거하다

We are proud of our zero defect policy in our factories, where employees ------- inspect all of our products.
(A) exactly (B) carefully

8 monitor closely
자세히 관찰하다

기출 closely read
자세히 읽다

work closely with
~와 긴밀하게 일하다

The performance of interns at the newspaper company is ------- monitored by its senior editorial staff.
(A) substantially (B) closely

9 rise considerably
상당히 상승하다

기출 vary considerably 상당히 다양하다

expand considerably 상당히 확장되다

Sales of Trine Automotive's new hybrid sedan have been ------- rising thanks to the car's high fuel efficiency.
(A) considerably (B) deeply

만점 TIP
- 부사 considerably는 주로 증감이나 변화를 나타내는 동사들과 함께 쓰여 very처럼 수량이나 정도가 크다는 것을 나타낸다. 형용사를 수식할 때는 주로 비교급과 함께 쓰인다.

10 go smoothly

● 순조롭게 진행되다

기출 **progress smoothly**
순조롭게 진행되다

run smoothly
부드럽게 작동하다

Thanks to Ms. Chamberline's assistance, my transition to London went -------.
(A) personally   (B) smoothly

11 thoroughly investigate

● 철저하게 조사하다

기출 **thoroughly examine**
철저하게 검사하다

thoroughly wash
철저하게 세척하다

A team of government inspectors is ------- investigating all potential causes of the accident at the construction site.
(A) hopefully   (B) thoroughly

12 strongly encourage

● 강력하게 권고하다

기출 **speak strongly**
강력하게 말하다

strongly agree with
~에 전적으로 동의하다

Due to scheduled repair work, motorists are ------- encouraged to avoid the Campton Bridge this afternoon.
(A) closely   (B) strongly

13 temporarily close

● 일시적으로 폐쇄하다

기출 **temporarily** halt
일시적으로 중단하다

temporarily out of stock
일시적으로 품절인

temporarily unavailable
일시적으로 이용할 수 없는

> Residents are reminded that Madison Park is ------- closed due to flooding since Friday.
> (A) temporarily   (B) potentially

14 rise dramatically

● 급격히 상승하다

기출 increase **dramatically**
급격히 증가하다

dramatically affect
상당한 영향을 미치다

> Sales of the Vision Pro VR device have ------- rose since the manufacturer released a well-received game.
> (A) accidentally   (B) dramatically

15 rapidly expand

● 빠르게 확장하다

기출 **rapidly** grow 빠르게 성장하다
progress **rapidly** 빠르게 진행되다
rapidly approach 빠르게 접근하다

> Rayon Electronics announced that it doubled its revenue this year while ------- expanding into the Asian electric vehicle markets.
> (A) rapidly   (B) highly

16 be conveniently located

● 편리하게 위치해 있다

기출 be **conveniently** situated in the city
도시에 편리하게 위치해 있다

be **conveniently** accessible by bus
버스로 편리하게 접근 가능하다

The venue for the upcoming convention is ------- located near the local airport, which is also close to your hotel.
(A) regularly   (B) conveniently

17 significantly increase

● 상당히 증가시키다

기출 **significantly** speed up
상당히 속도를 높이다

be **significantly** changed
상당히 변경되다

The new version of our accounting software would ------- increase our work efficiency and accuracy.
(A) significantly   (B) proficiently

18 fasten tightly

● 단단하게 고정하다

기출 fit **tightly**
딱 맞다

be screwed on **tightly**
나사로 단단하게 고정되다

press A **tightly**
A를 힘껏 누르다

When you replace the filter, please turn it clockwise until it is ------- fastened.
(A) tightly   (B) steadily

19 be tentatively scheduled

- 임시로 일정이 잡히다

  기출 **tentatively** reschedule
  임시로 일정을 재조정하다

  > The Annual Medical Technology Convention has been ------- scheduled for the first weekend of September.
  >
  > (A) tentatively (B) punctually

  만점 TIP
  - 부사 tentatively는 temporarily와 바꿔 쓸 수 있다.

20 officially assume

- 공식적으로 (역할을) 맡다

  기출 **officially** begin
  공식적으로 시작하다

  officially open
  정식으로 개장하다

  > Mr. Hill has ------- assumed the role of project manager and is in the process of selecting individuals to join his team.
  >
  > (A) officially (B) extremely

21 be urgently needed

- 긴급히 필요하다

  기출 be **urgently** seeking
  긴급히 찾고 있다

  > Now that the demand for our new SUV has doubled, overtime is ------- needed from our assembly line workers.
  >
  > (A) closely (B) urgently

22 securely store

- 안전하게 보관하다

  기출 be placed **securely**
  안전한 곳에 놓아두다

  be **securely** fastened
  단단히 고정되다

  attach A **securely** to B
  A를 B에 확실히 부착하다

  > Customers must make sure that their belongings are ------- stored in the lockers we provide.
  > (A) securely   (B) severely

23 be formally announced

- 정식으로 발표되다

  기출 be **formally** introduced
  정식으로 소개되다

  formally open
  정식으로 개장하다

  > Ms. Hanning's promotion will be ------- announced at a board meeting sometime next week.
  > (A) primarily   (B) formally

24 respond favorably

- 호의적으로 반응하다

  기출 react **favorably** to
  ~에 호의적으로 반응하다

  be viewed **favorably**
  호평을 받다

  > Lions Telecommunication has always responded ------- to customer requests for improved services.
  > (A) probably   (B) favorably

25 regularly check

- 정기적으로 확인하다

  기출 **regularly** order 정기적으로 주문하다
  regularly participate in ~에 정기적으로 참가하다
  be **regularly** shipped 정기적으로 배송되다

  All employees must ------- check their hard drives for viruses to ensure that important files are protected.
  (A) regularly　　　　(B) mainly

26 be known widely

- 널리 알려지다

  기출 be **widely** respected
  널리 존경받다
  be **widely** recognized as
  ~로 널리 인정받다

  Simcom Systems Inc. has been known ------- as the most innovative computer manufacturer for more than 30 years.
  (A) widely　　　　(B) smartly

27 process efficiently

- 효율적으로 처리하다

  기출 run a business **efficiently**
  사업을 효율적으로 운영하다
  produce goods **efficiently**
  상품을 효율적으로 생산하다
  track shipments **efficiently**
  배송을 효율적으로 추적하다

  Our improved e-commerce software will help your employees process customer orders more -------.
  (A) efficiently　　　　(B) knowingly

28 be strictly forbidden

- 엄격히 금지되다

  기출 be **strictly** prohibited 엄격히 금지되다
  be **strictly** followed 엄격히 준수되다
  be **strictly** controlled 엄격히 통제되다

  It is our policy that food and beverages are ------- forbidden in the Aberdeen Historical Museum.
  (A) strictly　　　　(B) hastily

29 mistakenly believe

- 착각하다

  기출 **mistakenly** think
  　　　잘못 생각하다

  　　　mistakenly delete
  　　　실수로 삭제하다

  Mr. Horton ------- believed that the order had already been processed.
  (A) mistakenly　　　(B) fortunately

30 enthusiastically applaud

- 열렬히 환호하다

  기출 **enthusiastically** welcome
  　　　열렬히 환영하다

  　　　enthusiastically approve
  　　　흔쾌히 승인하다

  　　　enthusiastically announce
  　　　아주 기쁜 마음으로 발표하다

  The audience ------- applauded the White Lions at the end of the performance.
  (A) probably　　　(B) enthusiastically

31 actively seek

● 적극적으로 찾다

기출 **actively** promote 적극적으로 홍보하다
be **actively** engaged in ~에 적극적으로 참여하다

> Hondix Automotive is ------- seeking new methods for reducing energy consumption in its vehicles.
> (A) actively   (B) lately

32 successfully complete

● 성공적으로 완료하다

기출 **successfully** manage
성공적으로 관리하다

successfully negotiate
성공적으로 협상하다

> Mr. Harrison ------- completed the long-term maintenance contract with Heritage Global Inc.
> (A) directly   (B) successfully

33 effectively communicate

● 효과적으로 소통하다

기출 deal with **effectively**
효과적으로 처리하다

effectively manage
효과적으로 관리하다

effectively market
효과적으로 광고하다

> Many entertainment companies use social networking services to ------- communicate with their potential customers.
> (A) effectively   (B) formerly

34 **substantially reduce**

● 상당히 줄이다

기출 increase employee productivity **substantially**
직원 생산성을 상당히 향상시키다

substantially expand its coverage
보장범위를 상당히 확대하다

Our new sports beverage, PowerBottle, can help you ------- reduce your weight while keeping your energy levels high.

(A) unnecessarily (B) substantially

35 **be accidentally discovered**

● 우연히 발견되다

기출 **accidentally** delete
우연히 삭제하다

An ancient residential site was ------- discovered during the construction of a sports stadium.

(A) urgently (B) accidentally

36 **politely ask for**

● 정중하게 ~을 요청하다

기출 **politely** offer
정중하게 제안하다

speak **politely**
예의 바르게 말하다

Upon arriving at the hotel, Mr. Forster ------- asked for a larger room.

(A) politely (B) regularly

37 rise sharply

• 급격히 상승하다

기출 fall **sharply** 급격히 하락하다

The recent hiring of temporary workers has had a positive impact on productivity, which is now rising -------.

(A) sharply　　　　(B) accurately

38 vote unanimously

• 만장일치로 투표하다

기출 **unanimously** approve 만장일치로 승인하다

The board members voted ------- to appoint Ms. Chadwick as the new Chief Operating Officer.

(A) wishfully　　　　(B) unanimously

39 be periodically updated

• 주기적으로 갱신되다

기출 be adjusted **periodically**
주기적으로 조정되다

check the inventory **periodically**
재고를 주기적으로 확인하다

Please be reminded that during peak seasons, our room rates are ------- updated based on availability.

(A) recently　　　　(B) periodically

40 gradually expand

• 점진적으로 확장하다

기출 replace A **gradually** 점진적으로 A를 교체하다
gradually phase out 점차 단계적으로 폐지하다

Rather than hiring twenty employees next month, the HR manager has suggested expanding the workforce ------- over the next six months.

(A) potentially　　　　(B) gradually

DAILY QUIZ

콜로케이션과 그에 알맞은 뜻을 연결해 보세요.

1. securely store • • (A) 상당히 상승하다
2. carefully inspect • • (B) 안전하게 보관하다
3. rise considerably • • (C) 신중하게 검사하다

빈칸에 알맞은 단어를 선택하세요.

4. buy vegetables -------
   채소를 지역에서 구매하다

5. ------- speed up
   상당히 속도를 높이다

6. ------- examine
   철저하게 검사하다

(A) thoroughly
(B) locally
(C) significantly
(D) formally

앞서 배운 콜로케이션들의 뜻을 생각하면서, 다음 문제를 풀어보세요.

7. Once you have arrived at Riceman Labs, proceed ------- to the security office and obtain an ID card.

   (A) regularly   (B) directly
   (C) closely   (D) firmly

8. Bikram Gas Ltd. board members voted ------- to reject the merger proposal put forward by Hyderabad Energy.

   (A) resourcefully (B) unanimously
   (C) extremely   (D) commonly

정답 1 (B) 2 (C) 3 (A) 4 (B) 5 (C) 6 (A) 7 (B) 8 (B)

1 call in sick

- 아파서 결근하다

> Can anyone come in to work this morning? We have a huge order to fill, and two employees scheduled for today have **called in sick**.
>
> 오늘 아침에 출근할 수 있는 사람이 있나요? 채워야 하는 주문량이 너무 많은데, 오늘 근무 예정인 직원 두 명이 아파서 결근을 했습니다.

2 publicize

- v. ~을 홍보하다

> The marketing team worked very hard to **publicize** the newly launched product and ensure it gains widespread attention in the market.
>
> 마케팅팀은 새로 출시된 제품을 홍보하고 그 제품이 시장에서 폭넓은 관심을 끌도록 하기 위해 열심히 노력했습니다.

만점 TIP

• 관련 기출

　public relations 홍보 (활동)

3 honor

- v. ~에게 영광을 베풀다, 수여하다
- n. 존경, 공경

> The company **honored** Ms. Rodriguez with a prize for her outstanding sales achievements during the annual reception.
>
> 회사는 매년 열리는 연회에서 로드리게즈 씨의 뛰어난 판매 성과에 대해 상을 수여했습니다.

만점 TIP

• 기출 Paraphrasing

　위 예문의 내용을 한 문장으로 She was given an award.(상을 받았다.)와 같이 표현할 수 있습니다.

4 close a deal

deal n. 거래, 계약

● 계약을 체결하다, 거래를 성사시키다

> After months of negotiations, we successfully **closed a deal** with BJ Capital.
> 수개월 간의 협상 끝에 BJ 캐피탈 사와 성공적으로 계약을 체결하였습니다.

만점 TIP
• 관련 기출
　negotiate a deal 거래를 협상하다

5 well-suited

● a. 적합한, 잘 어울리는

> Ms. Lane's strong communication skills and attention to detail make her **well-suited** for the role of project manager.
> 레인 씨의 훌륭한 의사소통 능력과 세부사항에 대한 주의는 그녀를 프로젝트 매니저의 역할에 적합하게 합니다.

6 hiring decision

● 채용 결정

> In our company, **hiring decisions** require unanimous approval from the hiring committee.
> 우리 회사에서, 채용 결정을 하려면 채용 위원회의 만장일치 승인이 필요합니다.

7 good fit

● 적임자, 꼭 맞는 것

> When making hiring decisions, we consider whether the candidate is a **good fit** for our long-term goals.
> 채용 결정을 할 때, 우리는 그 지원자가 우리의 장기적인 목표에 적임자인지를 고려합니다.

만점 TIP
• 기출 Paraphrasing
　good fit → perfect candidate (가장 훌륭한 후보)

8 work ethic

● 직업의식, 근면함

Jane's strong **work ethic** is evident in her dedication to completing tasks ahead of schedule.

제인의 강한 직업의식은 예정보다 빨리 일을 완수하려는 그녀의 헌신에서 잘 드러납니다.

9 invaluable

● a. 귀중한, 매우 유용한

The mentorship I received from my supervisor during my early career was **invaluable** in shaping my professional development.

경력 초기에 상사로부터 받은 멘토링은 저의 직업적 발전을 형성하는 데 매우 유용하였습니다.

10 be nominated

nominee n. 지명된 사람, 후보

● (수상) 후보자로 지명되다

The CEO **has been nominated** for the Business Leader of the Year Award, recognizing her outstanding leadership qualities.

그 CEO는 올해의 비즈니스 리더 상 후보에 올랐는데, 이는 그녀의 뛰어난 리더십 자질을 인정하는 것입니다.

만점 TIP

• 관련 기출

nominate A for B A를 B의 후보로 지명하다, 추천하다

11 probationary period

● 수습 기간, 시험 채용 기간

The **probationary period** typically lasts for three months, during which employees receive training and feedback.

수습 기간은 일반적으로 3개월 동안 지속되며, 이 기간 동안 직원들은 교육과 피드백을 받습니다.

12 supervise

supervisor n. 감독관, 관리자

- v. ~을 관리 감독하다

> The project manager will **supervise** the construction project, ensuring it stays on schedule and within budget.
>
> 프로젝트 관리자는 건설 프로젝트가 일정대로, 그리고 예산 내에서 유지되도록 감독할 것입니다.

만점 TIP
- 기출 Paraphrasing
  supervise → oversee (관리 감독하다)

13 referral

- n. 소개, 추천(서), 위탁

> His **referral** letter from a previous employer praised his strong work ethic, boosting his chances of landing the job.
>
> 이전 고용주가 보낸 그의 추천서는 그의 강한 직업의식을 칭찬했고, 이것은 그의 취업 기회를 증진시켰습니다.

만점 TIP
- 서비스나 업체 등을 추천하는 것도 referral이라고 표현합니다.

14 turnout

- n. 참가자의 수, 참석률

> The **turnout** at the charity event exceeded our expectations, with hundreds of people in attendance.
>
> 수백 명이 참석한 가운데 자선 행사의 참석률은 우리의 예상을 뛰어넘었습니다.

15 outing

- n. 야유회, 나들이

> Everyone was looking forward to the annual company **outing**, which included a picnic and games at the park.
>
> 모두가 매년 열리는 회사 야유회를 고대하고 있었는데, 그것은 소풍과 공원에서의 게임을 포함합니다.

16 flexible

flexibility n. 융통성

- a. 융통성 있는

> Many companies are adopting **flexible** work arrangements, allowing employees to choose their hours and workplace location.
>
> 많은 기업들이 유연한 근무 방식을 채택하여 직원들이 근무 시간과 근무 장소를 선택할 수 있도록 하고 있습니다.

17 duration

- n. (지속되는) 기간

> Visitors will be provided with temporary ID badges to wear throughout the **duration** of their visits to our factory.
>
> 방문객들에게는 공장 방문 기간 동안 착용할 임시 신분증 배지가 제공될 것입니다.

18 time slot

- 시간대

> Attendees can sign up for their preferred **time slot** for the workshop on a first-come, first-served basis.
>
> 참가자들은 선착순으로 워크숍에 선호하는 시간대에 등록할 수 있습니다.

19 fill up

- 자리가 차다

> The conference room quickly **filled up** with attendees eager to hear the keynote speaker.
>
> 회의실은 기조연설자의 말을 듣고 싶어 하는 참석자들로 순식간에 가득 찼습니다.

20 up front

- 선불로

I appreciate your services and am willing to pay you **up front** for the project to expedite the process.
귀하의 서비스에 감사드리며, 프로젝트 진행 속도를 높이기 위해 기꺼이 선불로 비용을 지불하겠습니다.

21 award-winning

- a. 상을 받은

The **award-winning** marketing campaign significantly boosted our brand's visibility and sales.
상을 받은 그 마케팅 캠페인은 우리 브랜드의 인지도와 매출을 크게 높였습니다.

22 praise

- v. ~을 칭찬하다
- n. 찬사, 칭찬

The CEO **praised** the marketing department for their innovative campaigns that led us to exceed our sales goals for the year.
CEO는 마케팅 부서의 혁신적인 캠페인으로 인해 올해 영업 목표를 초과 달성했다고 그 부서를 칭찬했습니다.

23 benefits

benefit n. 혜택
v. ~에게 이득이 되다

- n. 복리 후생

Once the probationary three months are completed, workers will be eligible for full employee **benefits**.
수습 3개월이 끝나면, 직원들은 모든 직원 복리 후생을 받을 자격을 갖추게 될 것입니다.

24 in-house

a. 사내의

We boast an **in-house** design team that excels in transforming ideas into visually compelling graphics.
저희는 아이디어를 시각적으로 매력적인 그래픽으로 바꾸는 일에 탁월한 사내 디자인 팀을 보유하고 있습니다.

25 take on / take over

떠맡다, 인계받다

Despite her busy schedule, she **took on** more responsibilities at work to prove her dedication.
바쁜 스케줄에도 불구하고, 그녀는 자신의 헌신을 증명하기 위해 직장에서 더 많은 책임을 맡았습니다.

만점 TIP
- 기출 Paraphrasing
  take on[over] → assume (떠맡다), accept (받아들이다)

26 qualifications

qualified a. 자격을 갖춘

n. 자격 요건

After considering the candidates' work experience and **qualifications**, the directors recommended Ms. Wong for the position.
지원자들의 근무 경력과 자격 요건을 고려한 후에, 이사들은 웡 씨를 그 직책에 추천했습니다.

27 possess

possession n. 소유

v. ~을 갖추다

Applicants for the position of communications officer must **possess** a master's degree in marketing or a related field.
커뮤니케이션 책임자의 직책에 지원하는 사람들은 마케팅 또는 관련 분야에서 석사 학위를 소지해야 합니다.

28 compensation package

● (급여와 복리후생을 포함한) 총 보수

> The company's generous **compensation package** includes health insurance, retirement plans, and paid time off.
>
> 회사의 후한 총 보수에는 건강 보험, 퇴직금 제도, 그리고 유급 휴가가 포함되어 있습니다.

만점 TIP
- 관련 기출
  - perks n. (급료 이외의) 특전

29 responsibilities [duties/tasks] include

● 업무에는 ~이 포함된다

> As the project manager, your **responsibilities include** overseeing the project timeline, coordinating team efforts, and ensuring that project objectives are met.
>
> 프로젝트 관리자로서, 여러분의 업무에는 프로젝트 일정을 감독하고, 팀 작업을 조정하며, 프로젝트 목표가 달성되도록 하는 것이 포함됩니다.

30 credentials

● n. 자격 인증서, 자격증

> Based on your **credentials**, it's clear that you are highly qualified for the job.
>
> 귀하의 자격 인증서들을 볼 때, 귀하는 그 일에 매우 적합한 사람임이 분명합니다.

만점 TIP
- 관련 기출
  - credit n. 인정, 칭찬

31 familiarize

familiar a. 익숙한, 친숙한

v. ~에 익숙하게 하다

New employees should **familiarize** themselves with the workplace safety guidelines before starting their job.

신입 사원들은 업무를 시작하기 전에 작업장 안전 지침을 숙지해야 합니다.

32 assure A that절

A에게 ~라는 확신을 주다

The CEO **assured the employees that** the company's merger would benefit them eventually.

그 CEO는 회사의 합병이 결국 그들에게 이익이 될 것이라고 직원들에게 확신을 주었습니다.

> **만점 TIP**
>
> • 관련 기출
>
> Rest assured, + 내용 ~라는 점에 대해 안심하셔도 됩니다.
> reassure ~을 안심시키다

33 morale

n. 사기, 의욕

In order to boost employee **morale**, the company offered performance-based bonuses.

직원들의 사기를 진작시키기 위해, 회사는 성과 기반 보너스를 제의했습니다.

34 seasoned

● a. 경험 많은, 숙련된

> After years of experience in the industry, he was considered a **seasoned** professional in his field.
> 업계에서의 수년간의 경험 후에, 그는 그의 분야에서 숙련된 전문가로 여겨졌습니다.

35 deserve

● v. ~을 받을 만하다, 누릴 자격이 있다

> After years of hard work and dedication, Ms. Perry rightfully **deserves** the promotion.
> 수년간의 노력과 헌신 끝에, 페리 씨는 당연히 승진할 자격이 있습니다.

만점 TIP
- 관련 기출
  well-deserved 충분한 자격이 있는

36 accept

acceptable a. 받아들일 수 있는

● v. ~을 받아들이다, 수락하다

> After careful consideration, I have decided to **accept** the position as the marketing manager at this company.
> 심사숙고 끝에, 이 회사의 마케팅 매니저 자리를 수락하기로 했습니다.

37 indicate

● v. ~을 나타내다

> Please sign and return the attached document **indicating** your willingness to accept the position as sales associate.
> 판매원직 수락 의사를 나타내는 첨부 서류에 서명 후 반송해 주시기 바랍니다.

38 applaud

applause n. 박수(갈채)

v. 박수치다, ~에게 박수를 보내다

The manager **applauded** the entire department for their dedication and hard work in meeting the quarterly sales targets.

관리자는 분기별 매출 목표 달성을 위해 헌신하고 열심히 일한 부서 전체에게 박수를 보냈습니다.

39 reward

rewarding a. 보람 있는, 수익이 나는

v. ~에게 보상하다, 사례하다

n. 보상, 사례

In recognition of its huge success in the past year, the company will **reward** employees with a generous bonus and a paid vacation.

작년의 큰 성공을 인정하여, 회사는 직원들에게 후한 보너스와 유급 휴가로 보상할 것입니다.

만점 TIP

• 관련 기출
reward A with B   A에게 B로 보상하다
reward A for B   A에게 B한 것에 대해 보상하다

40 constraint

n. 제약

Due to budget **constraints**, there is a restriction on hiring new employees this year.

예산상의 제약 때문에, 올해는 신입 직원들을 채용하는 데 제약이 있습니다.

만점 TIP

• 기출 Paraphrasing
constraint → restriction (제한), limit (한계, 제한)

DAILY QUIZ

단어와 그에 알맞은 뜻을 연결해 보세요.

1. benefits •   • (A) 제약
2. constraint •   • (B) 사기, 의욕
3. morale •   • (C) 소개, 추천(서)
4. referral •   • (D) 복리후생

빈칸에 알맞은 단어를 선택하세요.

5. Mark's outstanding performance has earned him a promotion, and he has ------- a new position at the head office.
   마크는 탁월한 성과로 승진하여 본사의 새로운 직책을 수락했습니다.

   (A) indicate
   (B) accepted
   (C) familiarize
   (D) deserved

6. The marketing team ------- the credit for the recent successful product launch, showcasing their innovative strategies.
   마케팅팀은 혁신적인 전략을 선보인 최근의 성공적인 제품 출시에 대해 인정을 받을 만 했습니다.

7. On your first day, please ------- yourself with your workspace and computer system to ensure a smooth transition into your new role.
   첫날에는, 새로운 역할로 원활하게 전환할 수 있도록 작업 공간과 컴퓨터 시스템을 숙지하시기 바랍니다.

8. Please ------- your food preferences to assist us in arranging a menu that accommodates all types of diets.
   저희가 모든 유형의 식단을 충족하는 메뉴를 마련하는 데 도움이 되도록 선호하는 음식들을 알려주십시오.

정답 1 (D) 2 (A) 3 (B) 4 (C) 5 (B) 6 (D) 7 (C) 8 (A)

/ Week /
07 실전 TEST

MP3 바로듣기

강의 바로보기

LISTENING

• Part 3

1. What are the speakers discussing?

   (A) Developing a marketing initiative
   (B) Improving some workstations
   (C) Reviewing hiring policies
   (D) Organizing a workshop

2. What was the woman planning to do?

   (A) Schedule a property viewing
   (B) Distribute an employee survey
   (C) Restock some office supplies
   (D) Collect some measurements

3. What does the man request from the woman?

   (A) A summary of feedback
   (B) A link to a website
   (C) A set of instructions
   (D) A payment receipt

• Part 4

4. What problem does the speaker mention?

   (A) She forgot to make a reservation.
   (B) She cannot access a file.
   (C) Some documents were misplaced.
   (D) A website shows incorrect information.

5. What will the listeners most likely do tonight?

   (A) Attend a training session
   (B) Reserve a restaurant
   (C) Work extra hours
   (D) Review a document

6. Why will the speaker contact an expert?

   (A) To have some machines inspected
   (B) To complain about a schedule
   (C) To discuss an overseas venture
   (D) To make a process simpler

READING

• Part 5

7. The building site supervisor is delighted that the installation of security lighting is ------ complete.

   (A) yet
   (B) nearby
   (C) rarely
   (D) almost

8. The factory owner stated that meeting production targets ------ was the key to running a successful manufacturing company.

   (A) consistently
   (B) durably
   (C) politely
   (D) largely

9. Ms. Song will speak ------ with each department manager to ensure that they are aware of the new lunch break policy.

   (A) newly
   (B) totally
   (C) briefly
   (D) exactly

10. Sprint Sports Beverages has invested ------ in online advertising to reach new customers across the world.

    (A) randomly
    (B) instantly
    (C) roughly
    (D) heavily

11. The eco-friendly packaging has been ------ beneficial as it has helped us reach a wider range of consumers.

    (A) permissibly
    (B) lastly
    (C) diligently
    (D) markedly

12. To ensure the accuracy of our findings, the survey questions should remain ------ the same during the course of the month-long study.

    (A) expertly
    (B) helpfully
    (C) mutually
    (D) exactly

13. While removing a fallen tree, the emergency services had to ------ close two lanes of Highway 40.

    (A) conveniently
    (B) temporarily
    (C) experimentally
    (D) sufficiently

14. Local residents are delighted that Alloway Town Library is ------ expanding its collection of books.

    (A) strangely
    (B) equally
    (C) rapidly
    (D) hardly

Part 6

Questions 15-18 refer to the following letter.

Dear Mr. Sanchez,

Thank you for your letter regarding your recent visit to our newly opened Mexican restaurant.

First, let me offer my sincere apologies that the appetizer was not to your liking. Most people who visit our establishment enjoy spicy food, but we understand that **15.** ------- do not. For that reason, we offer all menu selections in mild, medium, and hot versions. This is something your server should have told you when you placed your order.

I also understand that you are disappointed we do not offer free refills on soft drinks. However, we felt it will allow us to keep prices reasonable and minimize waste. **16.** -------, we offer filtered ice water at no cost. We would like another chance to make you one of our many satisfied customers. So, I **17.** ------- a gift certificate for two free meals with drinks and dessert, which is valid at any of our locations. **18.** -------.

Sincerely,
Penelope Lopez, Customer Relations Specialist

15. (A) any
(B) some
(C) all
(D) one

16. (A) Likewise
(B) Otherwise
(C) For example
(D) Instead

17. (A) had been enclosing
(B) have enclosed
(C) enclosing
(D) was enclosed

18. (A) I hope you will join us for dinner in the near future.
(B) I look forward to hearing about your recommendations.
(C) Thank you for staying with us during these difficult times.
(D) We would be pleased to do business with your company again.

• **Part 7**

Questions 19-20 refer to the following letter.

Dear sir/madam,

As requested, I am writing to you regarding Matthew Bright, who recently submitted an application for the vacant position at Nexico Corporation. I strongly believe Matthew would be well suited to the role and a good fit for your company.

Matthew worked in the human resources department at my company for four years. In addition to his good university qualifications and work credentials, he possessed many of the qualities that are essential in an HR role. After 18 months of probationary period, Matthew underwent in-house management training and then took on the role of assistant manager. His responsibilities included supervising a team of five workers. After only two years in his management role, Matthew was nominated for, and won, our Manager of the Year award.

Lastly, I wish to praise the impressive work ethic Matthew displayed for the duration of his employment at my firm. I believe it would be a wise hiring decision to offer Matthew the role, and I am confident he would be an invaluable asset to your company.

19. What is the purpose of the letter?

(A) To inquire about an opening
(B) To arrange an interview
(C) To nominate an employee for an award
(D) To provide a job reference

20. What is true about Mr. Bright?

(A) He currently works at Nexico Corporation.
(B) He was recognized for his management ability.
(C) He has applied for several different job vacancies.
(D) He graduated from university 18 months ago.

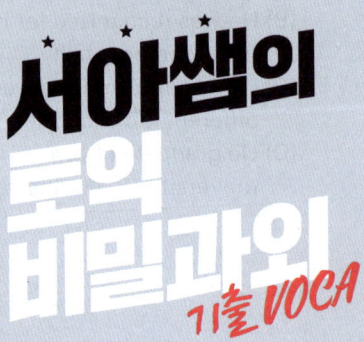

Week 08

Contents		Page	Date	Check
Day 01	Part 3, 4 기출 패러프레이징 ③	518	월 일	☐
Day 02	Part 5, 6 전치사	532	월 일	☐
Day 03	Part 5, 6 다품사	546	월 일	☐
Day 04	Part 5, 6 다의어	560	월 일	☐
Day 05	Part 7 독해가 쉬워지는 어휘 ④	574	월 일	☐
Week 08 실전 TEST		586	월 일	☐

기출 패러프레이징 ❸ Part 3, 4

1 show A around
- give A a tour
  A에게 구경시켜주다

● A에게 구경시켜주다

M: We plan to **show Mr. Kwon around** the recording studio once he arrives later this afternoon.

저희는 권 씨가 오늘 오후 늦게 도착하면 그에게 녹음실을 구경시켜드릴 계획입니다.

Q. 무엇을 할 것인가?
→ **Give** a client a tour

2 finalize
- finish 끝내다

● 마무리하다, 끝내다

W: Please be sure to **finish** writing the details for the conference schedule by tomorrow.

회의 일정에 대한 세부사항 작성을 내일까지 꼭 완료하시기 바랍니다.

Q. 무엇을 하라고 하는가?
→ **Finalize** a schedule

3 stop by
- visit 방문하다
- drop by, come by 들르다

● 들르다

M: I'm going to **stop by** the supplier's warehouse tomorrow to check out their storage situation.

내일 공급업체 창고에 들러 보관 상황을 확인할 예정입니다.

Q. 내일 무엇을 할 것인가?
→ **Visit** a warehouse

4 organize

- plan, arrange, prepare
계획하다, 준비하다

● ~을 조직하다, 준비하다

W: You did such an amazing job **organizing** the Leadership Conference. I want to thank you for your hard work in attracting over 300 attendees!

리더십 컨퍼런스 준비를 정말 잘 해내셨어요. 300명이 넘는 참석자를 유치하기 위해 열심히 노력해주셔서 감사합니다!

Q. 무엇에 대해 감사하는가?
→ **Planning** a large event

5 collaborate with

- work (together) with
~와 함께 작업하다
- in cooperation with
~와 협력하여

● ~와 협력하다

M: If you're feeling stuck, I recommend **working together with** Henson. He usually has great ideas when it comes to creating engaging presentations.

하다가 막히면, 헨슨 씨와 작업하시는 것을 추천합니다. 그는 매력적인 프레젠테이션을 만드는 일에 관한 한 거의 늘 좋은 아이디어를 가지고 있습니다.

Q. 무엇을 할 것을 권하는가?
→ **Collaborate with** a colleague

6 (job) opening

- vacancy 공석
- position 자리

● 공석, 빈 자리

W: I know you mentioned that there's a new **opening** in the sales department, too. I'll upload a post about it on our job board by the end of today.

영업부에도 공석이 생긴다고 말씀하셨지요. 오늘 중으로 채용 게시판에 관련된 글을 올리겠습니다.

Q. 무엇을 하겠다고 하는가?
→ Advertise a job **vacancy**

7 challenging

- difficult 어려운

어려운, 힘든

M: Our park also offers several hiking trails. Keep in mind though, they are **challenging** and meant for more experienced climbers.

저희 공원에는 여러 등산로가 있습니다. 하지만 이 등산로들은 어려워서, 경험이 풍부한 등산객들을 위한 것임을 명심하시기 바랍니다.

Q. 등산로에 대해 뭐라고 말하는가?
→ They are **difficult**.

8 purchase in bulk

- order more than ~ 이상을 주문하다
- large order 대량 주문
- in large quantities 대량으로

대량으로 구매하다

W: The cups are 8 dollars each, but if you **order more than 50**, you'll get 20 percent off of the total price.

컵이 각각 8달러인데요, 50개 이상 주문하시면 전체 금액에서 20% 할인을 받게 됩니다.

Q. 어떻게 할인을 받을 수 있는가?
→ By **placing a large order**
By **purchasing in bulk**
By **buying in large quantities**

9 verify

- confirm (사실임을) 확인하다

v. (사실인지) 확인하다, 확인해주다

M: Hi, this is Mark Shen. I just wanted to **confirm** that I will be able to meet you as scheduled tomorrow at 10 AM.

안녕하세요, 저는 마크 쉔입니다. 내일 오전 10시에 예정된대로 당신을 만날 수 있다는 걸 확인해드리고 싶었어요.

Q. 왜 전화했는가?
→ To **verify** an appointment

10 a form of identification

- photo ID 사진이 있는 신분증
- ID badge 신분증 명찰
- passport 여권
- driver's license 운전면허증

● 신분증

W: I'll just need to see some **photo ID** to verify your registration. Do you have your **passport** or **driver's license** with you?

귀하의 등록을 확인해드리기 위해 제가 사진이 부착된 신분증을 확인해야 합니다. 여권이나 운전 면허증을 갖고 계신가요?

Q. 무엇을 보여달라고 하는가?
→ **A form of identification**

11 expedited shipping

- express shipping 빠른 배송

● 급송, 신속 배송

M: Is there also an option for **express shipping**? I would like to receive the sunglasses as soon as possible.

급송도 가능한가요? 선글라스를 최대한 빨리 받고 싶습니다.

Q. 무엇을 요청하는가?
→ **Expedited shipping**

12 easy to use

- user-friendly 사용자 친화적인

● 사용하기 쉬운

W: Our remote controls are **user-friendly**. By offering a modern design with minimal buttons, you no longer have to struggle to perform simple functions.

저희 리모콘은 사용자 친화적입니다. 최소한의 버튼으로 이루어진 현대적인 디자인을 제공하므로 여러분은 더 이상 간단한 기능을 수행하는 데 어려움을 겪을 필요가 없습니다.

Q. 제품의 어떤 점을 강조하는가?
→ They are **easy to use**.

13 look into

• investigate 조사하다

● ~을 조사하다

M: I understand that you're calling to check what happened to your package. Please give me a minute to **look into** it.

귀하의 택배에 무슨 일이 있었는지 확인 차 전화하신 것으로 알고 있습니다. 잠시만 기다려주시면 제가 알아보겠습니다.

Q. 무엇을 하겠다고 하는가?
→ **Investigate** an order

14 accompany

• come along with 함께 가다

● ~와 동행하다

W: I need a photographer to **accompany** me to the excavation site. Do you think you can help me with hiring someone?

발굴 현장에 동행해 줄 사진작가가 필요합니다. 사람을 고용하는 것을 도와주실 수 있을까요?

Q. 무엇에 대해 도움을 요청하는가?
→ Finding someone to **come along with** her

15 schedule

• arrange, set (일정 등을) 잡다

● v. ~의 일정을 잡다

M: Our director wants to meet with the sellers in person next week. Can you **arrange** a time and place for them?

다음 주에 이사님께서 판매자분들을 직접 뵙고 싶어 하십니다. 시간과 장소를 잡아주실 수 있나요?

Q. 무엇을 해달라고 하는가?
→ **Schedule** a meeting

16 assemble

- put together
  조립하다, (이것저것을 모아) 만들다

● ~을 조립하다

W: My name is Kara, and I'm going to be training you on how to **put together** our lightweight bookshelves. These are our best-selling products.

제 이름은 카라이고, 저희 회사의 경량 책장을 조립하는 방법에 대해 알려드릴 예정입니다. 그것들은 저희가 가장 많이 판매하는 제품들입니다.

Q. 교육의 주된 내용은?
→ **Assembling** some furniture

17 proceed to

- head to, go to ~로 가다

● ~로 가다

M: If you've made an appointment online, please **proceed to** service window number 1 to receive assistance immediately.

온라인으로 예약하셨다면, 즉시 1번 창구로 가셔서 도움을 받으시기 바랍니다.

Q. 예약을 한 방문객들은 무엇을 해야 하는가?
→ **Go to** a specific service window

18 turn down

- reject 거절하다

● ~을 거절하다

W: I'm disappointed that the investors **turned down** our proposal. I thought the agreement would have a lot of potential.

투자자들이 우리의 제안을 거절한 것에 실망했습니다. 저는 그 계약에 많은 가능성이 있을 거라고 생각했습니다.

Q. 왜 실망했는가?
→ A proposal was **rejected**.

19 mandatory

- required 필수의

● 필수의, 의무적인

M: The seminar will focus on strategic development, so attendance for all employees is **mandatory**.

그 세미나는 전략적 개발에 초점을 맞출 것이기 때문에 전 직원이 의무적으로 참석해야 합니다.

Q. 세미나에 대해 뭐라고 하는가?
→ Attendance is **required**.

20 space

- room 방, 공간

● 공간

W: I heard we won't be able to hold client meetings here during the renovation. Why don't we call Meeting Solutions? They rent out meeting **rooms**.

개조 공사를 하는 동안 이곳에서 고객 미팅을 열 수 없을거라 들었습니다. 미팅 솔루션즈 사에 전화해보는 게 어떨까요? 거긴 회의실을 대여해 줍니다.

Q. 무엇을 제안하는가?
→ Renting some meeting **spaces**

21 resign

- step down, retire
물러나다, 퇴직하다

● 물러나다, 사임하다

M: It's unfortunate that Ms. Atkinson chose to **step down** from her position as CEO. She was a really inspiring figure.

앳킨슨 씨가 최고 경영자 자리에서 물러나기로 한 것은 유감스러운 일입니다. 그녀는 정말 영감을 주는 인물이었습니다.

Q. 왜 실망하는가?
→ A chief executive has **resigned**.

22 demonstrate

- show A how to
  A에게 ~하는 법을 알려주다

● 시연하다, 하는 법을 보여주다

W: Next, I'll **show you how to** use our hotel's reservation management system.

다음으로, 저희 호텔의 예약 관리 시스템을 이용하는 법을 보여드리겠습니다.

Q. 이어서 무엇을 할 것인가?
→ **Demonstrate** a computer program

23 can't find
can't locate

- misplace
  제자리에 두지 않아 찾지 못하다, 둔 곳을 잊다

● (어디에 있는지) 찾지 못하다

M: Have you perhaps seen where I put my briefcase? I **can't find** it anywhere in the office, but I need to use my laptop that's in there.

혹시 제가 서류 가방을 어디에 두었는지 보셨나요? 사무실 어디에서도 못 찾겠는데, 안에 있는 노트북을 사용해야 해요.

Q. 어떤 문제가 있는가?
→ He has **misplaced** his briefcase.

24 draft

- rough version 초안

● 초안

W: I'm still working on the **rough version** of the press release, but I should be able to send it to you for review by 3 o'clock at the latest.

제가 아직 보도자료 초안을 작성 중인데, 늦어도 3시까지는 검토를 위해 보내드릴 수 있을 것 같습니다.

Q. 3시까지 무엇을 하겠다고 하는가?
→ Submit a **draft**

25 be familiar with
- know A well A를 잘 알다

● ~을 잘 알다

M: Ask Kate for some help. She's very **familiar with** the recruitment process.

케이트에게 도움을 요청하세요. 그녀가 채용 절차를 잘 알아요.

Q. 케이트에 대해 뭐라고 하는가?
➜ She **knows a procedure well**.

26 sample
- try 맛보다, 사용해보다

● v. ~을 시식하다

W: Bargain Market appreciates your business. Today only, customers can visit our snack aisle to **sample** our handmade dried fruits mix, made in-store daily.

바게인 마켓을 이용해 주셔서 감사합니다. 오늘 단 하루, 고객들은 저희의 간식 통로에 오셔서 매일 매장에서 만들어지는 수제 건과일 믹스를 시식할 수 있습니다.

Q. 고객들이 무엇을 할 수 있는가?
➜ **Try** some snacks

27 be prohibited
- be not allowed 허용되지 않다

● 금지되다

M: Wait, you're **not allowed** to park there. There's a sign that says that those spots are for emergency vehicles only.

잠시만요, 거기 주차하시면 안 됩니다. 저기에 비상 차량 전용이라고 쓰여 있는 표지판이 있어요.

Q. 주차에 대해 뭐라고 말하는가?
➜ It **is prohibited** in certain spots.

28 reception

- party 파티

• 파티, 연회

> W: There's a **reception** next week for me and some people transferring to the New York branch. I hope you can make it. It's next Friday.
>
> 저와 뉴욕 지사로 전근가는 몇몇 사람들을 위한 파티가 다음 주에 있어요. 당신도 참석하시면 좋겠어요. 다음 주 금요일입니다.
>
> Q. 금요일에 어떤 일이 있을 것인가? ➜ A **party**

29 unique

- special 특별한
- unlike other + 명사
  다른 ~와는 다르게

• 독특한

> M: I think Sona's Jewelry Shop would be the perfect vendor to work with. They make **unique** designs for their jewelry.
>
> 소나 주얼리 숍이 거래하기에 완벽한 판매자 같아요. 그들은 주얼리 제품으로 독특한 디자인을 만들어요.
>
> Q. 판매자에 대해 무엇을 마음에 들어 하는가?
> ➜ They create **special** designs.

30 adjacent

- close 가까운

• 인근의, 가까운

> W: I'll be staying in a hotel during the trip. It's **adjacent** to the beach, so I'm excited for that.
>
> 여행하는 동안 호텔에 묵을 예정입니다. 바닷가와 인접해 있어서 기대가 됩니다.
>
> Q. 호텔에 대해 왜 기대하고 있는가?
> ➜ It is **close** to a beach.

31 stay

- remain ~인 채로 있다

• ~인 채로 있다

> M: Our quarterly sales have **stayed** the same for three terms in a row now.
>
> 분기 매출이 3분기 연속으로 제자리 걸음을 하고 있습니다.
>
> Q. 무엇을 언급하는가?
> ➜ Some sales have **remained** the same.

32 be out of town

- be away on business
  출장 중이다

● (출장 등으로) 출타중이다

W: Actually, I **was out of town** for a client meeting all of last week, so I wasn't able to finish the task you assigned me.

사실은, 지난주 내내 고객 미팅 때문에 출타중이었어서 제게 할당해주신 업무를 다 못 끝냈어요.

Q. 왜 업무를 마치지 못했는가?
→ She was **away on business**.

33 be responsible for

- be in charge of
  맡다, 담당하다

● ~을 책임지다, ~을 담당하다

M: I'**m responsible for** planning the company's annual year-end party, and I need help hiring a band to play for us.

저는 회사의 연례 연말 파티를 계획하는 일을 맡고 있고, 우리를 위해 연주할 밴드를 고용하는 데 도움이 필요합니다.

Q. 무엇을 맡고 (**in charge of**) 있는가?
→ Organizing a party

만점 TIP
- 이와 같이 질문에 paraphrase되는 경우도 자주 등장합니다.

34 punctual

- be on time 시간을 잘 지키다

● 시간을 잘 지키는

W: I know a mechanic! I highly recommend Dave Burris because he'**s** always **on time** to all service calls.

제가 아는 정비사가 있어요! 데이브 버리스 씨를 적극 추천하는데요, 그는 항상 모든 서비스 요청에 대해 시간을 잘 지키기 때문이에요.

Q. 데이브 버리스에 대해 뭐라고 하는가?
→ He is **punctual**.

35 assist

- help, give A a hand
  도와주다

• 도와주다

M: Mark, I want you to meet Amelia. Amelia is starting work today. Could you show her around and **help** her find her way to her workstation?

마크 씨, 아멜리아 씨를 소개할게요. 아멜리아 씨는 오늘 첫 근무를 시작하십니다. 그녀에게 주변을 안내해주고 자리로 가는 길을 찾는 것을 도와주시겠어요?

Q. 요청하는 것은 무엇인가?
→ **Assist** a new employee

36 research

- do a search 조사하다

• 조사하다, 연구하다

W: I'll **do a search** into the market trends from the past year. That'll give us a good idea of where to direct our marketing efforts.

지난 한 해 동안의 시장 동향을 조사해 보겠습니다. 마케팅 활동을 어떤 방향으로 해야 할지에 대해 좋은 아이디어를 줄 것입니다.

Q. 여자는 무엇을 할 것인가?
→ Conduct some market **research**

37 save energy

- conserve energy
  에너지를 절약하다
- reduce energy consumption
  에너지 소비를 줄이다
- energy-efficient
  에너지 효율적인

• 에너지를 절약하다

M: Our client mentioned that she is passionate about **reducing** her **energy consumption**, so we should probably recommend her more **energy-efficient** appliances.

우리 고객이 에너지 소비를 줄이는데 열정을 가지고 있다고 언급했으므로, 우리는 아마도 그녀에게 더 에너지 효율적인 가전제품을 추천해야 할 것입니다.

Q. 고객이 관심 있어 하는 것은?
→ **Saving energy**

Week 08   529

38 surplus

- excess 과잉
- too many 너무 많은

• 잉여, 과잉

> W: Not as many customers came in today as we expected, so we have **too many** scones and donuts left over. What should we do with them?
>
> 오늘은 예상만큼 손님이 많이 오지 않아서 스콘과 도넛이 너무 많이 남았습니다. 이것들을 어떻게 해야 할까요?
>
> Q. 무엇에 대해 이야기하고 있는가?
> → Addressing a **surplus** of items

39 customer review

- what customers are saying 고객들이 말하는 바

• 고객 후기, 고객 평가

> M: See **what other customers are saying** about our premium beef selection at starfieldranchbeef.com.
>
> starfieldranchbeef.com에서 우리의 프리미엄 소고기 제품에 대한 고객 평가를 확인해 보십시오.
>
> Q. 웹사이트에서 무엇을 찾을 수 있는가?
> → **Customer reviews**

40 remove

- discard, get rid of, dispose of
  버리다, 폐기하다, 처분하다

• ~을 제거하다, 없애다

> W: Laura, don't forget to **discard** the food waste before leaving for the day. We don't want any bugs gathering in the kitchen overnight.
>
> 로라, 오늘 가기 전에 음식물 쓰레기 버리는 것을 잊지 마세요. 밤새 부엌에 벌레가 모이는 것을 원치 않습니다.
>
> Q. 무엇을 하라고 하는가?
> → **Remove** some trash

DAILY QUIZ

🎧 질문을 읽고 음원을 들은 뒤, 정답을 골라보세요.

1 What service does the woman describe?

(A) Express shipping
(B) Real-time tracking

M: Hi, I have a package that needs to be sent to New York City. My situation's quite urgent.
W: Alright, we do offer expedited shipping, but for an extra 12 dollars. Would that be okay?

2 Why does the woman reject the man's offer?

(A) She has a mandatory training to attend.
(B) She is extremely busy.

M: Would you like to come along with me to the reception organized for Mr. Chang's retirement? He's the founder of the marketing agency we collaborated closely with last year.
W: I'd love to accompany you, but I'll have to turn down the opportunity. My schedule is really packed this week.
M: Got it. I'll ask someone else if they'd like to attend the party.

3 According to the speaker, what can the listeners find on a Web site?

(A) Survey questions
(B) Customer reviews

W: Our mini refrigerators are perfect for single households and dorm rooms. Plus, they're easy to assemble and offer unique features, like a lockable door, customizable temperatures, and even an ice dispenser. Check out what customers are saying about our mini refrigerators on our Web site today.

정답 1 (A) 2 (B) 3 (B)

Day 02 전치사 Part 5, 6

1 according to

~에 따르면

[기출] **according to** survey results 설문조사 결과에 따르면
according to Ms. Val 벨 씨에 따르면

------ comment cards filled out last week, our new dessert menu is a huge success.
(A) According to (B) Instead of

2 on behalf of

~을 대표하여, 대신하여

[기출] **on behalf of** his team
그의 팀을 대표하여

on behalf of Mayor Dan
댄 시장을 대신하여

Philip Seyomour, the CFO of Azard Corporation, will accept the award ------ the company's founder.
(A) on behalf of (B) like

3 along with

~와 함께, ~을 따라서

[기출] **along with** your application 귀하의 지원서와 함께
along with Ms. Alexa 알렉사 씨를 따라서

------ your résumé, please provide a portfolio of your previous graphic design work.
(A) Except for (B) Along with

4 among

- ~ 중에서, ~ 사이에서

  기출 **among** the nominees
  지명자들 중에서

  collaboration **among** coworkers
  동료들 사이에서의 협동

  > Michael Watson's new movie set during World War II proved most popular ------- filmgoers aged over 30.
  > (A) outside (B) among

5 at least

- 적어도, 최소한

  기출 **at least** two years of relevant experience
  적어도 2년의 관련 경험

  > Reservations for tables on our outdoor patio must be placed ------- two months in advance.
  > (A) in case of (B) at least

6 beyond

- ~을 넘어서, 초과하여

  기출 **beyond** the entry gate 출입구를 넘어서

  > Only festival attendees with VIP passes are permitted ------- the barrier at the side of the stage.
  > (A) beyond (B) during

7 concerning

- ~에 관하여

  기출 **concerning** the training seminar
  교육 세미나에 관하여

  concerning the plans to merge with
  ~와 합병할 계획에 관하여

  > The energy company sent an e-mail to all customers ------- the recent increase in electricity rates.
  > (A) concerning (B) owing

8 despite

- ~에도 불구하고

  기출 **despite** losses in the second quarter
  2분기의 손실에도 불구하고

  despite several deadline extensions
  여러 번의 마감일 연장에도 불구하고

  The construction of the new bowling alley has been canceled ------- demand from local residents for new recreational facilities.
  (A) except   (B) despite

9 due to

- ~로 인해, ~ 때문에

  기출 **due to** inclement weather
  악천후로 인해

  due to scheduled maintenance
  예정된 유지보수 때문에

  The Eagle Run ski route is off-limits today ------- concerns about dangerous conditions.
  (A) due to   (B) as for

10 except

- ~을 제외하고

  기출 **except** a limited number of staff
  한정된 직원 수를 제외하고

  except personal checks
  개인 수표를 제외하고

  No one ------- the movie's director has been allowed to see the final few pages of the screenplay.
  (A) out of   (B) except

11 following

- ~ 후에, ~ 다음에

  기출 **following** widespread speculation
  추측들이 널리 퍼진 후에

  following the luncheon
  오찬 후에

  ------- the positive reviews of her debut music album, Greta Inglis embarked on a global tour.

  (A) Following   (B) Like

12 given

- ~을 감안하면

  기출 **given** his negotiation skills
  그의 협상 기술을 감안하면

  given her limited experience in law
  법 분야에서의 제한된 경험을 감안하면

  ------- the rise in fuel prices, more and more workers are choosing to commute by bicycle.

  (A) Provided   (B) Given

13 in accordance with

- ~에 따라서

  기출 **in accordance with** generally accepted standards
  일반적으로 수용되는 기준에 따라서

  Wootton Engineering conducts safety inspections ------- nationally implemented government guidelines.

  (A) as opposed to   (B) in accordance with

14 in addition to

● ~에 더하여, ~뿐만 아니라

기출 **in addition to** expanding our hours of operation
우리의 운영 시간을 연장하는 것에 더하여

in addition to excellent academic credentials
훌륭한 학업 자격뿐만 아니라

------- supplying a wide range of food and beverages, Marion Catering provides experienced serving staff.
(A) In addition to　　(B) As soon as

15 ahead of

● ~보다 앞서, 빨리

기출 one day **ahead of** the general public
일반 대중보다 하루 앞서

ahead of schedule
일정보다 빨리

The maintenance team is attempting to fix a problem with the exhibition center's audio system ------- next month's Business Software Convention.
(A) ahead of　　(B) along with

16 in the event of

● ~의 경우에

기출 **in the event of** heavy snowfall
폭설의 경우에

in the event of a computer system failure
컴퓨터 시스템 장애의 경우에

------- heavy rain, the arts and crafts fair will be held in Dingley Community Center instead of Fairland Park.
(A) As much as　　(B) In the event of

17 including

- ~을 포함하여

  기출 **including** tax
  세금을 포함하여

  including three new nominees
  새로운 세 명의 후보들을 포함하여

  > All Mayfair Hotel employees, ------- housekeeping staff, must attend the customer service workshop on May 6.
  > (A) about   (B) including

18 instead of

- ~ 대신에

  기출 **instead of** residential areas
  주거 지역 대신에

  instead of renewing their contract
  그들의 계약을 갱신하는 대신에

  > Due to delay in obtaining the necessary permit, construction of the shopping mall will begin next month ------- this month.
  > (A) instead of   (B) except for

19 opposite

- ~ 반대편의, ~ 맞은편의

  기출 stand **opposite** the marketing manager
  마케팅 부장과 반대편에 서다

  parking lot **opposite** the power plant
  발전소 맞은편의 주차장

  > As we are planning to renovate the west wing, all visitors should use the public parking lot ------- the company headquarters.
  > (A) opposite   (B) apart

20 owing to

● ~ 때문에

기출 **owing to** rising fuel prices
증가하는 연료 가격 때문에

owing to a flood from the nearby river
근처 강으로부터의 홍수 때문에

------- the high cost of the renovation project, company executives will not receive a year-end bonus.
(A) Owing to　　　(B) Such as

21 per

● ~당, ~마다

기출 one coupon **per** customer
손님당 하나의 쿠폰

For the time being, there is a limit of one free beverage ------- passenger.
(A) by　　　(B) per

22 pertaining to

● ~에 관계된, 속하는

기출 additional details **pertaining to** the workshop
워크숍에 관계된 추가 세부사항들

address issues **pertaining to** our products
우리 상품에 속한 문제들을 처리하다

Additional information ------- the workshop is detailed in the brochure that will be handed out shortly.
(A) pertaining to　　　(B) in spite of

23 prior to

- ~ 이전에

  기출 **prior to** the first meeting
  첫 회의 이전에

  prior to sending products
  제품들을 보내기 이전에

  To help new staff members prepare for their roles, the company handbook was sent to each member ------- the orientation session.
  (A) in favor of (B) prior to

24 rather than

- ~보다는 (차라리)

  기출 changes in some recipes **rather than** new packaging
  새로운 포장보다는 몇몇 요리법에서의 변화

  expand its floor **rather than** buying a new facility
  새로운 시설을 매매하기보다는 자사 건물의 층을 확장하다

  Ms. Jones would like to reschedule the sales meeting for next Wednesday ------- tomorrow.
  (A) rather than (B) just as

25 regarding

- ~에 관한

  기출 information **regarding** our new product line
  우리의 새로운 제품군에 관한 정보

  questions **regarding** access to the account
  계정 접근에 관한 질문들

  Feel free to contact your supervisor if you have any questions ------- the vacation leave or sick leave policies.
  (A) regarding (B) between

26 regardless of

- ~와 상관 없이

  기출 **regardless of** who is in the leading role
  누가 선도적인 역할을 하는지와 상관 없이

  regardless of Ms. Crude's absence
  크루드 씨의 부재와 상관 없이

  At Ricardo Furnishings, the standard delivery fee is $10, ------- the size of the order.
  (A) along with　　　(B) regardless of

27 unlike

- ~와 달리

  기출 **unlike** the previous edition
  이전 쇄와 달리

  unlike most other equipment
  대부분의 다른 장비와 달리

  ------- Ms. Verani, Ms. Cortez accepted the offer to transfer to the New Orleans office.
  (A) Unlike　　　(B) Opposed

28 up to

- ~까지

  기출 **up to** 14 days from the date of purchase
  구매일로부터 14일까지

  up to 2,000 additional workers
  2,000명의 추가 직원들까지

  Visit Montega Market and save ------- 50 percent on a wide variety of top fashion brands.
  (A) up to　　　(B) except for

29 within

- ~ 이내에

  기출 **within** the limits of our budget
  우리 예산의 한계 이내에

  within two business days
  영업일 2일 이내에

  > ACA Electronics will provide you with a full refund ------- three days of receiving the faulty, returned product.
  >
  > (A) into (B) within

30 throughout

- ~ 전반에 걸쳐, ~ 동안 쭉

  기출 be well known **throughout** the fashion industry
  패션 산업 전반에 걸쳐 잘 알려져 있다

  throughout the entire construction period
  전체 건축 기간 동안 쭉

  > According to the annual sales report, several problems occurred ------- the third financial quarter.
  >
  > (A) besides (B) throughout

31 in light of

- ~에 비추어 볼 때, ~을 고려하여

  기출 **in light of** the suspension of transport services
  운송 서비스의 중단에 비추어 볼 때

  in light of unforeseen circumstances
  예측하지 못한 상황들을 고려하여

  > ------- the complaints about our new appetizer menu, we have decided to revert to the original menu.
  >
  > (A) In spite of (B) In light of

32 on top of

- ~외에, ~의 위에

  기출 **on top of** their regular workload
  정규 업무량 외에

  on top of the standard manufacturer's warranty
  제조사의 표준 보증 외에

  > Our Platinum Membership includes full use of the sauna and spa ------- the standard access to the main exercise rooms.
  > (A) on top of　　　(B) in case of

33 in response to

- ~에 대응하여

  기출 **in response to** overwhelming demand
  압도적인 수요에 대응하여

  in response to customer suggestions
  고객 제안에 대응하여

  > ------- negative feedback about delivery times, we have decided to work with a different courier service.
  > (A) In response to　　　(B) In place of

34 on account of

- ~ 때문에

  기출 **on account of** the sensitive information
  민감한 정보 때문에

  > ------- the harmful chemicals they contain, the cleaning products should be stored out of reach of children.
  > (A) On account of　　　(B) Such as

35 other than

● ~ 외에, ~ 말고 다른

기출 **other than** the important planning procedures
중요한 기획 절차 외에

a supplier **other than** their electric utility company
전력 회사 말고 다른 공급사

> Starting next year, employees will be able to pay into a pension fund ------- that recommended by our company.
>
> (A) combined　　　(B) other than

36 contrary to

● ~와 반대로, ~에 반해서

기출 **contrary to** the information on the Web site
그 웹 사이트에 있는 정보와 반대로

> ------- the showtimes listed in the event program, the ballet performance will begin at 3 PM rather than 4 PM.
>
> (A) As long as　　　(B) Contrary to

37 in spite of

● ~에도 불구하고

기출 **in spite of** negative market predictions
부정적인 시장 예측에도 불구하고

in spite of increased volumes of
~의 증가된 양에도 불구하고

> The fireworks display at Cove Beach was a success ------- the poor weather.
>
> (A) in spite of　　　(B) as a result of

38 thanks to

- ~ 덕분에

  기출 **thanks to** last-minute negotiations
  막바지의 협상 덕분에

  Sales of the Ronin 5 smartphone have doubled this month ------- Mr. Ronstein's exceptional marketing strategy.
  (A) thanks to (B) in addition to

39 as a result of

- ~의 결과로서

  기출 **as a result of** scheduled renovations
  예정된 보수공사의 결과로서

  as a result of an excellent training program
  우수한 교육 프로그램의 결과로서

  ------- the popularity of the new Thunder Flyer roller coaster, the theme park has broken its record for quarterly ticket sales.
  (A) On behalf of (B) As a result of

40 toward

- ~을 향하여, ~쯤

  기출 **toward** a specific financial goal
  특정 재무 목표를 향하여

  toward the end of the month
  월말쯤

  The architect intends to unveil his first draft of the building blueprint ------- the end of next week.
  (A) toward (B) against

DAILY QUIZ

단어와 그에 알맞은 뜻을 연결해 보세요.

1 up to •   • (A) ~에 따라서

2 in accordance with •   • (B) ~을 제외하고

3 except •   • (C) ~까지

빈칸에 알맞은 단어를 선택하세요.

4 ------- several deadline extensions
   여러 번의 마감일 연장에도 불구하고

5 collaboration ------- coworkers
   동료들 사이에서의 협동

(A) on account of
(B) despite
(C) among
(D) instead of

6 ------- renewing their contract
   그들의 계약을 갱신하는 대신에

앞서 배운 단어들의 뜻을 생각하면서, 다음 문제를 풀어보세요.

7 ------- the British Restaurant Guide, Humberside Bistro has the most extensive dessert menu in the country.

   (A) Whereas   (B) According to
   (C) Because   (D) Instead of

8 Ryler Laboratories will purchase a brand-new security system ------- repair the existing devices.

   (A) as such   (B) rather than
   (C) with regard to   (D) for example

정답 1 (C) 2 (A) 3 (B) 4 (B) 5 (C) 6 (D) 7 (B) 8 (B)

Day 03 다품사 Part 5, 6

1 change
n. 변경, 변화
v. 변경하다, 바꾸다

As a result of the ------- to our work schedule, some employees will be required to come to work one hour earlier than usual.
(A) changes   (B) positions

In order to expedite deliveries to our customers, we have recently ------- the shipping service we use.
(A) differed   (B) changed

2 advance
n. 향상, 전진
n. 우선, (때의) 진행
v. 발전하다, 나아가다

Satellite navigation devices are more precise than ever before due to recent ------- in GPS technology.
(A) advances   (B) promotions

Goron Electronics has increased its number of sales staff in ------- of the official launch of the new smartphone.
(A) growth   (B) advance

The seminar series at Arklay Institute will help individuals ------- in the field of marketing.
(A) advance   (B) remind

3 potential
n. 잠재력, 가능성
a. 잠재적인, 가능성 있는

Hampton Corporation has enormous ------- to increase its market share in the country.
(A) potential   (B) proposal

Coller Kitchenware has distributed over five hundred product catalogs to ------- clients in the area.
(A) motivated   (B) potential

4 standard
n. 기준, 표준
a. 일반적인, 표준의

All appliances and procedures in our kitchens must comply with the government's health and safety -------.
(A) details   (B) standards

In an effort to compete with other hotels in the city, Magnum Hotel's ------- room rates will be decreased.
(A) standard   (B) partial

5 surplus
n. 과잉 (재고), 흑자
a. 남는, 초과하는

In order to sell its ------- of computer monitors, Horizon Electronics has lowered the price of the products.
(A) substitute   (B) surplus

------- stock will be sold at 50 percent off in order to make room for our new merchandise.
(A) Surplus   (B) Brief

6 forward
ad. 앞으로
v. (제3자에게) 전송하다

The CEO confirmed that Ollay Logistics Inc. will move ------- with its plan to relocate its headquarters to Seattle.
(A) forward   (B) altogether

Inquiries regarding job vacancies should be ------- to Patricia Rumson in the HR department.
(A) located   (B) forwarded

7 once
ad. 한때, 한 번
conj. 일단 ~하면, ~하자마자

------- the most popular neighborhood in Bayville, Garland Heights is now full of abandoned buildings.
(A) Once   (B) Since

------- the clients arrive at the manufacturing plant, they will be given an extensive tour of the facility.
(A) Soon   (B) Once

8 later
ad. ~후에, 나중에
a. 추후의

The full line-up of performers for this summer's jazz music festival will be posted online ------- this week.
(A) next (B) later

Those who progress through the first round of interviews will be invited back for a final interview at a ------- date.
(A) final (B) later

9 following
prep. ~후에
a. 다음의, 뒤따르는

The film's launch has been pushed back ------- the negative feedback from the test screenings.
(A) because (B) following

Articles received after the deadline will not be published until the ------- month.
(A) following (B) remaining

10 secure
v. 확보하다, 보장하다
a. 안전한, 확실한

Mr. Halliday has arranged a product demonstration to ------- funding from local business owners.
(A) conduct (B) secure

Patient records at Belvedere Health Clinic are kept ------- at all times.
(A) imperative (B) secure

11 plus
prep. ~을 더하여
ad. 게다가

Purchase a premium ticket for any movie to receive a large popcorn ------- your choice of beverage for no extra charge.
(A) plus　　　　　　(B) whichever

You will receive 10% off of the purchase. -------, you will receive a free gift.
(A) However　　　　(B) Plus

12 several
a. 여러 가지의, 몇몇의
n. 몇 개

Martin Hodge has published more than twenty books covering ------- subjects related to sales.
(A) any　　　　　　(B) several

------- of our restaurant branches are likely to close down unless they become more profitable.
(A) Several　　　　(B) Either

13 alert
n. 경보, 경계
v. 알려주다, 경고하다

The continuous beeping noise from our smoke detectors functions as an ------- that the battery is almost depleted.
(A) example　　　　(B) alert

Should there be any turbulence during the flight, the pilot will ------- passengers immediately.
(A) alert　　　　　(B) inquire

14 near
a. 가까운
prep. ~ 근처에

Fiesta Mexican Restaurant announced that it will introduce several new vegetarian dishes in the ------- future.
(A) near (B) soon

If you would like to rent an audio guide, please visit the information center that is ------- the ticket office.
(A) next (B) near

15 original
a. 원래의, 진본의
n. 원본

The final draft of the blueprint for the new airport terminal is significantly different from the ------- design.
(A) original (B) similar

Photocopies of your documents will be kept at our office, but the ------- will be returned to you by recorded mail.
(A) interiors (B) originals

16 provided
v. 제공하다
conj. ~라면(that)

All technology conference attendees will be ------- with a name tag and an event program brochure.
(A) provided (B) required

All of our products may be returned for a refund within 21 days ------- they have not been used.
(A) provided that (B) as though

17 objective
n. 목표
a. 객관적인

Mr. Crenshaw's ------- is to attract prospective clients to our firm by impressing them with his presentation.
(A) evaluation (B) objective

The main aim of our Web site is to provide ------- information about news and current events.
(A) main (B) objective

18 permit
v. 허용하다, 허가하다
n. 허가증

Only those with Level 1 security clearance are ------- to use the research laboratory at Alvin Biotech Inc.
(A) given (B) permitted

The vendor ------- must be clearly displayed on the booth or cart that you will use at the food festival.
(A) request (B) permit

19 approach
v. 다가오다, 접근하다
n. 접근(법)

The scheduled launch date for the new cell phone model designed by Elektra Electronics is rapidly -------.
(A) setting (B) approaching

George Atwell's enthusiastic ------- to training new employees has earned him a good reputation within the company.
(A) approach (B) arrival

20 name
v. 직책에 임명하다
n. 이름, 명성

Sam Pickens was ------- as the new chairman of the board after Hank Tiller resigned from the post.
(A) named (B) granted

The Laguna Hotel announced that it is changing its ------- to Golden Palm Resort.
(A) address (B) name

21 attempt
v. 시도하다
n. 시도

Glint Manufacturing has ------- to recruit several Web designers but has yet to fill many of its vacancies.
(A) attempted   (B) persuaded

Ms. Nakatomi's latest ------- to start up her own business was unsuccessful due to insufficient investment.
(A) conclusion   (B) attempt

22 lack
v. ~이 없다, 부족하다
n. 부족, 결여

Unfortunately, we cannot offer you the position at this time because you ------- the required certification in computing.
(A) lack   (B) pass

The east wing reconstruction has been put on hold because of a ------- of funding from headquarters.
(A) response   (B) lack

23 lower
v. 줄이다, 낮추다
a. 더 낮은, 인하된

Providing employees with free exercise facilities can help ------- your company's healthcare costs.
(A) lower   (B) predict

Customers who make frequent international calls may be eligible for ------- rates on calls to certain countries.
(A) light   (B) lower

24 schedule
n. 일정
v. 일정을 잡다

Although an engine fault resulted in a brief stop for repairs, the train still arrived in Boston on -------.
(A) schedule   (B) appointment

Boats from the city quay to Gull Island are ------- to depart every 15 minutes during the peak tourism season.
(A) decided   (B) scheduled

25 increase
n. 인상, 상승
v. 인상하다, 상승하다

Customers of Westside Electric are disappointed that the company announced a 3 percent annual price -------.
(A) statistic   (B) increase

The Crowne Plaza Hotel has decided to ------- the rates of its suites starting from next year.
(A) increase   (B) remain

26 purchase
n. 구매(품)
v. 구매하다

Thank you for your recent ------- of our HQ104 photocopier.
(A) purchase   (B) visit

Theatergoers may ------- refreshments from the main lobby during the 30-minute intermission.
(A) purchase   (B) shop

Week 08 | Day 03 | Part 5, 6 대명사

27 process

n. 과정, 가공, 처리
v. 가공하다, 처리하다

The manufacturing ------- for Aleva kitchen appliances has been improved in order to boost production rates.
(A) location　　　　(B) process

Greenacre Inc. specializes in ------- recyclable items into affordable building materials.
(A) trading　　　　(B) processing

28 lease

v. 임대하다
n. 임대 (계약)

Anyone who wishes to ------- a cabin at Rosco Ski Resort must present a valid ID and pay a security deposit.
(A) turn　　　　(B) lease

The majority of tenants at Eastfield Condos have signed 18-month ------- for their apartments.
(A) leases　　　　(B) license

29 request

n. 요청
v. 요청하다

At your -------, Chad Publications can cancel your subscription to *Sports Time Monthly* immediately.
(A) claim　　　　(B) request

The finance department ------- that all employees submit expense reports by 5 PM on Fridays.
(A) requests　　　　(B) behaves

30 support

n. 지원, 지지, 도움, 후원
v. 지지하다, 지원하다

To express our gratitude to our investors for their valuable -------, we will invite them to our year-end banquet.
(A) transaction (B) support

Mr. Luiz designed the metal frame that ------- more than 250 lights above the theater's main stage.
(A) remarks (B) supports

31 notice

n. 안내, 알림
v. 알아차리다, 주목하다

Due to inclement weather, the trail to the mountain peak will not be accessible until further -------.
(A) attention (B) notice

When Ms. Jones read the job description, she ------- that she lacked several of the academic requirements.
(A) glanced (B) noticed

32 result

n. 결과
v. ~라는 결과를 낳다(in), ~에서 기인하다(from)

Simco Solutions analyzes the behavior and Web site preferences of Internet users and compiles the ------- for various clients.
(A) makers (B) results

Our decision to use cheaper materials will ------- in more affordable products for our customers.
(A) result (B) complete

33 award

v. 수여하다, 상을 주다
n. 상

Mr. Gray and Ms. Bailey have been ------- bonuses for their work in securing a contract with Hornet Systems.
(A) awarded (B) acknowledged

Margaret Harley has received numerous ------- for her performances in Broadway plays.
(A) replies (B) awards

34 offer

v. 제공하다
n. 제안, 제공

Ace Hotel's front desk staff now ------- guests a choice between a room service breakfast or a voucher for the buffet.
(A) offers (B) suggests

Our new client greatly appreciates our ------- to waive the fee for the initial consultation.
(A) offer (B) project

35 complete

v. (작성) 완료하다
a. 완료된

All employees should ------- the survey on our Web site at their earliest possible convenience.
(A) complete (B) participate

Once the first stage of construction is -------, a thorough safety inspection of the site will be conducted.
(A) whole (B) complete

36 open

v. 열다, 개장하다
a. 개장된, 영업 중인

Ray's Coffee & Donuts will ------- its 50th location in downtown Toronto this summer.
(A) expand (B) open

The waterpark will be ------- to visitors from 9 AM until 7 PM during the school holidays.
(A) open (B) entered

37 measure

n. 조치, 대책
v. 수치를 재다, 측정하다

Solaris Motors implements rigid safety ------- to ensure that factory workers are not at risk in the workplace.
(A) consents (B) measures

Prior to purchasing any of our custom curtains, you should ------- all of your windows accurately.
(A) expect (B) measure

38 benefit

v. 혜택을 얻다, 이득을 얻다
n. 혜택, 이득

Because college students can ------- from gaining work experience, many apply for our summer internship positions.
(A) benefit (B) assist

The ------- that the Platinum Membership offers to country club members include priority parking and full access to club facilities.
(A) interests (B) benefits

39 **experience**
n. 경력, 경험
v. 경험하다

Mr. Annit has extensive ------- in managing employees in various departments at Lord Services.
(A) permission　　(B) experience

Sanders Frozen Foods has ------- a sharp decrease in earnings since discontinuing its range of vegetarian meals.
(A) experienced　　(B) demanded

40 **particular**
n. 세부사항(복수형)
a. 특정한

The orientation session will include a 15-minute break so that attendees may read the ------- of their employment contracts.
(A) particulars　　(B) resolutions

Each month, the food subscription service delivers meals from a ------- region or country.
(A) granted　　(B) particular

DAILY QUIZ

앞서 배운 단어들의 뜻을 생각하면서, 다음 문제를 풀어보세요.

1. The assembly line machines in our new factory are so advanced that we need to explain our manufacturing process to ------- investors.

   (A) potential (B) vacant
   (C) complex   (D) limited

2. Our dentists currently have several free time slots as many patients have scheduled their appointments for ------- in the month.

   (A) later   (B) forward
   (C) along   (D) nearby

3. The beeping noise that is sometimes emitted from the car functions as an ------- that a collision is imminent.

   (A) allowance (B) example
   (C) alert   (D) authentication

4. Our factory's productivity steadily ------- by 25 percent between September and December.

   (A) distributed (B) increased
   (C) presented   (D) attempted

5. To provide adequate information for those browsing the furniture auction site, sellers should ------- all items prior to posting them online.

   (A) expect (B) revise
   (C) allow   (D) measure

6. The mobile app developer announced the launch of several new projects ------- its merger with a competitor.

   (A) whenever (B) toward
   (C) following (D) usually

정답 1 (A) 2 (A) 3 (C) 4 (B) 5 (D) 6 (C)

Day 04 다의어 Part 5, 6

1 performance
❶ 성과, 실적, 성능
❷ 공연

Ms. Kang's extensive product knowledge is one of the reasons for her impressive sales -------.
(A) performance (B) department

Theatergoers are politely asked to take their seats ten minutes before the ------- begins.
(A) performance (B) contest

2 location
❶ 장소, 위치
❷ 지점, 사무소

Once a home-based business, Mr. Hewitt's computer repair firm now operates stores in eight -------.
(A) connections (B) locations

PC Wizard has opened retail ------- that stock high-end computer accessories.
(A) locations (B) expertise

3 application
❶ 지원(서), 신청(서)
❷ 적용(점), 응용

Please submit a completed ------- to the HR manager at Regatta Systems Inc. by 5 PM on December 5.
(A) process (B) application

Although all of our employees found the presentation interesting, most of them felt that it had almost no ------- to their daily work.
(A) application (B) detail

4 operation

❶ 영업, 운영
❷ 작동, 조작

After being in business for 25 years, Goodfellow Bakery on Main Street will cease -------.
(A) availability (B) operation

The job of the audio technician at Sema Concert Hall is to check the ------- of every sound system in the music venue.
(A) operation (B) influence

5 reservation

❶ 예약
❷ 주저함, 내키지 않음

It is recommended to call La Chez Rouge at least a month in advance to make a ------- for a table.
(A) placement (B) reservation

Ms. Shapiro has ------- about moving Bizwell Telecom's head office to the suburbs of Ashville.
(A) reservations (B) specializations

6 assembly

❶ 조립
❷ 모임

Although the components are manufactured in Taiwan, the ------- of Typhoon dishwashers is carried out in Australia.
(A) assembly (B) meeting

Next Wednesday, the staff ------- will be held in the third floor conference room at 8:30 AM.
(A) assembly (B) complement

7 initiative

❶ 계획, 법안
❷ 적극성, 진취성

All residents have shown support for the ------- to provide free broadband Internet service to the county's public schools.
(A) initiative (B) bonus

Ms. Gillie displayed a great deal of ------- in learning to speak French prior to her important business trip to Paris.
(A) expectations (B) initiative

8 direction

❶ 길안내, 지시
❷ 지휘, 감독

For ------- to all major tourist attractions in the city, please download the Shanghai Tourism mobile application.
(A) experiments (B) directions

The employee relations division, under the ------- of Lorne Crane, has been credited with maintaining a high level of staff satisfaction.
(A) direction (B) suggestion

9 closely

❶ 긴밀하게
❷ 자세히

Mr. Higson's marketing division worked ------- with graphic designers to develop the new advertising campaign.
(A) heavily (B) closely

Our technical support agents are skilled at listening ------- to properly resolve customer issues.
(A) closely (B) perfectly

10 rather

❶ 다소, 꽤
❷ 차라리

Redding Industries' decision to file for bankruptcy was ------- sudden and left many shareholders distressed.
(A) rather (B) further

The sales director would ------- reschedule the meeting until all the missing data has been obtained.
(A) yet (B) rather

11 apply

❶ 적용하다, 응용하다
❷ 바르다

The business seminar was very informative and gave attendees several skills to ------- to their own work.
(A) apply (B) select

Remove all dirt and dust before ------- new varnish to your wooden decking.
(A) applying (B) showing

12 critical

❶ 중요한
❷ 비판적인

It is ------- that factory workers follow the instructions in this safety manual as written.
(A) actual (B) critical

Mr. Fulcher is ------- of interviewees who do not put in adequate research or preparation.
(A) critical (B) urgent

13 appointment

❶ 예약, 약속
❷ 임명

When booking patient -------, please note whether it will be their first visit to our dental clinic.
(A) circumstances (B) appointments

The ------- of a new CFO signals the company's intention to rapidly increase its revenue and profits.
(A) appointment (B) reservation

14 enter
❶ 출입하다, 들어가다
❷ 입력하다

All attendees are required to put on a wristband prior to ------- the festival site.
(A) stepping　　　(B) entering

To receive news about special offers, please ------- both your mobile phone number and e-mail address.
(A) join　　　(B) enter

15 develop
❶ 개발하다, 수립하다
❷ 발전시키다

The Francis Institute grant is designed to help entrepreneurs ------- their business plans.
(A) proceed　　　(B) develop

Toronto-based Eva Electronics has ------- strong relationships with several technology firms in Asia.
(A) led to　　　(B) developed

16 view
❶ 경치, 경관
❷ 견해, 관점

All rooms at Wallaga Bay Beach Resort offer a spectacular ------- of the ocean and coastline.
(A) site　　　(B) view

Opinions expressed in the Readers' Letters section of the newspaper do not necessarily reflect the ------- of our publication.
(A) differences　　　(B) views

17 consider

❶ 여기다, 간주하다
❷ 고려하다, 검토하다

The board members of Shatara Inc. ------- a high standard of customer service to be the company's top priority.
(A) consider   (B) refer

Employees who are ------- applying for the position in the accounting department should send an e-mail to Mr. Rico.
(A) considering   (B) specifying

18 promote

❶ 홍보하다
❷ 승진시키다

Blue Line Technologies has hired actor Ken Lorde to ------- its new range of tablet computers.
(A) promote   (B) impress

Karl Simmons has been ------- to Chief Financial Officer at Sandringham Catering Company.
(A) promoted   (B) agreed

19 reach

❶ 도달하다, ~에 가다
❷ 연락하다

Burton Marketing has hired several online marketing experts as part of its effort to ------- new customers.
(A) reach   (B) accept

Our customer service team can be ------- 24 hours a day either by phone or by using our online chat.
(A) applied   (B) reached

20 cover
❶ (보상 범위에) 포함하다, (비용을) 부담하다
❷ (주제) ~을 다루다

Employees should note that the cost for the Willow Valley excursion ------- accommodations and meals for three days.
(A) applies (B) covers

Ms. Jones gave each new employee a handout outlining the main topics that she will ------- during the orientation.
(A) cover (B) wrap

21 responsibility
❶ 책임
❷ (담당) 업무, 직무

It is each passenger's ------- to take care of their personal belongings during the city bus tour.
(A) permission (B) responsibility

------- of the senior event coordinator include contacting clients and submitting regular project updates.
(A) Promotions (B) Responsibilities

22 order
❶ 주문하다
❷ 지시하다

Ms. Ling will take a full inventory before she ------- more laboratory supplies.
(A) contains (B) orders

Pacific Industries has ------- an extensive review of the company's health and safety procedures.
(A) ordered (B) limited

23 acquire

❶ 인수하다
❷ 얻다, 획득하다

- When ALG Software ------- Digital Dream Games in November, all workers will work together at a newly constructed head office.
  (A) merges   (B) acquires

- We offer a wide variety of gifts and rewards to customers who ------- enough loyalty points.
  (A) acquire   (B) perform

24 assemble

❶ 조립하다
❷ 모으다, 모이다

- To satisfy increasing demand, factory workers will ------- more than five hundred new automobiles this week.
  (A) assemble   (B) carry

- Before he creates our promotional materials, Mr. Teller will ------- a team of experienced writers.
  (A) achieve   (B) assemble

25 conclude

❶ 종료하다, 끝내다
❷ 결론을 내리다

- The mobile phone launch event will last for approximately one hour and ------- with a demonstration of the device.
  (A) reserve   (B) conclude

- The financial advisors ------- that the company could significantly reduce its shipping expenses.
  (A) concluded   (B) completed

Week 08   567

26 receipt

❶ 영수증
❷ 수령

Sales executives who travel to conventions and conferences should turn in ------- for reimbursement.
(A) procedures   (B) receipts

Upon ------- of the faulty device, we will contact you with an estimated timeframe for repairs.
(A) request   (B) receipt

27 occasion

❶ 상황
❷ 특별한 사건

The band can create a setlist of songs that is ideal for any -------.
(A) occasion   (B) chance

Corden City was established 250 years ago, so the city council will mark this important ------- with a street festival.
(A) introduction   (B) occasion

28 reserve

❶ 예약하다
❷ (권한을) 보유하다

If you wish to ------- a table in our rooftop dining area, please contact us at least two weeks in advance.
(A) reserve   (B) appoint

Scando Travel Agency ------- the right to cancel tour bookings if payment is not received by the specified deadline.
(A) collects   (B) reserves

29 reference
❶ 참고, 참조
❷ 추천(서)

We will hold on to your résumé for future -------, although we currently have no job openings that would suit you.
(A) reference (B) direction

Applicants should include a list of ------- with their application form, résumé, and cover letter.
(A) references (B) subjects

30 extend
❶ (기한을) 연장하다
❷ 전하다, 주다

The completion date for the renovation work at Ashford Shopping Mall has been ------- to May 2.
(A) extended (B) finished

The business owners ------- an invitation to several potential investors who were interested in touring the manufacturing facility.
(A) extended (B) assigned

31 term
❶ (계약) 조건
❷ 임기

If you agree to the ------- of the contract, please sign both copies and send one copy to our Carolton office by mail.
(A) terms (B) views

During his ------- as the mayor of Leewood, George Ralston made numerous improvements to the town's transportation systems.
(A) vicinity (B) term

32 position

❶ 직책, 직급
❷ 위치, 자리

The company's CEO aims to fill the marketing director ------- before the end of the month.
(A) position   (B) employment

By hiring renowned chef Angela Booth and revising its menu, Loyola Bistro will rise to the top ------- among local restaurants.
(A) position   (B) record

33 shift

❶ (교대) 근무
❷ 변화, 전환

When applying for the assembly line operator vacancy, be advised that the role includes weekend -------.
(A) shifts   (B) entries

In a surprising ------- in its marketing approach, Swift Sportswear will no longer seek endorsements from famous athletes.
(A) shortage   (B) shift

34 issue

❶ (잡지) 호, 쇄
❷ 문제

We apologize that last month's ------- of *High Fashion Magazine* contained inaccurate information about designer Marika Hemsworth.
(A) page   (B) issue

Local council members are available to discuss a wide range of resident -------, from road repairs to noise complaints.
(A) issues   (B) positions

35 replacement
❶ 교환(품), 대체(품)
❷ 후임

Customers seeking a refund or ------- should submit an electronic form through our Web site.
(A) replacement (B) direction

At Mr. Barringer's retirement dinner, he introduced his ------- and discussed her notable business achievements.
(A) replacement (B) development

36 leave
❶ 떠나다
❷ 남겨두다

Gym members should ensure they have placed all of their belongings in a locker before ------- the dressing room.
(A) leaving (B) managing

At the end of the meeting, Ms. Dawson ------- additional copies of the presentation handouts on a desk.
(A) remained (B) left

37 take
❶ 데려가다, 가져가다
❷ (시간이) 걸리다, 사용하다

Mr. Jones offered to ------- the new recruits on a tour of the factory and its adjoining office buildings.
(A) take (B) tell

Drivers working for Big Apple Taxis typically ------- about 45 minutes for their lunch break.
(A) last (B) take

38 return
❶ 반품하다
❷ 돌아오다

Since the bookcase Ms. Garfield purchased was too wide, she ------- it to the furniture store.
(A) tailored (B) returned

Participants will receive a Certificate of Achievement within 7 days of ------- from the workshop.
(A) working (B) returning

39 determine
❶ 결정하다, 확정하다
❷ 알아내다

Our hotel can provide videos of each room to help event organizers ------- the most suitable room for their event.
(A) broaden (B) determine

Engineers are still attempting to ------- the cause of malfunction on the assembly line.
(A) develop (B) determine

40 consult
❶ 상담하다
❷ 참조하다

When making a critical department decision, Mr. Wallace finds it useful to ------- his employees for their opinions.
(A) consult (B) request

Please ------- the in-flight magazine to browse the full range of available snacks and beverages.
(A) consult (B) look

DAILY QUIZ

앞서 배운 단어들의 뜻을 생각하면서, 다음 문제를 풀어보세요.

1. Whenever products are being prepared for shipping, it is the warehouse manager's ------- to check for defects.

   (A) condition (B) responsibility
   (C) appointment (D) promotion

2. Many property Web sites include a mortgage calculator to help homebuyers ------- the approximate amount of money they could borrow.

   (A) broaden (B) determine
   (C) renovate (D) combine

3. Lee Valley Country Club members must submit an extension ------- for the premium membership every year.

   (A) performance (B) application
   (C) donation (D) activity

4. Although some of the individual components are produced in China, the ------- of GoFit running machines takes place in the UK.

   (A) user (B) demonstration
   (C) assembly (D) purchase

5. In accordance with the ------- of this agreement, you are required to submit your freelance work assignments no later than 5 PM each day.

   (A) opinions (B) terms
   (C) designs (D) applications

6. It is ------- that residents be reminded about the water usage restrictions that will come into effect next week.

   (A) sudden (B) critical
   (C) specific (D) cautious

정답 | 1 (B) 2 (B) 3 (B) 4 (C) 5 (B) 6 (B)

Day 05 독해가 쉬워지는 어휘 ❹ Part 7

1 reflect

v. ~을 반영하다

Although recent transactions are not **reflected** in the balance shown on the statement, they will be updated in the next billing cycle.

최근 거래 내역 건들이 명세서에 보여진 잔액에 반영되어 있지 않지만, 그것들은 다음 번 청구서 발송 주기 때 업데이트 될 것입니다.

2 top-notch

a. 최고의, 일류의

Experience our **top-notch** customer service, where dedicated support teams are committed to promptly addressing your needs.

전담 지원팀이 귀하의 요구 사항을 신속하게 해결하기 위해 전념하는 최고의 고객 서비스를 경험해 보세요.

3 congested

congestion n. 혼잡

a. 붐비는, 혼잡한

During rush hour, the city's highways become **congested**, causing delays for commuters.

출퇴근 혼잡 시간 동안에는, 도시의 고속도로가 붐벼서 통근자들을 지연시킵니다.

> 만점 TIP
> • 관련 기출
>   traffic congestion 교통 체증

4 **contemporary**

- a. 현대의

  The interior designer advises clients about the latest **contemporary** home decor and design concepts.
  그 인테리어 디자이너는 고객들에게 최신의 현대적인 실내 장식과 디자인 컨셉에 대해 조언해 줍니다.

5 **impending**

- a. 임박한, 곧 닥칠

  The team worked tirelessly to prepare for the **impending** product launch.
  그 팀은 임박한 제품 출시에 대비하기 위해 부단히 노력했습니다.

6 **house**

- v. ~에게 거처를 제공하다, ~을 수용하다

  The newly built complex will **house** both residential apartments and commercial spaces.
  새로 건설되는 단지에는 주거용 아파트와 상업 공간이 모두 들어설 예정입니다.

7 **respective**

respectively ad. 각각

- a. 각자의, 각각의

  The innovation team consisted of three members, all experts in their **respective** fields: software development, hardware design, and user experience.
  혁신팀은 세 명으로 구성되어 있는데, 이들 모두는 각자의 분야인 소프트웨어 개발, 하드웨어 설계, 그리고 사용자 경험에서 전문가입니다.

8 beforehand

ad. 사전에, 미리

If you want to secure a spot in the workshop, you should register **beforehand**.
워크숍에 자리를 확보하고 싶다면, 미리 등록을 해야 합니다.

9 take advantage of

~을 이용하다

While staying at our resort, guests may **take advantage of** diverse outdoor activities, such as hiking, snorkeling, and other water sports.
저희 리조트에 머무시는 동안 고객들은 하이킹, 스노클링, 기타 수상 스포츠와 같은 다양한 야외 활동을 이용하실 수 있습니다.

10 solid

a. 단단한, 견고한, 확실한

The startup's innovative approach to technology is expected to produce **solid** returns for its early investors.
그 신생 기업의 혁신적인 기술 접근 방식은 초기 투자자들에게 확실한 수익을 가져다 줄 것으로 기대됩니다.

11 associated with

~와 관련된

The anxiety and stress **associated** with public speaking can be significantly reduced through effective preparation and practice.
사람들 앞에서 말하는 것과 관련된 불안과 스트레스는 효과적인 준비와 연습을 통해 크게 줄어들 수 있습니다.

만점 TIP

• 기출 Paraphrasing
　associated with → related to (~와 관련 있는)

12 commercial

- a. 상업의, 상업용의
  n. 상업용 광고

  > The real estate agency provides expert advice for clients interested in both residential and **commercial** properties.
  > 그 부동산 중개업소는 주거용과 상업용 건물 모두에 관심 있는 고객들을 위해 전문적인 조언을 제공하고 있습니다.
  >
  > The new **commercial** for the product highlights its innovative features and benefits.
  > 그 제품의 새 광고는 제품의 혁신적인 특징과 이점을 잘 설명하고 있습니다.

  만점 TIP
  - 관련 기출
    resident n. 주민, 거주자

13 utilities

- n. 수도, 전기, 가스 등의 비용(= utility expenses)

  > The monthly rent for the apartment includes all **utilities**, such as water, electricity, and gas.
  > 아파트 월세에는 수도, 전기, 그리고 가스와 같은 모든 공공요금이 포함됩니다.

14 insulation

insulate v. 단열 처리를 하다

- n. 단열 처리

  > Proper **insulation** is essential for maintaining a comfortable temperature inside your home throughout the year.
  > 적절한 단열은 일 년 내내 여러분의 집 안에서 쾌적한 온도를 유지하는 데 필수적입니다.

  만점 TIP
  - 관련 기출
    ventilation 환기

15 enforce
enforcement n. 집행, 시행

- v. ~을 시행하다

> Strict parking rules are **enforced** to prevent congestion and ensure safety on the streets.
> 혼잡을 방지하고 도로의 안전을 확보하기 위해 엄격한 주차 규칙이 시행되고 있습니다.

16 be subject to + 명사

- ~의 대상이다, ~의 영향을 받게 되어 있다

> Please note that the schedule for the conference sessions **is subject to change**, so check for updates regularly.
> 컨퍼런스 세션의 일정은 변경의 대상이므로, 정기적으로 최신 소식을 확인하시기 바랍니다.

17 misleading

- a. 오해하게 하는

> The newspaper article was **misleading** because it contained inaccurate information about the company's financial performance.
> 그 신문 기사는 회사의 재무 실적에 대한 부정확한 정보를 담고 있어서 독자들을 오해하게 합니다.

18 earn
earnings n. 소득

- v. ~을 얻다, 받다, 벌다

> The recent survey results revealed that our product has **earned** the highest ratings for customer satisfaction among all competing brands.
> 최근 조사 결과 우리 제품은 경쟁 브랜드 중 가장 높은 고객 만족도 평가를 받았습니다.

19 critic

critical a. 비판적인
criticism n. 비판, 비평
criticize v. ~을 비판하다

- n. 비평가, 평론가

> Julien Clerc's debut performance was positively reviewed by the **critics**.
> 줄리앙 클레르의 데뷔 무대는 평론가들로부터 긍정적으로 평가 받았습니다.

20 complex

- n. 복합 단지[건물]

> The developer plans to build an apartment **complex** on the vacant lot at the corner of Main Street and Elm Avenue.
> 개발업자는 메인 스트리트와 엘름 애비뉴 모퉁이의 공터에 아파트 단지를 지을 계획입니다.

21 infrastructure

- n. 기본 시설, 사회[경제] 기반 시설

> The mayor announced a comprehensive plan to improve the city's **infrastructure**, including upgrading roads and public transportation.
> 시장은 도시의 기반 시설을 개선하기 위한 종합적인 계획을 발표했는데, 이는 도로와 대중교통을 개선하는 것을 포함하고 있습니다.

22 up and running

- 제대로 운영[작동]되는

> After a week of troubleshooting, we finally got the new software **up and running** smoothly.
> 일주일간의 문제 해결 끝에, 우리는 마침내 새 소프트웨어를 제대로 작동하게 만들었습니다.

만점 TIP

- 기출 Paraphrasing

  up and running → operational (운영 중인)

23 publication

publish v. ~을 출판하다

• n. 출판(물)

> We carefully evaluate all submitted articles, and only those that meet our quality standards are considered for **publication**.
>
> 저희는 제출된 모든 글들을 신중히 평가하며, 저희의 품질 기준을 충족하는 글들만 출간 대상으로 간주합니다.

24 spectacular

• a. 장관인, 극적인

> Families vacationing in Maui can enjoy **spectacular** views of the sunset from the beaches along the west coast.
>
> 마우이에서 휴가를 보내고 있는 가족들은 서쪽 해안을 따라 펼쳐진 해변에서 멋진 일몰 경관을 감상할 수 있습니다.

25 impede

• v. ~을 방해하다, 지체시키다

> The construction work on the main road has been causing significant delays and can **impede** the flow of local traffic during rush hours.
>
> 주요 도로 건설 공사는 극심한 지체를 발생시키고 있으며 출퇴근 시간에 지역의 교통 흐름을 방해할 수 있습니다.

26 be entitled to + 명사

• ~을 받을 자격이 되다

> Hotel guests who stay five consecutive nights in one year will **be entitled to** a complimentary room upgrade on their next visit.
>
> 1년에 5박을 연속으로 묵는 호텔 투숙객은 다음 방문 시 무료 객실 업그레이드를 받을 자격을 얻을 것입니다.

만점 TIP
- 「be eligible for + 명사」도 같은 의미로 쓰입니다.

27 on-site

- ad. 현장에서
- a. 현장의

> Visitors to the museum will find that audio guides can be purchased **on-site** to enhance their tour experience.
>
> 박물관 방문객들은 견학 경험을 향상시키기 위해 현장에서 오디오 가이드를 구입할 수 있다는 것을 알게 될 것입니다.

만점 TIP

• 기출 Paraphrasing
can be purchased on-site → be sold at the venue (현장에서 판매되다)

28 reconfiguration

- n. 구조 변경

> Considering the upcoming building **reconfiguration** project scheduled for next month, implementing telecommuting could be a solution for our company.
>
> 다음 달 예정된 건물 구조 변경 프로젝트를 고려할 때, 재택근무를 시행하는 것이 우리 회사에게 해결책이 될 수 있습니다.

만점 TIP

• 기출 Paraphrasing
building reconfiguration → change the layout of the building (건물의 배치를 바꾸다)

29 setback

- n. 차질

> The construction project experienced numerous **setbacks**, including unexpected weather delays and labor shortages.
>
> 건설 프로젝트는 예상치 못한 기상으로 인한 지연과 인력 부족 등 많은 차질을 겪었습니다.

30 on the premises
• 부지 내에, 관내에

The shopping mall has a strict policy in which any vehicles left **on its premises** overnight will be towed at the owner's expense.

그 쇼핑몰에는 하룻밤 사이에 부지 내에 남겨진 어떤 차량도 소유주의 비용으로 견인하도록 하는 엄격한 정책이 있습니다.

만점 TIP
• 관련 기출
  on-premises 부지 내의

31 voice
• v. 목소리를 내다, 말로 표하다

The construction of the new highway went ahead despite concerns **voiced** by environmental activists about its potential impact on local wildlife.

지역 야생 동물에 미칠 수 있는 영향에 대해 환경 운동가들이 표명한 우려에도 불구하고 새로운 고속도로 건설 공사가 진행되었습니다.

32 portray
portrait n. 묘사

• v. ~을 나타내다, 묘사하다

The marketing team worked hard to **portray** the brand as environmentally conscious and socially responsible.

마케팅 팀은 그 브랜드를 환경을 의식하고 사회적으로 책임감이 있는 것으로 묘사하기 위해 열심히 노력했습니다.

33 advocate

- v. ~을 지지하다, 옹호하다
- n. 옹호자, 지지자

> The environmentalist group **advocated** the use of renewable energy sources to reduce carbon emissions.
> 그 환경운동가 단체는 탄소 배출을 줄이기 위해 재생 가능한 에너지원의 사용을 지지했습니다.

34 divert

- v. ~을 우회시키다, 전환시키다

> During the road construction, drivers are **diverted** onto a different route while the crews work on widening the highway.
> 도로 공사 중에, 인부들이 고속도로를 확장하는 작업을 하는 동안 운전자들은 다른 경로로 우회합니다.

35 furnished

- a. 가구가 비치된

> The apartment for rent comes fully **furnished**, complete with modern appliances and stylish furniture.
> 임대 가능한 그 아파트는 가구가 완비되어 있는데, 현대적인 가전제품들과 멋진 가구를 완벽히 갖추고 있습니다.

36 identify

- v. ~이 무엇인지 확인하다

> During the upcoming meeting, we will **identify** the strengths and weaknesses of our current marketing strategy.
> 곧 있을 회의에서 우리는 현재 우리 마케팅 전략의 강점과 약점이 무엇인지 확인할 것입니다.

37 reportedly

ad. 전하는 바에 따르면, 소문에 의하면

> Profits **reportedly** fell after the market responded negatively to our decision to restructure the product lineup.
> 제품 라인업을 개편하기로 한 우리의 결정에 시장이 부정적인 반응을 보이자 수익이 감소한 것으로 전해졌습니다.

38 minimal

minimum a. 최저의, 최소한의
n. 최소한도

a. 최소한의

> Native wildflowers are a great choice for gardeners who want blossoms that require **minimal** care.
> 최소한의 관리만 필요한 꽃을 원하는 정원사들에게 토종 야생화는 아주 좋은 선택입니다.

만점 TIP

• 기출 Paraphrasing
  require minimal care → easy to maintain (관리하기 쉬운)

39 breakthrough

n. 돌파구, 획기적 발전

> **Breakthroughs** in manufacturing technology have boosted our production to five times the amount we had before.
> 제조 기술의 획기적인 발전이 우리의 생산량을 이전보다 5배 증가시켰습니다.

40 high-profile

a. 세간의 이목을 끄는, 유명한

> The **high-profile** merger between the two tech giants made headlines for weeks.
> 두 거대 기술 기업 간의 세간의 이목을 끄는 합병은 몇 주 동안 대서특필되었습니다.

DAILY QUIZ

단어와 그에 알맞은 뜻을 연결해 보세요.

1. setback • • (A) 비평가, 평론가
2. publication • • (B) 단열 처리
3. critic • • (C) 차질
4. insulation • • (D) 출판물

빈칸에 알맞은 단어를 선택하세요.

5. With the recent changes in company policy, all interns are now ------- to one week's paid vacation.
   최근 회사 정책이 변경됨에 따라 모든 인턴은 이제 1주일의 유급 휴가를 받을 수 있습니다.

   (A) entitled
   (B) enforced
   (C) voice
   (D) identify

6. Mr. Todd will ------- and resolve problems on the company's online network.
   토드 씨가 회사 온라인 네트워크 상의 문제를 파악하고 해결할 것입니다.

7. The company's confidentiality policy is strictly -------, so do not share any sensitive information with external parties.
   회사의 비밀유지 정책이 엄격하게 시행되므로, 민감한 정보를 외부인과 공유하지 마십시오.

8. It is important to create an environment where employees feel comfortable to ------- concerns about their workload.
   직원들이 자신의 업무량에 대한 우려 사항을 편안하게 말할 수 있는 환경을 조성하는 것이 중요합니다.

정답 1 (C) 2 (D) 3 (A) 4 (B) 5 (A) 6 (D) 7 (B) 8 (C)

/ Week / 08 실전 TEST

LISTENING

• Part 3

1. Who most likely is the woman?

    (A) A volunteer
    (B) A doctor
    (C) A technician
    (D) A photographer

2. What does the man say about some employees?

    (A) They are busy with a new project.
    (B) They need to work faster.
    (C) They do not know a system well.
    (D) They will show the woman around.

3. What will the woman need to provide?

    (A) A draft of a proposal
    (B) A form of identification
    (C) Some keys
    (D) Some price quotes

• Part 4

4. What does the speaker want the listeners to do a search on?

    (A) Raw materials
    (B) Neon signs
    (C) Wooden furniture
    (D) Paint colors

5. According to the speaker, what has been difficult lately?

    (A) Scheduling an appointment
    (B) Filling a job opening
    (C) Attracting customers
    (D) Reducing energy consumption

6. What does the speaker suggest listeners do?

    (A) Sample a new menu item
    (B) Buy a product elsewhere
    (C) Submit a request
    (D) Verify an account number

READING

Part 5

7. The board will resume its monthly employee evaluations ------- Mr. Prestwick gets back from Boston on March 2.

    (A) that
    (B) once
    (C) as well
    (D) then

8. Mr. Wenders, ------- his personal assistant, will travel to Tokyo this weekend to meet with our Japanese clients.

    (A) as soon as
    (B) in order to
    (C) along with
    (D) in case of

9. Reed Corporation's employee carpooling ------- will not only benefit the environment but also strengthen staff relationships.

    (A) initiative
    (B) object
    (C) impression
    (D) preview

10. We collaborate with several charities to work ------- a common goal of improving the lives of local residents.

    (A) of
    (B) near
    (C) outside
    (D) toward

11. Daisy Landscaping performs a variety of services at ------- rates than most other companies in the industry.

    (A) cleaner
    (B) easier
    (C) lighter
    (D) lower

12. Several hiking trails in the national park are inaccessible ------- the recent heavy rain, making them hazardous.

    (A) past
    (B) due to
    (C) much
    (D) having

13. Because of a delay in payroll processing, some payments might not ------- our staff until Friday morning.

    (A) arrive
    (B) prefer
    (C) cover
    (D) reach

14. Ms. Montague has the ------- required to effectively reduce the company's annual expenditure.

    (A) impression
    (B) advancement
    (C) experience
    (D) decision

Part 6

Questions 15-18 refer to the following e-mail.

To: Graham Vaughn <gvaughn@wizmail.com>
Subject: Your complaint

Dear Ms. Vaughn,

I am writing in reply to the feedback form you filled out on your flight from Rome to New York last week. I want to assure you that I **15.** ------- the matter fully, and I have given your complaint serious consideration.

After receiving the flight report, I forwarded the information **16.** ------- the regional director. He found that the flight path could have been altered to lessen the impact of the turbulence.

We would like to offer you either a 50 percent refund of your flight ticket price or a voucher for an upgrade to business class on your next flight with us.
17. -------. **18.** ------- Blue Mountain Air, I wish to apologize for the problems you experienced on board our aircraft.

Yours sincerely,

Peter Tobin, Customer Service Manager
Blue Mountain Air

---

15. (A) investigate
(B) have investigated
(C) will investigate
(D) have been investigated

16. (A) with
(B) over
(C) among
(D) to

17. (A) You will be assured that our flights offer premium comfort.
(B) I would like to know which option you would prefer.
(C) The change in the route will be effective immediately.
(D) Please be sure to bring your passport when you check in.

18. (A) On behalf of
(B) In case of
(C) As a result
(D) As if

Part 7

Questions 19-20 refer to the following article.

New Langford Announces Major Construction Plan

March 18 - (New Langford) City officials announced an urban renewal project set to transform Waterford district. The area was formerly a prosperous commercial center and home to many high-profile retail outlets. However, businesses have gradually moved away from the area due to rising rental rates.

Following the impending demolition of several abandoned buildings, two spectacular apartment complexes will be constructed. Once complete, the apartments will be fully furnished and utilities will be included in the monthly rent. Additionally, an extensive shopping mall will be built on Havers Avenue. The mall will have an ice rink and cinema on the premises and should be up and running by next summer, provided there are no setbacks.

Critics of the plan have warned of congested roads. Former mayor John Bishop voices as an advocate for preserving New Langford's heritage. Mr. Bishop said, "The city council should divert these funds towards routine maintenance of existing infrastructure and restore historic buildings."

19. What is the article mainly about?

(A) A proposal to expand a shopping mall
(B) The development of a city neighborhood
(C) An increase in property prices in New Langford
(D) The demolition of local apartment buildings

20. What is indicated about Mr. Bishop?

(A) He no longer lives in New Langford.
(B) He is opposed to the council's plans.
(C) He is the owner of a local business.
(D) He previously worked for a construction firm.

*2025 히트브랜드 대상
토익 강사 부문 1위

서아쌤의
토익
비밀과외
기출 VOCA

온라인 강의

토익 강사 1위

토익 강사 1위
20만 유튜버 서아쌤!
**VOCA 초밀착
케어 강의로
밀리지 않고 끝까지!**

**PART 1~7까지
모든 파트 어휘 포함!
하루 약 30분으로
VOCA 학습 끝!**

기출 문제 1500제 및
PART 5, 6 어휘
실전테스트 제공!
**상세한 해설로
VOCA 완전 정복!**

시원스쿨랩 사이트에서(lab.siwonschool.com)
유료로 수강 가능합니다.

서아쌤 토익 비밀과외
환급 Package

토익 유튜버 20만

토익 강사 1위
* 2025 희망브랜드 대상 1위 토익강사 부문

토익 입문부터 실전까지 **3주 완성**
서아쌤의 밀착관리로 **목표 달성하고 100% 환급까지!**

목표 달성하면 **수강료 100% 환급**	환급 대신 연장도 가능! **수강일 +90일 연장** 	토익 3주 완성 **강의 +교재 포함** 
* 교재비/결제수수료/제세공과금 제외 유의사항 참고		
기본 다지기 필수 강의 **처음토익 강의 제공**	온라인 모의고사 **3회분+해설강의 무료제공** 	토익+취업까지 책임지는 **취업영어 강의 무료제공** 

Premium Benefit

유튜브에선 경험할 수 없는!
서아쌤 밀착관리 카톡 온라인 스터디

학원과 다를 바 없는 빈틈없는 학습관리
서아쌤 부가 **학습자료 최대 4종**

시원스쿨LAB(lab.siwonschool.com)에서 패키지를 신청하실 수 있습니다. 제공되는 혜택은 기간에 따라 다를 수 있습니다.

시원스쿨 LAB

Week 01
정답 및 해설

Day 01 사람 사진 빈출 어휘

DAILY QUIZ

1. (A) The woman is standing in line at the register.
(B) **The woman is examining some clothing on a rack.**
(A) 여자가 계산대에 줄을 서고 있다.
(B) 여자가 옷걸이의 옷을 살펴보고 있다.
어휘 stand in line 줄을 서다 register 계산대 examine ~을 살펴보다 clothing 옷 rack 옷걸이

2. (A) A woman is cutting open a box.
(B) **A woman is kneeling on the floor.**
(A) 여자가 상자를 뜯고 있다.
(B) 여자가 바닥에 무릎을 꿇고 있다.
어휘 cut open ~을 뜯다, 절개하다 kneel 무릎을 꿇다 floor 바닥

3. (A) **A worker is wiping a table.**
(B) A server is delivering a food order.
(A) 직원이 테이블을 닦고 있다.
(B) 서빙 직원이 주문한 음식을 나르고 있다.
어휘 wipe ~을 닦다 server (식당의) 서빙 직원 deliver ~을 배달하다, 나르다 food order 주문한 음식

4. (A) Some people are walking toward a doorway.
(B) **Some pedestrians are crossing the street.**
(A) 몇몇 사람들이 출입구 쪽으로 걷고 있다.
(B) 몇몇 보행자들이 길을 건너고 있다.
어휘 toward ~ 쪽으로 doorway 출입구 pedestrian 보행자 cross the street 길을 건너다

5. (A) She's sipping from a cup.
(B) **She's facing a computer monitor.**
(A) 여자가 컵으로 조금씩 마시고 있다.
(B) 여자가 컴퓨터 모니터를 향해 있다.
어휘 sip 조금씩 마시다 face ~을 향하다

6. (A) **Some people are wearing helmets.**
(B) Some people are putting on jackets.
(A) 몇몇 사람들이 헬멧을 착용한 상태이다.
(B) 몇몇 사람들이 재킷을 입는 중이다.
어휘 wear ~을 착용하다 (상태) put on ~을 착용하다 (동작)

Day 02 명사 ①

표제어 문제 정답 및 해석

1. (A)	2. (A)	3. (B)	4. (B)	5. (B)
6. (A)	7. (B)	8. (A)	9. (A)	10. (B)
11. (A)	12. (A)	13. (B)	14. (B)	15. (A)
16. (A)	17. (B)	18. (A)	19. (B)	20. (A)
21. (B)	22. (A)	23. (B)	24. (B)	25. (A)
26. (A)	27. (A)	28. (A)	29. (B)	30. (B)
31. (B)	32. (B)	33. (B)	34. (B)	35. (A)
36. (B)	37. (A)	38. (B)	39. (A)	40. (A)

1. 핸드폰으로 또는 저희 앱을 통해 주문하실 때, 귀하의 피자 배달에 30분에서 45분의 여유를 주시기 바랍니다.
2. AMJ 메뉴팩쳐링 사에서 조립 라인 근로자들은 공장에서 안전 장비를 사용하도록 교육 받는다.
3. 타코 퀸 사는 프랜차이즈 소유주들이 식당을 차리는 데 필요한 모든 자원들을 공급한다.
4. 기업 웹 사이트에 대한 고객 후기의 추가는 회사

의 평판을 증진시키는 데 도움을 줄 수 있다.
5. 대부분의 지원자들은 패션 산업에서 적어도 3년의 경력을 가지고 있다.
6. 현대 그래픽 디자인 소프트웨어에 대한 지식은 온라인 컨텐츠 편집자 직무의 자격요건이다.
7. 지난 여름, 수많은 매우 유망한 지원자들이 우리 회사의 인턴 프로그램에 지원했다.
8. 마가렛 레인스 씨는 최근에 로스엔젤레스로 이사 갔고, 그 도시에서 적극적으로 일자리를 찾는 중이다.
9. 직원들이 법인카드를 사용하기 전에 회계부서로부터 공식적인 승인은 필수적이다.
10. 사무실 컴퓨터에 채팅 프로그램을 설치한 이후로, 라이더 주식회사는 직원 생산성에서의 걱정스러운 감소를 겪어왔다.
11. 시립 도서관의 확장에 대한 로우 씨의 제안은 도시의 기획부에 의해 받아들여졌다.
12. 약 250개의 매장뿐만 아니라, 프리미어 몰은 영화관과 여러 다른 시설들을 갖추고 있다.
13. 포트만 호텔에서 귀하의 객실에 체크인하실 때, 보증금이 지불되어야 합니다.
14. 고급 마케팅 워크숍에 등록된 후에, 마이크 씨는 그의 다양한 능력을 넓힐 수 있는 기회에 대해 그의 상사에게 감사했다.
15. 모든 주방 직원들은 식당의 주문을 준비할 때 적절한 절차를 반드시 따라야 한다.
16. 운영비를 줄이려는 노력의 일환으로, 우리는 현재 플라스틱 포장을 더 가격이 알맞은 종이 박스로 바꾸는 중이다.
17. 공학용 계산기를 사용하기 전에, 박스 뒤에 인쇄된 상세한 설명서를 읽어보십시오.
18. 트리톤 엔지니어링 사는 아펙스 원 사무실 건물의 엘리베이터의 유지보수에 대한 5년 계약에 동의했다.
19. 브램블 비스트로는 식사를 하는 사람들에게 어떠한 메인 코스 음식이라도 무료 디저트를 주문할 수 있도록 하는 홍보 행사를 운영 중이다.
20. 매장 입구 근처에 전시되어 있는 대부분의 상품은 겨울 세일의 일부로서 할인되었다.
21. 귀하께서 사전 등록 기간 동안 저희 체육관에 가입하신다면, 귀하께서는 월 회원 요금의 25퍼센트 할인을 받으실 것입니다.
22. 인사부장은 관리자 직책으로의 승진에 적합한 6명의 직원들의 목록을 모았다.
23. 투어 버스에서 내릴 때 개인 소지품을 안전하게 지키는 것은 각 탑승객의 책임이다.
24. 1년 보증 기간 내에, 고객들은 어떠한 타서스 노트북 컴퓨터에 대한 환불 또는 교환을 요청할 수 있다.
25. 저희 기관은 다양한 스타트업 기업체들에 소중한 재정적 지원을 제공합니다.
26. 퍼니 프루트 팜은 여러 배송 회사들과 상호 이익인 계약을 협상해 왔다.
27. 허드몬트 투자 사의 회계 감사는 3주의 기간 동안 수행될 것이다.
28. 참석자들은 매표소에서 그들의 입장권을 얻기 위해 사진이 부착된 유효한 신분증을 제시하도록 요구된다.
29. 직원들이 회사를 떠날 때, 노트북, 플래시 드라이브, 그리고 그 밖의 회사 재산은 반드시 반납되어야 한다.
30. 그린에이커 정원사 총회는 참석자들에게 전문적인 조언을 들을 기회를 준다.
31. 15살에서 25살 사이 나이대의 비디오 게임을 하는 사람들이 모바일 게임에 대한 증가하는 선호를 보이고 있다.
32. 레이놀즈 씨는 그가 새로운 지사를 감독하기 위한 경영 전문지식을 가지고 있지 않다는 것을 인정했다.
33. 저희 온라인 경매를 통해 판매된 모든 상품들은 거의 새 상태이며, 30일 동안 환불이 가능한 보증서가 딸려 있습니다.
34. 그 섬의 동해안은 관광객들에게 쇼핑과 관광에 대한 수많은 선택지들을 제공한다.
35. 저희는 훌륭한 고객 서비스를 제공하고 싶기 때문에, 모든 문의는 즉각적으로 처리되어야 합니다.
36. 오늘 아침 발표된 성명에서, 그랙슬리 사의 대표이사는 회사의 전국적인 채용 프로그램에 대해 간략히 설명했다.
37. 의회는 스카이웨이 스타디움 반대편의 부지에 대한 최선의 사용 방법에 대해 제안사항들을 모으기 위해 온라인 여론 조사를 게시했다.

38. 모든 근로자들은 연장된 점심 휴게시간을 가지기 전에 부장님의 허가를 받아야 합니다.
39. 건물 관리자는 공동 구역에 대한 새로운 청소 일정에 관한 주민들의 협조에 감사하고 있습니다.
40. 케네디 비즈니스 협회의 회원들은 모든 세미나에 대해 반값 입장 허가를 받는다.

DAILY QUIZ

7.
해석 딕시 쇼핑몰에 있는 에스컬레이터들은 정기적인 유지보수 작업을 거치는 동안 전원이 꺼져 있을 것이다.
해설 빈칸에 쓰일 어휘는 에스컬레이터라는 기계가 정기적으로 거칠 수 있는 일을 나타내야 하므로 '유지(보수)' 등을 뜻하는 (B)가 정답이다.
어휘 undergo ~을 거치다, 겪다 routine 정기적인 preference 선호(하는 것) maintenance 유지(보수) instruction 지시, 안내 transfer 이동, 전근

8.
해석 회사의 정책에 따르면, 바구니와 쇼핑 카트, 그리고 기타 슈퍼마켓의 자산은 매장 주차장 외부로 가져갈 수 없다.
해설 빈칸에는 바구니와 쇼핑 카트 등의 물품을 아우를 수 있는 것으로서 매장 주차장 밖으로 가져갈 수 없는 모든 물품을 나타낼 어휘가 필요하므로 '재산, 대지'를 뜻하는 (C)가 정답이다.
어휘 according to ~에 따르면 policy 정책, 방침 property 재산, 대지 competitor 경쟁사, 경쟁자

Day 03 명사 ②

표제어 문제 정답 및 해설

1. (B)	2. (A)	3. (A)	4. (A)	5. (B)
6. (B)	7. (B)	8. (B)	9. (A)	10. (B)
11. (B)	12. (A)	13. (B)	14. (A)	15. (A)
16. (B)	17. (B)	18. (B)	19. (B)	20. (B)
21. (B)	22. (A)	23. (A)	24. (B)	25. (A)
26. (B)	27. (B)	28. (B)	29. (A)	30. (B)
31. (A)	32. (A)	33. (B)	34. (B)	35. (B)
36. (B)	37. (B)	38. (B)	39. (B)	40. (A)

1. 도서관 회원들의 하나의 공통된 불만사항은 충분한 단체 학습 공간이 없다는 것이다.
2. 귀하께서 저희 비즈니스 경영 워크숍에 참석하고 싶으시다면, 5월 31일까지 온라인 등록 양식을 작성 완료해주십시오.
3. 알파 스포츠웨어는 자사의 새로운 텔레비전 광고에 관한 부정적인 의견을 받아왔다.
4. 해외 투자의 전문가인 아서 샌더스 씨는 국제적인 기업들의 주식을 구매하면서부터 부유해졌다.
5. 가수 리차드 프린스 씨는 그의 아이의 출생이 새로운 앨범에 대한 영감의 주요 원천이었다고 말했다.
6. 건강 보건 담당 공무원이 우리 주방의 연례 점검을 수행하기 위해 오늘 식당을 방문할 것이다.
7. 론델 씨는 모든 20개의 지사들로부터 매출 보고서를 받은 후에 회사의 연례 수치에 대해 보고할 것이다.
8. 소비자들의 증가하는 수요에 응답하여, 라이젠 가전제품은 자사의 냉장고의 생산을 두 배로 만들었다.
9. 맹그로브 비치 리조트는 제트스키와 스노클링과 같은 다양한 수상 활동 선택지들을 제공한다.
10. 새로운 펀랜드 복합단지는 이번 여름에 개장할 때 광범위하게 다양한 오락시설들을 제공할 것이다.

11. 산체스 씨는 다음 주에 밀란에서 카트리나 벨라스케스 패션 쇼에 참석하도록 초대를 받았다.
12. 블루파이어 게임회사는 아시아 시장으로의 확장의 일환으로 타네카 소프트웨어 사를 인수하는 것을 희망한다.
13. 회사에서의 30년 근무에 감사하여, 프리멕스 사는 리차드 씨에게 비싼 손목시계를 선물로 주었다.
14. 예이츠 씨는 우리 회사에 대한 그녀의 뛰어난 노력과 헌신의 보상으로 개선된 계약을 제안받았다.
15. 다음 달의 국내 음악 시상식은 11번 채널에서 전국적으로 방송될 것이다.
16. 지난주에 마닐라에서 컨퍼런스에 참석했던 영업 임원들은 환급을 위해 영수증을 제출해야 한다.
17. 9월마다, 리치필드 협회는 성공적인 비즈니스 소유주들에 의해 진행되는 일련의 워크숍을 주최한다.
18. 니트로 비버리지 사는 올해 자사의 국내 시장 점유율을 증가시키는 것을 가장 높은 우선순위로 두었다.
19. 올크로프트에 있는 그린그로 슈퍼마켓의 지점은 지난 6개월 동안 맥스 할그레이브스 씨의 관리 하에 있다.
20. 제약 컨퍼런스 등록비는 숙소와 교통 비용을 포함한다.
21. 모바일 게임 개발자들 사이의 증가하는 경쟁은 게임의 품질에서의 상당한 향상으로 이어졌다.
22. 헤리티지 트러스트는 기관에 소중한 기부를 해준 모든 사람들에게 감사를 표했다.
23. 레인 씨의 보고서는 기술의 간결한 설명뿐만 아니라 그것의 이점의 철저한 분석을 포함한다.
24. 5번가는 도시에서 골동품 매장들의 밀도가 가장 높은 본거지이다.
25. 만약 귀하께서 교통편이 필요하시다면, 총회 웹사이트에서 셔틀버스 일정을 보시기 바랍니다.
26. 800달러를 넘는 액수에 대한 모든 모바일 거래는 은행 앱을 사용함으로써 승인 받아야 한다.
27. 직원 회의 중에, 포브스 씨는 운영 부장 직무에 지원한다는 그의 의사를 알렸다.
28. 매장 할인을 이용하길 원하신다면, 리츠 백화점 멤버십에 오늘 가입하세요.
29. 여러 주요 버스 노선 근처에 위치해 있어, 대중교통으로의 어드벤처 랜드의 접근성은 그 장소를 편리한 목적지로 만든다.
30. 말로위 씨는 이메일로 고객 불만사항에 응답하는 업무를 받았다.
31. 이 점검의 목적은 공장이 전면 가동 중이며 완전히 효율적으로 운영하고 있다는 것을 보증하기 위해서이다.
32. 싱 씨는 지난 20년 동안 우리 회사에 인상깊은 헌신을 보여주었다.
33. 음악 페스티벌이 온라인 매표 체계의 어려움 때문에 연기되었다.
34. 핏메이트 스마트워치는 심박수, 호흡율, 그리고 수면 패턴을 추적 관찰하는 능력을 지녔다.
35. 첸의 국수 가게는 더 가격이 저렴한 배달 서비스로 수익성 있는 전환을 했다.
36. 저희는 10년 동안 영업을 해왔고, 이 중요한 사건을 기념하기 위해, 11월 22일에 파티를 주최할 것입니다.
37. 펠버그 씨의 관광 여행 일정표는 여러 유명한 박물관과 미술관에 방문하는 것을 포함한다.
38. 과잉 재고를 판매하려는 노력의 일환으로, 스미스 캠핑 굿즈는 최대 50퍼센트까지 일부 가격을 할인하고 있다.
39. 펨브로크 시장의 많은 성과는 환경 친화적인 모노레일 체계를 실행한 것을 포함한다.
40. 라이델 사의 많은 제조 기계들은 안전 규정을 준수하기 위해 변경되어야 했다.

DAILY QUIZ

7.

해석 그레이 씨는 40년간의 회사 재직을 인정받아 금시계를 제공받았다.

해설 빈칸 앞뒤에 각각 위치한 전치사 in, of와 어울리는 어휘가 필요하므로 이 둘과 함께 '~을 인정하여'라는 의미를 구성할 때 사용하는 (C)가 정답이다.

어휘 be presented with ~을 제공받다 in recognition of ~을 인정하여 service 재직,

근무 achievement 성취, 업적

8.
해석 마이클 아코나 씨는 케냐와 우간다 같은 여행 목적지에서 야생 동물 보호 운동을 조직적으로 펼친다.

해설 빈칸에는 예시를 나타내는 such as 뒤에 위치하는 어휘들이 속할 수 있는 범주에 해당되는 어휘가 와야 한다. 케냐와 우간다와 같은 국가명을 나타낼 수 있는 '(여행) 목적지, 도착지'를 뜻하는 (C)가 정답이다.

어휘 coordinate ~을 조직적으로 펼치다, 조정하다 conservation 보호, 보존 effort (조직적인) 운동, 활동 destination (여행) 목적지, 도착지 initiative (조직적인) 계획, 운동

Day 04 명사 + 명사 콜로케이션

표제어 문제 정답 및 해석

1. (B)	2. (A)	3. (B)	4. (A)	5. (B)
6. (B)	7. (B)	8. (B)	9. (B)	10. (B)
11. (B)	12. (B)	13. (B)	14. (B)	15. (A)
16. (B)	17. (B)	18. (B)	19. (B)	20. (B)
21. (A)	22. (B)	23. (B)	24. (A)	25. (A)
26. (A)	27. (A)	28. (A)	29. (A)	30. (B)
31. (A)	32. (B)	33. (B)	34. (A)	35. (B)
36. (A)	37. (A)	38. (B)	39. (B)	40. (B)

1. 제품 설명서는 자세히 설명된 조립 설명서와 그림들을 포함한다.
2. 지원금에 대한 신청서를 제출하기 전에, 예산 요건을 충족했는지 확인하시기 바랍니다.
3. 작년에 성과 기반의 급여 인상을 도입한 이래로, 허자 테크놀로지 사는 직원 생산성의 극적인 증가를 경험해왔다.
4. 이사회는 매달 5,000달러를 출장 비용으로 할당하기로 합의했다.
5. 몇 달 간의 준비 끝에, 시청이 건축 허가를 발급하자마자 마침내 건설 프로젝트가 착수되었다.
6. 그 IT팀은 회사 본사에 있는 중앙 통제 시스템을 업그레이드할 계획이다.
7. 존스 씨는 업계에서 15년 이상의 경력을 갖춘 생산 관리자 직책에 가장 적합한 지원자이다.
8. 오래된 기계의 교체는 이미 우리의 조립 과정의 효율을 10퍼센트까지 높였다.
9. 증가하는 운영비로 인해, 블루스카이 항공사는 일부 아시아 노선의 운항을 중단하기로 결정했다.
10. 에드워드 씨는 부동산 중개인에게 그가 300명의 직원들을 수용하기에 충분한 사무 공간이 필요하다는 것을 말했다.
11. 도시 지역에서의 인구 증가는 공공 서비스에 대한 더 큰 수요로 이어졌다.
12. 기획 위원회는 화요일에 상급 관리자 직책의 후보자를 논의하기 위해 모일 것이다.
13. 모든 카예 백화점 직원들에게, 휴가 요청은 반드시 인사부에서 승인되어야 한다.
14. 시 박람회에 다시 참석하고 싶은 음식 판매자들은 허가증을 위해 갱신 지원서를 제출해야 한다.
15. 스텐하우스 가구 사는 시의 경계 외부로 배달되는 주문들에 더 높은 서비스 요금을 부과한다.
16. 글렌필드 시 의회는 도시 개선 프로젝트를 위한 대규모의 자금을 확보했다.
17. 컨퍼런스 등록은 5월 4일에 시작해 월말까지 계속 이어질 것이다.
18. 최근 자동차 부품 가격의 급작한 인상은 2주 이상의 운송 지연이라는 결과를 낳았다.
19. 목요일에 라일리 씨가 공식적으로 승진되면, 즉시 관리 직무를 맡게 될 것이다.
20. 회사의 개인정보 보호정책에 따르면, 고객 정보는 절대 제3자와 공유되지 않는다.
21. 만료 일자가 저희 웹 사이트의 각 구독자 계정 페이지에 명확하게 명시되어 있습니다.
22. 티렐 씨는 비용을 낮추기 위한 노력의 일환으로 배송 계약을 재협상했다.

23. 인사부장은 모든 신입사원들이 그들의 직무에 완전히 준비되는 것을 확실히 하기 위해 네 개의 교육 시간 일정을 잡았다.
24. 엑스셀 디지털 솔루션 사는 다양한 업계의 고객들을 위한 성공적인 온라인 홍보 캠페인을 만들었다.
25. 더 생산적인 근무 환경을 만들기 위해, 비트포 테크놀로지 사는 모든 직원들에게 새로운 인체공학적 사무실 가구를 제공했다.
26. 방문객들이 건축 현장에 들어가는 것을 허가받기 전에, 필수 안전 장비를 반드시 착용해야 한다.
27. 프라이벳 미술관에서의 미술 전시회 개막식 밤에, 린다 카렌자 씨는 참석자들에게 그녀의 작품에 대해 말했다.
28. 이번 주말의 올해의 젊은 영화제작자 시상식은 시포스 강당에서 개최될 것이다.
29. 고객 충성도를 향상시키기 위해, 마제스틱 케이터링 사는 현재 장기 고객들에게 할인을 제공한다.
30. 최근 여러 희귀 식품에 대한 엄격한 정부 규제가 그것들의 가격이 급등하는 것을 야기했다.
31. 바 씨는 예산 분배 계획을 마무리하기 위해 영업부, 마케팅부, 그리고 인사부의 재정적인 필요성을 결정할 것이다.
32. 모든 직원들은 식당의 보건안전 규정을 준수해야 하며, 그렇지 않으면 규제 조치가 취해질 것입니다.
33. 바닥 보수공사가 약 3개월 정도 걸릴 것이며, 건물의 바닥 면적을 15퍼센트 증가시킬 것이다.
34. 카릴토 토레스 씨는 인도네시아나 말레이시아와 같은 관광지로 가는 음식을 주제로 한 여행들을 기획한다.
35. 일정 금액을 초과하는 특정 은행 거래들에 대해, 저희는 고객들이 은행 관리자와 직접 만날 것을 요청드립니다.
36. 대사관은 모든 여권 갱신과 재발급에 대해 처리 비용을 부과한다.
37. 배송 영수증을 제출하기 전에, 목록에 들어있는 모든 상품들이 좋은 상태인지 확인하시기 바랍니다.
38. 대표이사가 12월 29일에 있는 연말 연회에서 우리의 연례 매출 수치를 발표할 것이다.
39. 재택근무 선택권은 많은 직원들에게 집 또는 다른 원격 위치에서 일할 수 있는 유연성을 제공한다.
40. 모든 밥스 버거 지점의 직원들은 점심을 위한 2시간의 식사 시간이 주어진다.

DAILY QUIZ

7.

해석 고객님들께서는 저희 유제품의 어느 것이든지 소비하시기 전에 유통 기한을 확인하셔야 합니다.

해설 빈칸에는 고객들이 유제품을 소비할 때 확인해야 하는 대상을 나타내면서 빈칸 앞에 제시된 명사와 의미상 어울리는 어휘가 필요하므로 expiration과 함께 '유통 기한, 만료 일자'라는 의미를 가지는 (C)가 정답이다.

어휘 expiration date 유통 기한, 만료 일자 dairy product 유제품

8.

해석 웰링 씨는 샌디아고 사무실로부터 온 데이터를 취합한 후에 우리의 일 매출 수치를 발표할 것이다.

해설 빈칸에는 동사 announce의 목적어 역할을 할 수 있으면서 다른 사무실로부터 받아야 하는 대상을 나타낼 수 있는 어휘가 와야 하므로 빈칸 앞에 제시된 명사 sales와 함께 '매출 수치'를 뜻하는 (D)가 정답이다.

어휘 sales figure 매출 수치 compile ~을 취합하다, 모으다 measure 조치 instruction 지시

Day 05 기출 동의어 ①

표제어 문제 정답

1. (B)	2. (B)	3. (B)	4. (B)	5. (B)
6. (A)	7. (B)	8. (A)	9. (B)	10. (A)
11. (A)	12. (A)	13. (A)	14. (B)	15. (B)
16. (A)	17. (B)	18. (B)	19. (B)	20. (B)
21. (B)	22. (B)	23. (B)	24. (A)	25. (B)
26. (B)	27. (B)	28. (A)	29. (A)	30. (A)

DAILY QUIZ

1.
해석 IT 부서는 서버 다운으로 인해 긴급한 상황에 직면해 있어, 주요 서비스들을 복구하기 위해 즉각적인 주의가 필요합니다. 그 팀은 문제를 해결하고 중단 시간을 최소화하기 위해 부단히 노력하고 있습니다.
해설 서버 다운으로 인해 중요한 서비스 복구를 위한 즉각적인 주의가 필요하다고 하므로 '중대한, 긴급한' 상황임을 알 수 있다. 따라서 이러한 의미를 지닌 (C)가 정답이다.
어휘 face ~에 직면하다 server outage 서버 다운 require ~을 필요로 하다 immediate attention 즉각적인 관심 restore ~을 복원하다, 복구하다 tirelessly 지치지 않고 resolve ~을 해결하다 downtime 컴퓨터가 작동하지 않는 시간 essential 필수적인 urgent 긴급한

2.
해석 다가오는 테니스 선수권 대회는 전국에서 수천 명의 테니스 팬들을 끌어 모을 것이라고 예상되면서 엄청난 기대를 불러일으키고 있습니다. 최고의 선수들이 챔피언이 되기 위해 경쟁하는 가운데, 관중들은 스릴 넘치는 경기와 숨막히는 기술 발휘를 보길 열망하고 있습니다.
해설 엄청난 기대를 불러 일으키는 테니스 선수권 대회는 전국 각지로부터 테니스 팬들을 끌어들일 것으로 예상되는 대회이므로 (B)가 정답이다.
어휘 upcoming 다가오는, 곧 있을 immense 거대한, 대단한 anticipation 기대감 compete for ~을 갖기 위해 경쟁하다 title (스포츠) 타이틀, 챔피언십 spectator 관중 be eager to do 몹시 ~하고 싶어하다 thrilling 스릴 있는 match 경기 breathtaking 매우 멋진 display n. 보여주기

3.
해석 저희 매장에서는 고객들이 적절한 가격에 최고의 제품과 서비스를 누리도록 하는 것에 자부심을 갖고 있습니다. 저희의 가격은 합리적이고 신중하게 책정되어 고객에게 최고의 가치를 제공합니다.
해설 가격이 적절하고(affordable), 신중하게 책정되었다는(carefully evaluated) 내용에서 가격이 합리적이라는 것을 알 수 있으므로 (B)가 정답이다.
어휘 take pride in ~에 자부심을 갖다 ensure that 반드시 ~하도록 하다 fair 가격이 합리적인 evaluate ~을 평가하다, 감정하다 utmost 최고의 clientele 의뢰인들, 고객들 objective 객관적인 generous 후한

Week 01 실전 TEST

1. (C)	2. (C)	3. (B)	4. (D)	5. (A)
6. (A)	7. (D)	8. (C)	9. (C)	10. (A)
11. (B)	12. (D)	13. (C)	14. (B)	15. (A)
16. (C)	17. (C)	18. (C)		

1. (A) They're facing each other.

(B) They're preparing some food.
(C) **The man is pouring some liquid into a cup.**
(D) The woman is sipping from a mug.
(A) 사람들이 서로 마주보고 있다.
(B) 사람들이 음식을 준비하고 있다.
(C) 남자가 컵에 액체를 따르고 있다.
(D) 여자가 머그잔에 든 것을 조금씩 마시고 있다.

어휘 face ~을 마주보다 prepare ~을 준비하다 pour A into B A를 B에 따르다 liquid 액체 sip from ~에 든 것을 조금씩 마시다

2. (A) The man is trimming some bushes.
(B) The man is loading some logs into a vehicle.
(C) **The man is pushing a wheelbarrow.**
(D) The man is wearing a safety helmet.
(A) 남자가 일부 관목을 다듬고 있다.
(B) 남자가 일부 통나무를 차량에 싣고 있다.
(C) 남자가 외바퀴 손수레를 밀고 있다.
(D) 남자가 안전모를 착용한 상태이다.

어휘 trim ~을 다듬다, ~을 손질하다 bush 관목, 덤불 load A into B A를 B에 싣다 vehicle 차량 wheelbarrow 외바퀴 손수레 wear (상태) ~을 착용하다

3. (A) They're watering some plants.
(B) **They're working in a garden.**
(C) The woman is putting on her boots.
(D) The man is sweeping the ground.
(A) 사람들이 일부 식물에 물을 주고 있다.
(B) 사람들이 정원에서 일하고 있다.
(C) 여자가 장화를 착용하는 중이다.
(D) 남자가 땅바닥을 빗자루로 쓸고 있다.

어휘 water v. ~에 물을 주다 put on (동작) ~을 착용하다 sweep ~을 빗자루로 쓸다

4. (A) He's cutting down a tree.
(B) He's inserting a cord into an outlet.
(C) He's pointing at the ceiling.
(D) **He's kneeling down on the floor.**
(A) 남자가 나무를 잘라 쓰러뜨리고 있다.
(B) 남자가 전기코드를 콘센트에 삽입하고 있다.
(C) 남자가 천장을 가리키고 있다.
(D) 남자가 바닥에 무릎을 꿇고 있다.

어휘 cut down ~을 잘라 쓰러뜨리다 insert A into B A를 B에 삽입하다 outlet 콘센트 point at ~을 가리키다 ceiling 천장 kneel down 무릎을 꿇다

5.
해석 잭슨 & 리 헬스 서플라이 사는 구매 3일 이내에 자사의 영양 보충제에 대한 배송을 보장한다.
해설 빈칸에 들어갈 어휘는 제품 구매 후 3일 이내에 이뤄지며 회사가 보장할 수 있는 대상을 나타내야 하므로 '배송, 배달'을 의미하는 (A)가 정답이다.
어휘 assure ~을 보장하다, 장담하다 nutritional 영양상의 supplement 보충(제) delivery 배송, 배달 advance 발전, 진보 expense 지출(액), 경비

6.
해석 월간 직원 교육 워크숍을 확립하겠다는 뷰몬트 씨의 제안이 오늘 아침 이사회 임원들로부터 승인을 받았다.
해설 빈칸에는 동사 received의 목적어 역할로서 제안사항에 대해 이사회로부터 받을 수 있는 것을 나타내야 하므로 '승인'을 의미하는 (A)가 정답이다.
어휘 establish ~을 확립하다, 설립하다 approval 승인 invitation 초대(장) election 선거, 투표

7.

해설 지메네즈 씨와 우 씨는 올해의 직원 워크숍을 위한 장소 및 활동들과 관련해 서로 동의한다.

해설 빈칸에는 특정 대상에 대한 두 사람 사이의 의견 일치를 나타낼 수 있는 어휘가 필요하므로 '동의, 합의'라는 의미의 (D)가 정답이다.

어휘 regarding ~와 관련해 comprehension 이해(력) verification 입증, 확인 fulfillment 이행, 완수 agreement 동의, 합의, 계약

8.

해설 문스터 주식회사는 직원들에게 다양한 승진 기회와 주기적인 교육을 제공한다.

해설 빈칸에는 빈칸 앞뒤의 부정관사 a와 전치사 of와 함께 회사가 제공하는 다양한 것을 나타낼 수 있는 어휘가 필요하다. 따라서 a와 of와 결합해 '다양한'이라는 의미를 구성하는 (C)가 정답이다.

어휘 career advancement 승진 position 직책, 일자리 variety 다양성 promotion 승진, 홍보

9.

해설 쉐라톤 로드는 하트포드의 도시에서 고급 식당들이 가장 많이 밀집해 있는 중심지이다.

해설 빈칸에는 빈칸 앞에 위치한 최상급 largest의 수식을 받아 한 지역에 여러 식당들이 모여 있는 상태를 나타낼 수 있는 어휘가 필요하므로 '밀집, 밀도, 집중' 등을 의미하는 (C)가 정답이다.

어휘 home to ~의 중심지, 본고장 fine 고급의 dining establishment 식당 appointment 예약, 약속 concentration 밀집, 밀도, 집중

10.

해설 파이브 스타즈 사는 어떤 경우에도 적절한 공연 목록의 다양한 노래들을 준비할 수 있다.

해설 빈칸에는 다양한 노래들이 사용될 수 있는 상황을 나타낼 어휘가 필요하므로 '경우, 사건' 등을 뜻하는 (A)가 정답이다.

어휘 setlist 공연 목록 appropriate 적절한 occasion 경우, 사건 vacancy 공석

11.

해설 로퍼 주식회사는 스팽딩 스트리트의 길먼 빌딩에 새로운 사무 공간을 낸다고 발표했다.

해설 빈칸에는 빈칸 앞에 제시된 명사와 함께 새로 개장한 대상이 되는 장소 어휘가 필요하다. 따라서 office와 함께 '사무 공간'을 뜻하는 (B)가 정답이다.

어휘 opening 개장 brand-new 새로운 office space 사무 공간

12.

해설 라일리 메뉴팩쳐링 사에서 조립 라인 관리자 직책을 위한 면접이 일주일 내내 진행될 것이다.

해설 빈칸에는 빈칸 앞에 제시된 명사와 함께 면접이 진행되어야 하는 이유를 나타낼 어휘가 필요하므로 manager와 함께 '관리자 직책'을 뜻하는 (D)가 정답이다.

어휘 hold an interview 면접을 진행하다 all week 일주일 내내 assembly 조립 manager position 관리자 직책 outline 개요 arrangement 예약, 준비

13-16.

수신: <manager@housingconnection.com>
제목: 구매 가능한 아파트

담당자분께,

저는 지난주 대학신문에 있었던 귀사의 광고에 **13** 응답하여 이메일을 씁니다. 저는 귀사가 학생들을 위해 알맞은 가격의 주택 선택지를 찾아주는 것을 전문으로 한다는 것을 알고 있고, 귀사의 서비스를 이용하는 것에 관심이 있습니다. **14** 저에게는 몇 개의 기준이 있습니다.

첫째로, 저는 현재 차량을 소유하고 있지 않기 **15** 때문에 캠퍼스에서 걸어갈 수 있는 위치의 아파트가 필요합니다. 다음으로, 저는 두 명의 친구와 함께 임대료를

나눠 내고 싶기 때문에, 침실이 3개인 아파트가 이상적일 것입니다. 마지막으로, 저희 부모님 집에 고양이가 있는데, 저는 내년에 이 고양이를 데려오고 싶습니다.

만약 제가 적합한 장소를 찾는 것을 도와주실 수 있다고 생각하시면, 이 주소로 회신을 보내주십시오. 저는 또한 귀하가 보통 상담에 대해 어떤 유형의 16 요금을 청구하는지도 알고 싶습니다. 귀하로부터의 연락을 기다리고 있겠습니다.

안녕히 계십시오,

레지 맥도날드

어휘 edition (신문, 잡지의) 판, 호 specialize in ~을 전문으로 하다 within walking distance 걸어갈 수 있는 위치에, 도보 거리에 rent 임대료 ideal 이상적인 suitable 적합한 typically 보통, 전형적으로 charge ~을 청구하다

13.

해설 빈칸 앞뒤에 전치사 in과 to가 있으므로 빈칸은 전치사의 목적어 역할을 할 명사 자리이다. 따라서 선택지 중 명사인 (B)와 (C) 중에서 골라야 하는데, response가 '~에 응답하여'라는 뜻으로 사용될 때는 셀 수 없으므로 (C)가 정답이다.

14. (A) 저는 지금까지 그 서비스에 만족합니다.
(B) 저에게는 몇 개의 기준이 있습니다.
(C) 그 기사를 보내주셔서 감사합니다.
(D) 그 아파트는 점검을 위한 준비가 되어 있습니다.

해설 빈칸 다음 문단에서 글쓴이는 First, Next, Finally와 같은 부사를 이용하여, 원하는 아파트의 조건을 순서대로 설명하고 있다. 따라서 그 조건을 구체적으로 언급하기 전에, 선택 기준을 가지고 있음을 먼저 언급하는 것이 자연스러우므로 (B)가 정답이다.

어휘 so far 지금까지 criteria 기준(criterion의 복수형) inspection 점검, 조사

15.

해설 빈칸 앞뒤로 두 개의 완전한 절이 제시되어 있고, 빈칸 앞에는 도보 거리를, 빈칸 뒤에서는 자동차가 없다는 사실을 언급하고 있으므로 자동차가 없는 것이 도보 거리의 아파트를 원하는 이유라고 생각할 수 있다. 따라서 이유를 나타내는 접속사 (A)가 정답이다.

어휘 as ~ 때문에 though 비록 ~일지라도 therefore 그러므로, 따라서 due to ~로 인해

16.

해설 빈칸에는 빈칸 뒤에 있는 동사 charge의 목적어 역할을 할 수 있는 어휘가 들어가야 하는데, charge가 '(요금, 비용을) 청구하다'라는 의미이므로 '요금, 수수료'라는 의미의 (C)가 정답이다.

어휘 property 재산, 소유권 fee 요금, 수수료

17-18.

볼텍스 엔터테인먼트의 대표이사,
새로운 비행기를 구입하다

글: 콜린 모로우

로스앤젤레스 (7월 30일) - 음악과 영화제작사인 볼텍스 엔터테인먼트의 대표이사 마틴 비아누찌 씨가 슬립스트림 500 전용기를 구입하고, "비아누찌 원"이라고 이름 지었다. 그는 어제 시상식을 위해 뉴욕으로 비행할 때 이 비행기에 처음으로 탑승했다.

이 "비아누찌 원"은 총 13,900파운드의 추진력을 만들어내는 2개의 랜킨 마크 엔진을 자랑한다. 비록 이 비행기의 강력한 엔진이 다른 비행기들의 엔진보다 더 많은 소음을 낼지라도, 새롭게 갖춰진 고급 흡음 시스템 때문에 기내에서는 소음을 전혀 들을 수가 없다. 이 비행기는 승무원과 승객들을 가득 태웠을 때, 8,065km까지의 인상적인 거리를 이동할 수 있다.

17 비아누찌 씨의 새로운 비행기는 그의 예전 비행기만큼 많은 좌석이 있지는 않지만, 매우 다양한 현대식 편의시설과 기술들이 함께 제공된다. 하지만 이 비행기를 18 운행하는 데 드는 총 비용은 연간 약 1백만 달러가 될 것이다.

어휘 name ~의 이름을 짓다 board ~에 탑승하다 boast ~을 자랑하다 thrust power 추진력 lb 파운드(중량의 단위) cabin 기내, 선실 newly-equipped 새롭게 갖춰진 sound-absorbing 흡음의 distance 거리 up to ~까지 seat 좌석이 있다 come with ~이 함께 제공되다, ~이 딸려오다 a wide array of 매우 다양한

17. 비아누찌 씨의 새로운 비행기는 이전 비행기와 어떻게 다른가?
(A) 더 강력한 엔진을 가지고 있다.
(B) 기내에서 더 많은 소리가 난다.
(C) 더 오랜 시간 동안 비행할 수 있다.
(D) 더 적은 승객을 수용한다.

해설 지문의 마지막 문단에 '그의 예전 비행기만큼 많은 좌석이 있지는 않다'는 내용이 언급되어 있다. 따라서 (D)가 정답이다.

어휘 duration 시간, 기간 accommodate ~을 수용하다

18. 세 번째 단락, 세 번째 줄에 있는 단어 "running" 과 의미가 가장 가까운 것은 무엇인가?
(A) 여행하는
(B) 탑승하는
(C) 작동시키는
(D) 승인하는

해설 제시된 단어가 포함된 문장의 의미가 '그 비행기를 운행하는 총 비용이 연간 1백만 달러가 될 것'이라는 의미이므로 '작동시키는, 운영하는'이라는 뜻의 (C)가 정답이다.

Week 02
정답 및 해설

Day 01 사물 사진 빈출 어휘

1. **(A) Clothing is hanging on racks.**
   (B) Some furniture is being arranged.
   (A) 옷이 옷걸이에 걸려 있다.
   (B) 가구가 정리되고 있다.

   어휘 clothing 옷 rack 옷걸이 arrange ~을 정리하다

2. (A) A pathway leads to a parking area.
   (B) There are some mountains in the distance.
   (A) 길이 주차장으로 이어져 있다.
   (B) 멀리 산이 있다.

   어휘 pathway (작은) 길 lead to ~로 이어지다 parking area 주차 구역, 주차장 in the distance 멀리

3. (A) Some shelves are stocked with boxes.
   (B) Some bookshelves are separated by an aisle.
   (A) 몇몇 선반들이 상자들로 채워져 있다.
   (B) 몇몇 책장들이 통로로 나뉘어 있다.

   어휘 be stocked with ~로 채워지다, 구비되다 be separated by ~로 나뉘다

4. **(A) Some tools are propped against a wall.**
   (B) A wheelbarrow is being pushed.
   (A) 연장들이 벽에 기대어져 있다.
   (B) 외바퀴 손수레가 밀리고 있다.

   어휘 be propped against ~에 기대어 있다 wheelbarrow 외바퀴 손수레

5. **(A) Some buildings are located near some hills.**
   (B) A stone bridge is being built over a river.
   (A) 몇몇 건물들이 언덕 근처에 위치해 있다.
   (B) 돌로 된 다리가 강 위에 건설되는 중이다.

   어휘 be located 위치하다 near ~ 근처에 hill 언덕 be built 건설되다

6. (A) A potted plant has been set on the floor.
   (B) Documents are stacked on a desk.
   (A) 화분이 바닥에 놓여 있다.
   (B) 서류들이 책상 위에 쌓여 있다.

   어휘 potted plant 화분 be set 놓이다 floor 바닥, 마루 be stacked 쌓여 있다

Day 02 명사 ③

표제어 문제 정답 및 해석

1. (A)	2. (B)	3. (B)	4. (A)	5. (B)
6. (A)	7. (A)	8. (A)	9. (A)	10. (B)
11. (A)	12. (B)	13. (B)	14. (A)	15. (B)
16. (A)	17. (A)	18. (A)	19. (B)	20. (B)
21. (A)	22. (B)	23. (B)	24. (A)	25. (A)
26. (B)	27. (B)	28. (B)	29. (A)	30. (B)
31. (B)	32. (B)	33. (B)	34. (A)	35. (A)
36. (B)	37. (A)	38. (B)	39. (A)	40. (B)

1. 저희 품질 보증 담당자는 제품들이 고객들에게 배송되어 나가기 전에 어떠한 제조상의 결함을 확인합니다.
2. 지난 10년 동안, 인도네시아에 있는 우리 공장에서의 팜 오일 생산량은 두 배 이상이 되었다.
3. 저희 웹 사이트는 유럽 전역에 걸쳐 다양한 지점들에서 저희가 판매하는 모든 제품들의 완전한 목록을 포함하고 있습니다.

4. 의사소통을 더 편리하게 만들기 위해, 참석자들은 접수 데스크에서 이름표를 찾아가야 한다.
5. 귀하께서 어떠한 제레트론 기기에 문제가 있으시다면, 저희 기술 지원팀에게 연락해주십시오.
6. 체육관의 사우나 시설이 보수 공사를 위해 폐쇄될 것이며, 6월 초에 재개장할 것으로 예상됩니다.
7. 고객들이 우리 메일링 목록에서 없어지길 원하는 경우에, 그분들의 세부정보를 저희 마케팅팀에 건네주시기 바랍니다.
8. 올해의 브리지워터 마라톤에서, 참가자의 수가 20,000명을 넘을 것 같다.
9. 제품 개발팀은 우리의 새로운 태블릿 컴퓨터의 겉 케이스를 디자인하는 최종 단계에 있다.
10. 호웰 씨의 시장 경향에 대한 지식이 EXA 소프트웨어 사가 업계에서 경쟁자들보다 월등히 앞서 있도록 했다.
11. 브라운 씨는 다가오는 프로젝트를 이끌 기회를 받을 사람으로 여먼 씨를 추천했다.
12. 호텔 관리인은 시설 관리팀이 더 효율적으로 일일 근무를 완료해야 된다고 주장했다.
13. 고급 교육 코스 덕분에, 우리는 생산 시간을 25퍼센트 줄였다.
14. 회사의 설립자는 새로운 고객들을 공항에서 시내 지역에 있는 호텔로 이동시키기 위해 준비했다.
15. 샹그릴라 식당에서, 저희는 음식, 서비스 그리고 분위기가 귀하의 기대치를 능가하는 것을 확실히 하도록 열심히 일하고 있습니다.
16. 귀하께서 연례 유지보수 서비스를 취소하고 싶으시다면, 저희 고객 지원팀에 서면 확인증을 제공해주셔야 합니다.
17. 모든 사업체들은 정부의 '그리너 퓨처' 안내서에 목록화된 규정들을 따라야 한다.
18. 저희 웹 사이트에 귀하의 상품을 등록함으로써, 귀하께서는 노트북 컴퓨터에 대한 3년 보증 기한을 연장하실 수 있습니다.
19. 제이콥스 씨가 컨퍼런스로 떠나 있는 동안, 부팀장 도킨스 씨가 사무실에서 가장 많은 권한을 가지고 있다.
20. 이 직원 오리엔테이션은 시리우스 IT 솔루션 사의 일자리에 대한 모든 측면을 다룰 것이다.

21. 매우 숙련된 기술자만 2일 내에 제조 로봇을 수리할 수 있을 것이다.
22. 직원 참석자 수의 분석은 연례 생산성 목표에 확실히 도달하기 위해 필수적이다.
23. 화상회의는 전 세계에 근거지를 둔 동료직원들과 논의를 하는 데 효과적인 수단이다.
24. 건물 관리자는 옥상 공간을 사용할 방법을 결정할 때 세입자들의 의견을 고려할 것이다.
25. 스포츠 행사를 위한 주최 도시는 사회 기반 시설과 치안을 포함한 여러 요인들에 근거하여 선택되었다.
26. 수습 기간의 완료 후에, 합격한 직원들은 정규직 계약을 제공받을 것이다.
27. 테스커 씨를 제외하고, 거의 모든 이사회 임원들이 텍사스로 이전하자는 제안에 찬성했다.
28. 급여 담당 부장은 이번 주 매일 오후 4시 이후에 급여와 관련된 문제들에 대한 상담이 가능할 것이다.
29. 우리 본사의 증축이 도시 건물 규정에 따라 건축되어야 하는 것이 중요하다.
30. 올해의 영화상의 후보들이 25명의 유명 영화 평론가로 구성된 패널에 의해 고려될 것이다.
31. 살라 테크놀로지 사의 연말 연회에서의 로스 오길비 씨의 연설은 회사의 성공에 대한 직원들의 자신감을 증가시켰다.
32. 이것은 귀하의 주차 구역이 D5에서 E3으로 변경되었음을 상기시켜드리는 글입니다.
33. 개업 기념 행사를 준비하면서, 스타버스트 몰 소유자들은 지역 유명인들에게 초대장을 보내고 있다.
34. BC 하이킹 탐험대는 참가자들이 적절히 수분을 섭취하고 부상으로부터 자유로운 상태인 것을 보장하기 위해 모든 예방 조치를 취한다.
35. 연예인 광고는 그 회사의 세계적인 마케팅 전략의 주된 구성 요소이다.
36. 수영장이 청소를 위해 폐쇄될 동안, 저희는 귀하의 인내에 감사드리며, 호텔의 다른 편의시설을 즐기시도록 권고 드립니다.
37. 4번가에 대해 제안된 확장은 시내 도로들에서의 정체를 상당히 줄일 것이다.
38. 그 예술 비평가는 폴 누난의 작품과 루카 베르고

39. 수입 석유의 가격이 계속 급등하고 있기 때문에, 유럽의 운전자들은 중대한 연료의 부족 현상에 대해 대비해야 한다.
40. 바커 씨가 오늘 오후 3시 정각에 열릴 예정인 기자회견 참석을 요청하셨습니다.

DAILY QUIZ

7.

해석 모든 새롭게 설치된 일렉트라 보일러들은 기술적 결함을 보장해주는 연장된 보증 기한이 함께 딸려 온다.

해설 빈칸 뒤에 제시된 기술적 결함을 보장해주는 주체를 나타낼 수 있는 어휘가 와야 하므로 '보증(기한)'을 뜻하는 (D)가 정답이다.

어휘 installed 설치된 come with ~가 함께 딸려오다 extended 연장된 cover ~을 보장하다 fault 결함 operation 운영, 작동 warranty 보증(기한)

8.

해석 뷰캐넌 시장은 소규모의 공개 토론회를 선호하는데, 그것이 지역 유권자들과 더 나은 관계를 발전시키는 것을 도와주기 때문이다.

해설 빈칸에 공개 토론회가 주는 효과와 관련해 전치사 with와 어울리는 어휘가 필요하므로 '관계, 연결(성)'이라는 의미의 (B)가 정답이다.

어휘 small-scale 소규모의 public forum 공개 토론회 constituent 유권자 connection 관계, 연결(성) profession 직업

Day 03 명사 ④

표제어 문제 정답 및 해석

1. (B)	2. (B)	3. (B)	4. (B)	5. (B)
6. (A)	7. (A)	8. (A)	9. (B)	10. (A)
11. (A)	12. (B)	13. (A)	14. (B)	15. (B)
16. (A)	17. (B)	18. (B)	19. (A)	20. (B)
21. (B)	22. (A)	23. (B)	24. (B)	25. (B)
26. (B)	27. (A)	28. (B)	29. (B)	30. (B)
31. (A)	32. (B)	33. (B)	34. (B)	35. (A)
36. (B)	37. (B)	38. (A)	39. (B)	40. (A)

1. 임대 계약을 갱신하는 것을 원하지 않는 부동산 임차인들은 반드시 임대인에게 서면 통지를 보내야 한다.
2. 올백 씨는 인기 있는 팟캐스트 출연의 결과로써 그의 음악 앨범 판매의 증가를 경험했다.
3. 다이어 씨는 다음 주 월요일에 패스트푸드 할인점이 개장하기 전에 10개의 직책을 채워야 한다는 압박에 시달린다.
4. 뮤직 페스티벌에 대한 입장권 판매로부터 온 모든 수익금의 일부가 자선단체에 기부될 것이다.
5. 예정된 유지보수로 인해, 내일 오전 11시에 사무실의 인터넷 연결의 일시적인 중단이 있을 것입니다.
6. 정부 관계 기관은 최근에 윌트쉬어 풀 무역 사에 대해 조사를 수행했다.
7. 시장 조사 그룹은 신제품의 디자인, 기능성, 그리고 다른 요소를 고려할 것이다.
8. 벨라 비스트로에서의 음식은 많은 칭찬을 받았지만, 좌석이 한 번에 15명의 식사 손님들로 제한되어 있다.
9. 그래픽 디자인 컨설턴트는 우리의 웹 사이트의 강화가 온라인 매출을 상당히 신장시킬 수 있다고 생각한다.
10. 클리어몬트 컨벤션 센터와의 인접성으로 인해, 아이리스 호텔은 출장자들에게 인기 있는 선택권이다.

11. 랭 박사의 마운틴 고릴라의 번식 습성에 대한 견해는 <바이오사이언스 먼슬리>의 최신 호에 발표되었다.
12. 야구선수들은 종종 무패의 기록을 유지하고 있는 그들의 수석 코치에게 경의를 표한다.
13. 파트타이머 근로자들은 월간 회사 회의에 참석할 의무가 없지만, 여전히 참석하는 것이 강력하게 권고된다.
14. 킹 버거의 최고 운영 책임자는 청소년기부터 회사에서 일하기 시작했기 때문에 사업체에 대한 특이한 관점을 가지고 있다.
15. 건물의 보안 사무실에 접근하기 위해 번호의 올바른 순서가 키패드에 입력되어야 한다.
16. 새로운 모뎀이 24시간 이내에 귀하의 소유물이 될 것이고, 저희 기술자들이 그것을 무료로 설치해드릴 것입니다.
17. 마리오 알베로의 최신 투자 기업은 식당과 영화관의 조합이다.
18. 그 직책에 지원하는 사람들은 그들이 필수적인 기술을 가지고 있다는 증거를 보여줄 수 있도록 포트폴리오를 제출해야 한다.
19. 다른 기업들 간의 고객 정보의 공유를 금지하는 규정이 올해에 효력이 발생할 것이다.
20. 알버타 정유회사는 국내 유통 네트워크를 개선하기 위해 다음 5년 동안에 캐나다 전역에 걸쳐 새로운 관들을 설치할 것이다.
21. 저희 웹 사이트는 모든 EZ 전자 주방 용품의 크기와 기술적인 상세 요건을 분명하게 보여주고 있습니다.
22. 특정 외국 제품들의 수입에 가해진 무역 제한이 국내 경제를 신장시키기 위해 시행되었다.
23. 알비온 철도회사는 선로 유지보수로 인해 발생된 열차 서비스에서 최근 중단에 대해 승객들에게 사과했다.
24. 로날드 이브스는 런던의 도시 풍경으로부터 받은 영감을 통해 수채화 그림을 그렸다.
25. 고객 충성도를 강화하기 위해, 엑스 사무용품 사는 여러 혜택들이 있는 멤버십 프로그램을 도입할 것이다.
26. 하이츠 모터스 사의 하이브리드 자동차의 경우에 그랬던 것처럼, 첫 완전 전기 자동차는 전 세계에서 훌륭한 평을 받았다.
27. 저희 인사부의 장으로서, 호크 씨의 직무들 중 하나는 직원들의 의욕을 향상시키는 것입니다.
28. 저희는 식당을 방문해주시는 분들께 훌륭한 첫 인상을 남기고 싶으니 열정으로 모든 식사 손님들을 맞이해주십시오.
29. 자사의 홍보 자료에서, 젠 풀 파이버 사는 무선 인터넷 서비스의 속도와 신뢰도를 강조한다.
30. 도시의 설립을 기념하기 위해, 시장은 기념비적인 건물의 건설을 승인했다.
31. 귀하의 편의를 위해, 저희는 이 이메일에 귀하의 송장의 전자 사본을 첨부했습니다.
32. 많은 집주인들은 내구성 때문에 트루그레인의 원목 바닥재를 설치하는 것을 선택하고 있다.
33. 호텔 투숙객들은 가파른 급경사가 많기 때문에 근처 숲을 걸을 때 주의를 기울이도록 권고 받는다.
34. 국립 항공청의 장은 새로운 항공기의 안전에 대한 철저한 평가를 요청했다.
35. 어떠한 추가적인 수정을 하기 원할 경우에 대비해, 귀하의 기사를 편집팀의 켄 그림쇼 씨에게 제출하시기 바랍니다.
36. 스피디 잇츠와 고 그럽의 비교는 평균 배달 시간이 스피디 잇츠에게 훨씬 더 적었다는 것을 보여주었다.
37. 전국 육상 위원회에서 온 대표단이 클락슨 경기장의 적합성을 평가할 것이다.
38. 이전 후에, 사터 가구회사의 본사는 뉴욕 시티 밖으로 약 20킬로미터 떨어진 곳에 위치해 있을 것이다.
39. 길드 출판사의 편집자 직책은 창의력에 대한 안목과 세부사항에 대한 훌륭한 집중력을 필요로 한다.
40. 우리가 요청했던 기한 연장을 받을 수 없었기 때문에 매출 보고서의 마감일이 이번 주 금요일까지이다.

DAILY QUIZ

7.
해석 카르멘 엑스포 센터는 여러 5성급 호텔들과의 인접성으로 인해 사업 총회들을 위한 완벽한 장소이다.
해설 빈칸 다음에 위치한 전치사 to와 어울려 특정 건물이 지닌 위치적인 특성을 나타낼 어휘가 필요하므로 '인접(성), 근접'을 뜻하는 (B)가 정답이다.
어휘 venue (행사) 장소 accomplishment 성취, 업적 proximity 인접(성), 근접 competence 능숙함 opposition 반대

8.
해석 프로스트 출판사에서는, 자사의 직원들이 지닌 긍정적인 업무 태도를 대단히 중요하게 여기므로, 모든 업무에 대해 열정을 갖고 접근하도록 노력하시기 바랍니다.
해설 빈칸이 속한 so절은 명령문 형태로 업무를 접하는 방식을 알리는 내용이므로 with의 목적어로 쓰일 어휘는 사람의 마음가짐이나 태도와 관련되어야 한다. 따라서 '열정, 열광'을 의미하는 (D)가 정답이다.
어휘 greatly 대단히, 매우 value ~을 중요하게 여기다 attitude 태도 approach ~에 접근하다 task 업무, 일 comparison 비교, 대조 allocation 할당(량) enthusiasm 열정, 열광

Day 04 명사＋전치사 콜로케이션

표제어 문제 정답 및 해석

1. (A)	2. (A)	3. (A)	4. (A)	5. (B)
6. (A)	7. (B)	8. (B)	9. (B)	10. (B)
11. (A)	12. (B)	13. (A)	14. (A)	15. (B)
16. (A)	17. (B)	18. (B)	19. (B)	20. (B)
21. (A)	22. (A)	23. (B)	24. (B)	25. (A)
26. (B)	27. (B)	28. (B)	29. (A)	30. (A)
31. (A)	32. (A)	33. (A)	34. (B)	35. (B)
36. (B)	37. (B)	38. (B)	39. (A)	40. (B)

1. 오로지 정회원들만 수영장에 있는 스파와 사우나 시설에 대한 이용권을 받는다.
2. 우리의 식사 손님들은 점심시간 뷔페의 도입에 대한 많은 관심을 보여주었다.
3. 마틴 씨에게 12월의 귀하의 근무 가능 시간에 대한 어떠한 조정사항이라도 알려주시기 바랍니다.
4. 페리 운항 일정에 어떠한 변동사항이 있을 경우에는, 저희가 귀하께 미리 연락을 드릴 것입니다.
5. 저렴한 비용의 식물성 섬유는 전통적인 의류 소재들에 대한 훌륭한 대안이라는 것이 증명되었다.
6. 홍 씨와 시펄리 씨는 올해의 회사 워크숍 장소에 대해 합의했다.
7. 직원들을 동기 부여하는 것에 대한 트레이너 씨의 효과적인 접근법은 생산성에서의 20퍼센트 증가라는 결과를 낳았다.
8. 이 쿠폰은 다른 어떠한 상품권이나 할인 코드와 함께 사용될 수 없습니다.
9. 회계부장의 요청에 따라, 직원들은 개인적 지출에 대해 회사 신용카드를 사용할 수 없다.
10. 지역 오락 서비스들에 대한 자료는 주로 고객 설문조사를 통해 취합되었다.
11. 회사 재고 체계의 사소한 변경은 수요일 아침 회의 동안 다뤄질 것이다.
12. 앤더슨 씨는 도시의 시장으로부터 지역사회에 대한 그의 귀중한 공헌에 대한 인정을 받을 것이다.

13. 갈비스턴 프레시 프로듀스 사는 펜리스 지역의 소비자들에게 해당 지역에서의 최근 배송 서비스의 중단에 대해 사과했다.
14. 유럽 시장으로의 최근 확장으로 인해, 에라스무스 자동차 사는 자사의 수익이 거의 두 배가 되었음을 확인했다.
15. 제출된 피드백 양식들에 기반하여, 대부분의 우리 직원들은 그들의 지점장에 대한 신뢰를 가지고 있다.
16. 그 인테리어 디자이너는 우리가 최근에 구매한 사무 공간에 대한 몇몇 개선을 권고했다.
17. 모든 제조 과정은 반드시 정부 보건안전기준을 준수해야 한다.
18. 이 미납 안내를 잘못 받았다고 생각하신다면, 저희 고객 계정팀에 연락해주시기 바랍니다.
19. 포장 재료 비용의 증가로 인해, 시맨 파인 푸드 사는 자사의 가격을 인상할 수밖에 없었다.
20. 웨이퍼럴 인은 기차역과의 인접성 때문에 관광객들이 머물기에 이상적인 장소이다.
21. 지점장으로서, 랭 씨는 사무 업무를 위임하는 것에 대한 주도권을 가져야 한다.
22. 크릭 소프트웨어 사의 이사회 임원들은 지역 모바일 어플리케이션 개발사와 합병하는 것에 대한 조사를 시작했다.
23. 여행 일정에 대한 어떠한 변경사항이라도 저희 웹 사이트에 즉시 게시될 것입니다.
24. 재정적 문제들의 직면에 있어서의 설립자의 고집이 결국 그가 성공적인 섬유회사를 설립하는 데 도움이 되었다.
25. 고객들이 사우스 로드에 있는 오락 복합건물의 청사진에 대한 수정을 요구했다.
26. 저희 체육관 회원들의 불만에 대한 응답으로, 저희는 더 다양한 운동 수업을 제공하기로 결정했습니다.
27. 서머 솔스티스 음악 페스티벌의 기획자들은 행사에서 제공되었던 편의시설에 대한 피드백을 구하고 있습니다.
28. 베일리빌에 있는 우리의 새 사무실로 이전하는 동안, 여러 장비들이 보관 중일 것입니다.
29. 영업에서 일자리를 찾고 있는 사람들에 대한 중요한 필수요건은 효과적으로 소통하는 능력이다.
30. 배우 댄 하그레이브스 씨는 그의 팬들과의 연결성을 느낄 기회를 주기 때문에 팬미팅에 참석하는 것을 즐긴다.
31. 와이엇 교수는 교육 분야에 대한 그의 놀랄 만한 공헌을 인정하는 스탠튼 상을 받았다.
32. 바니 씨는 그녀의 새로운 화장품 매장을 위한 가장 이상적인 장소에 대한 조사를 실시할 것이다.
33. 정부 소음 규제 지침을 준수하여, 건설 현장에서의 작업은 오후 5시에 반드시 중단되어야 한다.
34. 청소 용품들은 피부를 자극할 수 있으므로 반드시 주의 깊게 다뤄져야 한다.
35. 코 씨의 부재의 결과로, 인사부는 지난 두 달 동안 맥스 베이리스 씨의 관리 하에 있었다.
36. 다가오는 비즈니스 시상식에 대비하여, 에드워드 씨는 연설을 연습하고 있다.
37. 이 계약 조건 하에서, 귀하의 구독을 취소하기를 희망하신다면, 적어도 3일 전에 저희에게 미리 알려주셔야 합니다.
38. 광고 캠페인을 취소한 세라핌 주식회사의 결정은 전체적인 수익의 감소로 이어졌다.
39. 회사 본사의 새로운 위치에 대한 합의의 실패는 제안된 사업 합병을 위험에 처하게 할 수 있다.
40. 데이토나 비치 리조트에서, 안내 데스크 직원들은 열정으로 모든 투숙객들을 맞이하도록 권고된다.

DAILY QUIZ

7.

해석 그 슈퍼마켓의 자체 브랜드의 세탁 세제는 시장에서 앞서가는 제품들에 대한 적당한 가격의 대안이다.

해설 빈칸에 들어갈 어휘는 laundry detergent와 동일한 대상으로서 빈칸 뒤에 제시된 전치사 to와 어울려야 하므로 to와 함께 '~에 대한 대안'이라는 의미의 (C)가 정답이다.

어휘 laundry 세탁 detergent 세제
alternative to ~에 대한 대안 leading 앞서가는, 선도적인 exchange 교환(품)

8.

해석 공항과 버스 터미널에 인접성을 고려하면, 캔튼 전시장이 국제무역박람회를 위한 이상적인 장소이다.

해설 빈칸에는 빈칸 뒤에 제시된 전치사 to와 함께 특정 장소가 무역박람회의 행사 장소로서 이상적인 이유를 나타낼 수 있어야 하므로 '~와의 인접성'이라는 뜻의 (B)가 정답이다.

어휘 considering ~을 고려하면 proximity to ~와의 인접성 exhibition 전시 trade expo 무역박람회 sequence 순서

Day 05 기출 동의어 ②

표제어 문제 정답

1. (A)	2. (A)	3. (A)	4. (B)	5. (B)
6. (B)	7. (B)	8. (B)	9. (B)	10. (A)
11. (B)	12. (A)	13. (A)	14. (A)	15. (B)
16. (A)	17. (A)	18. (B)	19. (B)	20. (B)
21. (B)	22. (B)	23. (B)	24. (B)	25. (B)
26. (B)	27. (B)	28. (A)	29. (A)	30. (B)

DAILY QUIZ

1.

해석 잡지는 다음 호에서 그 화가의 최신 전시를 다루며 독점 인터뷰도 특집으로 선보일 예정이다. 독자들은 생생한 사진과 상세한 해설을 통해 시각적으로 놀라운 전시 쇼케이스를 기대할 수 있다.

해설 잡지가 화가의 전시를 다룰 것이라는 것은 해당 내용을 '싣다, 포함하다'라는 뜻이므로 (A)가 정답이다.

어휘 cover ~을 다루다, 포함하다 latest 최신의 feature ~을 특집으로 싣다 exclusive 독점의 as well 또한, 역시 visually 시각적으로 stunning 굉장히 멋진 showcase 공개 (행사) vivid 생생한 commentary 해설 wrap ~을 싸다 insure 보험에 들다

2.

해석 우리는 가격이 적당하고 실용적일 뿐만 아니라 에너지 정책 및 보존법에서 정한 가전제품의 에너지 효율 기준을 충족하는 세탁기를 만듭니다.

해설 동사 meet는 필요나 요구사항, 기준 등을 목적어로 할 때 '~을 충족시키다'라는 뜻이다. 따라서 (B)가 정답이다.

어휘 washer 세탁기 practical 실용적인 meet the standards 기준을 충족하다 energy efficiency 에너지 효율 home appliance 가정용 기기 set by ~에 의해 정해진 touch ~에 닿다 satisfy ~을 충족시키다

3.

해석 귀하의 조경 필요 사항을 위해 저희 서비스를 선택해 주셔서 감사합니다. 저희는 귀하의 비즈니스를 소중히 여기며 귀하의 기대를 뛰어넘는 뛰어난 결과를 제공하기 위해 최선을 다하고 있습니다.

해설 서비스를 제공하는 업체에서 고객의 비즈니스를 value한다는 것은 '소중히 여기다'라는 뜻이므로 이러한 의미를 가지는 (B)가 정답이다.

어휘 landscaping 조경 be committed to -ing ~하는 데 전념하다 deliver ~을 내놓다 outstanding 훌륭한 exceed ~을 능가하다 expectation 기대 estimate ~을 평가하다 appreciate ~을 소중히 여기다

Week 02 실전 TEST

1. (D)	2. (A)	3. (D)	4. (D)	5. (C)
6. (C)	7. (D)	8. (B)	9. (C)	10. (B)
11. (B)	12. (B)	13. (A)	14. (D)	15. (B)
16. (D)	17. (A)	18. (D)		

1.
(A) Some windows are being installed.
(B) Shopping baskets are stacked by a window.
(C) Some drawers have been left open.
(D) Products are displayed on shelves.

(A) 몇몇 창문이 설치되는 중이다.
(B) 쇼핑용 바구니가 창가에 쌓여 있다.
(C) 몇몇 서랍이 열린 채로 있다.
(D) 상품들이 선반마다 진열되어 있다.

어휘 install ~을 설치하다 stack ~을 쌓다 drawer 서랍 be left 형용사 ~한 채로 있다 display ~을 진열하다, ~을 전시하다

2.
(A) Some boats are docked in a harbor.
(B) Some boats are filled with supplies.
(C) Some people are boarding a boat.
(D) Some people are swimming in the ocean.

(A) 몇몇 보트들이 항구에 정박되어 있다.
(B) 몇몇 보트들이 물품으로 가득 차 있다.
(C) 몇몇 사람들이 보트에 탑승하고 있다.
(D) 몇몇 사람들이 바다에서 수영하고 있다.

어휘 dock ~을 정박하다, ~을 부두에 대다 harbor 항구 be filled with ~로 가득 차 있다 supplies 물품, 용품 board ~에 탑승하다

3.
(A) A door has been propped open.
(B) An entrance is blocked by a bench.
(C) Some signs are posted on a wall.
(D) Some potted plants have been placed outside.

(A) 문 하나가 지지대를 받친 상태로 열려 있다.
(B) 출입문 하나가 벤치로 가로막혀 있다.
(C) 몇몇 안내 표지가 한쪽 벽에 게시되어 있다.
(D) 몇몇 화분에 심은 식물이 밖에 놓여 있다.

어휘 be propped open 지지대를 받친 상태로 열려 있다 be blocked by ~로 가로막혀 있다 post v. ~을 게시하다, ~을 내걸다 potted plant 화분에 심은 식물 place ~을 놓다, ~을 두다

4.
(A) A man is standing in front of a desk.
(B) A man is writing on a notepad.
(C) A light fixture has been hung from the ceiling.
(D) A clock is mounted above a whiteboard.

(A) 한 남자가 책상 앞에 서 있다.
(B) 한 남자가 메모장에 뭔가 쓰고 있다.
(C) 조명 기구 하나가 천장에 매달려 있다.
(D) 시계가 화이트보드 위에 설치되어 있다.

어휘 in front of ~ 앞에 light fixture 조명 기구 be hung from ~에 매달려 있다 ceiling 천장 mount ~을 설치하다, ~을 장착하다

5.
해석 청소 로봇 제품이 여전히 시제품 단계에 있으며, 이번 달 기술 컨벤션에서 전시될 준비가 되어 있지 않다.

해설 빈칸 앞에 위치한 명사 prototype과 복합명사를 구성할 수 있는 어휘가 필요한데, 아직 전시될 준비가 되지 않았다는 말과 어울리려면 '시제품 단계'에 있는 제품이라는 의미가 되어야 적절하다. 따라서 '단계'를 의미하는 (C)가 정답이다.

어휘 prototype 시제품, 원형 제품 exhibit ~을 전시하다 portion 부분, 일부 stage 단계 compartment (차량 등의) 짐칸, 보관함

6.
해석 국가 안전 규정은 모든 건설 근로자들이 건축 현장 내에서 안전모를 착용할 것을 요구한다.
해설 빈칸 앞에 위치한 명사 safety와 복합명사를 구성할 수 있는 어휘가 필요한데, 어떤 것이 시행되도록 요구할 수 있는 것이 빈칸에 필요하므로 '규정, 규칙, 규제' 등을 의미하는 (C)가 정답이다.
어휘 safety 안전 require that ~라는 것을 요구하다 construction 건설 protective helmet 안전모 building site 건축 현장 regulation 규정, 규칙, 규제 process 과정

7.
해석 그 연구의 결과는 에핑 지역 거주민들이 그들의 지역 의회 의원들에 대한 확신이 거의 없다는 것을 보여주었다.
해설 빈칸 앞뒤에 있는 동사 have 및 전치사 in과 어울리면서 특정 지역의 의회 의원들에 대한 주민들의 감정이나 생각을 나타내 줄 수 있는 어휘가 필요하므로 '확신, 자신감' 등의 뜻인 (D)가 정답이다.
어휘 few 거의 없는 council member 지역 의회 의원 honesty 정직함, 솔직함 strength 장점, 힘 motivation 동기 confidence 확신, 자신감

8.
해석 월그렌 사의 대표이사 젠슨 씨는 회사의 업무 정책에 대한 그 어떤 수정사항에 대해 승인하는 것을 책임지고 있다.
해설 빈칸에는 대표이사가 회사 업무 정책에 대해 승인할 수 있는 대상이 될 수 있는 어휘가 필요하므로 '수정, 개정'이라는 의미의 (B)가 정답이다.
어휘 be responsible for ~을 책임지다 approve ~을 승인하다 turn 차례, 순서 revision 수정, 개정

9.
해석 스톡홀름 대표단이 우리의 생산 시설을 방문할 때, 마티네즈 씨는 그들에게 자동차 제조 방법을 보여줄 것이다.
해설 빈칸에는 생산 시설을 방문하는 주체를 나타낼 수 있는 사람명사 어휘가 와야 하므로 '대표단'이라는 의미를 가진 (C)가 정답이다.
어휘 production 생산 manufacture ~을 제조하다 automobile 자동차 deviation 일탈, 탈선 precision 정확, 정밀 delegation 대표단 translation 번역

10.
해석 그 감독의 최신 영화는 1950년대의 미국 고전 영화의 몇몇 기본적인 요소들을 사용한다.
해설 빈칸에는 빈칸 앞에 위치한 형용사 fundamental의 수식을 받을 수 있으면서 영화에 사용될 수 있는 대상을 나타낼 수 있는 것이 필요하므로 '요소'를 뜻하는 (B)가 정답이다.
어휘 fundamental 기본적인, 근본적인 element 요소 similarity 유사성

11.
해석 중국에서의 잠재적 투자자들의 요청에 따라, 제조 공장에 대한 견학이 다음 달로 연기되었다.
해설 빈칸에는 어떤 일이 연기된다는 결과를 가져올 수 있는 어휘가 필요하므로 빈칸 뒤에 제시된 At the 및 of와 함께 '~의 요청에 따라'라는 의미를 구성하는 (B)가 정답이다.
어휘 at the request of ~의 요청에 따라 prospective 잠재적인, 장래의 postpone ~을 연기하다 following 다음의 effect 효과 certainty 확실한 것, 확실성 necessity 필요, 불가피한 것

12.
해석 아이스드 트리츠 사의 소유주는 최신 얼린 요거트의 맛에 대한 피드백을 기다리고 있다.
해설 빈칸에는 빈칸 뒤에 제시된 전치사 on과 함께 새로운 맛에 대해 소유주가 기다리는 대상을 나타낼 수 있는 어휘가 와야 한다. 따라서 문맥상 '맛에 대한 피드백, 의견'이 자연스러우므로 '피드백, 의견'을 의미하는 (B)가 정답이다.
어휘 feedback on ~에 대한 피드백, 의견 flavor

맛 frozen 얼린, 냉동의 statement 진술(서)
conduct 수행, 행동

13-16.

수신: 전 보안 직원들
날짜: 8월 16일
회신: 새로운 보안 조치들

많은 여러분들이 이미 아시다시피, 우리는 최근에 일련의 보안 위반을 겪어 왔습니다. 대부분은 심각한 문제로 이어지지는 않았지만, 마지막 사고는 거의 우리에게 수백만 달러의 **13** 상당하는 설계도의 비용이 발생할 뻔 하였습니다. 다행히, 우리는 그것들이 경쟁사들의 손에 떨어지기 전에 회수할 수 있었습니다. **14** 따라서, 우리는 새로운 보안 정책들을 실행할 것입니다.

우선, 여러분은 이제 반드시 우리 시설에 들어오는 모든 사람의 신분증을 스캔해야 합니다. **15** 예외는 없을 것입니다. 이것은 심지어 최고위 직급의 직원들에게도 해당됩니다. 또한, 모든 컴퓨터들은 반드시 적절한 보안 소프트웨어가 설치되어 있는지 확실하게 확인되어야 합니다. 마지막으로, 퇴근 시간 이후에, 보안 직원은 반드시 아무도 **16** 서면 허가 없이 늦게 남아 있지 않도록 확실하게 전체 시설을 확인해야 합니다.

여러분의 규칙 준수에 미리 감사드립니다.

그레그 데이비슨, 최고 보안 담당자

어휘 suffer ~을 겪다 breach 위반, 침해 lead to ~로 이어지다 blueprint 설계도, 청사진 first of all 우선 scan ~을 스캔하다, 자세히 보다 highest-ranking 최고위 직급의 ensure that ~라는 것을 확실하게 하다 proper 적절한 stay late 늦게 남아 있다 permission 허가 compliance (규칙) 준수, 지킴

13.

해설 빈칸 뒤 금액이 제시되어 있으므로 이 금액 표현과 함께 '얼마 어치, 얼마의 가치'라는 뜻으로 쓰이는 (A)가 정답이다.

어휘 worth 가치가 있는 valued 소중한 priced 가격이 책정된

14.

(A) 이런 서류들을 대체하는 것은 어려울 것입니다.
(B) 따라서, 우리는 새로운 보안 정책들을 실행할 것입니다.
(C) 그래서, 정보를 공유하기 전에 주의 깊게 생각하시기 바랍니다.
(D) 이 심각한 문제에 관심을 가져 주셔서 감사드립니다.

해설 빈칸 앞에는 최근 일련의 보안 문제들을, 다음 문단부터는 새로운 보안 강화 정책들을 나열하고 있다. 따라서 새로운 보안 정책들을 실행한다는 사실을 알리는 내용이 필요하므로 (B)가 정답이다.

어휘 therefore 따라서 implement ~을 실행하다 security 보안 attention 관심

15.

해설 빈칸 앞에는 모든 사람의 신분증을 확인한다는 내용이, 빈칸 뒤에는 이것이 최고위급 직원들에게도 해당된다고 언급되어 있다. 따라서 빈칸 앞에 위치한 no와 함께 '예외는 없다'는 내용이 오는 것이 적절하므로 '예외, 제외'라는 의미의 (B)가 정답이다.

어휘 submission 제출, 복종 exception 예외, 제외 transaction 거래 correlation 상호관계

16.

해설 빈칸 앞뒤에 전치사와 명사가 있으므로 빈칸은 명사를 수식할 수 있는 형용사 자리이다. 따라서 (B)와 (D) 중에서 정답을 골라야 하는데, 빈칸 뒤의 '허가'라는 의미의 permission이 있으므로 이는 사람에 의해 허가된 것임을 알 수 있다. 따라서 '서면의'라는 의미의 과거분사 (D)가 정답이다.

17-18.

아르고 솔루션 사, 목표에 도달하다

디트로이트 (9월 7일) - 아르고 솔루션 사는 기술 분야의 일자리에 요구되는 기술을 배우는 것을 희망하는 사람들을 위한 컴퓨터 프로그래밍 워크숍을 실시하겠다는 목표를 달성했다. **17** 아르고 사는 업무용 스프레드시트와 데이터베이스 프로그램을 제작하는 것을 전문으로 하는 곳이다.

디트로이트와 시카고, 그리고 세인트루이스의 지방 정부들의 재정적 도움을 통해, 몇몇 회사들은 유용한 새 기술을 배우려는 사람들에게 기회를 제공하기 위해 다양한 전문 능력 개발 워크숍을 준비하고 있다. 아르고 솔루션 사의 경우, 이 회사의 워크숍은 디트로이트에 있는 본사에서 매주 월요일에 개최된다.

"자금의 제공자들에 의해 제시된 **18** 조건에 따라, 저희는 연중 주기적으로 운영되는 종합적인 교육 활동을 제공해야 했습니다"라고 아르고 솔루션 사의 레온 도렌즈 대표이사가 말했다. "저희는 현재 제공 중인 워크숍을 자랑스럽게 생각하며, 이것들은 가장 경험 많고 숙련된 저희 프로그래머들의 일부가 진행하고 있습니다."

이런 교육 활동에 합류할뿐만 아니라, 이 회사는 자사의 제품에 대한 수요가 급격히 증가함에 따라 올 하반기에 본사에서 약 100명의 신입사원들을 채용할 계획이다.

(C) 지역 학교들을 위한 노트북 컴퓨터
(D) 시장 조사 보고서

해설 첫 단락 마지막 문장에서 아르고 사가 업무용 스프레드시트와 데이터베이스 프로그램을 만든다고 언급되어 있으므로 (A)가 정답이다.

18. 세 번째 단락 첫 번째 줄에 있는 단어 "terms"와 의미가 가장 가까운 것은 무엇인가?
(A) 생각
(B) 지속 시간
(C) 상표
(D) 조건

해설 제시된 단어 terms는 자금을 제공해주는 당사자가 정한 것으로서 따라야 하는 대상으로 언급되어 있다. 따라서 지원에 필요한 조건을 나타내는 의미로 사용되었음을 알 수 있으므로 '조건'이라는 뜻의 (D)가 정답이다.

어휘 reach ~에 도달하다 required 필요한, 필수적인 sector 분야, 부문 specialize in ~을 전문으로 하다 spreadsheet 스프레드시트(표 계산 소프트웨어) professional development 전문 능력 개발 in the case of ~의 경우에 term (계약 등의) 조건 set out ~을 제시하다, 시작하다 comprehensive 종합적인 run 운영되다 throughout ~ 동안 쭉 be led by A A가 진행하다 in addition to ~뿐만 아니라 demand 수요 sharply 급격히

17. 아르고 솔루션 사는 무엇을 만드는가?
(A) 사무용 소프트웨어
(B) 대학 교재

Week 03
정답 및 해설

Day 01 LC가 잘 들리는 어휘 ①

DAILY QUIZ

7. When will the office renovation be completed?
(A) Not until the end of May.
(B) Yes, I just completed the form.
(C) It's on the fourth floor.

사무실 보수작업이 언제 완료되나요?
(A) 5월 말은 되어야 합니다.
(B) 네, 방금 서식을 작성했어요.
(C) 4층에 있어요.

어휘 renovation 보수 작업 complete ~을 완료하다 not until + 일시 ~는 되어야 하다 complete a form 서식을 작성하다

8. We need to come up with a new marketing strategy.
(A) Yes, I need to go shopping.
(B) It's on the market.
(C) There's a meeting scheduled for tomorrow.

우리는 새로운 마케팅 전략을 생각해 내야 합니다.
(A) 네, 저는 쇼핑을 다녀와야 해요.
(B) 시중에 판매되고 있어요.
(C) 회의가 내일로 예정되어 있어요.

어휘 come up with ~을 생각해 내다 strategy 전략 scheduled for + 일시 ~로 일정이 잡힌

Day 02 동사 ①

표제어 문제 정답 및 해석

1. (B)	2. (A)	3. (A)	4. (B)	5. (B)
6. (A)	7. (B)	8. (A)	9. (B)	10. (B)
11. (A)	12. (B)	13. (B)	14. (A)	15. (A)
16. (B)	17. (A)	18. (A)	19. (A)	20. (A)
21. (B)	22. (A)	23. (A)	24. (A)	25. (A)
26. (B)	27. (A)	28. (A)	29. (A)	30. (A)
31. (A)	32. (A)	33. (A)	34. (A)	35. (A)
36. (A)	37. (A)	38. (B)	39. (A)	40. (A)

1. 직원들은 출장에 대한 출장비 보고서를 제출하는 것이 요구된다.
2. 콜린 코스메틱스 사에 합류하는 것에 관심이 있으시다면, 귀하의 이력서를 회사의 본사로 제출해주십시오.
3. 다가오는 기술 컨벤션에 등록하실 때, 귀하의 이메일 주소를 확실히 포함하시기 바랍니다.
4. 일단 소유주가 그 디자인을 승인하면 호텔의 접수 구역의 보수공사가 시작될 것이다.
5. 회사 창립자 팀 제프리 씨는 연말 연회 중에 은퇴하려는 결정을 발표할 예정이다.
6. 모든 상표들이 올바르게 인쇄되었는지 확실히 확인 해주시기 바랍니다.
7. 덥고 맑은 날씨 때문에, 이번 주말의 해변 파티는 붐빌 것으로 예상된다.
8. 고객들은 웹 사이트에서 그들의 소포를 추적할 수 있고, 배달 기사가 소포를 배송할 대략적인 시간을 볼 수 있다.
9. 내년에, 알렌비 시리얼 사는 더 많은 고객들을 끌어들이기 위해 자사의 제품 종류를 확대할 것이다.
10. 마케팅에서의 자격사항을 갖춘 것은 우리 회사에서 일자리를 제안받을 지원자의 기회를 향상시킵니다.
11. 오후 동안, 고객서비스 부장은 전화나 이메일로

고객불만을 종종 대응한다.
12. 오전 명이 넘는 쇼핑객들이 지난달 레드몬드 백화점에서 짧은 고객 설문조사에 참가하도록 요청받았다.
13. 에저만 사의 이사회 임원들은 관리팀에 팔리 씨를 승진 대상으로 추천했다.
14. 새로운 회사는 이전 회사의 브랜딩 및 홍보 자료의 대부분을 보관할 것이다.
15. 빌리지 패션의 새로운 의류 제품군에 대한 고객 의견은 다른 연령대 사이에서 매우 다양하다.
16. 그 패스트푸드 회사는 현재 북미 전역의 장소들에서 250개가 넘는 식당들을 운영한다.
17. 제임슨 씨는 우리에게 웨스트필드 몰의 손님들에게 전단지를 배포할 것을 요청했다.
18. 대표이사의 은퇴가 내일 언론 브리핑에서 발표될 것으로 예상된다.
19. 그린칩 인베스트먼트 사는 기술 업계에서 작은 규모의 업체들을 창업하는 사업가들을 돕는다.
20. 콘서트홀의 무대가 두 달 전 지어졌지만, 행사 장소 관리자는 음향 시스템을 어제서야 설치했다.
21. 귀하의 성과 평가 날짜 및 시간을 확인하시려면 1월 8일자의 앤더슨 씨의 이메일을 참조해주시기 바랍니다.
22. 국제선 여행객들은 출발시간 최소 3시간 전에 공항에 도착하는 것이 권고됩니다.
23. 과거에, 우리는 직원들에게 보건 안전 교육을 제공하는 것을 지점장들에게 의존했다.
24. 킹 타코 직원들은 인사부 사무실에 방문함으로써 작업복 교체품을 얻을 수 있다.
25. 메잇랜드 엔지니어링 사의 대변인은 바바라 스몰링 씨가 인사부장으로써 크레이그 스티븐스 씨를 대체할 것이라고 말했다.
26. 최고운영책임자는 최근 회사의 반품 및 교환 정책을 수정하기로 결정했다.
27. 리차드 씨에게 3층 회의실 예약이 승인됐다고 알려주시기 바랍니다.
28. 경쟁사와 경쟁하기 위해서는, 에스트로 사는 25세에서 35세 나이대의 고객들을 겨냥하는 새로운 방법을 찾아야 한다.
29. 밀라노에 새로운 지점을 설립하면서, 로미가 패션 사는 유럽 시장에 큰 영향을 미치기를 희망한다.

30. 드레이크 씨는 이번 달에 후반 명망 있는 상을 수상할 때 그의 혁신적인 디자인으로 인정받게 될 것이다.
31. 기술자들은 셀웨이 다리의 기반을 강화하기 위한 가장 효율적인 방법을 알아내기 위해 여전히 노력하고 있다.
32. 센트라코프 사는 월말까지 채우기를 희망하는 네 개의 기술 지원 일자리가 있습니다.
33. 이번 주의 치솟는 기온에, 많은 지역 매장들이 손님들을 끌어들이기 위해 무료 다과를 제공하고 있다.
34. 부동산 시장 전문가들은 주요 도시들의 주택 가격이 향후 5년 동안 계속 상승할 것으로 예측한다.
35. 새로운 의정서는 마크톤 프로덕션 사의 제조 공장에서의 폐기물의 안전한 처리를 보장하기 위해 시행되었다.
36. 신입사원들은 정규직을 배정받기 전에 3개월의 교육과 수습기간을 거친다.
37. 코왈스키 씨는 팀민 씨가 다음 달 초에 새로운 생산 시설을 견학할 수 있도록 준비할 것이다.
38. 버웰 사의 MX5 스포츠카는 시속 300 킬로미터를 넘어서며, 특히 효율적인 연비를 증명했다.
39. 특정 디자인의 결점으로 인해, 우리의 신제품 출시가 6월 30일까지 연기되었다.
40. 앨런 건강식품 사는 유통망을 확대하기 위한 일환으로, 최근 3개의 창고를 인수했다.

DAILY QUIZ

7.

해석 고객 만족을 보장하기 위해, 밀리아노 백화점은 최대 30일 이전까지 구매된 모든 제품에 대해 환불 및 교환을 제공한다.

해설 빈칸에는 빈칸 뒤에 제시된 customer satisfaction을 목적어로 가져 백화점이 환불 및 교환을 제공하는 목적을 나타낼 어휘가 필요하다. 따라서 환불 및 교환을 제공하는 것은 고객 만족을 보장하기 위한 것이므로 '~을 보장하다, 확실히 하다'라는 의미의 (D)가 정답이다.

어휘 up to 최대 ~까지 appraise ~을 평가하다

grant ~을 승인하다, 인정하다 ensure ~을 보장하다, 확실히 하다

8.
해석 계약 조건에 만족하신다면, 고용 계약서 2부에 모두 서명하신 후, 1부를 오길비에 씨에게 제출해 주시기 바랍니다.

해설 빈칸 뒤에 위치한 one of them은 언급된 2부의 계약서 중 하나를 의미하고, 빈칸에는 계약서에 서명한 후에 할 수 있는 일을 나타낼 어휘가 필요하므로 '~을 제출하다'를 뜻하는 (B)가 정답이다.

어휘 term (계약서 등의) 조건, 조항 submit ~을 제출하다 yield (결과, 수익 등) ~을 내다, 산출하다 alert ~에게 알리다, 경고하다

Day 03 동사 ②

표제어 문제 정답 및 해석

1. (A)	2. (A)	3. (B)	4. (B)	5. (B)
6. (B)	7. (A)	8. (B)	9. (B)	10. (A)
11. (A)	12. (B)	13. (A)	14. (B)	15. (B)
16. (A)	17. (A)	18. (B)	19. (B)	20. (B)
21. (B)	22. (A)	23. (B)	24. (A)	25. (B)
26. (B)	27. (B)	28. (B)	29. (A)	30. (B)
31. (B)	32. (B)	33. (A)	34. (A)	35. (B)
36. (A)	37. (A)	38. (B)	39. (A)	40. (A)

1. 구입하신 누트리카인드 야채 주스 캔을 힘껏 흔들지 않는다면, 음료의 맛에 영향을 미칠 수도 있습니다.
2. 비티엑스 모터스 사는 에너지 소비가 적은 차량들의 증가하는 수요를 충족하기 위해 하이브리드 차량들을 개발하고 있다.
3. 근무 책임자들은 반드시 필요하다고 여겨지는 경우가 아니라면, 직원들이 지나치게 긴 휴식을 취하지 못하도록 해야 한다.
4. 재규어 슈즈 사의 광고팀은 낮은 매출 수치를 영업부의 노력 부족 탓으로 돌렸다.
5. <고독한 유령>의 감독은 이 영화에서 얻은 수익의 20 퍼센트를 저소득층 가정에게 기부하겠다고 발표했다.
6. 저희 컴퓨터 전문가들은 고객님들의 기기가 최적으로 작동되도록 하기 위해 다양한 업그레이드를 수행할 준비가 되어 있습니다.
7. 그의 현재 직무에서, 후퍼 씨는 여러 부서들의 프로젝트를 조정하는 것에 책임이 있다.
8. 몇몇 상황에서는, 안내 데스크 직원이 체크아웃 시간이 조정되도록 준비해드릴 수 있습니다.
9. 김 씨의 직무는 고객들의 불만에 응대하고 그것을 해결하는 것을 포함한다.
10. 그 직책에 대한 귀하의 지원서를 수령했음을 알려드리고자 이 이메일을 씁니다.
11. 루모플로우 테크놀로지 사의 수퍼 브라이트 조명은 어떤 작업환경도 향상시킬 것을 보장합니다.
12. 인사부장으로서, 맥키 씨는 새로운 직원들을 채용하고, 그들과 연봉을 협상할 것이다.
13. 안전 감사관들이 모든 필요조건을 충족한다고 보증한 이후에, 그 공장은 생산을 시작할 것이다.
14. 승무원들은 구명조끼를 올바르게 착용하는 방법을 시연할 수 있어야 한다.
15. 틸 씨는 이제 사무실이 같은 층에 위치하므로, 이스턴 씨와 더 자주 협력하기를 희망한다.
16. 호그 씨는 저녁식사 메뉴 및 오락 등과 같은 송년회의 여러 세부사항들에 대해 여전히 마무리를 해야 한다.
17. 론튼 시는 주민들이 겪고 있는 수도 공급 문제를 평가하기 위해 배관공들을 파견할 것이다.
18. 올해 신규 구독자 수가 지난 1월 계획했던 수치를 뛰어넘었다.
19. 방문객들은 미술관 전 구역에서 플래시를 사용한 사진 촬영이 엄격히 금지된다는 점에 유의하시기 바랍니다.
20. 계정 비밀번호는 생년월일과 같은 쉽게 추측 가능한 정보를 포함해서는 안 된다.
21. 시카고 총회 일자가 편의상 윌모어 씨의 그 도시 고객과의 회의 일자와 겹친다.

22. 퀸시 씨는 그녀의 직원들이 그들의 영업 목표를 달성할 수 있게 동기부여하도록 항상 노력한다.
23. 최근 연구는 아침을 정기적으로 먹는 사람들이 아침을 거르는 사람들보다 더 건강한 경향이 있다는 결과를 보여준다.
24. 과학자 질 골드스테인 씨가 다음 주 환경 총회에서 라피도 주식회사를 대표할 것이다.
25. 일부 분석가들은 자동차 산업으로 확장하려는 그 회사의 계획이 실패할 것이라고 주장한다.
26. 시장 조사는 고객들이 믿을 수 있는 제품을 합리적인 가격에 판매하는 가게들을 단골로 이용할 가능성이 더 있음을 보여준다.
27. 그 회사가 어느 정도로 경제 불황에서 회복했는지는 향후 몇 주간 분명해질 것이다.
28. 그 도시는 잠깐 들렀다 가는 전통적인 역할을 넘어 대규모 관광지로 발전했다.
29. 로봇 기술은 제조업 및 의료 산업과 같은 다양한 분야에서 활용되고 있다.
30. 그 기기는 배터리 수명을 연장하기 위해 사용하지 않을 때는 항상 전원이 꺼져있어야 한다.
31. 약간의 교통 체증 감소는 도시의 교통 체계에 대한 우려를 경감하는 데 거의 도움이 되지 않았다.
32. 사용된 배터리는 투명 비닐봉지에 담아서 재활용 쓰레기통 옆에 놓아두어야 하는 점을 유의해 주십시오.
33. 얼어붙을 것 같은 기온이 오늘의 야외 음악 축제 참가자 수가 저조한 이유를 설명한다.
34. 이번 주말 전에 자신이 근무한 시간을 회계부에 알려 주시기 바랍니다.
35. 데이지 레스토랑은 더 많은 식사 손님들을 끌어들이고자 광범위한 개조를 겪을 예정이다.
36. 대표이사는 최근 회사의 인사부를 확장하는 제안을 발표했다.
37. 이번 분기에 매출의 상당한 증가에도 불구하고 마젠타 전자의 수익은 같은 수준을 유지하고 있다.
38. 이사회는 퇴임하는 시몬스 씨를 대신해, 레윈슨 씨를 신임 최고운영자로 임명했다.
39. 교육 워크숍에 자리를 확실히 확보할 수 있도록, 관심 있는 분들은 4월 16일 금요일까지 등록하시기를 권고합니다.
40. 핏텍 사는 착용자의 심장박동과 혈압을 관찰할 수 있는 새로운 종류의 스마트워치들을 개발했다.

DAILY QUIZ

7.

해석 RJT 엔터테인먼트 사는 행사의 인기 상승을 수용하기 위해 여름 시즌 뮤직 페스티벌을 로슨 공원으로 옮길 것이다.

해설 빈칸 이하 부분은 행사 장소를 옮긴 이유를 나타내야 하는데, 인기 상승과 관련해 취할 수 있는 조치를 나타내기에 적절한 어휘가 필요하므로 '~을 수용하다'라는 뜻인 (D)가 정답이다.

어휘 relocate A to B A를 B로 옮기다, 이전하다 allocate ~을 할당하다 incapacitate ~을 무력화하다 accommodate ~을 수용하다, 충족하다

8.

해석 그 주의 교통국은 지역 공원에서 자전거를 타는 것을 금지할 권리를 가지고 있다.

해설 빈칸에는 교통국이 지역 공원에서 자전거를 타는 것에 대해 행할 수 있는 권리를 나타낼 어휘가 필요하므로 '~을 금지하다'의 뜻인 (A)가 정답이다.

어휘 cycling 자전거 타기 prohibit ~을 금지하다 bother ~을 신경 쓰다

Day 04 동사 + 명사 콜로케이션

표제어 문제 정답 및 해석

1. (A)	2. (A)	3. (B)	4. (A)	5. (B)
6. (A)	7. (B)	8. (A)	9. (A)	10. (B)
11. (A)	12. (B)	13. (A)	14. (B)	15. (B)
16. (A)	17. (B)	18. (B)	19. (B)	20. (B)
21. (A)	22. (A)	23. (B)	24. (A)	25. (A)
26. (A)	27. (B)	28. (A)	29. (A)	30. (B)
31. (A)	32. (B)	33. (A)	34. (B)	35. (B)
36. (A)	37. (B)	38. (A)	39. (A)	40. (B)

1. 광범위한 마케팅 캠페인에도 불구하고, 새로운 엘바 휴대폰의 매출은 소비자의 기대를 충족하지 못했다.
2. 트링켓 주식회사는 사무실에서 직원 사기를 증진시킬 금전적 인센티브를 제공하는 정책을 도입했다.
3. SJ 전자는 운송 수단군을 업그레이드한 후 비용을 30퍼센트까지 줄였다.
4. 콜 센터 관리자인 밥 미쉘 씨가 다음 주 수요일에 고객 서비스에 대한 세미나를 이끌 것이다.
5. 피드백 양식에 있는 의견들은 우리의 메뉴의 채식 친화적인 요리에 대한 높은 선호도를 나타낸다.
6. 회사 창립자는 모든 주주들에게 새 공장을 견학하는 것을 제안했다.
7. 많은 수의 사전 티켓 판매량 때문에, 포터 씨는 뮤직 페스티벌을 연기하자는 제안을 거절했다.
8. 모든 신입 직원들은 각자의 부서장들에게 보고하기 전에 교육 시간에 반드시 참석해야 한다.
9. 바이오센스 사는 현재 자사 실험실의 연구원 직무에 대한 지원서를 받고 있다.
10. 미제노 그래픽 디자인 사는 로꼬 코퍼레이트 케이터링 사와의 약정을 갱신하기로 결정했다.
11. 리딕 진료소에 도착하기 전에 휴대폰이나 이메일로 예약을 확정해주시기 바랍니다.
12. 이링 출판사는 생산성을 향상시키기 위해 구조조정을 할 것이다.
13. 최소 두 가지 언어에 능통한 것은 로이스턴 여행사에 고용될 기회를 향상시킨다.
14. 이코노미석 또는 일등석으로 비행하든 간에, 알파인 항공사 승객들은 높은 품질의 서비스를 받을 자격이 있다.
15. 어떠한 혼선도 피하기 위해, 모든 이용자들은 프로그램을 시작하기 전에 설명서를 검토해야 합니다.
16. 자선단체 모금 행사에서, 여러 기관들의 회원들은 도날드슨 씨의 후한 기부액에 대해 감사를 표했다.
17. 스프리츠 백화점의 고객 서비스팀은 문제들을 즉각적이고 효율적으로 해결하도록 교육 받았다.
18. 다야츠 모터스 사의 기술자들은 다가오는 국제 자동차 쇼에서 그들의 새로운 고급 세단의 능력을 보여줄 것이다.
19. 다음 주 목요일에, 두 회사의 최고 운영 책임자들이 합작 투자에 관한 약정에 서명할 것이다.
20. 처리를 신속하게 하기 위해, 간단히 체크아웃 웹 페이지의 빠른 배송을 클릭하십시오.
21. 반스 씨는 새로운 임금 체계에 대한 문제를 다루기 위해 오늘 오후 1시부터 4시 사이에 그의 시간을 비워둘 것이다.
22. 주문을 받는 것이 가능한 전자기기를 사용하는 식당의 수가 증가하고 있다.
23. 일단 필수 서류들이 제출되고 검토되면, 지점장이 지불을 허가할 것이다.
24. 안전한 작업 환경을 보장하기 위해 새 조립 라인 기계를 작동할 때 안전 규정을 준수해 주십시오.
25. 테빗 씨는 로마스 씨가 9월에 은퇴한 후, 마케팅 이사 직함을 달 것이다.
26. 솔에일 비치 리조트는 주로 그곳이 제공하는 풍부한 활동과 편의시설로 인해 평판을 얻었다.
27. 존스 씨는 그녀의 동료가 프로젝트 일정표를 수정하기로 동의한 이후 그와의 분쟁을 해결했다.
28. 워크숍 참석자들은 고도의 제조 방식을 사용해 전자 부품 생산을 가속화하는 방법을 배울 것이다.
29. 렙콘 주식회사는 자사 직원들 사이에서 전문적인 모습을 유지하기 위해 복장 규정을 시행한다.

30. 여름 동안, 베닝 엔터프라이즈 사는 잠재적인 지원자들과 소통하고 그들의 질문에 답하기 위해 채용 설명회를 개최한다.
31. 마케팅부는 회사의 온라인 광고 전략에 대한 변화를 알릴 계획이다.
32. 아파트 건물 세입자들은 개인 주차 공간에 대한 요청사항을 1월 31일까지 제출해야 한다.
33. 저희는 고객들과 직접 이야기하는 것처럼 전화상으로도 똑같이 편안한 영업사원 직무에 대한 지원자를 찾고 있습니다.
34. 두발 씨는 더 많은 사무용품을 주문하기 전에 재고를 확인할 것이다.
35. 생산성을 증진시키기 위해, 코로나 랜드스케이핑 사는 장비를 업그레이드하고, 유동적인 근무 시간을 제공하는 것을 계획한다.
36. 퍼스트 리쿠르트먼트 사는 다양한 직무를 충원하기 위해 숙련된 직원들을 고용하도록 회사들을 돕는다.
37. 그린웨이 슈퍼마켓은 매달 마지막 일요일에 다양한 제품에 대한 할인을 제공한다.
38. 히친스 은행의 고객 지원팀에 연락하실 때마다 귀하의 계좌번호를 꼭 포함해주십시오.
39. 로이스 씨는 지난 분기의 그의 뛰어난 성과 때문에 승진했다.
40. 단체 관광객들은 버스를 떠날 때마다 안내 책자를 가져가야 한다.

DAILY QUIZ

7.
해석 직장에 지각을 하지 않는 것은 애들러 리걸 사에서 인턴 직원이 정규직 자리를 제공받을 수 있는 기회를 향상시킨다.
해설 빈칸에는 지각을 하지 않는 것과 정규직 자리를 제공받는 기회 사이의 관계를 나타낼 수 있는 어휘가 필요하므로 빈칸 뒤에 있는 chances와 함께 '기회를 향상시키다'를 뜻하는 (D)가 정답이다.
어휘 be late for work 직장에 지각하다
improve a chance 기회를 향상시키다

full-time position 정규직 자리 verify ~을 입증하다, 증명하다

8.
해석 잠재적인 통근의 어려움 때문에, 모건 씨는 회사의 본사를 교외 지역으로 이전하자는 제안을 거절했다.
해설 빈칸에는 통근 문제를 원인으로 들어 회사의 본사를 교외 지역으로 이전하자는 제안에 대한 모건 씨의 행위를 나타낼 수 있는 어휘가 필요하므로 빈칸 뒤에 있는 proposals와 함께 '제안을 거절하다'를 뜻하는 (B)가 정답이다.
어휘 commuting 통근 suburbs 교외 지역 observe ~을 관찰하다, 준수하다 reject a proposal 제안을 거절하다

Day 05 기출 동의어 ③

표제어 문제 정답

1. (A)	2. (B)	3. (B)	4. (B)	5. (A)
6. (B)	7. (A)	8. (B)	9. (B)	10. (B)
11. (A)	12. (A)	13. (A)	14. (B)	15. (B)
16. (B)	17. (B)	18. (A)	19. (B)	20. (B)
21. (B)	22. (B)	23. (B)	24. (B)	25. (A)
26. (B)	27. (B)	28. (B)	29. (A)	30. (B)

DAILY QUIZ

1.
해석 저희 팀은 30분 내에 컴퓨터 소프트웨어 설치를 수행할 수 있습니다. 새 프로그램 설치, 기존 소프트웨어 업데이트, 혹은 설치 문제 해결 등 어떤 작업이 필요하시더라도 저희는 이를 효율적으로 수행할 수 있는 전문 지식을 보유하고 있습니다.
해설 perform은 '(기술이 필요한) 어떤 일을 수행하

다'라는 뜻으로, 30분 내에 컴퓨터 소프트웨어 설치 작업을 '수행했다'는 것은 설치 작업을 '완료했다'는 의미로 볼 수 있으므로 (C)가 정답이다.

어휘 **installation** 설치 **existing** 기존의 **troubleshoot** 고장을 해결하다 **expertise** 전문성 **get A done** A를 끝내다 **efficiently** 효율적으로 **entertain** ~을 즐겁게 하다 **function** v. 기능하다

2.

해석 과열을 방지하기 위해 기계의 온도 센서를 정기적으로 확인하십시오. 설정 조정에 도움이 필요하시다면 기술자의 전화번호는 555-1648입니다.

해설 기계의 온도 센서를 '정기적인 간격으로' 확인하라고 안내하고 있다. 따라서 '주기적인'이라는 뜻의 (C)가 정답이다.

어휘 **interval** 간격 **prevent A from -ing** A가 ~하는 것을 막다 **adjust** ~을 조정하다 **orderly** 질서정연한 **customary** 관례적인 **periodic** 주기적인 **even** 고른, 평평한

3.

해석 그 프로젝트는 시기적절하게, 지연 없이 완료되어 팀의 효율성과 헌신을 보여주었습니다. 이러한 성과는 고객의 기대를 충족시켰을 뿐만 아니라 업계에서 팀의 신뢰성에 대한 명성을 강화했습니다.

해설 in a timely fashion은 '시기적절하게'라는 뜻으로, 여기서 fashion은 '방식'을 의미하므로 이러한 의미를 지닌 (D)가 정답이다.

어휘 **in a timely fashion[manner]** 시기적절하게 **showcase** ~을 보여주다 **efficiency** 효율성 **dedication** 헌신 **expectation** 기대 **strengthen** ~을 강화하다 **reputation** 명성 **reliability** 신뢰성 **manner** 방식

Week 03 실전 TEST

1. (A)	2. (C)	3. (C)	4. (A)	5. (B)
6. (B)	7. (A)	8. (C)	9. (A)	10. (A)
11. (A)	12. (B)	13. (A)	14. (C)	15. (A)
16. (B)	17. (B)	18. (D)	19. (D)	20. (A)
21. (B)	22. (C)	23. (B)	24. (B)	

1. Won't white paint be used to redesign our walls?
   (A) It's up to the manager to choose.
   (B) That's a wonderful color.
   (C) It's in the cupboards.

우리 벽들을 다시 디자인하는 데 흰색 페인트가 사용되지 않을까요?
(A) 그건 부장님께서 선택하시기에 달려 있어요.
(B) 아주 멋진 색이네요.
(C) 그건 찬장 안에 있어요.

어휘 **up to** ~에게 달려 있는 **choose** ~을 선택하다

2. When will the shipment of napkins be delivered?
   (A) Due to inventory shortages.
   (B) There's a restaurant across the street.
   (C) I haven't placed an order yet.

언제 냅킨 발송 제품이 배송될까요?
(A) 재고 부족 문제 때문에요.
(B) 길 건너편에 레스토랑이 하나 있어요.
(C) 제가 아직 주문하지 않았습니다.

어휘 **shipment** 발송(품), 배송(품) **due to** ~ 때문에 **inventory** 재고 (목록) **shortage** 부족 **place an order** 주문하다

3. Who's monitoring the musical rehearsal tomorrow?
  (A) The performance will begin soon.
  (B) At 5 o'clock on Wednesday.
  (C) That assignment hasn't been given out.

  누가 내일 뮤지컬 리허설을 감독하나요?
  (A) 공연이 곧 시작될 겁니다.
  (B) 수요일 5시에요.
  (C) 그 업무는 아직 공표되지 않았습니다.

  어휘 **monitor** v. ~을 감독하다, ~을 관찰하다
  rehearsal 리허설, 예행 연습 **performance** 공연, 연주(회) **assignment** (할당되는) 업무
  give out ~을 공표하다, ~을 주다

4. I'm having trouble finding information on this apartment listing.
  (A) Oh, I can help you with that.
  (B) They made a checklist.
  (C) A one-bedroom unit.

  제가 이 아파트 목록에서 정보를 찾는 데 어려움을 겪고 있어요.
  (A) 아, 제가 그 부분을 도와 드릴 수 있습니다.
  (B) 그분들이 점검 목록을 만들었어요.
  (C) 침실 한 개짜리 세대입니다.

  어휘 **have trouble -ing** ~하는 데 어려움을 겪다
  listing 목록, 명단 **unit** (아파트 등의) 한 세대, (상점 등의) 점포

5. Is the presentation going to be ready by tomorrow?
  (A) A well-known keynote speaker.
  (B) No, we're currently behind schedule.
  (C) In conference room B.

  발표가 내일까지 준비될 예정인가요?
  (A) 잘 알려진 기조 연설자요.
  (B) 아뇨, 저희가 현재 일정보다 뒤쳐져 있습니다.
  (C) 대회의실 B에서요.

  어휘 **keynote speaker** 기조 연설자 **currently** 현재 **behind schedule** 일정보다 뒤쳐진

6. Where can I find the closest post office?
  (A) Every weekend until 6.
  (B) I'm afraid it's already closed for the day.
  (C) Have you checked the tracking number?

  어디에서 가장 가까운 우체국을 찾을 수 있나요?
  (A) 매 주말 6시까지요.
  (B) 오늘은 이미 문을 닫은 것 같아요.
  (C) 추적 번호를 확인해 보셨나요?

  어휘 **I'm afraid (that)** (부정적인 일에 대해) ~인 것 같습니다, 유감이지만 ~입니다

7. Will the refreshments be catered or should I stop by the store tomorrow?
  (A) Jeremy found a caterer.
  (B) Before next week.
  (C) They're all out of stock.

  다과가 출장 요리 업체에 의해 제공되나요, 아니면 제가 내일 상점에 들어야 하나요?
  (A) 제레미 씨가 출장 요리 업체를 하나 찾았어요.
  (B) 다음 주가 되기 전에요.
  (C) 그것들은 전부 품절입니다.

  어휘 **refreshments** 다과, 간식 **cater** ~에 출장 요리를 제공하다 **stop by** ~에 들르다 **caterer** 출장 요리 업체 **out of stock** 품절인, 매진된

8. Who's supposed to contact the potential sponsors?
  (A) For a music festival.
  (B) We signed a new contract.
  (C) Janelle is in charge of that.

누가 잠재 후원자들에게 연락하기로 되어 있나요?
(A) 음악 축제를 위해서요.
(B) 저희가 새 계약서에 서명했습니다.
(C) 자넬 씨가 그 일을 책임지고 있어요.

어휘 **be supposed to do** ~하기로 되어 있다, ~해야 하다 **potential** 잠재적인 **sponsor** 후원자 **sign a contract** 계약서에 서명하다 **in charge of** ~을 책임지고 있는

9. How often do you commute to the office?
(A) Twice a week.
(B) Usually at around 10 o'clock.
(C) At the Long Beach branch.

얼마나 자주 사무실로 통근하시나요?
(A) 일주일에 두 번이요.
(B) 보통 10시쯤에요.
(C) 롱 비치 지사에서요.

어휘 **commute to** ~로 통근하다, ~로 통학하다

10. Would you be willing to pick up the clients from the airport?
(A) Yes, I'd be happy to.
(B) A business class ticket.
(C) 24 miles from here.

공항에서 고객들을 모시고 와 주시겠어요?
(A) 네, 기꺼이 그렇게 하겠습니다.
(B) 비즈니스 클래스 한 장이요.
(C) 여기서부터 24마일이요.

어휘 **pick up** (차로) ~을 데려오다

11.
해설 벤트너 씨는 우리에게 그랜드 래피즈 몰에서 쇼핑객들에게 홍보 전단지를 배포할 것을 요청했다.
해설 빈칸에는 빈칸 뒤에 제시된 홍보 전단지에 대해 벤트너 씨가 요청한 행위를 나타낼 수 있는 어휘가 필요하므로 '~을 배포하다, 유통하다, 분배하다'라는 뜻의 (A)가 정답이다.

어휘 **flyer** 전단지 **distribute** ~을 배포하다, 유통하다, 분배하다 **relate** 관련시키다

12.
해설 라킨 시장은 밀튼 애비뉴에 추가적인 버스 정류장을 설치하자는 요청에 반대했다.
해설 빈칸에는 빈칸 앞에 위치한 명사 calls를 수식할 수 있으면서 시장이 반대한 요청의 내용을 나타낼 수 있어야 한다. 따라서 '추가 버스 정류장을 설치한다'는 의미가 자연스러우므로 '~을 설치하다'라는 뜻의 (B)가 정답이다.

어휘 **call** 요청, 요구 **embark** 승선하다 **transport** ~을 운송하다, 수송하다 **install** ~을 설치하다

13.
해설 아스트로 체육관 회원들은 프론트 데스크 직원과 이야기를 함으로써 그들의 사물함을 위한 자물쇠를 얻을 수 있다.
해설 빈칸 뒤에 제시된 명사 padlocks는 프론트 데스크 직원과 이야기해서 얻을 수 있는 대상이므로 '~을 얻다, 획득하다'라는 뜻의 (A)가 정답이다.

어휘 **padlock** 자물쇠 **locker** 사물함 **obtain** ~을 얻다, 획득하다

14.
해설 기부할 계획인 사용하지 않을 의류를 가져오셨다면, 안내 구역에 위치한 수거함에 넣어 주시기 바랍니다.
해설 빈칸에는 원하지 않은 의류로 할 수 있는 일을 나타낼 수 있으면서 특정 장소에 놓는 행위와 어울리는 어휘가 필요하므로 '~을 기부하다'를 뜻하는 (C)가 정답이다.

어휘 **bring in** ~을 가져오다, 챙겨 오다 **unwanted** 원하지 않는 **place A in B** A를 B에 넣다, 두다 **collection bin** 수거함 **assemble** ~을 조립하다 **donate** ~을 기부하다

15.
해설 비록 회사 소유주는 귀하께서 늦어도 5월 5일에

는 근무를 시작하시길 원하지만, 타당한 사유가 있다면 기꺼이 협의하실 것입니다.
해설 빈칸에는 회사에서 원하는 근무 시작일과 관련해 타당한 사유가 있을 경우 일을 시작하는 날짜를 조정할 수 있다는 의미의 어휘가 필요하므로 '협의하다, 협상하다'를 뜻하는 (A)가 정답이다.
어휘 no later than + 날짜 늦어도 ~까지는 be willing to do 기꺼이 ~하다, ~할 의향이 있다 valid 타당한, 유효한 negotiate ~을 협의하다, 협상하다 ascertain ~을 확인해 내다, 확정하다 contradict ~을 반박하다, 부정하다

16.
해설 알피 씨는 오늘 오후에 부서 회의 동안 고객 데이터베이스를 업데이트하는 방법에 대해 시연할 것이다.
해설 빈칸에는 알피 씨가 회의에서 고객 데이터베이스를 업데이트하는 방법에 대해 취할 수 있는 행위를 나타낼 어휘가 필요하므로 '~을 시연하다, 입증하다'라는 뜻의 (B)가 정답이다.
어휘 demonstrate ~을 시연하다, 입증하다 attempt ~을 시도하다

17.
해설 에르고핏 인터네셔널 사는 건강에 좋은 자세를 촉진하는 사무용 장비와 가구를 제조한다.
해설 빈칸에는 회사가 제조하는 장비와 가구 등을 사용하는 목적을 나타낼 수 있는 어휘가 필요하므로 빈칸 뒤에 제시된 a healthy posture와 함께 '건강에 좋은 자세를 촉진하다'라고 해석하는 것이 자연스럽다. 따라서 '~을 촉진하다, 격려하다, 권고하다'라는 의미의 (B)가 정답이다.
어휘 furnishings 가구 posture 자세 anticipate ~을 예상하다 encourage ~을 촉진하다, 격려하다, 권고하다 succeed 성공하다, 뒤를 잇다

18.
해설 밋첨 비지니스 솔루션 사는 시간제 근무자들을 포함해 모든 직원들을 대상으로 복장 규정을 시행하고 있다.
해설 빈칸에는 회사가 전 직원들을 대상으로 회사의 복장 규정과 관련하여 할 수 있는 행위를 나타낼 어휘가 필요하므로 빈칸 뒤에 위치한 dress code와 함께 '복장 규정을 시행하다'를 뜻하는 (D)가 정답이다.
어휘 enforce dress code 복장 규정을 시행하다

19-22.

록하트 씨께,

19 이번 주 금요일로 예정되어 있는 회의의 세부사항들을 확인하기 위해 연락 드립니다. 저는 우리가 캔튼 호텔의 식당에서 1시에 만나는 것으로 알고 있습니다. 몬티 워렌 씨와 마사 솔로몬 씨를 포함한 마케팅팀이 참석할 것입니다. 유감스럽게도, 미쉘 골드버그 씨는 일정 **20** 충돌로 저희와 함께 하지 못할 것입니다.

저희는 다가오는 몇 달 간의 매출을 향상시킬 기술들을 논의하기를 바라며, 귀하의 생각을 몹시 듣고 싶습니다. 귀하가 풍부한 경험을 가지고 있다는 것을 알고 있으며, 저희 팀이 귀하의 전문지식 **21** 으로부터 크게 혜택을 얻을 수 있을 것이라 생각합니다. 저희의 현재 전략의 장점과 단점을 확인할 수 있을 것이며, 저희의 시장 점유율을 **22** 향상시키는 데 도움이 될 계획을 수립할 수 있을 것이라 확신합니다.

이번 회의와 앞으로의 서신 교환을 고대하고 있습니다.

안녕히 계십시오.

사만다 카스텐

어휘 in attendance 참석한 upcoming 다가오는 be eager to do 몹시 ~하고 싶다 a wealth of 풍부한 benefit from ~로부터 혜택을 얻다 hugely 크게, 엄청나게 expertise 전문지식 identify ~을 확인하다 strength 장점, 강점 weakness 단점, 약점 market share 시장 점유율 correspondence 서신 교환

19. (A) 제가 머무는 동안 숙소를 마련해 주셔서 감사드리고 싶습니다.
(B) 다가오는 회의를 위해 장소 예약을 진행해 주십시오.
(C) 저희는 영업 회의 의제에 추가할 항목들을 많이 가지고 있습니다.
(D) 이번 주 금요일로 예정되어 있는 회의의 세부사항들을 확인하기 위해 연락 드립니다.

해설 빈칸 뒤에 제시된 문장에 회의의 세부사항인 장소와 시간이 언급되기 때문에 회의의 세부사항을 확인하기 위함이라는 글의 목적을 담은 내용의 (D)가 정답이다.

어휘 arrange ~을 마련하다, 준비하다 proceed with ~을 진행하다 scheduled for ~로 예정된

20.

해설 빈칸 앞에 전치사와 -ing 형태의 명사가 있으므로 빈칸은 전치사의 목적어 역할을 하면서, scheduling과 복합명사를 구성할 수 있는 명사 자리이다. 또한, 빈칸 앞에 부정관사가 있으므로 단수명사 (A)가 정답이다.

어휘 conflict 충돌

21.

해설 빈칸 앞에 동사 benefit이 제시되어 있고, 빈칸 뒤에 혜택을 주는 대상이 있으므로 빈칸에는 '~로부터'라는 뜻을 가져 출처를 나타낼 수 있는 (B)가 정답이다.

22.

해설 빈칸 앞에 현재의 전략의 장점과 단점을 확인한다는 내용이 있으므로 빈칸에는 시장 점유율을 대상으로 계획을 수립하는 이유를 나타낼 어휘가 필요하다. 따라서 '~을 향상시키다, 개선시키다'라는 의미의 (C)가 정답이다.

어휘 grant ~을 주다, 수여하다 improve ~을 향상시키다, 개선시키다

23-24.

수신: ahayat@winfieldhotel.com
발신: lhaines@fyrefly.com
날짜: 4월 16일
제목: 예약번호 458278
첨부: 예약_확인서.docx

하야트 씨께,

저희 호텔 예약에 대한 예약 확인서(예약 번호 458278)가 오늘 도착했으며, 여기에는 저희가 예약하지 않았던 여러 퀸 사이즈 침대들이 있는 객실이 포함되어 있습니다. 저희는 다가오는 컨퍼런스를 위해 덴버 지역에 머무르는 동안 3개의 객실만 필요합니다. 제가 저희 회사 법인카드 잔액을 확인해 보니, 저희에게 4개의 객실에 대한 비용이 청구된 것 같습니다. 저는 귀하께서 저희 예약 내용에서 이 부분을 취소해 주시리라 23 생각하며, 이는 귀하의 동료 직원들 중 한 분이 실수를 하신 것이 분명합니다. 24 하지만, 저는 저희 법인카드에서 잘못된 청구를 제거하려면 어떻게 해야 하는지 알고 싶습니다.

안녕히 계십시오.

링컨 하인즈
파이어플라이 주식회사

어휘 multiple 여럿의, 다양한 reserve ~을 예약하다 upcoming 다가오는, 곧 있을 balance 잔액, 잔고 it appears that ~인 것 같다 be charged for ~에 대한 비용이 청구되다 assume (that) (~라고) 생각하다 in error 실수로, 잘못하여 wrong charge 잘못된 청구, 청구 오류

23. 첫 번째 단락의 다섯 번째 줄에 있는 단어 "assume"과 의미가 가장 가까운 것은 무엇인가?
(A) 수집하다
(B) 생각하다
(C) 처리하다
(D) 받아들이다

해설 제시된 단어 assume 뒤에 잘못된 예약 부분을 상대가 취소해 줄 것이라고 생각한다는 내용이

쓰여 있으므로 '생각하다, 가정하다'라는 의미로 사용되었음을 알 수 있다. 따라서 (B)가 정답이다.

24. 하인즈 씨는 무슨 정보를 요청하는가?
(A) 예약을 연장하는 방법
(B) 환불을 받는 방법
(C) 예약을 취소하는 방법
(D) 비용을 지불하는 방법

해설 지문 후반부에 잘못 예약된 부분을 취소해줄 것이라 생각한다면서 법인카드 청구 오류를 처리하려면 어떻게 해야 하는지 알고 싶다고 환불 방법을 문의하고 있으므로 (B)가 정답이다.

어휘 extend ~을 연장하다 make a payment 비용을 지불하다

Week 04
정답 및 해설

Day 01 LC가 잘 들리는 어휘 ②

DAILY QUIZ

7. Why did Ms. Jones miss the meeting?
(A) It'll be held in conference room B.
(B) Because she got stuck in traffic.
(C) 20 copies for the meeting.

존스 씨는 왜 회의에 못 왔나요?
(A) B 회의실에서 열릴 예정입니다.
(B) 교통 체증에 꼼짝 못했기 때문이에요.
(C) 회의 자료 20부입니다.

어휘 miss ~을 놓치다, ~에 참석하지 못하다
be stuck in traffic 교통 체증에 갇히다
copy 사본

8. Why don't you take a vacation?
(A) It takes 8 hours by flight.
(B) To a beach resort.
(C) I'm in the middle of a big project right now.

휴가를 떠나시는 게 어때요?
(A) 비행기로 8시간 걸려요.
(B) 해변가 리조트로요.
(C) 제가 지금 중요한 프로젝트를 하는 중이에요.

어휘 in the middle of ~하는 중인

Day 02 동사 ③

표제어 문제 정답 및 해석

1. (A)	2. (A)	3. (B)	4. (A)	5. (A)
6. (B)	7. (B)	8. (A)	9. (B)	10. (A)
11. (B)	12. (A)	13. (A)	14. (B)	15. (A)
16. (A)	17. (A)	18. (A)	19. (B)	20. (B)
21. (B)	22. (A)	23. (B)	24. (A)	25. (A)
26. (A)	27. (A)	28. (B)	29. (A)	30. (A)
31. (A)	32. (B)	33. (B)	34. (A)	35. (B)
36. (B)	37. (A)	38. (B)	39. (A)	40. (A)

1. 조립 라인 관리자들은 제품들이 품질 기준을 충족하는 것을 확실히 하기 위해 그것들을 자주 점검한다.
2. 새로운 서비스에 대한 모든 문의는 저희 고객 서비스 직원들에 의해 신속하게 처리되고 있습니다.
3. 손목시계에 대한 줄어든 수요의 결과로, 프레스티지 사는 작년에 자사 최저 매출액을 기록했다.
4. 험블 인더스트리스 사는 내년에 자사의 넥서스 전자레인지 제품군의 생산을 중단할 예정이라고 보고했다.
5. 하마토 씨는 제7차 연례 건축 총회에서 올해의 건축가상을 받는 것으로 선정되었다.
6. 그라인드 사이클 사는 포장에서 자전거 부품을 꺼낼 때, 제공된 제품 목록을 확인할 것을 권고한다.
7. 인사부가 취업박람회의 모든 발표자들에게 개인의 이름이 보이는 명찰을 제공할 것입니다.
8. 닐스 정비소에서는 보통 2주 이내에 파손된 차량들을 완전히 수리한다.
9. 론슨 디지털 사의 최신 노트북 출시가 자사 공장의 광범위한 침수로 인해 연기되었다.
10. 올해의 햄튼 영화제는 지역 독립 영화 제작자들이 만든 여러 영화들을 특별히 포함할 것이다.
11. 지역 주민들의 불만사항을 다루기 위해, 시 의회는 다음 달에 공청회를 개최할 것이다.

12. 스핑크스 주식회사는 자사의 홍보 자료를 개선하기 위해 새로운 그래픽 디자이너를 채용하기를 원한다.
13. 해이스팅 주식회사는 자사의 새로운 태블릿 컴퓨터 제품군으로 유럽 시장에 접근하기를 희망한다.
14. 눈보라가 지나가는 대로 라일리 철도의 정상적인 기차 운행 서비스가 재개될 것이다.
15. 아틀레티코 사는 모든 주요 운동복 매장에서 새로운 러닝화 제품군을 곧 출시할 것이다.
16. 악천후는 도시의 30퍼센트 도처에 걸쳐 전력 중단을 야기했다.
17. 귀하의 배송 정보를 입력함으로써, 콜스틴 딜리버리 사가 귀하의 주문품을 배송하는 데 걸리는 시간을 추정하실 수 있습니다.
18. 객실을 예약하시거나 저희 숙박시설에 대해 더 많은 정보를 알아보시기 위해 웹 사이트를 방문하십시오.
19. 코놀리 씨는 8월에 카디프 지사에서 뉴포트 지사로 전근할 것이다.
20. 총 씨와 그의 팀은 시장 연구 데이터의 광범위한 분석을 실시할 것이다.
21. 그 세미나는 모든 종류의 사업에 적용될 수 있는 경영 기술을 개발하는 것에 초점을 맞춘다.
22. 마케팅 워크숍에 귀하의 자리를 보장하기 위해, 4월 12일까지 온라인으로 등록하셔야 합니다.
23. 이 상품권은 소지자가 모든 조커 레스토랑에서 식사를 할 때 동일한 가격의 추가 식사를 제공합니다.
24. 연차를 신청하고 싶으시다면, 내선번호 102번으로 인사부에 연락하시길 바랍니다.
25. 사이드 요리를 다른 것으로 교환하고 싶은 식사 손님들은 종업원에게 말해야 합니다.
26. 자사의 새로운 휴대폰을 성공작으로 확실히 만들기 위해, 스와이프 전자는 세계적인 마케팅 캠페인을 개시할 것이다.
27. 우리 회사의 따뜻한 음료 종류에 대한 수요는 보통 여름철에는 하락하지만, 10월을 시작으로 다시 회복한다.
28. 대표이사는 이번 주 이사회 회의에서 회사의 지속적인 성장을 위한 그의 계획을 공유할 것이다.
29. 주문을 제때 처리하기 위해서, 저희는 이번 주에 직원들의 점심 휴식시간을 30분으로 줄일 수밖에 없습니다.
30. 피니건 씨에 의해 배부된 회람은 회사의 새로운 마케팅 전략 및 매출 목표를 요약한다.
31. 체스터 시의 시장은 새로운 놀이공원의 건설이 지역 관광에 긍정적으로 영향을 미칠 것이라고 생각한다.
32. 고용 위원회는 레이놀즈 씨가 연례 지출을 줄이는 것을 약속했기 때문에, 그에게 재무부장 직책을 제안하기로 결정했다.
33. 안티 바이러스 소프트웨어에 대한 문제를 접한 사용자들은 문제 해결 가이드를 참고할 것을 권고 받는다.
34. 그 요리법에서 낮은 칼로리를 선호하신다면, 크림을 저지방 요거트로 대체하셔도 됩니다.
35. 러닝머신에 있는 모든 전기 부품들은 적어도 3년 동안 기능이 지속될 것으로 보증됩니다.
36. 연구소로의 접근 권한을 얻기 위해서는, 보안 출입증을 입구에 있는 경비원에게 제시해야 한다.
37. 달링 씨는 디트로이트 교외에 새로운 제조 공장을 건설하는 데 대해 지지를 표했다.
38. 프로비전 사의 새로운 게임기가 매장에서 매진된 후에, 이 제품의 가격이 온라인 시장에서 거의 두 배가 되었다.
39. 심사위원들은 올해의 영국 체조 경기 우승자들을 발표하기 전에 두 시간 동안 숙고했다.
40. 프랭클린 과학 박물관은 일주일 내내 오전 10시에서 오후 8시까지 방문객들을 맞이한다.

DAILY QUIZ

7.

해석 행사 주최자가 대체 행사장을 선정하지 않는다면, 멜로디 뮤직 페스티벌은 올해 개최되지 못할 수도 있다.

해설 빈칸에는 행사 주최자가 행사를 개최하기 위해 대체 행사장과 관련해 할 수 있는 행위를 나타낼 어휘가 필요하므로 '~을 선정하다, 선택하다'를 뜻하는 (B)가 정답이다.

어휘 unless ~하지 않는다면, ~가 아니라면
alternative 대체의, 대안의 distribute ~을 나눠주다, 배포하다 select ~을 선정하다, 선택하다 withdraw ~을 인출하다, 철회하다

8.

해석 프레시디오 이벤트 사가 자사의 요금을 보장하기 때문에, 우리는 제안된 예산 안에서 자선행사를 기획할 수 있었다.

해설 빈칸 뒤에 제시된 '요금'이라는 명사를 목적어로 취하면서 행사를 정해진 예산 안에서 할 수 있게 하는 행위를 나타낼 수 있는 어휘가 필요하므로 '~을 보장하다, 보증하다'라는 뜻의 (A)가 정답이다.

어휘 rate 요금, 비율 fundraiser 자선행사, 모금행사 guarantee ~을 보장하다, 보증하다 advise ~을 충고하다, 조언하다

Day 03 동사 ④

표제어 문제 정답 및 해석

1. (B)	2. (A)	3. (A)	4. (B)	5. (B)
6. (B)	7. (B)	8. (B)	9. (B)	10. (A)
11. (A)	12. (A)	13. (B)	14. (A)	15. (B)
16. (B)	17. (A)	18. (A)	19. (B)	20. (B)
21. (B)	22. (A)	23. (A)	24. (B)	25. (B)
26. (A)	27. (B)	28. (A)	29. (B)	30. (B)
31. (A)	32. (B)	33. (A)	34. (B)	35. (A)
36. (B)	37. (B)	38. (A)	39. (A)	40. (B)

1. 비행편이 정원 이상으로 예약되면서 블랙 씨의 항공권 비용이 환불되었다.
2. 그 컨벤션 센터는 오전 9시부터 오후 6시 사이 모든 차량에 대해 주차 요금을 청구한다.
3. 매장 개업이 확실히 성공하도록 하기 위해, 우리는 유능한 행사 기획자를 채용할 계획이다.
4. 판매자들은 자신의 간판대나 부스에 업체명과 판매 허가증이 둘 다 잘 보이게 진열해야 한다.
5. 지역사회 센터에 있는 하모니 페스티벌 미술관에 작품을 전시하는데 관심이 있으신 분은 휴즈 씨에게 연락하시기 바랍니다.
6. 귀하의 스탠튼 도서관 회원카드가 발급되었으며, 3일 내에 도착할 것입니다.
7. 우리의 세미나가 신입직원들이 자신감을 얻는 데 도움이 되는 것으로 보여진다.
8. 뛰어난 디자인과 믿을 만한 직원들로 잘 알려진 가몬드 인테리어 사는 거주용과 사업용 건물을 둘 다 보수한다.
9. 로마 파스타의 모든 지점에서 무료 디저트로 교환될 수 있는 상품권을 동봉했으니 확인해보십시오.
10. 모바일 메일 사는 스마트폰 사용자들이 단 하나의 어플리케이션을 이용해 최대 10개의 다른 이메일 계정을 확인할 수 있게 해준다.
11. 사소한 결함들에 대해 몇 차례 보고가 있기는 했지만, 헨리 테크놀로지 사는 새로운 냉장고 제품군의 출시를 진행할 것이다.
12. 시에라 체육관에 대한 귀하의 회원권을 취소하고 싶으시다면, 저희 고객 지원팀으로 이메일을 주시기 바랍니다.
13. 카터 진료소는 환자들의 사생활을 보호하기 위해 모든 직원들에게 동의서에 서명할 것을 요구한다.
14. 어떠한 도난이나 사고를 피하기 위하여, 아파트 건물 관리인은 모든 세입자들에게 복도에 개인 물품을 두지 말 것을 상기시켰다.
15. 에버스 씨는 각 부서장들에게 새로운 교대근무 일정 절차에 대해 설명할 것이다.
16. 7월 29일에, 엘바 씨는 문테로 제약회사의 대표이사로서의 취임 20주년을 기념할 것이다.
17. 귀하의 장치를 설치하는 것에 도움이 필요하시다면, 저희 기술 지원팀에 전화주시는 것을 주저하지 마십시오.
18. 주주총회에서, 펭 씨는 다음 해를 위한 회사의 목표와 확장 계획을 설명했다.
19. 셔틀버스는 매 30분마다 공항에서 출발하며, 맥시 호텔과 에버크레스트 인에 정차합니다.
20. 청사진의 초안에 기반해, 아카디아 영화관은 쇼

핑몰의 최고층 전체를 사용할 것이다.
21. 로드리고 씨는 직원 오리엔테이션 프로그램의 모든 면을 감독하도록 요청 받았다.
22. 개선된 생산 라인 기술은 제조 공장이 생산율을 세 배로 만들 수 있도록 할 것이다.
23. 모든 민턴 사의 직원들은 무료로 고급 영업 워크숍에 등록할 수 있다.
24. 마무리 발언에서, 신임 대표이사는 새로운 도전을 고대하고 있다고 덧붙였다.
25. 휴스턴 씨는 드모인으로 회사의 본사를 이전하는 것의 수많은 이점을 간략히 설명했다.
26. 유명한 건축 회사가 150년 된 리치몬드 극장을 원래의 상태로 복원하기로 계약을 맺었다.
27. 컴퓨터 바이러스의 위험을 줄이기 위해, 새로운 정책들은 전 직원이 안티 바이러스 소프트웨어를 설치하도록 의무화하고 있다.
28. 급여는 전문 지식과 경력에 기반해 다를 것이다.
29. 팔 벨리 베버리지 사는 강력한 고객층을 유지하고 있으며, 내년에는 해외로 확장할 계획이다.
30. 합격자는 인사 분야에서의 최소 4년의 경력과 전문 지식을 보유해야 한다.
31. 비록 인근의 여러 건물들이 철거 예정이지만, 시 의회는 그 오래된 극장은 보존될 것이라고 약속했다.
32. 에이펙스 스포츠웨어 사는 인력감축 중이며, 가장 인기가 없는 의류 제품군의 생산을 중단할 것이다.
33. 기술 회사의 창립자는 훌륭한 고객 서비스를 제공하는 것의 중요성을 강조했다.
34. 생산 라인에서 작업이 재개되기 전에, 기계적인 문제가 추가적으로 분석되어야 한다.
35. 벨몬트 소방서 주변의 많은 거리들에서 주차가 제한된다.
36. 피니건 씨는 지역 자선단체를 위해 만 달러 이상을 모금한 것에 대해 시 의회의 추천을 받았다.
37. 유명 야구선수 조니 레드몬드 씨가 우리 회사의 스포츠 의류를 홍보하기로 동의했다.
38. 저희 건강식품 제품들은 녹색의 '정부 인증' 상표를 통해 쉽게 구분될 수 있습니다.
39. 케인 씨를 잠정적인 공동작업자로 평가하기 위해, 우리는 그에게 이전 사진 작업물의 포트폴리오를

제출할 것을 요청했다.
40. 저희는 승객 여러분께서 비행기가 이륙하는 동안 자리에서 떠나는 것을 자제해주실 것을 요청드립니다.

DAILY QUIZ

7.

해석 크로포드 씨는 자신의 회사에 영향을 미치는 모든 재무 사안들을 감독하기 위해 높이 평가 받는 회계사를 고용했다.

해설 빈칸에는 빈칸 뒤에 제시된 명사구 all financial matters를 목적어로 취해 회계사가 하는 일을 나타낼 수 있는 어휘가 필요하다. 따라서 모든 재무와 관련된 일들을 감독한다는 의미가 되어야 자연스러우므로 '~을 감독하다'를 뜻하는 (C)가 정답이다.

어휘 **highly regarded** 높이 평가 받는 **accountant** 회계사 **matter** 사안, 문제 **affect** ~에 영향을 미치다 **accumulate** ~을 축적하다, 모으다 **oversee** ~을 감독하다

8.

해석 내일 있을 세미나는 영업사원들이 잠재 고객들을 찾고, 그들에게 다가가 관계를 맺는 능력을 평가하는 데 있어 도움이 될 것이다.

해설 빈칸에는 영업 사원들이 세미나에서 도움을 받을 수 있는 일을 나타낼 어휘가 필요한데, 영업 사원들의 능력과 관련된 행위를 나타내야 하므로 '~을 평가하다'를 뜻하는 (D)가 정답이다.

어휘 **identify** ~을 찾아 내다, 알아보다 **approach** ~에게 다가가다 **engage with** ~와 관계를 맺다 **succeed** 성공하다, ~의 후임이 되다 **evaluate** ~을 평가하다

Day 04 동사 + 전치사 콜로케이션

표제어 문제 정답 및 해석

1. (A) 2. (B) 3. (A) 4. (B) 5. (A)
6. (A) 7. (A) 8. (A) 9. (B) 10. (A)
11. (A) 12. (A) 13. (B) 14. (B) 15. (B)
16. (B) 17. (B) 18. (B) 19. (B) 20. (A)
21. (A) 22. (A) 23. (A) 24. (A) 25. (A)
26. (A) 27. (A) 28. (A) 29. (A) 30. (A)
31. (A) 32. (A) 33. (B) 34. (A) 35. (A)
36. (A) 37. (A) 38. (B) 39. (B) 40. (B)

1. 지난 몇 년간, 레드힐 지역은 조용한 거주 구역에서 인기 있는 쇼핑 지역으로 진화했다.
2. 세입자 연합 회의에서, 조직 회장은 종종 임대료에 대한 회원들의 질문에 응답한다.
3. 겔프 매뉴팩처링 사의 최고 운영 책임자는 생산 과정을 더 효율적으로 만들기 위한 방법들을 찾고 있다.
4. 치과 수술에 대한 예약 시간을 변경하고 싶으시다면, 이 문자 메시지에 답장해주십시오.
5. 아무도 워크숍에 등록하지 않으면, 워크숍은 사전 공지 없이 취소될 것입니다.
6. 다가오는 시의 토론회에 참가하고 싶은 지역 주민들은 시 의회 웹 사이트에서 등록해야 한다.
7. 영국 운동복 회사 살웨이 사는 자사가 북미로 확장하는 것을 계획하고 있다는 것을 기자회견에서 발표했다.
8. 비용 효율이 더 좋은 제품 포장은 감소된 제품 가격이라는 결과를 낳을 것이다.
9. 그 세미나는 직원들 및 고객들과 강력한 업무 관계를 쌓는 것에 주력한다.
10. 경영진은 레벨 1 안전 자격을 획득하지 않은 모든 직원들에게 보건 안전 워크숍에 등록할 것을 요청한다.
11. 허가 받은 마고 소프트웨어의 판매자 목록에 대해, 사용자 안내서 10 페이지를 참조하십시오.
12. 그 소셜 미디어 플랫폼의 창립자 샘 싱씨는 조 파간 씨의 인기 있는 팟캐스트의 두 시간짜리 방송에 나왔다.
13. 킷슨 씨와 협의할 필요가 있다면, 그의 개인 비서와 약속을 잡으시기 바랍니다.
14. 각각의 루모스 손전등은 어떤 제조사 결함도 보장하는 2년의 보증서가 딸려 온다.
15. 피오나 미들턴 씨는 대표이사 자리를 스틸먼 씨로부터 넘겨받을 가장 유력한 후보로 떠올랐다.
16. 코세이르 택배 서비스 사는 릴라이언트 배송 회사와 내년 초에 합병할 것이다.
17. 우리 주방에 있는 모든 가전기기들은 식당 산업의 공동 안전 규정들을 반드시 지켜야 한다.
18. 할로 자선단체는 전 세계에 근거지를 둔 25,000명이 넘는 회원들로 구성된다.
19. 선스포츠 사의 새로운 티셔츠와 수영복 제품군의 출시는 여름 연휴와 겹칠 것이다.
20. 귀하의 기사의 길이와 형식이 작성 안내서에 있는 지침을 따르도록 확실히 하시기 바랍니다.
21. 휴대폰 메세지 어플리케이션들은 사용자들이 가족 및 친구들과 쉽게 소통할 수 있게 해준다.
22. 그 다큐멘터리는 기술 회사가 파산한 이유를 밝히는 것에 집중할 것이다.
23. 비록 여러 결함들이 테스트 단계 동안 언급되었지만, 우리에겐 제품 출시 일정에 맞춰 진행하는 것이 중요하다.
24. 몇 주 동안 의류 매장을 오후 7시까지 개장한 이후, 소유주는 원래의 영업 시간으로 되돌아가기로 결정했다.
25. 그 영화감독은 모든 의료 장면들이 정확하게 묘사되도록 마조리 어빈 박사와 협력했다.
26. 애스콧 쇼핑몰의 새로운 매장들 중 하나인 애티카 프린트는 사진을 포스터나 인쇄된 유화로 변환하는 것을 전문으로 한다.
27. 그 직무를 위한 면접 단계로 가기 전에, 라글란 씨는 우선 여러 다른 경험이 많은 지원자들과 경쟁해야 한다.
28. 코벤 시 시장은 뮤직 페스티벌을 개최하는 것이 쓰레기의 증가로 이어지진 않을 것이라고 주장했다.
29. 홀든 씨는 회계부가 추가 인턴을 고용하는 것을

정답 및 해설 43

주의깊게 살펴야 한다고 생각한다.
30. 오크뷰 시티 농장을 방문할 때 동물들에게 먹이를 주는 것을 자제해주시기 바랍니다.
31. 케시 24시간 식당의 직원들은 순환 교대근무로 일하며, 오후 10시부터 오전 6시 사이에 추가 급여를 받는다.
32. 차량의 전면유리에 카메라가 확실히 붙을 수 있도록 카메라의 흡착판을 유리에 대고 단단히 누르십시오.
33. 로슨 씨는 보통 현지 지역에 근거지를 둔 고객들과만 만났지만, 제너 씨와 이야기하기 위해 로스앤젤레스로 출장가는 것에 동의했다.
34. 야구장에서 떠나기 전에, 제공된 쓰레기통에 자신의 쓰레기를 넣어주시기 바랍니다.
35. 앤더슨 씨의 신생 회사 출시는 여러 투자자들의 재정적인 지원에 의존할 것이다.
36. <베드포드 타임즈>는 언론계에서 경력을 쌓고자 하는 숙련된 대학 졸업생들을 찾도록 채용 회사를 고용했다.
37. 로잘리타 커피숍은 애들레이드 대학과 가까운 접근성에서 이익을 얻고 있다.
38. 앤디 첸 씨는 패티그루 씨가 출산 휴가 중인 동안에 임시 지점장으로서 근무할 것을 요청받았다.
39. 릴리패드 비스트로는 더 넓은 고객층에 매력적으로 다가가기 위해 채식 요리들을 도입했다.
40. 하트맨 씨의 재정 고문과 상담한 이후, 그는 전망이 있는 새로운 기술 회사에 투자하기로 결정했다.

DAILY QUIZ

7.
해석 메이페어 월넛 옷장은 사전에 조립되어 오지 않으므로, 포함되어 있는 조립 설명서를 참조하시기 바랍니다.
해설 빈칸에는 빈칸 뒤에 위치한 전치사 to와 함께 문맥상 옷장을 구매한 고객들에게 요청하는 내용의 어휘가 와야 한다. 따라서 빈칸 뒤에 제시된 조립 설명서를 보라는 의미가 되어야 자연스러우므로 to와 함께 '~을 참조하다'라는 의미의

(A)가 정답이다.
어휘 pre-assembled 사전에 조립된 refer to ~을 참조하다 assembly 조립 instruction 설명서 adapt 적응하다

8.
해석 스키너 아일랜드로 향하는 마지막 페리는 항구에서 오후 4시에 출발할 것이다.
해설 빈칸 뒤에 항구라는 장소와 오후 4시라는 시간이 제시되어 있으므로 특정 목적지로 향하는 페리의 출발 장소와 시간임을 알 수 있다. 따라서 빈칸 뒤에 제시된 전치사 from과 함께 '~에서 출발하다, 떠나다'라는 뜻을 가진 (B)가 정답이다.
어휘 depart from ~에서 출발하다, 떠나다 harbor 항구 withdraw ~을 회수하다

Day 05 기출 동의어 ④

표제어 문제 정답

1. (A)	2. (B)	3. (B)	4. (B)	5. (A)
6. (A)	7. (A)	8. (A)	9. (A)	10. (B)
11. (A)	12. (A)	13. (A)	14. (A)	15. (B)
16. (B)	17. (B)	18. (B)	19. (A)	20. (B)
21. (A)	22. (A)	23. (A)	24. (A)	25. (A)
26. (A)	27. (A)	28. (A)	29. (A)	30. (B)

DAILY QUIZ

1.
해석 현재 많은 기업들이 에너지 효율적인 기술 구현, 일회용 플라스틱 사용 줄이기, 재활용 프로그램을 운영에 통합하는 등 환경친화적인 관행을 채택하고 있습니다.

해설 에너지 효율적인 기술 구현, 일회용 플라스틱 줄이기, 재활용 프로그램 등은 일회성 이벤트가 아니라 습관적으로 실시하는 '관행'이므로 이와 같은 의미를 지닌 (B)가 정답이다.

어휘 adopt ~을 채택하다 practice 관행 implement ~을 실행하다 energy-efficient 에너지 효율적인 single-use 일회용의 incorporate ~을 포함시키다 regular action 정기적인 실행 profession 직업

2.

해석 당사의 고객 지원팀은 최근의 서비스 마비에 대한 귀하의 우려 사항을 처리하고 불편을 최소화할 수 있도록 신속한 해결 방법을 제공하기 위해 노력할 것이니, 안심하시기 바랍니다.

해설 고객 지원팀이 고객의 우려 사항을 address 한다는 것은 우려 사항에 응대하여 이를 해결하는 것이다. 따라서 '~에 대응하다, ~을 응대하다'라는 뜻을 지닌 (B)가 정답이다.

어휘 Rest assured 안심하세요 address 문제 상황 등을 다루다 concern 우려 disruption 방해, 지장 swift 신속한 resolution 해결 supervise ~을 관리 감독하다 respond to ~에 대응하다

3.

해석 그 회사는 다음 달 새로운 스마트폰 라인을 출시할 계획으로, 모바일 기술의 최신 발전 사항을 경험하고 싶어 하는 기술 애호가들 사이에서 기대감을 불러일으키고 있습니다.

해설 여기서 roll out은 '제품 등을 출시하다'라는 의미로 쓰였으므로 '~을 선보이다, 소개하다'라는 뜻을 지닌 (D)가 정답이다.

어휘 roll out ~을 출시하다 anticipation 기대, 예상 tech enthusiast 기술의 열렬한 지지자 eager to do ~할 것을 갈망하는 advancement 발전, 진보 spread ~을 펼치다 introduce ~을 선보이다, 소개하다

Week 04 실전 TEST

1. (C)	2. (B)	3. (A)	4. (C)	5. (A)
6. (C)	7. (C)	8. (C)	9. (B)	10. (B)
11. (C)	12. (C)	13. (A)	14. (C)	15. (B)
16. (B)	17. (A)	18. (A)	19. (D)	20. (C)
21. (A)	22. (B)	23. (D)	24. (C)	

1.
When should we vacate the hotel room?
(A) I'll make a reservation.
(B) It has a 4-star rating.
(C) Noon at the latest.

언제 저희가 호텔 객실을 비워야 하나요?
(A) 제가 예약할게요.
(B) 그곳은 4성급이에요.
(C) 늦어도 정오까지입니다.

어휘 vacate (방, 건물 등) ~을 비우다, ~에서 나가다 make a reservation 예약하다 rating 등급, 평점, 순위 at the latest 늦어도

2.
I recommend taking a train rather than driving yourself.
(A) The train arrived at 9.
(B) Thanks, I'll consider that option.
(C) I'd like a roundtrip ticket.

직접 운전하는 것보다 기차를 타시기를 추천합니다.
(A) 그 기차는 9시에 도착했어요.
(B) 감사합니다, 그 옵션을 고려해 볼게요.
(C) 왕복 티켓으로 주세요.

어휘 recommend -ing ~하기를 추천하다 rather than ~보다는, ~하지 않고 consider ~을 고려하다

정답 및 해설 45

3. Where should we place our belongings?
   (A) **In the overhead compartments.**
   (B) They're packed up in cardboard boxes.
   (C) She went to check the lost and found.

   어디에 저희 개인 물품을 놓아야 하나요?
   (A) 머리 위쪽에 있는 짐칸에요.
   (B) 그것들은 판지 상자로 포장되어 있어요.
   (C) 그녀는 분실물 보관소에 확인하러 갔어요.

   어휘 place v. ~을 놓다, ~을 두다 belongings 개인 물품, 소지품 overhead compartments 머리 위쪽에 있는 짐칸 pack up ~을 포장하다, ~을 꾸리다 the lost and found 분실물 보관소

4. Ms. Feinstein will be arriving shortly.
   (A) Please provide your registration number.
   (B) No, the bus has already left.
   (C) **Great, I'll notify our guests.**

   파인스타인 씨께서 곧 도착하실 겁니다.
   (A) 등록 번호를 제공해 주시기 바랍니다.
   (B) 아뇨, 그 버스는 이미 떠났어요.
   (C) 잘됐네요, 우리 손님들께 알려 드릴게요.

   어휘 registration 등록 notify ~에게 알리다

5. What should we do about the leak in the roof?
   (A) **I'll call a local plumber.**
   (B) My apartment is four-stories tall.
   (C) Sometime next week.

   지붕에 새는 부분을 어떻게 해야 하나요?
   (A) 제가 지역 배관공에게 전화할게요.
   (B) 제 아파트는 4층 높이입니다.
   (C) 다음 주 중으로요.

   어휘 leak (물, 가스 등의) 새는 부분, 누출 local 지역의, 현지의 plumber 배관공

6. Ms. Ohori is interviewing candidates for the assistant manager position.
   (A) No, I don't need any assistance.
   (B) You should check the meeting room.
   (C) **Have you sent her all the résumés?**

   오호리 씨께서 부책임자 직책에 대한 지원자들을 면접하고 계십니다.
   (A) 아뇨, 저는 도움이 전혀 필요하지 않습니다.
   (B) 그 회의실을 확인해 보셔야 해요.
   (C) 그분께 모든 이력서를 보내 드리셨나요?

   어휘 candidate 지원자, 후보자 position 직책, 일자리 assistance 도움, 지원 résumé 이력서

7. Can you work the night shift on Tuesday?
   (A) They're hosting a large event downtown.
   (B) By Tuesday at noon.
   (C) **No, I already have plans.**

   화요일에 야간 교대 근무로 일하실 수 있으세요?
   (A) 그분들이 시내에서 큰 행사를 주최해요.
   (B) 화요일 정오까지요.
   (C) 아뇨, 저는 이미 계획이 있습니다.

   어휘 shift 교대 근무(조) host ~을 주최하다

8. When can I visit the property?
   (A) The real estate agency.
   (B) For a tour of the factory.
   (C) **Tomorrow afternoon.**

   언제 제가 그 건물을 방문할 수 있나요?
   (A) 부동산 중개업소요.
   (B) 공장 견학을 위해서요.
   (C) 내일 오후에요.

   어휘 property 건물, 부동산

9. We need to close the shop early tomorrow to take inventory.
(A) A box of printer paper.
(B) Ok, I'll post a sign at the entrance.
(C) They're out of stock.

우리가 재고 조사를 하기 위해 내일 일찍 매장 문을 닫아야 합니다.
(A) 프린터 용지 한 상자요.
(B) 네, 제가 출입구에 안내 표지를 게시할게요.
(C) 그것들은 품절입니다.

어휘 take inventory 재고 조사를 하다, 재고 목록을 만들다 post ~을 게시하다, ~을 내걸다

10. Have you filled the order for the office supplies?
(A) The store on Main Street.
(B) I took care of it yesterday.
(C) You need to fill out this form.

그 사무용품에 대한 주문을 처리하셨나요?
(A) 메인 스트리트에 있는 매장이요.
(B) 제가 어제 처리했습니다.
(C) 이 양식을 작성하셔야 합니다.

어휘 fill the order 주문을 처리하다 supplies 용품, 물품 take care of ~을 처리하다, ~을 다루다 fill out ~을 작성하다 form 양식, 서식

11.
해석 미드랜드 은행은 자사의 온라인 뱅킹팀을 위해 경력이 있는 웹 디자이너를 고용하기를 희망한다.
해설 '온라인 뱅킹팀을 위해 웹 디자이너를 고용하는 것을 바란다'는 맥락이 자연스러우므로 '~을 고용하다, 채용하다'를 의미하는 (C)가 정답이다.
어휘 experienced 경력이 있는 enter ~에 접속하다 hire ~을 고용하다, 채용하다 lead ~을 이끌다

12.
해석 곧 다가올 회사 출장에 대한 구체적인 세부사항을 위해, 행정 사무실에 있는 램모어 씨에게 연락해 주십시오.
해설 빈칸에는 특정 정보를 얻기 위해서 빈칸 뒤에 제시된 대상에게 취할 행위를 나타낼 어휘가 필요하므로 '~에게 연락하다'라는 뜻의 (C)가 정답이다.
어휘 specific 구체적인 administration 행정 appeal 관심을 끌다 identify ~을 확인하다, 찾다 contact ~에게 연락하다

13.
해석 구매품을 다른 상품으로 교환하기를 원하는 리버사이드 백화점 고객들은 유효한 영수증을 제시해야 한다.
해설 빈칸에는 영수증을 제시해야 하는 이유를 나타내면서 백화점 고객이 구매품과 다른 상품에 대해 취할 수 있는 행위를 나타낼 어휘가 필요하다. 따라서 '구매품을 다른 상품으로 교환하기를 원하는'의 맥락이 되어야 자연스러우므로 '(같은 종류로) 교환하다'라는 의미의 (A)가 정답이다.
어휘 valid 유효한, 타당한 exchange (같은 종류로) 교환하다 display ~을 전시하다

14.
해석 연휴 기간의 수요를 충족하기 위해, 헤론 백화점은 추가 영업 보조사원들을 채용할 필요가 있다.
해설 빈칸에는 수요에 대응하기 위해 빈칸 뒤에 위치한 추가 영업 보조사원에 대해 백화점이 취해야 할 행위를 나타낼 어휘가 필요하므로 '~을 채용하다'라는 뜻의 (C)가 정답이다.
어휘 meet ~을 충족하다 demand 수요 conclude ~을 끝마치다, 결론을 내리다 recruit ~을 채용하다

15.
해석 홀브룩 그룹의 신축 호텔에 대한 마케팅 자료는 호텔의 가격 적정성과 편리한 위치를 강조하고 있다.
해설 빈칸에는 호텔이 마케팅 자료에서 가격 적정성과 편리한 위치에 대해 취할 수 있는 행위를 나타낼 어휘가 필요하므로 '~을 강조하다'라는 뜻의 (B)가 정답이다.

어휘 **affordability** 가격 적정성 **emphasize** ~을 강조하다 **influence** ~에 영향을 미치다 **accessorize** ~에 장식물을 달다

16.
해석 메이포드 에너지 사는 현재 소비자 설문조사 결과를 분석할 마케팅 컨설턴트를 찾고 있다.
해설 빈칸에는 마케팅 컨설턴트가 소비자 설문조사 결과에 대해 취할 행위를 나타낼 어휘가 필요하므로 '~을 분석하다'라는 뜻의 (B)가 정답이다.
어휘 **decline** 감소하다, 거절하다 **analyze** ~을 분석하다 **advise** 조언하다, 충고하다 **conduct** ~을 수행하다

17.
해석 모든 자쯔 전자의 가전기기에는 모든 부품에 대한 수리 및 교체 작업을 포함하는 2년의 품질 보증서가 딸려 온다.
해설 빈칸에는 빈칸 뒤에 위치한 전치사 with와 함께 쓰일 수 있으면서 가전기기와 보증서 사이의 관계를 나타낼 수 있는 어휘가 필요하다. 따라서 가전기기를 구매할 때 품질 보증서가 포함된다는 맥락이 자연스러우므로 with와 함께 '~가 딸려 오다'의 뜻인 (A)가 정답이다.
어휘 **appliance** 가전기기 **come with** ~가 딸려 오다 **warranty** 품질 보증(서) **replacement** 교체(품) **part** 부품

18.
해석 원더월드 테마 파크 방문자들은 공원의 탈것들을 즐기는 동안 휴대전화를 사용하는 것을 자제하라는 주의를 받는다.
해설 빈칸에는 방문객들이 놀이기구 탑승 중 휴대전화를 사용하는 것에 대해 취해야 할 행위를 나타낼 어휘가 필요하므로 빈칸 뒤에 제시된 전치사 from과 함께 '~을 자제하다, 삼가다'라는 뜻의 (A)가 정답이다.
어휘 **be reminded to do** ~라는 주의를 받다 **ride** 탈것 **refrain from** ~을 자제하다, 삼가다 **forbid** ~을 금하다 **retreat** 후퇴하다

19-22.

> **애니멀 디펜스 재단**
>
> 저희 애니멀 디펜스 재단의 목표는 지역 내의 그 어떤 야생동물도 불법 사냥에 의해 부당하게 해를 입지 않도록 보호하는 것입니다. 저희는 **19** 끊임 없이 버크셔 카운티에 있는 삼림 구역과 하천을 순찰하고 있습니다. **20** 이로써 사냥꾼들이 해당 구역에 출입하는 것을 막을 수 있습니다. 그리고 저희는 그들의 출현을 지역 당국에 보고합니다.
>
> 지역에 기반을 둔 단체 **21** 로서, 저희 애니멀 디펜스 재단은 지역 주민들의 도움에 의존하고 있습니다. 저희는 지역 야생동물을 **22** 보호하는 데 여러분의 지원을 필요로 합니다. 여러분의 지역에서 불법 사냥이 발생되고 있다고 생각하시는 경우, 555-3878로 연락 주십시오.

어휘 **ensure that** ~을 보장하다, ~하는 것을 확실히 하다 **wildlife** 야생동물 **wrongfully** 부당하게 **through** ~을 통해 **illegal** 불법적인 **patrol** ~을 순찰하다 **woodland** 삼림 **stream** 개천, 시내 **presence** 출현, 존재 **authorities** 당국 **locally founded** 지역을 기반으로 한 **depend on** ~에 의존하다 **occur** 발생되다, 일어나다

19.
해설 주어 We와 동사 patrol 사이에 위치한 빈칸은 동사를 수식하는 부사 자리이므로 (D)가 정답이다.

20.
(A) 최근 수자원 보존 법안이 통과되었습니다.
(B) 마침내, 저희는 환경 교육 기회를 제공합니다.
(C) 이로써 사냥꾼들이 해당 구역에 출입하는 것을 막을 수 있습니다.
(D) 저희 단체는 지역에서 공중 위생에 전념하고 있습니다.

해설 빈칸 바로 앞에 삼림 구역과 하천을 순찰한다는 내용이 있으므로 이를 This로 지칭하여 순찰 활동의 긍정적인 효과를 나타내는 (C)가 정답이다.

어휘 water conservation 수자원 보존 be dedicated to ~에 전념하다 public health 공중 위생

21.
해설 빈칸 뒤의 명사구 a locally founded group과 콤마 뒤에 위치한 주어 the Animal Defense Foundation이 동일한 대상이므로 자격이나 신분 등을 나타내는 전치사 (A)가 정답이다.

어휘 as (자격, 신분) ~로서 through ~을 통해

22.
해설 앞 문단에 단체가 야생동물이 불법 사냥에 의한 피해를 입지 않도록 하는 일을 한다고 했으므로 '~을 보호하다'라는 뜻의 (B)가 정답이다.

23-24.

수신: 폴 설리반 <psullivan@htchemicals.com>
발신: 어니 홉스 <ehobbs@htchemicals.com>
주제: 회신: 열쇠 분실
날짜: 4월 23일

안녕하세요, 폴 씨,

당신이 비품을 구하는데 그렇게 어려움을 겪고 있으시다니 유감입니다. 저는 우리 건물의 모든 방과 사무실에 대한 마스터 키를 가지고 있기 때문에, 항상 열쇠를 가지고 있습니다. 제가 **23** 지금 예비 열쇠를 접수원 책상의 서랍 안에 넣어 두었으니, 당신의 비서가 필요로 하는 것을 오늘 아무 때나 **24** 가져갈 수 있습니다.

저희가 비품실을 잠가두는 것은 직원들 때문이 아니라 주로 늦은 밤 용역원들이 물건들을 가져가기 때문입니다. 그 방을 잠그는 것이 직원들의 직무를 수행하는 동안 문제를 일으키는 줄은 몰랐습니다.

각 부장님들이 필요로 하는 사항을 처리할 수 있도록 열쇠의 복사본을 만들어 드릴까요? 아니면 아마도 제가 매일 아침 그 방의 문을 열고, 하루가 끝날 때 다시 잠가서 하루 종일 열려 있게 해야 할 것 같습니다.

안녕히 계십시오,

어니

어휘 missing 잃어버린 have trouble (in) ~ing ~하는데 어려움을 겪다 place ~을 놓다, 두다 back-up 예비 drawer 서랍 pick up ~을 가져가다 mainly 주로 janitorial 용역의, 잡역의 in the course of ~하는 동안, ~하는 중에 take care of ~을 처리하다, 신경 쓰다 lock A up A를 잠그다

23. 어니 씨는 문제를 어떻게 해결했는가?
(A) 각각의 관리자에게 열쇠를 하나씩 주었다.
(B) 새로운 용역 서비스를 찾았다.
(C) 개인적으로 비품을 나누어 주었다.
(D) 열쇠를 접수원 책상에 넣어두었다.

해설 첫 번째 문단에서 어니 씨는 항상 마스터키를 가지고 있기 때문에, 접수원 책상에 방금 키를 넣어두었다고 언급하고 있으므로 (D)가 정답이다.

24. 첫 번째 문단의 네 번째 줄에 "pick up"과 의미가 가장 가까운 것은 무엇인가?
(A) 만나다
(B) 수확하다
(C) 얻다
(D) 배달하다

해설 제시된 단어 pick up이 포함된 문장은 열쇠를 특정 장소에 두었으니 언제든 가져가라는 맥락이므로 '~을 얻다, 가지다'라는 의미의 (C)가 정답이다.

Week 05
정답 및 해설

Day 01 LC가 잘 들리는 어휘 ③

DAILY QUIZ

7. Did you get your prescription filled?
(A) **Yes, I just picked it up from the pharmacy.**
(B) It's around the corner.
(C) Dr. Keller will see you now.

처방약을 조제 받으셨나요?
(A) 네, 방금 약국에서 받아왔어요.
(B) 모퉁이를 돌면 있어요.
(C) 켈러 선생님이 지금 진료를 봐 주실 겁니다.

어휘 **fill a prescription** 처방전대로 약을 조제하다 **pick up** ~을 가져오다

8. Why was the product line discontinued?
(A) About a month ago.
(B) It received bad reviews.
(C) Production has increased by 20 percent.

왜 그 제품군이 단종되었죠?
(A) 약 한 달 전에요.
(B) 좋지 않은 후기들을 받아왔어요.
(C) 생산량이 20퍼센트 증가했습니다.

어휘 **product line** 제품군 **discontinue** ~을 단종시키다 **production** 생산량

Day 02 형용사 ①

표제어 문제 정답 및 해석

1. (A)	2. (B)	3. (B)	4. (A)	5. (B)
6. (A)	7. (A)	8. (A)	9. (A)	10. (B)
11. (A)	12. (A)	13. (A)	14. (A)	15. (B)
16. (A)	17. (B)	18. (A)	19. (A)	20. (A)
21. (A)	22. (A)	23. (A)	24. (A)	25. (A)
26. (B)	27. (A)	28. (A)	29. (A)	30. (A)
31. (A)	32. (A)	33. (A)	34. (A)	35. (A)
36. (B)	37. (A)	38. (A)	39. (A)	40. (B)

1. 3개의 오후 시간 자리는 타인 강을 따라 보트 투어하는 것을 희망하는 누구든지 이용할 수 있다.
2. 매주 열리는 농산물 직판장은 주민들에게 낮은 가격에 지역 농부들로부터 신선한 농산물을 구매할 기회를 제공한다.
3. <메타 문 크로니클스>는 올해의 비디오 게임상의 가장 최근 수상작이다.
4. 귀하의 전기 요금 고지서에 명시된 금액은 늦어도 6월 14일까지가 지불 기한입니다.
5. 모든 페리 출발 시간은 기상 여건에 따라 변경될 수 있습니다.
6. 에르고 솔루션 사는 자세와 혈액 순환을 개선하기 위해 고안된 사무실 책상과 의자를 제조한다.
7. <더 터닝 오브 더 리브스>는 아직까지 작가 리차드 딘의 가장 성공적인 소설이다.
8. 다가오는 몇 달 동안, 그 회계사는 우리의 사업 비용을 줄일 추가적인 방법들을 찾기를 희망한다.
9. 지역 주민들은 시 의회가 공사 제안에 관한 그들의 우려를 들었다는 것을 듣고 기뻐했다.
10. 현재 저희 메뉴에 있는 여러 요리들이 식사 손님들의 피드백에 기반해 단종될 수 있습니다.
11. 다음 달에, 세나 씨는 샌프란시스코에 본사를 둔 기술 회사에 합류할 것이다.
12. 저희의 새로운 요가 수업에 참석하는 데 관심이 있는 체육관 회원들은 웹 사이트에서 등록하실

수 있습니다.

13. 브라운 씨는 꽤 많은 은행 대출을 받을 필요가 있음에도 불구하고, 가능한 어떠한 방법으로든 그의 사업을 시작할 계획이다.
14. 허니듀 놀이공원의 반값 입장권은 한정된 시간에만 이용 가능합니다.
15. 인공 지능의 출현은 AX 미술관에서의 현재 예술 박람회의 주요한 주제이다.
16. 건설 허가증에 대한 신청서를 제출할 때 모든 필요한 서류들을 포함하고 있도록 확실히 해주십시오.
17. 올해의 뮤직 페스티벌은 작년의 페스티벌보다 45명 더 많은 공연자들을 특징으로 할 것이다.
18. 저희의 새로운 운동화의 종류가 10대들에게 점점 더 인기 있어지고 있습니다.
19. <비즈니스 위클리>의 최신 기사에 따르면, 가장 효과적인 마케팅 전략들 중 하나는 소셜 미디어 광고이다.
20. 10년 전 설립 이후로, 에본 메뉴펙처링 사는 마이크로칩의 선도적인 생산 회사가 되었다.
21. 다가오는 축제 쇼핑 기간 동안 젤라틀리 씨는 수요를 감당하기 위해 더 많은 파트타이머 근로자들을 고용할 계획이다.
22. 아몬드 호텔은 컨퍼런스 센터에서 열리는 행사에 참석하는 것을 계획하는 사람들에게 아주 편리한 위치에 있다.
23. 컨퍼런스 회의록과 발표 자료 슬라이드는 행사 후에 저희 웹 사이트에서 이용 가능할 것입니다.
24. 벤트론 사에 의해 제조된 텐트들은 다양한 색상과 크기로 나온다.
25. 애쉬크로프트 시 의회는 버스 정류장 뒤에 있는 부지를 85개 주택들을 포함한 주거 구역으로 전환하는 것을 계획한다.
26. 면접 날짜와 시간이 괜찮은지를 확실히 하시고, 어떤 변경이라도 희망하신다면 저희에게 연락해 주시기 바랍니다.
27. 저희의 테라스용 가구는 알맞은 보호용 니스를 사용하여 올바르게 유지되지 않는다면 곰팡이에 취약합니다.
28. 회사의 정책에 따라, 귀하는 제때에 부서장에게 휴가 신청서를 제출해야 합니다.
29. 유로 철도 웹 사이트의 오류는 여러 기차들의 잘못된 출발 시간의 게시라는 결과를 낳았다.
30. 온수 욕조에 들어가기 전, 물을 귀하가 원하는 온도로 설정하기 위해 리모콘을 사용하세요.
31. 대부분의 지역 주민들은 지하철 시스템이 도시에서 가장 믿을 만한 대중교통 형태라는 것에 동의한다.
32. 인사부장은 직원들이 인트라넷을 통해 연차를 요청할 수 있도록 하는 효율적인 시스템을 만들었다.
33. 교육 워크숍에 참석할 수 없는 직원들은 이메일로 발표 자료 슬라이드를 받을 것이다.
34. 실험실 관리자 직책에 대한 지원자들은 생명 공학 학위 또는 관련된 연구 영역을 가지고 있어야 한다.
35. 오후 7시 이후에 근무하는 공장 직원들은 초과근무 수당의 자격이 있다.
36. 그 회사는 6개월의 운영 내에 초기의 창업 비용을 충당하는 것을 예상한다.
37. 귀하의 구매품에 완전히 만족하지 않으신다면, 10일 이내에 환불을 위해 그것을 반품하실 수 있습니다.
38. 비록 직원들을 교육 과정에 등록시키는 것이 비싸지만, 대표이사는 그것이 회사 전체에 이득일 것이라고 생각한다.
39. 부동산 중개인에 따르면, 그 사무실 건물은 적어도 150명의 직원들을 위한 충분한 공간을 가지고 있다.
40. 새로운 직원 장려책은 전체 직원 생산성에 대한 매우 유익한 효과를 가졌다.

DAILY QUIZ

7.

해석 밀튼 고등학교 근처에 있는 보행자 전용 다리는 위험한 빙판 때문에 이용할 수 없다.

해설 빈칸에는 위험한 빙판으로 인한 결과와 관련된 어휘가 빈칸에 쓰여야 알맞으므로 not과 결합해 '이용할 수 없는, 접근할 수 없는'이라는 의미를 구성할 수 있는 (B)가 정답이다.

어휘 **pedestrian footbridge** 보행자 전용 다리
black ice (도로 표면의 잘 보이지 않는) 빙판
raised 높이 올린, 높은 **accessible** 이용 가능한, 접근 가능한 **profitable** 수익성이 있는

8.

해석 해안가 지역에 대한 제안된 시안은 시청 웹 사이트에서 온라인으로 볼 수 있다.

해설 빈칸에는 해안가 지역에 대해 제안된 시안과 시청 웹 사이트라는 특정 장소의 관계를 나타낼 어휘가 필요한데, 의미상 웹 사이트는 디자인을 볼 수 있는 장소이므로 '이용할 수 있는, 구할 수 있는'이라는 의미의 (A)가 정답이다.

어휘 **waterfront** 해안가 **available** 이용할 수 있는, 구할 수 있는, 시간이 나는
considerable 상당한

Day 03 형용사 ②

표제어 문제 정답 및 해석

1. (A)	2. (B)	3. (A)	4. (B)	5. (B)
6. (A)	7. (B)	8. (A)	9. (A)	10. (B)
11. (A)	12. (B)	13. (A)	14. (B)	15. (A)
16. (A)	17. (B)	18. (A)	19. (A)	20. (B)
21. (A)	22. (B)	23. (B)	24. (A)	25. (A)
26. (A)	27. (A)	28. (A)	29. (A)	30. (A)
31. (B)	32. (B)	33. (A)	34. (A)	35. (A)
36. (B)	37. (B)	38. (A)	39. (A)	40. (B)

1. 진료소 직원들은 병원의 정책에 따라 모든 환자의 정보를 기밀로 유지해야 한다.
2. 커피 컵의 배송이 부적절하게 포장된 상품들로 인해 손상된 채 도착했다.
3. 유효한 주차 허가증이 분명히 보인다면, 차량들은 동쪽 주차장에만 주차되어질 수 있다.
4. 벤슨 씨는 투숙객들이 룸서비스 메뉴에 대한 변경을 찬성할 것 같다고 생각한다.
5. 제임스 멧칼프가 주연한 새로운 영화는 다수의 비평가들로부터 대개 긍정적인 후기를 받았다.
6. 이번 주말에 회사 하이킹에 합류하는 모든 사람들은 적절한 신발을 착용하고 자외선 차단제를 바르도록 안내되었다.
7. 다양한 기본 모델들의 도입으로 인해, 휴대전화는 마침내 거의 모든 사람들에게 가격이 적당해졌다.
8. 코로나 커피숍은 인상적인 종류의 페이스트리와 샌드위치를 취급한다.
9. 독립 영화 페스티벌의 심사 위원은 여러 유명한 감독들과 영화배우들을 포함할 것이다.
10. 교육 워크숍은 오후 2시 30분에 잠깐의 다과 시간을 위해 중단될 것이다.
11. 에어로 테크놀로지 사는 전 세계에서 사용되는 독특한 모바일 어플리케이션을 개발하는 것으로 유명하다.
12. 그 국립공원의 웹 사이트는 등산 코스의 길이와 난이도에 관한 정확한 정보를 제공한다.
13. 시 의회는 좋지 않은 날씨에도 불구하고 그 거리 퍼레이드가 계획된 대로 개최될 것이라고 여전히 확신한다.
14. 보어햄 주식회사는 엑세터에 있는 새로운 공장을 위해 250명 이상의 숙련된 직원들을 채용할 계획이 있다.
15. 힌클리 도서관의 회원들은 반납 기한이 지난 책들에 대한 비용 청구가 있을 것이라는 점에 유의하실 필요가 있습니다.
16. 시리우스 텔레콤은 귀하의 브로드밴드 서비스에 계속되는 중단에 대해 사과드리고 싶습니다.
17. 시장 전문가들은 가격이 적절한 TV 스트리밍 서비스에 대한 증가하는 수요에 주목해 왔다.
18. 모든 총회 참석자들은 다양한 도심 호텔로부터 무료 교통편을 이용할 수 있다.
19. 관리 직책은 온라인에 공석을 게시하기보다는 내부 채용을 통해 채워질 것이다.
20. 리젠트 호텔의 로비는 투숙객을 위한 여러 편안한 소파와 안락의자를 포함하고 있다.
21. 제프 브라이트맨은 그의 첫 영화 전체를 감독하기를 간절히 바라는 숙련된 뮤직 비디오 감독이다.

22. 전문적이고 잘 고안된 웹 사이트는 어떠한 사업체든지 성공하기 위해 필수적이다.
23. 루이즈 씨는 모든 직원들이 새로운 데이터베이스 시스템에 익숙해질 때까지 주간 교육 워크숍을 계속 시행할 것이다.
24. 줌바 레스토랑의 종업원들은 지역 재료와 와인에 대해 매우 박식하다.
25. 부동산 시장 전문가들은 글렌 벨리와 주변 지역에서의 주택 가격의 꾸준한 상승에 주목해왔다.
26. 예상치 못한 출장 지연으로 인해, 일본 고객들이 오후 4시까지 공장에 도착하지 않을 것이다.
27. 티아라 케이터링 사는 자사의 우수한 메뉴와 훌륭한 고객 서비스로 유명하다.
28. 에벌리 지사의 연례 수익이 마침내 우리의 플래그십 매장의 수익과 동등해졌다.
29. 살라자르와 인디고 사에 의해 출시된 새로운 휴대전화는 비교할 만한 특징들과 가격의 가치를 제공한다.
30. 그 대표이사는 제조 공장이 4월 20일까지 완전히 가동될 것으로 예상한다.
31. 그 고객은 공항 청사진에 대한 건축가의 제안된 변경사항에 만족한다.
32. 직원 야유회의 목적지는 재무부장에 의해 할당된 예산에 많이 의존한다.
33. 우수한 근로 윤리와 생산성을 보여준 직원들은 연례 보너스로 보상 받는다.
34. 그 두 후보자 사이에 명백한 차이가 없다.
35. 50명의 파트타임 직원들이 12월 전반에 걸쳐 계절적 요구에 대처하는 것을 돕기 위해 우리 지사에 고용되었다.
36. 리지백 등산화는 자사의 내구성이 좋은 밑창 덕분에 오랜 등산에 적합하다.
37. 우리 직원들의 직무 분장과 관련된 일련의 교육 워크숍은 1월 동안 개최될 것이다.
38. 시드마우스 콘서트 센터는 그 장소 뒤에 있는 비어 있는 부지를 매입함으로써 주차 수용력을 확장하는 것을 희망한다.
39. 새로운 사무실 정책의 일부로서, 직원들은 매달 마지막 금요일에 편안한 복장을 입을 수 있습니다.
40. 배드민턴 클럽에 가입하기 전에, 각각의 잠재적인 회원들은 우선 연습 시간에 참석해야 한다.

DAILY QUIZ

7.
해석 세계적으로 유명한 감독으로서, 로이드 씨는 연극계에 대한 우수한 공헌으로 널리 인정받아 왔다.
해설 빈칸에는 로이드 씨가 연극계에서 인정받는 이유를 나타낼 수 있는 어휘가 필요하므로 '우수한, 특출난, 예외적인'이라는 뜻의 (D)가 정답이다.
어휘 director 감독 recognized 인정받은, 알려진 contribution 공헌 theater 연극계 severe 극심한, 심한 established 확실히 자리를 잡은, 존경받는 abnormal 비정상적인 exceptional 우수한, 특출난, 예외적인

8.
해석 사우스 스트리트 주차장에 차량을 주차하시려면, 운전자들께서는 반드시 유효한 컨트리 클럽 회원 카드를 보이도록 놓아두시기 바랍니다.
해설 빈칸에는 주차 가능한 차량임을 입증하기 위한 회원 카드의 특성을 나타낼 어휘가 쓰여야 하므로 '유효한'을 뜻하는 (A)가 정답이다.
어휘 display ~을 보이도록 놓아두다, 전시하다 valid 유효한 gradual 점진적인 prolific (작가 등이) 다작하는, (동식물) 다산하는

Day 04 형용사+명사 콜로케이션

표제어 문제 정답 및 해석

1. (B)	2. (B)	3. (A)	4. (B)	5. (B)
6. (B)	7. (B)	8. (A)	9. (A)	10. (A)
11. (A)	12. (B)	13. (B)	14. (B)	15. (A)
16. (B)	17. (A)	18. (B)	19. (B)	20. (A)
21. (A)	22. (B)	23. (B)	24. (A)	25. (A)
26. (A)	27. (B)	28. (B)	29. (B)	30. (B)
31. (A)	32. (B)	33. (B)	34. (A)	35. (A)
36. (B)	37. (A)	38. (B)	39. (A)	40. (B)

1. 직원들은 개인 사유로 회사 자산을 사용하는 것이 허용되지 않는다.
2. 대부분의 운전자들은 그것들이 소비하는 과도한 양의 휘발유 때문에 볼콘 자동차의 SUV 차종에 관심이 없다.
3. 리버사이드 호텔의 다수가 올해 성수기 동안 최대 수용 인원으로 운영될 것으로 예상된다.
4. 로건 농장은 가장 신선한 채소들을 고객들에게 제공하는 것을 자랑스럽게 여긴다.
5. 글론팅 씨는 시골의 아름다운 경치를 즐기기 때문에 출장 때 기차 타는 것을 선호한다.
6. 올리버 하디 씨는 회사에 상당한 기여를 해왔으며, 그의 최근 승진은 매우 당연한 것이다.
7. 우리의 여름 패키지 상품은 기업과 기관들을 위한 많은 야외 활동들을 제공한다.
8. 맨리 인더스트리 사는 효율을 증가시키기 위해 자사의 생산 관행에 폭넓은 변화를 줄 것이다.
9. 레이 존스 체육관 회원들은 경험이 풍부한 강사들에 의해 진행되는 아주 다양한 헬스 강좌들에 대한 독점적인 이용권을 얻는다.
10. AK 전자는 고객들에게 추가 비용 없이 연장된 품질 보증 기간을 제공하는 것을 결정했다.
11. 사회 기반 시설의 개발은 재정적 자원과 헌신적인 인력 관점에서 모두 중대한 투자를 필요로 한다.
12. S&B 리테일 그룹은 고객 만족과 충성도를 향상시키는 것에 대한 귀중한 제안들을 구하고 있습니다.
13. 귀하의 완성된 입사 지원서를 인사팀 사무실에 8월 15일까지 이메일로 제출해주십시오.
14. 로건 로지스틱스는 최근 배송물을 실시간으로 추적하는 고급 기술을 채택했다.
15. 직원들은 소셜 미디어에서 자신의 일에 대한 어떤 정보도 공유하기 전에 사전 허가를 받아야 한다.
16. 우리는 현재 우리 지점 사무실에서 근무할 매우 경험이 많은 기술직 직원 몇 분을 채용하고 있습니다.
17. 산업안전부는 올슨 메뉴팩처링 사에 있는 기계의 정기 점검을 수행할 것이다.
18. 블루 스카이라인은 운동화와 풋볼 저지와 같은 아주 다양한 스포츠 용품들을 제공한다.
19. 최신 교육 일정이 일정 충돌로 인해 회사 웹 사이트에 다시 게시되었습니다.
20. 임시 직원들은 기밀인 고객 데이터베이스에 대해 제한된 접근 권한만이 주어진다.
21. 본 약정에 대한 추가 세부사항은 부록에 제공된 보충 정보를 참조하십시오.
22. 밀헤이븐 시 의회는 주민들에게 그들의 의견을 나눌 수 있는 기회를 주기 위해 공청회를 개최할 것이다.
23. 그 회사 안내서는 직원들이 매일 충족하도록 예상되는 높은 기준들을 간략하게 서술한다.
24. 도미니크 사토 씨는 직무에 대한 모범적인 성과로 올해의 직원상의 영광을 가졌다.
25. 다이아몬드 그룹의 헌신적인 직원들이 지난주 가장 높은 매출을 기록했다.
26. 저희의 새로운 상품은 귀하의 컴퓨터와 모니터 모두에 대한 손해를 보상하는 종합적인 제품 보증을 포함합니다.
27. 고메즈 씨는 스토리텔링 기술에 대한 보기 드문 기여로 명망 있는 국제 작가상을 받았다.
28. 저희의 고객 서비스 센터에서의 과도한 통화량으로 인해, 귀하께서는 전화 교환원과 이야기하기 위해 기다리실 필요가 있을 수도 있습니다.
29. 내일 직원 회의의 주요 목표는 내년을 위한 매출 목표를 설정하는 것입니다.

30. 래리 윌킨스 씨가 우리의 제조 과정에 빠른 변화를 일으킨 공로로 상을 받을 것으로 예상된다.
31. 스위트 사운드 사의 연구팀은 자신들이 개발한 자동차 스테레오 시스템의 혁신적인 디자인에 대한 공로를 인정받았다.
32. 인터넷은 지식의 확산에 지속적인 영향을 끼친 가장 위대한 발명으로 여겨진다.
33. 로이 벤슨 박사는 새로운 엔진 개발에 대한 뛰어난 기여에 대해 상을 받았다.
34. 생산 부장 직책을 위한 자격을 갖춘 모든 지원자들은 이력서를 10월 15일까지 제출해야 한다.
35. 연극 공연에 참가하는 배우들에 대한 상세 정보가 소책자에 포함되어 있습니다.
36. 우리의 목표는 가장 합리적인 가격에 최고 품질의 제품과 서비스를 제공하는 것이다.
37. 스마트 잇츠는 이전에 식품 유통 분야에서 근무했던 분들께 경쟁력 있는 급여를 제공합니다.
38. 저희의 모든 신상품은 2년의 품질 보증이 딸려 있으며, 추가 비용 없이 어떠한 결함 있는 상품들도 교체해 드릴 것입니다.
39. 어떤 오해도 피하기 위해 서명하기 전에 동봉된 계약서를 매우 신중하게 읽어보십시오.
40. 시장 조사 시험의 최종 단계에, 환자들은 플라스틱 말보다 나무로 된 게임 말을 선호했다.

DAILY QUIZ

7.

해석 그 잡지의 구독자들은 이스틀리 뮤직 홀에서의 라이브 공연과 같은 행사에 대한 독점적인 이용권을 얻는다.

해설 빈칸에는 빈칸 뒤에 제시된 명사 access를 수식하면서 잡지 구독자들이 누릴 수 있는 혜택을 나타낼 수 있는 어휘가 필요하므로 access와 함께 '독점적인 이용(권)'이라는 의미의 (A)가 정답이다.

어휘 **exclusive access** 독점적인 이용(권) **unknown** 알려지지 않은

8.

해석 브리타니 푸드 사는 합리적인 가격에 질 높은 서비스를 제공하는 곳으로 알려져 있기 때문에 로건 홀 컨퍼런스 센터와 출장 요리 제공 계약을 체결했다.

해설 빈칸에는 빈칸 뒤에 제시된 명사 price를 수식해 가격 수준을 나타낼 수 있는 어휘가 필요하므로 price와 함께 '합리적인 가격'이라는 의미인 (B)가 정답이다.

어휘 **be awarded a contract with** ~와 계약을 체결하게 되다 **brief** 간략한, 잠시 동안의 **reasonable price** 합리적인 가격 **sudden** 갑작스러운

Week 05 실전 TEST

1. (A)	2. (C)	3. (B)	4. (B)	5. (A)
6. (A)	7. (B)	8. (A)	9. (C)	10. (A)
11. (C)	12. (B)	13. (C)	14. (A)	15. (A)
16. (D)	17. (B)	18. (A)	19. (B)	20. (A)
21. (A)	22. (A)	23. (D)	24. (B)	

1. Wasn't Carol organizing the company party?
(A) Yes, I'll see if that's still happening.
(B) To celebrate our product launch.
(C) We had a delicious meal.

캐롤 씨께서 회사 파티를 준비하고 계시지 않나요?
(A) 네, 제가 그게 여전히 열리는지 확인해 볼게요.
(B) 우리 제품 출시를 기념하기 위해서요.
(C) 저희는 맛있는 식사를 했습니다.

어휘 **organize** ~을 준비하다, ~을 조직하다 **see if** ~인지 확인하다 **celebrate** ~을 기념하다, ~을

축하하다 launch 출시, 공개, 발표

2. We should prepare disposable cups for guests.
(A) I've set up tables and chairs.
(B) Each pack contains 40 pieces.
(C) We were told to cut back on using plastics.

우리가 손님들을 위해 일회용 컵을 준비해야 합니다.
(A) 제 탁자와 의자들을 설치해 두었습니다.
(B) 각각의 팩에 40개가 들어 있습니다.
(C) 플라스틱 사용을 줄이라는 지시를 받았습니다.

어휘 prepare ~을 준비하다 disposable 일회용의 set up ~을 설치하다, ~을 설정하다 contain ~을 담고 있다, ~을 포함하다 cut back on ~을 줄이다

3. Is Ms. Perez going to be our guest speaker?
(A) An audio system malfunction.
(B) No, she'll be out of town.
(C) We look forward to it.

페레즈 씨께서 우리의 초청 연사가 되시는 건가요?
(A) 오디오 시스템 오작동 문제요.
(B) 아뇨, 그분께서는 다른 지역에 가 계실 거예요.
(C) 저희는 그것을 고대하고 있습니다.

어휘 malfunction 오작동, 작동 불량 look forward to ~을 고대하다

4. Did Oliver get transferred to another store?
(A) I can transfer your call.
(B) Yes, because he recently moved.
(C) Bus 408 stops over there.

올리버 씨가 다른 매장으로 전근되신 건가요?
(A) 전화를 돌려 드릴 수 있습니다.
(B) 네, 그분이 최근에 이사했기 때문입니다.
(C) 408번 버스가 저기 저쪽에 서요.

어휘 get p.p. ~되다 transfer ~을 전근시키다, (받은 전화를) 돌려 주다, 연결시키다 recently 최근에

5. Make sure to switch off all appliances before leaving.
(A) Of course, I'll follow the instructions.
(B) It is a new model.
(C) No, not until lunch time.

나가시기 전에 반드시 모든 기기의 스위치를 끄시기 바랍니다.
(A) 물론이죠, 지시 사항을 따르겠습니다.
(B) 그건 새 모델이에요.
(C) 아뇨, 점심 시간이나 되어야 합니다.

어휘 make sure to do 반드시 ~하도록 하다 switch off ~의 스위치를 끄다 appliance (가전) 기기, 기구 follow ~을 따르다, ~을 준수하다 instructions 지시, 안내, 설명

6. When will you upload the poster I designed?
(A) Probably on Monday at the latest.
(B) On our social media page.
(C) I bought a toaster oven.

언제 제가 디자인한 포스터를 업로드하실 건가요?
(A) 아마 늦어도 월요일일 거예요.
(B) 우리 소셜 미디어 페이지에요.
(C) 제가 토스터 오븐을 구입했어요.

어휘 at the latest 늦어도

7. What is the reason for canceling your magazine subscription?
(A) The printing company.

정답 및 해설 57

(B) I don't have time to read anymore.
(C) Several fashion trends.

귀하의 잡지 구독 서비스를 취소하신 이유가 무엇인가요?
(A) 인쇄업체요.
(B) 더 이상 읽을 시간이 없습니다.
(C) 여러 패션 트렌드요.

어휘 **subscription** 구독, 서비스 가입

8. May I get an itemized bill for the repairs?
(A) Sure, give me one second.
(B) I can't afford that price.
(C) The auto shop down the street.

수리 작업에 대한 요금 명세서를 받아 볼 수 있을까요?
(A) 그럼요, 잠시만요.
(B) 저는 그 가격을 감당할 수 없어요.
(C) 길 저쪽에 있는 자동차 정비소요.

어휘 **itemized bill** (항목별로 나눈) 요금 명세서 **repair** 수리 **can't afford** (가격 등) ~을 감당할 수 없다, ~에 대한 여유가 없다

9. Who approved the budget proposal?
(A) It's due on Friday.
(B) About 8 thousand dollars.
(C) The department head.

누가 예산 제안서를 승인했나요?
(A) 금요일이 기한입니다.
(B) 약 8천 달러입니다.
(C) 부장님께서요.

어휘 **approve** ~을 승인하다 **due** ~가 기한인 **department head** 부서장, 부서 책임자

10. When will the film festival be held this year?
(A) In the springtime, like always.
(B) He's a famous director.

(C) At the city convention center.

그 영화제가 올해 언제 개최되나요?
(A) 봄철에요, 늘 그랬던 것처럼요.
(B) 그는 유명 감독이에요.
(C) 시립 컨벤션 센터에서요.

어휘 **hold** ~을 개최하다 **like always** 늘 그렇듯이, 언제나처럼

11.
해석 문베일 호텔은 투숙객들에게 무료 와이파이 서비스와 24시간 운영하는 비즈니스 센터를 포함한 다양한 편의시설을 제공한다.
해설 빈칸에는 빈칸 뒤에 위치한 명사 amenities를 수식하면서 와이파이 서비스와 비즈니스 센터 등 편의시설의 특징을 나타내야 하므로 '다양한'이라는 뜻의 (C)가 정답이다.
어휘 **24-hour** 24시간 운영하는 **descriptive** 서술하는, 묘사하는 **instructed** 교육을 받은 **various** 다양한 **alert** 기민한

12.
해석 더 가격이 알맞은 공급업체로 변경하기로 한 결정이 우리의 월간 지출 비용에 바람직한 영향을 미치고 있다.
해설 빈칸에는 빈칸 뒤에 위치한 명사 impact를 수식해 더 가격이 알맞은 공급업체로 변경하기로 한 결정이 불러올 영향의 특성을 나타낼 어휘가 와야 한다. 따라서 '바람직한, 원하는' 등을 의미하는 (B)가 정답이다.
어휘 **switch to** ~로 변경하다, 바꾸다 **have an impact on** ~에 영향을 미치다 **expense** 지출 (비용), 경비 **eventful** 다사다난한 **desired** 바람직한, 원하는 **diligent** 근면한

13.
해석 환경 단체들은 시장이 터스커 강 지역의 정화 운동에 대한 충분한 자금을 할당해 주기를 바라고 있다.
해설 빈칸에는 빈칸 뒤에 위치한 명사 funding을 수식해 자금의 양 등을 설명할 수 있는 어휘가 필

요하므로 '충분한'을 뜻하는 (C)가 정답이다.
어휘 **allocate** ~을 할당하다, 배정하다 **cleanup** 정화, 청소 **effort** (조직적인) 운동, 노력 **intentional** 의도적인, 고의의 **sufficient** 충분한

14.
해석 식탁이 배송되자마자 손상된 것으로 보였기 때문에, 강 씨는 그 상품이 다시 가져 가져야 된다고 요구했다.
해설 빈칸에는 소비자가 제품이 다시 가져 가져야 한다고 요구할 수 있는 조건에 해당되는 상태를 나타낼 어휘가 쓰여야 알맞으므로 '손상된'을 의미하는 (A)가 정답이다.
어휘 **appear** ~처럼 보이다 **upon** ~하자마자 **damaged** 손상된 **organized** 체계적인, 조직화된 **assembled** 조립된

15.
해석 체육관의 모든 회원들을 수용하기 위해, 스타 피트니스는 모든 신체 단련 수준에 적절한 새 요가 강좌들을 추가했다.
해설 빈칸에는 빈칸 앞에 위치한 명사구 yoga classes를 뒤에서 수식해 그 특성을 나타낼 어휘가 필요한데, 빈칸 뒤에 위치한 전치사 for와 어울려야 하므로 '적절한, 적합한'을 의미하는 (A)가 정답이다.
어휘 **appropriate** 적절한, 적합한 **adjacent (to)** (~에) 인접한, 가까운 **mutual** 상호간의, 서로의

16.
해석 박물관의 최근 보수공사 기간 내내 방문객의 수가 꾸준히 유지되었다.
해설 빈칸에는 박물관의 보수공사 기간 내에 방문객의 수의 상태를 나타낼 수 있는 어휘가 필요하므로 '꾸준한'이라는 의미의 (D)가 정답이다.
어휘 **the number of** ~의 수 **throughout** ~ 내내, ~ 도처에서 **distinct** 뚜렷한, 분명한 **proper** 적절한, 제대로의 **steady** 꾸준한

17.
해석 웰컴 팩에 있는 보충 정보는 신입직원들이 우리의 회사 업무 환경에 더 쉽게 자리잡도록 도움을 줄 수 있다.
해설 빈칸에는 빈칸 뒤에 위치한 명사 information을 수식해 신입직원들이 회사에 더 쉽게 자리잡을 수 있도록 도울 수 있는 정보의 특징을 나타내야 하므로 information과 함께 '보충 정보'라는 뜻의 (B)가 정답이다.
어휘 **supplemental information** 보충 정보 **settle into** ~에 자리잡다 **arbitrary** 제멋대로인 **superfluous** 불필요한

18.
해석 엘리자베스 바커 씨는 비평가들의 극찬을 받은 소설 <써머 어페어>로 명망 있는 상을 받았다.
해설 빈칸에는 빈칸 뒤의 명사 award를 수식하며 비평가들의 극찬을 받을 정도의 소설이 받는 상의 특징을 설명할 수 있는 어휘가 필요하다. 따라서 award와 함께 '명망 있는 상'이라는 의미의 (A)가 정답이다.
어휘 **be presented with** (상 등) ~을 받다 **prestigious award** 명망 있는 상 **critically acclaimed** 비평가들의 극찬을 받은 **repetitive** 반복적인 **prolific** 다작하는 **laborious** 힘든

19-22.

로스앤젤레스, 4월 23일 – 지역 방송국인 JSV 텔레비전은 올해 지금까지 수백만 달러의 손실을 봤는데, 기록적인 2분기 손실이 2천 2백만 달러에 이르고, 심지어는 올해 말 파산에 직면할 수도 있다. 수익의 하락은 미디어 기업들의 세계적인 감소와 어려운 경제 상황 **19** 탓일 수 있다.

20 수익의 하락에도 불구하고, JSV 텔레비전은 최근에 일간 신문사를 인수했다. 이러한 인쇄 매체로의 이동은 최근의 한 회의에서 그 매입에 반대 목소리를 냈던 몇몇 주주들의 걱정을 샀다.

JSV 텔레비전은 캘리포니아 주에서 가장 큰 민영 텔레

비전 방송국이고, 해리 스미슨 씨에 의해 1964년 **22** **설립**된 이후로 업계에서 **21** **선도적인** 회사들 중 하나가 되었다. 이 회사는 현재 6,800명의 직원을 고용하고 있다.

어휘 millions 수백만 so far 지금까지 record 기록적인 bankruptcy 파산 downturn 하락 be attributed to ~의 탓으로 돌리다, ~때문이다 worry ~을 걱정시키다 voice ~의 목소리를 내다 privately owned 민영의, 사적으로 소유된

19.
해설 빈칸 앞에는 '수익 감소'라는 결과가, 빈칸 뒤에는 전치사 to와 함께 감소의 원인 두 가지가 언급되고 있다. 따라서 be동사 및 to와 함께 '~의 탓으로 돌리다'라는 의미를 구성하는 (A)가 정답이다.

어휘 committed 헌신하는, 전념하는

20.
(A) 업계 분석가들은 부진한 경제가 곧 회복될 것이라고 예측한다.
(B) 수익의 하락에도 불구하고, JSV 텔레비전은 최근에 일간 신문사를 인수했다.
(C) 미디어 기업들은 사람들이 미디어를 소비하는 방식에 적응할 방법을 찾을 필요가 있다.
(D) 그것은 많은 소비자들이 더 싼 요금제를 선호하여 그들의 서비스를 그만두는 것을 보았다.

해설 빈칸 바로 앞 문단은 한 방송국 수익 감소에 관한 내용인데, 빈칸 뒤의 문장에서 인쇄 매체로의 이동이라는 내용이 언급되어 있다. 따라서 빈칸에는 인쇄 매체에 관련된 내용이 와야 하므로 수익 하락에도 불구하고 인쇄 매체인 일간 신문사를 인수했다는 내용이 가장 적절하다. 따라서 (B)가 정답이다.

어휘 sluggish 부진한 acquire ~을 인수하다, 얻다 adapt to ~에 적응하다 drop one's service 서비스를 그만두다 in favor of ~을 선호하여 plan 요금제

21.
해설 빈칸에는 빈칸 뒤에 companies를 수식하면서 빈칸 앞에 JSV 텔레비전이 가장 큰 민영 방송국이라는 문맥에 맞는 JSV 텔레비전의 특성을 나타낼 수 있는 어휘가 필요하므로 '선도적인, 주도적인'이라는 의미의 (A)가 정답이다.

어휘 leading 선도적인, 주도적인 accustomed 익숙한 originated 기원한 moving 움직이는

22.
해설 빈칸 앞에는 전치사 since와 소유격 its가, 빈칸 뒤에는 전치사구가 있으므로 빈칸은 명사 자리이다. 선택지 중 명사는 (A)와 (C)인데, (C)는 '설립자'라는 의미를 가져 해석상 어색하므로 '설립 이후로'라는 의미가 되는 (A)가 정답이다.

23-24.

풀치 씨께,

지난주 화요일 총회에서 가졌던 논의에 대한 후속 조치로 귀하께 연락 드립니다. 제가 언급했던 것처럼, 저는 리저소프트라고 불리는 모바일 어플리케이션 개발 회사의 설립자이고, **23** **제 사업에 기꺼이 투자해주실 분들을 찾고 있습니다.**

만약 저희가 충분한 투자금을 확보한다면, 저희는 이지틱스라는 행사 티케팅 어플리케이션을 우선적으로 처리할 것입니다. 이 프로젝트의 상황은 현재 30퍼센트 완성되었습니다. **24** **저희는 예산 범위 내에서 프로젝트의 첫 단계를 완성하기 위해 호라이즌 IT 솔루션스 사에게 프로그래밍 하청을 주었습니다.** 저희 이사진들은 프로그래밍의 마지막 단계를 위해 호라이즌 사와 계약을 갱신하는 것에 만장일치로 동의했습니다.

귀하께서 저희 회사에 투자하시는 것에 관심이 있으시다면, 귀하의 자본금은 우선적으로 이지틱스를 마케팅하는 것에 할당될 것입니다. 저희는 주기적으로 프로젝트에 대한 최신 보고서를 제공할 것이며, 귀하께서는 초기 투자금과 배당금을 2년 이내에 상환하는 것을 예상하실 수 있습니다.

이러한 흥미로운 기회에 관해 귀하로부터 곧 소식을 들을 수 있기를 바랍니다.

안녕히 계십시오.

카일 글래스
설립자 및 회장, 리저소프트 주식회사

할 것이라는 계획을 언급하고 있으므로 (B)가 정답이다.

어휘 work on ~에 대해 작업하다
overspending 낭비 represent 참석하다, 대표하다

어휘 follow up on ~에 대한 후속 조치를 하다
willing to do 기꺼이 ~하다 provided that 만약 ~한다면 secure ~을 확보하다
adequate 충분한, 적절한 prioritize ~을 우선적으로 처리하다 status 상황, 상태 subcontract ~에게 하청을 주다
unanimously 만장일치로 renew the contract 계약을 갱신하다 allocate ~에 할당하다 primarily 주로 up-to-date 최신의 anticipate ~을 예상하다, 기대하다
repayment dividends 배당금

23. 이 편지의 주된 목적은 무엇인가?
(A) 풀시 씨에게 일자리를 제공하기 위해
(B) 회사 합병을 마무리짓기 위해
(C) 한 프로젝트의 성공을 기념하기 위해
(D) 재정적 지원을 구하기 위해

해설 첫 번째 문단에서 글쓴이는 자신을 한 모바일 어플리케이션 개발 회사의 설립자로 소개하면서 사업에 투자해줄 사람을 찾고 있다고 밝히고 있다. 따라서 재정적인 도움을 요청하고 있다는 (D)가 정답이다.

어휘 finalize ~을 마무리 짓다, 끝내다 merger 합병

24. 리저소프트 주식회사에 대해 사실인 것은 무엇인가?
(A) 성공적인 운동 어플리케이션을 개발했다.
(B) 낭비 없이 한 프로젝트에 대해 작업해오고 있다.
(C) 과거에 풀시 씨와 협력한 적이 있다.
(D) 곧 있을 총회에 참석할 것이다.

해설 두 번째 문단에서 글쓴이는 예산 범위 내에서 하청을 통해 프로그래밍의 첫 단계 작업을 완료했고, 마지막 작업을 위해 그 업체와 계약을 갱신

Week 06
정답 및 해설

Day 01 기출 패러프레이징 ①

DAILY QUIZ

1.

남: 죄송합니다만, 저희가 지금 구매 가능한 참나무 테이블이 하나도 없습니다. 다음 주에 새로 배송을 받을 거예요.
여: 전시품은 구매 가능한가요?
남: 저희 매니저님께 확인해 보겠습니다.

Q. 무엇이 문제인가?
(A) 일부 물건들이 없어졌다.
(B) 일부 제품들이 재고가 떨어졌다.

어휘 oak 참나무 available 구매 가능한, 이용할 수 있는 shipment 수송품, 적하물 floor model 전시품 check with + 사람 ~에게 확인해보다 missing 잃어버린, 없어진 out of stock 재고가 없는

2.

남: 제 급여에 대해 자동 예금을 개설하려고 하는데, 어떻게 하는지 모르겠어요.
여: 급여팀의 사만다 씨에게 얘기해 보세요. 그녀가 설명을 해 줄 수 있을 겁니다.
남: 알겠습니다. 점심 식사 후에 가서 만나 봐야겠어요.

Q. 여자는 남자에게 무엇을 할 것을 제안하는가?
(A) 동료에게 연락하기
(B) 상사에게 보고하기

어휘 set up ~을 개설하다 automatic 자동의 deposit 예금 paycheck 급여 Payroll 급여 담당 부서 instruction (무엇을 하거나 사용하는 데 필요한) 설명 contact ~에게 연락하다 report to ~에게 보고하다 supervisor 상사

3.

안녕하세요, 저는 메이플 스트리트 23번지의 아파트 4B호에 사는 제인 도우라고 합니다. 제 냉장고가 제대로 작동하지 않고 있어서 즉시 살펴 볼 필요가 있어요. 가능한 한 빨리 수리 기술자를 보내서 이 문제를 해결하도록 해주세요.

Q. 화자는 무엇에 대해 전화하는가?
(A) 프로젝트 지연
(B) 고장 난 기기

어휘 refrigerator 냉장고 function v. 기능하다, 작동하다 properly 제대로 require ~을 필요로 하다 immediate 즉각적인 attention 관심 repair person 수리 기술자 address (문제 등을) 처리하다 delay 지연, 지체 broken 고장 난 appliance 가정용 기기

Day 02 형용사 ③

표제어 문제 정답 및 해석

1. (B)	2. (B)	3. (B)	4. (B)	5. (B)
6. (A)	7. (B)	8. (A)	9. (A)	10. (A)
11. (B)	12. (A)	13. (B)	14. (A)	15. (B)
16. (B)	17. (B)	18. (B)	19. (A)	20. (B)
21. (A)	22. (A)	23. (A)	24. (A)	25. (A)
26. (B)	27. (A)	28. (A)	29. (B)	30. (A)
31. (A)	32. (A)	33. (B)	34. (A)	35. (A)
36. (A)	37. (B)	38. (A)	39. (A)	40. (B)

1. 손상된 성당 지붕의 수리는 상당한 시간과 비용을 필요로 할 것이다.
2. 헨리 씨는 사무실 직원들에게 금고에 민감한 정보를 포함하는 모든 서류들을 저장하도록 지시했다.
3. 펄시벌 비스트로에 있는 전용 식사 공간은 최대 20명의 모임을 위한 충분한 장소를 제공한다.
4. 스타릿 기업은 다양한 국적과 배경의 사람들을

특징으로 하는 다양한 인력을 채용한다.
5. 저희는 배송 중에 깨지기 쉬운 제품들이 손상되지 않는 것을 확실히 하기 위해 특별한 포장 재료를 사용합니다.
6. 저희는 새로운 운동 수업에 관해 회원들로부터 전망이 좋은 피드백들을 많이 받아왔습니다.
7. 그 경매가 많은 참석자들을 끌어들였지만, 대부분은 어떤 입찰도 부르는 것을 꺼려했다.
8. 트리온 컨설팅 사는 고객들에게 혁신적이지만 실용적인 해결책을 제공하는 것을 전문으로 한다.
9. 프렛 씨가 연차이지만, 그녀는 긴급한 문제가 있다면 전화로 연락될 수 있다.
10. 크리거 씨는 영국 전역에 걸쳐 20개의 코드모 버거 지점을 개장할 그의 야심찬 계획을 간략하게 말할 것이다.
11. 모든 이사회 임원들이 올해 수입이 20억 달러로 두 배 증가할 수 있다는 기대를 하고 있다.
12. 보수 공사 동안에 개인 독서 공간이 이용할 수 없다는 사실을 도서관 회원들에게 알려드리게 되어 유감입니다.
13. 맷 로저스 씨는 3년 연속으로 올해의 작곡가 상을 받았다.
14. 수많은 지역 주민들이 근처 건설 현장에서 나온 끊임없이 지속되는 소음에 대해 불만을 제기해왔다.
15. 첫 시즌 동안 <서클 오브 프렌즈>를 본 사람이 거의 없었지만, 다음 시즌들은 아주 많은 시청자들을 끌여들였다.
16. 귀하의 노트북을 보호하기 위해, 충전재가 들어 있는 견고한 휴대용 가방을 권해드립니다.
17. 남부 전력 고객들은 그들의 월간 에너지 고지서에 전례 없는 인상에 격분했다.
18. 컨벤션 센터에 가까운 에펙스 호텔의 전략적 위치는 그곳을 출장 여행객들에게 인기 있게 만든다.
19. 데스몬드 아쿰바 씨에 의해 쓰여진 새로운 연극은 대다수의 연극 비평가들로부터 가혹한 후기를 받았다.
20. 몇몇 직원들은 연봉 협상의 결과에 실망한 채로 남겨졌다.
21. 직원 카페테리아는 작업조가 새로운 의자와 탁자를 설치하는 동안에 이용할 수 없을 것이다.
22. 다음 달부터, 모든 연체된 요금 지불은 10퍼센트의 관리비의 대상이 될 것입니다.
23. 마커스 토프트 씨는 <엘든 오크스> 텔레비전 쇼에서의 최상의 공연으로 상을 받았다.
24. 육상 위원회는 로스앤젤레스에서 행사를 개최하자는 매우 설득력 있는 주장을 했다.
25. 쿼텟 사의 신형 디지털 카메라는 매우 다양한 환경에서 사용되기에 충분히 다양한 기능들을 지니고 있다.
26. 지원서 양식에 어떠한 세부정보라도 정확하지 않다면, 귀하께서는 행사에 대한 매점 허가증을 발급받을 수 없을 것입니다.
27. 직원들은 월요일 오전 8시 45분에 주간 지점 회의에 참석하는 것이 의무적이라는 것을 상기했다.
28. 이사회 임원들은 새로운 제조 공장의 수익성에 대해 낙관적이다.
29. 존슨 냉장고 사는 고기와 유제품과 같이 상하기 쉬운 상품의 운송을 위해 고안된 용기들을 생산한다.
30. 모든 참가자들은 오전 9시 정각에 호텔 로비에서 출발할 예정인 도시 투어를 위해 시간을 엄수하도록 노력해야 합니다.
31. 새로운 휴대전화 모델의 출시가 제품 테스터들로부터의 호의적이지 않은 피드백 때문에 연기되었다.
32. 샤프 씨는 불만족스러운 고객들이 포함된 민감한 문제들을 처리하는 데 능숙하다.
33. 6개월 전에 회사에 합류한 이후로, 로페즈 씨는 영업팀의 믿을 만한 구성원으로 그 자신을 증명해왔다.
34. 버드 피크 폭포로의 당일 여행은 호텔의 정기적인 셔틀 버스 서비스 덕분에 쉽게 일정을 관리할 수 있다.
35. 월포드 과학 박물관의 새로운 상호적인 전시회는 모든 가족들을 위해 기억할 만한 경험을 제공하는 것을 약속드립니다.
36. 몇몇 직원들은 임시로 고용될 것이고, 그들 중 몇몇은 3월에 정규직 계약을 제안받을 것이다.
37. 분기 재정 보고서는 새로운 광고 캠페인이 매출에 부정적인 영향을 끼쳤다는 것을 보여준다.
38. 투숙객들은 호텔 접수 구역에서 지역 명소에 대한

유익한 소책자를 가져갈 수 있다.
39. 로열티 포인트와 할인 코드는 저희 웹 사이트에서 교환 가능합니다.
40. 주주들은 회사를 캘리포니아에서 텍사스로 이전하자는 만장일치의 결정에 도달했다.

DAILY QUIZ

7.
해석 모든 가능한 연회 장소들 중에, 더 메이플 라운지가 우리 필요에 충분한 유일한 곳으로 보인다.
해설 빈칸에는 빈칸 뒤에 제시된 전치사 for와 어울리면서 더 메이플 라운지가 연회 장소로서 가지는 특징을 나타낼 수 있는 어휘가 와야 하므로 '충분한, 적절한'의 의미의 (D)가 정답이다.
어휘 banquet 연회 tentative 잠정적인 extensive 광범위한 adequate 충분한, 적절한

8.
해석 긴급한 조치를 필요로 하는 기술적 문제들은 상대적으로 사소한 다른 문제들보다 먼저 처리되어야 한다.
해설 빈칸에는 빈칸 뒤의 명사 attention을 수식하며, 문제가 먼저 처리되어야 하는 이유를 나타내는 어휘가 필요하다. 따라서 '긴급한' 등의 의미인 (D)가 정답이다.
어휘 attention 조치, 관심 relatively 상대적으로 fluent 유창한 absent 부재한, 결석한 urgent 긴급한

Day 03 형용사 ④

표제어 문제 정답 및 해설

1. (B)	2. (A)	3. (B)	4. (A)	5. (B)
6. (B)	7. (A)	8. (A)	9. (B)	10. (B)
11. (A)	12. (B)	13. (A)	14. (A)	15. (B)
16. (A)	17. (A)	18. (A)	19. (B)	20. (A)
21. (A)	22. (A)	23. (B)	24. (B)	25. (B)
26. (A)	27. (B)	28. (B)	29. (B)	30. (A)
31. (B)	32. (A)	33. (B)	34. (B)	35. (A)
36. (B)	37. (A)	38. (B)	39. (B)	40. (A)

1. 많은 온라인 후기들은 그 식당에서 종업원들이 식사 손님들의 요구에 얼마나 주의를 기울이는지를 언급한다.
2. 근로 계약의 종료 최소 30일 전에 고지하는 것은 필수적이다.
3. 브릿지 씨는 사무실 공간의 개조 이후로, 직원 생산성에서의 뚜렷한 향상에 주목했다.
4. 윈터 씨는 올해의 젊은 작가상의 자랑스러운 수상자였다.
5. 도슨 국립 공원은 등산객들이 길을 잃지 않도록 확실히 하기 위해 뚜렷한 등산로 표시들을 추가했다.
6. 새로운 영화 스트리밍 플랫폼인 플릭스 스타는 10,000개 이상의 영화들의 방대한 목록을 자랑한다.
7. 비용이 많이 드는 기계 고장을 예방하기 위해, 에어컨 시스템에 대한 청소 지침을 따르는 것이 바람직하다.
8. 그 대표이사는 지난주의 자선 모금 행사에서의 상당한 액수의 기부에 대해 호그 씨에게 사적으로 감사했다.
9. 새로운 데이터베이스 시스템에 대해 여전히 익숙하지 않은 직원들은 내일 오후 2시에 워크숍에 참석하도록 요청된다.
10. 그라우스 산의 정상으로의 산책길은 특별히 힘들

지 않고, 모든 나이대의 사람들에게 적합하다.
11. 11월 10일이 서머빌 쇼핑몰의 대개장을 위한 임시 일자로 선택되었다.
12. 국제 금융 총회의 기조 연설자는 유명한 사업가인 알렌 케인 씨일 것입니다.
13. 여러 공장 직원들은 그들이 반드시 수행해야 하는 업무의 반복적인 특성으로부터 초래된 근육통에 대해 불평했다.
14. 우리의 새로운 자동차에 대한 많은 선주문 수치는 지금까지 매우 고무적이다.
15. 그린 힐스는 훌륭한 공원과 학교들 덕분에 가족들을 위한 매우 매력적인 동네가 되었다.
16. 그 파일을 다운로드하기 전에, 직원들은 그 형식이 그들의 모바일 기기와 호환되는지 확인해야 한다.
17. 그 시장은 도시가 육상 행사를 개최하기 위해 선택되도록 확실히 하기 위해 그의 영향력을 최대로 사용하는 것을 목표로 한다.
18. 저희 웹 사이트는 터틀 아일랜드로의 귀하의 방문이 순조롭도록 하기 위해 여러 유용한 팁들을 포함하고 있습니다.
19. 저희 웹 사이트에 회원으로 등록하시자마자, 귀하께서는 변경해야 하는 임시 비밀번호를 받으실 것입니다.
20. 글렌 씨가 밋첨 기업에 합류한 이후로, 그 회사는 연례 지출에서의 30퍼센트의 주목할 만한 감소를 목격했다.
21. 모든 공장 근로자들은 위험한 기계를 가동할 때 보호 마스크 및 장갑을 착용하는 것이 요구된다.
22. 고용 위원회는 결국 오랜 숙고 끝에 헬렌 존스 씨에게 계약을 제안하기로 결정했다.
23. 새로운 환경에 적응하는 것은 힘들 수 있으니, 어떤 도움이라도 필요하시다면 언제든지 저에게 물어보는 것을 주저하지 마십시오.
24. 팻슨 교통공사의 여러 새로운 버스 노선들이 9월에 운영될 것입니다.
25. 작가 스테판 랭 씨의 가장 인기 있는 소설의 최신판은 편집자의 서문을 포함할 것이다.
26. 모든 공장 근로자들은 항상 첨부된 안전 지침을 따라야 한다.
27. 폴리 과학 박물관은 모든 연령대의 방문객들이 흥미롭게 여길 상호작용하는 전시회들이 많이 있다.
28. 우리 이메일 서비스 이용자들은 하루에 받는 스팸 이메일의 양이 압도적인 것에 항상 불평하고 있다.
29. 이 달의 콘서트 시리즈는 세계에서 가장 뛰어난 많은 음악가들을 특집으로 할 것이다.
30. 재포장 과정 동안에, 직원 주차장의 지정된 구역만 사용할 수 있을 것입니다.
31. 모든 메츠 렌탈 사의 차량들은 최고급 인공위성 길 안내 시스템을 완벽하게 갖추고 있습니다.
32. 과도한 소음은 사무실 환경에서의 주된 방해를 일으킬 수 있고, 이는 감소된 생산성으로 이어진다.
33. 인테리어 디자이너인 존 리 씨는 바닥 공간의 경제적인 활용으로 유명하다.
34. 수바루 자동차 사는 대가족들에게 적합한 더 넓은 자동차들을 생산하는 것으로 유명하다.
35. 저희 프랭클린 가스 서비스 사의 창립 20주년 기념 행사에 여러 재능 있는 지역 음악가분들을 모시게 되어 운이 좋다고 생각합니다.
36. 트로이 메뉴펙쳐링 사는 랜드리 씨의 팀이 가장 덜 생산적이며 추가 교육이 필요하다는 것을 알아냈다.
37. 엘링턴 주식회사의 증가하는 직원들의 요구를 충족하기 위해, 회사는 새로운 직원 식당의 건설을 승인했다.
38. 새로운 자부 250 노트북이 다른 컴퓨터들과 비슷하게 보임에도 불구하고, 그것은 지금까지 시장에서 가장 가볍다.
39. 모닝 썬 항공사는 가족들과 5명 또는 그 이상의 단체 고객에 대해 다수의 목적지로 향하는 할인 항공편을 제공하고 있다.
40. 인사부는 고위 경영진과 직원들 사이의 의사소통을 용이하게 하는 데 중요한 역할을 한다.

DAILY QUIZ

7.

해석 각 부장들은 로든 파이낸셜 사에 고용된 이후 지정된 주차 공간을 배정받는다.

해설 빈칸에는 빈칸 뒤에 제시된 복합명사 parking

space를 수식하면서, 고용 이후 부장들이 배정받는 주차장의 특징을 설명할 수 있는 어휘가 필요하므로 '지정된'이라는 의미의 (D)가 정답이다.

어휘 assign ~을 배정하다 moderate 완화되다, 누그러뜨리다 tolerate ~을 용인하다, 참다 designated 지정된

8.

해석 창 씨는 까다로운 상사임에도 불구하고, 그는 여전히 대부분의 직원들에게 인기가 있다.

해설 빈칸에는 빈칸 뒤에 제시된 명사 supervisor를 수식하면서, 창 씨의 특징을 설명할 수 있는 어휘가 필요하다. 문맥상 '부정적인 성격에도 불구하고 대부분의 직원들에게 인기 있다'는 의미가 되어야 자연스러우므로 '까다로운, 힘든'이라는 의미의 (A)가 정답이다.

어휘 well-liked 인기 있는 demanding 까다로운, 힘든 collective 집단의, 공동의

Day 04 형용사+전치사 콜로케이션

표제어 문제 정답 및 해석

1. (B) 2. (A) 3. (A) 4. (B) 5. (B)
6. (B) 7. (A) 8. (B) 9. (A) 10. (A)
11. (B) 12. (A) 13. (A) 14. (B) 15. (A)
16. (A) 17. (B) 18. (B) 19. (A) 20. (A)
21. (A) 22. (A) 23. (A) 24. (A) 25. (B)
26. (A) 27. (B) 28. (B) 29. (A) 30. (A)
31. (B) 32. (A) 33. (A) 34. (A) 35. (A)
36. (B) 37. (B) 38. (A) 39. (A) 40. (B)

1. 휴가에 대한 모든 요청은 검토의 대상이며, 주로 직급에 의해 결정된다.
2. 인사부장의 직무를 맡은 이후로, 다이아스 씨는 우리 직원들의 요구에 대해 매우 빠른 반응을 보여왔다.
3. 대부분의 청자들에게, 그 밴드에 의해 공연된 커버 곡들이 원래의 버전과 동일하게 들렸다.
4. 모든 로데오 버거 직원들은 교대 근무 마다 1시간의 식사 휴게시간의 자격이 있다.
5. 라트너 씨는 엣지몬트 호텔의 연회장이 우리의 필요에 충분한 단 하나의 장소라고 생각한다.
6. 귀하의 면접 동안, 귀하께서 지원하신 직무와 관련이 있는 정보만을 공유하도록 노력해주십시오.
7. 광고 예산의 대다수가 TV 상업 광고 시리즈를 개발하는 데에 바쳐졌다.
8. 회사의 올해의 직원상에 대한 자격이 있기 위해서는, 5일 이상 결근을 하면 안 된다.
9. 리모델링 작업은 윌밍턴 호텔의 메인 로비를 투숙객들에게 더 매력적이게 만들 것이다.
10. 선글라스의 진열이 계단대 바로 옆에 준비되어서, 쇼핑객들의 눈에 아주 잘 보인다.
11. 그 식당 소유주는 종업원들이 우리 식사 손님들의 요구에 주의를 기울일 것을 요청했다.
12. 한 개의 로봇의 설치와 유지보수는 5명의 직원들의 연봉을 지불하는 것과 동등하다.
13. 공청회 동안, 대부분의 지역 주민들은 버려진 극장의 제안된 철거에 동의하는 것처럼 보였다.
14. 보호 코팅이 처리되지 않은 목재는 습기로부터의 손상에 더 취약하다.
15. 환불을 위해 파손되지 않은 제품을 반품할 때, 고객들은 어떠한 배송 비용에 대해도 책임이 있을 것이다.
16. 우리 인테리어 디자인팀이 사무실 배치에 대해 변경하기 전에, 우리는 이 디자인이 고객들에게 받아들여질 수 있는지를 확실히 할 필요가 있다.
17. 컨트리 클럽의 새로운 회원들은 주차 허가증을 신청해야 하는데, 이것은 6개월 동안 유효하다.
18. 오전 9시에 출발하는 투어에 관심이 있는 호텔 투숙객들은 프론트 데스크 직원에게 알려주셔야 합니다.
19. 에딘버러에 본사를 둔 사타이어 항공사는 암스테르담과 브뤼셀로의 저비용 항공편을 제공하고 있다.
20. 역할극 활동을 위해, 워크숍 참석자들은 그들의 직업 분야에 기반해 그룹으로 분리되었다.
21. 오리엔테이션 시간에, 신입사원들은 특정 부서에

배정될 것이다.
22. 모든 조립 라인 직원들은 공장의 안전 규정을 알고 있는 것으로 예상된다.
23. 루니 씨는 애플비 씨가 특히 공개 연설에 능숙하다고 생각한다.
24. 그 시제품에 추가 수정을 할 것인지에 대한 결정은 고객 피드백에 달려있다.
25. 드월 치과의 새로운 치과의사인 히난 씨는 월요일에 오전 9시부터 예약이 가능할 것이다.
26. A1 레스토랑의 요리사들은 어떠한 식사 손님의 선호에 맞는 주문 제작 요리를 할 수 있다.
27. 오락 시설 복합단지를 건설하는 비용이 높음에도 불구하고, 시 의회 의원들은 그 프로젝트가 경제에 이로울 것이라는 점에 동의했다.
28. 50달러 쿠폰은 힐리 체육관에서 회원권 갱신 비용에 적용될 수 있다.
29. 우롱 지역에 익숙한 많은 환경 과학자들은 몇 달 동안 기온이 계속해서 상승할 것이라고 예측한다.
30. 타란트 씨는 회사 직원들에게 지불되는 연장근무 수당을 줄이는 것에 회의적이었는데, 많은 직원들이 퇴사할 것이라고 생각했기 때문이다.
31. 귀하의 차량이 주차비에서 면제되었는지 확인하시기 위해, 안내판을 참조하십시오.
32. 여행 가이드의 최신 판이 지난 버전과 유사함에도 불구하고, 그것은 도시의 개선된 지도를 포함하고 있다.
33. 청 씨는 그 직무에 대한 가장 자격을 잘 갖춘 후보자로 선정되기 전에 이번 주에 일련의 면접들을 볼 것이다.
34. 귀하의 새로운 하이브 홈 난방 허브는 모든 하이브 라디에이터 스마트 밸브 장치와 호환됩니다.
35. 에드몬드 아서튼 씨에 의해 촬영된 새로운 다큐멘터리는 여행과 탐험에 대해 열정적인 사람들에게 특히 매력적으로 다가갈 것이다.
36. 잔지바 비치 리조트는 귀하의 피드백에 감사하며, 귀하의 다음 방문에 귀하를 환영하기를 고대합니다.
37. 아주 긴 배터리 수명과 극도로 강력한 운영 체제는 지오 3 휴대전화를 다른 선도적인 모델들보다 우수하게 만든다.
38. 롤린스 씨는 작년에 최고 재무 관리자 직책을 맡은 이후로 회사의 연 매출이 20퍼센트 증가한 것에 대해 공로를 인정받고 있다.
39. 일링 현대 미술관의 소유주들은 그들이 어떤 예술 작품을 전시할지에 대해 까다롭다.
40. 젤 스키 리조트에 있는 모든 별장들은 온수 욕조와 바베큐장을 갖추고 있다.

DAILY QUIZ

7.
해석 오전 요가 수업에 관심이 있는 호텔 투숙객들은 누구든지 오전 7시에 헬스장으로 오십시오.
해설 빈칸 뒤에 제시된 전치사 in과 함께 쓰이면서 특정 시간에 헬스장으로 가야 하는 투숙객의 특징을 나타내야 하므로 in과 함께 '~에 관심이 있는'을 의미하는 (C)가 정답이다.
어휘 **interested in** ~에 관심이 있는 **connected** 관련이 있는 **contained** 억제하는, 침착한

8.
해석 최근 취합된 시장 조사 결과에 근거한 그 보고서는 우리의 현재 프로젝트와 관련이 있는 세부사항들만을 포함하고 있다.
해설 빈칸 뒤 전치사 to와 함께 쓰이면서 현 프로젝트와 세부사항의 연관성을 나타낼 수 있는 '~와 관련이 있는'의 의미인 (C)가 정답이다.
어휘 **compile** ~을 취합하다, 편집하다 **relevant to** ~와 관련이 있는 **acceptable** 수용 가능한, 만족스러운 **certain** 확실한

Week 06 실전 TEST

1. (B)	2. (A)	3. (C)	4. (A)	5. (D)
6. (D)	7. (D)	8. (D)	9. (C)	10. (B)
11. (D)	12. (C)	13. (C)	14. (B)	15. (B)
16. (D)	17. (C)	18. (D)	19. (D)	20. (C)

1-3.

M: Julie, **1** are you excited for the annual awards banquet? Everyone has been talking about it.
W: I heard the venue is bigger than ever this year!
M: That's right. And **2** our company was able to hire a luxury caterer at a reasonable rate, too.
W: That's great to hear. Have you decided how you're getting to the event yet?
M: I'll probably take public transportation. There's a bus that goes straight there.
W: Wow, that's nice! I had planned to drive there myself, but **3** I was concerned about the potential traffic congestion in that area.

남: 줄리 씨, 연례 시상식 연회가 기대되세요? 모든 사람이 계속 그 이야기를 하고 있어요.
여: 제가 듣기로는 행사장이 올해 그 어느 때보다 더 크다고 하던데요!
남: 맞아요. 그리고 우리 회사에서 합리적인 요금으로 고급 출장 요리 업체도 고용할 수 있었어요.
여: 그 얘기를 들으니 기쁘네요. 행사장에 어떻게 가실지 혹시 결정하셨나요?
남: 저는 아마 대중 교통을 이용할 것 같아요. 그곳으로 곧장 가는 버스가 있거든요.
여: 와우, 잘됐네요! 저는 직접 차를 운전해서 갈 계획이었는데, 그 지역의 잠재적인 교통 혼잡 문제가 걱정되었어요.

어휘 annual 연례적인 banquet 연회 venue 행사장, 개최 장소 than ever 그 어느 때보다 hire ~을 고용하다 caterer 출장 요리 업체 reasonable 합리적인 rate 요금, 비율, 속도, 등급 get to ~로 가다 be concerned about ~을 걱정하다, ~을 우려하다 potential 잠재적인 traffic congestion 교통 혼잡

1. 화자들이 무엇을 이야기하고 있는가?
(A) 기술 컨퍼런스
(B) 연례 행사
(C) 제품 출시
(D) 고용 계약
Paraphrase annual awards banquet
→ yearly event

2. 남자가 출장 요리 업체와 관련해 무엇을 언급하는가?
(A) 예약하기에 가격이 알맞은 곳이었다.
(B) 현장에 많은 직원들이 있을 것이다.
(C) 음식 수준이 뛰어나다.
(D) 무제한 다과를 제공할 것이다.
어휘 affordable 가격이 알맞은 reserve ~을 예약하다 on site 현장에 outstanding 뛰어난, 우수한 unlimited 무제한의 refreshments 다과, 간식
Paraphrase at a reasonable rate
→ affordable

3. 여자는 무엇을 우려하는가?
(A) 행사장을 찾는 일
(B) 마감 기한을 충족하는 일
(C) 교통 체증에 갇혀 있는 일
(D) 예산 범위 내에 머물러 있는 일
어휘 meet ~을 충족하다 get stuck in traffic 교통 체증에 갇히다 budget 예산
Paraphrase traffic congestion
→ Getting stuck in traffic

4-6.

4 Welcome to your first day at the CGJ BioTech summer internship. You'll be mainly tasked with assignments in the laboratory, but there will be times where we'll need you to help make social media content to help promote our research projects. Also, **5** our safety regulations have been revised recently. Please remember that when in the lab, loose clothing is not recommended, and long pants and close-toed shoes must be worn at all times. Now, **6** I'm going to give you a tour of our facilities and show you our state-of-the-art equipment.

CGJ 바이오테크 여름 인턴 프로그램의 첫째 날에 오신 것을 환영합니다. 여러분께서는 실험실 내에서의 할당 업무를 주로 맡으시게 되겠지만, 우리 연구 프로젝트를 홍보하는 데 도움이 될 수 있도록 소셜 미디어 콘텐츠를 만드는 데 도움을 주실 필요가 있는 시간도 있을 것입니다. 또한, 우리 안전 규정이 최근에 변경되었습니다. 실험실에 계실 때, 헐렁한 옷차림은 권장되지 않으며, 긴 바지와 발가락 부분이 막힌 신발을 반드시 항상 착용하셔야 한다는 점을 기억하시기 바랍니다. 이제, 제가 우리 시설을 견학시켜 드리고 최신 장비도 보여 드리겠습니다.

어휘 be tasked with ~에 대한 업무를 맡다 assignment (할당되는) 업무 laboratory 실험실(= lab) promote ~을 홍보하다 regulation 규정, 규제 revise ~을 변경하다, ~을 수정하다 recently 최근에 loose 헐렁한 close-toed 발가락 부분이 막힌 at all times 항상 facility 시설(물) state-of-the-art 최신의 equipment 장비

4. 청자들은 누구인가?
(A) 신입 인턴들
(B) 잠재 투자자들
(C) 연구 참가자들
(D) 보안 직원들

어휘 potential 잠재적인 investor 투자자 participant 참가자

5. 최근에 무엇이 변경되었는가?
(A) 공사 제안서
(B) 환급 정책
(C) 사무실 평면도
(D) 일부 안전 지침

어휘 proposal 제안(서) reimbursement (비용) 환급 policy 정책, 방침 floorplan 평면도
Paraphrase safety regulations
→ safety guidelines

6. 화자가 곧이어 무엇을 할 것인가?
(A) 기계 이용법을 시연하는 일
(B) 점검을 위해 제품 하나를 따로 챙겨두는 일
(C) 고객 문의 사항을 처리하는 일
(D) 근무지 견학을 제공하는 일

어휘 demonstrate ~을 시연하다 how to do ~하는 법 set aside ~을 따로 챙겨두다, ~을 한쪽으로 치워 놓다 inspection 점검 handle ~을 처리하다, ~을 다루다 inquiry 문의
Paraphrase give you a tour of our facilities
→ Give a tour of a workplace

7.
해석 최근에 고용된 영업팀 부장은 입사 첫 달에 250명의 신규 고객을 유치하겠다는 야심찬 목표를 갖고 있었다.
해설 빈칸에는 빈칸 뒤에 제시된 명사 target을 수식해 250명의 신규 고객을 유치하는 목표가 지니는 특징을 나타내야 하므로 '야심찬'을 뜻하는 (D)가 정답이다.
어휘 prosperous 번영한, 번창한 spacious 넓은 ambitious 야심찬

8.
해석 직원들의 능력과 경험은 우리 회사에 중요하므

로, 모든 구직 지원자들에 대한 취업 이력 확인은 의무적이다.
해설 빈칸 앞에는 직원들의 능력과 경험이 중요하다는 내용이 있으므로 빈칸 뒤에 제시된 지원자들의 고용 이력을 확인하는 일이 꼭 필요하다는 것을 알 수 있다. 따라서 '의무적인'이라는 의미의 (D)가 정답이다.
어휘 liable ~하기 쉬운, ~할 것 같은 renewable 갱신 가능한, 재생 가능한 mandatory 의무적인

9.
해석 호텔 투숙객들께서는 저희의 예정된 공항 셔틀 버스를 승차하실 계획이 있다면 반드시 시간을 엄수하셔야 합니다.
해설 빈칸에는 예정된 셔틀 버스를 탈 의향이 있는 호텔 투숙객들이 지켜야 할 사항과 관련된 어휘가 와야 한다. 따라서 '시간을 엄수하는'이라는 의미를 나타내는 (C)가 정답이다.
어휘 board 승차하다, 승선하다 eventual 궁극적인, 최종의 immediate 즉각적인 punctual 시간을 엄수하는

10.
해석 더글라스 스포츠 센터는 또한 여러 행사를 연속해서 수용할 수 있는 엄청난 야외 운동 경기장도 가지고 있다.
해설 빈칸에는 빈칸 뒤에 제시된 명사구 outdoor sports field를 수식하면서 여러 행사를 연속으로 수용할 수 있는 규모를 나타낼 수 있는 어휘가 필요하므로 '엄청난 (양의), 방대한 (크기의)'이라는 뜻의 (B)가 정답이다.
어휘 consecutively 연속해서 alert 기민한, 조심성 있는 immense 엄청난 (양의), 방대한 (크기의)

11.
해석 올해 재즈 축제의 잠정적인 일자가 정해졌지만, 그것은 그 장소가 시간 내에 개조될 것인지에 달려 있다.
해설 빈칸 뒤에 축제 장소가 제시간에 개조가 완료되는지에 달려 있다는 내용이 언급되어 있으므로 축제 행사의 날짜가 확정된 것이 아니라는 것을 알 수 있다. 따라서 '잠정적인, 임시의'라는 의미의 (D)가 정답이다.
어휘 in time 시간 내에, 제시간에 pending 임박한 sudden 갑작스러운 tentative 잠정적인, 임시의

12.
해석 아미티지 씨에 의해 제안된 제조 공정은 운영 비용의 상당한 감소를 초래할 것이다.
해설 빈칸에는 제안된 제조 공정이 영향을 끼친 운영 비용의 감소 수준을 나타낼 어휘가 필요하므로 '(크기, 액수가) 상당한'이라는 의미의 (C)가 정답이다.
어휘 operating 운영 spacious 넓은 sizable (크기, 액수가) 상당한 durable 오래 가는, 내구성 있는

13.
해석 새로운 통역 서비스는 개리 프라이빗 렌터카를 외국 관광객들에게 더 매력적으로 만들 것이다.
해설 빈칸에는 새로 추가되는 서비스가 기업에 미치는 영향을 나타내는 어휘가 필요하므로 빈칸 뒤의 전치사 to와 함께 '~에게 매력적인'이라는 뜻의 (C)가 정답이다.
어휘 interpretation 통역 attractive to ~에게 매력적인 separated 분리된

14.
해석 4층에서 보수공사 중인 공간들은 1월 23일 월요일 오전 9시까지 회의를 위해 이용 가능할 것이다.
해설 빈칸 앞에 제시된 주어인 rooms가 빈칸 뒤에 언급된 특정 일시까지 이용 가능할 것이라고 해석하는 것이 자연스러우므로 빈칸 앞에 제시된 전치사 for와 함께 '~을 이용 가능한, ~을 위한 시간이 있는'이라는 뜻인 (B)가 정답이다.
어휘 available for ~을 이용 가능한, ~을 위한 시간이 있는 by ~까지 grateful 기쁜 generous 관대한

15-18.

수신: 신수케 이토 <s.Ito@bestapparel.com>
발신: 그랜트 우드 <gwood@mbtextiles.com>
주제: 견본들

이토 씨께,

저희는 귀하가 6월 20일에 보내주신 문의를 환영하는 바이며, 저희 상품에 대한 귀하의 관심에 감사드립니다. 오늘 저희의 카탈로그와 몇몇의 견본들이 속달 우편 **15** 으로 귀하에게 보내질 것입니다. 안타깝게도, 저희는 현재 전체 종류의 견본들을 귀하께 보낼 수가 없지만, 견본들은 완제품과 같은 고품질입니다.

16 귀하가 저희 상품을 보실 수 있는 방법에 대해 한 가지 생각이 있습니다. 저희의 해외 담당 이사인 김 씨께서 다음 달 초에 일본에 계실 것이며, 귀하를 기꺼이 방문하실 것입니다. 그는 다양한 저희 상품을 가지고 있을 것이며, 귀하가 그것들을 보면, 재료의 품질과 높은 수준의 솜씨가 그들이 구매하는 제품들에 대해 **17** 까다로운 사람들에게 매력적일 것이라는 점에 동의하시리라 생각합니다.

저희는 귀하로부터의 주문을 **18** 받을 수 있기를 아주 많이 기대하고 있습니다.

안녕히 계십시오.

그랜트 우드

어휘 make an inquiry 문의하다 finished product 완제품 call on ~을 방문하다 craftsmanship 솜씨, 장인정신 appeal to ~에게 매력적이다

15.

해설 빈칸 앞에 이메일의 작성자가 견본들을 보낸다는 내용이, 빈칸 뒤에 속달 우편이 제시되어 있으므로 속달 우편이 견본들을 보내는 수단임을 알 수 있다. 따라서 '~으로, ~을 사용하여'라는 의미의 (B)가 정답이다.

16.

(A) 저희는 귀하가 저희의 본사로 오시기를 바랍니다.
(B) 저희 제품이 내일 귀하에게 발송될 것입니다.
(C) 저희 제품에 대한 피드백을 보내주셔서 감사합니다.
(D) 귀하가 저희 상품을 보실 수 있는 방법에 대해 한 가지 생각이 있습니다.

해설 빈칸 앞 문단에서 '전체 견본들을 보내주지 못하지만, 일부 견본들은 보내주겠다'는 내용이 언급되어 있고, 빈칸 뒤에 '해외 담당 이사가 방문해서 다양한 제품을 보여줄 것이다'라는 내용이 언급되어 있다. 따라서 빈칸에는 '제품을 볼 수 있는 방법에 대한 생각이 있다'라는 내용의 (D)가 정답이다.

17.

해설 빈칸에는 빈칸 앞에 제시된 자사 재료의 품질과 높은 수준의 솜씨가 제품을 구매하는 사람들에게 매력적일 것이라는 내용이 언급되어 있으므로 빈칸에는 고객들에 대한 특성을 설명할 수 있는 어휘가 와야 한다. 따라서 전치사 about과 함께 '~에 대해 까다로운'의 의미를 가진 (C)가 정답이다.

어휘 selective about ~에 대해 까다로운
curious 호기심이 많은 prominent 저명한

18.

해설 빈칸 앞에 look forward to가 제시되어 있으므로 전치사 to 뒤에 올 수 있는 동명사 (D)가 정답이다.

19-20.

http://www.heavenlycatering.com/aboutus

| 소개 | 서비스 | **19** 갤러리 | 연락처 | 후기 |

헤븐리 케이터링 사는 7년 동안 영업 중이며, 요리 솜씨에 대한 명성을 얻은 후로 현재는 광범위한 고객층을 자랑합니다. 저희는 모든 식단 선호도를 수용하여 요청 시에 맞춤 메뉴를 제공하고, 요리에 잠재적인 알레르기 유발 항원의 존재를 나타낸 스티커를 사용해 분명하게 라벨을 붙이고 있습니다. **19** 저희가 제공하는 음식들을 미리 보시려면, 저희의 가장 인기 있는 요리들 중 일부를 소개하는 갤러리를 방문하실 것을 권고 드립니다.

최근 몇년 동안, 저희는 더욱 환경 친화적이도록 노력해오고 있습니다. 비록 어떠한 정부 기준의 위반도 없었지만, 저희는 합성 구성품들을 사용하는 것을 중지하기로 결정하고, **20** 에너지 효율적인 주방 기구들을 설치했습니다. 이러한 접근은 또한 소형 휴대용 런치 박스 제품군에도 적용되었습니다.

저희 제품과 서비스에 관해 문의사항이 있으시다면, 저희에게 연락주세요! 첫 고객님은 첫 케이터링 서비스에 대해 50달러를 절약하실 수 있습니다.

어휘 in business 영업 중인 boast ~을 자랑하다 culinary 요리의 customized 맞춤의 upon request 요청 시에 dietary preference 식단 선호도 presence 존재(감) allergen 알레르기 유발 항원 urge ~을 권고하다, 촉구하다 showcase ~을 소개하다 in violation of ~을 위반하여 synthetic 합성의 approach 접근(법) compact 소형 portable 휴대용의

19. 헤븐리 케이터링 사에 대해 사실인 것은 무엇인가?
(A) 10년 전에 설립되었다.
(B) 여러 사업 지점을 운영한다.
(C) 현재 새로운 직원들을 채용 중이다.
(D) 자사 웹 사이트에 음식 사진을 포함한다.

해설 첫 번째 문단 마지막 줄에 헤븐리 케이터링 사가 제공하는 음식을 미리 보려면, 인기 있는 메뉴를 보여주는 갤러리를 방문해달라고 언급하고 있는데, 지문 상단에 GALLERY 탭을 확인할 수 있으므로 (D)가 정답이다.

20. 헤븐리 케이터링 사는 환경을 돕기 위해 무엇을 했는가?
(A) 자선 기부금을 냈다.
(B) 배송 서비스를 변경했다.
(C) 새로운 장비를 설치했다.
(D) 금속 식기류를 도입했다.

해설 두 번째 문단에 헤븐리 케이터링 사는 환경에 대한 정부 규정을 위반한 적이 없지만, 환경친화적이기 위해 합성 구성품들의 사용을 중단하고, 에너지 효율적인 주방 기구들을 설치했다는 내용이 나와 있다. 따라서 환경을 위해 새 장비를 설치했다는 내용의 (C)가 정답이다.

어휘 charitable 자선의 cutlery 식기류

Week 07
정답 및 해설

Day 01 기출 패러프레이징 ②

DAILY QUIZ

1.

남: 안녕하세요, 캔디스 씨, 우리 공장의 손 비누 생산 수준이 지난주에 많이 증가해서 용기 공급이 벌써 부족해지고 있어요. 병을 더 주문해 주실 수 있나요?
여: 물론이죠, 그런데 어느 공급업체에 연락해야 하나요?
남: 지난번에 이용했던 공급업체를 이용합시다. 거기가 매우 효율적이었어요.

Q. 화자들은 어디에서 일하겠는가?
(A) 제조 시설에서
(B) 식료품점에서

어휘 production 생산 level 수준 hand soap 손 비누 factory 공장 increase 증가하다 supply 공급 dispenser (손잡이를 눌러 안에 든 것을 사용할 수 있는) 용기 bottle 병 get low 줄어들다 place an order for ~을 주문하다 supplier 공급업체(=provider) contact ~에게 연락하다 go with ~로 결정하다 efficient 효율적인 manufacturing facility 제조 시설 grocery store 식료품점

2.

남: 실례합니다만, 가장 가까운 지하철역까지 가는 길을 아십니까?
여: 물론이죠. 저기 은행 보이세요? 은행 방향으로 걷다가 교차로에서 좌회전하면 세 블록 정도 더 가서 세븐 씨즈 역이 나옵니다.

Q. 남자는 왜 여자에게 말을 거는가?
(A) 기차표를 예약하기 위해
(B) 길 안내를 요청하기 위해

어휘 how to get to ~로 가는 길 turn left 좌회전하다 intersection 교차로 be about three blocks further down 3블럭 정도 더 가면 있다 reserve ~을 예약하다 ask for ~을 요청하다 directions 길 안내

3.

안녕하세요, 프랭클린 도서관에서 전화 드린 수민입니다. 귀하께서 연례 도서 리뷰 콘테스트의 우승자로 선정되셨음을 알려드리게 되어 기쁘게 생각합니다. 축하드립니다! 도서관 운영 시간 중에 도서관에 들러 주시면 지역 영화관에서 사용 가능한 상품권인 상품을 수령하실 수 있습니다.

Q. 화자는 청자가 무엇을 받을 것이라고 말하는가?
(A) 식당 쿠폰
(B) 영화관 상품권

어휘 be happy to do ~하게 되어 기쁘다 notify A that절 A에게 ~에 대해 알리다 winner 우승자 book review 도서 후기 contest 대회 Congratulations 축하합니다 pick up ~을 수령하다 prize 상품 gift certificate 상품권 valid 유효한 cinema 영화관 stop by ~에 들르다 hours of operation 운영 시간 movie theater 영화관 voucher 상품권

Day 02 부사 ①

표제어 문제 정답 및 해석

1. (A)	2. (A)	3. (B)	4. (A)	5. (A)
6. (A)	7. (A)	8. (B)	9. (B)	10. (A)
11. (A)	12. (B)	13. (A)	14. (B)	15. (B)
16. (A)	17. (A)	18. (B)	19. (A)	20. (A)
21. (B)	22. (B)	23. (A)	24. (A)	25. (A)
26. (A)	27. (A)	28. (B)	29. (A)	30. (A)
31. (B)	32. (A)	33. (A)	34. (A)	35. (A)
36. (A)	37. (A)	38. (A)	39. (A)	40. (A)

1. 그레이브 씨가 연차인 동안에, 주간 업무 일정은 존스 씨에 의해 대신 만들어질 것이다.
2. 제프리는 이미 월 매출 목표를 넘었다. 따라서 그는 보너스를 받게 될 것이다.
3. 필 씨는 모금 행사를 위한 장소를 예약했다. 그리고 나서 손님들에게 발송할 초대장을 만들었다.
4. 저희는 연말 전까지 유통망을 확장하는 것을 계획하고 있습니다. 현재, 우리는 디트로이트 지역 내에 기반을 둔 고객들에게만 배송하고 있습니다.
5. 우리 레스토랑의 이름의 변경에 관한 결정이 되면, 우리 메뉴들도 그에 맞춰 변경될 것이다.
6. 음악가 빌 메디슨의 노래들은 상을 받은 TV 시리즈에 특별히 포함된 후에 점점 더 인기 있어졌다.
7. 올해 뮤직 페스티벌에 있는 모든 참석자들은 안전하게 그리고 책임감 있게 행동하도록 상기시켰다.
8. 수석 건축가는 쇼핑몰 청사진에 더 많은 구조를 추가하는 것이 재정적으로 실현 불가능하다는 것을 내비쳤다.
9. 샌드윅 씨는 그의 이미 수익성이 있는 사업체에서 수입을 증가시킬 새로운 방법들을 찾았다.
10. 여행객들은 도시의 버스 투어에 합류함으로써 여러 관광지를 쉽게 방문할 수 있다.
11. 두 달의 협상 후에, 아처 건설 사는 새로운 국제공항을 건설할 계약을 마침내 따냈다.
12. 도시의 연례 영화 페스티벌의 지연은 주로 안전 점검에 실패한 제안된 행사 장소로 인한 것이었다.
13. 생산 효율성을 최대화하기 위해, 그 공장 관리인은 조립 라인에 있는 직원들을 계속해서 동기부여 해야 한다.
14. 흠이 있는 보안 카메라들의 문제는 우리가 3층 엘리베이터를 수리한 직후에 주의를 기울일 것이다.
15. 우리의 새로운 롤러코스터의 추가 덕분에, 입장권 판매가 지난 여름과 비교하여 거의 3배가 되었다.
16. 베수비어스 소프트웨어 회사는 최근에 도시의 외곽에 있는 공업 단지로 이전했다.
17. 모든 공장 방문객들은 도착하는 즉시 안전 장비를 착용해야 한다.
18. 우리의 맛있는 소스들의 종류는 평범한 식사를 기억에 남을만한 식사 경험으로 다르게 바꿔줄 수 있다.
19. 그린웨이 슈퍼마켓에 있는 모든 선반들은 고객들이 필요한 물품들을 항상 찾을 수 있도록 확실히 하기 위해 자주 재고가 채워진다.
20. 게임 일정과 결과는 보통 그 야구팀의 웹 사이트에 게시된다.
21. 해안 지역의 기온은 몇 주 미리 떨어질 것으로 예상된다.
22. 졸라 스마트폰에 대한 수요는 기기의 디자인이 작년에 변경된 이후로 분명히 감소해왔다.
23. 서던 치킨에서의 신입직원들은 두 개의 근무복을 처음에 제공받지만, 추가의 근무복은 요청 시에 받을 수 있다.
24. 편랜드 장난감 가게의 대개장은 구체적으로 학교 방학 첫 날에 열릴 것으로 일정이 잡혔다.
25. 그레인저 씨는 일관성 있게 뛰어난 영업 성과에 대해 연례 시상식에서 인정 받았다.
26. 새로운 겨울 자켓의 진열은 고객의 관심을 끌기 위해 입구에 가까운 곳에 의도적으로 정리되어 있다.
27. 그 감독은 영화 시사회를 떠나기 전에 아주 잠깐 관객들에게 말했다.
28. 부동산 시장 전문가들은 주택 가격이 아마도 다음 5년 동안 상당히 증가할 것이라고 생각한다.
29. 그 대표이사는 비용을 줄이기 위해 약간 더 저렴한 포장 재료를 사용하는 것을 제안했다.
30. 자코비 주식회사의 회장 출신인 에드워드 존스 씨는 그의 새로운 기술 회사의 출시를 발표했다.
31. 귀하의 기차표를 인쇄하여 그것을 역에 있는 직원에게 제시해주십시오. 대신, 전자 티켓 버전을 보여주셔도 됩니다.
32. 지난달에 설립된 이래로, 볼니콘 사는 주로 한국에 기반을 둔 회사들로부터 많은 주문을 받고 있다.
33. 등산객들은 양쪽이 가파른 절벽인 산등성이 등산길을 따라 조심스럽게 걸을 것이 권고됩니다.
34. 하몬 씨는 회사가 인력에서의 증가된 수요에 대처하는 것을 돕기 위해 적어도 10명의 새로운 영업직원들을 이상적으로 고용할 것이다.
35. 그레타 모팻 씨는 재활용된 나무로 수제 가구를 능숙하게 만드는 것으로 유명하다.

36. 메즈다 자동차 회사에 의해 제조된 새로운 차는 긴 로드 트립을 가는 것을 즐기는 중규모의 가족들에게 완벽하게 적합하다.
37. 귀하의 새로운 핏마스터 러닝머신을 조립하기 위해서, 간단히 사용자 매뉴얼에 있는 설명서를 따르세요.
38. 길만 백화점은 12월 24일이 특히 바쁜 쇼핑날이기 때문에 오후 10시까지 문을 연 상태일 것이다.
39. 스포츠 경연대회의 개막식이 이번 주 금요일 오후 7시에 정확히 시작할 것이다.
40. 우리의 로스앤젤레스 주 지점과 같이, 샌프란시스코의 새로운 옷 매장은 마찬가지로 고객의 요청에 따라 옷을 주문 제작한다.

DAILY QUIZ

7.
해석 라이젠 전자는 최근에 새 본사를 로스앤젤러스 시내로 이전했다.
해설 빈칸에는 빈칸 뒤에 제시된 동사 relocated를 수식해 새 본사를 이전한 시점을 나타낼 수 있는 어휘가 와야 하므로 '최근(에)'를 뜻하는 (C)가 정답이다.
어휘 **relocate to** ~로 이전하다 **severely** 심각하게 **recently** 최근(에) **exactly** 정확히

8.
해석 관객들이 <갤럭시 원>의 시범 상영에 대해 긍정적으로 반응했는데, 이는 이 영화는 그에 맞춰 추가 촬영이나 편집이 필요하지 않다는 것을 의미한다.
해설 시범 상영에서 긍정적인 반응이 있었다는 것은 추가 촬영 또는 편집이 필요하지 않을 것이라는 결과를 가져오므로 빈칸에는 결과적으로 발생된 일과 관련된 의미의 어휘가 와야 한다. 따라서 '그에 맞춰, (상황에) 따라서' 등의 의미의 (A)가 정답이다.
어휘 **audiences** 관객, 청중 **respond** 반응하다, 응답하다 **test screening** 시범 상영(회) **shot** 촬영 **edit** 편집 **therefore** 그에 맞춰, (상황에) 따라서 **rather** 다소, 오히려

Day 03 부사 ②

표제어 문제 정답 및 해설

1. (A)	2. (A)	3. (B)	4. (B)	5. (B)
6. (A)	7. (B)	8. (A)	9. (A)	10. (A)
11. (B)	12. (A)	13. (A)	14. (B)	15. (A)
16. (A)	17. (A)	18. (B)	19. (A)	20. (A)
21. (B)	22. (A)	23. (A)	24. (A)	25. (A)
26. (A)	27. (A)	28. (A)	29. (B)	30. (A)
31. (A)	32. (A)	33. (B)	34. (A)	35. (A)
36. (A)	37. (A)	38. (A)	39. (B)	40. (A)

1. 인공 지능에 대한 다가오는 세미나는 피니 기술 협회의 회원들에게 독점적으로 공개될 것이다.
2. 안타깝게도, 박물관의 주된 전시회장이 3월 1일까지 방문객들에게 폐쇄될 것이다.
3. 에드워드 씨는 자전거로 통근하는 것을 선호하며, 드물게 대중교통이나 자차를 사용한다.
4. 비행기표는 적어도 출발일의 2주 전에 취소 요청이 된다면 전액 환불될 수 있다.
5. 귀하의 구매품의 크기로 인해, 두 개의 포장 상자가 3월 5일에 귀하의 주소로 따로 배송될 것입니다.
6. 우리 온라인 포럼에 있는 사용자들에 의해 게시된 의견들이 반드시 우리 기관의 의견을 반영하는 것은 아니다.
7. 저희가 그 부동산에 대해 요청하는 가격을 정확하게 목록화했는지 확인하기 위해 부동산 중개인과 연락하십시오.
8. 머스코카 지역으로의 여행은 다음 며칠 동안 눈이 아주 많이 내릴 것으로 예상되고 있기 때문에 권고되지 않는다.
9. 시마 헬스 푸드와 플로우 선박 사이의 사업 계약은 서로 이익이 될 것이다.

10. 라이젠 4 스마트폰의 매출은 수많은 배터리 문제의 보고에도 불구하고 상당히 꾸준한 상태이다.
11. 마리오 피자의 월간 수입이 계속 증가한다면, 그 사업은 마침내 수익성이 있을 것이다.
12. 이번 여름 드물게 높은 기온 때문에, 그 회사는 자사의 사무실에 에어컨을 설치했다.
13. 맨체스터로 가는 기차가 기술적 결함으로 인해 예기치 않게 지연되었다.
14. 팜 스프링 리조트는 광범위한 종류의 편의시설을 가지고 있는데, 이는 가족들과 혼자 다니는 여행객들 모두를 위한 완벽한 선택으로 만들어 준다.
15. 벨몬트 비스트로의 소유주는 수많은 불만족하는 고객들의 피드백을 받은 후에 오징어 요리를 완전히 없애기로 결정했다.
16. 아파트 건물에서 모든 공동 구역은 하루에 2번 능숙한 유지보수팀에 의해 정기적으로 청소되고 있다.
17. 모든 구매에 대해 5퍼센트 할인을 받기 위해 회원권에 등록하세요. 추가적으로, 회원이 되시면 온라인 주문에 대한 무료 배송 혜택을 드립니다.
18. 바디 씨는 면접 동안에 이사회 임원들에게 깊은 인상을 주었고, 최고 재무 관리자 직책을 그 후에 제안받았다.
19. 피칸 호텔에서 디럭스 스위트 객실에 체크인하는 투숙객들은 스파클링 와인 1병과 과일 한 그릇을 관례상 받는다.
20. 우리가 받은 피드백에 기반하면, 고객들은 우리 웹 사이트의 새로운 레이아웃을 명백하게 좋아한다.
21. 영업에서의 경험이 거의 없기 때문에, 엣킨슨 씨는 면접관에게 깊은 인상을 남기기 위해 회사의 제품 종류에 대한 그녀의 지식에 오로지 의존했다.
22. 연례 블루포드 예술 축제는 9월의 마지막 주말에 전통적으로 개최된다.
23. 베로나 레스토랑에 있는 단독 식사 공간은 회사 연회 행사 장소로서의 우리의 요구를 충분히 충족할 것이다.
24. 세미나 중에 강당을 나가고 싶으시다면, 가능한 한 조용하게 나가십시오.
25. 반품과 환불에 관한 정책은 저희 웹 사이트에 명확하게 설명되어 있습니다.
26. 저희 웹 사이트를 통해 들어온 모든 주문들은 구매 48시간 이내에 일반적으로 배송된다.
27. 광범위한 광고 캠페인에도 불구하고, 새로운 게임기는 어느 정도 성공적이었다고 증명되었을 뿐이다.
28. 시몬 에거스 씨는 새로운 제품 개발팀의 리더로서 임시로 임명되었다.
29. 강력한 리더십과 능숙한 직원들은 사업이 성공하기 위해서 똑같이 필수적이다.
30. 가필드 극장에서 현재 상영되는 새로운 연극은 정확히 2시간 동안 진행된다.
31. 원격 재택 근무는 여러 산업군에서 점점 더 흔해지는 중인데, 특히 고객 서비스와 고객 지원에 초점을 맞춘 산업군에서 그렇다.
32. 무대가 도시의 연례 축제를 대비하기 위해 데이비스 플라자에서 현재 공사 중이다.
33. 일정에서 몇몇 약속을 취소한 후, 존스 씨는 주주 총회에 분명 참석할 수 있을 것이다.
34. 엘렌비 씨는 퍼펙트 가든 사에 의해 수행된 조경 작업에 몹시 기뻐하고 있다.
35. 새로운 고속도로는 공항과 시내 지역 사이의 더 빠른 경로를 제공한다. 또한, 지역 도로에서 교통 체증을 상당히 줄여준다.
36. 비치 타월이 모든 호텔 투숙객들에게 완전히 무료로 제공됩니다.
37. 개정된 정책에 대해 질문은 귀하께 곧 연락하게 될 인사부장에게 보내주시기 바랍니다.
38. 에어컨이 제대로 유지 보수되었다는 것을 가정하면, 그것은 적어도 25년 동안 효과적으로 작동해야 한다.
39. 4층 컨퍼런스 공간은 직원 오리엔테이션을 위해 가끔 사용되지만, 보통 중요한 고객 미팅을 위해 사용된다.
40. 고객들은 새로운 소파의 색상이 우리 웹 사이트에 있는 사진과 비교하여 눈에 띄게 다르다는 것에 불평해왔다.

DAILY QUIZ

7.
해석 음반회사에서 고인이 된 그 가수의 마지막 녹음 자료를 수집했으며, 곧 그것을 완전한 앨범의 형태로 출시할 것이다.
해석 빈칸에는 빈칸 뒤에 제시된 조동사 will과 동사 release 사이에 위치해 미래시제를 나타낼 수 있는 어휘가 와야 한다. 따라서 '곧, 조만간'이라는 뜻의 (D)가 정답이다.
어휘 recording 녹음(된 것) late 고인이 된 soon 곧, 조만간

8.
해석 중동에서의 여러 무역 계약의 종결은 올해 예치치 않게 연료비를 상승시키는 것을 야기할지도 모른다.
해석 빈칸에는 빈칸 앞에 제시된 동사 rise를 수식하여 연료비 상승의 폭을 나타낼 어휘가 필요하므로 '예치치 않게, 뜻밖에'라는 의미의 (B)가 정답이다.
어휘 agreement 계약, 합의 cause A to do A가 ~하도록 야기하다 unexpectedly 예치치 않게, 뜻밖에 apparently 명백하게, 분명하게

Day 04 동사 + 부사 콜로케이션

표제어 문제 정답 및 해석

1. (B)	2. (B)	3. (A)	4. (B)	5. (A)
6. (A)	7. (B)	8. (B)	9. (A)	10. (B)
11. (B)	12. (B)	13. (A)	14. (B)	15. (A)
16. (B)	17. (A)	18. (A)	19. (A)	20. (A)
21. (B)	22. (A)	23. (B)	24. (B)	25. (A)
26. (A)	27. (A)	28. (A)	29. (A)	30. (B)
31. (A)	32. (B)	33. (A)	34. (B)	35. (B)
36. (A)	37. (A)	38. (B)	39. (B)	40. (B)

1. 서울 뮤직 페스티벌은 자랑스럽게도 올해 많은 떠오르는 가수들을 특별히 포함할 것이다.
2. 메리 베이커리는 지역에서 생산된 신선한 재료들을 사용하는 것을 자랑스럽게 여깁니다.
3. 저희 건물 주 출입구에 도착하시자마자, 보안 데스크로 곧장 가십시오.
4. 고객 관리 직원들은 반드시 고객들의 모든 우려 사항에 즉시 반응해야 하며, 어떤 문제라도 관심을 가지고 해결해야 한다.
5. 정부 규제로 인해 전에는 이용할 수 없었던 드론을 사용한 음식 배달 서비스는 이제 인기를 얻고 있다.
6. 더 많은 급행 노선을 추가했으므로, 통근자들은 그들의 목적지까지 빠르게 이동할 수 있다.
7. 저희는 직원들이 저희의 모든 제품을 신중하게 검사하는 곳인 공장에서의 무결함 정책에 대해 자랑스럽게 여깁니다.
8. 신문사에서 인턴들의 성과는 선임 편집 직원들에 의해 자세히 관찰되고 있다.
9. 그 자동차의 높은 연비 덕분에 트라인 자동차 사의 신형 하이브리드 세단의 매출이 상당히 상승하고 있다.
10. 챔벌라인 씨의 도움 덕분에, 저의 런던으로의 전근은 매우 순조롭게 진행되었습니다.

11. 정부 조사단이 건설 현장에서 모든 잠재적 사고 원인들에 대해 철저하게 조사하고 있다.
12. 예정된 보수 작업으로 인해, 운전자들은 오늘 오후에 캠튼 다리를 피해가시는 것이 강력하게 권고됩니다.
13. 주민들께서는 메디슨 공원이 침수로 인해 금요일 이후로 일시적으로 폐쇄되었음에 유의하시기 바랍니다.
14. 제조사가 호평을 받은 게임을 출시한 이후로 비전 프로 VR 기기의 판매가 급격히 상승해왔다.
15. 레이온 전자는 아시아 전기 자동차 시장으로 빠르게 확장하면서 올해 자사의 수익이 두 배가 되었다는 것을 발표했다.
16. 다가오는 총회의 행사 장소는 지역 공항 근처에 편리하게 위치해 있으며, 또한 귀하의 호텔과도 가깝습니다.
17. 우리 회계 소프트웨어의 새로운 버전은 우리의 작업 효율성과 정확성을 상당히 증가시킬 것이다.
18. 필터를 교체할 때, 단단히 고정될 때까지 시계 방향으로 돌려주십시오.
19. 연례 의료 기술 총회가 9월 첫 주말에 임시로 일정이 잡혔다.
20. 힐 씨는 프로젝트 관리직을 공식적으로 맡게 되었고, 자신의 팀에 합류할 사람들을 선정하는 과정에 있다.
21. 우리의 새로운 SUV 차량의 수요가 두배가 되었으므로, 조립 라인 근로자들로부터의 초과근무가 긴급히 필요하다.
22. 고객 여러분은 개인 소지품이 저희가 제공하는 보관함에 안전하게 보관되도록 확실히 해주시기 바랍니다.
23. 해닝 씨의 승진은 다음 주 중에 이사회 회의에서 정식으로 발표될 것이다.
24. 라이언스 텔레커뮤니케이션은 개선된 서비스에 대한 고객 요청들에 대해 항상 호의적으로 반응해왔다.
25. 전 직원은 중요한 파일들이 보호되는 것을 확실히 하기 위해 그들의 하드 드라이브에 바이러스가 있는지 정기적으로 확인해야 한다.
26. 심콤 시스템 사는 30년 넘게 가장 혁신적인 컴퓨터 제조사로 널리 알려져 왔다.
27. 저희의 개선된 전자상거래 소프트웨어는 귀사의 직원들이 고객 주문을 더 효율적으로 처리하도록 도울 것입니다.
28. 애버딘 역사 박물관 안에서 음식이나 음료가 엄격히 금지되는 것이 저희 정책입니다.
29. 홀튼 씨는 주문이 이미 처리되었다고 착각했다.
30. 청중들은 공연 마지막에 화이트 라이언즈에게 열렬히 환호했다.
31. 혼딕스 자동차 사는 자사 차량의 에너지 소비량을 줄이기 위한 새로운 방법들을 적극적으로 찾고 있다.
32. 해리슨 씨는 헤리티지 글로벌 사와의 장기 유지 보수 계약을 성공적으로 완료했다.
33. 많은 엔터테인먼트 회사들이 잠재 고객들과 효과적으로 소통하기 위해 사회관계망서비스들을 이용한다.
34. 우리의 새 스포츠 음료인 파워바틀은 여러분의 에너지 수준을 높게 유지하면서 체중을 상당히 줄이도록 도울 수 있습니다.
35. 고대의 주거 현장이 스포츠 경기장의 건축 동안에 우연히 발견되었다.
36. 호텔에 도착하자마자, 포스터 씨는 더 큰 객실을 정중하게 요청했다.
37. 최근의 임시 직원 채용이 생산성에 긍정적 영향을 주고 있으며, 생산성이 급격히 상승하고 있다.
38. 이사회 임원들은 채드윅 씨를 새로운 최고 운영 책임자로 임명하는 것에 대해 만장일치로 투표했다.
39. 성수기 동안 저희 객실 요금이 이용 가능성에 기반하여 주기적으로 갱신된다는 것에 유의하시기 바랍니다.
40. 다음 달에 20명의 직원을 고용하기보다는, 인사부장은 다음 6개월 동안 인력을 점진적으로 확장하는 것을 제안했다.

DAILY QUIZ

7.

해석 일단 라이스맨 랩스에 도착하시면, 곧장 경비실로 가셔서 신분증을 받으시기 바랍니다.

해설 빈칸에는 빈칸 앞뒤에 제시된 동사 proceed 와 전치사 to 사이에 위치해 회사 도착 이후의 이동 방법과 관련된 어휘가 와야 한다. 따라서 proceed와 to와 함께 '~로 곧장 가다'를 뜻하는 (B)가 정답이다.

어휘 once 일단 ~하면, ~하자마자 **proceed directly to** ~로 곧장 가다 **security office** 경비실 **firmly** 굳게, 단호히

8.

해설 비크람 가스 유한회사의 이사진은 하이데라바드 에너지 사가 내놓은 합병 제안을 거절하는 것을 만장일치로 투표했다.

해설 빈칸에는 빈칸 앞에 위치한 동사 voted를 수식해 이사진이 표결한 방식을 나타내야 하므로 vote와 함께 '만장일치로 투표하다'를 뜻하는 (B)가 정답이다.

어휘 **vote unanimously** 만장일치로 투표하다 **reject** ~을 거절하다, 거부하다 **merger** 합병 **put forward** (의견 등) ~을 내놓다, 제안하다 **resourcefully** 자원이 풍부하게

Week 07 실전 TEST

1. (B)	2. (D)	3. (B)	4. (D)	5. (C)
6. (D)	7. (D)	8. (A)	9. (C)	10. (D)
11. (D)	12. (D)	13. (B)	14. (C)	15. (B)
16. (D)	17. (B)	18. (A)	19. (D)	20. (B)

1-3.

W: Mark, did you talk to our supervisor about replacing our team's desks yet? **1** It's about time we upgraded our workspace.
M: I mentioned it to him, but he hasn't given us approval yet.
W: I see. **2** I was going to measure and gather the dimensions of our current desks, but I'll hold off for now.
M: Yeah, our boss still needs some time to approve the request. In the meantime, let's research some furniture companies to offer as options.
W: That sounds like a good idea. I know one that's well known for selling eco-friendly products.
M: Awesome! **3** Can you send me the link to its website? I'll start compiling a list of sellers.

여: 마크 씨, 혹시 우리 팀 책상들을 교체하는 일과 관련해 부장님과 이야기해 보셨나요? 우리 업무 공간을 업그레이드해야 할 때가 되었어요.
남: 언급해 드리긴 했는데, 아직 승인해 주시지 않았어요.
여: 알겠어요. 현재의 책상들에 대한 치수를 측정해 취합하려고 했었는데, 지금으로서는 미뤄야겠네요.
남: 네, 부장님께서 그 요청을 승인하시는 데 여전히 시간이 좀 필요하세요. 그 사이에, 선택 사항으로 제시할 몇몇 가구 회사들을 조사해 봐요.
여: 좋은 생각인 것 같아요. 친환경 제품을 판매하는 것으로 잘 알려진 곳을 한 군데 알아요.
남: 잘됐네요! 그 웹사이트 링크를 보내 주시겠어요? 제가 판매업체 목록을 작성하기 시작할게요.

어휘 **supervisor** 상사, 책임자 **replace** ~을 교체하다 **It's about time** + 과거동사 ~할 때가 되었다 **approval** 승인 **measure** ~을 측정하다, ~을 재다 **gather** ~을 취합하다, ~을 모으다 **dimensions** 치수, 크기 **current** 현재의 **hold off** 미루다 **approve** ~을 승인하다 **request** 요청 **in the meantime** 그 사이에, 그러는 동안 **well known** 잘 알려진 **eco-friendly** 친환경의 **compile** (자료 등을 모아) ~을 정리하다, ~을 편집하다

1. 화자들이 무엇을 이야기하고 있는가?
(A) 마케팅 계획을 발전시키는 일
(B) 일부 업무 공간을 개선하는 일
(C) 고용 정책을 검토하는 일

(D) 워크숍을 마련하는 일

어휘 initiative n. 계획 hiring 고용 policy 정책, 방침 organize ~을 마련하다, ~을 조직하다
Paraphrase upgraded our workspace → Improving some workstations

2. 여자는 무엇을 할 계획을 세우고 있었는가?
(A) 건물을 둘러보는 일정을 잡는 일
(B) 직원 설문 조사지를 배부하는 일
(C) 몇몇 사무용품을 보충하는 일
(D) 몇몇 치수 정보를 취합하는 일

어휘 property 건물, 부동산 viewing 둘러보기 distribute ~을 배부하다 survey 설문 조사(지) restock ~을 보충하다, ~을 다시 채우다 supplies 용품, 물품 collect ~을 취합하다, ~을 모으다
Paraphrase measure and gather the dimensions → Collect some measurements

3. 남자는 여자에게 무엇을 요청하는가?
(A) 의견 요약본
(B) 웹사이트 링크
(C) 일련의 지시 사항
(D) 지불 영수증

4-6.

I'm holding this meeting because we've received customer complaints about **4** how our hotel website sometimes displays inaccurate information about our seasonal discounts. It has been brought to my attention that there is a malfunction in the software program that we use, so **5** we may need to work overtime tonight to get it fixed as soon as possible. On a similar note, I want us to consult with a web design specialist to improve our reservations page. **6** We need to make sure that the booking process isn't too complicated.

제가 이 회의를 개최하는 이유는 어떻게 우리 호텔 웹사이트가 때때로 계절 할인 서비스와 관련해 부정확한 정보를 보이는 지와 관련해 고객 불만 사항을 접수했기 때문입니다. 우리가 이용하는 소프트웨어 프로그램에 오작동 문제가 있다는 사실에 주목하게 되었기 때문에, 우리가 가능한 한 빨리 이를 바로잡기 위해 오늘밤 야근을 해야 할 수도 있습니다. 한 가지 비슷한 얘기를 하자면, 저는 우리 예약 페이지를 개선하기 위해 웹 디자인 전문가와 상의하기를 원합니다. 우리는 반드시 예약 과정이 너무 복잡하지 않도록 해야 합니다.

어휘 hold ~을 개최하다 complaint 불만, 불평 display ~을 보이다 inaccurate 부정확한 It has been brought to my attention that ~라는 사실에 주목하게 되었습니다 malfunction 오작동, 작동 불량 get A p.p. A를 ~되게 하다 fix ~을 바로잡다, ~을 고치다 on a similar note 한 가지 비슷한 얘기를 하자면 consult with ~와 상의하다 improve ~을 개선하다 make sure that 반드시 ~하도록 하다 process 과정 complicated 복잡한

4. 화자가 어떤 문제를 언급하는가?
(A) 예약하는 것을 잊었다.
(B) 파일에 접근할 수 없다.
(C) 일부 문서들이 분실되었다.
(D) 웹사이트가 부정확한 정보를 나타낸다.

어휘 access ~에 접근하다, ~을 이용하다 misplace ~을 분실하다, ~을 둔 곳을 잊다
Paraphrase displays inaccurate information → shows incorrect information

5. 청자들이 오늘밤 무엇을 할 것 같은가?
(A) 교육 시간에 참석하는 일
(B) 레스토랑을 예약하는 일
(C) 추가 근무를 하는 일
(D) 문서를 검토하는 일

어휘 extra 추가의, 별도의

Paraphrase work overtime → Work extra hours

6. 화자는 왜 전문가에게 연락할 것인가?
(A) 일부 기계를 점검 받기 위해
(B) 일정에 대해 불만을 제기하기 위해
(C) 해외 사업을 논의하기 위해
(D) 과정을 더 단순하게 만들기 위해

어휘 expert 전문가 have A p.p. A를 ~되게 하다 inspect ~을 점검하다 complain about ~에 대해 불만을 제기하다 overseas 해외의 venture (모험적) 사업

Paraphrase make sure that the booking process isn't too complicated → make a process simpler

7.
해석 건축 현장 감독관은 보안 등의 설치가 거의 완료되어 기쁘다.
해설 빈칸에는 보안 등의 설치가 완료되는 정도를 나타낼 수 있는 어휘가 필요하므로 '거의' 등의 의미를 가진 (D)가 정답이다.
어휘 supervisor 감독관 installation 설치 security lighting 보안 등 yet 하지만 rarely 거의 ~않다 almost 거의

8.
해석 공장 소유주는 지속적으로 생산 목표를 충족하는 것이 성공적인 제조 회사를 운영하는 데 있어 핵심이었다고 말했다.
해설 빈칸에는 생산 목표를 충족하는 방식을 나타낼 어휘가 필요한데, 성공적인 회사 운영과 관련되어야 하므로 '지속적으로, 일관성 있게'라는 의미의 (A)가 정답이다.
어휘 state that ~라고 말하다, 언급하다 key to ~에 있어서의 핵심 run ~을 운영하다 consistently 지속적으로, 일관성 있게 durably 내구성 있게, 튼튼하게 largely 대체로, 주로

9.
해석 송 씨는 새로운 점심시간 정책을 알고 있는지 확실히 하기 위해 각 부서장과 잠깐 이야기할 것이다.
해설 빈칸에는 동사 speak을 수식해 송 씨가 각 부서장들과 얘기하는 방식을 나타낼 어휘가 필요하므로 '잠깐, 간략히'의 의미를 가진 (C)가 정답이다.
어휘 be aware of ~을 알고 있다 totally 완전히, 전적으로 briefly 잠깐, 간략히

10.
해석 스프린트 스포츠 베버리지 사는 전 세계에 걸쳐 새로운 고객들에게 도달하기 위해 온라인 광고에 아주 많이 투자해 왔다.
해설 빈칸에는 빈칸 앞에 위치한 동사 has invested를 수식해 투자하는 행위에 대해 설명할 수 있어야 하는데 의미상 '아주 많이 투자해 왔다'고 해석하는 것이 자연스러우므로 '아주 많이, 심하게, 대단히'라는 뜻의 (D)가 정답이다.
어휘 invest in ~에 투자하다 reach ~에 도달하다, 다다르다 randomly 무작위로 instantly 즉시 roughly 대략, 약 heavily (아주) 많이, 심하게, 대단히

11.
해석 환경 친화적인 포장은 우리가 더 다양한 고객층에게 도달하는 데 도움을 줌으로써 눈에 띄게 유익했다.
해설 빈칸에는 빈칸 뒤에 제시된 형용사 beneficial을 수식하면서 환경 친화적인 포장이 고객층에게 도달하는 데 도움이 된 정도를 나타낼 수 있는 어휘가 와야 하므로 '눈에 띄게, 현저하게'라는 뜻의 (D)가 정답이다.
어휘 beneficial 유익한 reach ~에 도달하다 permissibly 허용되어 diligently 부지런하게 markedly 눈에 띄게, 현저하게

12.

해석 결과의 정확성을 보장하기 위해, 조사 질문들은 한 달의 연구 기간 동안 정확히 동일하게 유지되어야 한다.

해설 빈칸에는 빈칸 뒤에 제시된 the same을 수식해 조사 질문들의 유지되어야 하는 정도를 나타낼 수 있는 어휘가 필요하므로 '정확히'라는 뜻의 (D)가 정답이다.

어휘 accuracy 정확성 findings (연구) 결과 the same 동일한 expertly 능숙하게 mutually 상호 exactly 정확히

13.

해석 쓰러진 나무를 제거하는 동안, 긴급 구조대는 40번 고속도로의 2개 차선을 일시적으로 폐쇄해야 했다.

해설 빈칸에는 빈칸 뒤에 제시된 동사 close를 수식하여 보수공사 또는 비상사태 등의 이유로 항상 차량이 다녀야 하는 고속도로를 폐쇄하는 기간을 나타내야 하므로 close와 함께 '일시적으로 폐쇄하다'라는 의미의 (B)가 정답이다.

어휘 fallen 쓰러진 emergency services 긴급 구조대 temporarily close 일시적으로 폐쇄하다 experimentally 시험적으로 sufficiently 충분하게

14.

해석 지역 주민들은 알로웨이 마을 도서관이 빠르게 도서 모음을 빠르게 확장하고 있는 것에 기뻐하고 있다.

해설 빈칸에는 빈칸 뒤에 나와 있는 현재진행형 expanding을 수식해 도서관이 도서 수집을 확대하는 속도를 나타낼 수 있는 어휘가 필요하므로 is expanding과 함께 '빠르게 확장하다'라는 뜻의 (C)가 정답이다.

어휘 rapidly expand 빠르게 확장하다 hardly 거의 ~ 않다

15-18.

산체스 씨께,

새로 개장한 멕시코 식당에 귀하의 최근 방문에 관해 편지를 보내주셔서 감사합니다.

먼저, 에피타이저가 귀하의 취향에 맞지 않았던 점에 대해 진심 어린 사과를 드립니다. 저희 음식점을 방문하신 대부분 손님들은 매운 음식을 즐기지만, **15** 몇몇 분들은 아닐 수 있다는 점을 이해합니다. 그 이유로, 저희는 모든 메뉴에 순한 맛, 중간 맛, 매운 맛의 선택권을 제공하고 있습니다. 이는 귀하께서 주문을 할 때 귀하의 종업원이 말씀드렸어야 하는 것입니다.

또한, 저희가 탄산음료에 대해 무료 리필을 제공해드리지 않는다는 것에 실망하신 것도 이해합니다. 하지만, 저희는 그것이 저희로 하여금 가격을 합리적으로 유지하게 하고 낭비를 최소화할 것이라고 생각했습니다. **16** 그 대신, 저희는 정수된 얼음물을 무료로 제공하고 있습니다. 저희는 귀하를 저희에게 만족한 많은 손님들 중 한 분으로 만들기 위한 또 다른 기회를 원합니다. 그래서, 저희 지점 중 어느 곳에서나 유효한 음료와 디저트를 포함한 2인 무료 식사상품권을 편지에 **17** 동봉합니다. **18** 저희는 가까운 미래에 귀하께서 저희 음식점에서 저녁 식사를 하시길 바랍니다.

안녕히 계십시오.

페넬로페 로페즈, 고객관리 전문가

어휘 regarding ~ 관해 sincere 진심 어린, 진심의 to one's liking ~의 취향에 맞는 establishment 매장, 시설 selection 선택권 mild (맛이) 순한 server (식당의) 종업원 waste 낭비, 쓰레기 filtered 정수된 gift certificate 상품권

15.

해설 빈칸 앞에 '대부분의 사람들은 ~하다'라는 내용과, 상반접속사 but이 제시되어 있으므로 빈칸에는 Most people과 대조를 이루는 부분적인 표현이 와야 한다. 따라서 '대부분은 ~하지만, 몇몇은 아니다'라는 흐름이 적절하므로 '몇몇'을 나타내는 복수 부정대명사 (B)가 정답이다.

16.

해설 빈칸 앞에서는 '무료로 음료를 리필해주지 않는다'는 내용이 언급되어 있고, 빈칸 뒤에는 '정수된 얼음물은 무료로 제공한다'는 내용이 있으므로, 음료 대신 얼음물을 제공한다는 것을 알 수 있다. 따라서 '대신에'라는 의미의 (D)가 정답이다.

어휘 likewise 마찬가지로 otherwise 그렇지 않으면 for example 예를 들어 instead 대신(에)

17.

해설 빈칸 앞에 주어인 I가 있고, 빈칸 뒤에 명사 목적어가 있으므로 빈칸은 능동태 동사 자리이다. 또한, 산체스 씨가 편지를 읽기 전에 상품권을 동봉했으므로 현재완료시제 (B)가 정답이다.

18. (A) 저희는 가까운 미래에 귀하와 귀하의 초대 손님이 저희 음식점에서 저녁 식사를 하시길 바랍니다.
(B) 저는 귀하의 추천에 대해 듣기를 기대합니다.
(C) 이런 어려운 시기에 저희와 머물러 주셔서 감사 드립니다.
(D) 저희가 귀사와 다시 거래를 하게 되면 기쁠 것입니다.

해설 빈칸 앞에 식사권을 동봉하였다는 내용이 언급되었으므로 빈칸에는 이 식사권에 관한 내용이 언급된 문장이 와야 한다. 따라서 '가까운 미래에 저녁 식사를 하길 기대한다'는 내용인 (A)가 정답이다.

어휘 in the near future 가까운 미래에

19-20.

관계자분께,

[19] 요청에 따라, 최근에 넥시코 주식회사에 공식에 대한 지원서를 제출한 메튜 브라이트 씨에 관해 귀하께 편지를 씁니다. 저는 메튜 씨가 그 직무에 적합하고, 귀사에 적임자라고 굳게 믿고 있습니다.

메튜 씨는 제 회사에서 인사부에서 4년 동안 근무했습니다. 그의 훌륭한 학력 자격 요건과 직무 자격증 외에도, 그는 인사 직무에서 필수적인 많은 자질들을 갖추고 있었습니다. 18개월의 수습 기간 후에, 메튜 씨는 사내 관리 교육을 들었고, 그리고 나서 부관리자 직책을 맡았습니다. 그의 업무에는 5명의 직원들로 구성된 하나의 팀을 감독하는 것을 포함합니다. [20] 2년의 관리 직무 후에, 메튜 씨는 올해의 관리자 상에 지명되었고, 그리고 그 상을 수상했습니다.

마지막으로, 저는 메튜 씨가 저의 회사에서 그의 고용 기간 동안 보여준 인상 깊은 직업 윤리를 칭찬하고 싶습니다. 메튜 씨에게 그 직무를 제안하는 것이 현명한 고용 결정일 것이라 생각되며, 그가 귀사에 귀중한 자산이 될 것이라는 것에 확신합니다.

어휘 as requested 요청에 따라 regarding ~에 관해 strongly 굳게, 강력하게 well suited 적합한, 잘 어울리는 good fit 적임자, 꼭 맞는 것 qualification 자격 요건 credential 자격증 possess ~을 갖추다, 소유하다 probationary period 수습 기간 undergo ~을 받다, 겪다 in-house 내부의 take on ~을 맡다, 떠맡다 supervise ~을 감독하다 nominate ~을 지명하다 praise ~을 칭찬하다 work ethic 직업 윤리 duration 기간 wise 현명한 asset 자산

19. 편지의 목적은 무엇인가?
(A) 일자리 공석에 대해 문의하기 위해
(B) 면접을 준비하기 위해
(C) 상을 위해 직원을 지명하기 위해
(D) 일자리 추천서를 제공하기 위해

해설 지문 첫 문단에 요청에 따라 최근 넥시코 주식회사에 공석에 대한 지원서를 제출한 메튜 브라이트 씨에 관해 편지를 쓴다고 언급되어 있고, 브라이트 씨가 해당 직무와 귀사에 적임자일 것이라 생각한다는 내용이 있으므로 추천서 제공을 위해 편지를 썼음을 알 수 있다. 따라서 (D)가 정답이다.

20. 브라이트 씨에 대해 사실인 것은 무엇인가?
(A) 현재 넥시코 주식회사에서 일하고 있다.
(B) 관리 능력에 대해 인정받았다.
(C) 여러 다른 일자리 공석에 지원했다.
(D) 18개월 전에 대학을 졸업했다.

해설 두 번째 문단 마지막 문장에서 브라이트 씨가 관리 직무를 맡은지 2년 만에 올해의 관리자 상에 지명되었고, 수상했다는 내용이 있으므로 관리 능력을 인정받았다는 내용의 (B)가 정답이다.

어휘 be recognized for ~에 대해 인정받다

Week 08
정답 및 해설

Day 01 기출 패러프레이징 ③

DAILY QUIZ

1.

남: 안녕하세요, 뉴욕시로 보내야 할 소포가 있습니다. 제 상황이 꽤 급해요.
여: 알겠습니다, 저희가 빠른 배송을 제공해 드리지만 12달러를 추가로 지불하셔야 합니다. 괜찮으시겠어요?

Q. 여자는 어떤 서비스를 설명하는가?
(A) 빠른 배송
(B) 실시간 위치 추적

어휘 expedited shipping 신속 배송 for an extra 12 dollars 12달러를 추가하여

2.

남: 장 씨를 위한 은퇴식 연회에 저와 함께 가시겠어요? 그는 작년에 우리가 긴밀히 협력했던 마케팅 대행사의 창립자입니다.
여: 저도 동행하고 싶지만 이 기회를 거절해야 할 것 같아요. 이번 주는 일정이 정말 빡빡하거든요.
남: 알겠습니다. 다른 사람에게 파티에 참석하고 싶은지 물어 볼게요.

Q. 여자는 왜 남자의 제안을 거절하는가?
(A) 참석해야 할 필수 교육이 있다.
(B) 매우 바쁘다.

어휘 reception 연회, 파티 collaborate with ~와 협력하다 closely 긴밀하게 accompany ~와 동행하다 turn down ~을 거절하다 packed 꽉 찬

3.

저희 미니 냉장고는 1인 가구와 기숙사 방에 적합합니다. 또한 조립이 쉬우며 잠글 수 있는 도어, 맞춤 설정 가능한 온도, 얼음 디스펜서 등의 고유한 기능도 제공합니다. 오늘 저희 웹사이트에서 저희 미니 냉장고에 대한 고객들의 의견을 확인해 보세요.

Q. 화자에 따르면, 청자들이 웹사이트에서 찾을 수 있는 것은 무엇인가?
(A) 설문 조사 질문
(B) 고객 후기

어휘 single household 1인 가구 dorm 기숙사 assemble ~을 조립하다 customizable 맞춤형의, 주문에 따라 만들 수 있는 review 후기, 평

Day 02 전치사

표제어 문제 정답 및 해석

1. (A)	2. (A)	3. (B)	4. (B)	5. (B)
6. (A)	7. (A)	8. (B)	9. (A)	10. (B)
11. (A)	12. (B)	13. (B)	14. (A)	15. (A)
16. (B)	17. (B)	18. (B)	19. (B)	20. (A)
21. (B)	22. (A)	23. (B)	24. (B)	25. (A)
26. (B)	27. (B)	28. (B)	29. (B)	30. (B)
31. (B)	32. (A)	33. (B)	34. (A)	35. (B)
36. (B)	37. (B)	38. (A)	39. (B)	40. (A)

1. 지난주에 작성한 의견 카드에 따르면, 우리의 새로운 디저트 메뉴는 큰 성공작이었다.
2. 아자드 사의 최고 재무 관리자인 필립 세이오무어 씨는 회사의 설립자를 대신하여 상을 받을 것이다.
3. 귀하의 이력서와 함께, 이전 그래픽 디자인 작업물의 포트폴리오를 제공해주십시오.
4. 마이클 왓슨의 2차 세계대전 동안의 새로운 영화

배경은 30세 이상의 영화관람객들 사이에서 가장 인기있는 것으로 증명됐다.
5. 저희의 야외 테라스의 테이블 예약은 적어도 2달 전에 미리 되어야 합니다.
6. VIP 패스를 가진 축제 참석자들만이 무대 옆에 있는 벽을 넘는 것이 허용된다.
7. 에너지 회사는 모든 고객들에게 전기 요금의 최근 인상에 관하여 이메일을 보냈다.
8. 새로운 볼링장의 건설은 새로운 오락 시설에 대한 지역 주민들의 수요에도 불구하고 취소되었다.
9. 이글 런 스키 슬로프는 오늘 위험한 기상 조건에 대한 우려로 인해 출입 금지이다.
10. 그 영화 감독을 제외하고 아무도 영화대본의 마지막 몇 페이지를 보는 것이 허용되지 않았다.
11. 그레타 잉글리스의 데뷔 음악 앨범에 대한 긍정적인 평가 후에, 그녀는 월드 투어에 나섰다.
12. 연료 가격의 상승을 감안하면, 더욱 더 많은 직원들이 자전거로 통근을 하는 것을 선택할 것이다.
13. 우튼 엔지니어링 사는 국가적으로 시행되는 정부 지침에 따라서 안전 점검을 수행한다.
14. 다양한 음식과 음료를 제공하는 것에 더하여, 마리온 케이터링 사는 경험이 많은 종업원들을 제공한다.
15. 유지보수팀은 다음 달의 비즈니스 소프트웨어 총회보다 앞서 전시회장의 오디오 시스템에 대한 문제를 고치려고 시도하고 있다.
16. 폭우의 경우에, 예술 공예 박람회는 페어랜드 공원 대신에 딩글리 커뮤니티 센터에서 개최될 것이다.
17. 시설관리 직원들을 포함하여 모든 메이페어 호텔 직원들은 5월 6일에 고객 서비스 워크숍에 반드시 참석해야 한다.
18. 필요한 허가를 얻는 것에 대한 지연으로 인해, 그 쇼핑몰의 건축은 이번 달 대신에 다음 달에 시작할 것이다.
19. 서동을 개조하는 것을 계획하고 있으므로, 모든 방문객들은 회사 본사 반대편의 공공 주차장을 사용해야 한다.
20. 보수 공사 프로젝트의 높은 비용 때문에, 회사 임원들은 연말 보너스를 못 받을 것이다.
21. 당분간, 각 승객마다 하나의 무료 음료의 제한이 있을 것이다.
22. 워크숍에 관계된 추가 정보는 곧 나누어 드릴 소책자에 상세히 설명되어 있습니다.
23. 새로운 직원들이 그들의 직무에 준비되는 것을 돕기 위해, 회사 안내서가 오리엔테이션 시간 이전에 각 직원들에게 보내졌다.
24. 존스 씨는 영업회의를 내일 개최하기보다는 차라리 다음주 수요일로 일정을 재조정하고 싶어 한다.
25. 휴가나 병가 정책에 관한 어떤 질문이라도 있으시다면, 귀하의 상사에게 언제든 연락하시기 바랍니다.
26. 리카르도 가구 사에서, 주문품의 크기와 상관 없이 표준 배송비는 10달러이다.
27. 베라니 씨와 달리, 코르테즈 씨는 뉴올리언스 지사로의 전근이라는 제안을 받아들였다.
28. 몬테나 마켓을 방문하시고, 다양한 최고의 패션 브랜드들에 대해 최대 50퍼센트까지 절약해보세요.
29. ACA 전자는 결함 있는 반품된 상품을 받은 3일 이내에 전액 환불을 귀하께 제공할 것입니다.
30. 연례 매출 보고서에 따르면, 3분기 금융분기 전반에 걸쳐 쭉 여러 문제들이 발생했다.
31. 우리의 새로운 에피타이저 메뉴에 대한 불만 사항을 고려하여, 우리는 원래 메뉴로 되돌아가기로 결정했다.
32. 저희 플래티늄 멤버십은 주요 운동 시설로의 표준 이용권 외에 사우나와 스파의 완전한 사용을 포함합니다.
33. 배송 시간에 대한 부정적인 피드백에 대응하여, 우리는 다른 배송 서비스 사와 일하기로 결정했다.
34. 청소 제품들이 포함한 유해한 화학약품 때문에, 그것들은 아이들의 손에 닿지 않는 곳에 보관되어야 한다.
35. 내년부터, 직원들은 회사에 의해 추천된 연금 기금 외에 다른 것에 납입할 수 있을 것이다.
36. 행사 프로그램에 목록화된 공연 시작 시간과 반대로, 발레 공연은 오후 4시보다는 오후 3시에 시작할 것이다.
37. 코브 해변에서의 불꽃놀이는 좋지 않은 날씨에도 불구하고 성공작이었다.

38. 로닌 5 스마트폰의 매출은 론스테인 씨의 이례적인 마케팅 전략 덕분에 이번 달에 두 배가 되었다.
39. 새로운 썬더 플라이어 롤러 코스터의 인기의 결과로서, 그 놀이공원은 분기별 입장권 판매에 대한 기록을 깼다.
40. 그 건축가는 건물 청사진의 초안을 다음 주 말쯤 공개할 계획이다.

DAILY QUIZ

7.
해석 영국 식당 가이드에 따르면, 험버사이드 비스트로는 국내에서 가장 광범위한 디저트 메뉴를 가지고 있다.
해설 빈칸 뒤에 명사가 있으므로 빈칸에 들어갈 알맞은 전치사를 찾아야 한다. 주절이 험버사이드 비스트로에 가장 광범위한 디저트가 있다는 내용이므로, British Restaurant Guide에 주절의 내용이 담겨 있다는 것을 알 수 있다. 따라서 '~에 따르면'이라는 의미의 출처를 나타내는 전치사 (B)가 정답이다.
어휘 according to ~에 따르면

8.
해석 라일러 연구소는 기존의 기기들을 수리하기 보다는 완전히 새로운 보안 시스템을 구입할 것이다.
해설 빈칸 앞뒤로 각각 동사 purchase와 repair가 이끄는 두 개의 동사구가 위치해 있고, '수리를 하기 보다는 새로운 것을 구입할 것'이라는 의미가 되어야 자연스러우므로 '~보다는 (차라리)'의 뜻을 가진 (B)가 정답이다.
어휘 rather than ~보다는 (차라리) with regard to ~에 관해서는

Day 03 다품사

표제어 문제 정답 및 해설

1. (A), (B)	2. (A), (B), (A)	3. (A), (B)	4. (B), (A)
5. (B), (A)	6. (A), (B)	7. (A), (B)	8. (B), (B)
9. (B), (A)	10. (B), (B)	11. (A), (B)	12. (B), (A)
13. (B), (A)	14. (A), (B)	15. (A), (B)	16. (A), (A)
17. (B), (A)	18. (B), (B)	19. (B), (A)	20. (A), (B)
21. (A), (B)	22. (A), (B)	23. (A), (B)	24. (A), (B)
25. (A), (B)	26. (A), (A)	27. (B), (B)	28. (B), (B)
29. (B), (A)	30. (A), (B)	31. (B), (B)	32. (A), (B)
33. (A), (B)	34. (B), (A)	35. (A), (B)	36. (B), (A)
37. (B), (B)	38. (A), (B)	39. (B), (A)	40. (A), (B)

1. 우리의 근무 일정의 변경에 따른 결과로, 몇몇 직원들은 평소보다 한 시간 일찍 출근해야 할 것이다.
   우리 고객들에게 신속하게 배달을 하기 위해, 우리는 최근 사용하던 배송 서비스를 변경했다.
2. 위성 내비게이션 기기들은 GPS 기술의 최신 향상으로 인해 과거 그 어느 때보다 더 정확하다.
   고론 전자는 새로운 스마트폰의 공식 출시에 우선하여 영업사원의 수를 늘렸다.
   아크레이 협회의 세미나 시리즈는 마케팅 분야에서 개인들이 발전하도록 도울 것이다.
3. 햄튼 주식회사는 국내에서 자사의 시장 점유율을 높일 수 있는 엄청난 잠재력을 가지고 있다.
   콜라 키친웨어 사는 지역 내에서 잠재 고객들에게 500개가 넘는 제품 카탈로그를 배포했다.
4. 우리 주방에서의 모든 기구와 절차는 정부 보건 안전 기준을 따라야만 한다.
   도시 내의 다른 호텔들과의 경쟁하기 위한 노력의 일환으로, 메그넘 호텔의 일반 객실 요금이 감소될 것이다.
5. 컴퓨터 모니터의 과잉 재고를 팔기 위해서, 호라이즌 전자는 그 제품의 가격을 낮췄다.

새로운 상품을 위한 공간을 만들기 위해 남은 재고는 50퍼센트 인하된 가격에 판매될 것이다.

6. 대표이사는 올레이 로지스틱스 사가 본사를 시애틀로 이전한다는 계획을 앞으로 추진할 것이라는 것을 확실히 했다.
   일자리 공석에 관한 문의들은 인사부의 패트리시아 럼슨 씨에게 전송되어야 한다.

7. 한때 베일빌에서 가장 인기 있는 지역이었던, 갈랜드 하이츠는 현재 버려진 건물들로 가득차 있다.
   일단 고객들이 제조 공장에 도착하면, 시설의 광범위한 견학을 할 것이다.

8. 이번 여름 재즈 음악 축제를 위한 공연자들의 전체 라인업이 이번 주 후반에 온라인에 게시될 것이다.
   1차 면접을 거친 사람들은 추후 일자에 최종 면접을 위해 다시 초대될 것이다.

9. 영화의 개봉이 시범 상영에서 부정적인 피드백이 있은 후에 뒤로 밀렸다.
   마감기한 후에 받은 기사들은 다음 달까지 출간되지 않을 것이다.

10. 할리데이 씨는 지역 사업체 소유주들로부터 자금을 확보하기 위해 상품 시연회를 준비했다.
    벨베데레 진료소에서의 환자 기록은 항상 안전하게 유지된다.

11. 추가 요금 없이 선택하신 음료에 더하여 큰 사이즈의 팝콘을 받기 위해 어떤 영화든지 프리미엄 티켓을 구매하십시오.
    귀하께서는 구매품에 대해 10퍼센트 할인을 받으실 것입니다. 게다가, 무료 선물도 받으실 것입니다.

12. 마틴 호지 씨는 매출과 관련된 여러 주제들을 포함한 20권 이상의 책들을 출간했다.
    저희 식당 지점들 중 몇 개는 더욱 더 수익성이 있게 되지 않는다면, 폐업될 것 같습니다.

13. 흡연 감지기로부터의 계속되는 삐 하는 소리는 배터리가 거의 고갈되었다는 경보로서 기능한다.
    비행 중 어떠한 난기류가 있다면, 기장은 즉시 승객들에게 알려줄 것이다.

14. 피에스타 멕시칸 레스토랑은 가까운 미래에 여러 새로운 채식 메뉴를 소개할 것이라고 발표했다.

오디오 가이드를 대여하고 싶으시다면, 매표소 근처에 있는 안내소를 방문해주십시오.

15. 새로운 공항 터미널에 대한 청사진의 최종 시안은 원래 디자인과 상당히 다르다.
    귀하의 서류의 복사본은 저희 사무실에 보관될 것이지만, 원본은 기록된 우편 주소로 귀하께 다시 반환될 것입니다.

16. 모든 기술 컨퍼런스 참석자들은 이름표와 행사 프로그램 소책자를 제공 받을 것이다.
    우리의 모든 제품들은 사용되지 않았다면 21일 이내에 환불을 위해 반품될 수 있습니다.

17. 크렌쇼 씨의 목표는 그의 발표로 잠재 고객들에게 깊은 인상을 줌으로써 우리 회사로 그들을 끌어들이는 것이다.
    우리 웹 사이트의 주된 목표는 뉴스와 현재 사건들에 관한 객관적인 정보를 제공하는 것이다.

18. 1급 보안 인가 등급을 가진 직원들만이 엘빈 바이오에 사에서 연구실을 사용하는 것이 허용된다.
    판매 허가증은 음식 축제에서 귀하께서 사용하는 부스나 카트에 분명히 보여져야 한다.

19. 일렉트라 전자에 의해 디자인된 새로운 핸드폰 모델의 예정된 출시일이 빠르게 다가오고 있다.
    조지 엣웰 씨의 신입직원들을 교육시키려는 열정적인 접근은 그가 회사 내에서 좋은 평판을 얻게 해주었다.

20. 샘 피킨스 씨는 행크 틸러 씨가 자리에서 물러난 후에 새 이사장으로 임명되었다.
    라구나 호텔은 골든 팜 리조트로 자사의 이름을 바꿀 것임을 발표했다.

21. 글린트 메뉴팩처링 사는 여러 웹 디자이너를 채용하려고 시도했지만, 아직도 많은 공석을 채우지 못하고 있다.
    자신의 사업을 시작하려는 나카토미 씨의 최근 시도는 불충분한 투자로 인해 성공적이지 못했다.

22. 안타깝게도, 저희는 귀하께서 컴퓨터 사용 능력에 대한 필수 자격증이 없으시기 때문에 이번에 귀하께 그 직책을 제안할 수 없습니다.
    동관의 재건축이 본사로부터의 자금 부족 때문에 보류되고 있다.

23. 직원들에게 무료 운동 시설을 제공하는 것은 회사의 의료보장 비용을 줄이는 데 도움이 될 수 있다.

자주 국제 전화를 하는 고객들께서는 특정 국가로의 통화를 더 낮은 요금으로 이용하실 수 있습니다.

24. 비록 엔진 결함이 수리를 위해 잠깐의 정지라는 결과를 낳았지만, 기차는 여전히 일정대로 보스턴에 도착했다.
도시 부두가에서 걸 아일랜드로 가는 배들은 여행 성수기 동안 매 15분마다 출발하도록 일정이 잡혀 있다.

25. 웨스트사이드 전기의 고객들은 회사가 3퍼센트의 연례 가격 인상을 발표한 것에 대해 실망했다.
크라운 플라자 호텔은 내년부터 스위트 객실의 요금을 인상하는 것을 결정했다.

26. 최근 저희 HQ104 복사기 구매에 감사드립니다.
30분의 중간 휴식 시간 동안 극장 방문객께서는 메인 로비에서 다과를 구매하실 수 있습니다.

27. 알레바 주방기기의 제조 과정은 생산율을 신장시키기 위해 개선되었다.
그린에이커 사는 재활용이 가능한 제품들을 가격이 적당한 건축 자재로 가공하는 것을 전문으로 한다.

28. 로스코 스키 리조트에서의 객실을 임대하기 희망하는 분은 유효한 신분증을 제시하고, 보증금을 지불하셔야 합니다.
이스트필드 아파트의 세입자 대다수는 그들의 아파트에 대해 18개월의 임대 계약에 서명했다.

29. 귀하의 요청에 따라, 채드 출판사는 <월간 스포츠 타임>에 대한 귀하의 구독을 즉시 취소할 것입니다.
재무부는 모든 직원들이 지출 보고서를 매주 금요일 오후 5시까지 제출할 것을 요청한다.

30. 저희 투자자들의 소중한 지원에 대해 감사를 표하기 위해, 저희는 연말 연회에 그분들을 초대할 것입니다.
루이즈 씨는 극장의 주 무대 위에 250개 이상의 조명을 지지하는 금속틀을 디자인했다.

31. 악천후로 인해, 정상으로 가는 등산로가 추후 안내 때까지 접근할 수 없을 것이다.
존스 씨가 직무 설명을 읽었을 때, 그녀는 여러 학력의 필수조건이 부족하다는 것을 알아차렸다.

32. 심코 솔루션사는 인터넷 사용자들의 행동과 웹 사이트 선호도를 분석하고 다양한 고객들을 위해 그 결과를 편집한다.
더 싼 재료를 사용하려는 우리의 결정은 우리 고객들을 위한 더 가격이 알맞은 제품들이라는 결과를 낳을 것이다.

33. 그레이 씨와 베일리 씨는 홀넷 시스템 사와의 계약을 따낸 그들의 성과에 대한 보너스를 받았다.
마가렛 할리 씨는 브로드웨이 연극에서 그녀의 작품들로 수많은 상을 받아왔다.

34. 에이스 호텔의 프런트 데스크 직원은 이제 투숙객들에게 룸서비스 조식 또는 뷔페 상품권 중 선택권을 제공한다.
우리의 새로운 고객은 첫 상담에 대한 요금을 면제해준다는 우리의 제안에 대단히 감사하고 있다.

35. 모든 직원들은 가능한 한 빨리 웹 사이트에서 설문조사를 완료해야 한다.
건축의 첫 단계가 완료되자마자, 부지에 대한 철저한 안전 점검이 시행될 것이다.

36. 레이 커피 앤 도넛은 이번 여름에 토론토 시내에서 50번째 지점을 열 것이다.
그 워터파크는 학교 휴일 동안 오전 9시부터 오후 7시까지 방문객들에게 개장될 것이다.

37. 솔라리스 자동차 사는 공장 직원들이 직장에서 위험에 처하지 않는 것을 확실히 하기 위해 엄격한 안전 조치를 시행한다.
어떤 맞춤 커튼이든지 구매하시기 전에, 귀하께서는 귀하의 모든 창문의 수치를 정확하게 재야 합니다.

38. 대학교 학생들이 근무 경험으로부터 혜택을 얻을 수 있기 때문에, 많은 학생들이 우리의 여름 인턴십 직책에 지원한다.
플래티늄 회원권이 컨트리 클럽 회원들에게 제공하는 혜택들은 우선 주차와 클럽 시설에 대한 전체 이용권을 포함한다.

39. 아닛 씨는 로드 서비스 사에서 다양한 부서 내에서 직원들을 관리하는 것에 대한 폭넓은 경력을 가지고 있다.
샌더스 냉동 식품은 채식 식사 세트를 단종한 이후로 수익에서의 급격한 감소를 경험했다.

40. 오리엔테이션 시간은 참석자들이 채용 계약의 세

부사항을 읽을 수 있도록 15분의 휴식시간을 포함할 것이다.
각 달에, 음식 구독 서비스는 특정 지역 또는 국가로부터의 식사를 배달한다.

DAILY QUIZ

1.
해석 우리 새 공장의 조립라인 기계들은 매우 발전되어서 우리는 제조 과정을 잠재적인 투자자들에게 설명할 필요가 있다.
해설 빈칸에는 빈칸 뒤의 명사 investor를 수식하면서 발전된 기계의 제조 과정을 설명하는 대상을 나타낼 수 있는 어휘가 필요한데 이는 미래의 잠재적인 투자자가 되어야 자연스럽다. 따라서 '잠재적인, 가능성 있는'이라는 의미의 (A)가 정답이다.
어휘 **potential** 잠재적인, 가능성 있는 **vacant** 비어 있는

2.
해설 많은 환자들이 그들의 예약을 월말로 잡았기 때문에 저희 치과의사들은 현재 빈 예약 시간대가 몇 개 있습니다.
해설 빈칸에는 환자들이 잡은 예약 시간에 대한 시점을 나타내면서 이에 따라 치과의사들이 가지는 빈 예약 시간대의 시점을 나타낼 수 있는 어휘가 필요하다. 따라서 '~후에, 나중에'라는 의미의 (A)가 정답이다.
어휘 **slot** 시간(대), 자리 **later** ~후에, 나중에

3.
해석 자동차로부터 때때로 나는 삐 소리는 충돌이 곧 발생될 상태임을 알리는 경보의 기능을 한다.
해설 빈칸에는 차에서 나는 삐 소리가 충돌이 곧 발생한다는 것을 알리는 기능의 특성을 나타낼 수 있는 어휘가 필요하므로 '경보, 경계'의 의미의 (C)가 정답이다.
어휘 **emit** (소리, 열, 가스 등) ~가 나다, ~을 내다 **collision** 충돌 **imminent** 곧 발생될, 임박한

alert 경보, 경계 **authentication** 인증, 증명

4.
해석 우리 공장의 생산성은 9월과 12월 사이에 꾸준히 25퍼센트까지 상승했다.
해설 빈칸에는 빈칸 앞에 위치한 부사 steadily의 수식을 받으면서 공장의 생산성과 25 percent라는 수치의 관계를 나타낼 수 있는 어휘가 필요하므로 '상승하다, 인상하다'의 의미인 (B)가 정답이다.
어휘 **steadily** 꾸준히 **distribute** ~을 분배하다, 유통시키다 **increase** 상승하다, 인상하다

5.
해석 가구 경매 사이트를 둘러보는 사람들에게 적절한 정보를 제공하기 위해, 판매자들은 모든 물품을 온라인에 게시하기 전에 수치를 측정해야 한다.
해설 빈칸에는 온라인에 가구에 대한 정보를 제공하기 전에 판매자들이 해야 하는 행위를 나타낼 어휘가 필요하다. 따라서 '(수치를) 측정하다, 수치를 재다'라는 의미인 (D)가 정답이다.
어휘 **adequate** 적절한, 충분한 **measure** (수치를) 측정하다, 수치를 재다

6.
해석 모바일 앱 개발사는 경쟁사와의 합병 후 여러 새로운 프로젝트의 착수를 발표했다.
해설 빈칸 앞뒤로 명사구가 제시되어 있으므로 빈칸에는 이 둘을 연결할 수 있는 전치사가 필요하다. 선택지 중 전치사는 (B)와 (C)인데, 의미상 '합병 이후 새로운 프로젝트의 시작을 발표했다'라고 해석하는 것이 시간 순서상 자연스러우므로 '~후(에)'라는 의미의 (C)가 정답이다.
어휘 **toward** ~을 향해 **following** ~후(에)

Day 04 다의어

표제어 문제 정답 및 해석

1. (A), (A) 2. (B), (A) 3. (B), (A) 4. (B), (A)
5. (B), (A) 6. (A), (A) 7. (A), (B) 8. (B), (A)
9. (B), (A) 10. (A), (B) 11. (A), (A) 12. (B), (A)
13. (B), (A) 14. (B), (B) 15. (A), (B) 16. (B), (A)
17. (A), (A) 18. (A), (A) 19. (A), (B) 20. (B), (A)
21. (B), (B) 22. (A), (B) 23. (B), (A) 24. (A), (B)
25. (B), (A) 26. (B), (A) 27. (A), (B) 28. (A), (B)
29. (A), (B) 30. (A), (B) 31. (A), (B) 32. (A), (B)
33. (A), (B) 34. (A), (B) 35. (A), (B) 36. (A), (B)
37. (B), (B) 38. (B), (B) 39. (A), (B) 40. (A), (B)

1. 강 씨의 광범위한 제품에 대한 지식이 그녀의 인상적인 판매 성과의 이유들 중 하나이다.
   극장 관객들은 공연이 시작되기 10분 전에 자리에 앉으시도록 정중히 요청됩니다.
2. 한때 재택 사업이었던, 휴잇 씨의 컴퓨터 수리 회사는 현재 8개의 장소에서 매장을 운영 중이다.
   PC 위저드 사는 고급 컴퓨터 부대용품들을 갖춘 소매점을 개장했다.
3. 작성 완료된 지원서를 레가타 시스템 사의 인사부장에게 12월 5일 오후 5시까지 제출해주시기 바랍니다.
   모든 직원들이 그 발표가 흥미롭다고 생각했지만, 대부분은 그들의 일상 업무에의 적용점이 거의 없다고 느꼈다.
4. 25년 동안의 영업 이후, 메인 스트리트에 있는 굿 펠로우 베이커리는 영업을 중단할 것이다.
   세마 콘서트 홀의 음향 기술자의 직무는 음악 공연장소에 있는 모든 음향 시스템의 작동을 확인하는 것이다.
5. 라 체즈 루즈에 자리를 예약하려면, 적어도 한 달 전에 미리 전화하는 것이 권고된다.
   샤피로 씨는 비즈웰 통신사의 본사를 애쉬빌 교외 지역으로 이동하는 것에 대해 주저하고 있다.
6. 구성품이 대만에서 제조되지만, 타이푼 식기세척기의 조립은 호주에서 진행된다.
   다음 주 수요일, 직원 모임이 오전 8시 30분에 3층에 있는 회의실에서 열릴 예정이다.
7. 모든 주민들이 카운티의 공립 학교들에게 무료 광대역 인터넷 서비스를 제공하려는 계획을 지지했다.
   길리 씨는 파리로의 중요한 출장에 앞서 프랑스어를 배우는 데 엄청난 적극성을 보였다.
8. 도시 내 모든 주요 관광지들의 길안내를 위해, 상하이 관광 모바일 어플리케이션을 다운 받으시기 바랍니다.
   론 크레인씨의 지휘 하에 있는 노무 부서는 높은 수준의 직원 만족도를 유지한 공이 크다고 여겨진다.
9. 힉슨 씨의 마케팅 부서는 새로운 광고 캠페인을 개발하기 위해 그래픽 디자이너들과 긴밀하게 일했다.
   저희 기술 지원 직원들은 고객 문제를 적절히 해결하기 위해 자세히 듣는 것에 능숙합니다.
10. 레딩 인더스트리 사의 파산 신청 결정은 다소 갑작스러운 일이었으며, 많은 주주들을 고민에 빠뜨렸다.
    영업이사는 누락된 데이터가 모두 입수될 때까지 차라리 회의의 일정을 재조정할 것이다.
11. 그 사업 세미나는 매우 유익했고, 각자의 업무에 적용할 여러 기술들을 참석자들에게 주었다.
    나무 갑판에 새 광택제를 바르기 전에 모든 흙과 먼지를 제거하십시오.
12. 공장 근로자들은 안전 지침서에 적힌 지시를 따르는 것이 중요하다.
    풀처 씨는 적절한 조사 또는 준비를 하지 않은 면접자들에 대해 비판적이다.
13. 환자 예약을 받을 때에는, 우리 치과에 처음 방문하는 것인지에 대한 여부를 적어주시기 바랍니다.
    새로운 최고 재무 책임자의 임명은 자사의 수익과 이익을 빠르게 증가시키려는 회사의 의도를 암시한다.
14. 모든 참석자들은 페스티벌 장소로 출입하기 전에 손목밴드를 착용할 것이 요구된다.

특가 판매에 대한 소식을 받기 위해서는, 귀하의 휴대전화 번호와 이메일 주소를 모두 입력하시기 바랍니다.

15. 프란시스 협회 보조금은 사업가들이 그들의 사업 계획을 개발하는 것을 돕기 위해 고안되었다.

    토론토에 본사를 둔 에바 전자는 아시아에 있는 여러 기술 회사와 공고한 관계를 발전시켜왔다.

16. 왈라가 베이 비치 리조트에 있는 모든 객실은 장관을 이루는 바다와 해안가 경치를 제공한다.

    신문의 독자 의견란에 나타난 의견들이 반드시 저희 출판물의 견해를 반영하는 것은 아닙니다.

17. 샤타라 주식회사의 이사진들은 높은 수준의 고객 서비스를 회사의 최우선사항으로 여긴다.

    회계부의 그 직무에 지원하는 것을 고려하는 직원들은 리코 씨에게 이메일을 보내야한다.

18. 블루 라인 테크놀로지 사는 자사의 신형 태블릿 컴퓨터 제품군을 홍보하기 위해 배우 켄 로드 씨를 고용했다.

    칼 시몬스 씨는 샌드링햄 케이터링 회사의 최고 재무 책임자로 승진되었다.

19. 버튼 마케팅 사는 신규 고객들에게 도달하기 위한 노력의 한 부분으로 여러 온라인 마케팅 전문가들을 고용했다.

    저희 고객 서비스팀은 전화나 자사 온라인 채팅 둘 중에 하나를 이용해 24시간 내내 연락될 수 있습니다.

20. 직원 여러분께서는 윌로우 밸리 야유회의 비용에 3일 간의 숙박 및 식사 비용이 포함된다는 점을 유념하시기 바랍니다.

    존스 씨는 오리엔테이션 동안에 자신이 다룰 주요 주제들에 대해 간략히 설명하는 유인물을 각 신입 직원들에게 주었다.

21. 도시 버스 투어 중에 개인 소지품을 챙기는 것은 각 승객들의 책임입니다.

    상급 행사 담당자의 업무는 고객과 연락하는 것과 정기적인 프로젝트 상황 업데이트를 제출하는 것을 포함한다.

22. 링 씨는 실험실 물품을 더 주문하기 전에 전체 재고를 확인할 것이다.

    퍼시픽 인더스트리 사는 회사의 보건안전 절차에 대한 광범위한 검토를 지시했다.

23. ALG 소프트웨어 사가 11월에 디지털 드림 게임 사를 인수할 때, 모든 직원들은 새로 건축된 본사에서 함께 근무할 것이다.

    저희는 충분한 로열티 포인트를 얻으신 고객들께 매우 다양한 선물과 보상을 제공합니다.

24. 증가하는 수요를 만족시키기 위해, 공장 직원들은 이번 주에 500대 이상의 새 자동차를 조립할 것이다.

    텔러 씨가 우리의 홍보 자료를 만들기 전에, 그는 숙련된 작가들을 한 팀으로 모을 것이다.

25. 휴대폰 출시 행사는 대략 한 시간 정도 지속될 것이고, 기기의 시연으로 종료될 것이다.

    재정 고문들은 회사가 운송 비용을 상당히 줄일 수 있을 것이라고 결론을 내렸다.

26. 총회와 컨퍼런스에 가는 영업 이사들은 환급을 위해 영수증을 제출해야 한다.

    결함이 있는 기기의 수령 즉시, 저희가 수리를 위한 예상 시간에 대해 연락 드리겠습니다.

27. 그 밴드는 어떤 상황에도 이상적인 노래들의 공연 목록을 만들 수 있다.

    코든 시는 250년 전에 설립되었는데, 시 의회가 이 특별한 사건을 거리 페스티벌로 기념할 것이다.

28. 저희 옥상 식사 자리의 테이블을 예약하고 싶으시다면, 적어도 2주 전에 미리 저희에게 연락 주십시오.

    스칸도 여행사는 비용을 명시된 마감일까지 받지 못한다면 여행 예약들을 취소할 권한을 보유한다.

29. 현재 저희가 귀하께 적합한 채용 공고를 보유하고 있지 않지만, 다음을 위한 참고로 귀하의 이력서를 보관할 것입니다.

    지원자들은 지원서와 이력서, 그리고 자기소개서와 함께 추천서 목록을 포함해야 한다.

30. 애쉬포드 쇼핑몰의 보수공사 완료일자는 5월 2일로 기한이 연장되었다.

    사업 소유주들은 제조 시설을 견학하는 데 관심이 있던 여러 잠재적인 투자자들에게 초대장을 전했다.

31. 계약 조건에 동의하시는 경우, 두 개의 사본에 모두 서명하신 후 우편을 통해 한 부를 저희 캐롤턴

사무실로 보내주십시오.
리우드 시 시장으로서의 그의 임기 동안, 조지 랄스턴 씨는 마을 대중교통 체계에 대해 수많은 개선을 했다.

32. 회사의 대표이사는 이달 말 전에 마케팅 이사 직책을 충원하는 것이 목표이다.
유명한 요리사 안젤라 부스 씨를 고용하고 메뉴를 수정함으로써, 로욜라 비스트로는 지역 식당들 사이에서 정상의 위치로 올라갈 것이다.

33. 조립 라인 기사 공석에 지원하실 때에, 그 직무가 주말 교대 근무를 포함한다는 것을 알아두시기 바랍니다.
마케팅 접근법에서의 놀라운 변화로, 스위프트 스포츠웨어 사는 더 이상 유명 운동선수의 홍보를 추구하지 않는다.

34. 저희는 <하이 패션 매거진>의 지난달 호가 디자이너 마리카 헴스워스 씨에 대한 부정확한 정보를 포함한 것을 사과 드립니다.
지방 의회 의원들은 도로 보수부터 소음 불만사항까지 다양한 주민 문제를 논의할 수 있다.

35. 환불이나 교환을 원하는 고객들은 우리 웹 사이트를 통해 전자 서식을 제출해야 한다.
배링거 씨의 은퇴 저녁식사에서, 그는 그의 후임을 소개하며 그녀의 주목할 만한 사업 성과들을 소개했다.

36. 체육관 회원들은 탈의실을 떠나기 전에, 그들의 모든 소지품을 사물함에 넣은 것을 확실히 해야 한다.
회의 끝에, 도슨 씨는 책상에 발표 자료 몇 부를 추가로 남겨두었다.

37. 존스 씨는 신입 직원들을 공장 및 그에 인접한 사무실 건물들의 견학에 데려갈 것을 제안했다.
빅 애플 택시에서 일하는 기사들은 보통 그들의 점심 휴식 시간으로 약 45분이 걸린다.

38. 가필드 씨가 구입한 책장이 너무 넓었기 때문에, 그녀는 그것을 가구 매장에 반품했다.
참가자들은 워크숍에서 돌아온 7일 이내로 수료 증명서를 받을 것이다.

39. 저희 호텔은 행사 기획자들이 행사를 위한 가장 적합한 객실을 결정하는 것을 돕도록 각 객실에 대한 영상을 제공할 수 있습니다.

기술자들은 여전히 조립 라인의 오작동 원인을 알아내기 위해 시도하고 있다.

40. 부서의 중요한 결정을 내릴 때, 월레스 씨는 그의 직원들에게 의견에 대해 상담하는 것이 유용하다는 것을 안다.
이용 가능한 간식과 음료의 전체 제품군을 보기 위해서는 기내의 잡지를 참조해주시기 바랍니다.

DAILY QUIZ

1.
해석 제품들이 배송을 위해 준비될 때마다, 결함을 확인하는 것은 창고 관리자의 담당 업무이다.
해설 빈칸에는 특정 직책을 가진 사람과 결함이 있는지 확인하는 일의 연결성을 나타낼 어휘가 필요하므로 '담당 업무, 직무'를 뜻하는 (B)가 정답이다.
어휘 responsibility 담당 업무, 직무

2.
해석 많은 부동산 웹 사이트는 주택 구매자들이 빌릴 수 있는 근사치의 금액을 알아내는 데 도움을 주는 주택담보대출 계산기를 포함하고 있다.
해설 빈칸에는 주택 구매자들이 주택을 구매할 때 부동산 웹 사이트를 통해 그들이 빌릴 수 있는 금액에 대해 도움을 받을 수 있는 행위를 나타내는 어휘가 필요하므로 '~을 알아내다'라는 뜻의 (B)가 정답이다.
어휘 mortgage 주택담보대출 approximate 근사치의, 거의 유사한 amount 양 broaden ~을 넓히다 determine ~을 알아내다

3.
해석 리 벨리 컨트리 클럽 회원들은 프리미엄 회원권을 위해 반드시 매년 연장 신청서를 제출해야 한다.
해설 빈칸에는 회원권 연장을 위해 제출해야 하는 대상을 나타낼 수 있는 어휘가 필요하므로 '신청(서), 지원(서)'를 의미하는 (B)가 정답이다.
어휘 application 신청(서), 지원(서)

4.

해석 비록 일부 개별 부품들이 중국에서 생산되지만, 고핏 러닝머신의 조립은 영국에서 실시된다.

해설 빈칸에는 개별 부품이 다른 곳에서 제조되는 것과 대비되는 일을 나타내면서, 제품 생산 과정의 하나에 해당되는 어휘가 필요하므로 '조립'을 뜻하는 (C)가 정답이다.

어휘 take place (일, 행사 등이) 일어나다, 발생되다 assembly 조립

5.

해석 이 계약 조건에 따라, 귀하께서는 프리랜서 작업 과제를 늦어도 매일 오후 5시까지 제출하시는 것이 요구됩니다.

해설 빈칸에는 작업 과제를 특정 시간에 제출해야 하는 것의 근거를 나타낼 수 있는 어휘가 필요하므로 '(계약) 조건'이라는 뜻의 (B)가 정답이다.

어휘 in accordance with ~에 따라 terms (계약) 조건

6.

해석 주민들이 다음 주에 시행되는 수도 사용 제약에 대해 유념하는 것은 중요하다.

해설 빈칸에는 다음 주에 시행될 예정인 제약에 대해 유념하는 것의 특성을 나타낼 수 있는 어휘가 필요하므로 '중요한'이라는 의미의 (B)가 정답이다.

어휘 come into effect 효력을 발생하다 critical 중요한 cautious 신중한

Week 08 실전 TEST

1. (C)	2. (C)	3. (B)	4. (D)	5. (C)
6. (B)	7. (B)	8. (C)	9. (A)	10. (D)
11. (D)	12. (B)	13. (D)	14. (C)	15. (B)
16. (D)	17. (B)	18. (A)	19. (B)	20. (B)

1-3.

W: Excuse me, I'm from Gateway Technologies, the security management company that operates at this hospital. I was told that **1** I'm supposed to assist the IT department with some wiring and cabling. Do you know where I should go?

M: Oh, you must be responsible for the tech support we've been needing for our security system. **2** None of our staff are familiar with connecting the various components, so we need your help. Thanks for finally stopping by.

W: Thanks for being patient! I was out of town for the past week.

M: We understand. Anyway, the IT department is adjacent to the intensive care unit. **3** You'll need to show your photo ID or else you'll be prohibited from entering.

여: 실례지만, 저는 이 병원에서 운영되고 있는 보안 관리 업체인 게이트웨이 테크놀로지 사에서 온 사람입니다. 제가 일부 배선 및 케이블 관련 작업에 대해 IT부를 지원해야 한다는 얘기를 들었습니다. 제가 어디로 가야 하는지 아시나요?

남: 아, 저희 보안 시스템에 계속 필요로 하고 있던 기술 지원 업무를 책임지고 계신 분이 틀림없는 것 같네요. 저희 직원들 중에는 다양한 부품을 연결하는 일에 익숙한 사람이 아무도 없기 때문에, 도움이 필요합니다. 드디어 들러 주셔서 감사합니다.

여: 참고 기다려 주셔서 감사합니다! 제가 지난 한 주

동안 다른 지역에 가 있었습니다.
남: 알겠습니다. 어쨌든, IT부는 중환자실과 가까운 곳에 있습니다. 사진이 있는 신분증을 제시하셔야 하는데, 그렇지 않으면 출입이 금지될 것입니다.

어휘 **be supposed to do** ~해야 하다, ~하기로 되어 있다 **component** 부품 **adjacent to** ~와 가까운, ~에 인접한 **be prohibited from -ing** ~하는 것이 금지되다

1. 여자는 누구일 것 같은가?
(A) 자원봉사자
(B) 의사
(C) 기술자
(D) 사진가

2. 남자가 일부 직원들과 관련해 무슨 말을 하는가?
(A) 새 프로젝트로 바쁘다.
(B) 더 빨리 일해야 한다.
(C) 시스템을 잘 알지 못한다.
(D) 여자에게 곳곳을 둘러보게 해 줄 것이다.

Paraphrase None of our staff are familiar with connecting the various components → do not know a system well

3. 여자는 무엇을 제공해야 하는가?
(A) 제안서 초안
(B) 한 가지 형태의 신분증
(C) 몇몇 열쇠들
(D) 몇몇 가격 견적서

Paraphrase photo ID → A form of identification

4-6.

Alright everyone, we're very close to finalizing our remodeling plans. As one of the last steps, 4 I want each of you to research the best paint colors that will give our space a vibrant and welcoming atmosphere. 5 Attracting customers to visit our café has been challenging with more and more coffee shops opening up near us lately. Also, I've noticed that there's been a surplus of packaged cookies that we keep having to discard every month. 6 How about we stop purchasing them online in bulk and instead get them from the supermarket from now on?

좋습니다, 여러분, 우리 보수 공사 계획을 최종 확정하는 데 아주 가까워진 상태입니다. 마지막 단계들 중의 하나로, 저는 여러분 각자가 우리 공간에 활기차고 따뜻하게 맞이하는 분위기를 제공해 줄 최상의 페인트 색상을 조사해 주셨으면 합니다. 우리 카페를 방문하도록 고객들을 끌어들이는 것이 최근에 우리 근처에 문을 여는 커피 매장들이 점점 더 많아지면서 어려운 일이 되었습니다. 또한, 우리가 매달 계속 폐기 처분해야 하는 여분의 포장 쿠키가 있었다는 사실도 알게 되었습니다. 그것들을 온라인에서 대량으로 구매하는 것을 중단하고, 대신 지금부터는 슈퍼마켓에서 구입하면 어떨까요?

어휘 **finalize** ~을 최종 확정하다 **vibrant** 활기찬 **welcoming** 따뜻하게 맞이하는 **atmosphere** 분위기 **with A -ing** A가 ~하면서, A가 ~하는 채로 **surplus** 여분, 과잉 **discard** 폐기 처분하다 **in bulk** 대량으로

4. 화자는 청자들에게 무엇에 대해 조사하기를 원하는가?
(A) 원자재
(B) 네온 사인
(C) 목재 가구
(D) 페인트 색상

5. 화자의 말에 따르면, 최근에 무엇이 어려웠는가?
(A) 예약 일정을 잡는 일
(B) 공석을 충원하는 일
(C) 고객을 끌어들이는 일
(D) 에너지 소비를 줄이는 일

6. 화자는 청자들에게 무엇을 하도록 권하는가?
(A) 새 메뉴 항목을 시식해 보는 일
(B) 제품을 다른 곳에서 구입하는 일
(C) 요청서를 제출하는 일
(D) 계좌 번호를 확인해 주는 일

어휘 **sample** v. ~을 시식하다, ~을 시음하다
Paraphrase instead get them from the supermarket from now on → Buy a product elsewhere

7.
해석 프레스트윅 씨가 3월 2일에 보스턴에서 돌아오면 이사회가 월간 직원 평가를 재개할 것이다.
해설 빈칸 앞뒤로 주어와 동사가 각각 포함된 절이 위치해 있으므로 빈칸은 접속사 자리이며, 프레스트윅 씨가 돌아오는 것이 직원 평가를 재개하는 조건에 해당하므로 '(일단) ~하면, ~하자마자'라는 의미로 조건을 나타낼 때 사용하는 (B)가 정답이다.
어휘 **resume** ~을 재개하다 **evaluation** 평가(서) **once** (일단) ~하면, ~하자마자

8.
해석 웬더스 씨는, 그의 개인 비서와 함께, 우리의 일본 고객들과 만나기 위해 이번 주말에 도쿄로 출장을 갈 것이다.
해설 빈칸 뒤에 명사가 위치해 있으므로 빈칸은 전치사 자리인데, 빈칸 뒤에 제시된 내용이 도쿄로 출장갈 것이라는 의미이므로 웬더스 씨의 개인 비서는 그 출장을 함께 가는 대상임을 알 수 있다. 따라서 '~와 함께'라는 의미의 (C)가 정답이다.
어휘 **along with** ~와 함께, ~을 따라서 **in case of** ~인 경우에 대비하여

9.
해석 리드 주식회사의 직원 카풀 계획은 환경에 이로울뿐만 아니라, 직원 간의 관계도 강화할 것이다.
해설 빈칸에는 빈칸 앞에 위치한 명사구 employee carpooling과 복합명사를 구성하며, 직원의 카풀이 미래에 환경과 관계에 있어서 가져올 긍정적인 부분을 설명할 수 있어야 하므로 '계획'을 뜻하는 (A)가 정답이다.
어휘 **strengthen** ~을 강화하다, 더 튼튼하게 하다 **initiative** 계획, 법안 **impression** 인상, 감명

10.
해석 우리는 지역 주민들의 삶을 개선시킨다는 공통의 목표를 향하여 일하는 여러 자선단체들과 협업한다.
해설 빈칸에는 빈칸 앞에 제시된 동사 work와 함께 쓰여 '공통의 목표를 향하여 일한다'는 문맥이 되어야 자연스러우므로 '~을 향하여'라는 뜻의 (D)가 정답이다.
어휘 **charity** 자선단체 **toward** ~을 향하여, ~쯤

11.
해석 데이지 랜드스케이핑 사는 업계에서 대부분의 다른 회사들보다 더 낮은 요금으로 다양한 서비스를 실시한다.
해설 빈칸에는 빈칸 뒤에 제시된 명사 rates를 수식해 그 수준과 관련된 의미를 나타낼 수 있는 어휘가 필요하므로 '더 낮은, 인하된'을 뜻하는 (D)가 정답이다.
어휘 **rate** 요금 **lower** 더 낮은, 인하된

12.
해석 국립 공원의 여러 등산로가 최근 폭우로 인해 위험해져 접근할 수 없다.
해설 빈칸 앞에 완전한 절이, 빈칸 뒤에 명사구가 있으므로 빈칸은 전치사 자리이다. 따라서 선택지 중 전치사인 (A)와 (B) 중에서 정답을 골라야 하는데, 빈칸 뒤에 제시된 폭우가 등산로에 접근할

수 없는 원인에 해당되므로 '~로 인해, ~ 때문에'
라는 뜻의 (B)가 정답이다.

어휘 hiking trail 등산로 inaccessible 접근할
수 없는 hazardous 위험한 due to ~로
인해, ~ 때문에

13.

해석 급여 지급 처리의 지연 때문에, 일부 지급금은
금요일 오전이 되어야 직원들에게 갈 것이다.

해설 빈칸에는 빈칸 뒤에 제시된 특정 시점까지 급여
의 상태에 대해 설명할 수 있는 어휘가 필요하므
로 '지급금이 직원들에게 가다'라고 해석하는 것
이 자연스럽다. 따라서 '~에 가다, 도달하다'라
는 의미를 갖는 (D)가 정답이다.

어휘 not A until B B나 되어야 A하다 reach ~에
가다, 도달하다

14.

해석 몬태규 씨는 회사의 연간 지출을 효과적으로 줄
이기 위해 요구되는 경력을 갖고 있다.

해설 빈칸에는 주어진 몬태규 씨가 가지고 있는 회사
의 지출을 줄이기 위해 필요한 대상을 나타낼 수
있는 어휘가 필요하므로 '경력, 경험'이라는 의미
의 (C)가 정답이다.

어휘 effectively 효과적으로 expenditure 지출
advancement 발전, 승진

15-18.

수신: 그라함 본 <gvaughn@wizmail.com>
제목: 귀하의 불만사항

본 씨께,

지난주 귀하가 탑승하신 로마를 출발하여 뉴욕으로 향
하는 비행편에 대해 작성하신 피드백 양식에 답변을 보
내 드립니다. 저는 그 문제를 충분히 15 조사하였고,
진지하게 귀하의 불만사항을 숙고하였다는 점을 확실
히 알려드리고 싶습니다.

비행 보고서를 받은 후, 저는 지역 관리자 16 에게 그
정보를 전달했습니다. 그는 난기류의 영향을 줄이기 위
해 항로를 변경할 수 있었다는 것을 밝혀냈습니다.

저희는 귀하에게 비행기표 가격의 50퍼센트를 환불해
드리거나, 다음 번 저희 항공을 이용하실 경우 비지니
스석으로 업그레이드 하실 수 있는 상품권 중 하나를
제공해드리고자 합니다. 17 귀하가 어느 선택사항을
선호하는지 알고 싶습니다. 블루 마운틴 항공사 18
를 대표하여, 귀하께서 저희 기내에 탑승하여 겪으신
문제에 대해 사과 드리고 싶습니다.

안녕히 계십시오.

피터 토빈, 고객서비스부장
블루 마운틴 항공사

어휘 in reply to ~에 대한 답변으로 assure A
that A에게 ~임을 확실히 알려주다 forward
~을 전달하다, 보내다 path 경로, 길 alter ~을
변경하다 lessen ~을 줄이다 turbulence
난기류 on board 탑승하여

15.

해설 빈칸 앞에 비행편에 탑승한 고객이 피드백을 남
긴 후에 그것에 대해 '조사했다'는 흐름이 자연
스러우므로 빈칸에는 과거시제나 현재완료시제
가 와야 한다. 빈칸 뒤 and로 이어진 문장에서
have given이라는 현재완료시제가 쓰였으므로
(B)가 정답이다.

16.

해설 빈칸 앞에 '정보를 전달했다'는 내용이, 빈칸 뒤
에 그 대상이 제시되어 있으므로 '~에게'라는 의
미의 (D)가 정답이다.

17.
(A) 귀하는 저희의 비행기가 우수한 안락함을
제공해드린다는 점을 확신하실 것입니다.
**(B) 귀하가 어느 선택사항을 선호하는지 알고
싶습니다.**
(C) 항로의 변경은 즉시 시행될 것입니다.
(D) 체크인 시에 반드시 귀하의 여권을 가지고
오시기 바랍니다.

해설 빈칸 앞 문장에서 50퍼센트 환불이나 좌석 업그
레이드 상품권이라는 선택지를 제안하였으므로
이와 이어지는 옵션 선택을 언급한 (B)가 정답이

다.

어휘 **effective** 시행되는, 효력이 있는

18.

해설 빈칸 뒤에 고유명사가 제시되어 있으므로 빈칸은 전치사 자리인데, 이 이메일의 작성자인 고객서비스 부장이 회사를 대신하여 사과의 말을 전하고 싶다고 하는 것이 자연스러우므로 '~을 대신하여, 대표하여'라는 의미의 (A)가 정답이다.

어휘 **on behalf of** ~을 대신하여, 대표하여 **in case of** ~하는 경우에 대비하여 **as if** 마치~인 것처럼

19-20.

뉴 랭포드 시가 주요한 건설 계획을 발표하다

3월 18일 – (뉴 랭포드) 19 시 공무원들이 워터포드 구역을 완전히 바꿔놓을 준비를 하는 도시 갱생 프로젝트를 발표했다. 이 지역은 예전에 번영하는 상업용 센터였으며, 세간의 이목을 끄는 많은 소매점들의 고향이었다. 하지만, 사업체들은 증가하는 임대료로 인해 그 지역에서 점차 떠나갔다.

여러 버려진 건물들의 임박한 철거 이후, 두 개의 장관인 아파트 복합단지가 건설될 것이다. 일단 완성이 되면, 그 아파트들은 가구를 완벽히 갖추고 있을 것이며, 수도, 전기, 가스 등의 비용이 월 임대료에 포함될 것이다. 추가적으로, 광범위한 쇼핑몰이 하버스 에비뉴에 지어질 것이다. 그 쇼핑몰은 부지 내에 아이스링크와 영화관을 갖추고 있을 것이고, 차질이 없다면, 다음 여름까지 제대로 운영될 것이다.

이 계획의 비평가들은 혼잡한 도로를 경고해왔다. 20 전 시장이었던 존 비숍 씨는 뉴 랭포드 시의 유산을 보호하는 것에 대한 옹호자로서 목소리를 내고 있다. 비숍 씨는 "시 의회는 이러한 자금을 현존하는 사회 기반 시설의 정기적인 유지보수를 향해 방향을 바꿔야 하며, 역사적 건물들을 복원해야 한다."라고 말했다.

어휘 **transform** ~을 완전히 바꿔 놓다
prosperous 번영하는 **high-profile** 세간의 이목을 끄는 **move away from** ~에서 떠나가다, 이동하다 **following** ~ 이후

impending 임박한 **demolition** 철거, 폭파 **abandoned** 버려진 **spectacular** 장관인 **on the premises** 부지에 **up and running** 제대로 운영되는 **setback** 차질 **advocate** 옹호자 **divert** ~의 방향을 바꾸다

19. 이 기사는 주로 무엇에 관한 것인가?
(A) 쇼핑몰을 확장하자는 제안
(B) 도시 지역의 개발
(C) 뉴 랭포드 시에서의 부동산 가격 상승
(D) 지역 아파트 건물의 철거

해설 첫 번째 문단에서 시의 공무원들이 도시 지역을 바꿔 놓을 갱생 프로젝트를 발표했다고 언급되어 있으므로 도시 지역 개발에 대한 내용의 (B)가 정답이다.

어휘 **neighborhood** 지역, 지방

20. 비숍 씨에 대해 알려진 것은 무엇인가?
(A) 더 이상 뉴 랭포드 시에 살지 않는다.
(B) 시의 계획에 반대한다.
(C) 한 지역 사업체의 소유주이다.
(D) 이전에 건설 회사에서 일했다.

해설 마지막 문단에서 전 시장이었던 비숍 씨는 자금을 기존 건물에 대한 정기 유지보수와 역사적 건물들을 복원하는 비용으로 써야 한다고 주장하며, 시의 유산을 보호하자는 입장이므로 시의 개발 계획에 반대하고 있는 것을 알 수 있다. 따라서 (B)가 정답이다.

어휘 **no longer** 더 이상 ~않다

*2025 히트브랜드 대상
토익 강사 부문 1위

서아쌤의
토익
비밀과외

기출 VOCA

온라인 강의

토익 강사
1위

토익 강사 1위
20만 유튜버 서아쌤!
**VOCA 초밀착
케어 강의로
밀리지 않고 끝까지!**

**PART 1~7까지
모든 파트 어휘 포함!
하루 약 30분으로
VOCA 학습 끝!**

**기출 문제 1500제 및
PART 5, 6 어휘
실전테스트 제공!**
상세한 해설로
VOCA 완전 정복!

시원스쿨랩 사이트에서(lab.siwonschool.com)
유료로 수강 가능합니다.

서아쌤 토익 비밀과외
환급 Package

토익 유튜버 20만
토익 강사 1위
*2025 핏스브랜드 대상 1위 토익강사 부문

토익 입문부터 실전까지 3주 완성
서아쌤의 밀착관리로 목표 달성하고 100% 환급까지!

목표 달성하면 수강료 **100% 환급** *교재비/결제수수료/제세공과금 제외 유의사항 참고	 **환급 대신 연장도 가능!** 수강일 **+90일 연장**	 **토익 3주 완성** 강의 **+교재 포함**
기본 다지기 필수 강의 처음토익 강의 제공	 **온라인 모의고사** 3회분+해설강의 무료제공	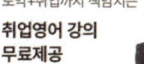  **토익+취업까지 책임지는** 취업영어 강의 무료제공

Premium Benefit

유튜브에선 경험할 수 없는!
서아쌤 밀착관리 카톡 온라인 스터디

학원과 다를 바 없는 빈틈없는 학습관리
서아쌤 부가 학습자료 최대 4종

시원스쿨LAB(lab.siwonschool.com)에서 패키지를 신청하실 수 있습니다. 제공하는 혜택은 기간에 따라 다를 수 있습니다.

시원스쿨 LAB